SPANISH

for

EVERYONE

FIRST EDITION

COLLINS
REFERENCE

First Edition 2009

© HarperCollins Publishers 2009

HarperCollins Publishers
10 East 53rd Street
New York
NY 10022

ISBN 978-0-06-177438-6

www.harpercollins.com

HarperCollins books may be purchased for
educational, business, or sales promotional use.
For information please write:
Special Markets Department
HarperCollins Publishers
10 East 53rd Street
New York
NY 10022

Printed in the United States of America

Reprint 10 9 8 7 6 5 4 3 2 1 0

Typeset by Davidson Pre-Press, Glasgow, UK

Acknowledgements

We would like to thank those authors and publishers who kindly gave permission for
copyright material to be used in the Collins Word Web. We would also like to thank
Times Newspapers Ltd for providing valuable data.

HARPERCOLLINS SPANISH FOR EVERYONE.

Based on *Collins Easy Learning Spanish Grammar*, *Collins Easy Learning Spanish Verbs*
and *Collins Easy Learning Spanish Words*

PUBLISHING DIRECTOR
Catherine Love

MANAGING EDITOR
Gaëlle Amiot-Cadey

PROJECT MANAGER
John Whitlam

CONTRIBUTORS
Beatriz Jarman
Steve Spencer
John Whitlam

SERIES EDITOR
Rob Scriven

Contents

Note on trademarks

Entered words which we have reason to believe constitute trademarks have been designated as such. However, neither the presence nor the absence of such designation should be regarded as affecting the legal status of any trademark.

Foreword for language teachers

Spanish for Everyone is designed to be used with both young and adult learners, as a group reference book to complement your course book during classes, or as a recommended text for self-study and homework/coursework.

The text specifically targets learners from beginner to intermediate level, and therefore its structural content and vocabulary have been matched to the relevant specifications.

The approach aims to develop knowledge and understanding of grammar and your learners' ability to apply it by:

- defining parts of speech at the start of each major section with examples in English to clarify concepts
- minimizing the use of grammar terminology and providing clear explanations of terms within the text and in the **Glossary**
- illustrating points with examples (and their translations) based on topics and contexts which are relevant to beginner and intermediate course content

The text helps your students develop positive attitudes to grammar learning by:

- giving clear, easy-to-follow explanations
- prioritizing content according to relevant specifications for learner levels
- sequencing points to reflect course content, e.g. verb tenses
- highlighting useful **Tips** to deal with common difficulties
- summarizing **Key points** at the end of sections to consolidate learning

In addition to fostering success and building a thorough foundation in Spanish grammar, the optional **Grammar Extra** sections will encourage and challenge your learners to further their studies to higher and advanced levels.

The blue pages in the middle section of the book contain **Verb Tables** and a **Verb Index** which students can use as a reference in their work.

Finally, the **Vocabulary** section in the last part of the book provides thematic vocabulary lists which can either be used for self-study or as an additional teaching resource.

Introduction for students

Whether you are starting to learn Spanish for the very first time, brushing up on topics you have studied in class, or preparing for a test, *Spanish for Everyone* is here to help. This easy-to-use guide takes you through all the basics you will need to speak and understand modern, everyday Spanish.

Newcomers can sometimes struggle with the technical terms they come across when they start to explore the grammar of a new language. *Spanish for Everyone* explains how to come to grips with all the parts of speech you will need to know, using simple, jargon-free language.

The text is divided into sections, each dealing with a particular area of grammar. Each section can be studied individually, as numerous cross-references in the text guide you to relevant points in other sections of the book for further information.

Every major section begins with an explanation of the area of grammar covered in the pages that follow. For quick reference, these definitions are also collected together on pages viii–xii in a glossary of essential grammar terms.

> **What is a verb?**
> A **verb** is a 'doing' word which describes what someone or something does, what someone or something is, or what happens to them. For example: *be*, *sing*, *live*.

Each grammar point in the text is followed by simple examples of real Spanish, complete with English translations, thus helping you to understand the rules. Underlining has been used in examples throughout the text to highlight the grammatical point being explained.

➤ In orders and instructions telling someone <u>TO DO</u> something, the pronoun is attached to the end of the verb to form one word.

Ayúda<u>me</u>.   Help me.

Acompáña<u>nos</u>.   Come with us.

In Spanish, as with any foreign language, there are certain pitfalls which have to be avoided. **Tips** and **Information** notes throughout the text are useful reminders of the things that often trip learners up.

Tip

Don't forget to use personal **a** before indefinite pronouns referring to people when they are the object of a verb.

¿Viste <u>a</u> alguien?　　　Did you see anybody?

No vi <u>a</u> nadie.　　　I didn't see anybody.

Key points sum up all the important facts about a particular area of grammar, saving you time when you are reviewing and helping you focus on the main grammatical points.

Key points

✔ Like other adjectives, Spanish indefinite adjectives (such as **otro** and **todo**), must agree with what they describe.

✔ They go before the noun to which they relate.

If you think you would like to continue your Spanish studies at a higher level, check out the **Grammar Extra** sections. These are intended for advanced students who are interested in knowing a little more about the structures they will come across beyond their current level.

Grammar Extra!

por is often combined with other Spanish prepositions and words, usually to show movement.

Saltó <u>por encima</u> de la mesa.　　She jumped over the table.

Nadamos <u>por debajo del</u> puente.　We swam under the bridge.

Pasaron <u>por delante de la iglesia</u>.　They went past the church.

The blue pages in the middle of the book contain **Verb Tables**, where 83 important Spanish verbs (both regular and irregular) are fully conjugated. Examples show you how to use these verbs in a sentence. You can look up any common verb in the **Verb Index** on pages 464–468 to find a cross-reference to a model verb.

Finally, the **Vocabulary** section at the end of the book is divided into 50 topics, followed by a list of supplementary vocabulary.

Glossary Of Grammar Terms

ABSTRACT NOUN a word used to refer to a quality, idea, feeling or experience, rather than a physical object. For example: *size, reason, happiness*. Compare with **concrete noun**.

ACTIVE a form of the verb that is used when the subject of the verb is the person or thing doing the action. For example: *They sold a lot of books*. Compare with **passive**.

ADJECTIVE a 'describing' word that tells you more about a person or thing, such as their appearance, color, size or other qualities. For example: *pretty, interesting, big*.

ADVERB a word usually used with verbs, adjectives or other adverbs that gives more information about when, where, how or in what circumstances something happens or to what degree something is true. For example: *quickly, happily, now, extremely, very*.

AGREE (to) in the case of adjectives and pronouns, to have the correct word ending or form according to whether what is referred to is masculine, feminine, singular or plural; in the case of verbs, to have the form that goes with the person or thing carrying out the action.

APOSTROPHE s an ending ('s) added to a noun to show who or what someone or something belongs to. For example: *Danielle's dog, the doctor's wife, the book's cover*.

ARTICLE a word such as *the, a* and *an*, which is used in front of a noun. See also **definite article**, **indefinite article**.

AUXILIARY VERB a verb such as *be, have* or *do* used with a main verb to form tenses, negatives and questions.

BASE FORM the form of the verb without any endings added to it. For example: *walk, have, be, go*.

CARDINAL NUMBER a number used in counting. For example: *one, seven, ninety*. Compare with **ordinal number**.

CLAUSE a group of words containing a verb.

COMPARATIVE an adjective or adverb with *-er* on the end of it or *more* or *less* in front of it that is used to compare people, things or actions. For example: *slower, less important, more carefully*.

COMPOUND NOUN a word for a living being, thing or an idea, which is made up of two or more words. For example: *can-opener, train station*.

CONCRETE NOUN a word that refers to an object you can touch with your hand, rather than to a quality or an idea. For example: *ball, map, apples*. Compare with **abstract noun**.

CONDITIONAL a verb form used to talk about things that would happen or would be true under certain conditions. For example: *I would help you if I could*. It is also used to say what you would like or need. For example: *Could I have the check, please?*

CONJUGATE (to) to give a verb different endings according to whether you are referring to *I, you, they* and so on, and according to whether you are referring to the present, past or future. For example: *I have, she had, they will have*.

CONJUGATION a group of verbs that have the same endings as each other or change according to the same pattern.

CONJUNCTION a word such as *and, because* or *but* that links two words or phrases of a similar type or two parts of a sentence. For example: *Diane and I have been friends for years; I left because I was bored*.

CONSONANT a letter that isn't a vowel. For example: *b, f, m, s, v* and so on. Compare with **vowel**.

CONTINUOUS TENSE a verb tense formed using *to be* and the *-ing* form of the main verb. For example: *They're swimming* (present continuous); *He was eating* (past continuous).

DEFINITE ARTICLE the word *the*. Compare with **indefinite article**.

DEMONSTRATIVE ADJECTIVE a word such as *this, that, these* or *those* used with a noun to refer to particular people or things. For example: *this woman, that dog*.

DEMONSTRATIVE PRONOUN a word such as *this, that, these* or *those* used instead of a noun to point out people or things. For example: *That looks fun*.

DIRECT OBJECT a noun or pronoun used with verbs to show who or what is acted on by the verb. For example, in *He wrote a letter* and *He wrote me a letter, letter* is the direct object. Compare **indirect object**.

DIRECT OBJECT PRONOUN a word such as *me, him, us* and *them* which is used instead of a noun to stand in for the person or thing most directly affected by the action expressed by the verb. Compare with **indirect object pronoun**.

ENDING a form added to a verb (for example, *go → goes*) and to adjectives and nouns depending on whether they refer to masculine, feminine, singular or plural things.

EXCLAMATION a word, phrase or sentence that you use to show you are surprised, shocked, angry and so on. For example: *Wow!; How dare you!; What a surprise!*

FEMININE a form of noun, pronoun or adjective that is used to refer to a living being, thing or an idea that is not classed as masculine.

FUTURE a verb tense used to talk about something that will happen or will be true.

GENDER whether a noun, pronoun or adjective is feminine or masculine.

GERUND a verb form in English ending in *-ing*. For example: *eating, sleeping*.

IMPERATIVE the form of a verb used when giving orders and instructions. For example: *Shut the door!; Sit down!; Don't go!; Let's eat*.

IMPERFECT one of the verb tenses used to talk about the past, especially in descriptions, and to say what was happening or used to happen. For example: *He was tall and thin; We were living in Mexico at the time; I used to walk to school*. Compare to **preterite**.

IMPERSONAL VERB a verb whose subject is *it*, but where the *it* does not refer to any specific thing. For example: *It's raining; It's 10 o'clock*.

INDEFINITE ADJECTIVE one of a small group of adjectives used to talk about people or things in a general way, without saying who or what they are. For example: *several, all, every*.

INDEFINITE ARTICLE the words *a* and *an*. Compare with **definite article**.

INDICATIVE ordinary verb forms that aren't subjunctive, such as the present, preterite or future. Compare with **subjunctive**.

INDEFINITE PRONOUN a small group of pronouns such as *everything, nobody* and *something*, which are used to refer to people or things in a general way, without saying exactly who or what they are.

INDIRECT OBJECT a noun or pronoun used with verbs to show who benefits or is harmed by an action. For example, in *I gave the carrot to the rabbit*, *the rabbit* is the indirect object and *the carrot* is the direct object. Compare with **direct object**.

INDIRECT OBJECT PRONOUN a pronoun used with verbs to show who benefits or is harmed by an action. For example, in *I gave him the carrot* and *I gave it to him*, *him* is the indirect object and the *carrot* and *it* are the direct objects. Compare with **direct object pronoun**.

INDIRECT QUESTION a question that is embedded in another question or instruction such as *Can you tell me what time it is?*; *Tell me why you did it*. Also used for reported speech such as *He asked me why I did it*.

INDIRECT SPEECH the words you use to report what someone has said when you aren't using their actual words. For example: *He said that he was going out*. Also called **reported speech**.

INFINITIVE a form of the verb that hasn't any endings added to it and doesn't relate to any particular tense. In English the infinitive is usually shown with *to*, as in *to speak, to eat*.

INTERROGATIVE ADJECTIVE a question word used with a noun. For example: *What instruments do you play?*; *Which shoes do you like?*

INTERROGATIVE PRONOUN a word such as *who, whose, whom, what* or *which* when it is used instead of a noun to ask questions. For example: *What's that?*; *Who's coming?*

INTRANSITIVE VERB a type of verb that does not take a direct object. For example: *to sleep, to rise, to swim*. Compare with **transitive verb**.

INVARIABLE used to describe a form which does not change.

IRREGULAR VERB a verb whose forms do not follow a general pattern. Compare with **regular verb**.

MASCULINE a form of noun, pronoun or adjective that is used to refer to a living being, thing or idea that is not classed as feminine.

NEGATIVE a question or statement which contains a word such as *not, never* or *nothing*, and is used to say that something is not happening, is not true or is absent. For example: *I never eat meat; Don't you love me?* Compare with **positive**.

NOUN a 'naming' word for a living being, thing or an idea. For example: *woman, desk, happiness, Andrew*.

NOUN GROUP, NOUN PHRASE a word or group of words that acts as the subject or object of a verb, or as the object of a preposition. For example: *my older sister; the man next door; that big house on the corner*.

NUMBER used to say how many things you are referring to or where something comes in a sequence. See also **ordinal number** and **cardinal number**. Also the condition of being singular or plural.

OBJECT a noun or pronoun that refers to a person or thing that is affected by the action described by the verb. Compare with **direct object**, **indirect object** and **subject**.

OBJECT PRONOUN one of the set of pronouns including *me, him* and *them*, which are used instead of the noun as the object of a verb or preposition. Compare with **subject pronoun**.

ORDINAL NUMBER a number used to indicate where something comes in an order or sequence. For example: *first, fifth, sixteenth*. Compare with **cardinal number**.

PART OF SPEECH a word class. For example: *noun*, *verb*, *adjective*, *preposition*, *pronoun*.

PASSIVE a form of the verb that is used when the subject of the verb is the person or thing that is affected by the action. For example: *A lot of books were sold.*

PAST PARTICIPLE a verb form which is used to form perfect and pluperfect tenses and passives. For example: *watched*, *swum*. Some past participles are also used as adjectives. For example: *a broken watch*.

PAST PERFECT see **pluperfect**.

PERFECT a verb form which is used to talk about what has or hasn't happened. For example: *I've broken my glasses; We haven't spoken about it.*

PERSON one of the three classes: the first person (*I*, *we*), the second person (*you* singular and *you* plural), and the third person (*he*, *she*, *it* and *they*).

PERSONAL PRONOUN one of the group of words including *I*, *you* and *they* which are used to refer to you, the people you are talking to, or the people or things you are talking about.

PLUPERFECT one of the verb tenses used to describe something that <u>had</u> happened or <u>had</u> been true at a point in the past. For example: *I'd forgotten to finish my homework.* Also called **past perfect**.

PLURAL the form of a word which is used to refer to more than one person or thing. Compare with **singular**.

POSITIVE a positive sentence or instruction is one that does not contain a negative word such as *not*. Compare with **negative**.

POSSESSIVE ADJECTIVE a word such as *my*, *your*, *his*, *her*, *its*, *our* or *their*, used with a noun to show who it belongs to.

POSSESSIVE PRONOUN a word such as *mine*, *yours*, *hers*, *his*, *ours* or *theirs*, used instead of a noun to show who something belongs to.

PREPOSITION a word such as *at*, *for*, *with*, *into* or *from*, which is usually followed by a noun, pronoun or, in English, a word ending in *-ing*. Prepositions show how people and things relate to the rest of the sentence. For example: *She's <u>at</u> home; a tool <u>for</u> cutting grass; It's <u>from</u> David.*

PRESENT a verb form used to talk about what is true at the moment, what happens regularly, and what is happening now. For example: *I'm a student; I <u>travel</u> to college by train; I'm <u>studying</u> languages.*

PRESENT PARTICIPLE a verb form in English ending in *-ing*. For example: *eating*, *sleeping*.

PRETERITE a Spanish verb form used to talk about actions that were completed in the past. It often corresponds to the ordinary past tense in English. For example: *I bought a new bike; Mary went to the shops on Friday; I typed two reports yesterday.*

PRONOUN a word which you use instead of a noun, when you do not need or want to name someone or something directly. For example: *it, you, none.*

PROPER NOUN the name of a person, place, organization or thing. Proper nouns are always written with a capital letter. For example: *Kevin, Seattle, Europe, Empire State Building.*

QUESTION WORD a word such as *why*, *where*, *who*, *which* or *how*, that is used to ask a question.

RADICAL-CHANGING VERBS in Spanish, verbs which change their stem or root in certain tenses and for certain persons.

REFLEXIVE PRONOUN a word ending in -self or -selves, such as myself or themselves, which refers back to the subject. For example: He hurt _himself_; Take care of _yourself_.

REFLEXIVE VERB a verb where the subject and object are the same, and where the action 'reflects back' on the subject. A reflexive verb is used with a reflexive pronoun such as myself, yourself or herself. For example: I washed myself; He cut himself.

REGULAR VERB a verb whose forms follow a general pattern or the normal rules. Compare with **irregular verb**.

RELATIVE PRONOUN a word such as that, who or which, when it is used to link two parts of a sentence together.

REPORTED SPEECH see **indirect speech**.

SENTENCE a group of words which usually has a verb and a subject. In writing, a sentence begins with a capital letter and ends with a period, question mark or exclamation point.

SIMPLE TENSE a verb tense in which the verb form is made up of one word, rather than being formed from to have and a past participle or to be and an -ing form. For example: She _plays_ tennis; He _wrote_ a book.

SINGULAR the form of a word which is used to refer to one person or thing. Compare with **plural**.

STEM the main part of a verb to which endings are added.

SUBJECT a noun or pronoun that refers to the person or thing doing the action or being in the state described by the verb. For example: _My cat_ doesn't drink milk. Compare with **object**.

SUBJECT PRONOUN a word such as I, he, she and they which carries out the action described by the verb. Pronouns stand in for nouns when it is clear who is being talked about. For example: My brother isn't here at the moment. _He_'ll be back in an hour. Compare with **object pronoun**.

SUBJUNCTIVE a verb form used in certain circumstances to indicate some sort of feeling, or to show doubt about whether something will happen or whether something is true. It is only used occasionally in modern English. For example: If I _were_ you, I wouldn't bother; So _be_ it.

SUPERLATIVE an adjective or adverb with -est on the end of it or most or least in front of it that is used to compare people, things or actions. For example: thin_nest_, _most_ quickly, _least_ interesting.

SYLLABLE consonant+vowel units that make up the sounds of a word. For example: ca-the-dral (3 syllables), im-po-ssi-ble (4 syllables).

TENSE the form of a verb which shows whether you are referring to the past, present or future.

TRANSITIVE VERB a type of verb that takes a direct object. For example: to spend, to raise, to waste. Compare with **intransitive verb**.

VERB a 'doing' word which describes what someone or something does, is, or what happens to them. For example: be, sing, live.

VOWEL one of the letters a, e, i, o or u. Compare with **consonant**.

Nouns

> **What is a noun?**
> A **noun** is a 'naming' word for a living being, thing or idea. For example:
> *woman, desk, happiness, Andrew*.

Using nouns

➤ In Spanish, all nouns are either <u>masculine</u> or <u>feminine</u>. This is called their <u>gender</u>. Even words for things have a gender.

➤ Whenever you are using a noun, you need to know whether it is masculine or feminine as this affects the form of other words used with it, such as:

  ● adjectives that describe it
  ● articles (such as **el** or **una**) that go before it

⇨ *For more information on **Articles** and **Adjectives**, see pages 10 and 19.*

➤ You can find information about gender by looking the word up in a dictionary. When you come across a new noun, always learn the word for *the* or *a* that goes with it to help you remember its gender.

  ● **el** or **un** before a noun tells you it is masculine
  ● **la** or **una** before a noun tells you it is feminine

➤ We refer to something as <u>singular</u> when we are talking about just one of them, and as <u>plural</u> when we are talking about more than one. The singular is the form of the noun you will usually find when you look a noun up in the dictionary. As in English, nouns in Spanish change their form in the plural.

➤ Adjectives, articles and pronouns are also affected by whether a noun is singular or plural.

> *Tip*
> Remember that you have to use the right word for *the*, *a* and so on according to the gender of the Spanish noun.

Gender

1 Nouns referring to people

➤ Most nouns referring to men and boys are <u>masculine</u>.

<u>el</u> hombre	the man
<u>el</u> rey	the king

➤ Most nouns referring to women and girls are <u>feminine</u>.

<u>la</u> mujer	the woman
<u>la</u> reina	the queen

➤ When the same word is used to refer to either men/boys or women/girls, its gender usually changes depending on the sex of the person it refers to.

<u>el</u> estudiante	the (male) student
<u>la</u> estudiante	the (female) student
<u>el</u> artista	the (male) artist
<u>la</u> artista	the (female) artist

Grammar Extra!

Some words for people have only <u>one</u> possible gender, whether they refer to a male or a female.

<u>la</u> persona	the (male *or* female) person
<u>la</u> víctima	the (male *or* female) victim

➤ In English, we can sometimes make a word masculine or feminine by changing the ending, for example, *policeman* and *policewoman* or *prince* and *princess*. In Spanish, very often the ending of a noun changes depending on whether it refers to a man or a woman.

<u>el</u> americano	the American (*male*)
<u>la</u> americana	the American (*female*)
<u>el</u> empleado	the employee (*male*)
<u>la</u> empleada	the employee (*female*)
<u>el</u> anfitrión	the host
<u>la</u> anfitriona	the hostess

> **Tip**
>
> Note that a noun ending in **-o** is usually <u>masculine</u> and a noun ending in **-a** is usually <u>feminine</u>.

⇨ For more information on **Masculine and feminine forms of words**, *see page* 5.

2 <u>Nouns referring to animals</u>

➤ In English we can choose between words like *bull* or *cow*, depending on the sex of the animal. In Spanish too there are sometimes separate words for male and female animals.

el toro	the bull
la vaca	the cow

➤ Sometimes, the same word with different endings is used for male and female animals.

el perro	the (male) dog
la perra	the (female) dog, bitch
el gato	the (male) cat
la gata	the (female) cat

> **Tip**
>
> When you do not know or care what sex the animal is, you can usually use the masculine form as a general word.

➤ Words for other animals don't change according to the sex of the animal. In these instances, you only need to learn the Spanish word with its gender, which always remains the same.

el sapo	the toad
el hámster	the hamster
la ardilla	the squirrel
la tortuga	the turtle

3 <u>Nouns referring to things</u>

➤ In English, we call all things – for example, *table, car, book, apple* – 'it'. In Spanish, however, things are either <u>masculine</u> or <u>feminine</u>. As things don't divide into sexes the way humans and animals do, there are no physical clues to help you determine their gender in Spanish. Try to learn the gender as you learn the word.

➤ There are lots of rules to help you. Certain endings are usually found on masculine nouns, while other endings are usually found on feminine nouns.

4 Nouns

➤ The following ending is usually found on <u>masculine nouns</u>.

Masculine ending	Examples
-o	el libro the book el periódico the newspaper EXCEPTIONS: la mano the hand la foto the photo la moto the motorcycle

➤ The following types of word are also masculine.

- the names of the days of the week and the months of the year

  Te veo el lunes.   I'll see you on Monday.

- the names of languages

  el inglés   English
  el español   Spanish
  El japonés es difícil.   Japanese is difficult.

- the names of rivers, mountains and seas

  el Amazonas   the Amazon
  el Everest   Everest
  el Atlántico   the Atlantic

➤ The following endings are usually found on <u>feminine nouns</u>.

Feminine ending	Examples
-a	la casa the house la cara the face EXCEPTIONS: el día the day el mapa the map el planeta the planet el tranvía the streetcar, and many words ending in -ma (el problema the problem, el programa the program, el sistema the system, el clima the climate)
-ción -sión	la lección the lesson la estación the station; the season la expresión the expression
-dad -tad -tud	la ciudad the city la libertad freedom la multitud the crowd

For further explanation of grammatical terms, please see pages viii-xii.

Grammar Extra!

Some words have different meanings depending on whether they are masculine or feminine.

Masculine	Meaning	Feminine	Meaning
el capital	the capital (meaning *money*)	la capital	the capital (meaning *city*)
el frente	the front	la frente	the forehead
el policía	the police officer (*male*)	la policía	the police (force); the police officer (*female*)
el guía	the guide (*man*)	la guía	the guidebook; the guide (*woman*)

Invirtieron mucho capital.   They invested a lot of capital.
Viven en la capital.   They live in the capital.

4   Masculine and feminine forms of words

➤ Like English, Spanish sometimes has very different words for males and females.

     el hombre   the man
     la mujer   the woman

     el rey   the king
     la reina   the queen

➤ Many Spanish words can be used to talk about men or women simply by changing the ending. For example, if the word for the male ends in -o, you can almost always make it feminine by changing the -o to -a.

     el amigo   the (male) friend
     la amiga   the (female) friend

     el hermano   the brother
     la hermana   the sister

     el empleado   the (male) employee
     la empleada   the (female) employee

     el viudo   the widower
     la viuda   the widow

i Note that some words referring to people end in -a in the masculine as well as in the feminine. Only the article (el or la, un or una) can tell you what is the gender of the noun.

     el dentista   the (male) dentist
     la dentista   the (female) dentist

     el deportista   the sportsman
     la deportista   the sportswoman

➤ Many masculine nouns ending in a consonant (any letter other than a vowel) become feminine by adding an -**a**.

<u>el</u> **español**	the Spanish man
<u>la</u> **española**	the Spanish woman
<u>el</u> **profesor**	the (male) teacher
<u>la</u> **profesora**	the (female) teacher

Típ

If the last vowel of the masculine word has an accent, this is dropped in the feminine form.

<u>un</u> **inglés**	an Englishman
<u>una</u> **inglesa**	an Englishwoman
<u>un</u> **león**	a lion
<u>una</u> **leona**	a lioness

▷ *For more information about **Spelling** and **Stress**, see pages 198 and 202.*

Key points

✔ The ending of a Spanish word often helps you determine its gender: for instance, if a word ends in -**o**, it is probably masculine; if it ends in -**a**, it is probably feminine.

✔ These endings generally mean that the noun is feminine: -**ción**, -**sión**, -**dad**, -**tad**, -**tud**.

✔ Days of the week and months of the year are masculine. So are languages, mountains and seas.

✔ You can change the ending of some nouns from -**o** to -**a** to make a masculine noun feminine.

Forming plurals

Plurals ending in -s and -es

➤ In English we usually make nouns plural by adding an -s to the end (*garden* → *gardens*; *house* → *houses*), although we do have some nouns which are <u>irregular</u> and do not follow this pattern (*mouse* → *mice*; *child* → *children*).

> *Tip*
>
> Remember that you have to use **los** (for <u>masculine nouns</u>) or **las** (for <u>feminine nouns</u>) with plural nouns in Spanish. Any adjective that goes with the noun also has to agree with it, as does any pronoun that replaces it.
>
> ➪ *For more information on* **Articles**, **Adjectives** *and* **Pronouns**, *see pages 10, 19 and 41.*

➤ To form the plural in Spanish, add **-s** to most nouns ending in a vowel (*a, e, i, o* or *u*) which doesn't have an accent.

el libro	the book
los libro<u>s</u>	the books
el hombre	the man
los hombre<u>s</u>	the men
la profesora	the (female) teacher
las profesora<u>s</u>	the (female) teachers

➤ Add **-es** to singular nouns ending in a consonant (any letter other than a vowel).

el profesor	the (male) teacher
los profesor<u>es</u>	the (all male or male and female) teachers
la ciudad	the town/city
las ciudad<u>es</u>	the towns/cities

ⓘ Note that some foreign words (that is, words which have come from another language, such as English) ending in a consonant just add **-s**.

el coñac	the brandy
los coñac<u>s</u>	the brandies
el mail	the email
los mail<u>s</u>	the emails

➤ Words ending in **-s** which have an unstressed final vowel do not change in the plural.

el paraguas	the umbrella
los paraguas	the umbrellas
el lunes	(on) Monday
los lunes	(on) Mondays

⇨ *For more information on* **Stress***, see page 202.*

➤ Some singular nouns ending in an accented vowel add **-es** in the plural while other very common ones add **-s**.

el rubí	the ruby
los rubíes	the rubies
el café	the coffee
los cafés	the coffees
el sofá	the sofa
los sofás	the sofas

Grammar Extra!

When nouns are made up of two separate words, they are called <u>compound nouns</u>, for example, **el abrelatas** (meaning *the can-opener*) and **el hombre rana** (meaning *the deep sea diver*). Some of these nouns don't change in the plural, for example, **los abrelatas**, while others do, for example, **los hombres rana**. It is always best to check in a dictionary to see what the plural is.

---

2 **Spelling changes with plurals ending in -es**

➤ Singular nouns which end in an accented vowel and either **-n** or **-s** drop the accent in the plural.

la canción	the song
las canciones	the songs
el francés	the Frenchman
los franceses	the French

➤ Singular nouns of more than one syllable which end in **-en** and don't already have an accent, add one in the plural.

el examen	the exam
los exámenes	the exams
el origen	the origin
los orígenes	the origins

For further explanation of grammatical terms, please see pages viii-xii.

➤ Singular nouns ending in **-z** change to **-ces** in the plural.

la luz	the light
las lu<u>ces</u>	the lights
la vez	the times
las ve<u>ces</u>	the times

⇨ *For further information on **Spelling** and **Stress**, see pages 198 and 202.*

3 Plural versus singular

➤ A few words relating to clothing that are plural in English can be singular in Spanish.

<u>un</u> calzoncillo	(a pair of) underpants
<u>un</u> pantalón	(a pair of) pants
<u>un</u> short	(a pair of) shorts

➤ A few common words behave differently in Spanish from the way they behave in English.

un mueble	a piece of furniture
unos muebles	some furniture
una noticia	a piece of news
unas noticias	some news
un consejo	a piece of advice
unos consejos	some advice

Key points

✔ Add **-s** to form the plural of a noun ending in an unaccented vowel.

✔ Add **-es** to form the plural of most nouns ending in a consonant.

✔ Drop the accent when adding plural **-es** to nouns ending in an accented vowel + **-n** or **-s**.

✔ Add an accent when adding plural **-es** to words of more than one syllable ending in **-en**.

✔ Change **-z** to **-ces** when forming the plural of words like **luz**.

✔ A few common words are plural in English but not in Spanish.

Articles

Different types of article

➤ There are two types of article:

- the <u>definite</u> article: *the* in English. This is used to identify a particular thing or person.

   I'm going to <u>the</u> supermarket.
   That's <u>the</u> woman I was talking to.

- the <u>indefinite</u> article: *a* or *an* in English, whose plural is *some* or *any* (or no word at all). This is used to refer to something unspecific, or that you do not really know about.

   Is there <u>a</u> supermarket near here?
   I need <u>a</u> day off.

For further explanation of grammatical terms, please see pages viii-xii.

The definite article: el, la, los and las

1 __The basic rules__

➤ In English, there is only <u>one</u> definite article: *the*. In Spanish, you have to choose between <u>four</u> definite articles: **el**, **la**, **los** and **las**. Which one you choose depends on the noun which follows.

➤ In Spanish, all nouns (including words for things) are either masculine or feminine – this is called their <u>gender</u>. And, just as in English, they can also be either singular or plural. You must bear this in mind when deciding which Spanish word to use for *the*.

➪ *For more information on **Nouns**, see page 1.*

➤ **el** is used before <u>masculine singular nouns</u>.

el hombre	the man
el periódico	the newspaper

➤ **la** is used before <u>feminine singular nouns</u>.

la mujer	the woman
la revista	the magazine

Tip

To help you speak and write correct Spanish, always learn the <u>article</u> or the <u>gender</u> together with the noun when learning vocabulary. A good dictionary will also give you this information.

➤ **los** and **las** are used before <u>plural nouns</u>. **los** is used with masculine plural words, and **las** is used with feminine plural words.

<u>los</u> hombres	the men
<u>las</u> mujeres	the women
<u>los</u> periódicos	the newspapers
<u>las</u> revistas	the magazines

i Note that you use **el** instead of **la** immediately before a feminine singular word beginning with **a** or **ha** when the stress falls on the beginning of the word. This is because **la** sounds wrong before the '*a*' sound. <u>BUT</u> if you add an adjective in front of the noun, you use **la** instead, since the two 'a' sounds do not come next to each other.

<u>el</u> agua	the water
<u>el</u> hacha	the ax
<u>la</u> misma agua	the same water
<u>la</u> mejor hacha	the best ax

2 a and de with the definite article

➤ If **a** is followed by **el**, the two words become **al**.

al cine	to the movies
al empleado	to the employee
al hospital	to the hospital
Vio **al** mesero.	He saw the waiter.

➤ If **de** is followed by **el**, the two words become **del**.

del departamento	of/from the apartment
del autor	of/from the author
del presidente	of/from the president

3 Using the definite article

➤ **el**, **la**, **los** and **las** are often used in Spanish in the same way as *the* is used in English. However, there are some cases where the article is used in Spanish but not in English.

➤ The definite article IS used in Spanish:

- when talking about people, animals and things in a general way

Me encantan los animales.	I love animals.
Están subiendo los precios.	Prices are going up.
No me gusta el café.	I don't like coffee.
El chocolate engorda.	Chocolate is fattening.

- when talking about abstract qualities, for example, *time, hope, darkness, violence*

El tiempo es oro.	Time is money.
Admiro la sinceridad en la gente.	I admire honesty in people.

ℹ️ Note that the definite article is NOT used in certain set phrases consisting of **tener** and a noun or after certain prepositions.

tener hambre	to be hungry	(*literally: to have hunger*)
sin duda	no doubt	(*literally: without doubt*)
con cuidado	carefully	(*literally: with care*)

➪ *For more information on **Prepositions**, see page 180.*

- when talking about colors

    El azul es mi color favorito.   Blue is my favorite color.

- when talking about parts of the body – you do not use *my, your, his* and so on as you would in English

    Tiene <u>los</u> ojos verdes.   He has green eyes.

    No puedo mover <u>las</u> piernas.   I can't move my legs.

[*i*] Note that possession is often shown by a personal pronoun in Spanish.

    <u>Me</u> duele la rodilla.   <u>My</u> knee hurts.

    Láva<u>te</u> las manos.   Wash <u>your</u> hands.

⇨ *For more information on **Personal pronouns**, see page 42.*

- when using someone's title – for example, *Doctor, Mr.* – but talking <u>ABOUT</u> someone rather than to them.

    <u>El</u> doctor Vidal no está.   Dr. Vidal isn't here.

    <u>El</u> señor Pelayo vive aquí.   Mr. Pelayo lives here.

- when talking about institutions, such as school or church

    en <u>el</u> colegio   at school

    en <u>la</u> universidad   at college

    en <u>la</u> iglesia   at church

    en <u>la</u> cárcel   in prison

- when talking about meals, games or sports

    <u>La</u> cena es a las nueve.   Dinner is at nine o'clock.

    Me gusta <u>el</u> tenis.   I like tennis.

    No me gusta <u>el</u> ajedrez.   I don't like chess.

- when talking about days of the week and dates, where we use the preposition *on* in English

    Te veo <u>el</u> lunes.   I'll see you <u>on</u> Monday.

    <u>Los</u> domingos vamos al cine.   We go to the movies <u>on</u> Sundays.

    Nací <u>el</u> 17 de marzo.   I was born <u>on</u> March 17.

- when talking about the time

    Es <u>la</u> una.   It's one o'clock.

    Son <u>las</u> tres.   It's three o'clock.

    Son <u>las</u> cuatro y media.   It's half past four.

- when talking about prices and rates
  Cuestan dos dólares la docena.   They cost two dollars a dozen.
  Cobra 200 pesos la hora.   He charges 200 pesos an hour.

Key points

✔ Before masculine singular nouns → use **el**.

✔ Before feminine singular nouns → use **la**.

✔ Before feminine singular nouns starting with stressed **a** or **ha** → use **el**.

✔ Before masculine plural nouns → use **los**.

✔ Before feminine plural nouns → use **las**.

✔ a + el → al

✔ de + el → del

✔ There are some important cases when you would use a definite article in Spanish when you wouldn't in English. For example, when talking about:
  - things in a general way
  - abstract qualities
  - colors
  - parts of the body
  - someone with a title in front of their name
  - institutions
  - meals, games or sports
  - the time, days of the week and dates (*using the preposition <u>on</u> in English*)
  - prices and rates

The indefinite article: un, una, unos and unas

1 The basic rules

➤ In English, the indefinite article is *a*, which changes to *an* when it comes before a vowel or a vowel sound (for example, *an apple*). In the plural, we use *some* or *any*.

➤ In Spanish, you have to choose between <u>four</u> indefinite articles: **un**, **una**, **unos** and **unas**. Which one you choose depends on the noun that follows.

➤ In Spanish, all nouns (including words for things) are either masculine or feminine – this is called their <u>gender</u>. And, just as in English, they can also be either singular or plural. You must bear this in mind when deciding which Spanish word to use for *a*.

⇨ *For more information on* **Nouns**, *see page 1.*

➤ **un** is used before <u>masculine singular nouns</u>.

<u>un</u> hombre	a man
<u>un</u> periódico	a newspaper

➤ **una** is used before <u>feminine singular nouns</u>.

<u>una</u> mujer	a woman
<u>una</u> revista	a magazine

➤ **unos** is used before <u>masculine plural nouns</u>.

<u>unos</u> hombres	some men
<u>unos</u> periódicos	some newspapers

➤ **unas** is used before <u>feminine plural nouns</u>.

<u>unas</u> mujeres	some women
<u>unas</u> revistas	some magazines

ⓘ Note that you use **un** instead of **una** immediately before a feminine singular word beginning with **a** or **ha** when the stress falls on the beginning of the word. This is because **una** sounds wrong before the '*a*' sound.

un ave	a bird
un hada	a fairy

2 Using the indefinite article

➤ The indefinite article is often used in Spanish in the same way as it is in English. However, there are some cases where the article is not used in Spanish but is in English, and vice versa.

➤ The indefinite article is <u>NOT</u> used in Spanish:

- when you say what someone's job is

Es profesor.	He's <u>a</u> teacher.
Mi madre es enfermera.	My mother is <u>a</u> nurse.

- after **tener**, **buscar**, or **llevar (puesto)** when you are only likely *to have*, *be looking for* or *be wearing* one of the items in question

No tengo celular.	I don't have <u>a</u> cell phone.
¿Llevaba sombrero?	Was he wearing <u>a</u> hat?

i Note that when you use an adjective to describe the noun, you <u>DO</u> use an article in Spanish too.

Es <u>un</u> excelente médico.	He's <u>an</u> excellent doctor.
Tiene <u>una</u> novia peruana.	He has a Peruvian girlfriend.
Llevaba <u>un</u> sombrero de paja.	He was wearing a straw hat.

➤ The indefinite article is <u>NOT</u> used in Spanish with the words **otro**, **cierto**, **cien**, **mil**, **sin**, and **qué**.

otro libro	another book
cierta calle	<u>a</u> certain street
cien soldados	<u>a</u> hundred soldiers
mil años	<u>a</u> thousand years
sin casa	without <u>a</u> house
¡Qué sorpresa!	What <u>a</u> surprise!

Key points

✔ Before masculine singular nouns → use **un**.

✔ Before feminine singular nouns → use **una**.

✔ Before feminine singular nouns starting with stressed **a** or **ha** → use **un**.

✔ Before masculine plural nouns → use **unos**.

✔ Before feminine plural nouns → use **unas**.

✔ You do not use an indefinite article in Spanish for saying what someone's job is.

✔ You do not use an indefinite article in Spanish with the words **otro**, **cierto**, **cien**, **mil**, **sin**, and **qué**.

For further explanation of grammatical terms, please see pages viii-xii.

The article lo

➤ Unlike the other Spanish articles, and articles in English, **lo** is <u>NOT</u> used with a noun.

➤ **lo** can be used with a masculine singular adjective or past participle (the **-ado** and **-ido** forms of regular verbs) to form a noun.

<u>Lo único</u> que no me gusta ...	The only thing I don't like ...
Eso es <u>lo importante</u>.	That's the important thing.
<u>Lo bueno</u> es que ...	The good thing is that ...
Sentimos mucho <u>lo ocurrido</u>.	We are very sorry about what happened.

⇨ *For more information on the **Past participle**, see page 118.*

➤ **lo** is also used in a number of very common phrases:

- **a lo mejor**   maybe, perhaps

  <u>A lo mejor</u> no lo sabe.   Maybe he doesn't know.

- **por lo menos**   at least

  Hubo <u>por lo menos</u> cincuenta   At least fifty people were injured.
  heridos.

- **por lo general**   generally

  <u>Por lo general</u> me acuesto   I generally go to bed early.
  temprano.

➤ **lo** can also be used with **que** to make **lo que** (meaning *what*).

Vi <u>lo que</u> pasó.	I saw what happened.
<u>Lo que</u> más me gusta es nadar.	What I like best is swimming.

Grammar Extra!

lo can be used with **de** followed by a noun phrase to refer back to something the speaker and listener both know about.

Lo de tu hermano me preocupa mucho.	That business with your brother worries me a lot.
Lo de ayer es mejor que lo olvides.	It would be best to forget <u>what happened yesterday</u>.

lo can be used with an adjective followed by **que** to emphasize how big/small/beautiful and so on something is or was. The adjective must agree with the noun it describes.

No sabíamos <u>lo antigua que</u> era la casa.	We didn't know <u>how old</u> the house was.
No te imaginas <u>lo simpáticos que</u> son.	You can't imagine <u>how nice</u> they are.

lo can also be used in a similar way with an adverb followed by **que**.

Sé <u>lo mucho que</u> te gusta la música.	I know <u>how much</u> you like music.

Key points

- ✔ **lo** is classed as an article in Spanish, but is not used with nouns.
- ✔ You can use **lo** with a masculine adjective or past participle to form a noun.
- ✔ You also use **lo** in a number of common phrases.
- ✔ **lo que** can be used to mean *what* in English.

For further explanation of grammatical terms, please see pages viii-xii.

Adjectives

> **What is an adjective?**
> An **adjective** is a 'describing' word that tells you more about a person or thing, such as their appearance, color, size or other qualities. For example: *pretty*, *blue*, *big*.

Using adjectives

➤ Adjectives are words like *smart*, *expensive* and *good* that tell you more about a noun (a living being, thing or idea). They can also tell you more about a pronoun, such as *he* or *they*. Adjectives are sometimes called 'describing words'. They can be used right next to a noun they are describing, or can be separated from the noun by a verb like *be*, *look*, *feel* and so on.

    a <u>smart</u> girl
    an <u>expensive</u> car
    a <u>good</u> idea

⇨ *For more information on **Nouns** and **Pronouns**, see pages 1 and 41.*

➤ In English, the only time an adjective changes its form is when you are making a comparison.

    She's <u>smarter</u> than her brother.
    That's the <u>best</u> idea you've ever had!

➤ In Spanish, however, most adjectives <u>agree</u> with what they are describing. This means that their endings change depending on whether the person or thing you are referring to is masculine or feminine, singular or plural.

un hombre <u>alto</u>	a tall man
una mujer <u>alta</u>	a tall woman
unos hombres <u>altos</u>	some tall men
unas mujeres <u>altas</u>	some tall women

➤ In English adjectives come <u>BEFORE</u> the noun they describe, but in Spanish you usually put them <u>AFTER</u> it.

    una casa <u>blanca</u>   a <u>white</u> house

⇨ *For more information on **Word order with adjectives**, see page 24.*

Making adjectives agree

1 Forming feminine adjectives

➤ The form of the adjective shown in dictionaries is generally the masculine singular form. This means that you need to know how to change its form to make it agree with the person or thing it is describing.

➤ Adjectives ending in -o in the masculine change to -a for the feminine.

Mi padre es <u>mexicano</u>.	My father is Mexican.
Mi madre es <u>mexicana</u>.	My mother is Mexican.

➤ Adjectives ending in any vowel other than -o (that is: *a*, *e*, *i* or *u*) or ending in a vowel with an accent on it do <u>NOT</u> change for the feminine.

el vestido <u>verde</u>	the green dress
la blusa <u>verde</u>	the green blouse
un pantalón <u>caqui</u>	some khaki pants
una camisa <u>caqui</u>	a khaki shirt
un médico <u>iraquí</u>	an Iraqi doctor
una familia <u>iraquí</u>	an Iraqi family

➤ Adjectives ending in a consonant (any letter other than a vowel) do <u>NOT</u> change for the feminine except in the following cases:

● Adjectives of nationality or place ending in a consonant add -a for the feminine. If there is an accent on the final vowel in the masculine, they lose this in the feminine.

un periódico <u>inglés</u>	an English newspaper
una revista <u>inglesa</u>	an English magazine
el equipo <u>francés</u>	the French team
la cocina <u>francesa</u>	French cooking
el vino <u>español</u>	Spanish wine
la lengua <u>española</u>	the Spanish language

i Note that these adjectives do not start with a capital letter in Spanish.

● Adjectives ending in -or in the masculine usually change to -ora for the feminine.

un niño <u>encantador</u>	a charming little boy
una niña <u>encantadora</u>	a charming little girl

ⓘ Note that a few adjectives ending in **-or** used in comparisons – such as **mejor** (meaning *better* or *best*), **peor** (meaning *worse* or *worst*), **mayor** (meaning *older* or *bigger*), **superior** (meaning *upper* or *top*), **inferior** (meaning *lower* or *inferior*) as well as **exterior** (meaning *outside* or *foreign*) and **posterior** (meaning *rear*) do not change in the feminine.

● Adjectives ending in **-án**, **-ón** and **-ín** in the masculine change to **-ana**, **-ona** and **-ina** (without an accent) in the feminine.

un gesto <u>burlón</u>	a mocking gesture
una sonrisa <u>burlona</u>	a mocking smile
un hombre <u>parlanchín</u>	a talkative man
una mujer <u>parlanchina</u>	a talkative woman

➤ Adjectives ending in a consonant which do not fall into the above categories do <u>NOT</u> change in the feminine.

un muchacho <u>joven</u>	a young boy
una muchacha <u>joven</u>	a young girl
un final <u>feliz</u>	a happy ending
una infancia <u>feliz</u>	a happy childhood

2 **Forming plural adjectives**

➤ Adjectives ending in an unaccented vowel (*a, e, i, o* or *u*) in the singular add **-s** in the plural.

el <u>último</u> tren	the last train
los <u>últimos</u> trenes	the last trains
una casa <u>vieja</u>	an old house
unas casas <u>viejas</u>	some old houses
una chica muy <u>habladora</u>	a very talkative girl
unas chicas muy <u>habladoras</u>	some very talkative girls
una pintora <u>francesa</u>	a French (woman) painter
unas pintoras <u>francesas</u>	some French (women) painters
una mesa <u>verde</u>	a green table
unas mesas <u>verdes</u>	some green tables

➤ Adjectives ending in a consonant in the masculine or feminine singular add **-es** in the plural. If there is an accent on the <u>FINAL</u> syllable in the singular, they lose it in the plural.

un chico muy <u>hablador</u>	a very talkative boy
unos chicos muy <u>habladores</u>	some very talkative boys
un pintor <u>francés</u>	a French painter
unos pintores <u>franceses</u>	some French painters

un examen <u>fácil</u>	an easy exam
unos exámenes <u>fáciles</u>	some easy exams
la tendencia <u>actual</u>	the current trend
las tendencias <u>actuales</u>	the current trends

➤ **-z** at the end of a singular adjective changes to **-ces** in the plural.

un día <u>feliz</u>	a happy day
unos días <u>felices</u>	happy days

Tip

When an adjective describes a mixture of both masculine and feminine nouns, use the <u>masculine plural</u> form of the adjective.

El pan y la fruta son <u>baratos</u>.   Bread and fruit are cheap.

Grammar Extra!

Adjectives ending in an accented vowel in the singular add **-es** in the plural.

un médico iraní	an Iranian doctor
unos médicos iraníes	some Iranian doctors

---

3   Invariable adjectives

➤ A small number of adjectives do not change in the feminine or plural. They are called <u>invariable</u> because their form <u>NEVER</u> changes, no matter what they are describing. These adjectives are often made up of more than one word – for example **azul marino** (meaning *navy blue*) – or come from the names of things – for example **naranja** (meaning *orange*).

las chaquetas <u>azul marino</u>	navy-blue jackets
los vestidos <u>naranja</u>	orange dresses

4   Short forms for adjectives

➤ The following adjectives drop the final **-o** before a <u>masculine singular</u> noun.

bueno	→	buen	→	un <u>buen</u> libro	a good book
malo	→	mal	→	<u>mal</u> tiempo	bad weather
alguno	→	algún	→	<u>algún</u> libro	some book
ninguno	→	ningún	→	<u>ningún</u> hombre	no man
uno	→	un	→	<u>un</u> día	one day

For further explanation of grammatical terms, please see pages viii-xii.

| primero | → | primer | → | el <u>primer</u> hijo | the first child |
| tercero | → | tercer | → | el <u>tercer</u> hijo | the third child |

ℹ️ Note that the adjectives **alguno** and **ninguno** add accents when they are shortened to become **algún** and **ningún**.

➤ **grande** (meaning *big* or *great*) is shortened to **gran** before a <u>singular noun</u>.

| **un gran actor** | a great actor |
| **una gran sorpresa** | a big surprise |

➤ **ciento** (meaning *a hundred*) changes to **cien** before all <u>plural nouns</u> as well as before **mil** (meaning *thousand*) and **millones** (meaning *millions*).

| **cien años** | a hundred years |
| **cien millones** | a hundred million |

ℹ️ Note that you use the form **ciento** before other numbers.

| **ciento tres** | one hundred and three |

➡️ *For more information on **Numbers**, see page 208.*

Grammar Extra!

➤ **cualquiera** drops the final **a** before any noun.

| <u>cualquier</u> día | any day |
| a <u>cualquier</u> hora | any time |

Key points

✔ Most Spanish adjectives change their form according to whether the person or thing they are describing is masculine or feminine, singular or plural.

✔ In Spanish, adjectives usually go after the noun they describe.

✔ Don't forget to make adjectives agree with the person or thing they describe – they change for the feminine and plural forms:

un hombre americano
una mujer americana
unos hombres americanos
unas mujeres americanas

✔ Some adjectives never change their form.

✔ Some adjectives drop the final -o before a masculine singular noun.

✔ **grande** and **ciento** also change before certain nouns.

Word order with adjectives

➤ When adjectives are used right beside the noun they are describing, they go <u>BEFORE</u> it in English. Spanish adjectives usually go <u>AFTER</u> the noun.

una corbata <u>azul</u>	a <u>blue</u> tie
una palabra <u>española</u>	a <u>Spanish</u> word
la página <u>siguiente</u>	the <u>following</u> page
la hora <u>exacta</u>	the <u>precise</u> time

➤ When you have two or more adjectives after the noun, you use **y** (meaning *and*) between the last two.

un hombre alto <u>y</u> delgado	a tall, thin man

➤ A number of types of Spanish adjectives go <u>BEFORE</u> the noun:

- demonstrative adjectives
  <u>este</u> sombrero   this hat

- possessive adjectives (**mi**, **tu**, **su** and so on)
  <u>mi</u> padre   my father

- numbers
  <u>tres</u> días   three days

- interrogative adjectives
  <u>¿qué</u> hombre?   which man?

- indefinite adjectives
  <u>cada</u> día   every day

- shortened adjectives
  <u>mal</u> tiempo   bad weather

For further explanation of grammatical terms, please see pages viii-xii.

➤ Some adjectives can go both <u>BEFORE</u> and <u>AFTER</u> the noun, but their meaning changes depending on where they go.

Adjective	Before Noun	Examples	After Noun	Examples
antiguo	former	un antiguo colega a former colleague	old, ancient	la historia antigua ancient history
diferente	various	diferentes idiomas various languages	different	personas diferentes different people
grande	great	un gran pintor a great painter	big	una casa grande a big house
medio	half	medio melón half a melon	average	el ingreso medio the average income
mismo	same	la misma respuesta the same answer	self, very, precisely	yo mismo myself eso mismo precisely that
nuevo	new (= *taking the place of an old one*)	mi nuevo profesor my new teacher	(brand) new (= *recently made, built, etc.*)	una bicicleta nueva a (brand) new bike
pobre	poor (= *wretched*)	esa pobre mujer that poor woman	poor (= *not rich*)	un país pobre a poor country
viejo	old (= *long-standing*)	un viejo amigo an old friend	old (= *aged*)	esas toallas viejas those old towels

Key points
✔ Most Spanish adjectives go after the noun.
✔ Certain types of adjectives go before the noun.
✔ Some adjectives can go before or after the noun – the meaning changes according to the position in the sentence.

Comparatives and superlatives of adjectives

1   Making comparisons using comparative adjectives

> **What is a comparative adjective?**
> A **comparative adjective** in English is one with -er on the end of it or
> more or less in front of it, which is used to compare people or things.
> For example: shorter, less important, more beautiful.

➤ In Spanish, to say something is cheaper, more expensive and so on, you use
  más (meaning more) before the adjective.

Esta bicicleta es <u>más barata</u>.	This bicycle is cheaper.
La verde es <u>más cara</u>.	The green one is more expensive.

➤ To say something is less expensive, less beautiful and so on, you use **menos**
  (meaning less) before the adjective.

La azul es <u>menos cara</u>.	The blue one is less expensive.

➤ To introduce the person or thing you are making the comparison with,
  use **que** (meaning than).

Es <u>más</u> alto <u>que</u> mi hermano.	He's taller than my brother.
La otra bicicleta es <u>más</u> cara <u>que</u> esta.	The other bicycle is more expensive than this one.
Esta bicicleta es <u>menos</u> cara <u>que</u> la otra.	This bicycle is less expensive than the other one.

Grammar Extra!

When than in English is followed by a verbal construction, use <u>de lo que</u> rather than
que alone.

    Está <u>más</u> cansada <u>de lo que</u> parece.   She is more tired than she seems.

---

2   Making comparisons using superlative adjectives

> **What is a superlative adjective?**
> A **superlative adjective** in English is one with -est on the end of it or
> most or least in front of it, which is used to compare people or things.
> For example: thinnest, most beautiful, least interesting.

➤ In Spanish, to say something is *the cheapest*, *the most expensive* and so on, you use **el/la/los/las** (+ noun) + **más** + adjective.

el caballo más viejo	the oldest horse
la casa más antigua	the oldest house
los hoteles más baratos	the cheapest hotels
las manzanas más caras	the most expensive apples
¿Quién es el más alto?	Who's the tallest?

➤ To say something is *the least expensive*, *the least intelligent* and so on, you use **el/la/los/las** (+ noun) + **menos** + adjective.

el hombre menos simpático	the least likeable man
la niña menos habladora	the least talkative girl
los temas menos interesantes	the least interesting topics
el problema menos urgente	the least urgent problem
¿Quién es el menos trabajador?	Who's the least hardworking?

Tip

In phrases like *the most popular girl in the school* and *the tallest man in the world*, you use **de** to translate *in*.

el hombre más alto del mundo   the tallest man in the world

---

3   **Irregular comparatives and superlatives**

➤ Just as English has some irregular comparative and superlative forms – *better* instead of '*more good*', and *worst* instead of '*most bad*' – Spanish also has a few irregular forms.

Adjective	Meaning	Comparative	Meaning	Superlative	Meaning
bueno	good	mejor	better	el mejor	the best
malo	bad	peor	worse	el peor	the worst
grande	big	mayor	older	el mayor	the oldest
pequeño, chico	small	menor	younger	el menor	the youngest

El tuyo es mejor que el mío.	Yours is better than mine.
Es el mejor de todos.	It's the best of them all.
Hoy me siento peor.	I feel worse today.
la peor alumna de la clase	the worst student in the class

i Note that **mejor**, **peor**, **mayor** and **menor** don't change their endings in the feminine. In the plural, they become **mejores**, **peores**, **mayores** and **menores**. Don't forget to use **el**, **la**, **los** or **las** as appropriate, depending on whether the person or thing described is masculine or feminine, singular or plural.

Tip

más grande and **más pequeño/más chico** are used mainly to talk about the actual size of something.

Este plato es <u>más grande</u> que aquel.	This plate is bigger than that one.
Mi casa es <u>más pequeña/más chica</u> que la tuya.	My house is smaller than yours.

mayor and **menor** are used mainly to talk about age.

mis hermanos <u>mayores</u>	my older brothers
la hija <u>menor</u>	the youngest daughter

---

4 Other ways of making comparisons

➤ To say *as ... as* (for example, *as pretty as, not as pretty as*) you use **tan ... como** in Spanish.

Pedro es <u>tan</u> alto <u>como</u> Miguel.	Pedro is as tall as Miguel.
No es <u>tan</u> atractiva <u>como</u> su madre.	She isn't as attractive as her mother.
No es <u>tan</u> grande <u>como</u> yo creía.	It isn't as big as I thought.

Grammar Extra!

In some expressions, you use **tanto** with a noun rather than **tan** with an adjective. This is because in Spanish you would use a noun where in English we would use an adjective.

Pablo tiene <u>tanto</u> miedo <u>como</u> yo.	Pablo is as frightened as I am.
Yo no tengo <u>tanta</u> hambre <u>como</u> tú.	I'm not as hungry as you are.

➤ To make an adjective stronger, you can use **muy** (meaning *very*).

Este libro es <u>muy</u> interesante.	This book is very interesting.

For further explanation of grammatical terms, please see pages viii-xii.

Grammar Extra!

For even more emphasis, you can attach -ísimo (meaning *really* or *extremely*) to the end of an adjective. Drop the final vowel if the adjective already ends in one. For example, **delgado** (meaning *thin*) becomes **delgadísimo** (meaning *really thin*).

Se compró un traje <u>carísimo</u>.	He bought himself a really expensive suit.
Es <u>delgadísima</u>.	She's extremely thin.

If you attach -ísimo, you need to drop any other accent. For example, **fácil** (meaning *easy*) becomes **facilísimo** (meaning *extremely easy*) and **rápido** (meaning *fast*) becomes **rapidísimo** (meaning *extremely fast*).

Es <u>facilísimo</u> de hacer.	It's really easy to make.
Iban <u>rapidísimo</u>.	They were going extremely fast.

When the adjective ends in **-co**, **-go** or **-z**, spelling changes are required to keep the same sound. For example, **rico** (meaning *rich*) becomes **riquísimo** (meaning *extremely rich*) and **feroz** (meaning *fierce*) becomes **ferocísimo** (meaning *extremely fierce*).

Se hizo <u>riquísimo</u>.	He became extremely rich.
un tigre <u>ferocísimo</u>	an extremely fierce tiger

⇨ *For more information on* **Spelling** *and* **Stress**, *see pages 198 and 202.*

Key points

✔ Comparative adjectives in Spanish are formed by:
- **más** + adjective + **que**
- **menos** + adjective + **que**

✔ Superlative adjectives in Spanish are formed by:
- **el/la/los/las** + **más** + adjective
- **el/la/los/las** + **menos** + adjective

✔ There are a few irregular comparative and superlative forms in Spanish.

✔ You can use **tan ... como** to say *as ... as*.

✔ To make an adjective stronger, use **muy**.

Demonstrative adjectives

> **What is a demonstrative adjective?**
> In English, a **demonstrative adjective** is a word such as *this*, *that*, *these*
> or *those* which is used with a noun to point out a particular thing or
> person. For example, _this_ woman, _that_ dog.

1 Using demonstrative adjectives

➤ Just as in English, Spanish demonstrative adjectives go <u>BEFORE</u> the noun.
   Like other adjectives in Spanish, they have to change for the feminine and
   plural forms.

	Masculine	Feminine	Meaning
Singular	este	esta	this
	ese	esa	that (*close by*)
	aquel	aquella	that (*further away*)
Plural	estos	estas	these
	esos	esas	those (*close by*)
	aquellos	aquellas	those (*further away*)

➤ Use **este/esta/estos/estas** (meaning *this/these*) to talk about things and
   people that are near <u>you</u>.

<u>**Este**</u> bolígrafo no escribe.	This pen isn't working.
Traje <u>**estos**</u> libros.	I brought these books.

➤ Use **ese/esa/esos/esas** and **aquel/aquella/aquellos/aquellas**
   (meaning *that/those*) to talk about things that are further away.

<u>**Esa**</u> revista es muy mala.	That magazine is very bad.
¿Conoces a <u>**esos**</u> señores?	Do you know those gentlemen?
No le gusta <u>**aquella**</u> muñeca.	She doesn't like that doll.
¿Ves <u>**aquellos**</u> árboles?	Do you see those trees (over there)?

2 ese or aquel?

➤ In English we use *that* and *those* to talk about anything that is not near by,
   but in Spanish you need to be a bit more precise.

For further explanation of grammatical terms, please see pages viii-xii.

➤ Use **ese/esa/esos/esas**:

- to talk about things and people that are nearer to the person you are talking to than to you

<u>ese</u> libro que estás leyendo	that book you are reading
¿Cuánto te costó <u>esa</u> falda?	How much did that skirt cost you?

- to talk about things and people that aren't very far away

No me gustan <u>esos</u> cuadros.	I don't like those pictures.

➤ Use **aquel/aquella/aquellos/aquellas** to talk about things that are further away from you and the person you are speaking to

Me gusta más <u>aquella</u> mesa.	I prefer that table (over there).

Grammar Extra!

You should use **ese/esa/esos/esas** when you are referring back to something which has already been mentioned in the conversation.

¿1999? No me acuerdo de dónde pasamos las vacaciones <u>ese</u> año.	1999? I can't remember where we went on vacation that year.

You should use **aquel/aquella/aquellos/aquellas** when you refer to something for the first time in the conversation.

<u>aquellas</u> vacaciones que pasamos en Francia	that vacation we had in France

---

Key points

✔ <u>this</u> + noun = **este/esta** + noun

✔ <u>these</u> + noun = **estos/estas** + noun

✔ <u>that</u> + noun = **ese/esa** + noun (*when the object is not far away from you or the person you're talking to*)

✔ <u>that</u> + noun = **aquel/aquella** + noun (*when the object is more distant*)

✔ <u>those</u> + noun = **esos/esas** + noun (*when the objects are not far away from you or the person you're talking to*)

✔ <u>those</u> + noun = **aquellos/aquellas** + noun (*when the objects are more distant*)

Interrogative adjectives

> **What is an interrogative adjective?**
> An **interrogative adjective** is a question word or expression used with a noun, such as *which, what, how much* and *how many*. For example: *Which shirt are you going to wear?*; *How much time do we have?*

➤ In Spanish the interrogative adjectives are **qué** (meaning *which* or *what*) and **cuánto/cuánta/cuántos/cuántas** (meaning *how much/how many*). Note that, like all other question words in Spanish, **qué** and **cuánto** have accents on them.

➤ **¿qué?** (meaning *what?* or *which?*) doesn't change for the feminine and plural forms.

¿Qué clase de diccionario necesitas?	What kind of dictionary do you need?
¿Qué instrumentos tocas?	Which instruments do you play?
¿Qué ofertas has recibido?	What offers have you received?
¿Qué libro te gusta más?	Which book do you like best?

➤ **¿cuánto?** means the same as *how much?* in English. It changes to **¿cuánta?** in the feminine form.

¿Cuánto dinero te queda?	How much money do you have left?
¿Cuánta fruta compraste?	How much fruit did you buy?

[*i*] Note that with **gente** (meaning *people*), which is a feminine singular noun, **cuánta** must be used.

¿Cuánta gente vino?	How many people came?

➤ **¿cuántos?** means the same as *how many?* in English. It changes to **¿cuántas?** in the feminine plural.

¿Cuántos primos tienes?	How many cousins do you have?
¿Cuántas personas van a venir?	How many people are coming?

> *Tip*
> Don't forget to add the opening, upside-down question mark in Spanish questions.

For further explanation of grammatical terms, please see pages viii-xii.

Grammar Extra!

In English we can say, *Tell me what time it is*, *He asked me how much sugar there was* and *I don't know which dress to choose* to express doubt, report a question, or ask a question in a roundabout or indirect way. In Spanish you can use **qué** and **cuánto/cuánta/cuántos/cuántas** in the same way.

Dime <u>qué</u> hora es.	Tell me what time it is.
Me preguntó <u>cuánto</u> dinero tenía.	He asked me how much money I had.
No sé <u>qué</u> vestido ponerme.	I don't know which dress to wear.
No sé a <u>qué</u> hora llegó.	I don't know what time she arrived.
Dime <u>cuántas</u> postales quieres.	Tell me how many postcards you'd like.

Adjectives used in exclamations

➤ In Spanish ¡qué...! is often used where, in English, we might say *What a ...!*

¡<u>Qué</u> **lástima!**	What a pity!
¡<u>Qué</u> **sorpresa!**	What a surprise!

Tip

Don't forget to add the opening, upside-down exclamation point in Spanish exclamations.

Grammar Extra!

¡**qué**...! combines with **más** or **tan** and an adjective in Spanish to mean *What (a)...!* in English.

¡Qué hombre **más insoportable!**	What an intolerable man!
¡Qué tiempo **más horrible!**	What terrible weather!
¡Qué gente **tan simpática!**	What nice people!

In Spanish **cuánto/cuánta/cuántos/cuántas** can be used to mean *What a lot of ...!* in English.

¡**Cuánto dinero!**	What a lot of money!
¡**Cuánta gente!**	What a lot of people!
¡**Cuántos CDs!**	What a lot of CDs!
¡**Cuánto tiempo!**	What a long time!

For further explanation of grammatical terms, please see pages viii-xii.

Possessive adjectives (1)

> **What is a possessive adjective?**
> In English a **possessive adjective** is one of the words *my, your, his, her, its, our* or *their* used with a noun to show that one person or thing belongs to another.

➤ Like other adjectives in Spanish, possessive adjectives change for the plural and sometimes for the feminine forms.

Singular		Plural		Meaning
masculine	feminine	masculine	feminine	
mi	mi	mis	mis	my
tu	tu	tus	tus	your (*belonging to someone you address as* **tú**)
su	su	sus	sus	his; her; its; your (*belonging to someone you address as* **usted**)
nuestro	nuestra	nuestros	nuestras	our
vuestro*	vuestra*	vuestros*	vuestras*	your (*belonging to people you address as* **vosotros/vosotras**)
su	su	sus	sus	their; your (*belonging to people you address as* **ustedes**)

➪ *These forms are not normally used in Latin America, where the pronoun **ustedes** is used instead of **vosotros**. For more information on **Ways of saying 'you' in Spanish**, see page 44.*

¿Dónde está <u>tu</u> hermana?	Where's your sister?
José perdió <u>sus</u> llaves.	José lost his keys.
¿Dónde están <u>nuestros</u> pasaportes?	Where are our passports?
¿Por qué no traen a <u>sus</u> hijos?	Why don't you bring your children?
Mis tíos van a vender <u>su</u> casa.	My uncle and aunt are going to sell their house.

Típ

Possessive adjectives agree with what they describe <u>NOT</u> with the person who owns that thing.

Pablo trajo <u>su</u> diccionario.	Pablo brought his dictionary.
Pablo trajo <u>sus</u> diccionarios.	Pablo brought his dictionaries.

i Note that possessive adjectives aren't normally used with parts of the body. You usually use the <u>definite article</u> instead.

Tiene <u>los</u> ojos verdes.	He has green eyes.
No puedo mover <u>las</u> piernas.	I can't move my legs.

⇨ *For more information on **Articles**, see page 10.*

Tip

As **su** and **sus** can mean *his, her, its, your* or *their*, it can sometimes be a bit confusing. When you need to avoid confusion, you can use the Spanish equivalent of *of him* and so on.

<u>su</u> casa	→	la casa <u>de él</u>	his house (*literally: the house of him*)
<u>sus</u> amigos	→	los amigos <u>de usted</u>	your friends (*literally: the friends of you*)
<u>sus</u> padres	→	los padres <u>de ellos</u>	their parents (*literally: the parents of them*)
<u>su</u> abrigo	→	el abrigo <u>de ella</u>	her coat (*literally: the coat of her*)

⇨ *For more information on **Personal pronouns**, see page 42.*

Key points

✔ The Spanish possessive adjectives are:
  • **mi/tu/su/nuestro/vuestro** (in Spain)/**su** with a masculine singular noun
  • **mi/tu/su/nuestra/vuestra** (in Spain)/**su** with a feminine singular noun
  • **mis/tus/sus/nuestros/vuestros** (in Spain)/**sus** with a masculine plural noun
  • **mis/tus/sus/nuestras/vuestras** (in Spain)/**sus** with a feminine plural noun

✔ Possessive adjectives come before the noun they refer to. They agree with what they describe, rather than with the person who owns that thing.

✔ Possessive adjectives are not usually used with parts of the body. Use **el/la/los** or **las** as appropriate instead.

✔ To avoid confusion, it is sometimes clearer to use **el coche de él/ella/ellas/ellos/usted** and so on rather than **su coche**.

For further explanation of grammatical terms, please see pages viii-xii.

Possessive adjectives (2)

➤ In Spanish, there is a second set of possessive adjectives, which mean (of) mine, (of) yours and so on. Like other adjectives in Spanish, they change in the feminine and plural forms.

Singular		Plural		Meaning
masculine	feminine	masculine	feminine	
mío	mía	míos	mías	mine/of mine
tuyo	tuya	tuyos	tuyas	yours/of yours (*belonging to tú*)
suyo	suya	suyos	suyas	his/of his; hers/of hers; of its; yours/of yours (*belonging to usted*)
nuestro	nuestra	nuestros	nuestras	ours/of ours
vuestro*	vuestra*	vuestros*	vuestras*	yours/of yours (*belonging to vosotros/as*)
suyo	suya	suyos	suyas	theirs/of theirs; yours/of yours (*belonging to ustedes*)

⇨ * These forms are not normally used in Latin America, where the pronoun **ustedes** is used instead of **vosotros**. For more information on **Ways of saying 'you' in Spanish**, see page 44.

un amigo <u>mío</u>	a (male) friend of mine, one of my (male) friends
una revista <u>tuya</u>	a magazine of yours, one of your magazines
una tía <u>suya</u>	an aunt of his/hers/theirs/yours, one of his/her/their/your aunts
unas amigas <u>nuestras</u>	some (female) friends of ours, some of our friends
¿De quién es esta bufanda? – Es <u>mía</u>.	Whose scarf is this? – It's mine.

ℹ️ Note that unlike the other possessive adjectives, these adjectives go <u>AFTER</u> the noun they describe.

un primo <u>mío</u>	a (male) cousin of mine, one of my cousins

Tip

Possessive adjectives agree with what they describe <u>NOT</u> with the person who owns that thing.

Estos guantes son <u>míos</u>.   These gloves are mine.

Grammar Extra!

mío/mía and so on are also used in exclamations and when addressing someone. In this case they mean the same as *my* in English.

¡Dios <u>mío</u>!	My God!
amor <u>mío</u>	my love, (my) darling
Muy señor <u>mío</u>	Dear Sir (*in very formal letters*)

Indefinite adjectives

> **What is an indefinite adjective?**
> An **indefinite adjective** is one of a small group of adjectives used to talk about people or things in a general way without saying exactly who or what they are. For example: *several*, *all*, *every*.

➤ In English indefinite adjectives do not change, but in Spanish most indefinite adjectives change for the feminine and plural forms.

Singular		Plural		Meaning
masculine	**feminine**	**masculine**	**feminine**	
algún	alguna	algunos	algunas	some; any
cada	cada			each; every
mismo	misma	mismos	mismas	same
mucho	mucha	muchos	muchas	a lot of, much, many
otro	otra	otros	otras	another; other
poco	poca	pocos	pocas	little; few
tanto	tanta	tantos	tantas	so much; so many
todo	toda	todos	todas	all; every
		varios	varias	several

<u>algún</u> día	some day
<u>algunas</u> personas	some people
el <u>mismo</u> día	the same day
las <u>mismas</u> películas	the same movies
<u>otro</u> tren	another train
<u>otra</u> manzana	another apple
<u>poca</u> agua	(a) little water
<u>pocos</u> amigos	few friends

🛈 Note that you can never use **otro** (meaning *other* or *another*) with **un** or **una**.

¿Me das <u>otra</u> manzana?	Will you give me another apple?
¿Tienes <u>otro</u> suéter?	Do you have another sweater?

> *Tip*
> *Some* and *any* are usually not translated before nouns that you can't count, like bread, butter, water.
>
> | | |
> |---|---|
> | **Hay pan en la mesa.** | There's some bread on the table. |
> | **¿Quieres café?** | Would you like some coffee? |
> | **¿Hay leche?** | Is there any milk? |
> | **No hay mantequilla.** | There isn't any butter. |

➤ todo/toda/todos/todas (meaning *all* or *every*) can be followed by:

- a definite article (**el, la, los, las**)

Bailaron <u>toda la</u> noche.	They danced all night.
Vengo <u>todos los</u> días.	I come every day.

- a demonstrative adjective (**este, ese, aquel** and so on)

Planché <u>toda esta</u> ropa.	I ironed all these clothes.

- a possessive adjective (**mi, tu, su** and so on)

Voy a invitar a <u>todos mis</u> amigos.	I'm going to invite all my friends.

- a place name

Lo sabe <u>todo Bogotá</u>.	All of Bogotá knows it.

⇨ *For more information on **Articles**, **Demonstrative adjectives** and **Possessive adjectives**, see pages 10, 30 and 35.*

➤ As in English, Spanish indefinite adjectives come <u>BEFORE</u> the noun they describe.

las <u>mismas</u> películas	the same movies

> **Key points**
> ✔ Like other adjectives, Spanish indefinite adjectives (such as **otro** and **todo**) must agree with what they describe.
> ✔ They go before the noun to which they relate.

Pronouns

> **What is a pronoun?**
> A **pronoun** is a word you use instead of a noun, when you do not need
> or want to name someone or something directly. For example: *it*, *you*,
> *none*.

➤ There are several different types of pronoun:
- Personal pronouns such as *I*, *you*, *he*, *her* and *they*, which are used
  to refer to you, the person you are talking to, or other people and
  things. They can be either subject pronouns (*I*, *you*, *he* and so on) or
  object pronouns (*him*, *her*, *them*, and so on).
- Possessive pronouns like *mine* and *yours*, which show who someone or
  something belongs to.
- Indefinite pronouns like *someone* or *nothing*, which refer to people or
  things in a general way without saying exactly who or what they are.
- Relative pronouns like *who*, *which* or *that*, which link two parts of a
  sentence together.
- Interrogative pronouns like *who*, *what* or *which*, which are used in
  questions.
- Demonstrative pronouns like *this* or *those*, which point things or people
  out.
- Reflexive pronouns, a type of object pronoun that forms part of
  Spanish reflexive verbs like **levantarse** (meaning *to get up* or *to stand up*)
  or **llamarse** (meaning *to be called*).

⇨ *For more information on* **Reflexive verbs**, *see page* 92.

➤ Pronouns often stand in for a noun to save repeating it.
> I finished my homework and gave <u>it</u> to my teacher.
> Do you remember Jack? I saw <u>him</u> this past weekend.

➤ Word order with personal pronouns is usually different in Spanish and
English.

Personal pronouns: subject

> **What is a subject pronoun?**
> A **subject pronoun** is a word such as *I*, *he*, *she* and *they*, that carries out the action expressed by the verb. Pronouns stand in for nouns when it is clear who or what is being talked about. For example: *My brother isn't here at the moment. He'll be back in an hour.*

1 **Using subject pronouns**

➤ Here are the Spanish subject pronouns:

Singular	Meaning	Plural	Meaning
yo	I	**nosotros** (*masculine*)/ **nosotras** (*feminine*)	we
tú	you	**vosotros** (*masculine*)/ **vosotras** (*feminine*)*	you
él	he	**ellos** (*masculine*)	they
ella	she	**ellas** (*feminine*)	they
usted (Vd.)	you	**ustedes** (Vds.)	you

⇨ *__Vosotros__ and **vosotras** are not normally used in Latin America, where* **ustedes** *is used instead. For more information on **Ways of saying 'you' in Spanish**, see page 44.*

ⓘ *Note that there is an accent on* **tú** (*you*) *and* **él** (*he*) *so that they are not confused with* **tu** (*your*) *and* **el** (*the*).

> *Tip*
> The abbreviations **Vd.** and **Vds.** are often used instead of **usted** and **ustedes**.

➤ In English, we use subject pronouns all the time – *I walk, you eat, they are going*. In Spanish, you don't need them if the verb endings and context make it clear who the subject is. For example **hablo español** can only mean *I speak Spanish* since the **-o** ending on the verb is only used with *I*. Similarly, **hablamos francés** can only mean *we speak French* since the **-amos** ending is only used with *we*. So the subject pronouns are not needed in these examples.

Tengo un hermano.	<u>I</u> have a brother.
Tenemos dos perros.	<u>We</u> have two dogs.

For further explanation of grammatical terms, please see pages viii–xii.

➤ Spanish subject pronouns are normally only used:

- for emphasis

¿Y <u>tú</u> qué piensas?	What do <u>you</u> think about it?
<u>Ellos</u> sí que llegaron tarde.	<u>They</u> really did arrive late.

- for contrast or clarity

<u>Yo</u> estudio español pero <u>él</u> estudia francés.	<u>I</u> study Spanish but <u>he</u> studies French.
<u>Él</u> llamó pero <u>ella</u> no.	<u>He</u> called but <u>she</u> didn't.

- after **ser** (meaning *to be*)

Soy <u>yo</u>.	It's <u>me</u>.
¿Eres <u>tú</u>?	Is that <u>you</u>?

- in comparisons after **que** and **como**

Enrique es más alto que <u>yo</u>.	Enrique is taller than <u>I</u> am *or* than me.
Antonio no es tan alto como <u>tú</u>.	Antonio isn't as tall as <u>you</u> (are).

⇨ *For more information on **Making comparisons**, see page 26.*

- on their own without a verb

¿Quién dijo eso? – <u>Él</u>.	Who said that? – <u>He</u> did.
¿Quién quiere venir? – <u>Yo</u>.	Who wants to come? – <u>I</u> do.

- after certain prepositions

Es para <u>ella</u>.	It's for <u>her</u>.

⇨ *For more information on **Pronouns after prepositions**, see page 54.*

ℹ️ Note that *it* used as the subject, and *they* referring to things, are <u>NEVER</u> translated into Spanish.

¿Qué es? – Es una sorpresa.	What is it? – <u>It</u>'s a surprise.
¿Qué son? – Son abrelatas.	What are they? – <u>They</u> are can openers.

2 Ways of saying 'you' in Spanish

➤ In English, we have only <u>one</u> way of saying *you*. In Spanish, there are <u>several</u> words to choose from. The word you use depends on:
  - whether you are talking to one person or more than one person
  - whether you are talking to a friend or family member, or someone else.

➤ If you are talking to one person <u>you know well</u>, such as a friend, a young person or a relative, use **tú**.

➤ If you are talking to one person <u>you do not know so well</u>, such as your teacher, your boss or a stranger, use the polite form, **usted**.

➤ If you are talking to <u>more than one person</u> you know well, use **ustedes** in Latin America. Use **vosotros** (or **vosotras**, if you are talking to women only) in Spain.

➤ Use **ustedes** everywhere if you are talking to more than one person <u>you do not know so well</u>.

> *Tip*
>
> Remember that adjectives describing **tú** and **usted** should be feminine if you're talking to a woman or girl, while adjectives describing **ustedes** should be feminine plural if you're talking to women or girls only.

3 Using the plural subject pronouns

➤ When you are talking about males only, use **nosotros**, **vosotros** (in Spain only) or **ellos**.

> <u>Nosotros</u> no somos italianos.   <u>We</u> are not Italian.

➤ When you are talking about females only, use **nosotras**, **vosotras** (in Spain only) or **ellas**.

> Hablé con mis hermanas.   I spoke to my sisters.
> <u>Ellas</u> estaban de acuerdo   <u>They</u> agreed with me.
> conmigo.

➤ When you are talking about both males and females, use **nosotros**, **vosotros** (in Spain) or **ellos**.

> Martín y Raquel no llegaron   Martín and Raquel didn't arrive
> hasta la medianoche.   till midnight.
> <u>Ellos</u> sí que llegaron tarde.   <u>They</u> really did arrive late.

For further explanation of grammatical terms, please see pages viii-xii.

Key points

✔ The Spanish subject pronouns are: **yo**, **tú**, **él**, **ella**, **usted** in the singular, and **nosotros/nosotras**, **vosotros/vosotras** (in Spain only), **ellos/ellas**, **ustedes** in the plural.

✔ Don't use the subject pronouns with verbs except for emphasis or clarity.

✔ Make sure you choose the correct form of the verb.

✔ Do use the subject pronouns:
  • after **ser** (meaning *to be*)
  • in comparisons after **que** and **como**
  • in one-word answers to questions.

✔ Choose the word for *you* carefully. Remember to think about how many people you are talking to and your relationship with them when deciding between **tú**, **usted** and **ustedes** (or **vosotros/vosotras** in Spain only).

✔ *It* as the subject of the verb, and *they* when it refers to things are **NOT** translated in Spanish.

✔ Use masculine plural forms (**nosotros**, **vosotros** (in Spain only), **ellos**) for groups made up of men and women.

✔ Remember to make any adjectives describing the subject agree.

Personal pronouns: direct object

> **What is a direct object pronoun?**
> A **direct object pronoun** is a word such as *me*, *him*, *us* and *them*, which is used instead of the noun to stand in for the person or thing most directly affected by the action expressed by the verb.

1 | Using direct object pronouns

➤ Direct object pronouns stand in for nouns when it is clear who or what is being talked about, and save having to repeat the noun.

   I've lost my glasses. Have you seen <u>them</u>?
   'Have you met Jo?' – 'Yes, I really like <u>her</u>!'

➤ Here are the Spanish direct object pronouns:

Singular	Meaning	Plural	Meaning
me	me	nos	us
te	you (*relating to* **tú**)	los	you (*relating to* **ustedes** *when there are males in the group*)
		las	you (*relating to* **ustedes** *when there are no males in the group*)
		os*	you (*relating to* **vosotros/vosotras**)
lo	him it (*masculine*) you (*relating to* **usted** *– masculine*)	los	them (*relating to* **ellos**)
la	her it (*feminine*) you (*relating to* **usted** *– feminine*)	las	them (*relating to* **ellas**)

*Not normally used in Latin America.

Te quiero.	I love you.
No **los** toques.	Don't touch them.

[i] Note that you cannot use the Spanish direct object pronouns on their own without a verb or after a preposition such as **a** or **de**.

➪ *For more information on* **Pronouns after prepositions**, *see page 54.*

2   Word order with direct object pronouns

➤ The direct object pronoun usually comes <u>BEFORE</u> the verb.

¿Las ves?	Can you see them?
¿No me oyen?	Can't you hear me?
Tu hija no nos conoce.	Your daughter doesn't know us.
¿Lo has visto?	Have you seen it?

➤ In orders and instructions telling someone <u>TO DO</u> something, the pronoun is attached to the end of the verb to form one word.

Ayúdame.	Help me.
Acompáñanos.	Come with us.

i Note that you will often need to add a written accent to preserve the spoken stress when attaching pronouns to the end of verbs.

⇨ *For more information on **Stress**, see page 202.*

➤ In orders and instructions telling someone <u>NOT TO DO</u> something, the pronoun is <u>NOT</u> attached to the end of the verb.

No los toques.	Don't touch them.

➤ If the pronoun is the object of an infinitive (the *to* form of the verb) or a gerund (the *-ing* form of the verb), you always attach the pronoun to the end of the verb to form one word, unless the infinitive or gerund follows another verb. Again, you may have to add a written accent to preserve the stress.

Se fue después de arreglarlo.	He left after fixing it.
Practicándolo, aprenderás.	You'll learn by practicing it.

⇨ *For more information on **Verbs** and **Gerunds**, see pages 69 and 128.*

➤ Where an infinitive or gerund follows another verb, you can put the pronoun either at the end of the infinitive or gerund, or before the other verb.

Vienen a vernos *or*	
Nos vienen a ver.	They are coming to see us.
Está comiéndolo *or*	
Lo está comiendo.	He's eating it.

⇨ *For further information on the **Order of object pronouns**, see page 52.*

3 Special use of lo

➤ **lo** is sometimes used to refer back to an idea or information that has already been introduced. The word *it* is often missed out in English.

¿Va a venir María? – No <u>lo</u> sé.	Is María coming? – I don't know.
Ya habían comido pero no nos <u>lo</u> dijeron.	They had already eaten, but they didn't tell us.

Key points

✔ The Spanish direct object pronouns are: **me**, **te**, **lo**, **la** in the singular, and **nos**, **os** (in Spain only), **los**, **las** in the plural.

✔ The object pronoun usually comes before the verb.

✔ Object pronouns are attached to the end of infinitives, gerunds or verbs instructing someone to do something.

✔ If an infinitive or gerund follows another verb, you can choose whether to attach the object pronoun to the end of the infinitive or gerund or to put it before the first verb.

✔ **lo** is sometimes used to refer back to an idea or information that has already been introduced.

For further explanation of grammatical terms, please see pages viii-xii.

Personal pronouns: indirect object

> **What is an indirect object pronoun?**
> An **indirect object pronoun** is used instead of a noun to show the person or thing an action is intended to benefit or harm, for example, *me* in *He gave me a book.*; *Can you get me a towel?*; *He wrote to me*.

1 Using indirect object pronouns

➤ It is important to understand the difference between direct and indirect object pronouns in English, as they can have different forms in Spanish.

➤ You can usually test whether an object is a direct object or an indirect one by asking questions about the action using *what* and *who*:

- an indirect object answers the question *who ... to?* or *who ... for?*, equally *what ... to?* or *what ... for?*

  He gave me a book. → *Who did he give the book to?* → me
  (=*indirect object pronoun*)
  Can you get me a towel? → *Who can you get a towel for?* → me
  (=*indirect object pronoun*)
  We got some paint for it. → *What did you get the paint for?* → it
  (=*indirect object pronoun*)

- If something answers the question *what* or *who*, then it is the direct object and <u>NOT</u> the indirect object.

  He gave me a book. → *What did he give me?* → a book
  (=*direct object*)
  I saw Mandy. → *Who did you see?* → Mandy
  (=*direct object*)
  We got some paint for it. → *What did you get?* → some paint
  (=*direct object*)

i Note that a verb won't necessarily have both a direct and an indirect object.

➤ Here are the Spanish indirect object pronouns:

Singular	Meaning	Plural	Meaning
me	me, to me, for me	nos	us, to us, for us
te	you, to you, for you (*relating to* **tú**)	les os*	you, to you, for you (*relating to* **ustedes**) you, to you, for you (*relating to* **vosotros/vosotras**)
le	him, to him, for him her, to her, for her it, to it, for it you, to you, for you (*relating to* **usted**)	les	them, to them, for them you, to you, for you (*relating to* **ustedes**)

Not normally used in Latin America.

➤ The pronouns shown in the table are used instead of using the prepositions **a** or **para** with a noun.

> **Mandó una carta <u>a todos los socios</u>.** She sent a letter to all the members. → <u>Les</u> **mandó una carta.** She sent them a letter.
>
> **Compra un regalo <u>para tu hermana</u>.** Buy your sister a present. →
> **Cómpra<u>le</u> un regalo.** Buy her a present.

➤ Some Spanish verbs like **mirar** (meaning *to look at*), **esperar** (meaning *to wait for*) and **buscar** (meaning *to look for*) take a direct object, because the Spanish construction is different from the English.

Grammar Extra!

You should usually use direct object pronouns rather than indirect object pronouns when replacing the personal **a** + <u>noun</u>.

> **Vi <u>a Teresa</u>.** → <u>La</u> **vi.**   I saw Teresa. → I saw her.

⇨   *For more information on* **Personal a**, *see page 184.*

---

2 | <u>Word order with indirect object pronouns</u>

➤ The indirect object pronoun usually comes <u>BEFORE</u> the verb.

Sofía <u>le</u> escribió.	Sofía wrote to him.
¿<u>Le</u> escribió Sofía?	Did Sofía write to him?
Carlos no <u>nos</u> habla.	Carlos doesn't speak to us.
¿Qué <u>te</u> pedían?	What were they asking you for?

➤ In orders and instructions telling someone <u>TO DO</u> something, the pronoun is attached to the end of the verb to form one word.

> **Contésta<u>me</u>.**   Answer me.
> **Di<u>me</u> la respuesta.**   Tell me the answer.

ⓘ Note that you will often need to add a written accent to preserve the spoken stress.

⇨ *For more information on **Stress**, see page 202.*

➤ In orders and instructions telling someone <u>NOT TO DO</u> something, the pronoun is <u>NOT</u> attached to the end of the verb.

> **No <u>me</u> digas la respuesta.**   Don't tell me the answer.

➤ If the pronoun is the object of an infinitive (the *to* form of the verb) or a gerund (the *-ing* form of the verb), you always attach the pronoun to the end of the verb to form one word, unless the infinitive or gerund follows another verb. Again, you may have to add a written accent to preserve the stress.

> **Dar<u>le</u> tu dirección no fue**   It wasn't very smart to give him
> **muy prudente.**   your address.
> **Gritándo<u>le</u> así lo vas a**   You'll frighten him by shouting at
> **asustar.**   him like that.

➤ Where an infinitive or gerund follows another verb, you can put the pronoun either at the end of the infinitive or gerund, or before the other verb.

> **Quiero decir<u>te</u> algo.** *or*   I want to tell you something.
> **<u>Te</u> quiero decir algo.**
> **Estoy escribiéndo<u>le</u>.** *or*   I am writing to him/her.
> **<u>Le</u> estoy escribiendo.**

⇨ *For further information on the **Order of object pronouns**, see page 52.*

Key points
✔ The Spanish indirect object pronouns are: **me**, **te**, **le** in the singular, and **nos**, **os** (in Spain only), **les** in the plural.
✔ They can replace the prepositions **a** or **para** (meaning *to* or *for*) + noun.
✔ Like the direct object pronoun, the indirect object pronoun usually comes before the verb.
✔ Object pronouns are attached to the end of infinitives, gerunds or verbs instructing someone to do something.
✔ If an infinitive or gerund follows another verb, you can choose whether to attach the object pronoun to the end of the infinitive or gerund or to put it before the first verb.

Order of object pronouns

➤ Two object pronouns are often used together in the same sentence (for example: *he gave me them* or *he gave them to me*). In Spanish, you should always put the indirect object pronoun <u>BEFORE</u> the direct object pronoun.

Indirect		Direct
me	<u>BEFORE</u>	lo
te		la
nos		los
os (*in Spain only*)		las

Ana <u>nos lo</u> mandará mañana.	Ana will send it to us tomorrow.
¿<u>Te los</u> mostró mi hermana?	Did my sister show them to you?
No <u>me lo</u> digas.	Don't tell me (that).
No quiere prestár<u>nosla</u>.	He won't lend it to us.

➤ You have to use **se** instead of **le** (*to him, to her, to you*) and **les** (*to them, to you*) before the object pronouns **lo**, **la**, **los**, or **las**.

<u>Se</u> lo di ayer.	I gave it to him/her/you/them yesterday.
<u>Se</u> las enviaré.	I'll send them to him/her/you/them.

Key points

✔ When combining two object pronouns, put the indirect object pronoun before the direct object pronoun.

✔ Use **se** as the indirect object pronoun rather than **le** or **les** when there is more than one object pronoun.

For further explanation of grammatical terms, please see pages viii-xii.

Further information on object pronouns

➤ The object pronoun **le** can mean (to) him, (to) her and (to) you; **les** can mean (to) them and (to) you, and **se** can mean all of these things, which could lead to some confusion.

➤ To make it clear which one is meant, **a él** (meaning to him), **a ella** (meaning to her), **a usted** (meaning to you) and so on can be added to the phrase.

A ella le escriben mucho.	They write to her often.
Se lo van a mandar pronto a ellos.	They will be sending it to them soon.

➤ When a noun object comes before the verb, the corresponding object pronoun must be used too.

A tu hermano lo conozco bien. I know your brother well.
(literally: Your brother I know him well.)
A María la vemos algunas veces. We sometimes see María.
(literally: María, we see her sometimes.)

➤ Indirect object pronouns are often used in constructions with the definite article and parts of the body or items of clothing to show who they belong to. In English, we use a possessive adjective.

La chaqueta le quedaba grande.	His jacket was too big for him.
Me dio la mano.	He held my hand/shook my hand.

⇨ *For more information on **The definite article** and **Possessive adjectives**, see pages 11, 35 and 37.*

➤ Indirect object pronouns can also be used in certain common phrases which use reflexive verbs.

Se me perdieron las llaves.	I lost my keys.

⇨ *For more information on **Reflexive verbs**, see page 92.*

ⓘ Note that in Spain, you will often hear **le** and **les** used instead of **lo** and **los** as direct object pronouns when referring to men and boys.

Pronouns after prepositions

➤ In English, we use *me, you, him* and so on after a preposition (for example: *he came <u>toward me</u>; it's <u>for you</u>; books <u>by him</u>*). In Spanish, there is a special set of pronouns which are used after prepositions.

➤ In Spanish, the pronouns used after a preposition are the same as the subject pronouns, except for the forms **mí** (meaning *me*), **ti** (meaning *you*), and **sí** (meaning *himself, herself, yourself, themselves, yourselves*).

Singular	Meaning	Plural	Meaning
mí	me	nosotros	us (*masculine*)
ti	you	nosotras	us (*feminine*)
él	him	vosotros*	you (*masculine*)
ella	her	vosotras*	you (*feminine*)
usted (Vd.)	you	ellos	them (*masculine*)
sí	himself	ellas	them (*feminine*)
	herself	ustedes (Vds.)	you
	yourself	sí	themselves yourselves

*Not normally used in Latin America, where **ustedes** is used instead.

Pienso <u>en ti</u>.	I think about you.
¿Son <u>para mí</u>?	Are they for me?
No he sabido nada <u>de él.</u>	I haven't heard from him.
Es <u>para ella</u>.	It's for her.
Venían <u>hacia nosotros</u>.	They were coming toward us.
Volvió <u>sin ellos</u>.	He came back without them.
Volaban <u>sobre ustedes</u>.	They were flying above you.

⚠ Note that **mí**, **sí** and **él** each have an accent, to distinguish them from **mi** (meaning *my*), **si** (meaning *if*), and **el** (meaning *the*), but **ti** does not have an accent.

➤ These pronouns are often used for emphasis.

¿A <u>ti</u> no te escriben?	Don't they write to <u>you</u>?
Me lo manda a <u>mí</u>, no a <u>ti</u>.	She's sending it to <u>me</u>, not to you.

➤ **con** (meaning *with*) is combined with **mí**, **ti** and **sí** to form:

- **conmigo**   with me

  Ven <u>conmigo</u>.   Come with me.

For further explanation of grammatical terms, please see pages viii–xii.

- **contigo**   with you
  Me gusta estar <u>contigo</u>.   I like being with you.
- **consigo**   with himself/herself/yourself/themselves/yourselves
  Lo trajeron <u>consigo</u>.   They brought it with them.

➤ **entre, hasta, salvo, menos** and **según** are always used with the <u>subject pronouns</u> (**yo** and **tú**), rather than with the object pronouns (**mí** and **ti**).

- **entre**   between, among
  <u>entre</u> tú y yo   between you and me
- **hasta**   even, including
  <u>Hasta</u> yo puedo hacerlo.   Even I can do it.
- **menos**   except
  todos <u>menos</u> yo   everybody except me
- **salvo**   except
  todos <u>salvo</u> yo   everyone except me
- **según**   according to
  <u>según</u> tú   according to you

⇨ *For more information on **Subject pronouns**, see page 42.*

Key points

✔ Most prepositions are followed by the forms: **mí, ti, sí** and so on.

✔ **entre, hasta, menos, salvo** and **según** are followed by the subject pronouns **yo** and **tú**.

✔ **con** is combined with **mí, ti** and **sí** to form **conmigo, contigo** and **consigo**.

Possessive pronouns

> **What is a possessive pronoun?**
> A **possessive pronoun** is one of the words *mine, yours, hers, his, ours* or *theirs*, which are used instead of a noun to show that one person or thing belongs to another. For example: *Ask Carole if this pen is <u>hers</u>.; <u>Mine</u>'s <u>the blue one</u>*.

➤ Here are the Spanish possessive pronouns:

Masculine singular	Feminine singular	Masculine plural	Feminine plural	Meaning
el mío	la mía	los míos	las mías	mine
el tuyo	la tuya	los tuyos	las tuyas	yours (*belonging to tú*)
el suyo	la suya	los suyos	las suyas	his; hers; its; yours (*belonging to usted*)
el nuestro	la nuestra	los nuestros	las nuestras	ours
el vuestro*	la vuestra*	los vuestros*	las vuestras*	yours (*belonging to vosotros/vosotras*)
el suyo	la suya	los suyos	las suyas	theirs; yours (*belonging to ustedes*)

⇨ *Not normally used in Latin America, where* **el suyo**, **la suya**, *etc. are used instead. For more information on* **Ways of saying 'you' in Spanish**, *see page 44*.

Pregúntale a Cristina si este abrigo es <u>el suyo</u>.	Ask Cristina if this coat is hers.
¿Qué equipo ganó, <u>el suyo</u> o <u>el nuestro</u>?	Which team won – theirs or ours?
Mi perro es más joven que <u>el tuyo</u>.	My dog is younger than yours.
Daniel pensó que esos libros eran <u>los suyos</u>.	Daniel thought those books were his.
Si no tienes lápices, te prestaré <u>los míos</u>.	If you haven't got any pencils, I'll lend you mine.
Nuestros productos compiten con <u>los suyos</u>.	Our products compete with yours.

Tip

In Spanish, possessive pronouns agree with what they describe, <u>NOT</u> with the person who owns that thing. For example, **el suyo** can mean *his*, *hers*, *yours* or *theirs*, but can only be used to replace a masculine singular noun.

ℹ️ Note that the prepositions **a** and **de** combine with the article **el** to form **al** and **del**. For example: **a** + **el mío** becomes **al mío**, and **de** + **el mío** becomes **del mío**.

Prefiero tu barrio <u>al mío</u>.	I prefer your neighborhood to mine.
Su vestido se parece <u>al tuyo</u>.	Her dress is similar to yours.
Mi abrigo estaba al lado <u>del suyo</u>.	My coat was next to hers/his/yours.
El colegio de Lupe está cerca <u>del nuestro</u>.	Lupe's school is near ours.

➤ Instead of **el suyo/la suya/los suyos/las suyas**, it is sometimes clearer to say **el/la/los/las de usted**, **el/la/los/las de ustedes**, **el/la/los/las de ellos** and so on. You choose between **el/la/los/las** to agree with the noun that is being referred to.

mi casa y <u>la de</u> ustedes	my house and yours

➤ **el/la/los/las de** can also be used with a name or other noun that is referring to somebody.

El dibujo de Juan no está mal pero yo prefiero <u>el de</u> Ana.	Juan's drawing is not bad, but I prefer Ana's.
Nuestro jardín no es tan grande como <u>el de</u> los vecinos.	Our yard isn't as big as the neighbors'.

Key points

✔ The Spanish possessive pronouns are **el mío**, **el tuyo**, **el suyo**, **el nuestro**, **el vuestro** (in Spain only) and **el suyo** when they stand in for a masculine noun. If they stand in for a feminine or a plural noun, their forms change accordingly.

✔ In Spanish, the pronoun you choose has to agree with the noun it replaces and <u>not</u> with the person who owns that thing.

✔ **el/la/los/las de** are used with a noun or pronoun to mean the *one(s) belonging to ...*

Indefinite pronouns

> **What is an indefinite pronoun?**
> An **indefinite pronoun** is one of a small group of pronouns, such as *everything*, *nobody* and *something*, which are used to refer to people or things in a general way, without saying exactly who or what they are.

➤ Here are the most common Spanish indefinite pronouns:

- **algo**   something, anything

Tengo <u>algo</u> para ti.	I have something for you.
¿Viste <u>algo</u>?	Did you see anything?

- **alguien**   somebody, anybody

<u>Alguien</u> me lo dijo.	Somebody told me.
¿Viste a <u>alguien</u>?	Did you see anybody?

> *Típ*
>
> Don't forget to use the personal **a** before indefinite pronouns that refer to people when they are used as the object of a verb.
>
> | | |
> |---|---|
> | ¿Viste <u>a</u> alguien? | Did you see anybody? |
> | No vi <u>a</u> nadie. | I didn't see anybody. |
>
> ⇨ *For more information on **Personal a**, see page 184.*

- **alguno/alguna/algunos/algunas**   some, a few

<u>Algunos</u> de los niños ya saben leer.	Some of the children can already read.

- **cada uno/una**   each (one), everybody

Le dio una manzana a <u>cada uno</u>.	She gave each one an apple.
<u>Cada uno</u> pidió lo que quiso.	Everybody ordered what they wanted.

- **cualquiera**   anybody; any

<u>Cualquiera</u> puede hacerlo.	Anybody can do it.
<u>Cualquiera</u> de las explicaciones vale.	Any of the explanations is valid.

- **mucho/mucha/muchos/muchas**   much; many

<u>Muchas</u> de las casas no tenían jardín.	Many of the houses didn't have a yard.

- **nada**   nothing, anything

  ¿Qué tienes en la mano? — **Nada**.

  What do you have in your hand? — Nothing.

  No dijo <u>nada</u>.

  He didn't say anything.

- **nadie**   nobody, anybody

  <u>Nadie</u> nos vio.

  Nobody saw us.

  No quiere ver a <u>nadie</u>.

  He doesn't want to see anybody.

Tip

Don't forget to use the personal **a** before indefinite pronouns that refer to people when they are used as the object of a verb.

¿Viste <u>a</u> alguien?   Did you see anybody?

No vi <u>a</u> nadie.   I didn't see anybody.

⇨ *For more information on **Personal** a, see page 184.*

- **ninguno/ninguna**   none, any

  ¿Cuántas tienes? – <u>Ninguna</u>.   How many do you have? – None.

  No me queda <u>ninguno</u>.   I haven't any left *or* I have none left.

- **otro/otra/otros/otras**   another one; others

  No me gusta este modelo. ¿Tienes <u>otro</u>?   I don't like this model. Do you have another?

(i) Note that you can never put **un** or **una** before **otro** or **otra**.

- **poco/poca/pocos/pocas**   little; few

  sólo unos <u>pocos</u>   only a few

- **tanto/tanta/tantos/tantas**   so much; so many

  ¿Se oía mucho ruido? – No <u>tanto</u>.   Was there a lot of noise? – Not so much.

- **todo/toda/todos/todas**   all; everything

  Lo estropeó <u>todo</u>.   He spoiled everything.

  <u>Todo</u> va bien.   It's all going well.

- **uno ... el otro/una ... la otra**   (the) one ... the other

  <u>Uno</u> dijo que sí y <u>el otro</u> que no.   One said yes while the other said no.

- **unos ... los otros/unas ... las otras**   some ... the others

  <u>Unos</u> son de oro, <u>los otros</u> de plata.   Some are gold, the others silver.

- **varios/varias**   several

Varios de ellos me gustan mucho.	I like several of them very much.

> *Tip*
>
> Don't forget to make those pronouns that have feminine and plural forms agree with the noun they refer to.
>
> | | |
> |---|---|
> | **Toma esta goma, yo tengo <u>otra</u>.** | Take his eraser, I have another one. |

ⓘ Note that **algo**, **alguien** and **alguno** can <u>NEVER</u> be used after a negative such as **no**. Instead you must use the appropriate negative pronouns, **nada**, **nadie**, **ninguno**.

<u>No</u> veo a <u>nadie</u>.	I can't see anybody.
<u>No</u> tengo <u>nada</u> que hacer.	I don't have anything to do.

➤ You use **nada**, **nadie** and **ninguno** on their own, without **no**, to answer questions.

¿Qué pasa? – **<u>Nada</u>**.	What's happening? – Nothing.
¿Quién llamó? – **<u>Nadie</u>**.	Who called? – Nobody.
¿Cuántos quedan? – **<u>Ninguno</u>**.	How many are left? – None.

➤ You also use **nada**, **nadie** and **ninguno** on their own, without **no**, when they come before a verb.

<u>Nada</u> lo asusta.	Nothing frightens him.
<u>Nadie</u> dijo nada.	Nobody said anything.
<u>Ninguno</u> de mis amigos quiso venir.	None of my friends wanted to come.

⇨ *For more information on **Negatives**, see page 159.*

Key points

✔ Where indefinite pronouns have alternative endings, they must agree with the noun they refer to.

✔ *Anything* is usually translated by **algo** in questions and by **nada** in sentences containing **no**.

✔ *Anybody* is usually translated by **alguien** in questions and by **nadie** in sentences containing **no**.

✔ When **nada**, **nadie** or **ninguno** come <u>after</u> the verb, remember to put **no** before it. When they come <u>before</u> the verb, don't use **no**.

Relative pronouns

What is a relative pronoun?

In English, a **relative pronoun** is a word such as *who*, *which* or *that* (and the more formal *whom*) which can be used to introduce information that makes it clear which person or thing is being talked about. For example: *The man <u>who</u> has just come in is Ann's boyfriend.*; *The vase <u>that</u> you broke was quite valuable.*

Relative pronouns can also introduce additional information about someone or something. For example: *Peter, <u>who</u> is a brilliant painter, wants to study art.*; *Jane's house, <u>which</u> was built in 1890, needs a lot of repairs.*

---

1 ## Relative pronouns referring to people

➤ In English, we use the relative pronouns *who*, *whom* and *that* to talk about people. In Spanish, **que** is used.

el hombre <u>que</u> vino ayer	the man <u>who</u> came yesterday
Mi hermano, <u>que</u> tiene veinte años, es mecánico.	My brother, <u>who</u> is twenty, is a mechanic.
el hombre <u>que</u> vi en la calle	the man (<u>that</u>) I saw in the street

---

Tip

In English, we often leave out the relative pronouns *who*, *whom* and *that*. For example, we can say both *the friends <u>that</u> I see most*, or *the friends I see most*.

In Spanish, you can <u>NEVER</u> leave out **que** in this way.

➤ When the relative pronoun is used with a <u>preposition</u>, use **el/la/los/las que** or **quien/quienes** which must agree with the noun it replaces; **el que** changes for the feminine and plural forms, **quien** changes only in the plural.

➤ Here are the Spanish relative pronouns referring to people that are used after a preposition:

	Masculine	Feminine	Meaning
Singular	el que quien	la que quien	who, that, whom
Plural	los que quienes	las que quienes	who, that, whom

las mujeres con <u>las que</u> or con <u>quienes</u> estaba hablando	the women (that) she was talking to
La chica de <u>la que</u> or de <u>quien</u> te hablé llega mañana.	The girl (that) I told you about is arriving tomorrow.
los niños de <u>los que</u> or de <u>quienes</u> te ocupas	the children (that) you take care of

[*i*] Note that when **de** is used with **el que**, they combine to become **del que**. When **a** is used with **el que**, they combine to become **al que**.

el hombre <u>del que</u> te hablé	the man I told you about
Vive con un hombre <u>al que</u> adora.	She lives with a man she adores.

Tip

In English, we often put prepositions at the end of the sentence (for example: *the man she was talking to*). In Spanish, you can <u>never</u> put a preposition at the end of a sentence.

el hombre <u>con el que</u> or <u>con quien</u> estaba hablando	the man she was talking to

⇨ *For more information on* **Prepositions**, *see page 180.*

---

[2] **Relative pronouns referring to things**

➤ In English, we use the relative pronouns *which* and *that* to talk about things. In Spanish, **que** is used.

la novela <u>que</u> ganó el premio	the novel <u>that</u> or <u>which</u> won the prize
el CD <u>que</u> compré	the CD (<u>that</u> or <u>which</u>) I bought

---

Tip

In English, we often leave out the relative pronouns *which* and *that*. For example, we can say both *the house <u>which</u> we want to buy*, or *the house we want to buy*.

In Spanish, you can <u>NEVER</u> leave out **que** in this way.

➤ When the relative pronoun is used with a preposition, use **el/la/los/las que**, which must agree with the noun it replaces. Here are the Spanish relative pronouns referring to things that are used after a preposition:

	Masculine	Feminine	Meaning
Singular	el que	la que	which, that
Plural	los que	las que	which, that

la iglesia a <u>la que</u> siempre va	the church (that or which) she always goes to
los temas de <u>los que</u> habla	the subjects he talks about

📋 Note that when **de** is used with **el que**, they combine to become **del que**. When **a** is used with **el que**, they combine to become **al que**.

el programa <u>del que</u> te hablé	the program I told you about
el banco <u>al que</u> fuiste	the bank you went to

➤ The neuter form **lo que** is used when referring to the whole of the previous part of the sentence.

No había nadie, <u>lo que</u> me pareció raro.	There was nobody there, which I thought was strange.

➪ *For more information on **lo que**, see page 17.*

Tip

In English, we often put prepositions at the end of the sentence (for example: *the church she always goes to*). In Spanish, you can <u>never</u> put a preposition at the end of a sentence.

la iglesia <u>a la que</u> siempre va	the church she always goes <u>to</u>
la película <u>de la que</u> te hablaba	the movie I was telling you <u>about</u>

Grammar Extra!

In English, we can use *whose* to show possession (for example: *the woman whose son is ill*). In Spanish, you use **cuyo/cuya/cuyos/cuyas**; **cuyo** is actually an adjective and must agree with the noun it describes <u>NOT</u> with the person who owns that thing.

La mujer, <u>cuyo</u> nombre era Antonia, estaba jubilada.	The woman, whose name was Antonia, was retired.
el señor en <u>cuya</u> casa me alojé	the gentleman whose house I stayed in

In your reading, you may come across the forms **el cual/la cual/los cuales/las cuales**, which are a more formal alternative to **el que/la que/los que/las que** after a preposition.

las mujeres con <u>las cuales</u> estaba hablando	the women (that or who) she was talking to
la ventana desde <u>la cual</u> nos observaban	the window from which they were watching us

In other cases, where the pronoun does not immediately follow the person or thing it refers to, **el cual/la cual/los cuales/las cuales** are also useful to make it clear who you are talking about.

El padre de Elena, <u>el cual</u> tiene mucho dinero, es ...	Elena's father, who has a lot of money, is ...

---

3 | <u>Other uses of</u> el que, la que, los que, las que

➤ You can use **el que, la que, los que, las que** to mean *the one(s) (who/which)* or *those who*.

Esa película es <u>la que</u> quiero ver.	That movie is the one I want to see.
<u>los que</u> quieren irse	those who want to leave

> ### Key points
> ✔ **que** can refer to both people and things in Spanish.
> ✔ In English we often leave out the relative pronouns *who, which* and *that*, but in Spanish you can never leave out **que**.
> ✔ After a preposition you use **el que/la que/los que/las que** or **quien/quienes** if you are referring to people; you use **el que/ la que/los que/las que** if you are referring to things. **el que** and **quien** must agree with the nouns they replace.
> ✔ **a + el que → al que**
>   **de + el que → del que**
> ✔ In Spanish, <u>never</u> put the preposition at the end of a sentence.
> ✔ **el que/la que/los que** and **las que** are also used to mean *the one(s) who/which* or *those who*.

For further explanation of grammatical terms, please see pages viii–xii.

Interrogative pronouns

> **What is an interrogative pronoun?**
> In English, an **interrogative pronoun** is one of the words *who*, *which*, *whose*, *whom*, and *what* when they are used without a noun to ask questions.

➤ These are the interrogative pronouns in Spanish:

Singular	Plural	Meaning
¿qué?	¿qué?	what?
¿cuál?	¿cuáles?	which? which one(s)?; what?
¿quién?	¿quiénes?	who? (*as subject or after a preposition*)
¿cuánto?/¿cuánta?	¿cuántos?/¿cuántas?	how much? how many?

i Note that, in Spanish, question words have an accent on them.

1 ¿qué?

➤ ¿qué? is the equivalent of *what?* in English.

¿Qué están haciendo?	What are they doing?
¿Qué dices?	What are you saying?
¿Para qué lo quieres?	What do you want it for?

➤ You can use **¿por qué?** in the same way as *why?* in English.

¿Por qué no vienes?	Why don't you come?

2 ¿cuál?, ¿cuáles?

➤ ¿cuál? and ¿cuáles? are usually the equivalent of *which?* in English and are used when there is a choice between two or more things.

¿Cuál de estos vestidos te gusta más?	Which of these dresses do you like best?
¿Cuáles quieres?	Which (ones) do you want?

i Note that you don't use **cuál** before a noun; use **qué** instead.

¿Qué libro es más interesante? Which book is more interesting?

➪ *For more information on **Interrogative adjectives**, see page 32.*

3 qué es or cuál es?

➤ You should only use ¿qué es …? (meaning *what is…?*) and ¿qué son …? (meaning *what are…?*) when you are asking someone to define, explain or classify something.

| ¿Qué es esto? | What is this? |
| ¿Qué son los genes? | What are genes? |

➤ Use ¿cuál es …? and ¿cuáles son …? (also meaning *what is …?* and *what are …?*) when you want someone to specify a particular detail, number, name and so on.

| ¿Cuál es la capital de Venezuela? | What is the capital of Venezuela? |
| ¿Cuál es tu consejo? | What's your advice? |

4 ¿quién?

➤ ¿quién? and ¿quiénes? are the equivalent of *who?* in English when it is the subject of the verb or when used with a preposition.

¿Quién ganó la carrera?	Who won the race?
¿Con quiénes los viste?	Who did you see them with?
¿A quién se lo diste?	Who did you give it to?

➤ ¿a quién? and ¿a quiénes? are the equivalent of *who(m)?* when it is the object of the verb.

| ¿A quién viste? | Who did you see? *or* Whom did you see? |
| ¿A quiénes ayudaste? | Who did you help? *or* Whom did you help? |

➤ ¿de quién? and ¿de quiénes? are the equivalent of *whose?* in English.

| ¿De quién es este libro? | Whose is this book? *or* Whose book is this? |
| ¿De quiénes son estos coches? | Whose are these cars? *or* Whose cars are these? |

5 ¿cuánto?, ¿cuántos?

➤ ¿cuánto? (*masculine*) and ¿cuánta? (*feminine*) are the equivalent of *how much* in English. ¿cuántos? (*masculine plural*) and ¿cuántas? (*feminine plural*) are the equivalent of *how many?*

| ¿Cuánto es? | How much is it? |
| ¿Cuántos tienes? | How many do you have? |

For further explanation of grammatical terms, please see pages viii-xii.

Demonstrative pronouns

> **What is a demonstrative pronoun?**
> In English, a **demonstrative pronoun** is one of the words *this, that, these,* and *those* used instead of a noun to point people or things out. For example: *That looks fun.*

1 Using demonstrative pronouns

➤ These are the demonstrative pronouns in Spanish:

	Masculine	Feminine	Neuter	Meaning
Singular	este	esta	esto	this, this one
	ese	esa	eso	that, that one (*nearby*)
	aquel	aquella	aquello	that, that one (*further away*)
Plural	estos	estas		these, these ones
	esos	esas		those, those ones (*nearby*)
	aquellos	aquellas		those, those ones (*further away*)

i Note that the masculine and feminine forms of demonstrative pronouns used to be spelled with an accent on the first 'e', to distinguish them from demonstrative adjectives. The accented forms **éste**, **ésos**, **aquéllas**, etc. are still used by many people but the accent is only necessary in the rare cases when the sentence might otherwise be misunderstood.

➤ In Spanish, demonstrative pronouns have to agree with the noun that they are replacing.

¿Qué abrigo te gusta más? – <u>Este</u>.	Which coat do you like best? – This one.
<u>Estos</u> libros son míos y <u>esos</u> son tuyos.	These books are mine and those are yours.
<u>Esas</u> sandalias son de cuero pero aquellos no.	Those sandals are made of leather but those over there aren't.

2 ¿ese or aquel?

➤ In English we use *that* and *those* to talk about anything that is not nearby. In Spanish, you need to be a bit more precise.

➤ Use **ese/esa** and so on to indicate things and people that are nearer to the person you're talking to than to you.

Me gusta más <u>ese</u> que tienes en la mano.	I prefer the one you have in your hand.

➤ Use **ese/esa** and so on to indicate things and people that aren't very far away.

| ¡Qué bonitos vestidos! | What nice dresses! |
| Me gusta <u>ese</u> azul. | I like that blue one. |

➤ Use **aquel/aquella** and so on to talk about things that are further away.

| Mi casa es <u>aquella</u> al fondo de la calle. | My house is that one at the end of the street. |

➤ The neuter forms (**esto**, **eso**, **aquello**) are used to talk about an object you don't recognize or about an idea or statement.

¿Qué es <u>eso</u> que llevas en la mano?	What's that you have in your hand?
No puedo creer que <u>esto</u> me esté pasando a mí.	I can't believe this is really happening to me.
<u>Aquello</u> sí que me gustó.	I really did like that.

ⓘ Note that the neuter forms of demonstrative pronouns <u>NEVER</u> have an accent.

Key points

✔ In Spanish, demonstrative pronouns agree with the noun they are replacing.

✔ In Spanish you have to choose the correct pronoun to emphasize the difference between something that is near to you and something that is further away:

- **este/esta/estos** and **estas** (meaning *this/these*) are used to indicate things and people that are very close.
- **ese/esa/esos** and **esas** (meaning *that/those*) are used to indicate things and people that are near the person you are talking to or that aren't too far away.
- **aquel/aquella/aquellos/aquellas** (meaning *that/those*) are used to indicate things and people that are further away.

✔ The neuter pronouns (**esto**, **eso** and **aquello**) are used to talk about things you don't recognize or to refer to statements or ideas. They never have an accent.

Verbs

> **What is a verb?**
> A **verb** is a 'doing' word which describes what someone or something does, what someone or something is, or what happens to them. For example: *be*, *sing*, *live*.

Overview of verbs

➤ Verbs are frequently used with a noun, with somebody's name or, particularly in English, with a pronoun such as *I*, *you* or *she*. They can relate to the present, the past and the future; this is called their <u>tense</u>.

⇨ *For more information on **Nouns** and **Pronouns**, see pages 1 and 41.*

➤ Verbs are either:
  ● <u>regular</u>; their forms follow the normal rules
  ● <u>irregular</u>; their forms do not follow the normal rules

➤ Almost all verbs have a form called the <u>infinitive</u>. This is a base form of the verb (for example, *walk*, *see*, *hear*) that hasn't had any endings attached to it and doesn't relate to any particular tense. In English, the infinitive is usually shown with *to*, as in *to speak*, *to eat*, *to live*.

➤ In Spanish, the infinitive is always made up of just one word (never two, as in *to speak* in English) and ends in **-ar, -er** or **-ir**. For example: **habl<u>ar</u>** (meaning *to speak*), **com<u>er</u>** (meaning *to eat*) and **viv<u>ir</u>** (meaning *to live*). All Spanish verbs belong to one of these three types, which are called <u>conjugations</u>. We will look at each of these three conjugations in turn on the next few pages.

➤ Regular English verbs have other forms apart from the infinitive: a form ending in *-s* (*walks*), a form ending in *-ing* (*walking*), and a form ending in -ed (*walked*).

➤ Spanish verbs have many more forms than this, which are made up of endings attached to a <u>stem</u>. The stem of a verb can usually be worked out from the infinitive.

➤ Spanish verb endings change depending on who or what is doing the action and on when the action takes place. In fact, the ending is very often the only thing that shows you <u>who</u> is doing the action, as the Spanish equivalents of *I*, *you*, *he* and so on (**yo, tú, él** and so on) are not used very much. So, both **hablo** on its own and **yo hablo** mean *I speak*. Sometimes there is a name or a noun in the sentence to make it clear who is doing the action.

<u>José</u> **habla español.**   <u>José</u> speaks Spanish.

<u>El profesor</u> **habla español.**   <u>The teacher</u> speaks Spanish.

⇨ *For more information on **Subject pronouns**, see page 42.*

➤ Spanish verb forms also change depending on whether you are talking about the present, past or future, so **(yo) hablaré** means *I will speak* while **(yo) hablé** means *I spoke*.

➤ Some verbs in Spanish do not follow the usual patterns. These <u>irregular verbs</u> include some very common and important verbs like **ir** (meaning *to go*), **ser** and **estar** (meaning *to be*) and **hacer** (meaning *to do* or *to make*). Other verbs are only slightly irregular, changing their stems in certain tenses.

⇨ *For **Verb Tables**, see the middle section of this book.*

Key points
✔ Spanish verbs have different forms depending on who or what is doing the action and on the tense.

✔ Spanish verb forms are made up of a stem and an ending. The stem is usually based on the infinitive of the verb. The ending depends on who or what is doing the action and on when the action takes place.

✔ Regular verbs follow the standard patterns for **-ar**, **-er** and **-ir** verbs. Irregular verbs do not.

The present tenses

> **What are the present tenses?**
> The **present tenses** are the verb forms that are used to talk about what is true at the moment, what happens regularly and what is happening now. For example: I'm a student; I travel to college by train; I'm studying languages.

➤ In English, there are two tenses you can use to talk about the present:

- the present simple tense

  I live here.
  They get up early.

- the present continuous tense

  He is eating an apple.
  You aren't working very hard.

➤ In Spanish, there is also a present simple and a present continuous tense. As in English, the present simple in Spanish is used to talk about:

- things that are generally true

  En invierno hace frío.   It's cold in winter.

- things that are true at the moment

  Carlos no come carne.   Carlos doesn't eat meat.

- things that happen at intervals

  A menudo vamos al cine.   We often go to the movies.

➤ The present continuous tense in Spanish is used to talk about things that are happening right now or at the time of writing:

  Marta está viendo las noticias.   Marta is watching the news.

➤ However, there are times where the use of the present tenses in the two languages is not exactly the same.

➪ *For more information on the use of the* **Present tenses**, *see pages 79 and 85.*

The present simple tense

1   Forming the present simple tense of regular -ar verbs

➤ If the infinitive of the Spanish verb ends in **-ar**, it means that the verb belongs to the <u>first conjugation</u>. For example: **hablar**, **lavar**, **llamar**.

➤ To know which form of the verb to use in Spanish, you need to determine what the stem of the verb is and then attach the correct ending. The stem of regular **-ar** verbs in the present simple tense is formed by taking the <u>infinitive</u> and chopping off **-ar**.

Infinitive	Stem (without -ar)
hablar (to speak)	habl-
lavar (to wash)	lav-

➤ Now that you know how to find the stem of a verb you can attach the correct ending. The one you choose will depend on who or what is doing the action.

i   Note that as the ending generally makes it clear who is doing the action, you usually don't need to add a subject pronoun, such as **yo** (meaning *I*) or **tú** (meaning *you*), as well.

⇨   *For more information on* **Subject pronouns**, *see page 42.*

➤ Here are the present simple endings for regular **-ar** verbs:

Present simple endings	Present simple of hablar	Meaning: *to speak*
-o	(yo) habl<u>o</u>	I speak
-as	(tú) habl<u>as</u>	you speak
-a	(él/ella) habl<u>a</u>	he/she/it speaks
	(usted) habl<u>a</u>	you speak
-amos	(nosotros/nosotras) habl<u>amos</u>	we speak
-áis*	(vosotros/vosotras) habl<u>áis</u>*	you speak
-an	(ellos/ellas) habl<u>an</u> (ustedes) habl<u>an</u>	they speak you speak

*only used in Spain

➤ You use the **él/ella** (*third person singular*) form of the verb with nouns and with people's names, when you are just talking about one person, animal or thing.

> **Lydia estudi<u>a</u> medicina.**   Lydia studies *or* is studying medicine.
> **Mi profesor me ayud<u>a</u> mucho.**   My teacher helps me a lot.

For further explanation of grammatical terms, please see pages viii–xii.

➤ You use the **ellos/ellas** (*third person plural*) form of the verb with nouns and with people's names, when you are talking about more than one person, animal or thing.

Lydia y Carlos estudian medicina.	Lydia and Carlos study *or* are studying medicine.
Mis profesores me ayudan mucho.	My teachers help me a lot.

i Note that even though you use the **él/ella** and **ellos/ellas** forms of the verb to talk about things in Spanish, you should never include the pronouns **él**, **ella**, **ellos** or **ellas** themselves in the sentence when referring to things.

Funciona bien.	It works well.
Funcionan bien.	They work well.

⇨ For more information on **Ways of saying 'you' in Spanish**, see page 44.

> ### Key points
>
> ✔ Verbs ending in **-ar** belong to the first conjugation. Regular **-ar** verbs form their present tense stem by losing the **-ar**.
>
> ✔ The present tense endings for regular **-ar** verbs are: **-o**, **-as**, **-a**, **-amos**, **-áis** (in Spain), **-an**.
>
> ✔ You usually don't need to use a pronoun in Spanish as the ending of the verb makes it clear who or what is doing the action.

2 Forming the present simple tense of regular -er verbs

➤ If the infinitive of the Spanish verb ends in **-er**, it means that the verb belongs to the second conjugation. For example, **comer**, **depender**.

➤ The stem of regular **-er** verbs in the present simple tense is formed by taking the infinitive and chopping off **-er**.

Infinitive	Stem (without -er)
comer (*to eat*)	com-
depender (*to depend*)	depend-

➤ Now attach the correct ending, depending on who or what is doing the action.

i Note that as the ending generally makes it clear who is doing the action, you usually don't need to add a subject pronoun, such as **yo** (meaning *I*) or **tú** (meaning *you*), as well.

⇨ For more information on **Subject pronouns**, see page 42.

➤ Here are the present simple endings for regular **-er** verbs:

Present simple endings	Present simple of comer	Meaning: *to eat*
-o	(yo) com<u>o</u>	I eat
-es	(tú) com<u>es</u>	you eat
-e	(él/ella) com<u>e</u>	he/she/it eats
	(usted) com<u>e</u>	you eat
-emos	(nosotros/nosotras) com<u>emos</u>	we eat
-éis*	(vosotros/vosotras) com<u>éis</u>*	you eat
-en	(ellos/ellas) com<u>en</u>	they eat
	(ustedes) com<u>en</u>	you eat

*only used in Spain

➤ You use the **él/ella** (*third person singular*) form of the verb with nouns and with people's names, when you are just talking about one person, animal or thing.

Juan com<u>e</u> demasiado.	Juan eats too much.
Mi padre me deb<u>e</u> 150 pesos.	My father owes me 150 pesos.

➤ You use the **ellos/ellas** (*third person plural*) form of the verb with nouns and with people's names, when you are talking about more than one person, animal or thing.

Juan y Pedro com<u>en</u> demasiado.	Juan and Pedro eat too much.
Mis padres me deb<u>en</u> 150 pesos.	My parents owe me 150 pesos.

[*i*] Note that even though you use the **él/ella** and **ellos/ellas** forms of the verb to talk about things in Spanish, you should <u>never</u> include the pronouns **él**, **ella**, **ellos** or **ellas** themselves in the sentence when referring to things.

Vale mucho dinero.	It's worth a lot of money.

➪ *For more information on* **Ways of saying 'you' in Spanish**, *see page 44.*

see page 44.

> ### Key points
> ✔ Verbs ending in **-er** belong to the second conjugation. Regular **-er** verbs form their present tense stem by losing the **-er**.
> ✔ The present tense endings for regular **-er** verbs are: **-o**, **-es**, **-e**, **-emos**, **-éis** (in Spain), **-en**.
> ✔ You usually don't need to use a pronoun in Spanish as the ending of the verb makes it clear who or what is doing the action.

For further explanation of grammatical terms, please see pages viii-xii.

3 | Forming the present simple tense of regular -ir verbs

➤ If the infinitive of the Spanish verb ends in **-ir**, it means that the verb belongs to the <u>third conjugation</u>. For example: **vivir**, **recibir**.

➤ The stem of regular **-ir** verbs in the present simple tense is formed by taking the <u>infinitive</u> and chopping off **-ir**.

Infinitive	Stem (without -ir)
vivir (to live)	viv-
recibir (to receive)	recib-

➤ Now attach the correct ending depending on who or what is doing the action.

ⓘ Note that as the ending generally makes it clear who is doing the action, you usually don't need to add a subject pronoun, such as **yo** (meaning *I*) or **tú** (meaning *you*), as well.

⇨ For more information on **Subject pronouns**, see page 42.

➤ Here are the present simple endings for regular **-ir** verbs:

Present simple endings	Present simple of vivir	Meaning: *to live*
-o	(yo) viv<u>o</u>	I live
-es	(tú) viv<u>es</u>	you live
-e	(él/ella) viv<u>e</u>	he/she/it lives
	(usted) viv<u>e</u>	you live
-imos	(nosotros/nosotras) viv<u>imos</u>	we live
-ís*	(vosotros/vosotras) viv<u>ís</u>*	you live
-en	(ellos/ellas) viv<u>en</u>	they live
	(ustedes) viv<u>en</u>	you live

*only used in Spain

➤ You use the **él/ella** (*third person singular*) form of the verb with nouns and with people's names, when you are just talking about one person, animal or thing.

> **Javier viv<u>e</u> en Palenque.**   Javier lives in Palenque.
> **Mi padre recib<u>e</u> muchas cartas.**   My father gets a lot of letters.

➤ You use the **ellos/ellas** (*third person plural*) form of the verb with nouns and with people's names, when you are talking about more than one person, animal or thing.

> **Javier y Antonia viv<u>en</u> en Palenque.**   Javier and Antonia live in Palenque.

| Mis padres reciben muchas cartas. | My parents get a lot of letters. |

i Note that even though you use the **él/ella** and **ellos/ellas** forms of the verb to talk about things in Spanish, you should <u>never</u> include the pronouns **él**, **ella**, **ellos** or **ellas** themselves in the sentence when referring to things.

| Ocurre muy a menudo. | It happens very often. |

⇨ *For more information on **Ways of saying 'you' in Spanish**, see page 44.*

> **Key points**
> ✔ Verbs ending in **-ir** belong to the third conjugation. Regular **-ir** verbs form their present tense stem by losing the **-ir**.
> ✔ The present tense endings for regular **-ir** verbs are: **- o, -es, -e, -imos, -ís** (in Spain), **-en**.
> ✔ You usually don't need to use a pronoun in Spanish as the ending of the verb makes it clear who or what is doing the action.

4 Forming the present simple tense of less regular verbs

➤ Many Spanish verbs do not follow the regular patterns shown previously. There are lots of verbs that change their <u>stem</u> in the present tense when the stress is on the stem. This means that all forms are affected in the present simple <u>APART FROM</u> the **nosotros** and **vosotros** forms. Such verbs are often called <u>radical-changing verbs</u>, meaning root-changing verbs.

➤ For example, some verbs containing an **-o** in the stem change it to **-ue** in the present simple for all forms <u>APART FROM</u> the **nosotros/nosotras** and **vosotros/vosotras** forms.

	encontrar *to find*	recordar *to remember*	poder *to be able*	dormir *to sleep*
(yo)	encuentro	recuerdo	puedo	duermo
(tú)	encuentras	recuerdas	puedes	duermes
(él/ella/usted)	encuentra	recuerda	puede	duerme
(nosotros/as)	encontramos	recordamos	podemos	dormimos
(vosotros/as)*	encontráis*	recordáis*	podéis*	dormís*
(ellos/ellas/ustedes)	encuentran	recuerdan	pueden	duerme

*only used in Spain

For further explanation of grammatical terms, please see pages viii-xii.

➤ Other verbs containing an **-e** in the stem change it to **-ie** for all forms APART FROM the **nosotros/nosotras** and **vosotros/vosotras** forms.

	cerrar to close, to shut	pensar to think	entender to understand	perder to lose	preferir to prefer
(yo)	cierro	pienso	entiendo	pierdo	prefiero
(tú)	cierras	piensas	entiendes	pierdes	prefieres
(él/ella/usted)	cierra	piensa	entiende	pierde	prefiere
(nosotros/as)	cerramos	pensamos	entendemos	perdemos	preferimos
(vosotros/as)*	cerráis*	pensáis*	entendéis*	perdéis*	preferís*
(ellos/ellas/ustedes)	cierran	piensan	entienden	pierden	prefieren

*only used in Spain

➤ A few **-ir** verbs containing **-e** in the stem change this to **-i** in the present simple for all forms APART FROM the **nosotros/nosotras** and **vosotros/vosotras** forms.

	pedir to ask (for)	servir to serve
(yo)	pido	sirvo
(tú)	pides	sirves
(él/ella/usted)	pide	sirve
(nosotros/as)	pedimos	servimos
(vosotros/as)*	pedís*	servís*
(ellos/ellas/ustedes)	piden	sirven

*only used in Spain

➤ If you are not sure whether a Spanish verb belongs to this group of radical-changing verbs, you can look up the **Verb Tables** in the middle section of this book.

➡ *For more information on **Spelling**, see page 198.*

5 Forming the present simple tense of common irregular verbs

➤ There are many other verbs that do not follow the standard patterns in Spanish. These include some very common and important verbs such as **tener** (meaning *to have*), **hacer** (meaning *to do* or *to make*) and ir (meaning *to go*). These verbs are shown in full on the next page.

➤ Here are the present simple tense endings for **tener**:

	tener	**Meaning:** *to have*
(yo)	tengo	I have
(tú)	tienes	you have
(él/ella/usted)	tiene	he/she/it has, you have
(nosotros/nosotras)	tenemos	we have
(vosotros/vosotras)*	tenéis*	you have
(ellos/ellas/ustedes)	tienen	they have, you have

*only used in Spain

<u>Tengo</u> dos hermanas.	I have two sisters.
No <u>tengo</u> dinero.	I don't have any money.
¿Cuántas clases <u>tienes hoy</u>?	How many classes do you have today?
<u>Tiene</u> el pelo largo.	He has long hair.

➤ Here are the present simple tense endings for **hacer**:

	hacer	**Meaning:** *to do, to make*
(yo)	hago	I do, I make
(tú)	haces	you do, you make
(él/ella/usted)	hace	he/she/it does, he/she/it makes, you do, you make
(nosotros/nosotras)	hacemos	we do, we make
(vosotros/vosotras)*	hacéis*	you do, you make
(ellos/ellas/ustedes)	hacen	they do, they make, you do, you make

*only used in Spain

<u>Hago</u> la cena todos los días.	I make dinner every day.
No <u>hago</u> mucho deporte.	I don't play a lot of sports.
¿Qué <u>haces</u>?	What are you doing?
¿Qué <u>hace</u> tu padre?	What does your father do?

For further explanation of grammatical terms, please see pages viii-xii.

➤ Here are the present simple tense endings for **ir**:

	ir	Meaning: *to go*
(yo)	voy	I go
(tú)	vas	you go
(él/ella/usted)	va	he/she/it goes, you go
(nosotros/nosotras)	vamos	we go
(vosotros/vosotras)*	vais*	you go
(ellos/ellas/ustedes)	van	they go, you go

*only used in Spain

<u>Voy</u> a Miami.	I'm going to Miami.
¿Adónde <u>vas</u>?	Where are you going?
No <u>va</u> al colegio.	He doesn't go to school.
Nunca <u>van</u> al teatro.	They never go to the theater.

⇨ *For other irregular verbs in the present simple tense, see* **Verb Tables** *in the middle section of this book.*

6 | How to use the present simple tense in Spanish

➤ The present simple tense is often used in Spanish in the same way as it is in English, although there are some differences.

➤ As in English, you use the Spanish present simple to talk about:

- things that are generally true

  En verano <u>hace</u> calor.   It's hot in summer.

- things that are true now

  <u>Viven</u> en Guatemala.   They live in Guatemala.

- things that happen all the time or at certain intervals or that you do as a habit

  Marta <u>usa</u> lentes.   Marta wears glasses.
  Mi tío <u>viaja</u> mucho.   My uncle travels a lot.

- things that you are planning to do

  El domingo <u>jugamos</u> en León.   We're playing in León on Sunday.
  Mañana <u>voy</u> a Puebla.   I am going to Puebla tomorrow.

➤ There are some instances when you would use the present simple in Spanish, but you wouldn't use it in English:

- to talk about current projects and activities that may not actually be going on right at this very minute

¿_Llueve_?	Is it raining?

- when you use certain time expressions in Spanish, especially **desde** (meaning *since*), **desde hace** (meaning *for*) and **hace ... que** (meaning *for*) to talk about activities and states that started in the past and are still going on now

Jaime _estudia_ inglés _desde_ hace dos años.	Jaime has been learning English for two years.
Daniel _trabaja_ aquí _desde_ 1999.	Daniel has worked here since 1999.
Hace tres años _que vivo_ en California.	I've been living in California for three years.
Hace años _que_ no la _veo_.	I haven't seen her for years.

⇨ *For more information on the use of tenses with **desde**, see page 191.*

ser and estar

➤ In Spanish there are two irregular verbs, **ser** and **estar**, that both mean *to be*, although they are used very differently. In the present simple tense, they follow the patterns shown below.

Pronoun	ser	estar	Meaning: *to be*
(yo)	soy	estoy	I am
(tú)	eres	estás	you are
(él/ella/usted)	es	está	he/she/it is, you are
(nosotros/nosotras)	somos	estamos	we are
(vosotros/vosotras)*	sois*	estáis*	you are
(elllos/ellas/ustedes)	son	están	they/you are

*only used in Spain

➤ **ser** is used:

- with an adjective when talking about a characteristic or fairly permanent quality (for example: shape, size, height, color, material, nationality).

Mi hermano <u>es</u> alto.	My brother is tall.
María <u>es</u> inteligente.	María is intelligent.
<u>Es</u> americana.	She's American.
<u>Es</u> muy bonita.	She's very pretty.
<u>Es</u> rojo.	It's red.
<u>Es</u> de algodón.	It's made of cotton.
Sus padres <u>son</u> italianos.	His parents are Italian.
<u>Es</u> joven/viejo.	He's young/old.
<u>Son</u> muy ricos/pobres.	They're very rich/poor.

- followed by a noun or pronoun that tells you what someone or something is

Miguel <u>es</u> abogado.	Miguel is a lawyer.
<u>Soy</u> yo, Enrique.	It's me, Enrique.
Madrid <u>es</u> la capital de España.	Madrid is the capital of Spain.

- to say that something belongs to someone

La casa <u>es</u> de mis padres.	The house belongs to my parents.
<u>Es</u> mío.	It's mine.

- to talk about where someone or something comes from

Yo <u>soy</u> de Santa Clara.	I'm from Santa Clara.
Mi esposa <u>es</u> de La Habana.	My wife is from Havana.

- to say what time it is or what the date is

  Son las tres y media. It's half past three.

  Mañana es sábado. Tomorrow is Saturday.

- in calculations

  Tres y dos son cinco. Three and two are five.

  ¿Cuánto es? – Son veinte dólares. How much is it? It's twenty dollars.

- when followed by an infinitive

  Lo importante es decir la verdad. The important thing is to tell the truth.

➡️ *For more information on the **Infinitive**, see page 146.*

- to describe actions using the passive (for example *they are made, it is sold*)

  Son pintados a mano. They are hand painted.

➡️ *For more information on the **Passive**, see page 125.*

➤ **estar** is used:

- to talk about where something or someone is

  Estoy en casa. I'm at home.

  ¿Dónde está la estación? Where's the station?

  Está cerca de aquí. It's near here.

- with an adjective when there has been a change in the condition of someone or something or to suggest that there is something unexpected about them

  El café está frío. The coffee's cold.

  ¡Qué elegante estás con ese vestido! How elegant you look in that dress!

  Hoy estoy de mal humor. I'm in a bad mood today.

➡️ *For more information on **Adjectives**, see page 19.*

- with a past participle used as an adjective, to describe the state that something is in

  Las tiendas están cerradas. The stores are closed.

  No está terminado. It isn't finished.

  Las camas están hechas. The beds are made.

  Está roto. It's broken.

➡️ *For more information on **Past participles**, see page 118.*

For further explanation of grammatical terms, please see pages viii-xii.

- when talking about someone's health

¿Cómo **están**?	How are you?
Estamos todos bien.	We're all well.

- to form continuous tenses such as the present continuous tense

Está comiendo.	He's eating.
Estamos aprendiendo mucho.	We are learning a great deal.

⇨ *For more information on the **Present continuous**, see page 85.*

➤ Both **ser** and **estar** can be used with certain adjectives, but the meaning changes depending on which is used.

➤ Use **ser** to talk about <u>permanent</u> qualities.

Es muy viejo.	He's very old.
Juan **es** alto y delgado.	Juan is tall and slim.
Viajar **es** cansado.	Traveling is tiring.
La química **es** aburrida.	Chemistry is boring.

➤ Use **estar** to talk about <u>temporary</u> states or qualities.

Está muy viejo.	He's not young any more./ He's aged a lot.
¡**Estás** muy delgada!	You're looking very thin!/ You've lost a lot of weight!
Hoy **estoy** cansado.	I'm tired today.
Estoy aburrido.	I'm bored.

➤ **ser** is used with adjectives such as **importante** (meaning *important*) and **imposible** (meaning *impossible*) when the subject is *it* in English.

Es muy interesante.	It's very interesting.
Es imposible.	It's impossible.
Es fácil.	It's easy.

➤ **ser** is used in certain set phrases.

Es igual *or* **Es** lo mismo.	It's all the same.
Es para ti.	It's for you.

➤ **estar** is also used in some set phrases.

- estar de pie — to be standing

Juan **está** de pie.	Juan is standing.

- estar de vacaciones — to be on vacation

Mi jefe **está** de vacaciones.	My boss is on vacation.

- estar de viaje — to be on a trip

Mi padre **está** de viaje.	My father's on a trip.

- **estar de moda**   to be in fashion
  El negro está de moda.   Black is in fashion.
- **estar claro**   to be obvious
  Está claro que no entiendes.   It's obvious that you don't understand.

Grammar Extra!

Both **ser** and **estar** can be used with past participles.

Use **ser** and the past participle in passive constructions to describe an action.

   Son pintados a mano.   They are hand painted.

Use **estar** and the past participle to describe a state.

   Está terminado.   It's finished.

⇨ *For more information on **Past participles**, see page 118.*

Key points

✔ **ser** and **estar** both mean *to be* in English, but are used very differently.

✔ **ser** and **estar** are irregular verbs. You have to learn them.

✔ Use **ser** with adjectives describing permanent qualities or characteristics; with nouns or pronouns telling you who or what somebody or something is; with time and dates; and to form the passive.

✔ Use **estar** to talk about location and health; with adjectives describing a change of state; and with past participles used as adjectives to describe states.

✔ **estar** is also used to form present continuous tenses.

✔ **ser** and **estar** can sometimes be used with the same adjectives, but the meaning changes depending on which verb is used.

✔ **ser** and **estar** are both used in a number of set phrases.

The present continuous tense

➤ In Spanish, the present continuous tense is used to talk about something that is happening at this very moment.

➤ The Spanish present continuous tense is formed from the <u>present tense</u> of **estar** and the <u>gerund</u> of the verb. The gerund is the form of the verb that ends in **-ando** (for **-ar** verbs) or **-iendo** (for **-er** and **-ir** verbs) and is the same as the *-ing* form of the verb in English (for example, *walking, swimming*).

<u>Estoy</u> trabaj<u>ando</u>	I'm working.
No <u>estamos</u> discut<u>iendo</u>.	We aren't arguing.
¿<u>Estás</u> escuch<u>ando</u>?	Are you listening?

⇨ *For more information on **estar** and the **Gerund**, see pages 80 and 128.*

➤ To form the gerund of an **-ar** verb, drop the **-ar** ending of the infinitive and attach **-ando**:

Infinitive	Meaning	Stem (without -ar)	Gerund	Meaning
hablar	to speak	habl-	hab<u>lando</u>	speaking
trabajar	to work	trabaj-	trabaj<u>ando</u>	working

➤ To form the gerund of an **-er** or **-ir** verb, drop the **-er** or **-ir** ending of the infinitive and attach **-iendo**:

Infinitive	Meaning	Stem (without -er/-ir)	Gerund	Meaning
comer	to eat	com-	com<u>iendo</u>	eating
escribir	to write	escrib-	escrib<u>iendo</u>	writing

Tip

Only use the present continuous to talk about things that are in the middle of happening right now. Use the present simple tense instead to talk about activities that are current, but which may not be happening at this minute.

Lydia <u>estudia</u> medicina.	Lydia's studying medicine.

⇨ *For more information on the **Present simple tense**, see page 72.*

Key points

✔ Only use the present continuous in Spanish for actions that are happening right now.

✔ To form the present continuous tense in Spanish, take the present tense of **estar** and add the gerund of the main verb.

The imperative

> **What is the imperative?**
> An **imperative** is a form of the verb used when giving orders and instructions. For example: *Sit down!*; *Don't go!*; *Let's start!*

1 Using the imperative

➤ In Spanish, the form of the imperative that you use for giving instructions depends on:

- whether you are telling someone to do something or not to do something
- whether you are talking to one person or to more than one person
- whether you are on familiar or more formal terms with the person or people

➤ These imperative forms correspond to the familiar **tú** (and **vosotros/vosotras** in Spain), to the more formal **usted** and to **ustedes**, although you don't actually say these pronouns when giving instructions.

⇨ *For more information on **Ways of saying 'you' in Spanish**, see page 44.*

➤ There is also a form of the imperative that corresponds to *let's* in English.

2 Forming the imperative: instructions not to do something

➤ In orders that tell you <u>NOT</u> to do something and that have **no** in front of them in Spanish, the imperative forms for **tú**, **usted**, **nosotros/nosotras**, **vosotros/vosotras** and **ustedes** are all taken from a verb form called the <u>present subjunctive</u>. It's easy to remember because the endings for **-ar** and **-er** verbs are the opposite of what they are in the ordinary present tense.

⇨ *For more information on the **Present tense** and the **Subjunctive**, see pages 69 and 134.*

➤ In regular **-ar** verbs, you drop the **-as**, **-a**, **-amos**, **-áis** and **-an** endings of the present tense and replace them with: **-es**, **-e**, **-emos**, **-éis** and **-en**.

-ar verb	trabajar	to work
tú form	¡no trabajes!	Don't work!
usted form	¡no trabaje!	Don't work!
nosotros/as form	¡no trabajemos!	Let's not work!
vosotros/as form*	¡no trabajéis!*	Don't work!
ustedes form	¡no trabajen!	Don't work!

*only used in Spain

For further explanation of grammatical terms, please see pages viii-xii.

➤ In regular -**er** verbs, you drop the -**es**, -**e**, -**emos**, -**éis** and -**en** endings of the present tense and replace them with -**as**, -**a**, -**amos**, -**áis** and -**an**.

-er **verb**	comer	**to eat**
tú form	¡no comas!	Don't eat!
usted form	¡no coma!	Don't eat!
nosotros/as form	¡no comamos!	Let's not eat!
vosotros/as form*	¡no comáis!*	Don't eat!
ustedes form	¡no coman!	Don't eat!

*only used in Spain

➤ In regular -**ir** verbs, you drop the -**es**, -**e**, -**imos**, -**ís** and -**en** endings of the present tense and replace them with -**as**, -**a**, -**amos**, -**áis** and -**an**.

-ir **verb**	decidir	**to decide**
tú form	¡no decidas!	Don't decide!
usted form	¡no decida!	Don't decide!
nosotros/as form	¡no decidamos!	Let's not decide!
vosotros/as form*	¡no decidáis!*	Don't decide!
ustedes form	¡no decidan!	Don't decide!

*only used in Spain

➤ A number of irregular verbs also have irregular imperative forms. These are shown in the table below.

	dar **to give**	decir **to say**	estar **to be**	hacer **to do/make**	ir **to go**
tú form	¡no des! don't give!	¡no digas! don't say!	¡no estés! don't be!	¡no hagas! don't do/make!	¡no vayas! don't go!
usted form	¡no dé! don't give!	¡no diga! don't say!	¡no esté! don't be!	¡no haga! don't do/make!	¡no vaya! don't go!
nosotros form	¡no demos! let's not give!	¡no digamos! let's not say!	¡no estemos! let's not be!	¡no hagamos! let's not do/make!	¡no vayamos! let's not go!
vosotros form*	¡no deis!* don't give!	¡no digáis!* don't say!	¡no estéis!* don't be!	¡no hagáis!* don't do/make!	¡no vayáis!* don't go!
ustedes form	¡no den! don't give!	¡no digan! don't say!	¡no estén! don't be!	¡no hagan! don't do/make!	¡no vayan! don't go!
	poner **to put**	salir **to leave**	ser **to be**	tener **to have**	venir **to come**
tú form	¡no pongas! don't put!	¡no salgas! don't leave!	¡no seas! don't be!	¡no tengas! don't have!	¡no vengas! don't come!
usted form	¡no ponga! don't put!	¡no salga! don't leave!	¡no sea! don't be!	¡no tenga! don't have!	¡no venga! don't come!
nosotros form	¡no pongamos! let's not put!	¡no salgamos! let's not leave!	¡no seamos! let's not be!	¡no tengamos! let's not have!	¡no vengamos! let's not come!
vosotros form*	¡no pongáis!* don't put!	¡no salgáis!* don't leave!	¡no seáis!* don't be!	¡no tengáis!* don't have!	¡no vengáis!* don't come!
ustedes form	¡no pongan! don't put!	¡no salgan! don't leave!	¡no sean! don't be!	¡no tengan! don't have!	¡no vengan! don't come!

*only used in Spain

ⓘ Note that, for instructions NOT TO DO something, some of these irregular forms will be more predictable if you take the **yo** form of the present tense, drop the **-o** and attach the endings to this instead.

digo	I say	→	negative imperative stem	→	**dig-**
hago	I do	→	negative imperative stem	→	**hag-**
pongo	I put	→	negative imperative stem	→	**pong-**
salgo	I leave	→	negative imperative stem	→	**salg-**
tengo	I have	→	negative imperative stem	→	**teng-**
vengo	I come	→	negative imperative stem	→	**veng-**

3   Forming the imperative: instructions to do something

➤ In instructions telling you <u>TO DO</u> something, the forms for **usted**, **nosotros** and **ustedes** are exactly the same as they are in negative instructions (instructions telling you not to do something) except that there isn't a **no**.

	trabajar **to work**	comer **to eat**	decidir **to decide**
usted **form**	¡Trabaje!	¡Coma!	¡Decida!
nosotros/as **form**	¡Trabajemos!	¡Comamos!	¡Decidamos!
ustedes **form**	¡Trabajen!	¡Coman!	¡Decidan!

➤ In positive instructions (instructions telling you to do something), there are special forms of the imperative for **tú** and **vosotros/vosotras**.

➤ The **tú** form of the imperative is the same as the **tú** form of the ordinary present simple tense, but without the final **-s**.

trabajar	→	**¡Trabaja!**
to work		Work!
comer	→	**¡Come!**
to eat		Eat!
decidir	→	**¡Decide!**
to decide		Decide!

⇨ *For more information on the **Present simple tense**, see page 72.*

➤ The **vosotros/vosotras** form of the imperative, only used in Spain, is the same as the infinitive, except that you drop the final **-r** and attach **-d** instead.

trabajar	→	**Trabajad!**
to work		Work!
comer	→	**Comed!**
to eat		Eat!
decidir	→	**Decidid!**
to decide		Decide!

For further explanation of grammatical terms, please see pages viii–xii.

➤ In Spanish, there are a number of imperative forms that are irregular. The irregular imperative forms for **usted**, **nosotros/nosotras** and **ustedes** are the same as the irregular negative imperative forms without the **no**. The **tú** and **vosotros/vosotras** forms are different again.

.	dar to give	decir to say	estar to be	hacer to do/make	ir to go
tú **form**	¡da! give!	¡di! say!	¡está! be!	¡haz! do/make!	¡ve! go!
usted **form**	¡dé! give!	¡diga! say!	¡esté! be!	¡haga! do/make!	¡vaya! go!
nosotros/as **form**	¡demos! let's give!	¡digamos! let's say!	¡estemos! let's be!	¡hagamos! let's do/make!	¡vamos! let's go!
vosotros/as **form***	¡dad!* give!	¡decid!* say!	¡estad!* be!	¡haced!* do/make!	¡id!* go!
ustedes **form**	¡den! give!	¡digan! say!	¡estén! be!	¡hagan! do/make!	¡vayan! go!
	poner to put	salir to leave	ser to be	tener to have	venir to come
tú **form**	¡pon! put!	¡sal! leave!	¡sé! be!	¡ten! have!	¡ven! come!
usted **form**	¡ponga! put!	¡salga! leave!	¡sea! be!	¡tenga! have!	¡venga! come!
nosotros/as **form**	¡pongamos! let's put!	¡salgamos! let's leave!	¡seamos! let's be!	¡tengamos! let's have!	¡vengamos! let's come!
vosotros/as* **form**	¡poned!* put!	¡salid!* leave!	¡sed!* be!	¡tened!* have!	¡venid!* come!
ustedes **form**	¡pongan! put!	¡salgan! leave!	¡sean! be!	¡tengan! have!	¡vengan! come!

*only used in Spain

[*i*] Note that, in instructions <u>TO DO</u> something, the **nosotros/as** form for **ir** is **vamos**; in instructions <u>NOT TO DO</u> something, it is **no vayamos**.

| 4 | **Position of object pronouns**

➤ An object pronoun is a word that is used instead of a noun as the object of a sentence, like **me** (meaning *me* or *to me*), **la** (meaning *her/it*) or **les** (meaning *to them/to you*). In orders and instructions, the position of these object pronouns in the sentence changes depending on whether you are telling someone <u>TO DO</u> something or <u>NOT TO DO</u> something.

⇨ *For more information on **Object pronouns**, see page 46.*

➤ If you are telling someone <u>NOT TO DO</u> something, the object pronouns go <u>BEFORE</u> the verb.

¡No <u>me lo</u> mandes!	Don't send it to me!
¡No <u>me</u> molestes!	Don't disturb me!
¡No <u>los</u> castigue!	Don't punish them!
¡No <u>se la</u> devolvamos!	Let's not give it back to him/her/them!

➤ If you are telling someone <u>TO DO</u> something, the object pronouns are attached to the <u>END</u> of the verb. An accent is usually added to make sure that the stress in the imperative verb stays the same.

¡Explíca<u>melo</u>!	Explain it to me!
¡Perdóne<u>me</u>!	Excuse me!
¡Díga<u>me</u>!	Tell me!
¡Esperémos<u>la</u>!	Let's wait for her/it!

[*i*] Note that when there are two object pronouns, the indirect object pronoun always goes before the direct object pronoun.

➪ *For more information on* **Stress**, *see page 202.*

For more information on **Stress**, *see page 202.*

[5] **Other ways of giving instructions**

➤ For directions in instruction manuals, recipes and so on, the <u>infinitive</u> form is often used instead of the imperative.

<u>Ver</u> página 9.	See page 9.

➤ **vamos a** with the infinitive is often used to mean *let's*.

<u>Vamos a</u> ver.	Let's see.
<u>Vamos a</u> empezar.	Let's start.

Key points

✔ In Spanish, in instructions <u>not to do</u> something, the endings are taken from the present subjunctive. They are the same as the corresponding endings for -ar and -er verbs in the ordinary present tense, except that the -e endings are attached to the -ar verbs and the -a endings are attached to the -er and -ir verbs.

✔ For -ar verbs the forms are: **no hables** (tú form); **no hable** (usted form); **no hablemos** (nosotros/as form); **no habléis** (vosotros/as form)*; **no hablen** (ustedes form)

✔ For -er verbs the forms are: **no comas** (tú form); **no coma** (usted form); **no comamos** (nosotros/as form); **no comáis** (vosotros/as form)*; **no coman** (ustedes form)

✔ For -ir verbs the forms are: **no decidas** (tú form); **no decida** (usted form); **no decidamos** (nosotros/as form); **no decidáis** (vosotros/as form)*; **no decidan** (ustedes form)

✔ In instructions <u>to do</u> something, the forms for **usted**, **nosotros/as** and **ustedes** are the same as they are in instructions not to do something.

✔ The forms for **tú** and **vosotros/as*** are different:
  • the **tú** form is the same as the corresponding form in the ordinary present tense, but without the final **-s**: trabaja; come; decide
  • the **vosotros/as** form* is the same as the infinitive but with a final **-d** instead of the **-r**: trabajad; comed; decidid

✔ A number of verbs have irregular imperative forms.

✔ The object pronouns in imperatives go before the verb when telling someone not to do something; they are attached to the end of the verb when telling someone to do something.

*only used in Spain

Reflexive verbs

What is a reflexive verb?
A **reflexive verb** is one where the subject and object are the same, and where the action 'reflects back' on the subject. It is used with a reflexive pronoun such as *myself*, *yourself* and *herself* in English. For example: *I washed myself.*; *He cut himself.*

---

1 Using reflexive verbs in Spanish

➤ In Spanish, reflexive verbs are not only used to describe things you do to yourself, as they are in English. They often describe actions that involve a change of some sort, for example, going to bed, sitting down, getting angry, and so on, as well as other types of actions. The infinitive form of a reflexive verb has **se** attached to the end of it (for example: **secarse**, which means *to get dry* or *to dry oneself*). This is the way reflexive verbs are shown in dictionaries. **se** is called a reflexive pronoun.

Some of the most common reflexive verbs in Spanish are listed here.

acostarse	to go to bed
afeitarse	to shave
bañarse	to take a bath, to take a shower, to have a swim
dormirse	to go to sleep, to fall asleep
enojarse	to get angry
lavarse	to wash (yourself)
levantarse	to get up, to stand up
llamarse	to be called
secarse	to dry, to get dry, to dry yourself
sentarse	to sit down
vestirse	to get dressed

Siempre <u>nos acostamos</u> temprano.	We always go to bed early.
¿Por qué no <u>te afeitas</u>?	Why don't you shave?
Mi marido <u>se baña</u> por la mañana.	My husband takes a bath in the morning.
¡<u>Duérmete</u>!	Go to sleep!
<u>No te enojes</u> conmigo.	Don't be angry with me.
Mi hermano no <u>se lava</u>.	My brother doesn't wash.
<u>Me levanto</u> a las siete.	I get up at seven o'clock.
¿Cómo <u>te llamas</u>?	What's your name?
¡<u>Siéntense</u>!	Sit down!
<u>Me visto</u> en el baño.	I get dressed in the bathroom.

For further explanation of grammatical terms, please see pages viii–xii.

ℹ️ Note that **se**, **me** and so on are very rarely translated into English as *himself*, *myself* and so on.

➤ Many Spanish verbs can be used both as reflexive verbs and as ordinary verbs (without the reflexive pronoun). When they are used as ordinary verbs, the person or thing doing the action is not the same as the person or thing receiving the action, so the meaning is different.

Me lavo.	I wash (myself).
Lavo la ropa a mano.	I wash the clothes by hand.
Me llamo Antonio.	I'm called Antonio./ My name is Antonio.
¡**Llama** a la policía!	Call the police!
Me acuesto a las 11.	I go to bed at 11 o'clock.
Acuesta a Sarita.	Put Sarita to bed.

Grammar Extra!

With some verbs there is a small but important difference in meaning between the reflexive and non-reflexive forms.

Duermo.	I sleep.
Me duermo.	I go to sleep, I fall asleep.
Miguel va al cine todos los sábados.	Miguel goes to the movies every Saturday.
Miguel se va mañana.	Miguel's leaving tomorrow.

---

2   ## Forming the present tense of reflexive verbs

➤ When you use a reflexive verb in Spanish, the reflexive pronoun that goes with it varies according to the subject of the verb. The table on the next page shows you which reflexive pronoun to use.

Subject of the verb	Reflexive pronoun to use
(yo)	me
(tú)	te
(él) (ella) (uno) (usted) any singular noun	se
(nosotros/nosotras)	nos
(vosotros/vosotras)*	os*
(ellos) (ellas) (ustedes) Any plural noun or combination or singular or plural nouns joined with y	se

*only used in Spain

(Yo) <u>me</u> levanto temprano.	I get up early.
Pancho todavía no <u>se</u> afeita.	Pancho doesn't shave yet.
(Nosotros) <u>nos</u> vamos mañana.	We are leaving tomorrow.
Ana y Pedro <u>se</u> acuestan a las once.	Ana and Pedro go to bed at eleven.

➤ The present tense forms of a reflexive verb work exactly the same way as an ordinary verb, except that the reflexive pronoun is used as well.

⇨ *For more information on the **Present tense**, see page 69.*

➤ The following table shows the reflexive verb **levantarse** in full.

Reflexive forms of levantarse	Meaning
(yo) me levanto	I get up
(tú) te levantas	you get up
(él) se levanta (ella) se levanta (uno) se levanta se levanta (usted) se levanta	he gets up she gets up one gets up it gets up you get up
(nosotros/nosotras) nos levantamos	we get up
(vosotros/vosotras) os levantáis*	you get up
(ellos) se levantan (ellas) se levantan (ustedes) se levantan	they get up they get up you get up

*only used in Spain

➤ Some reflexive verbs, such as **acostarse**, are irregular. Some of these irregular verbs are shown in the **Verb tables** in the middle section of this book.

③ Position of reflexive pronouns

➤ In ordinary tenses such as the present simple, the reflexive pronoun goes <u>BEFORE</u> the verb.

<u>Me</u> acuesto temprano.	I go to bed early.
¿Cómo <u>se</u> llama usted?	What's your name?

➪ For more information on the **Present simple tense**, see page 72.

➤ When telling someone <u>NOT TO DO</u> something, you also put the reflexive pronoun <u>BEFORE</u> the verb.

No <u>te</u> levantes.	Don't get up.
¡No <u>se</u> vayan todavía!	Don't go yet!

➤ When telling someone <u>TO DO</u> something, you attach the reflexive pronoun onto the end of the verb.

¡Sién<u>te</u>nse!	Sit down!
¡Cálla<u>te</u>!	Be quiet!

➪ For more information on the **Imperative**, see page 86.

> **Típ**
>
> When attaching reflexive pronouns to the end of the imperative, you drop the final **-s** of the **nosotros** form and the final **-d** of the **vosotros** form, before the pronoun.
>
> | | |
> |---|---|
> | ¡Vámo<u>nos</u>! | Let's go! |
> | ¡Senta<u>os</u>! (*Spain only*) | Sit down! |

➤ You always attach the reflexive pronoun onto the end of infinitives and gerunds (the **-ando** or **-iendo** forms of the verb) unless the infinitive or gerund follows another verb.

Hay que relajar<u>se</u> de vez en cuando.	You have to relax from time to time.
Acostándo<u>se</u> temprano, se descansa mejor.	You feel more rested by going to bed early.

➤ Where the infinitive or gerund follows another verb, you can either attach the reflexive pronoun to the end of the infinitive or gerund or put it before the other verb.

Quiero bañar<u>me</u> *or* **<u>Me</u> quiero bañar.**	I want to take a bath.
Tienes que vestir<u>te</u> *or* **<u>Te</u> tienes que vestir.**	You must get dressed.
Está vistiéndo<u>se</u> *or* **<u>Se</u> está vistiendo.**	She's getting dressed.
¿Estás durmiéndo<u>te</u>? *or* **¿<u>Te</u> estás durmiendo?**	Are you falling asleep?

⇨ *For more information on **Gerunds**, see page 128.*

ℹ️ When attaching pronouns to the ends of verb forms, note that you will often have to add a written accent to preserve the stress.

⇨ *For more information on **Stress**, see page 202.*

4 Using reflexive verbs with parts of the body and clothes

➤ In Spanish, you often talk about actions to do with your body or your clothing using a reflexive verb.

<u>Se</u> está secando <u>el</u> pelo.	She's drying her hair.
<u>Nos</u> lavamos <u>los</u> dientes.	We brush our teeth.
<u>Se</u> está poniendo <u>el</u> abrigo.	He's putting on his coat.

ⓘ Note that in Spanish you do not use a possessive adjective such as *my* and *her* when talking about parts of the body. You use **el**, **la**, **los** and **las** with a reflexive verb instead.

> **Me** estoy lavando <u>las</u> manos.   I'm washing my hands.

⇨ *For more information on **Articles**, see page 10.*

5 | Other uses of the pronoun se

➤ In English, we often use a passive construction (for example: *goods <u>are</u> <u>transported</u> all over the world, most of our tea <u>is imported</u> from India and China*). In Spanish, this construction is not used very often. Instead, a construction with **se** is used.

Aquí <u>se vende</u> café.	Coffee <u>is sold</u> here.
Aquí <u>se venden</u> muchos libros.	Lots of books <u>are sold</u> here.
<u>Se habla</u> inglés.	English <u>is spoken</u> here.
En Suiza <u>se hablan</u> tres idiomas.	Three languages <u>are spoken</u> in Switzerland.

ⓘ Note that the verb has to be singular or plural depending on whether the subject is singular or plural.

⇨ *For more information on the **Passive**, see page 125.*

➤ **se** is also used in impersonal expressions. In this case, it often corresponds to *you* in English.

No <u>se puede</u> entrar.	You can't go in.
No <u>se permite</u>.	It isn't allowed.
¿Cómo <u>se dice</u> "siesta" en inglés?	How do you say "siesta" in English?
¿Cómo <u>se escribe</u> "Tarragona"?	How do you spell "Tarragona"?

⇨ *For more information on **Impersonal verbs**, see page 132.*

6 | Other uses of the pronoun se, nos and os

➤ **se**, **nos** and **os** (in Spain only), are all also used to mean *each other* and *one another*.

<u>Nos</u> escribimos.	We write to one another.
<u>Nos</u> queremos.	We love each other.
Rachel y Julie <u>se</u> odian.	Rachel and Julie hate each other.
No <u>se</u> conocen.	They don't know each other.

Key points

✔ A reflexive verb is made up of a reflexive pronoun and a verb.

✔ The reflexive pronouns are: **me**, **te**, **se**, **nos**, **os** (in Spain only), **se**.

✔ The reflexive pronoun goes before the verb, except when you are telling someone to do something and with infinitives and gerunds.

The future tense

> **What is the future tense?**
> The **future** tense is a verb tense used to talk about something that will happen or will be true in the future. For example: *He'll be here soon; I'll give you a call; What will you do?; It will be sunny tomorrow.*

1 Ways of talking about the future

➤ In Spanish, just as in English, you can often use the present tense to refer to something that is going to happen in the future.

> **La película <u>empieza</u> a las nueve.** The movie <u>starts</u> at nine o'clock.
> **Mañana <u>voy</u> a Madrid.** I <u>am going</u> to Madrid tomorrow.

➤ In English, we often use *going to* with an infinitive to talk about the immediate future or our future plans. In Spanish, you can use the present tense of **ir** followed by **a** and an infinitive.

> **<u>Va a</u> perder el tren.** He's going to miss the train.
> **<u>Va a</u> llevar una media hora.** It's going to take half an hour.
> **<u>Voy a</u> hacerlo mañana.** I'm going to do it tomorrow.

2 Forming the future tense

➤ In English, we can form the future tense by putting *will* or its contracted form *'ll* before the verb. In Spanish, you have to change the verb endings. So, just as **hablo** means *I speak*, **hablaré** means *I will speak* or *I shall speak*.

➤ To form the future tense of regular **-ar**, **-er** and **-ir** verbs, attach the following endings to the <u>infinitive</u> of the verb: **-é**, **-ás**, **-á**, **-emos**, **-éis**, **-án**.

➤ The following table shows the future tense of three regular verbs: **hablar** (meaning *to speak*), **comer** (meaning *to eat*) and **vivir** (meaning *to live*).

(yo)	hablar<u>é</u>	comer<u>é</u>	vivir<u>é</u>	I'll speak/eat/live
(tú)	hablar<u>ás</u>	comer<u>ás</u>	vivir<u>ás</u>	you'll speak/eat/live
(él) (ella) (usted)	hablar<u>á</u>	comer<u>á</u>	vivir<u>á</u>	he'll speak/eat/live she'll speak/eat/live it'll speak/eat/live you'll speak/eat/live
(nosotros/nosotras)	hablar<u>emos</u>	comer<u>emos</u>	vivir<u>emos</u>	we'll speak/eat/live
(vosotros/vosotras)*	hablar<u>éis</u>*	comer<u>éis</u>*	vivir<u>éis</u>*	you'll speak/eat/live
(ellos/ellas/ustedes)	hablar<u>án</u>	comer<u>án</u>	vivir<u>án</u>	they'll/you'll speak/eat/live

*only used in Spain

Hablaré con ella.	I'll speak to her.
Comeremos en casa de José.	We'll eat at José's.
No volverá.	He won't come back.
¿Lo entenderá?	Will she understand it?

ℹ️ Note that in the future tense only the **nosotros/nosotras** form doesn't have an accent.

> *Tip*
>
> Remember that Spanish has no direct equivalent of the word *will* in verb forms like *will rain* or *will look* and so on. Instead, you change the Spanish verb ending to form the future tense.

Grammar Extra!

In English, we sometimes use *will* with the meaning of *be willing to* rather than simply to express the future, for example, *Will you wait for me a moment?* In Spanish you don't use the future tense to say this; you use the present tense or the verb **querer** (meaning *to want*) instead.

| ¿Me esperas un momento, por favor? | Will you wait a moment for me, please? |
| ¿Te quieres callar? | Will you shut up? |

3 Verbs with irregular stems in the future tense

➤ There are a few verbs that **DO NOT** use their infinitives as the stem for the future tense. Here are some of the most common.

Verb	Stem	(yo)	(tú)	(él) (ella) (usted)	(nosotros) (nosotras)	(vosotros)* (vosotras)*	(ellos) (ellas) (ustedes)
decir to say	dir-	diré	dirás	dirá	diremos	diréis*	dirán
haber to have	habr-	habré	habrás	habrá	habremos	habréis*	habrán
hacer to do/make	har-	haré	harás	hará	haremos	haréis*	harán
poder to be able to	podr-	podré	podrás	podrá	podremos	podréis*	podrán
poner to put	pondr-	pondré	pondrás	pondrá	pondremos	pondréis*	pondrán
querer to want	querr-	querré	querrás	querrá	querremos	querréis*	querrán

For further explanation of grammatical terms, please see pages viii-xii.

Verb	Stem	(yo)	(tú)	(él) (ella) (usted)	(nosotros) (nosotras)	(vosotros)* (vosotras)*	(ellos) (ellas) (ustedes)
saber to know	sabr-	sabré	sabrás	sabrá	sabremos	sabréis*	sabrán
salir to leave	saldr-	saldré	saldrás	saldrá	saldremos	saldréis*	saldrán
tener to have	tendr-	tendré	tendrás	tendrá	tendremos	tendréis*	tendrán
venir to come	vendr-	vendré	vendrás	vendrá	vendremos	vendréis*	vendrán

*only used in Spain

Lo <u>haré</u> mañana.	I'll do it tomorrow.
No <u>podremos</u> hacerlo.	We won't be able to do it.
Lo <u>pondré</u> aquí.	I'll put it here.
<u>Saldrán</u> por la mañana.	They'll leave in the morning.
¿A qué hora <u>vendrás</u>?	What time will you come?

[i] Note that the verb **haber** is only used when forming other tenses, such as the perfect tense, and in the expression **hay** (meaning *there is* or *there are*).

⇨ For more information on the **Perfect tense** and on **hay**, see pages 118 and 133.

[4] **Reflexive verbs in the future tense**

➤ The future tense of reflexive verbs is formed in just the same way as for ordinary verbs, except that you have to remember to include the reflexive pronoun (**me**, **te**, **se**, **nos**, **os**, **se**).

    <u>Me levantaré</u> temprano.   I'll get up early.

Key points

✔ In Spanish, you can use the present tense to talk about something that will happen or be true, just as in English.

✔ You can use **ir a** with an infinitive to talk about things that will happen in the immediate future.

✔ In Spanish, there is no direct equivalent of the word *will* in verb forms like *will rain* and *will look*. Instead, you must change the verb endings.

✔ To form the future tense, attach the endings -é, -ás, á, -emos, -éis (in Spain), -án to the infinitive.

✔ Some verbs have irregular stems in the future tense. It is worth learning these.

The conditional

> **What is the conditional?**
> The **conditional** is a verb form used to talk about things that would happen or that would be true under certain conditions. For example: I _would_ help you if I could.
> It is also used to say what you would like or need. For example: _Could_ you help me, please?

1 Using the conditional

➤ In English, you can often recognize a conditional by the word _would_ or its contracted form _'d_.

I _would_ be sad if you left.
If you asked him, he_'d_ help you.

➤ You use the conditional for:

- saying what you would like to do

  Me **gustaría** conocerlo.   I'd like to meet him.

- making suggestions

  Podrías quedarte en su casa.   You could stay at their house.

- giving advice

  Deberías hacer más ejercicio.   You should exercise more.

- saying what you would do

  Te dije que te ayudaría.   I said I would help you.

> _Tip_
> There is no direct Spanish translation of _would_ in verb forms like _would be, would like, would help_ and so on. Instead, you change the Spanish verb ending.

2 Forming the conditional

➤ To form the conditional of regular **-ar**, **-er**, and **-ir** verbs, attach the following endings to the infinitive of the verb: **-ía**, **-ías**, **-ía**, **-íamos**, **-íais**, **-ían**.

➤ The following table shows the conditional tense of three regular verbs: **hablar** (meaning *to speak*), **comer** (meaning *to eat*) and **vivir** (meaning *to live*).

(yo)	hablaría	comería	viviría	I would speak/eat/live
(tú)	hablarías	comerías	vivirías	you would speak/eat/live
(él) (ella) (usted)	hablaría	comería	viviría	he would speak/eat/live she would speak/eat/live it would speak/eat/live you would speak/eat/live
(nosotros/nosotras)	hablaríamos	comeríamos	viviríamos	we would speak/eat/live
(vosotros/vosotras)*	hablaríais*	comeríais*	viviríais*	you would speak/eat/live
(ellos/ellas) (ustedes)	hablarían	comerían	vivirían	they would speak/eat/live you would speak/eat/live

*only used in Spain

Me <u>gustaría</u> ir a China.	I'd like to go to China.
Dije que <u>hablaría</u> con ella.	I said that I would speak to her.
<u>Debería</u> llamar a mis padres.	I should call my parents.

Tip

Don't forget to put an accent on the **í** in the conditional.

ℹ️ Note that the endings in the conditional tense are identical to those of the <u>imperfect tense</u> for **-er** and **-ir** verbs. The difference is that they are attached to a different stem.

⇨ *For more information on the **Imperfect tense**, see page 112.*

3 Verbs with irregular stems in the conditional

➤ To form the conditional of irregular verbs, use the same stem as for the <u>future tense</u>, then attach the usual endings for the conditional. The same verbs that are irregular in the future tense are irregular in the conditional.

Verb	Stem	(yo)	(tú)	(él) (ella) (usted)	(nosotros) (nosotras)	(vosotros)* (vosotras)*	(ellos) (ellas) (ustedes)
decir to say	dir-	diría	dirías	diría	diríamos	diríais*	dirían
haber to have	habr-	habría	habrías	habría	habríamos	habríais*	habrían
hacer to do/ make	har-	haría	harías	haría	haríamos	haríais*	harían
poder to be able to	podr-	podría	podrías	podría	podríamos	podríais*	podrían
poner to put	pondr-	pondría	pondrías	pondría	pondríamos	pondríais*	pondrían
querer to want	querr-	querría	querrías	querría	querríamos	querríais*	querrían
saber to know	sabr-	sabría	sabrías	sabría	sabríamos	sabríais*	sabrían
salir to leave	saldr-	saldría	saldrías	saldría	saldríamos	saldríais*	saldrían
tener to have	tendr-	tendría	tendrías	tendría	tendríamos	tendríais*	tendrían
venir to come	vendr-	vendría	vendrías	<u>vendría</u>	vendríamos	vendríais*	vendrían

*only used in Spain

➪ *For more information on the **Future tense**, see page 99.*

¿Qué <u>harías</u> tú en mi lugar?	What would you do if you were me?
¿<u>Podrías</u> ayudarme?	Could you help me?
Yo lo <u>pondría</u> aquí.	I would put it here.

ℹ️ Note that the verb **haber** is only used when forming other tenses, such as the perfect tense, and in the expression **hay** (meaning *there is/there are*).

➪ *For more information on the **Perfect tense** and on **hay**, see pages 118 and 133.*

For further explanation of grammatical terms, please see pages viii-xii.

4 | Reflexive verbs in the conditional

➤ The conditional of reflexive verbs is formed in the same way as it is for ordinary verbs, except that you have to remember to include the reflexive pronoun (**me, te, se, nos, os, se**).

> **Le dije que <u>me levantaría</u> temprano.**   I said I would get up early.

Key points

✔ In Spanish, there is no direct equivalent of the word *would* in verb forms like *would go* and *would look* and so on. Instead, you change the verb ending.

✔ To form the conditional tense, attach the endings **-ía, ías, -ía, -íamos, -íais** (in Spain), **-ían** to the infinitive. The conditional uses the same stem as the future.

✔ Some verbs have irregular stems which are used for both the conditional and the future. It is worth learning these.

The preterite

> **What is the preterite?**
> The Spanish **preterite** is a form of the verb that is used to talk about actions that were completed in the past. It often corresponds to the simple past in English, as in *I bought a new bike; Mary went shopping on Friday; I typed two reports yesterday.*

1 Using the preterite

➤ In English, we use the <u>simple past tense</u> to talk about actions:
  - that were completed at a certain point in the past
    I <u>bought</u> a dress yesterday.
  - that were part of a series of events
    I <u>got up, got dressed</u> and <u>made</u> breakfast.
  - that went on for a certain amount of time
    The war <u>lasted</u> for three years.

➤ In English, we also use the <u>simple past tense</u> to describe actions that occurred frequently (*Our parents <u>took</u> us swimming during our vacations*), and to describe settings (*It <u>was</u> a dark and stormy night*).

➤ In Spanish, the <u>preterite</u> is the most common tense for talking about the past. You use the preterite for actions:
  - that were completed at a certain point in the past

    Ayer <u>compré</u> un vestido.   I bought a dress yesterday.

  - that were part of a series of events

    Me <u>levanté</u>, me <u>vestí</u> y   I got up, got dressed and made
    <u>preparé</u> el desayuno.   breakfast.

  - that went on for a certain amount of time

    La guerra <u>duró</u> tres años.   The war lasted for three years.

➤ However, you use the <u>imperfect tense</u> for actions that happened frequently (where, in English, you could use *used to*) and for descriptions of settings.

⇨ *For more information on the **Imperfect tense**, see page 112.*

2 Forming the preterite of regular verbs

➤ To form the preterite of any regular **-ar** verb, you drop the **-ar** ending to form the stem and attach the endings: **-é, -aste, -ó, -amos, -asteis, -aron**.

➤ To form the preterite of any regular **-er** or **-ir** verb, you also drop the **-er** or **-ir** ending to form the stem and attach the endings: **-í, -iste, -ió, -imos, -isteis, -ieron**.

➤ The following table shows the preterite of three regular verbs: **hablar** (meaning *to speak*), **comer** (meaning *to eat*) and **vivir** (meaning *to live*).

(yo)	hablé	comí	viví	I spoke/ate/lived
(tú)	hablaste	comiste	viviste	you spoke/ate/lived
(él) (ella) (usted)	habló	comió	vivió	he spoke/ate/lived she spoke/ate/lived it spoke/ate/lived you spoke/ate/lived
(nosotros/nosotras)	hablamos	comimos	vivimos	we spoke/ate/lived
(vosotros/vosotras)*	hablasteis*	comisteis*	vivisteis*	you spoke/ate/lived
(ellos/ellas) (ustedes)	hablaron	comieron	vivieron	they spoke/ate/lived you spoke/ate/lived

*only used in Spain

Bailé con mi hermana. — I danced with my sister.
No hablé con ella. — I didn't speak to her.
Cenamos en un restaurante. — We had dinner in a restaurant.
¿Cerraste la ventana? — Did you close the window?

ℹ️ Note that Spanish has no direct translation of *did* or *didn't* in questions or negative sentences. You simply use a past tense and make it a question by making your voice go up at the end or changing the word order; you make it negative by adding **no**.

➪ *For more information on **Questions** and **Negatives**, see pages 162 and 159.*

Tip
Remember the accents on the **yo** and **él/ella/usted** forms of regular verbs in the preterite. Only an accent shows the difference, for example, between **hablo** *I speak* and **habló** *he spoke*.

3 | Irregular verbs in the preterite

➤ A number of verbs have very irregular forms in the preterite. The table shows some of the most common.

Verb	(yo)	(tú)	(él) (ella) (usted)	(nosotros) (nosotras)	(vosotros)* (vosotras)*	(ellos) (ellas) (ustedes)
andar to walk	anduve	anduviste	anduvo	anduvimos	anduvisteis*	anduvieron
conducir to drive	conduje	condujiste	condujo	condujimos	condujisteis*	condujeron
dar to give	di	diste	dio	dimos	disteis*	dieron
decir to say	dije	dijiste	dijo	dijimos	dijisteis*	dijeron
estar to be	estuve	estuviste	estuvo	estuvimos	estuvisteis*	estuvieron
hacer to do, to make	hice	hiciste	hizo	hicimos	hicisteis*	hicieron
ir to go	fui	fuiste	fue	fuimos	fuisteis*	fueron
poder to be able to	pude	pudiste	pudo	pudimos	pudisteis*	pudieron
poner to put	puse	pusiste	puso	pusimos	pusisteis*	pusieron
querer to want	quise	quisiste	quiso	quisimos	quisisteis*	quisieron
saber to know	supe	supiste	supo	supimos	supisteis*	supieron
ser to be	fui	fuiste	fue	fuimos	fuisteis*	fueron
tener to have	tuve	tuviste	tuvo	tuvimos	tuvisteis*	tuvieron
traer to bring	traje	trajiste	trajo	trajimos	trajisteis*	trajeron
venir to come	vine	viniste	vino	vinimos	vinisteis*	vinieron
ver to see	vi	viste	vio	vimos	visteis*	vieron

*only used in Spain

ⓘ Note that **hizo** (the **él/ella/usted** form of **hacer**) is spelled with a z.

⇨ *For more information on **Spelling**, see page 198.*

For further explanation of grammatical terms, please see pages viii–xii.

Fue a Madrid.	He went to Madrid.
Te vi en el parque.	I saw you in the park.
No vinieron.	They didn't come.
¿Qué hizo?	What did she do?
Se lo di a Teresa.	I gave it to Teresa.
Fue en 2007.	It was in 2007.

Típ

The preterite forms of **ser** (meaning *to be*) are the same as the preterite forms of **ir** (meaning *to go*).

➤ Some other verbs are regular <u>EXCEPT FOR</u> the **él/ella/usted** and **ellos/ellas/ustedes** forms (*third persons singular and plural*). In these forms the stem vowel changes.

Verb	(yo)	(tú)	(él) (ella) (usted)	(nosotros) (nosotras)	(vosotros)* (vosotras)*	(ellos) (ellas) (ustedes)
dormir to sleep	dormí	dormiste	durmió	dormimos	dormisteis*	durmieron
morir to die	morí	moriste	murió	morimos	moristeis*	murieron
pedir to ask for	pedí	pediste	pidió	pedimos	pedisteis*	pidieron
reír to laugh	reí	reíste	rió	reímos	reísteis*	rieron
seguir to follow	seguí	seguiste	siguió	seguimos	seguisteis*	siguieron
sentir to feel	sentí	sentiste	sintió	sentimos	sentisteis*	sintieron

*only used in Spain

ℹ️ Note that **reír** also has an accent in all persons apart from the **ellos/ellas/ustedes** forms. The accent is optional in the third person singular form (**rio** *or* **rió**).

Antonio durmió diez horas.	Antonio slept for ten hours.
Murió en 1066.	He died in 1066.
Pidió fajitas.	He ordered fajitas.
¿Los siguió?	Did she follow them?
Sintió un dolor en la pierna.	He felt a pain in his leg.
Nos reímos mucho.	We laughed a lot.
Juan no se rio.	Juan didn't laugh.

➤ **caer** (meaning *to fall*) and **leer** (meaning *to read*) have an accent in all persons <u>apart from</u> the **ellos/ellas/ustedes** form (*third person plural*). In addition, the vowel changes to **y** in the **él/ella/usted** and **ellos/ellas/ustedes** forms (*third persons singular and plural*).

Verb	(yo)	(tú)	(él) (ella) (usted)	(nosotros) (nosotras)	(vosotros)* (vosotras)*	(ellos) (ellas) (ustedes)
caer to fall	caí	caíste	cayó	caímos	caísteis*	cayeron
construir to build	construí	construiste	construyó	construimos	construisteis*	construyeron
leer to read	leí	leíste	leyó	leímos	leísteis*	leyeron

*only used in Spain

[ⓘ] Note that **construir** also changes to **y** in the **él/ella/usted** and **ellos/ellas/ustedes** forms (*third persons singular and plural*), but only has accents in the **yo** and **él/ella/usted** forms.

Se <u>cayó</u> por la ventana.	He fell out of the window.
Ayer <u>leí</u> un artículo muy interesante.	I read a very interesting article yesterday.
<u>Construyeron</u> una nueva autopista.	They built a new highway.

4   <u>Other spelling changes in the preterite</u>

➤ Spanish verbs that end in **-zar, -gar** and **-car** in the infinitive change the **z** to **c**, the **g** to **gu** and the **c** to **qu** in the **yo** form (*first person singular*).

Verb	(yo)	(tú)	(él) (ella) (usted)	(nosotros) (nosotras)	(vosotros)* (vosotras)*	(ellos) (ellas) (ustedes)
cruzar to cross	cru<u>c</u>é	cruzaste	cruzó	cruzamos	cruzasteis*	cruzaron
empezar to begin	empe<u>c</u>é	empezaste	empezó	empezamos	empezasteis*	empezaron
pagar to pay for	pa<u>gu</u>é	pagaste	pagó	pagamos	pagasteis*	pagaron
sacar to take out	sa<u>qu</u>é	sacaste	sacó	sacamos	sacasteis*	sacaron

*only used in Spain

For further explanation of grammatical terms, please see pages viii-xii.

Crucé el río.	I crossed the river.
Empecé a hacer mis deberes.	I began doing my homework.
No pagué la cuenta.	I didn't pay the bill.
Saqué las llaves del bolsillo.	I took my keys out of my pocket.

[*i*] Note that the change from **g** to **gu** and **c** to **qu** before **e** is to keep the sound hard.

⇨ *For more information on **Spelling**, see page 198.*

[5] **Reflexive verbs in the preterite**

➤ The preterite of reflexive verbs is formed the same way as for ordinary verbs, except that you have to remember to include the reflexive pronoun (**me**, **te**, **se**, **nos**, **os**, **se**).

Me levanté a las siete.	I got up at seven.

Key points

✔ The preterite is the most common way to talk about the past in Spanish.

✔ To form the preterite of regular -**ar** verbs, drop the -**ar** ending and attach the endings: -**é**, -**aste**, -**ó**, -**amos**, -**asteis** (in Spain), -**aron**.

✔ To form the preterite of regular -**er** and -**ir** verbs, drop the -**er** and -**ir** endings and attach the endings: -**í**, -**iste**, -**ió**, -**imos**, -**isteis** (in Spain), -**ieron**.

✔ There are a number of verbs which are irregular in the preterite. These forms have to be learned.

✔ With some verbs, the accents and spelling change in certain forms.

The imperfect tense

> **What is the imperfect tense?**
> The **imperfect tense** is one of the verb tenses used to talk about the past, especially in descriptions, and to say what was happening or used to happen. For example: *It was sunny at the weekend; We were living in Spain at the time; I used to walk to school.*

1 Using the imperfect tense

➤ In Spanish, the imperfect tense is used:

- to describe what things were like and how people felt in the past

Hacía calor.	It was hot.
No **teníamos** agua.	We didn't have any water.
Teníamos sed.	We were thirsty.

- to say what used to happen or what you used to do regularly in the past

Llamaba a su madre todos los días.	He used to call his mother every day.

- to describe what was happening or what the situation was when something else took place

Volvía del trabajo cuando la vi.	I was on my way back from work when I saw her.
Me **caí** cuando **cruzaba** la calle.	I fell down when I was crossing the street.

Grammar Extra!

Sometimes, instead of the ordinary imperfect tense being used to describe what was happening at a given moment in the past when something else occurred and interrupted it, the continuous form is used. This is made up of the imperfect tense of **estar** (**estaba**, **estabas** and so on), followed by the **-ando/-iendo** form of the main verb. The other verb – the one that relates the event that occurred – is in the preterite.

Inés **miraba** la televisión *or* Inés **estaba mirando** la televisión cuando sonó el teléfono.	Inés was watching television when the telephone rang.

➪ *For further information on the **Preterite**, see page 106.*

---

2 Forming the imperfect tense

➤ To form the imperfect of any regular -ar verb, you drop the -ar ending of the infinitive to form the stem and attach the endings: -aba, -abas, -aba, -ábamos, -abais, -aban.

➤ The following table shows the imperfect tense of one regular -ar verb: hablar (meaning *to speak*).

(yo)	hablaba	I spoke I was speaking I used to speak
(tú)	hablabas	you spoke you were speaking you used to speak
(él/ella/usted)	hablaba	he/she/it/you spoke he/she/it was speaking, you were speaking he/she/it/you used to speak
(nosotros/nosotras)	hablábamos	we spoke we were speaking we used to speak
(vosotros/vosotras)*	hablabais*	you spoke you were speaking you used to speak
(ellos/ellas/ustedes)	hablaban	they/you spoke they/you were speaking they/you used to speak

*only used in Spain

[*i*] Note that in the imperfect tense of -ar verbs, the only accent is on the nosotros/nosotras form

Hablaba francés e italiano.	He spoke French and Italian.
Jugaba al tenis cuando era joven.	He used to play tennis when he was young.
Notamos que olía a gas.	We noticed there was a smell of gas.

➤ To form the imperfect of any regular -er or -ir verb, you drop the -er or -ir ending of the infinitive to form the stem and attach the endings: -ía, -ías, -ía, -íamos, -íais, -ían.

➤ The following table shows the imperfect of two regular verbs: **comer** (meaning *to eat*) and **vivir** (meaning *to live*).

(yo)	comía	vivía	I ate/lived I was eating/living I used to eat/live
(tú)	comías	vivías	you ate/lived you were eating/living you used to eat/live
(él/ella/usted)	comía	vivía	he/she/it/you ate/lived he/she/it was eating/living, you were eating/living he/she/it was eating/living, you were eating/living
(nosotros/nosotras)	comíamos	vivíamos	we ate/lived we were eating/living we used to eat/live
(vosotros/vosotras)*	comíais*	vivíais*	you ate/lived you were eating/living you used to eat/live
(ellos/ellas/ustedes)	comían	vivían	they/you ate/lived they/you were eating/living they/you used to eat/live

*only used in Spain

[*i*] Note that in the imperfect tense of **-er** and **-ir** verbs, there's an accent on all the endings.

A veces, <u>comíamos</u> en casa de Pepe.	We sometimes used to eat at Pepe's.
<u>Vivía</u> con sus suegros.	He was living with his in-laws.
Cuando llegó el médico, ya se <u>sentían</u> mejor.	They were already feeling better when the doctor arrived.

Típ
The imperfect endings for **-er** and **-ir** verbs are the same as the endings used to form the conditional for all verbs. The difference is that, in the conditional, the endings are attached to the future stem.

⇨ *For more information on the **Conditional**, see page 102.*

For further explanation of grammatical terms, please see pages viii-xii.

3   Irregular verbs in the imperfect tense

➤ **ser**, **ir** and **ver** are irregular in the imperfect tense.

	ser	**Meaning:** to be
(yo)	era	I was
(tú)	eras	you were
(él/ella/usted)	era	he/she/it was, you were
(nosotros/nosotras)	éramos	we were
(vosotros/vosotras)*	erais*	you were
(ellos/ellas/ustedes)	eran	they were/you were

*only used in Spain

Era un muchacho muy simpático.   He was a very nice boy.

Mi madre **era** profesora.   My mother was *or* used to be a teacher.

	ir	**Meaning:** to go
(yo)	iba	I went/used to go/was going
(tú)	ibas	you went/used to go/were going
(él/ella/usted)	iba	he/she/it went/used to go/was going, you went/used to go/were going
(nosotros/nosotras)	íbamos	we went/used to go/were going
(vosotros/vosotras)*	ibais*	you went/used to go/were going
(ellos/ellas/ustedes)	iban	they/you went/used to go/were going

*only used in Spain

Iba a verla todos los días.   He would go *or* used to go and see her every day.

¿Adónde **iban**?   Where were they going?

	ver	**Meaning:** to see/to watch
(yo)	veía	I saw/used to see I watched/used to watch/was watching
(tú)	veías	you saw/used to see you watched/used to watch/were watching
(él/ella/usted)	veía	he/she/it saw/used to see he/she/it watched/used to watch/ was watching you saw/used to see you watched/used to watch/were watching
(nosotros/nosotras)	veíamos	we saw/used to see we watched/used to watch/were watching
(vosotros/vosotras)*	veíais*	you saw/used to see you watched/used to watch/were watching
(ellos/ellas/ustedes)	veían	they/you saw/used to see they/you watched/used to watch/ were watching

*only used in Spain

Lo <u>veíamos</u> a menudo.   We saw him *or* used to see him often.

<u>Veía</u> cada vez menos.   He could see less and less.

4   **Reflexive verbs in the imperfect tense**

➤ The imperfect of reflexive verbs is formed the same way as for ordinary verbs, except that you have to remember to include the reflexive pronoun (me, te, se, nos, os, se).

Antes <u>se levantaba</u> temprano.   He used to get up early.

Grammar Extra!

In Spanish, you also use the imperfect tense with certain time expressions, in particular with **desde** (meaning *since*), **desde hacía** (meaning *for*) and **hacía ... que** (meaning *for*) to talk about activities and states that had started previously and were still going on at a particular point in the past:

<u>Estaba</u> enfermo desde 2000.	He had been ill since 2000.
Lo <u>conocía</u> desde hacía tres meses.	She had known him for three months.
Hacía mucho tiempo que <u>salían</u> juntos.	They had been dating for a long time.
Hacía dos años que <u>vivíamos</u> en Nueva York.	We had been living in New York for two years.

Compare the use of **desde**, **desde hacía** and **hacía ... que** with the imperfect with that of **desde**, **desde hace**, and **hace ... que** with the present.

➪ *For more information on the use of tenses with* desde, *see page* 191.

Key points

✔ To form the imperfect tense of **-ar** verbs, drop the **-ar** ending and attach the endings: **-aba, -abas, -aba, -ábamos, -abais** (in Spain), **-aban**.

✔ To form the imperfect tense of **-er** and **-ir** verbs, drop the **-er** and **-ir** endings and attach the endings: **-ía, -ías, -ía, -íamos, -íais** (in Spain), **-ían**.

✔ **ser, ir** and **ver** are irregular in the imperfect.

The perfect tense

> **What is the perfect tense?**
> The **perfect** tense is a verb form used to talk about what has or hasn't happened. For example: *I've broken my glasses; We haven't spoken about it.*

1 Using the perfect tense

➤ In English, we use the perfect tense (*have*, *has* or their contracted forms *'ve* and *'s* followed by a past participle such as *spoken, eaten, lived, been*) to talk about what has or hasn't happened today, this week, this year or in our lives up to now.

➤ The Spanish perfect tense is used in a similar way.

He terminado el libro.	I've finished the book.
Nunca **ha estado** en Bolivia.	He's never been to Bolivia.
Ha vendido su caballo.	She has sold her horse.
Todavía no **hemos comprado** una impresora.	We still haven't bought a printer.
Ya se **han ido**.	They've already left.

Grammar Extra!

In some Latin American countries, the preterite is often used instead of the perfect tense in colloquial language. This is also true in English. So you may hear **¿Ya comiste?** (Did you eat yet?) instead of **¿Ya has comido?** (Have you eaten yet?), **Ya vi esa película.** (I already saw that movie.) instead of **Ya he visto esa película.** (I've already seen that movie.), etc.

2 Forming the perfect tense

➤ As in English, the perfect tense in Spanish has two parts to it. These are:

- the present tense of the verb **haber** (meaning *to have*)
- a part of the main verb called the past participle.

3 Forming the past participle

➤ To form the past participle of regular **-ar** verbs, drop the **-ar** ending of the infinitive and attach **-ado**.

    hablar (*to speak*) → **hablado** (*spoken*)

➤ To form the past participle of regular **-er** or **-ir** verbs, drop the **-er** or **-ir** ending of the infinitive and attach **-ido**.

    comer (*to eat*) → **comido** (*eaten*)
    vivir (*to live*) → **vivido** (*lived*)

For further explanation of grammatical terms, please see pages viii-xii.

4 The perfect tense of some regular verbs

➤ The following table shows how you can combine the present tense of **haber** with the past participle of any verb to form the perfect tense. In this case, the past participles are taken from the following regular verbs: **hablar** (meaning *to speak*); **trabajar** (meaning *to work*); **comer** (meaning *to eat*); **vender** (meaning *to sell*); **vivir** (meaning *to live*); **decidir** (meaning *to decide*).

	Present of haber	Past participle	Meaning
(yo)	he	hablado	I have spoken
(tú)	has	trabajado	you have worked
(él/ella/usted)	ha	comido	he/she/it has eaten, you have eaten
(nosotros/nosotras)	hemos	vendido	we have sold
(vosotros/vosotras)*	habéis*	vivido	you have lived
(ellos/ellas/ustedes)	han	decidido	they/you have decided

*only used in Spain

Has trabajado mucho.	You've worked hard.
No **he comido** nada.	I haven't eaten anything.

ℹ Note that you should not confuse **haber** with **tener**. Even though they both mean *to have*, **haber** is only used for forming tenses and in certain impersonal expressions such as **hay** and **había** meaning *there is, there are, there was, there were,* and so on.

➩ *For further information on **Impersonal verbs**, see page 132.*

5 Verbs with irregular past participles

➤ Some past participles are irregular. There aren't too many, so try to learn them.

abrir (*to open*)	→	**abierto** (*opened*)
cubrir (*to cover*)	→	**cubierto** (*covered*)
decir (*to say*)	→	**dicho** (*said*)
escribir (*to write*)	→	**escrito** (*written*)
freír (*to fry*)	→	**frito** (*fried*)
hacer (*to do, to make*)	→	**hecho** (*done, made*)
morir (*to die*)	→	**muerto** (*died*)
oír (*to hear*)	→	**oído** (*heard*)
poner (*to put*)	→	**puesto** (*put*)

romper (*to break*)	→	**roto** (*broken*)
ver (*to see*)	→	**visto** (*seen*)
volver (*to return*)	→	**vuelto** (*returned*)

<u>He abierto</u> una cuenta en el banco.	I've opened a bank account.
No <u>ha dicho</u> nada.	He hasn't said anything.
<u>Ha escrito</u> muchas novelas.	He has written many novels.
<u>Han muerto</u> tres personas.	Three people have died.
¿Dónde <u>has puesto</u> mis zapatos?	Where have you put my shoes?
Carlos <u>ha roto</u> el espejo.	Carlos has broken the mirror.
Jamás <u>he visto</u> una cosa parecida.	I've never seen anything like it.
¿<u>Ha vuelto</u> Ana?	Has Ana come back?

Tip

he/has/ha and so on must <u>NEVER</u> be separated from the past participle. Any object pronouns go before the form of **haber** being used, and <u>NOT</u> between the form of **haber** and the past participle.

No <u>lo</u> he visto.	I haven't seen it.
¿<u>Lo</u> has hecho ya?	Have you done it yet?

---

6 <u>Reflexive verbs in the perfect tense</u>

➤ The perfect tense of reflexive verbs is formed in the same way as it is for ordinary verbs. The reflexive pronouns (**me**, **te**, **se**, **nos**, **os**, **se**) come before **he**, **has**, **ha**, and so on. The table on the next page shows the perfect tense of **levantarse** in full.

(Subject pronoun)	Reflexive pronoun	Present tense of haber	Past Participle	Meaning
(yo)	me	he	levantado	I have gotten up
(tú)	te	has	levantado	you have gotten up
(él) (ella) (uno) (usted)	se	ha	levantado	he has gotten up she has gotten up one has gotten up it has gotten up you have gotten up
(nosotros) (nosotras)	nos	hemos	levantado	we have gotten up we have gotten up
(vosotros)* (vosotras)*	os*	habéis*	levantado	you have gotten up you have gotten up
(ellos) (ellas) (ustedes)	se	han	levantado	they have gotten up they have gotten up you have gotten up

*only used in Spain

Grammar Extra!

Don't use the perfect tense with **desde**, **desde hace** and **hace ... que** when talking about how long something has been going on for. Use the <u>present tense</u> instead.

<u>Está</u> enfermo desde julio.	He has been ill since July.
<u>Trabaja</u> conmigo desde hace tres meses.	She's been working with me for three months.
Hace mucho tiempo que <u>salen</u> juntos.	They have been dating for a long time.

⇨ *For more information on the **Present tense**, see page 72.*

➤ In European Spanish you <u>CAN</u> use the perfect tense in the negative with **desde** and **desde hace**.

No lo <u>he visto</u> desde hace mucho tiempo.	I haven't seen him for a long time.

Key points

✔ The Spanish perfect tense is formed using the present tense of **haber** and a past participle.

✔ In Spanish, the perfect tense is used in very much the same way as it is in English. In some Latin American countries, the preterite is often used instead of the perfect tense in colloquial language.

✔ The past participle of regular **-ar** verbs ends in **-ado**, and the past participle of regular **-er** and **-ir** verbs ends in **-ido**.

✔ Make sure you know the following irregular past participle forms: **abierto, cubierto, dicho, escrito, frito, hecho, muerto, puesto, roto, visto, vuelto**.

The pluperfect or past perfect tense

> **What is the pluperfect tense?**
> The **pluperfect** is a verb tense that is used to talk about what had happened or had been true at a point in the past. For example: *I'd seen the movie twice before*.

1 Using the pluperfect tense

➤ When talking about the past, we sometimes refer to things that had happened previously. To do this in English, we often use *had* followed by a past participle such as *seen*, *eaten*, *lived* or *been*. This tense is known as the pluperfect or past perfect tense.

➤ The Spanish pluperfect tense is used and formed in a similar way.

Ya <u>habíamos comido</u> cuando llegó.	We'd already eaten when he arrived.
Nunca lo <u>había visto</u> antes.	I'd never seen him before.

2 Forming the pluperfect tense

➤ Like the perfect tense, the pluperfect tense in Spanish has <u>two</u> parts to it:
- the imperfect tense of the verb **haber** (meaning *to have*)
- the past participle.

➡ *For more information on the **Imperfect tense** and **Past participles**, see pages 112 and 118.*

➤ The table below shows how you can combine the imperfect tense of **haber** with the past participle of any verb to form the pluperfect tense. Here, the past participles are taken from the following regular verbs: **hablar** (meaning *to speak*); **trabajar** (meaning *to work*); **comer** (meaning *to eat*); **vender** (meaning *to sell*); **vivir** (meaning *to live*); **decidir** (meaning *to decide*).

(Subject pronoun)	Imperfect of <u>haber</u>	Past Participle	Meaning
(yo)	había	hablado	I had spoken
(tú)	habías	trabajado	you had worked
(él/ella/usted)	había	comido	he/she/it/you had eaten
(nosotros/nosotras)	habíamos	vendido	we had sold
(vosotros/vosotras)*	habíais*	vivido*	you had lived
(ellos/ellas/ustedes)	habían	decidido	they/you had decided

*only used in Spain

For further explanation of grammatical terms, please see pages viii-xii.

No <u>había trabajado</u> antes.	He hadn't worked before.
<u>Había vendido</u> su caballo.	She had sold her horse.

➤ Remember that some very common verbs have irregular past participles.

abrir (*to open*)	→	**abierto** (*opened*)
cubrir (*to cover*)	→	**cubierto** (*covered*)
decir (*to say*)	→	**dicho** (*said*)
escribir (*to write*)	→	**escrito** (*written*)
freír (*to fry*)	→	**frito** (*fried*)
hacer (*to do, to make*)	→	**hecho** (*done, made*)
morir (*to die*)	→	**muerto** (*died*)
oír (*to hear*)	→	**oído** (*heard*)
poner (*to put*)	→	**puesto** (*put*)
romper (*to break*)	→	**roto** (*broken*)
ver (*to see*)	→	**visto** (*seen*)
volver (*to return*)	→	**vuelto** (*returned*)

No <u>había dicho</u> nada.	He hadn't said anything.
Tres personas <u>habían muerto</u>.	Three people had died.

Tip

había/habías/habían and so on must <u>NEVER</u> be separated from the past participle. Any object pronouns go before the form of **haber** being used, and <u>NOT</u> between the form of **haber** and the past participle.

No lo había visto.	I hadn't seen it.

---

3 | **Reflexive verbs in the pluperfect tense**

➤ The pluperfect tense of reflexive verbs is formed in the same way as it is for ordinary verbs. The reflexive pronouns (**me, te, se, nos, os, se**) come before **había, habías, había**, and so on. The table on the next page shows the pluperfect tense of **levantarse** in full.

(Subject pronoun)	Reflexive pronoun	Imperfect tense of haber	Past Participle	Meaning
(yo)	me	había	levantado	I had gotten up
(tú)	te	habías	levantado	you had gotten up
(él) (ella) (uno) (usted)	se	había	levantado	he had gotten up she had gotten up one had gotten up it had gotten up you had gotten up
(nosotros) (nosotras)	nos	habíamos	levantado	we had gotten up we had gotten up
(vosotros)* (vosotras)	os*	habíais*	levantado	you had gotten up you had gotten up
(ellos) (ellas) (ustedes)	se	habían	levantado	they had gotten up they had gotten up you had gotten up

*only used in Spain

Grammar Extra!

Don't use the pluperfect with **desde**, **desde hacía** and **hacía ... que** when talking about how long something had been going on. Use the <u>imperfect</u> instead.

<u>Estaba</u> enfermo desde 2000. — He had been ill since 2000.

<u>Trabajaba</u> conmigo desde hacía tres meses. — He had been working with me for three months.

Hacía mucho tiempo que <u>salían</u> juntos. — They had been dating for a long time.

➡ For more information on the **Imperfect tense**, see page 112.

Key points

✔ The Spanish pluperfect tense is formed using the imperfect tense of **haber** and a past particple.

✔ In Spanish, the pluperfect tense is used in very much the same way as it is in English.

✔ The past participle of regular -**ar** verbs ends in -**ado**, while that of regular -**er** and -**ir** verbs ends in -**ido**.

✔ Make sure you know the irregular forms: **abierto, cubierto, dicho, escrito, frito, hecho, muerto, puesto, roto, visto, vuelto**.

For further explanation of grammatical terms, please see pages viii-xii.

The passive

What is the passive?
The **passive** is a verb form that is used when the subject of the verb is the person or thing that is affected by the action. For example: *Mary is liked by everyone; Two children were hurt in an accident; The house was sold*.

1 Using the passive

➤ Verbs can be either active or passive.

➤ In a normal or active sentence, the subject of the verb is the person or thing doing the action described by the verb. The object of the verb is the person or thing that the verb most directly affects.

> They (*subject*) received (*active verb*) many letters of complaint (*object*).
> Someone (*subject*) hit (*active verb*) me (*object*).

➤ So long as the verb has an object, in English, as in Spanish, you can turn an active sentence around to make it a passive sentence by using *to be* followed by a past participle. In this case the person or thing directly affected by the action becomes the subject of the verb.

> Many letters of complaint (*subject*) were received (*passive verb*).
> I (*subject*) was hit (*passive verb*).

➤ In English, to show who or what is responsible for the action in a passive construction, you use *by*.

> I (*subject*) was hit (*passive verb*) by someone.

➤ You use the passive rather than the active when you want to focus attention on the person or thing affected by the action rather than the person or thing that carries it out.

> The man was arrested.

➤ You can also use the passive when you don't know who is responsible for the action.

> Several buses were vandalized.

2 Forming the passive

➤ In English, we use the verb *to be* with a past participle (*was painted, were seen, are made*) to form the passive. In Spanish, the passive is formed in exactly the same way, using the verb **ser** (meaning *to be*) and a past participle. When you say who the action is or was done by, you use the preposition **por** (meaning *by*).

➪ *For more information on the **Past participle**, see page 118.*

Es respetada <u>por</u> todos.	She is respected by everybody.
El cuadro fue pintado <u>por</u> uno de sus discípulos.	The picture was painted by one of his pupils.
Estas casas fueron construidas en 1956.	These houses were built in 1956.
El problema ya ha sido solucionado.	The problem has already been solved.
La película no había sido estrenada.	The movie hadn't been premiered.
El nuevo edificio va a ser inaugurado <u>por</u> el presidente.	The new building is going to be opened by the president.

(i) Note that the ending of the past participle agrees with the subject of the verb **ser** in exactly the same way as an adjective would.

➪ *For more information on **Adjectives**, see page 19.*

➤ Here is the preterite of the **-ar** verb **enviar** (meaning *to send*) in its passive form.

(Subject pronoun)	Preterite of ser	Past Participle	Meaning
(yo)	fui	enviado (masculine) enviada (feminine)	I was sent
(tú)	fuiste	enviado (masculine) enviada (feminine)	you were sent
(él) (ella) (usted)	fue	enviado enviada enviado (masculine) enviada (feminine)	he was sent she was sent you were sent
(nosotros) (nosotras)	fuimos fuimos	enviados enviadas	we were sent we were sent
(vosotros)* (vosotras)*	fuisteis*	enviados enviadas	you were sent you were sent
(ellos) (ellas) (ustedes)	fueron	enviados enviadas enviados (masculine) enviadas (feminine)	they were sent they were sent you were sent you were sent

*only used in Spain

➤ You can form other tenses in the passive by changing the tense of the verb **ser**.

Future:	**serán enviados**	they will be sent.
Perfect:	**eran enviados**	they were/used to be sent.

➤ Irregular past participles are the same as they are in the perfect tense.

⇨ *For more information on **Irregular past participles**, see page 119.*

3 ## Avoiding the passive

➤ Passives are not as common in Spanish as they are in English. Spanish native speakers usually prefer to avoid using the passive by:

- using the active construction instead of the passive

La policía <u>interrogó</u> al sospechoso.	The suspect was interrogated by the police.
Su madre le <u>regaló</u> un libro.	He was given a book by his mother.

- using an active verb in the third person plural

Ya <u>han</u> solucionado el problema.	The problem has already been solved.

- using a passive or impersonal construction with the pronoun **se** (as long as you don't need to say who the action is done by). Note the the verb is in the third person (singular or plural, depending on the subject).

<u>**En Brasil se habla** portugués.</u>	Portuguese is spoken in Brazil.
La casa <u>se construyó</u> en 1956.	The house was built in 1956.
Todos los libros <u>se vendieron</u>.	All the books were sold.
No <u>se había</u> estrenado la película.	The movie hadn't been premiered.
<u>**Se**</u> **cree que va a morir.**	It is thought he will die.

⇨ *For more information on **passive and impersonal** constructions with **se**, see pages 97 and 135.*

Tip

Active verbs often have both a direct object and an indirect object. He gave me (*indirect object*) a book (*direct object*).
In English, both of these objects can be made the subject of a passive verb. For example: <u>*I was given a book.*</u> or <u>*A book was given to me.*</u>
In Spanish, an indirect object can <u>NEVER</u> become the subject of a passive verb.

Key points

- ✔ The passive is formed using **ser** + past participle, sometimes followed by **por** (meaning *by*).
- ✔ The past participle must agree with the subject of **ser**.
- ✔ Passive constructions are not as common as they are in English. You can often avoid the passive by using the third person plural of the active verb or by using a construction with the pronoun **se**.

The gerund

> **What is a gerund?**
> The **gerund** is a verb form ending in -ing which is used to form verb tenses and which in English may also be used as an adjective and a noun. For example: *What are you doing?; the setting sun; Swimming is easy!*

1 Using the gerund

➤ In Spanish, the gerund is a form of the verb that usually ends in **-ando** or **-iendo** and is used to form continuous tenses.

Estoy trabajando.	I'm work**ing**.
Estamos comiendo.	We are eat**ing**.

➤ It is used with **estar** to form continuous tenses such as:

● the present continuous

Está planchando su camisa.	He's ironing his shirt.
Estoy escribiendo una carta.	I'm writing a letter.

⇨ *For more information on the **Present continuous**, see page 85.*

● the imperfect continuous

Estaba arreglando el carro.	She was fixing the car.
Estaban esperándonos.	They were waiting for us.

ℹ️ Note that, in Spanish, continuous tenses should only be used to describe actions that are or were happening at the precise moment to which you are referring.

Grammar Extra!

In continuous tenses, another verb, such as **ir** or **venir**, is sometimes used with a gerund instead of **estar**. These verbs emphasize the gradualness or the slowness of the process.

Iba aprendiendo poco a poco.	He was learning little by little.
Eso es lo que vengo diciendo desde el principio.	That's what I've been saying all along.

➤ The gerund is also used after certain other verbs:

● **seguir haciendo algo** and **continuar haciendo algo** are both used with the meaning of *to go on doing something* or *to continue doing something*.

For further explanation of grammatical terms, please see pages viii-xii.

| Siguió cantando *or* Continuó cantando. | He went on singing *or* He continued singing. |
| Siguieron leyendo *or* Continuaron leyendo. | They went on reading *or* They continued reading. |

- **llevar** with a time expression followed by the gerund is used to talk about how long someone has been doing something:

| Lleva dos años estudiando inglés. | He's heen studying English for two years. |
| Llevo una hora esperando aquí. | I've been waiting here for an hour. |

i Note that the present tense of **llevar** followed by a gerund means the same as the English *have/has been + -ing*.

➤ **pasar(se)** with a time expression followed by the gerund is used to talk about how long you've spent doing something.

| Pasé *or* Me pasé el fin de semana estudiando. | I spent the weekend studying. |
| Pasamos *or* Nos pasamos el día leyendo. | We spent the day reading. |

➤ Verbs expressing movement, such as **salir** (meaning *to come out* or *to go out*), **entrar** (meaning *to come in* or *to go in*), and **irse** (meaning *to leave*) are sometimes followed by a gerund such as **corriendo** (meaning *running*) or **cojeando** (meaning *limping*). In such cases, the English equivalent of **salir corriendo**, **entrar corriendo** or **irse cojeando**, would be *to run out*, *to run in* or *to limp off*.

| Salió corriendo. | He ran out. |
| Se fue cojeando. | He limped off. |

Típ

To talk about physical position, use a past participle not a gerund.

Estaba <u>acostado</u> en el sofá.	He was lying on the sofa.
Estaba <u>sentada</u>.	She was sitting down.
Lo encontré <u>tendido</u> en el suelo.	I found him lying on the floor.
La escalera estaba <u>apoyada</u> contra la pared.	The ladder was leaning against the wall.

⇨ *For more information on the **Past participles**, see page 118.*

➤ You will also come across the gerund used in other ways. For example:

| Los vimos jugando al fútbol. | We saw them playing football. |
| Estudiando, aprobarás. | If you study, you'll pass. |

2   Forming the gerund of regular verbs

➤ To form the gerund of regular **-ar** verbs, drop the **-ar** ending of the infinitive to form the stem, and attach **-ando.**

Infinitive	Stem	Gerund
hablar	habl-	hablando
trabajar	trabaj-	trabajando

➤ To form the gerund of regular **-er** and **-ir** verbs, drop the **-er** and **-ir** ending of the infinitive to form the stem, and attach **-iendo.**

Infinitive	Stem	Gerund
comer	com-	comiendo
vivir	viv-	viviendo

3   The gerund of irregular verbs

➤ Some verbs have an irregular gerund form. You have to learn these.

Infinitives	Meaning	Gerund	Meaning
decir	to say	diciendo	saying
dormir	to sleep	durmiendo	sleeping
freír	to fry	friendo	frying
morir	to die	muriendo	dying
pedir	to ask for	pidiendo	asking for
poder	to be able to	pudiendo	being able to
reír	to laugh	riendo	laughing
seguir	to follow	siguiendo	following
sentir	to feel	sintiendo	feeling
venir	to come	viniendo	coming
vestir	to dress	vistiendo	dressing

➤ In the next group of verbs there is a **y** rather than the normal **i**.

Infinitives	Meaning	Gerund	Meaning
caer	to fall	cayendo	falling
creer	to believe	creyendo	believing
leer	to read	leyendo	reading
oír	to hear	oyendo	hearing
traer	to bring	trayendo	bringing
ir	to go	yendo	going

For further explanation of grammatical terms, please see pages viii-xii.

Tip

In English, we often use *-ing* forms as adjectives (for example: *running water, shining eyes, the following day*). In Spanish, you cannot use the **-ando** and **-iendo** forms like this.
Instead, there are sometimes corresponding forms ending in **-ante** and **-iente** that can be used as adjectives.

agua <u>corriente</u>	running water
ojos <u>brillantes</u>	shining eyes
Al día <u>siguiente</u>, visitamos Cozumel.	The following day we visited Cozumel.

Similarly, in English, we often use the *-ing* forms as nouns. In Spanish you have to use the <u>infinitive</u> instead.

<u>Fumar</u> es malo para la salud.	<u>Smoking</u> is bad for you.

4   **Position of pronouns with the gerund**

➤ Object pronouns and reflexive pronouns are usually attached to the end of the gerund, although often, in continuous tenses, you can also put them before **estar**.

Estoy hablándote *or* **Te estoy hablando.**	I'm talking to you.
Está vistiéndose *or* **Se está vistiendo.**	He's getting dressed.
Estaban mostrándoselo *or* **Se lo estaban mostrando.**	They were showing it to him/her/them/you.

ⓘ Note that, when attaching pronouns to the end of a gerund, you will always have to add an accent to keep the stress in the same place.

⇨ *For more information on **Stress**, see page 202.*

Key points

✔ Use the gerund in continuous tenses with **estar** as well as after **seguir** and **continuar**.
✔ Gerunds for **-ar** verbs attach **-ando** to the stem of the verb.
✔ Gerunds for **-er** and **-ir** verbs usually attach **-iendo** to the stem of the verb.
✔ **-ando** and **-iendo** gerunds <u>cannot</u> be used as adjectives or nouns.
✔ You can attach pronouns to the end of the gerund, or sometimes put them before the previous verb.

Impersonal verbs

> **What is an impersonal verb?**
> An **impersonal verb** is a verb whose subject is *it*, but this '*it*' does not refer to any specific thing. For example: *It's going to rain; It's nine o'clock.*

1 Verbs that are always used impersonally

➤ There are some verbs, such as **llover** (meaning *to rain*) and **nevar** (meaning *to snow*), that are only used in the '*it*' form, the infinitive, and as a gerund (the *-ing* form of the verb). These are called <u>impersonal verbs</u> because there is no person, animal or thing performing the action.

Llueve.	It's raining.
Está lloviendo.	It's raining.
Va a llover.	It's going to rain.
Nieva.	It's snowing.
Está nevando.	It's snowing.
Nevaba.	It was snowing.
Estaba nevando.	It was snowing.
Mañana va a nevar.	It's going to snow tomorrow.

2 Verbs that are sometimes used impersonally

➤ There are also several other very common verbs that are sometimes used as impersonal verbs, for example **hacer**, **haber** and **ser**.

➤ **hacer** is used in a number of impersonal expressions relating to the weather:

<u>Hace</u> frío/calor.	It's cold/hot.
Ayer <u>hacía</u> mucho frío/calor.	It was very cold/hot yesterday.
<u>Hace</u> sol/viento.	It's sunny/windy.
Va a <u>hacer</u> sol/viento.	It's going to be sunny/windy.
<u>Hace</u> un tiempo horrible.	It's a horrible day./The weather's horrible.

➤ **hacer** is also used in combination with **que** and **desde** in impersonal time expressions, to talk about how long something has been going on or how long it has been since something happened.

<u>Hace</u> seis meses <u>que</u> vivo aquí. *or* Vivo aquí <u>desde hace</u> seis meses.	I've been living here for six months.
<u>Hace</u> tres años <u>que</u> estudio español *or* Estudio español <u>desde hace</u> tres años.	I've been studying Spanish for three years.

For further explanation of grammatical terms, please see pages viii-xii.

Hace mucho tiempo **que** no la veo *or* No la veo **desde hace** mucho tiempo.	I haven't seen her for ages *or* It's been ages since I saw her.
Hace varias semanas **que** no voy por allí *or* No voy por allí **desde hace** varias semanas.	I haven't been there for several weeks *or* It's been several weeks since I went there.

i Note in the above examples the use of the <u>present simple</u> in Spanish where in English we'd use the perfect tense or the past tense.

➤ **hacer** is also used impersonally in the expression (**me/te/le**) **hace falta**, which means *it is necessary* (*for me/you/him*).

Si <u>hace falta</u>, voy.	I'll go if necessary.
No <u>hace falta</u> llamar.	We/You/I don't need to call.
Me <u>hace falta</u> otro vaso más.	I need another glass.
No <u>hace falta</u> ser un experto.	You don't need to be an expert.
No <u>hacía falta</u>.	It wasn't necessary.

i Note that not all impersonal expressions in Spanish are translated into English using impersonal expressions.

➤ **haber** too can be used impersonally with the meaning *there is/there are*, *there was/there were*, *there will be*, and so on. It has the special form **hay** in the present. For the other tenses, you take the third person singular (the *'it'* form) of **haber** in the appropriate tense.

<u>Hay</u> un cine cerca de aquí.	There's a movie theater near here.
<u>Hay</u> dos supermercados.	There are two supermarkets.
No <u>hay</u> bares.	There are no bars.
<u>Había</u> mucho ruido.	There was a lot of noise.
<u>Había</u> muchos perros.	There were a lot of dogs.
<u>Hubo</u> un accidente.	There was an accident.
<u>Hubo</u> varios problemas.	There were several problems.
¿<u>Habrá</u> tiempo?	Will there be time?
¿<u>Habrá</u> suficientes sillas?	Will there be enough chairs?

i Note that you should <u>ALWAYS</u> use the singular form (never the plural), no matter how many things there are.

➤ **haber** is used in the construction **hay que** with an infinitive to talk about actions that need to be taken.

<u>Hay que</u> trabajar más.	We/You need to work harder.
<u>Hay que</u> ser respetuoso.	You/We/One must be respectful.
<u>Habrá</u> que decírselo.	We'll/You'll have to tell him.

➤ **ser** can be used in certain impersonal constructions with adjectives, for example:

- **es/era/fue** + adjective + infinitive

Es importante ahorrar dinero.	It's important to save money.
Fue ridículo hacer eso.	It was ridiculous to do that.
Sería mejor esperar.	It would be better to wait.

- **es/era/fue** + adjective + **que** + verb

Es cierto que tengo problemas.	It's true that I have problems.
Es verdad que trabaja mucho.	It's true that he works hard.

[*i*] Note that when they are used in the negative (**no es cierto que...**; **no es verdad que...**), these expressions have to be followed by the subjunctive.

➪ *For more information on the **Subjunctive**, see page 136.*

Grammar Extra!

When impersonal expressions that don't state facts are followed by **que** (meaning *that*) and a verb, this verb must be in the subjunctive.

For this reason, the following non-factual impersonal expressions are all followed by the subjunctive:

- **Es posible que...**   It's possible that... / ...might...
  Es posible que ganen.   They might win.
- **Es imposible que...**   It's impossible that... / ...can't possibly...
  Es imposible que lo sepan.   They can't possibly know.
- **Es necesario que...**   It's necessary that... / ...need to...
  No es necesario que vengas.   You don't need to come.
- **Es mejor que...**   ...be better to...
  Es mejor que no se entere.   It's better if he doesn't find out.

➪ *For more information on the **Subjunctive**, see page 136.*

➤ **ser** is also used impersonally with **de día** and **de noche** to say whether it's day or night.

Era de noche cuando llegamos.	It was night when we arrived.
Todavía es de día allí.	It's still day there.

➪ *For other time expressions with **ser**, see page 82.*

➤ **basta con** is used impersonally:

- with a following infinitive to mean *it's enough to/all you need do is*

Basta con llamar para reservar una mesa.	All you need to do is to call to reserve a table.

For further explanation of grammatical terms, please see pages viii-xii.

Basta con dar una vuelta por la ciudad para... You only need to take a walk around the city to ...

- with a <u>noun</u> or <u>pronoun</u> to mean *all you need is* or *all it takes is*

Basta con un error para que se enoje. All it takes is one mistake to make him angry.

➤ **(me) parece que** is used to give opinions.

<u>Parece que</u> va a llover. It looks as if it's going to rain.
<u>Me parece que</u> estás equivocado. I think that you are wrong.

i Note that when **(me) parece que** is used in the negative, the following verb has to be in the <u>subjunctive</u>.

⇨ *For more information on the **Subjunctive**, see page 136.*

➤ **vale la pena** is used to talk about what's worth doing.

Vale la pena. It's worth it.
No vale la pena. It's not worth it.
Vale la pena hacer el esfuerzo. It's worth making the effort.
No vale la pena gastar tanto dinero. It's not worth spending so much money.

Grammar Extra!

se is often used in impersonal expressions, especially with the verbs **creer**, **decir**, **poder**, and **tratar**. In such cases it often corresponds to *it*, *one* or *you* in English.

- **Se cree que...** It is thought *or* People think that...
  Se cree que es un mito. It is thought to be a myth.
- **Se dice que...** It is said *or* People say that...
  Se dice que es rico. He is said to be rich.
- **Se puede...** One can.../People can.../You can...
  Aquí se puede estacionar. One can park here.
- **Se trata de...** It's a question of.../It's about...
  No se trata de dinero. It isn't a question of money.
  Se trata de resolverlo. We must solve it.

⇨ *For more information on contructions with se, see page 97.*

Key points

✔ Impersonal verbs and expressions can only be used in the *'it'* form, the infinitive and the gerund.
✔ Impersonal expressions relating to the weather are very common.
✔ Although in English we use *there is* or *there are* depending on the number of people or things that there are, in Spanish **hay**, **había**, **hubo** and so on should be used in the singular form only.
✔ Some very common ordinary verbs are also used as impersonal verbs.

The subjunctive

> **What is the subjunctive?**
> The **subjunctive** is a verb form that is used in certain circumstances especially when expressing some sort of feeling or when there is doubt about whether something will happen or whether something is true. It is only used occasionally in modern English. For example: *If I were you, ...; So be it.; I wish you were here.*

1 Using the subjunctive

➤ Although you may not know it, you will already be familiar with many of the forms of the present subjunctive, as it is used when giving orders and instructions not to do something as well as in the **usted**, **ustedes** and **nosotros** forms of instructions to do something.

⇨ *For more information on* **Imperatives**, *see page 86.*

➤ In Spanish, the subjunctive is used after certain verbs and conjunctions when two parts of a sentence have different subjects.

Yo tengo miedo de que le ocurra algo.	I'm afraid <u>something</u> may (*subjunctive*) happen to him.

(The subject of the first part of the sentence is *I*; the subject of the second part of the sentence is *something*.).

➤ In English, in a sentence like *We want him/José to be happy*, we use an infinitive (*to be*) for the second verb even though *want* and *be happy* have different subjects (*we* and *him/José*).

➤ In Spanish, you cannot do this. You have to use the <u>subjunctive</u> for the second verb.

Queremos que nuestros hijos sean felices.	We want our children to be happy. (*Literally*: We want that our children (*subjunctive*) be happy.)
Queremos que (tú) seas feliz.	We want you to be happy. (*Literally*: We want that you (*subjunctive*) be happy.)

➤ You <u>CAN</u> use an infinitive for the second verb in Spanish when the subject of both verbs is the same.

Queremos ser felices.	We want to be happy.

2 | Recognizing the subjunctive

➤ The subjunctive has several tenses, the main ones being the present subjunctive and the imperfect subjunctive. The tense used for the subjunctive verb depends on the tense of the previous verb.

⇨ For more information on **Tenses with the subjunctive**, see page 141.

➤ In sentences containing two verbs with different subjects, you will find that the second verb is in the subjunctive when the first verb:

- expresses a wish

Quiero que <u>vengan</u>.	I want them to come.
Prefiero que te <u>quedes</u>.	I'd rather you stayed.
Deseamos que <u>tengan</u> éxito.	We want them to be successful.

- expresses an emotion

Siento mucho que no <u>puedas</u> venir.	I'm very sorry that you can't come.
Espero que <u>venga</u>.	I hope he comes.
Me sorprende que no <u>esté</u> aquí.	I'm surprised that he isn't here.
Me alegro de que te <u>gusten</u>.	I'm pleased that you like them.

➤ If the subject of both verbs is the <u>same</u>, an infinitive is used as the second verb instead of a subjunctive.

➤ Compare the following examples. In the examples on the left, both the verb expressing the wish or emotion and the second verb have the same subject, so the second verb is an <u>infinitive</u>. In the examples on the right, each verb has a different subject, so the second verb is in the <u>subjunctive</u>.

Infinitive construction	Subjunctive construction
Quiero <u>estudiar</u>. I want to study.	**Quiero que José <u>estudie</u>.** I want José to study.
Elena quiere <u>irse</u>. Elena wants to leave.	**Elena quiere que me <u>vaya</u>.** Elena wants me to leave.
Siento no <u>poder</u> venir. I'm sorry I can't come.	**Siento que no <u>puedas</u> venir.** I'm sorry that you can't come.
Me alegro de <u>poder</u> ayudar. I'm pleased to be able to help.	**Me alegro de que <u>puedas</u> ayudar.** I'm pleased you can help.

➤ You will also come across the verb + **que** + subjunctive construction (often with a personal object such as **me**, **te** and so on) when the first verb is one you use to ask or advise somebody to do something.

Sólo te pido que <u>tengas</u> cuidado.	I'm only asking you to be careful.
Te aconsejo que no <u>llegues</u> tarde.	I'd advise you not to be late.

➤ You will also come across the subjunctive in the following cases:

- after verbs expressing doubt or uncertainty, and verbs saying what you think about something that are used with **no**

Dudo que <u>tenga</u> tiempo.	I doubt I'll have time.
No creo que <u>venga</u>.	I don't think she'll come.
No pienso que <u>esté</u> bien.	I don't think it's right.

- in impersonal constructions that show a need to do something

¿Hace falta que <u>vaya</u> Jaime?	Does Jaime need to go?
No es necesario que <u>vengas</u>.	You don't need to come.

- in impersonal constructions that do not express facts

Es posible que <u>tengan</u> razón.	They may be right.

⇨ *For more information on **Impersonal verbs**, see page 132.*

Grammar Extra!

Use the <u>indicative</u> (that is, any verb form that isn't subjunctive) after impersonal expressions that state facts provided they are <u>NOT</u> in the negative.

Es verdad que <u>es</u> interesante.	It's true that it's interesting.
Es cierto que me <u>gusta</u> el café.	It's true I like coffee.
Parece que se <u>va</u> a ir.	It seems that he's going to go.

➤ The subjunctive is used after **que** to express wishes.

¡Que lo <u>pases</u> bien!	Have a good time!
¡Que te <u>diviertas</u>!	Have fun!

➤ The subjunctive is also used after certain conjunctions linking two parts of a sentence which each have different subjects.

- **antes de que** — before

¿Quieres decirle algo antes de que se <u>vaya</u>?	Do you want to say anything to him before he goes?

- **para que** — so that

Es para que te <u>acuerdes</u> de mí.	It's so that you'll remember me.

- **sin que** — without

Salimos sin que nos <u>vieran</u>.	We left without them seeing us.

⇨ *For more information on **Conjunctions**, see page 194.*

For further explanation of grammatical terms, please see pages viii-xii.

Tip

Use **para**, **sin** and **antes de** with the <u>infinitive</u> when the subject of both verbs is the <u>same</u>.

Fue en taxi para no <u>llegar</u> tarde. He went by taxi so that he wouldn't be late.

Pedro se fue sin <u>esperar</u>nos. Pedro left without waiting for us.

Cenamos antes de <u>ir</u> al teatro. We had dinner before we went to the theater.

3 Forming the present subjunctive

➤ To form the present subjunctive of most verbs, drop the **-o** ending of the **yo** form of the <u>present simple</u>, and attach a fixed set of endings.

➤ For **-ar** verbs, the endings are: **-e**, **-es**, **-e**, **-emos**, **-éis** (in Spain), **-en**.

➤ For both **-er** and **-ir** verbs, the endings are: **-a**, **-as**, **-a**, **-amos**, **-áis** (in Spain), **-an**.

➤ The following table shows the present subjunctive of three regular verbs: **hablar** (meaning *to speak*), **comer** (meaning *to eat*) and **vivir** (meaning *to live*).

Infinitive	(yo)	(tú)	(él) (ella) (usted)	(nosotros) (nosotras)	(vosotros)* (vosotras)*	(ellos) (ellas) (ustedes)
hablar to speak	hab<u>le</u>	hab<u>les</u>	hab<u>le</u>	hab<u>lemos</u>	hab<u>léis</u>*	hab<u>len</u>
comer to eat	com<u>a</u>	com<u>as</u>	com<u>a</u>	com<u>amos</u>	com<u>áis</u>*	com<u>an</u>
vivir to live	viv<u>a</u>	viv<u>as</u>	viv<u>a</u>	viv<u>amos</u>	viv<u>áis</u>*	viv<u>an</u>

*only used in Spain

Quiero que <u>comas</u> algo. I want you to eat something.

Me sorprende que no <u>hable</u> inglés. I'm surprised he doesn't speak English.

No es verdad que <u>trabajen</u> aquí. It isn't true that they work here.

➤ Some verbs have very irregular **yo** forms in the ordinary present tense and these irregular forms are reflected in the stem for the present subjunctive.

Infinitive	(yo)	(tú)	(él) (ella) (usted)	(nosotros) (nosotras)	(vosotros)* (vosotras)*	(ellos) (ellas) (ustedes)
decir to say	diga	digas	diga	digamos	digáis*	digan
hacer to do/make	haga	hagas	haga	hagamos	hagáis*	hagan
poner to put	ponga	pongas	ponga	pongamos	pongáis*	pongan
salir to leave	salga	salgas	salga	salgamos	salgáis*	salgan
tener to have	tenga	tengas	tenga	tengamos	tengáis*	tengan
venir to come	venga	vengas	venga	vengamos	vengáis*	vengan

*only used in Spain – note that this verb form has an accent.

Voy a limpiar la casa antes de que vengan.   I'm going to clean the house before they come.

Tip

The present subjunctive endings are the opposite of what you'd expect, as **-ar** verbs have endings starting with **-e**, and **-er** and **-ir** verbs have endings starting with **-a**.

4   **Forming the present subjunctive of irregular verbs**

➤ The following verbs have irregular subjunctive forms:

Infinitive	(yo)	(tú)	(él) (ella) (usted)	(nosotros) (nosotras)	(vosotros)* (vosotras)*	(ellos) (ellas) (ustedes)
dar to give	dé	des	dé	demos	deis*	den
estar to be	esté	estés	esté	estemos	estéis*	estén
haber to have	haya	hayas	haya	hayamos	hayáis*	hayan
ir to go	vaya	vayas	vaya	vayamos	vayáis*	vayan
saber to know	sepa	sepas	sepa	sepamos	sepáis*	sepan
ser to be	sea	seas	sea	seamos	seáis*	sean

*only used in Spain

No quiero que te vayas.   I don't want you to go.
Dudo que esté aquí.   I doubt if it's here.
No piensan que sea él.   They don't think it's him.
Es posible que haya problemas.   There may be problems.

For further explanation of grammatical terms, please see pages viii-xii.

➤ Verbs that change their stems (<u>radical-changing verbs</u>) in the ordinary present usually change them in the same way in the present subjunctive.

⇨ *For more information on **radical-changing verbs**, see page 76.*

Infinitive	(yo)	(tú)	(él) (ella) (usted)	(nosotros) (nosotras)	(vosotros)* (vosotras)*	(ellos) (ellas) (ustedes)
pensar to think	piense	pienses	piense	pensemos	penséis*	piensen
entender to understand	entienda	entiendas	entienda	entendamos	entendáis*	entiendan
poder to be able	pueda	puedas	pueda	podamos	podáis*	puedan
querer to want	quiera	quieras	quiera	queramos	queráis*	quieran
volver to return	vuelva	vuelvas	vuelva	volvamos	volváis*	vuelvan

*only used in Spain

No hace falta que <u>vuelvas</u>.	There's no need for you to come back.
Es para que lo <u>entiendas</u>.	It's so you'll understand.
Me alegro de que <u>puedas</u> venir.	I'm pleased you can come.

➤ Sometimes the stem of the **nosotros** and **vosotros** forms isn't the same as it is in the ordinary present tense.

Infinitive	(yo)	(tú)	(él) (ella) (usted)	(nosotros) (nosotras)	(vosotros)* (vosotras)*	(ellos) (ellas) (ustedes)
dormir to sleep	duerma	duermas	duerma	<u>durmamos</u>	<u>durmáis</u>*	duerman
morir to die	muera	mueras	muera	<u>muramos</u>	<u>muráis</u>*	mueran
pedir to ask for	pida	pidas	pida	<u>pidamos</u>	<u>pidáis</u>*	pidan
seguir to follow	siga	sigas	siga	<u>sigamos</u>	<u>sigáis</u>*	sigan
sentir to feel	sienta	sientas	sienta	<u>sintamos</u>	<u>sintáis</u>*	sientan

*only used in Spain

No quieren que sigamos cantando.	They don't want us to go on singing.

5   Tenses with the subjunctive

➤ If the verb in the first part of the sentence is in the <u>present, future</u> or <u>imperative</u>, the second verb will usually be in the <u>present subjunctive</u>.

Quiero (*present*) **que lo hagas** (*present subjunctive*).
I want you to do it.

Lo pondré (*future*) **en el closet para que no lo vea** (*present subjunctive*).
I'll put it in the closet so she won't see it.

Ven (*imperative*) **cuando quieras** (*present subjunctive*).
Come whenever you want.

➤ If the verb in the first part of the sentence is in the <u>conditional</u> or a <u>past tense</u>, the second verb will usually be in the <u>imperfect subjunctive</u>.

> **Me gustaría** *(conditional)* **que llegaras** *(imperfect subjunctive)* **temprano.** I'd like you to arrive early.
>
> **Les pedí** *(preterite)* **que me esperaran** *(imperfect subjunctive)*. I asked them to wait for me.

6   Indicative or subjunctive?

➤ Many expressions are followed by the <u>indicative</u> (the ordinary form of the verb) when they state facts, and by the <u>subjunctive</u> when they refer to possible or intended future events and outcomes.

➤ Certain conjunctions relating to time such as **cuando** (meaning *when*), **hasta que** (meaning *until*), **en cuanto** (meaning *as soon as*) and **mientras** (meaning *while*) are used with the <u>indicative</u> when the action has happened or when talking about what happens regularly.

> **¿Qué dijo cuando te <u>vio</u>?**   What did he say when he saw you?
>
> **Siempre lo veo cuando <u>voy</u>**   I always see him when I go to **a San Francisco.**   San Francisco.
>
> **Me quedé allí hasta que <u>volvió</u>**   I stayed there until Antonio came **Antonio.**   back.

➤ The same conjunctions are followed by the <u>subjunctive</u> when talking about a future time.

> **Dale recuerdos cuando**   Give him my regards when you **lo veas.**   see him.
>
> **Lo veré cuando vaya a**   I'll see him when I go to **San Francisco.**   San Francisco.
>
> **¿Por qué no te quedas aquí**   Why don't you stay here until **hasta que <u>vuelva</u> Antonio?**   Antonio comes back?

Grammar Extra!

aunque is used with the <u>indicative</u> (the ordinary verb forms) when it means *although* or *even though*. In this case, the second part of the sentence is stating a fact.

> **Me gusta el francés, aunque**   I like French, although I prefer **<u>prefiero</u> el alemán.**   German.
>
> **Aunque estaba cansada, seguí**   Although I was tired, I continued **trabajando.**   working.

aunque is used with the <u>subjunctive</u> when it means *even if*. Here, the second part of the sentence is not a fact.

> **Tienes que seguir aunque**   You have to go on, even if you are tired. **estés cansada.**

For further explanation of grammatical terms, please see pages viii-xii.

7 | Forming the imperfect subjunctive

➤ For all verbs, there are <u>two</u> imperfect subjunctive forms that are exactly the same in meaning.

➤ The stem for both imperfect subjunctive forms is the same: you drop the **-aron** or **-ieron** ending of the **ellos** form of the preterite and attach a fixed set of endings to what is left.

⇨ *For more information on the* **Preterite**, *see page 106.*

➤ For **-ar** verbs, the endings are: **-ara**, **-aras**, **-ara**, **-áramos**, **-arais** (in Spain), **-aran** *or* **-ase**, **-ases**, **-ase**, **-ásemos**, **-aseis** (in Spain), **-asen**. The first form is more common.

➤ For **-er** and **-ir** verbs, the endings are: **-iera**, **-ieras**, **-iera**, **-iéramos**, **-ierais** (in Spain), **-ieran** *or* **-iese**, **-ieses**, **-iese**, **-iésemos**, **-ieseis** (in Spain), **-iesen**. The first form is more common.

➤ The following table shows the imperfect subjunctive of three regular verbs: **hablar** (meaning *to speak*), **comer** (meaning *to eat*) and **vivir** (meaning *to live*).

Infinitive	(yo)	(tú)	(él) (ella) (usted)	(nosotros) (nosotras)	(vosotros)* (vosotras)*	(ellos) (ellas) (ustedes)
hablar to speak	hablara	hablaras	hablara	habláramos	hablarais*	hablaran
	hablase	hablases	hablase	hablásemos	hablaseis*	hablasen
comer to eat	comiera	comieras	comiera	comiéramos	comierais*	comieran
	comiese	comieses	comiese	comiésemos	comieseis*	comiesen
vivir to live	viviera	vivieras	viviera	viviéramos	vivierais*	vivieran
	viviese	vivieses	viviese	viviésemos	vivieseis*	viviesen

*only used in Spain

➤ Many verbs have irregular preterite forms which are reflected in the stem for the imperfect subjunctive. For example:

Infinitive	(yo)	(tú)	(él) (ella) (usted)	(nosotros) (nosotras)	(vosotros)* (vosotras)*	(ellos) (ellas) (ustedes)
dar to give	diera	dieras	diera	diéramos	dierais*	dieran
	diese	dieses	diese	diésemos	dieseis*	diesen
estar to be	estuviera	estuvieras	estuviera	estuviéramos	estuvierais*	estuvieran
	estuviese	estuvieses	estuviese	estuviésemos	estuvieseis*	estuviesen
hacer to do/ make	hiciera	hicieras	hiciera	hiciéramos	hicierais*	hicieran
	hiciese	hicieses	hiciese	hiciésemos	hicieseis*	hiciesen
poner to put	pusiera	pusieras	pusiera	pusiéramos	pusierais*	pusieran
	pusiese	pusieses	pusiese	pusiésemos	pusieseis*	pusiesen
tener to have	tuviera	tuvieras	tuviera	tuviéramos	tuvierais*	tuvieran
	tuviese	tuvieses	tuviese	tuviésemos	tuvieseis*	tuviesen
ser to be	fuera	fueras	fuera	fuéramos	fuerais*	fueran
	fuese	fueses	fuese	fuésemos	fueseis*	fuesen
venir to come	viniera	vinieras	viniera	viniéramos	vinierais*	vinieran
	viniese	vinieses	viniese	viniésemos	vinieseis*	viniesen

*only used in Spain

8   Forming the imperfect subjunctive of some irregular -ir verbs

➤ In some irregular -ir verbs – the ones that don't have an i in the **ellos** form of the preterite – -era, -eras, -era, -éramos, -erais, -eran or -ese, -eses, -ese, -ésemos, -eseis, -esen are added to the preterite stem instead of -iera and -iese and so on.

⇨ *For more information on the **Preterite**, see page 106.*

Infinitive	(yo)	(tú)	(él) (ella) (usted)	(nosotros) (nosotras)	(vosotros)* (vosotras)*	(ellos) (ellas) (ustedes)
decir to say	dijera	dijeras	dijera	dijéramos	dijerais*	dijeran
	dijese	dijeses	dijese	dijésemos	dijeseis*	dijesen
ir to go	fuera	fueras	fuera	fuéramos	fuerais*	fueran
	fuese	fueses	fuese	fuésemos	fueseis*	fuesen

*only used in Spain

ⓘ Note that the imperfect subjunctive forms of **ir** and **ser** are identical.

    Teníamos miedo de que se <u>fuera</u>. We were afraid he might leave.

    No podíamos creer que <u>fuera</u> él. We couldn't believe it was him.

For further explanation of grammatical terms, please see pages viii-xii.

9 **Present indicative or imperfect subjunctive after** si

➤ Like some other conjunctions, si (meaning *if*) is sometimes followed by the ordinary present tense (the <u>present indicative</u>) and sometimes by the <u>imperfect subjunctive</u>.

➤ si is followed by the <u>present indicative</u> when talking about likely possibilities.

Si <u>quieres</u>, te acompaño.	If you like, I'll come with you. *(and you might want me to come with you)*
Si venden periódicos, compra uno.	If they sell newspapers, get one. *(and they might sell newspapers)*

➤ si is followed by the <u>imperfect subjunctive</u> when talking about unlikely or impossible conditions.

Si <u>tuviera</u> más dinero, me lo compraría.	If I had more money, I'd buy it. *(but I haven't got more money)*
Si yo <u>fuera</u> tú, lo compraría.	If I were you, I'd buy it. *(but I'm not you)*

Tip

You probably need the imperfect subjunctive in Spanish after si if the English sentence has *would* in it.

Key points

✔ After certain verbs you have to use a subjunctive in Spanish when there is a different subject in the two parts of a sentence.

✔ A subjunctive is also found after impersonal expressions, as well as after certain conjunctions.

✔ The subjunctive can be avoided if the subject of both verbs is the same. An infinitive is normally used instead.

✔ The endings of the present subjunctive in regular -ar verbs are: -e, -es, -e, -emos, -éis (in Spain), -en.

✔ The endings of the present subjunctive in regular -er and -ir verbs are: -a, -as, -a, -amos, -áis (in Spain), -an.

✔ The endings of the imperfect subjunctive in regular -ar verbs are: -ara, -aras, -ara, -áramos, -arais (in Spain), -aran or -ase, -ases, -ase, -ásemos, -aseis (in Spain), -asen.

✔ The endings of the imperfect subjunctive in regular -er and -ir verbs are: -iera, -ieras, -iera, -iéramos, -ierais (in Spain), -ieran or -iese, -ieses, -iese, -iésemos, -ieseis (in Spain), -iesen.

✔ Some verbs have irregular subjunctive forms.

The Infinitive

> **What is the infinitive?**
> The **infinitive** is a form of the verb that hasn't had any endings added to it and doesn't relate to any particular tense. In English, the infinitive is usually shown with *to*, as in *to speak*, *to eat*, *to live*.

1 Using the infinitive

➤ In English, the infinitive is usually thought of as being made up of two words (for example: *to speak*). In Spanish, the infinitive consists of one word and is the verb form that ends in **-ar**, **-er** or **-ir** (for example: **hablar**, **comer**, **vivir**).

➤ When you look up a verb in the dictionary, you will find that information is usually listed under the infinitive form.

➤ In Spanish, the infinitive is often used in the following ways:

- after a preposition such as **antes de** (meaning *before*), **después de** (meaning *after*)

Después de comer, fuimos al club.	<u>After eating</u>, we went to the club.
Salió <u>sin hacer</u> ruido.	She went out <u>without making</u> a noise.
Siempre leo <u>antes de acostarme</u>.	I always read <u>before going to bed</u>.

[i] Note that in English we always use the *-ing* form of the verb after a preposition (for example: *before going*). In Spanish, you have to use the infinitive form after a preposition.

- in set phrases, particularly after adjectives or nouns

Estoy <u>encantada de poder</u> ayudarte.	I'm delighted to be able to help you.
Está <u>contento de vivir</u> aquí.	He's happy living here.
<u>Tengo ganas de salir</u>.	I feel like going out.
No <u>hace falta comprar</u> leche.	We/You don't need to buy any milk.
<u>Me dio</u> mucha <u>alegría verla</u>.	I was very pleased to see her.
<u>Me da miedo ir</u> sola.	I'm scared of going on my own.

- after another verb, sometimes as the object of it

<u>Tengo que llamar</u> a casa.	I have to call home.
<u>Prefiero esquiar</u>.	I prefer skiing.
<u>Me gusta escuchar</u> música.	I like listening to music.
<u>Nos encanta nadar</u>.	We love swimming.
<u>Odio esperar</u>.	I hate waiting.

i Note that, after verbs expressing like and dislike, the Spanish infinitive often corresponds to the *-ing* form in English.

- in instructions that are aimed at the general public – for example in cook books or on signs

<u>Cocer</u> a fuego lento.	Cook on a low heat.
Prohibido <u>sacar</u> fotos.	No photography.

- as a noun, where in English we would use the *-ing* form of the verb

Lo importante es <u>intentar</u>lo.	Trying is the important thing.

> ### Tip
> Be especially careful when translating the English *-ing* form. It is often translated by the infinitive in Spanish.

2 | Linking two verbs together

➤ There are three ways that verbs can be linked together when the second verb is an infinitive:

- with no linking word in between

¿Quieres venir?	Do you want to come?
Necesito hablar contigo.	I need to talk to you.

- with a preposition:

ir <u>a</u> hacer algo	to be going to do something
aprender <u>a</u> hacer algo	to learn to do something
dejar <u>de</u> hacer algo	to stop doing something
Voy <u>a</u> comprarme un celular.	I'm going to buy a cell phone.
Aprendimos <u>a</u> esquiar.	We learned to ski.
Quiere dejar <u>de</u> fumar.	He wants to stop smoking.

i Note that you have to learn the preposition required for each verb.

- in set structures

tener que hacer algo	to have to do something
Tengo que salir.	I've got to go out.
Tendrías que comer más.	You should eat more.
Tuvo que devolver el dinero.	He had to pay back the money.

3 Verbs followed by the infinitive with no preposition

➤ Some Spanish verbs and groups of verbs can be followed by an infinitive with no preposition:

- **poder** (meaning *to be able to, can, may*), **saber** (meaning *to know how to, can*), **querer** (meaning *to want*) and **deber** (meaning *to have to, must*)

No <u>puede venir</u>.	He can't come.
¿<u>Sabes esquiar</u>?	Can you ski?
<u>Quiere estudiar</u> medicina.	He wants to study medicine.
<u>Debes hacerlo</u>.	You must do it.

- verbs like **gustar** and **encantar**, where the infinitive is the subject of the verb

<u>Me gusta estudiar</u>.	I like studying.
<u>Nos encanta bailar</u>.	We love dancing.

- verbs that relate to seeing or hearing, such as **ver** (meaning *to see*) and **oír** (meaning *to hear*)

Nos <u>ha visto llegar</u>.	He saw us arrive.
Te <u>oí cantar</u>.	I heard you singing.

- the verbs **hacer** (meaning *to make*) and **dejar** (meaning *to let*)

¡No me <u>hagas reír</u>!	Don't make me laugh!
Mis padres no me <u>dejan salir</u> por la noche.	My parents don't let me go out at night.

- the following common verbs

decidir	to decide
desear	to wish, want
esperar	to hope
evitar	to avoid
necesitar	to need
odiar	to hate
olvidar	to forget
pensar	to think
preferir	to prefer
recordar	to remember
sentir	to regret

<u>Decidieron comprarse</u> una casa.	They decided to buy a house.
No <u>desea tener</u> más hijos.	She doesn't want to have any more children.
<u>Espero poder</u> ir.	I hope to be able to go.

For further explanation of grammatical terms, please see pages viii-xii.

<u>Evita gastar</u> demasiado dinero.	Avoid spending too much money.
<u>Necesito salir</u> un momento.	I need to go out for a moment.
<u>Olvidó dejar</u> su dirección.	She forgot to leave her address.
<u>Pienso hacer</u> enchiladas.	I'm thinking of making enchiladas.
<u>Siento molestarte</u>.	I'm sorry to bother you.

➤ Some of these verbs combine with infinitives to make set phrases with a special meaning:

- querer decir — to mean
  ¿Qué <u>quiere decir</u> eso? — What does that mean?

- dejar caer — to drop
  <u>Dejó caer</u> la bandeja. — She dropped the tray.

4 Verbs followed by the preposition a and the infinitive

➤ The following verbs are the most common ones that can be followed by **a** and the infinitive:

- verbs relating to movement such as **ir** (meaning *to go*) and **venir** (meaning *to come*)

Se va <u>a</u> comprar un caballo.	He's going to buy a horse.
Viene <u>a</u> vernos.	He's coming to see us.

- the following common verbs

aprender <u>a</u> hacer algo	to learn to do something
comenzar <u>a</u> hacer algo	to begin to do something
decidirse <u>a</u> hacer algo	to decide to do something
empezar <u>a</u> hacer algo	to begin to do something
llegar <u>a</u> hacer algo	to manage to do something
llegar <u>a</u> ser algo	to become something
probar <u>a</u> hacer algo	to try to do something
volver <u>a</u> hacer algo	to do something again

Me gustaría aprender <u>a</u> nadar.	I'd like to learn to swim.
No llegó <u>a</u> terminar la carrera.	He didn't manage to finish college.
Llegó <u>a</u> ser presidente.	He became president.
No vuelvas <u>a</u> hacerlo nunca más.	Don't ever do it again.

➤ The following verbs can be followed by **a** + a person's name or by **a** + a noun or pronoun referring to a person, and by **a** + infinitive. In the case of **a** + a person's name or **a** + a noun, this can also be placed after the **a** + infinitive.

ayudar <u>a</u> alguien <u>a</u> hacer algo	to help someone to do something
enseñar <u>a</u> alguien <u>a</u> hacer algo	to teach someone to do something
invitar <u>a</u> alguien <u>a</u> hacer algo	to invite someone to do something

Ayuda <u>a</u> mamá a poner la mesa.	Help Mom set the table.
¿Por qué no le enseñas a nadar a tu hermano?	Why don't you teach your brother to swim?
Los invité <u>a</u> cenar en casa.	I invited them over for dinner.

5   <u>Verbs followed by the preposition de and the infinitive</u>

➤ The following verbs are the most common ones that can be followed by de and the infinitive:

aburrirse <u>de</u> hacer algo	to get bored with doing something
acabar <u>de</u> hacer algo	to have just done something
acordarse <u>de</u> haber hecho/<u>de</u> hacer algo	to remember doing/to do something
alegrarse <u>de</u> hacer algo	to be glad to do something
dejar <u>de</u> hacer algo	to stop doing something
tener ganas <u>de</u> hacer algo	to feel like doing something
tratar <u>de</u> hacer algo	to try to do something
Me aburrí <u>de</u> jugar a las cartas.	I got bored with playing cards.
Acabo <u>de</u> comprar un celular.	I just bought a cell phone.
Acababan <u>de</u> llegar cuando...	They had just arrived when...
Me alegro <u>de</u> verte.	I'm glad to see you.
¿Quieres dejar <u>de</u> hablar?	Will you stop talking?
Tengo ganas <u>de</u> ir al cine.	I feel like going to the movies.

6   <u>Verbs followed by the preposition con and the infinitive</u>

➤ The following verbs are the most common ones that can be followed by con and the infinitive:

amenazar <u>con</u> hacer algo	to threaten to do someting
soñar <u>con</u> hacer algo	to dream of doing something
Amenazó <u>con</u> denunciarlos.	He threatened to report them.
Sueño <u>con</u> hacer un crucero.	I dream of going on a cruise.

7   <u>Verbs followed by the preposition en and the infinitive</u>

➤ The verb quedar is the most common one that can be followed by en and the infinitive:

quedar <u>en</u> hacer algo	to agree to do something
Habíamos quedado <u>en</u> encontrarnos a las ocho.	We had agreed to meet at eight.

For further explanation of grammatical terms, please see pages viii-xii.

Key points

✔ Infinitives are found after prepositions, set phrases and in instructions to the general public.

✔ They can also function as the subject or object of a verb, when the infinitive corresponds to the *-ing* form in English.

✔ Many Spanish verbs can be followed by another verb in the infinitive.

✔ Two verbs may be linked by nothing at all, or by **a**, **de** or another preposition.

✔ In Spanish, the construction does not always match the English. It's best to learn these constructions when you learn a new verb.

Prepositions after verbs

➤ In English, there are some phrases which are made up of verbs and prepositions (for example: *to accuse somebody of something*, *to look forward to something* and *to rely on something*).

➤ In Spanish, there are also lots of set phrases made up of verbs and prepositions. Often the prepositions in Spanish are not the same as they are in English, so you will need to learn them. Listed below are phrases using verbs and some common Spanish prepositions.

⇨ *For more information on verbs used with a preposition and the infinitive, see page 149.*

1   Verbs followed by a

➤ **a** is often the equivalent of the English word *to* when it is used with an indirect object after verbs like **enviar** (meaning *to send*), **dar** (meaning *to give*) and **decir** (meaning *to say*).

darle algo a alguien	to give something to someone
decirle algo a alguien	to say something to someone
enviarle algo a alguien	to send something to someone
escribirle algo a alguien	to write something to someone
mostrarle algo a alguien	to show something to someone

⇨ *For more information on **Indirect objects**, see page 49.*

> *Tip*
>
> There is an important difference between Spanish and English with this type of verb. In English, you can say either *I gave the keys to Susan* or *I gave Susan the keys*, leaving out the *to*.
> You can <u>NEVER</u> leave out **a** in Spanish in this way: *Le di las llaves a Susan*.

➤ Here are some verbs using **a** in Spanish that have a different construction in English.

asistir a algo	to attend something, to be at something
dirigirse a (un lugar)	to head for (a place)
dirigirse a alguien	to address somebody
llegar a (un lugar)	to arrive at (a place)
oler a algo	to smell of something
parecerse a alguien/algo	to look like somebody/something

subir(se) **a** un tren/un coche	to get on a train/into a car
subir(se) **a** un árbol	to climb a tree
tenerle miedo **a** alguien	to be afraid of somebody
Este perfume huele **a** jazmín.	This perfume smells of jasmine.
Se parece **a** tu hermana.	She looks like your sister.
Nunca le tuvieron miedo **a** su padre.	They were never afraid of their father.

➭ *For verbs such as* gustar, encantar *and* faltar, *see* **Verbal idioms** *on page 156.*

2 **Verbs followed by de**

➤ Here are some verbs using **de** in Spanish that have a different construction in English:

acordarse **de** algo/alguien	to remember something/somebody
alegrarse **de** algo	to be glad about something
bajarse **de** un tren/un coche	to get off a train/out of a car
darse cuenta **de** algo	to realize something
depender **de** algo/alguien	to depend on something/somebody
despedirse **de** alguien	to say goodbye to somebody
preocuparse **de** (*or* por) algo/alguien	to worry about something/somebody
quejarse **de** algo	to complain about something
reírse **de** algo/alguien	to laugh at something/somebody
salir **de** (un cuarto/un edificio)	to leave (a room/a building)
tener ganas **de** algo	to want something, to feel like something
tener miedo **de** algo	to be afraid of something
trabajar **de** (mecánico/secretario)	to work as (a mechanic/secretary)
tratarse **de** algo/alguien	to be a question of something/to be about somebody
Nos acordamos muy bien **de** aquellas vacaciones.	We remember that vacation very well.
Se bajó **del** tren.	He got off the train.
No depende **de** mí.	It doesn't depend on me.
No te rías **de** ella.	Don't laugh at her.

3 | Verbs followed by con

➤ Here are some verbs using **con** in Spanish that have a different construction in English:

comparar algo/a alguien con algo/alguien	to compare something/somebody with something/somebody
contar con alguien/algo	to rely on somebody/something
encontrarse con alguien	to meet somebody (*by chance*)
enojarse con alguien	to get annoyed with somebody
estar de acuerdo con alguien/algo	to agree with somebody/something
hablar con alguien	to talk to somebody
soñar con alguien/algo	to dream about somebody/something
Cuento contigo.	I'm relying on you.
Me encontré con ella al salir del banco.	I met her as I was leaving the bank.
¿Puedo hablar con usted un momento?	May I talk to you for a moment?

4 | Verbs followed by en

➤ Here are some verbs using **en** in Spanish that have a different construction in English:

entrar en (un edificio/ un cuarto)	to enter, go into (a building/a room)
pensar en algo/alguien	to think about *or* of something/somebody
trabajar en (una oficina/ una fábrica)	to work in (an office/a factory)
No quiero pensar en eso.	I don't want to think about that.

5 | Verbs followed by por

➤ Here are some verbs using **por** in Spanish that have a different construction in English:

interesarse por algo/alguien	to take an interest in something/somebody; to ask about something/somebody
preguntar por alguien	to ask for/about somebody
preocuparse por (*or* de) algo/alguien	to worry about something/somebody

For further explanation of grammatical terms, please see pages viii-xii.

| Se interesó <u>por</u> la marcha del proyecto. | He asked about the progress of the project. |
| Se preocupa mucho <u>por</u> su apariencia. | He worries a lot about his appearance. |

6 Verbs taking a direct object in Spanish but not in English

➤ In English there are a few verbs that are followed by *at*, *for* or *to* which, in Spanish, are not followed by any preposition other than the personal **a**.

➪ For more information on **Personal** *a*, see page 184.

mirar algo/a alguien	to look at something/somebody
escuchar algo/a alguien	to listen to something/somebody
buscar algo/a alguien	to look for something/somebody
pedir algo	to ask for something
esperar algo/a alguien	to wait for something/somebody
pagar algo	to pay for something

Mira esta foto.	Look at this photo.
Me gusta escuchar música.	I like listening to music.
Estoy buscando los lentes.	I'm looking for my glasses.
Pidió una taza de té.	He asked for a cup of tea.
Estamos esperando el tren.	We're waiting for the train.
Ya pagué el recibo del teléfono.	I've already paid the phone bill.
Estoy buscando a mi hermano.	I'm looking for my brother.

Key points

✔ The prepositions used with Spanish verbs are often very different from those used in English, so make sure you learn common expressions involving Spanish prepositions.

✔ In Spanish, the most common prepositions used with verbs are **a**, **de**, **con**, **en** and **por**.

✔ Some Spanish verbs are not followed by a preposition, but are used with a preposition in English.

Verbal Idioms

1 Present tense of gustar

➤ You will probably already have come across the phrase **me gusta...** meaning *I like...* . Actually, **gustar** literally means *to please*. If you remember this, you will be able to use **gustar** much more easily.

Me <u>gusta</u> **el chocolate.**	I like chocolate. (*literally: chocolate* <u>*pleases*</u> *me*)
Me <u>gustan</u> **los animales.**	I like animals. (*literally: animals* <u>*please*</u> *me*)
Nos <u>gusta</u> **el tenis.**	We like tennis. (*literally: tennis* <u>*pleases*</u> *us*)
Nos <u>gustan</u> **todos los deportes.**	We like all sports. (*literally: all sports* <u>*please*</u> *us*)

➤ Even though **chocolate**, **animales**, and so on, come after **gustar**, they are the <u>subject</u> of the verb (the person or thing performing the action) and, therefore, the endings of **gustar** change to agree with them.

➤ When the thing that you like is <u>singular</u>, you use **gusta** (*third person singular*), and when the thing that you like is <u>plural</u>, you use **gustan** (*third person plural*).

Le <u>gusta</u> **Colombia.**	He/She likes Colombia. (*literally: Colombia* <u>*pleases*</u> *him/her*)
Le <u>gustan</u> **los colombianos.**	He/She likes Colombians. (*literally: Colombians* <u>*please*</u> *him/her*)

i Note that **me**, **te**, **le**, **nos**, **os** and **les**, which are used with **gustar**, are indirect object pronouns.

➪ For more information on **Indirect object pronouns**, see page 49.

2 Other tenses of gustar

➤ You can also use **gustar** in other tenses.

Les <u>gustó</u> **la fiesta.**	They liked the party.
Les <u>gustaron</u> **los fuegos artificiales.**	They liked the fireworks.
Te <u>va a gustar</u> **la película.**	You'll like the movie.
Te <u>van a gustar</u> **las fotos.**	You'll like the photos.

➤ You can also use **más** with **gustar** to say what you prefer.

A mí me <u>gusta más</u> el rojo.	I prefer the red one. (*literally: the red one pleases me more*)
A mí me <u>gustan más</u> los rojos.	I prefer the red ones. (*literally: the red ones please me more*)

3	**Other verbs like** <u>gustar</u>

➤ There are several other verbs which behave in the same way as **gustar**:

- encantar

Me <u>encanta</u> el jazz.	I love jazz.
Me <u>encantan</u> los animales.	I love animals.

- faltar

Le <u>faltaba</u> un botón.	He had a button missing.
Le <u>faltaban</u> tres dientes.	He had three teeth missing.

- quedar

No les <u>queda</u> nada.	They have nothing left.
Sólo nos <u>quedan</u> dos capítulos.	We only have two chapters left.

- doler

Le <u>dolía</u> la cabeza.	His head hurt.
Le <u>dolían</u> las muelas.	His teeth hurt.

- interesar

Le <u>interesó</u> la oferta.	He was interested in the offer.
Siempre me <u>interesaron</u> estos temas.	I've always been interested in these issues.

- importar

No me <u>importa</u> el dinero.	Money doesn't matter to me.
Me <u>importan</u> mucho mis estudios.	My studies matter to me a lot.

- hacer falta

Nos <u>hace</u> falta una computadora.	We need a computer.
Nos <u>hacen</u> falta libros.	We need books.

Grammar Extra!

All of the examples above are in the third persons singular and plural as these are by far the most common. However, it is also possible to use these verbs in other forms.

Creo que le <u>gustas</u>.	I think he likes you. (*literally: I think you please him*)

---

4 **Verbal idioms used with another verb**

➤ In English, you can say *I like playing chess, we love swimming* and so on. In Spanish, you can also use another verb with most of the verbs similar to **gustar**. However, in Spanish, the verb form you use for the second verb is the <u>infinitive</u>.

Le <u>gusta jugar</u> tenis.	He/She likes playing tennis.
No me <u>gusta bailar</u>.	I don't like dancing.
Nos <u>encanta cocinar</u>.	We love cooking.
No me <u>importa tener</u> que esperar.	I don't mind having to wait.

⇨ *For more information on the **Infinitive**, see page 146.*

> **Key points**
> ✔ In Spanish, there are a number of common verbs which are used in the opposite way to English, for example, **gustar**, **encantar**, **hacer falta**, and so on. With all of these verbs, the object of the English verb is the subject of the Spanish verb.
> ✔ The endings of these verbs change according to whether the thing liked or needed and so on is singular or plural.
> ✔ All of these verbs can be followed by another verb in the infinitive.

Negatives

What is a negative?
A **negative** question or statement is one which contains a word such as *not*, *never* or *nothing* and is used to say that something is not happening, is not true or is absent.

1   <u>no</u>

➤ In English, we often make sentences negative by adding *don't*, *doesn't* or *didn't* before the verb. In Spanish you simply add **no** before the main verb.

Affirmative			Negative	
Trabaja.	He works.	→	**No** trabaja.	He doesn't work.
Comen.	They eat.	→	**No** comen.	They don't eat.
Salió.	She went out.	→	**No** salió.	She didn't go out.
Lo sabía.	I knew (it).	→	**No** lo sabía.	I didn't know (it).
Sabe nadar.	He can swim.	→	**No** sabe nadar.	He can't swim.

> *Tip*
>
> *don't*, *doesn't* and *didn't* do not have an equivalent in Spanish.
> You just add **no** to form the negative.

➤ When there is a subject (the person doing the action) in the sentence, put **no** between the subject and the verb.

Juan <u>no</u> vive aquí.	Juan doesn't live here.
Mi hermana <u>no</u> lee mucho.	My sister doesn't read much.
Mis padres <u>no</u> llamaron.	My parents didn't call.
Él <u>no</u> lo entenderá.	He won't understand.

[i] Note that the Spanish word **no** also means *no* in answer to a question.

➤ Where the subject is only shown by the verb ending, **no** goes before the verb.

<u>No</u> tenemos tiempo.	We don't have time.
Todavía <u>no</u> ha llegado.	He hasn't arrived yet.
<u>No</u> habíamos comido.	We hadn't eaten.
<u>No</u> va a llevar mucho tiempo.	It won't take long.

➤ If there are any object pronouns (for example: **me**, **te**, **lo**, **los**, **le** and so on) before the verb, **no** goes <u>BEFORE</u> them.

<u>No</u> la vi.	I didn't see her.
<u>No</u> me gusta el beisbol.	I don't like baseball.

➤ In phrases consisting only of *not* and another word, such as *not now* or *not me*, the Spanish **no** usually goes <u>AFTER</u> the other word.

Ahora <u>no</u>.	Not now.
Yo <u>no</u>.	Not me.
Todavía <u>no</u>.	Not yet.

➤ Some phrases have a special construction in Spanish.

Espero que sí.	I hope so.	→	**Espero que no.**	I hope not.
Creo que sí.	I think so.	→	**Creo que no.**	I don't think so.

2 | Other negative words

➤ In Spanish, you can form negatives using pairs and groups of words, as you can in English.

- **no ... nunca**   never *or* not ... ever
  <u>No</u> la veo <u>nunca</u>.   I never see her *or*
  I don't ever see her.

- **no ... jamás**   never *or* not ... ever
  <u>No</u> la veo <u>jamás</u>.   I never ever see her *or*
  I don't ever see her.

- **no ... nada**   nothing *or* not ... anything
  <u>No</u> dijo <u>nada</u>.   He said nothing *or*
  He didn't say anything.

- **no ... nadie**   nobody *or* not ... anybody
  <u>No</u> hablaron con <u>nadie</u>.   They spoke to nobody *or*
  They didn't speak to anybody.

- **no ... tampoco**   not ... either
  Yo <u>no</u> la vi. – Yo <u>tampoco</u>.   I didn't see her. – Neither did I.
  or I didn't either. *or* Nor did I.

  A él <u>no</u> le gusta el café y a mí   He doesn't like coffee and neither
  <u>tampoco</u>.   do I.

- **no ... ni ... ni**   neither ... nor
  <u>No</u> vinieron <u>ni</u> Carlos <u>ni</u> Ana.   Neither Carlos nor Ana came.

- **no ... más**   no longer *or* not .. any more
  <u>No</u> te veré <u>más</u>.   I won't see you any more.

- **no ... ningún/ninguna** + *noun*   no *or* not ... any
  <u>No</u> tiene <u>ningún</u> interés en ir.   She has no interest in going.

➤ In answers to questions or before a verb, most of these negative words can also be used without **no**.

¿Qué compraste? <u>Nada</u>.	What did you buy? Nothing.
¿Quién llamó? <u>Nadie</u>.	Who called? No one.
<u>Nunca</u> la veo.	I never see her.
<u>Nadie</u> nos ayudó.	No one helped us.
<u>Ni</u> Pedro <u>ni</u> Pablo fuman.	Neither Pedro nor Pablo smokes.

➤ Sometimes negative expressions combine with each other.

<u>Nunca</u> hacen <u>nada</u>.	They never do anything.
<u>Nunca</u> viene <u>nadie</u>.	No one ever comes.
<u>No</u> lo haré <u>nunca más</u>.	I'll never do it again.
<u>No</u> veo <u>nunca</u> a <u>nadie</u>.	I never see anyone.

[3] **Word order with negatives**

➤ In English you can put words like *never* and *ever* between *have/has/had* and the past participle, for example, *We <u>have</u> never <u>been</u> to Argentina*. In Spanish, you should <u>NEVER</u> separate **he**, **has**, **ha**, **había** and so on from the past participle of the verb.

<u>Nunca</u> hemos estado en Argentina.	We have never been to Argentina.
<u>Nunca</u> había visto <u>nada</u> así.	I had never seen anything like this.
<u>Ninguno</u> de nosotros había esquiado <u>nunca</u>.	None of us had ever skied.

⇨ *For more information on **Past participles**, see page 118.*

Key points

✔ The Spanish word **no** is equivalent to both *no* and *not* in English.

✔ You can make sentences negative by putting **no** before the verb (and before any object pronouns that are in front of the verb).

✔ Other negative words also exist, such as **nunca**, **nadie** and **nada**. Use them in combination with **no**, with the verb sandwiched in between. Most of them also work on their own, in answers to questions or <u>before</u> a verb.

✔ Never insert negative words, or anything else, between **he**, **has**, **ha**, **había** and so on and the past participle.

Questions

What is a question?
A **question** is a sentence which is used to ask someone about something and which often has the verb in front of the subject. Questions often include a question word such as *why*, *when*, *where*, *who*, *which* or *how*.

Asking questions in Spanish

In Spanish, there are three main ways of asking questions:

- by making your voice go up at the end of the sentence
- by changing normal word order
- by using a question word

> **Tip**
>
> Don't forget the opening question mark in written Spanish. It goes at the beginning of the question or of the question part of a sentence.
>
> **¿No quieres tomar algo?** Wouldn't you like something to eat or drink?
>
> **Eres cubano, ¿no?** You're Cuban, aren't you?

1 Asking a question by making your voice go up

➤ If you are expecting a *yes* or *no* answer, there is a very simple way of asking a question. You keep the word order exactly as it would be in a normal sentence but you turn it into a question by making your voice go up at the end.

¿Hablas español?	Do you speak Spanish?
¿Es profesor?	Is he a teacher?
¿Hay leche?	Is there any milk?
¿Te gusta la música?	Do you like music?

➤ When the subject (the person or thing doing the action) of the verb is a noun, pronoun or name, it can be placed before the verb, as in an ordinary sentence. The difference is that you turn the statement into a question by making your voice go up at the end.

¿Tu hermana compró pan?	Did your sister buy any bread?
¿Tú lo hiciste?	Did you do it?
¿Tu padre te vio?	Did your father see you?
¿Paula va a venir?	Is Paula coming?

For further explanation of grammatical terms, please see pages viii-xii.

2   Asking a question by changing word order

➤ When the subject of the verb is specified, another common way of asking questions is to change the word order so that the verb comes <u>BEFORE</u> the subject instead of after it.

¿Lo hiciste tú?	Did you do it?
¿Te vio tu padre?	Did your father see you?
¿Va a venir Paula?	Is Paula coming?

¿ Note that the position of object pronouns is not affected.

⇨ *For more information on **Word order with object pronouns**, see pages 47, 50 and 52.*

Grammar Extra!

If the verb has an object, such as *any bread* in *Did your sister buy any bread?*, the subject comes <u>AFTER</u> the object, provided the object is short.

¿Compró <u>pan</u> tu hermana?	Did your sister buy any bread?
¿Trajo la <u>cámara</u> tu novio?	Did your boyfriend bring the camera?

If the object is made up of several words, the subject goes <u>BEFORE</u> it.

Se compraron tus padres <u>aquella casa de que me hablaste</u>?	Did your parents buy that house you told me about?

When there is an adverbial phrase after the verb (*to the party*, *in Lima*), the subject can go <u>BEFORE OR AFTER</u> the adverbial phrase, depending on the emphasis of the question.

¿Viene <u>a la fiesta</u> Andrés? *or*	Is Andrés coming to the party?
¿Viene Andrés <u>a la fiesta</u>?	

---

3   Asking a question by using a question word

➤ Question words are words like *when, what, who, which, where* and *how* that are used to ask for information. In Spanish, <u>ALL</u> question words have an accent on them.

¿adónde?	where ... to?
¿cómo?	how?
¿cuál/cuáles?	which
¿cuándo?	when?
¿cuánto/cuánta?	how much?
¿cuántos/cuántas?	how many?
¿dónde?	where?
¿para qué?	what for?
¿por qué?	why?
¿qué?	what?, which?
¿quién?	who?

> **Típ**
>
> Be careful not to mix up **por qué** (meaning *why*) with **porque** (meaning *because*).

¿**Cuándo** se fue?	When did he go?
¿**Qué** te pasa?	What's the matter?
¿**Qué** vestido te vas a poner?	Which dress are you going to wear?
¿**Cuál** de los dos quieres?	Which do you want?
¿**Cuánto** café quieres?	How much coffee do you want?
¿**Cuánto** tiempo hace que esperas?	How long have you been waiting?

➪ *For more information on question words, see **Interrogative adjectives** on page 32 and **Interrogative pronouns** on page 65.*

➤ When a question starts with a question word that isn't the subject of the verb, the subject noun or pronoun (if expressed) goes <u>AFTER</u> the verb.

¿De qué color es <u>la alfombra</u>?	What color's the rug?
¿A qué hora empieza <u>el concierto</u>?	What time does the concert start?
¿Dónde están <u>tus pantalones</u>?	Where are your pants?
¿Adónde iba <u>tu padre</u>?	Where was your father going?
¿Cómo están <u>tus padres</u>?	How are your parents?
¿Cuándo volverán <u>los inspectores</u>?	When will the inspectors come back?

4 Which question word to use?

➤ **qué** or **cuál** or **cuáles** can be used to mean *which*:

- always use **qué** before a noun

¿<u>**Qué** vestido</u> te vas a poner?	<u>Which dress</u> are you going to wear?

- otherwise use **cuál** (*singular*) or **cuáles** (*plural*)

¿<u>**Cuál**</u> quieres?	<u>Which (one)</u> do you want?
¿<u>**Cuáles**</u> quieres?	<u>Which (ones)</u> do you want?

➤ **quién** or **quiénes** can be used to mean *who*:

- use **quién** when asking about one person

¿<u>**Quién**</u> ganó?	<u>Who</u> won?

- use **quiénes** when asking about more than one person

¿<u>**Quiénes**</u> estaban?	<u>Who</u> was there?

For further explanation of grammatical terms, please see pages viii-xii.

i Note that you need to put the personal **a** before **quién** and **quiénes** when they act as objects.

¿<u>A quién</u> viste?	<u>Who</u> did you see?

⇨ *For more information on **Personal a**, see page 184.*

➤ **de quién** and **de quiénes** are used to mean *whose*:
- use **de quién** when there is likely to be one owner
¿<u>De quién</u> es este abrigo?	<u>Whose</u> coat is this?
- use **de quiénes** when there is likely to be more than one owner
¿<u>De quiénes</u> son estos abrigos?	<u>Whose</u> coats are these?

i Note that, in Spanish, the structure is the equivalent of *Whose <u>is</u> this coat?/Whose <u>are</u> these coats?* Don't try putting ¿**de quién?** or ¿**de quiénes?** immediately before a noun.

➤ **qué**, **cómo**, **cuál** and **cuáles** can all be used to mean *what* although **qué** is the most common translation:
- use **cómo** not **qué** when asking someone to repeat something that you didn't hear properly
¿<u>Cómo</u>?	<u>What</u> (did you say)?
- use ¿**cuál es ... ?** and ¿**cuáles son ... ?** to mean *what is ... ?* and *what/are ... ?* when you aren't asking for a definition
¿<u>Cuál es</u> la capital de Francia?	<u>What's</u> the capital of France?
¿<u>Cuál es</u> su número de teléfono?	<u>What's</u> his telephone number?
- use ¿**qué es ... ?** and ¿**qué son ... ?** to mean *what is ... ?* and *what are ... ?* when you are asking for a definition
¿<u>Qué son</u> los genes?	<u>What are</u> genes?
- always use **qué** to mean *what* before another noun
¿<u>Qué hora</u> es?	<u>What time</u> is it?
¿<u>Qué materias</u> estudias?	<u>What subjects</u> are you studying?

Tip

You can finish an English question (or sentence) with a preposition such as *about*, for example, *Who did you write to?* *What are you talking about?*. In Spanish, you can <u>NEVER</u> end a question or sentence with a preposition.

¿<u>Con</u> quién hablaste?	Who did you speak <u>to</u>?

Grammar Extra!

All the questions we have looked at so far have been straight questions, otherwise known as <u>direct questions</u>. However, sometimes instead of asking directly (for example: *Where is it?* or *Why did you do it?*), we ask the question in a more roundabout way (for example: *Can you tell me where it is?* or *Please tell me why you did it*). These are called <u>indirect questions.</u>

In English indirect questions we say *where <u>it is</u>* instead of *where <u>is it</u>* and *why <u>you did it</u>* instead of *why <u>did you do it</u>*. In Spanish, however, you still put the subject <u>AFTER</u> the verb.

¿Sabes adónde <u>iba tu papá</u>?	Do you know where your dad was going?
¿Puedes decirme para qué <u>sirven los diccionarios</u>?	Can you tell me what dictionaries are for?

In Spanish, the subject also goes <u>AFTER</u> the verb when you report a question in indirect speech.

Quería saber adónde <u>iba mi papá</u>.	He wanted to know where my dad was going.

(i) Note that, in Spanish, you still put accents on question words even when they are in indirect and reported questions or when they come after expressions of uncertainty:

No sé <u>qué</u> hacer.	I don't know what to do.
No sabemos <u>por qué</u> se fue.	We don't know why he left.

5   Negative questions

➤ When you want to make a negative question, put **no** before the verb in the same way that you do in statements (non-questions).

¿<u>No</u> vienes?	Aren't you coming?
¿<u>No</u> lo viste?	Didn't you see it?

➤ You can also use **o no** at the end of a question in the same way that we can ask *or not* in English.

¿Vienes <u>o no</u>?	Are you coming <u>or not</u>?
¿Lo quieres <u>o no</u>?	Do you want it <u>or not</u>?

6   Short questions

➤ In English we sometimes check whether our facts and beliefs are correct by putting *isn't it?*, *don't they?*, *are they?* and so on at the end of a comment. In Spanish, you can add **¿no?** or **¿verdad?** in the same way.

Hace calor, ¿<u>no</u>?	It's hot, <u>isn't it</u>?
Te gusta, ¿<u>no</u>?	You like it, <u>don't you</u>?

For further explanation of grammatical terms, please see pages viii-xii.

No te vas a olvidar, ¿no?	You won't forget, <u>will you</u>?
No vino, ¿verdad?	He didn't come, <u>did he</u>?

7 Answering questions

➤ To answer a question which requires a *yes* or *no* answer, just use **sí** or **no**.

¿Te gusta? – Sí/No.	Do you like it? – Yes, I do/No, I don't.
¿Está aquí? – Sí/No.	Is he here? – Yes he is/No, he isn't.
¿Tienes prisa? – Sí/No.	Are you in a hurry? – Yes, I am/ No, I'm not.
No te acordaste, ¿verdad? – Sí/No.	You didn't remember, did you? - Yes, I did/No, I didn't.

➤ You can also often answer **sí** or **no** followed by the verb in question.

¿Tienes celular? – Sí, tengo.	Do you have a cell phone? – Yes, I do.
¿Vas a la fiesta? – No, no voy.	Are you going to the party? – No, I'm not.

Key points

✔ In Spanish, you ask a question by making your voice go up at the end of the sentence, by changing normal word order, and by using question words.

✔ Question words always have an accent on them.

✔ To make a negative question, add **no** before the verb.

✔ You can add ¿no? or ¿verdad? to check whether your facts or beliefs are correct.

Adverbs

What is an adverb?
An **adverb** is a word usually used with verbs, adjectives or other adverbs that gives more information about when, how, where, or in what circumstances something happens, or to what degree something is true. For example: *quickly, happily, now, extremely, very*.

How adverbs are used

➤ In general, adverbs are used together with verbs, adjectives and other adverbs (for example: *act quickly*; *smile cheerfully*; *rather long*; *a lot happier*; *really slowly*; *very well*).

➤ Adverbs can also relate to the whole sentence. In this case they often tell you what the speaker is thinking or feeling.

> Fortunately, Jan had already left.

How adverbs are formed

1   The basic rules

➤ In English, adverbs that tell you how something happened are often formed by adding -ly to an adjective (for example: *sweet → sweetly*). In Spanish, you form this kind of adverb by attaching **-mente** to the feminine singular form of the adjective.

Masculine adjective	Feminine adjective	Adverb	Meaning
lento	lenta	lentamente	slowly
normal	normal	normalmente	normally

> **Habla muy lentamente.**   He speaks very slowly.
> **¡Hazlo inmediatamente!**   Do it immediately!
> **Normalmente llego a las nueve.** I normally arrive at nine o'clock.

i Note that, in Spanish, adverbs <u>NEVER</u> change their endings to agree with anything.

Tip

You don't have to worry about adding or removing accents on the adjective when you attach **-mente**; they stay as they are.

> **fácil** easy   →   **fácilmente** easily

For further explanation of grammatical terms, please see pages viii-xii.

Grammar Extra!

When there are two or more adverbs joined by a conjunction such as **y** (meaning *and*) or **pero** (meaning *but*), omit the **-mente** ending on all but the last adverb.

> **Lo hicieron <u>lenta</u> pero <u>eficazmente</u>.** They did it slowly, but efficiently.

Use the form **recién**, rather than **recientemente** (meaning *recently*), before a past participle (the form of the verb ending in **-ado** and **-ido** in regular verbs).

> **El comedor está <u>recién</u> pintado.** The dining room has just been painted.

⇨ *For more information on **Past participles**, see page 118.*

In Spanish, adverbs ending in **-mente** are not as common as adverbs ending in *-ly* in English. For this reason, you will come across other ways of expressing an adverb in Spanish (for example: **con** used with a noun or **de manera** used with an adjective).

> **Maneja <u>con cuidado</u>.** Drive carefully.
> **Todos estos cambios ocurren <u>de manera natural</u>.** All these changes happen naturally.

---

2 Irregular adverbs

➤ The adverb that comes from **bueno** (meaning *good*) is **bien** (meaning *well*). The adverb that comes from **malo** (meaning *bad*) is **mal** (meaning *badly*).

> **Habla <u>bien</u> el español.** He speaks Spanish <u>well</u>.
> **Está muy <u>mal</u> escrito.** It's very <u>badly</u> written.

➤ Additionally, there are some other adverbs in Spanish which are exactly the same as the related masculine singular adjective:

- **alto** (adjective: *high, loud*; adverb: *high, loudly*)
  > **El avión volaba <u>alto</u> sobre las montañas.** The plane flew high over the mountains.
  > **Pepe habla muy <u>alto</u>.** Pepe talks very <u>loudly</u>.

- **bajo** (adjective: *low, quiet*; adverb: *low, quietly*)
  > **El avión volaba muy <u>bajo</u>.** The plane was flying very <u>low</u>.
  > **¡Habla <u>bajo</u>!** Speak <u>quietly</u>.

- **barato** (adjective: *cheap, inexpensive*; adverb: *cheaply, inexpensively*)
  > **Aquí se come muy <u>barato</u>.** You can eat really <u>inexpensively</u> here.

- **claro** (adjective: *clear*; adverb: *clearly*)
  > **Lo oí muy <u>claro</u>.** I heard it very <u>clearly</u>.

- **derecho** (adjective: *right, straight*; adverb: *straight*)
  > **Vino <u>derecho</u> hacia mí.** He came <u>straight</u> towards me.

- **fuerte**   (adjective: *loud*, *hard*; adverb: *loudly*, *hard*)

  Habla muy <u>fuerte</u>.   He talks very <u>loudly</u>.
  No lo golpees tan <u>fuerte</u>.   Don't hit it so <u>hard</u>.

- **rápido**   (adjective: *fast*, *quick*; adverb: *fast*, *quickly*)

  Manejas demasiado <u>rápido</u>.   You drive too <u>fast</u>.
  Lo hice tan <u>rápido</u> como pude.   I did it as <u>quickly</u> as I could.

i Note that, when used as adverbs, these words do <u>NOT</u> agree with anything.

⇨ *For more information on words that can be both adjectives and adverbs, see page 177.*

Grammar Extra!

Sometimes an <u>adjective</u> is used in Spanish where in English we would use an <u>adverb</u>.

  Esperaban <u>impacientes</u>.   They were waiting <u>impatiently</u>.
  Vivieron muy <u>felices</u>.   They lived very <u>happily</u>.

i Note that these Spanish <u>adjectives</u> describe the person or thing being talked about and, therefore, <u>MUST</u> agree with them.

Equally, you can often use an adverb or an adverbial expression.

  Esperaban <u>impacientemente</u> *or*
  <u>con impaciencia</u>.   They were waiting <u>impatiently</u>.

Key points
✔ To form adverbs in Spanish that tell you how something happens, you can usually attach **-mente** to the feminine singular adjective.
✔ Adverbs don't agree with anything.
✔ Some Spanish adverbs are irregular, just as they are in English.
✔ Some Spanish adverbs are identical in form to their corresponding adjectives; when used as adverbs, they never agree with anything.

For further explanation of grammatical terms, please see pages viii-xii.

Comparatives and superlatives of adverbs

1   Comparative adverbs

> **What is a comparative adverb?**
> A **comparative adverb** is one which, in English, has -er on the end of it or *more* or *less* in front of it. For example: *earlier, later, more/less often*.

➤ Adverbs can be used to make comparisons in Spanish, just as they can in English. The comparative of adverbs (*more often, more efficiently, faster*) is formed by using the same phrases as for adjectives:

- **más ... (que)**   more ... (than)
  más rápido (que)   faster (than), more quickly (than)
  Corre más rápido que tú.   He runs faster than you do.

- **menos ... (que)**   less ... (than)
  menos rápido (que)   less fast (than), less quickly (than)
  Lo hizo menos rápido que tú.   He did it less fast than you.

2   Superlative adverbs

> **What is a superlative adverb?**
> A **superlative adverb** is one which, in English, has -est on the end of it or *most* or *least* in front of it. For example: *soonest, most/least often*.

➤ In Spanish, the superlative of adverbs (*the most often, the most efficiently, the fastest*) is formed in the same way as is the comparative, using **más** and **menos**. In this case they mean *the most* and *the least*.

María es la que corre más rápido.	María is the one who runs (the) fastest.
la chica que sabe más	the girl who knows (the) most
la chica que sabe menos	the girl who knows (the) least
El que llegó menos tarde fue Miguel.	Miguel was the one who arrived least late.

> (*i*) Note that, even though comparative and superlative adverbs are usually identical in Spanish, you can tell which is which from the rest of the sentence.

3   Irregular comparative and superlative adverbs

➤ Some common Spanish adverbs have irregular comparative and superlatives.

Adverb	Meaning	Comparative	Meaning	Superlative	Meaning
bien	well	mejor	better	mejor	(the) best
mal	badly	peor	worse	peor	(the) worst
mucho	a lot	más	more	más	(the) most
poco	little	menos	less	menos	(the) least

La conozco <u>mejor</u> que tú.　　I know her <u>better</u> than you do.
¿Quién lo hace <u>mejor</u>?　　Who does it (the) <u>best</u>?
Ahora salgo <u>más/menos</u>.　　I go out <u>more/less</u> these days.

Tip

When saying *more than*, *less than* or *fewer than* followed by a number, use **más** and **menos** <u>de</u> rather than **más** and **menos que**.

　　más/menos <u>de</u> veinte cajas　　more/fewer than twenty boxes

---

[i] Note that, in Spanish, in phrases like *it's the least one can expect* or *it's the least I can do*, where the adverb is qualified by further information, you have to put **lo** before the adverb.

　　Es <u>lo menos que</u> se puede　　It's the least one can expect.
　　esperar.

4　**Other ways of making comparisons**

➤ In Spanish, there are other ways of making comparisons:

- **tanto como**　as much as

　　No lee <u>tanto como</u> tú.　　He doesn't read <u>as much as</u> you.

- **tan ... como**　as ... as

　　Vine <u>tan</u> pronto <u>como</u> pude.　　I came <u>as</u> fast <u>as</u> I could.

Key points

✔ **más** + adverb (+ **que**) = *more* + adverb + (*than*)
✔ **menos** + adverb (+ **que**) = *less* + adverb + (*than*)
✔ **más** + adverb = (*the*) *most* + adverb
✔ **menos** + adverb = (*the*) *least* + adverb
✔ There are a few irregular comparative and superlative adverbs.
✔ There are other ways of making comparisons in Spanish: **tanto como**, **tan ... como**.

Common adverbs

1 One-word adverbs not ending in -mente

➤ There are some common adverbs that do not end in **-mente**, most of which give more information about when or where something happens or to what degree something is true.

- **abajo**   down, below, downstairs
Ponlo aquí <u>abajo</u>.	Put it <u>down</u> here.
el departamento de <u>abajo</u>	the apartment <u>below</u>
<u>Abajo</u> están los dormitorios.	The bedrooms are <u>downstairs</u>.

- **adelante**   forward
Dio un paso <u>adelante</u>.	He stepped <u>forward</u>.
Siéntate más <u>adelante</u>.	Sit further <u>forward</u>.

- **adentro**   inside, indoors
Me llevó <u>adentro</u>.	He took me <u>inside/indoors</u>.

- **afuera**   outside, outdoors
Vayamos <u>afuera</u>.	Let's go <u>outside</u>.

- **ahí**   there
¡<u>Ahí</u> están!	<u>There</u> they are!

- **ahora**   now
¿Adónde vamos <u>ahora</u>?	Where are we going <u>now</u>?

- **allá**   there
<u>allá</u> arriba	up <u>there</u>

- **allí**   there
<u>Allí</u> está.	<u>There</u> it is.

- **anoche**   last night
<u>Anoche</u> llovió.	It rained <u>last night</u>.

- **anteanoche** *or* **antenoche**   the night before last
Llegaron <u>anteanoche</u>.	They arrived <u>the night before last</u>.

- **anteayer** *or* **antier**   the day before yesterday
<u>Anteayer</u> hubo tormenta.	There was a storm <u>the day before yesterday</u>.

- **antes**   before, beforehand
Llámalos <u>antes</u>.	Call them <u>beforehand</u>.

- **apenas**   hardly
<u>Apenas</u> podía levantarse.	He could <u>hardly</u> stand up.

- **aquí**   here
  Aquí está el informe.   Here's the report.

- **arriba**   up, above, upstairs
  Ponlo aquí arriba.   Put it up here.
  el departamento de arriba   the apartment above
  Arriba están los dormitorios.   The bedrooms are upstairs.

- **atrás**   (at the/in the) back
  Dio un paso atrás.   He stepped back.
  Siéntate más atrás.   Sit further back.

- **aun**   even
  Aun sentado me duele la   Even when I'm sitting down, my
  pierna.   leg hurts.

- **aún**   still, yet
  ¿Aún te duele?   Does it still hurt?

Tip

The following mnemonic (memory jogger) should help you remember when to use **aun** and when to use **aún**:
Even **aun** doesn't have an accent.
aún still has an accent.
aún hasn't lost its accent yet.

- **ayer**   yesterday
  Ayer fue mi cumpleaños.   It was my birthday yesterday.

- **casi**   almost
  Son casi las cinco.   It's almost five o'clock.

- **cerca**   near
  El colegio está muy cerca.   The school is very near.

- **claro**   clearly
  Lo oí muy claro.   I heard it very clearly.

- **debajo**   underneath
  Miré debajo.   I looked underneath.

- **dentro**   inside
  ¿Qué hay dentro?   What's inside?

- **despacio**   slowly
  Maneja <u>despacio</u>.   Drive <u>slowly</u>.

- **después**   afterwards
  <u>Después</u> estábamos muy   We were very tired <u>afterwards</u>.
  cansados.

- **detrás**   behind
  Vienen <u>detrás</u>.   They're following <u>behind</u>.

- **enfrente**   opposite
  la casa de <u>enfrente</u>   the house <u>opposite</u>

- **enseguida**   right away, immediately
  La ambulancia llegó <u>enseguida</u>. The ambulance arrived <u>right away</u>.

- **entonces**   then
  ¿Qué hiciste <u>entonces</u>?   What did you do <u>then</u>?

- **hasta**   even
  Estudia <u>hasta</u> cuando está de   He studies <u>even</u> when he's on
  vacaciones.   vacation.

- **hoy**   today
  <u>Hoy</u> no tenemos clase.   We don't have any classes <u>today</u>.

- **jamás**   never (ever)
  <u>Jamás</u> he visto nada parecido.   I've <u>never</u> seen anything like it.

- **lejos**   far
  ¿Está <u>lejos</u>?   Is it <u>far</u>?

- **luego**   then, later
  <u>Luego</u> nos fuimos a dormir.   <u>Then</u> we went to bed.

- **muy**   very
  Estoy <u>muy</u> cansada.   I'm <u>very</u> tired.

- **no**   no, not
  <u>No</u>, no me gusta.   <u>No</u>. I don't like it.

- **nunca**   never
  No viene <u>nunca</u>.   He <u>never</u> comes.
  <u>Nunca</u> nos vienes a ver.   You <u>never</u> come to see us.

- **pronto**   soon
  Llegarán <u>pronto</u>.   They'll be here <u>soon</u>.

- **quizás**   perhaps
  <u>Quizás</u> está cansado.   <u>Perhaps</u> he's tired.

ⓘ Note that, if referring to the future, you use the present
subjunctive after **quizás**.

> Quizás venga mañana. Perhaps he'll come tomorrow.

⇨ *For more information on the* **Subjunctive***, see page 136.*

- **sí** yes
  ¿Quieres un café? – Would you like a cup of coffee? –
  Sí, gracias. Yes, please.

- **siempre** always
  Siempre dicen lo mismo. They always say the same thing.

- **solo** only
  Solo hay que apretar este botón. You only have to press this button.

ⓘ Note that **solo** is sometimes spelled **sólo** to distinguish it from
the adjective, meaning *alone*. The accent is only necessary if there
is a risk that the sentence might be misunderstood.

- **también** also, too
  A mí también me gusta. I like it too.

- **tampoco** either, neither
  Yo tampoco lo compré. I didn't buy it either.
  Yo no la vi. – Yo tampoco. I didn't see her. – Neither did I.

- **tan** as, so
  Vine tan pronto como pude. I came as fast as I could.
  Hablas tan rápido que no You speak so fast that I can't
  te entiendo. understand you.

- **tarde** late
  Se está haciendo tarde. It's getting late.

- **temprano** early
  Tengo que levantarme I've got to get up early.
  temprano.

- **todavía** still, yet, even
  Todavía tengo dos. I've still got two.
  Todavía no han llegado. They haven't arrived yet.
  mejor todavía even better

- **ya** already
  Ya están aquí. They're already here.

For further explanation of grammatical terms, please see pages viii-xii.

2 | Words which are used both as adjectives and adverbs

➤ **bastante**, **demasiado**, **tanto**, **mucho** and **poco** can be used both as adjectives and as adverbs. When they are <u>adjectives</u>, their endings change in the feminine and plural to agree with what they describe. When they are <u>adverbs</u>, the endings don't change.

	Adjective use	Adverb use
bastante enough; quite a lot; quite	Hay <u>bastantes</u> libros. There are enough books.	Ya comiste <u>bastante</u>. You've had enough to eat. **Son** <u>bastante</u> ricos. They are quite rich.
demasiado too much (*plural*: too many); too	<u>demasiada</u> mantequilla too much butter <u>demasiados</u> libros too many books	Comí <u>demasiado</u>. I ate too much. **Llegamos** <u>demasiado</u> tarde. We arrived too late.
tanto as much (*plural*: as many); as often	Ahora no bebo <u>tanta</u> leche. I don't drink as much milk these days. Tengo <u>tantas</u> cosas que hacer. I have so many things to do.	Se preocupa <u>tanto</u> que no puede dormir. He worries so much that he can't sleep. **Ahora no la veo** <u>tanto.</u> I don't see her so often now.
mucho a lot (of), much (*plural*: many)	Había <u>mucha</u> gente. There were a lot of people. <u>muchas</u> cosas a lot of things	¿Lees <u>mucho</u>? Do you read a lot? ¿Está <u>mucho</u> más lejos? Is it much further?
poco little, not much, (*plural*: few, not many); not very	Hay <u>poca</u> leche. There isn't much milk. Tiene <u>pocos</u> amigos. He doesn't have many friends.	Habla muy <u>poco</u>. He speaks very little. **Es** <u>poco</u> sociable. He's not very sociable.

Tip

Don't confuse **poco**, which means *little, not much* or *not very*, with **un poco**, which means *a little* or *a bit*.

Come <u>poco</u>.　　　　　　　He doesn't eat <u>much</u>.

¿Me das un <u>poco</u>?　　　　Can I have <u>a bit</u>?

➤ **más** and **menos** can also be used both as adjectives and adverbs. However, they <u>NEVER</u> change their endings, even when used as adjectives.

	Adjective use	Adverb use
más more	No tengo <u>más</u> dinero. I don't have any more money. <u>más</u> libros more books	Es <u>más</u> inteligente que yo. He's more intelligent than I am. No le des <u>más</u>. Don't give her any more.
menos less; fewer	<u>menos</u> mantequilla less butter Había <u>menos</u> gente que ayer. There were fewer people than yesterday.	Estoy <u>menos</u> sorprendida que tú. I'm less surprised than you are. Trata de beber <u>menos</u>. Try and drink less.

3 Adverbs made up of more than one word

➤ Just as in English, some Spanish adverbs are made up of two or more words instead of just one.

a veces	sometimes
a menudo	often
de vez en cuando	from time to time
todo el tiempo	all the time
hoy en día	nowadays

> ### Key points
> ✔ In Spanish, there are a number of common adverbs which do not end in **-mente**.
> ✔ **bastante**, **demasiado**, **tanto**, **mucho** and **poco** can be used both as adjectives and as adverbs. Their endings change in the feminine and plural when they are adjectives, but when they are adverbs their endings <u>do not</u> change.
> ✔ **más** and **menos** can be both adjectives and adverbs – their endings <u>never</u> change.
> ✔ A number of Spanish adverbs are made up of more than one word.

For further explanation of grammatical terms, please see pages viii-xii.

Position of adverbs

1 Adverbs with verbs

➤ In English, adverbs can appear in various places in a sentence – at the beginning, in the middle or at the end.

> I'm <u>never</u> coming back.
> See you <u>soon</u>!
> <u>Suddenly</u>, the phone rang.
> I'd <u>really</u> like to come.

➤ In Spanish, the adverb can either go immediately <u>BEFORE</u> the verb or <u>AFTER</u> it.

> **<u>Todavía</u> estoy esperando.**   I'm still waiting.
> **<u>Siempre</u> le regalaban flores.** *or*   They always gave her flowers.
> **Le regalaban <u>siempre</u> flores.**

➤ When the adverb goes with a verb in the perfect tense or in the pluperfect, you can <u>NEVER</u> put the adverb between **haber** and the past participle.

> **Lo han firmado <u>ya</u>.** *or*   They have already signed it.
> **<u>Ya</u> lo han firmado.**
> **No había estado <u>nunca</u> en Italia.**   She'd never been to Italy.
> *or* **<u>Nunca</u> había estado en Italia.**

⇨ *For more information on the **Perfect tense**, see page 118.*

➤ Adverbs which explain how something is done are normally placed between the verb and its object.

> **Habla <u>bien</u> inglés.**   He speaks English well.
> **Le quitó <u>cuidadosamente</u>**   He carefully took the lid off.
> **la tapa.**

2 Adverbs with adjectives and adverbs

➤ The adverb normally goes <u>BEFORE</u> any adjective or adverb it is used with.

> **un sombrero <u>muy</u> bonito**   a very nice hat
> **hablar <u>demasiado</u> alto**   to talk too loudly

Key points

✔ In most cases, adverbs follow the verb.
✔ Adverbs can go before or after verbs.
✔ You can <u>never</u> separate **haber**, **he**, **ha** and so on from the following past participle (the **-ado/-ido** form of regular verbs).
✔ Adverbs generally come just before an adjective or another adverb.

Prepositions

What is a preposition?
A **preposition** is a word such as *at*, *for*, *with*, *into* or *from*, which is usually followed by a noun, pronoun or, in English, a word ending in *-ing*. Prepositions show how people and things relate to the rest of the sentence. For example: *She's at home.*; *a tool for cutting grass*; *It's from David.*

Using prepositions

➤ Prepositions are used in front of nouns and pronouns (such as *people*, *the man*, *me*, *him* and so on), and show the relationship between the noun or pronoun and the rest of the sentence. Although, in English, prepositions can be used before verb forms ending in *-ing*, in Spanish, they're followed by the infinitive – the form of the verb ending in **-ar**, **-er**, or **-ir**.

Le mostré la foto a Pedro.	I showed the photo to Pedro.
Ven con nosotros.	Come with us.
Sirve para limpiar zapatos.	It's for polishing shoes.

⇨ *For more information on **Nouns**, **Pronouns** and **Infinitives**, see pages 1, 41 and 146.*

➤ Prepositions are also used after certain adjectives and verbs, linking them to the rest of the sentence.

Estoy muy contento con tu trabajo.	I'm very happy with your work.
Estamos hartos de repetirlo.	We're fed up with repeating it.
Anoche soñé con Gustavo.	I dreamed about Gustavo last night.

➤ As in English, Spanish prepositions can be made up of several words instead of just one.

delante de	in front of
antes de	before

➤ In English we can end a sentence with a preposition such as *for*, *with* or *into*, even though some people think this is not good grammar. You can NEVER end a Spanish sentence with a preposition.

¿Para qué es?	What's it for?
la chica con la que hablaste	the girl you spoke to

For further explanation of grammatical terms, please see pages viii-xii.

Tip

As English speakers, the choice of an appropriate Spanish preposition is not always what we might expect. It is often difficult to identify a single English equivalent for a particular Spanish preposition, since prepositions are used so differently in the two languages. This means that you need to learn how they are used and use a dictionary to look up common phrases involving prepositions (such as *to depend on something* or *dressed in white*) in order to find an equivalent expression in Spanish.

a, de, en, para and por

1 **a**

> **Tip**
> When **a** is followed by **el**, the two words merge to become **al**.

➤ **a** can mean *to* with places and destinations.

Voy **a** la fiesta.	I'm going <u>to the</u> party.
Voy **al** médico.	I'm going <u>to the</u> doctor's.

> **Tip**
> **de** is also used with **a** to mean *from ... to ...*
>
> | | |
> |---|---|
> | **de** la mañana **a** la noche | <u>from</u> morning <u>to</u> night |
> | **de** 10 **a** 12 | <u>from</u> 10 <u>to</u> 12 |

➤ **a** can mean *to* with indirect objects.

Dale el dinero **a** María. Give the money <u>to</u> María.

➤ **a** can mean *to* after **ir** when talking about what someone is *going to* do.

Voy **a** verlo mañana. I'm going <u>to</u> see him tomorrow.

➤ **a** can mean *at* with times.

a las cinco	<u>at</u> five o'clock
a la una y media	<u>at</u> half past one
a medianoche	<u>at</u> midnight

➤ **a** can mean *at* with prices and rates.

a dos dólares el kilo	(<u>at</u>) two dollars a kilo
a 100 millas por hora	<u>at</u> 100 miles per hour

➤ **a** can mean *at* with ages.

a los 18 años <u>at</u> the age of 18

➤ **a** can mean *at* with places, but generally only after verbs suggesting movement.

Te voy a buscar **a** la estación.	I'll meet you <u>at</u> the station.
cuando llegó **al** aeropuerto	when he arrived <u>at</u> the airport

For further explanation of grammatical terms, please see pages viii-xii.

> **Tip**
> You can't use **a** to mean *at* when talking about a building, area, or village where someone is at a given moment. Use **en** instead.
>
> **Está <u>en</u> casa.**   He's <u>at</u> home.

➤ **a** can mean *onto*.

    Se cayó <u>al</u> suelo.   He fell <u>onto</u> the floor.

➤ **a** can mean *into*.

    traducir algo <u>al</u> inglés   to translate something <u>into</u> English

➤ **a** is also used to talk about distance.

    <u>a</u> pocas cuadras de aquí   just a few blocks from here

➤ **a** is also used after certain adjectives and verbs.

    parecido <u>a</u> esto   similar to this

➤ **a** can mean *from* after certain verbs.

    Se lo compré <u>a</u> mi hermano.   I bought it <u>from</u> my brother.
    Les robaba dinero <u>a</u> sus compañeros de clase.   He was stealing money <u>from</u> his classmates.

➪ For more information on **Prepositions after verbs**, see page 152.

➤ **a** is used in common phrases.

<u>a</u> final/finales/fines de mes	at the end of the month
<u>a</u> veces	at times
<u>a</u> menudo	often
<u>a</u> la puerta	at the door
<u>a</u> mano	by hand, to hand
<u>a</u> caballo	on horseback
<u>a</u> pie	on foot
<u>a</u> tiempo	on time
<u>al</u> sol	in the sun
<u>a</u> la sombra	in the shade

Grammar Extra!

a is often used to talk about the manner in which something is done.

<u>a</u> la inglesa	English style
<u>a</u> paso lento	slowly
poco <u>a</u> poco	little by little

The Spanish equivalent of the English construction *on* with a verb ending in *-ing* is **al** followed by the <u>infinitive</u>.

<u>al</u> levantarse	on getting up
<u>al</u> abrir la puerta	on opening the door

2 Personal <u>a</u>

➤ When the direct object of a verb is a specific person or pet animal, **a** is placed immediately before it.

Querían mucho <u>a</u> sus sobrinas.	They were very fond of their nieces.
Cuido <u>a</u> mi hermanita.	I look after my little sister.

i Note that personal **a** is <u>NOT</u> used after the verb **tener**.

Tienen dos hijos.	They have two children.

➪ For more information on **Direct objects**, *see page 46*.

3 <u>de</u>

> *Típ*
> When **de** is followed by **el**, the two words merge to become **del**.

➤ **de** can mean *from*.

Soy <u>de</u> Mérida.	I'm <u>from</u> Mérida.
un médico <u>de</u> Buenos Aires	a doctor <u>from</u> Buenos Aires

> *Típ*
> **de** is also used with **a** to mean *from ... to ...*
>
> | | |
> |---|---|
> | <u>de</u> la mañana <u>a</u> la noche | <u>from</u> morning <u>to</u> night |
> | <u>de</u> 10 <u>a</u> 12 | <u>from</u> 10 <u>to</u> 12 |

➤ **de** can mean *of*.

el presidente <u>de</u> Francia	the president <u>of</u> France
dos litros <u>de</u> leche	two liters <u>of</u> milk

➤ **de** shows who or what something belongs to.

el sombrero <u>de</u> mi padre	my father's hat (*literally: the hat <u>of</u> my father*)
la oficina <u>del</u> presidente	the president's office (*literally: the office <u>of</u> the president*)

➤ **de** can indicate what something is made of, what it contains or what it is used for.

un vestido <u>de</u> seda	a silk dress
una caja <u>de</u> cerillas	a box of matches
una taza <u>de</u> té	a cup of tea *or* a teacup
una silla <u>de</u> cocina	a kitchen chair
un traje <u>de</u> baño	a swimsuit

➤ **de** is used in comparisons when a number is mentioned.

Había más/menos <u>de</u> cien personas.	There were more/fewer than a hundred people.

🛈 Note that you do <u>NOT</u> use **que** with **más** or **menos** when there is a number involved.

➤ **de** can mean *in* after superlatives (*the most…, the biggest, the least…*).

la ciudad más/menos contaminada <u>del</u> mundo	the most/least polluted city <u>in</u> the world

⇨ *For more information on **Superlative adjectives**, see page 26.*

➤ **de** is used after certain adjectives and verbs.

Es fácil/difícil <u>de</u> entender.	It's easy/difficult to understand.
Es capaz <u>de</u> olvidarse.	He's quite capable of forgetting.

⇨ *For more information on **Prepositions after verbs**, see page 152.*

Grammar Extra!

de is often used in descriptions.

la mujer <u>del</u> sombrero verde	the woman <u>in</u> the green hat
un chico <u>de</u> ojos azules	a boy <u>with</u> blue eyes

---

4 en

➤ en can mean *in* with places.

en el campo	in the country
en Uruguay	in Uruguay
en la cama	in bed
con un libro en la mano	with a book in his hand

➤ en can mean *at* with places and with certain holidays.

en casa	at home
en el colegio	at school
en el aeropuerto	at the airport
en la parada de autobús	at the bus stop
en Navidad	at Christmastime

➤ en can mean *in* with months, years, and seasons, and when saying how long something takes or took.

en marzo	in March
en 2005	in 2005
Nació en invierno.	He was born in winter.
Lo hice en dos días.	I did it in two days.

ⓘ Note the following time phrase, which, in English, does not use *in*.

en este/ese *or* aquel momento	at this/that moment

> *Típ*
>
> When talking about parts of the day in Spanish, you can use either **en** or **por**:
>
> **en** *or* **por la mañana** in the morning
>
> **en** *or* **por la tarde** in the afternoon/evening
>
> **en** *or* **por la noche** at night
>
> In Spain, only **por** is used.

➤ en can mean *in* with languages and in common phrases indicating manner.

Está escrito en español.	It's written in Spanish.
en voz baja	in a low voice
en silencio	in silence

➤ **en** can mean *on*.

sentado <u>en</u> una silla	sitting <u>on</u> a chair
Lo dejé <u>en</u> la mesa.	I left it <u>on</u> the table.
Hay dos cuadros <u>en</u> la pared.	There are two pictures <u>on</u> the wall.

➤ **en** can mean *by* with most types of transportation.

<u>en</u> coche	<u>by</u> car
<u>en</u> avión	<u>by</u> plane
<u>en</u> tren	<u>by</u> train

➤ **en** can mean *into*.

No entremos <u>en</u> la casa.	Let's not go <u>into</u> the house.
Metió todo <u>en</u> la caja.	She put everything <u>into</u> the box.

➤ **en** is also used after certain adjectives and verbs.

Es muy buena/mala <u>en</u> geografía.	She is very good/bad at geography.
Fueron los primeros/últimos/ únicos <u>en</u> llegar.	They were the first/last/only ones to arrive.
No pienses <u>en</u> eso.	Don't think about that.

⇨ *For more information on* **Prepositions after verbs**, *see page 152.*

5 | **para**

➤ **para** can mean *for* with a person, destination or purpose.

<u>Para</u> mí un jugo de naranja.	An orange juice <u>for</u> me.
Mañana salen <u>para</u> Panamá.	They are leaving <u>for</u> Panamá tomorrow.
¿<u>Para</u> qué lo quieres?	What do you want it <u>for</u>?

ℹ️ Note that, in Spanish, you cannot end a sentence with a preposition as you can in English.

➤ **para** can mean *for* with time.

Es <u>para</u> mañana.	It's <u>for</u> tomorrow.
una habitación <u>para</u> dos noches	a room <u>for</u> two nights

➤ **para** is also used with an infinitive with the meaning of *(in order) to*.

Lo hace <u>para</u> ganar dinero.	He does it <u>to</u> earn money.
Lo hice <u>para</u> ayudarte.	I did it <u>to</u> help you.

> **Tip**
>
> **para mí/él/ella**, etc. can be used to mean *in my/his/her etc. opinion*.
>
> **Para mí, es estupendo.** In my opinion, it's great.

6 **por**

➤ **por** can mean *for* when it means *for the benefit of* or *because of*.

Lo hago por ellos.	I'm doing it for them.
por la misma razón	for the same reason

➤ **por** can mean *for* when it means *in exchange for*.

¿Cuánto me darán por este libro?	How much will they give me for this book?
Te lo cambio por este.	I'll swap you for this one.

➤ **por** can mean *by* in passive constructions.

descubierto por unos niños	discovered by some children
odiado por sus enemigos	hated by his enemies

➪ *For more information on the* **Passive**, *see page 125.*

➤ **por** can mean *by* with types of transportation when talking about freight.

mandar algo por barco	to send something by ship
por avión	by airmail
por correo aéreo	by airmail

➤ **por** can mean *along*.

Vaya por ese camino.	Go along that path.

➤ **por** can mean *through*.

por el túnel	through the tunnel

➤ **por** can mean *around*.

pasear por el campo	to walk around the countryside

➤ **por** is used to talk vaguely about where something or someone is.

Tiene que estar por aquí.	It's got to be around here somewhere.
Lo busqué por todas partes.	I looked for him everywhere.

➤ **por** (or **en**) is used with parts of the day.

<u>por</u> la mañana	<u>in</u> the morning
<u>por</u> la tarde	<u>in</u> the afternoon/evening
<u>por</u> la noche	<u>at</u> night

➤ **por** is used to talk about rates.

90 millas <u>por</u> hora	90 miles an hour
un cinco <u>por</u> ciento	five per cent

➤ **por** is used in certain phrases which talk about the reason for something.

¿<u>por</u> qué?	why?, for what reason?
<u>por</u> todo eso	because of all that
<u>por</u> lo que dice Mario	judging by what Mario says

➤ **por** is used to talk about how something is done.

llamar <u>por</u> teléfono	to telephone
Lo vi <u>por</u> la tele.	I saw it on TV.

Grammar Extra!

por is often combined with other Spanish prepositions and words, usually to show movement.

Saltó <u>por encima</u> de la mesa.	She jumped over the table.
Nadamos <u>por debajo del</u> puente.	We swam under the bridge.
Pasaron <u>por delante de</u> la iglesia.	They went past the church.

Key points

✔ **a**, **de**, **en**, **para** and **por** are the most frequently used prepositions which you will need to study carefully.

✔ Each of them has several possible meanings, which depend on the context they are used in.

Some other common prepositions

➤ In Spanish, the following prepositions are also frequently used.

- **antes de**   before

  <u>antes</u> de las 5   <u>before</u> 5 o'clock

(*i*) Note that, like many other Spanish prepositions, **antes de** is used before infinitives, whereas in English, we'd use the *-ing* form of the verb.

> **<u>Antes de abrir</u> el paquete,**   <u>Before opening</u> the package, read
> **lea las instrucciones.**   the instructions.

- **bajo**   below, under

  un grado <u>bajo</u> cero   one degree <u>below</u> zero
  <u>bajo</u> el puente   <u>under</u> the bridge

(*i*) Note that **debajo de** is more common than **bajo** when talking about the actual position of something.

> **<u>debajo de</u> la cama**   <u>under</u> the bed

- **con**   with

  Vino <u>con</u> su amigo.   She came <u>with</u> her friend.

(*i*) Note that **con** can be used after certain adjectives as well as in a few very common phrases.

> **enojado <u>con</u> ellos**   angry <u>with</u> them
> **un café <u>con</u> leche**   a (cup of) coffee with milk
> **un té <u>con</u> limón**   a (cup of) lemon tea

- **contra**   against

  Estaba apoyado <u>contra</u>   He was leaning <u>against</u> the wall.
  la pared.

  El domingo juegan <u>contra</u>   They play <u>against</u> Paraguay on
  Paraguay.   Sunday.

- **debajo de**   under

  <u>debajo de</u> la cama   <u>under</u> the bed

- **delante de**   in front of

  Iba <u>delante de</u> nosotros.   He was walking <u>in front of</u> us.

- **desde**   from, since

Desde aquí se puede ver.	You can see it <u>from</u> here.
<u>desde</u> otro punto de vista	<u>from</u> a different point of view
desde entonces	<u>from</u> then onwards
desde la una <u>hasta</u> las siete	<u>from</u> one o'clock <u>to</u> seven
desde la fiesta	<u>since</u> the party

Tip

Spanish uses the <u>present tense</u> with **desde** (meaning *since*) and the expressions **desde hace** and **hace ... que** (meaning *for*) to talk about actions that started in the past and are still going on.

<u>**Estoy**</u> aquí desde las diez.	I've been here since ten o'clock.
<u>**Estoy**</u> aquí desde hace dos horas. *or* Hace dos horas que <u>**estoy**</u> aquí.	I've been here for two hours.

⇨ *For more information on the **Present tense** and the **Perfect tense**, see pages 71 and 118.*

- **después de**   after

después del partido	<u>after</u> the game

ⓘ Note that, like many other Spanish prepositions, **después de** is used before infinitives, whereas in English we'd use the *-ing* form of the verb.

Después de lijarlo, se pinta.	<u>After sanding it down</u>, you paint it.

- **detrás de**   behind

Están <u>detrás de</u> la puerta.	They are <u>behind</u> the door.

- **durante**   during, for

<u>durante</u> la guerra	<u>during</u> the war
Caminaron <u>durante</u> 3 días.	They walked <u>for</u> 3 days.

- **entre**   between, among, amongst

<u>entre</u> 8 y 10	<u>between</u> 8 and 10
Hablaban <u>entre</u> sí.	They were talking <u>amongst</u> themselves.

- **hacia**   toward, around

Van <u>hacia</u> ese edificio.	They're heading <u>toward</u> that building.
<u>hacia</u> las tres	at <u>around</u> three (o'clock)
<u>hacia</u> finales de enero	<u>around</u> the end of January

---

Grammar Extra!

hacia can also combine with some adverbs to show movement in a particular direction.

hacia arriba	upwards
hacia abajo	downwards
hacia adelante	forwards
hacia atrás	backwards

- **hasta**   until, as far as, to, up to

<u>hasta</u> el jueves	<u>until</u> Thursday
Caminamos <u>hasta</u> el parque.	We walked <u>as far as</u> the park.
<u>desde</u> la una <u>hasta</u> las tres	<u>from</u> one o'clock <u>to</u> three
<u>Hasta</u> ahora no ha habido quejas.	There have been no complaints <u>up to</u> now.

i Note that there are some very common ways of saying goodbye using **hasta**.

¡<u>Hasta</u> luego!	See you!
¡<u>Hasta</u> mañana!	See you tomorrow!

- **sin**   without

<u>sin</u> agua/dinero	<u>without</u> any water/money
<u>sin</u> mi marido	<u>without</u> my husband

Tip

Whereas in English we say *without a doubt, without a hat* and so on, in Spanish the indefinite article isn't used after **sin**.

sin duda	without a doubt
sin sombrero	without a hat

⇨ *For more information on **Articles**, see page 10.*

---

i Note that, in Spanish, **sin** is used before infinitives, whereas in English, we would use the *-ing* form of the verb.

Se fue <u>sin decir</u> nada.	He left <u>without saying</u> anything.

- **sobre**   on, about
<u>sobre</u> la cama	<u>on</u> the bed
Ponlo <u>sobre</u> la mesa.	Put it <u>on</u> the table.
un libro <u>sobre</u> Shakespeare	a book <u>on</u> or <u>about</u> Shakespeare

➤ Spanish prepositions can be made up of more than one word (for example: **antes de**, **detrás de**). Here are some more common prepositions made up of two or more words:

- **a causa de**   because of
No salimos <u>a causa de</u> la lluvia.	We didn't go out <u>because of</u> the rain.

- **al lado de**   beside, next to
<u>al lado de</u> su novia	<u>next to</u> his girlfriend

- **cerca de**   near, close to
Está <u>cerca de</u> la iglesia.	It's <u>near</u> the church.

- **encima de**   on, on top of
Ponlo <u>encima de</u> la mesa.	Put it <u>on</u> the table.

- **por encima de**   above, over
Saltó <u>por encima de</u> la mesa.	He jumped <u>over</u> the table.

- **en medio de**   in the middle of
Está <u>en medio de</u> la plaza.	It's <u>in the middle of</u> the square.

- **junto a**   next to, alongside
<u>junto a</u> la ventana.	<u>next to</u> the window
trabajando <u>junto a</u> su esposa	working <u>alongside</u> his wife

- **junto con**   together with
Fue detenido <u>junto con</u> su hijo.	He was arrested <u>together with</u> his son.

- **lejos de**   far from
No está <u>lejos de</u> aquí.	It isn't <u>far from</u> here.

Grammar Extra!

In Latin American Spanish, you will often come across **abajo de**, **adelante de**, **adentro de**, **arriba de** and **atrás de** used instead of **debajo de**, **delante de**, **dentro de**, **encima de** and **detrás de** respectively. Although they are used very frequently, especially in the spoken language, they are considered incorrect by some people.

<u>abajo</u> de la cama	<u>under</u> the bed
<u>adelante</u> de papá	<u>in front</u> of Dad
<u>adentro</u> de la caja	<u>inside</u> the box
<u>arriba</u> de la mesa	<u>above</u> the table
<u>atrás</u> de la puerta	<u>behind</u> the door

Conjunctions

What is a conjunction?
A **conjunction** is a word such as *and*, *but*, *or*, *so*, *if* and *because*, that links two words or phrases of a similar type, or two parts of a sentence. For example: *Diane and I have been friends for years. I left because I was bored.*

y, o, pero, porque and si

➤ In Spanish, **y**, **o**, **pero**, **porque** and **si** are the most common conjunctions that you need to know:

- **y**　　and
  el perro y el gato　　　　　　the dog <u>and</u> the cat

[i] Note that you use **e** instead of **y** before words beginning with **i** or **hi** (but not **hie**).

　　Diana e Isabel　　　　　Diana <u>and</u> Isabel
　　madre e hija　　　　　　mother <u>and</u> daughter
　　BUT
　　árboles y hierba　　　　trees <u>and</u> grass

- **o**　　or
  papas o arroz　　　　　　potatoes <u>or</u> rice

[i] Note that you use **u** instead of **o** before words beginning with **o** or **ho**.

　　diez u once　　　　　　ten <u>or</u> eleven
　　minutos u horas　　　　minutes <u>or</u> hours

[i] Note that you use **ó** instead of **o** between numerals to avoid confusion with zero.

　　37 ó 38　　　　　　　　37 or 38

⇨ *For more information on **Numbers**, see page 208.*

- **pero**　　but
  Me gustaría ir, <u>pero</u> no puedo.　　I'd like to go, <u>but</u> I can't.

[i] Note that you use **sino** in direct contrasts after a negative.

　　No es española, <u>sino</u> italiana.　　She's not Spanish <u>but</u> Italian.

For further explanation of grammatical terms, please see pages viii-xii.

- **porque**   because
  Llamó <u>porque</u> necesita un libro.   He called <u>because</u> he needs a book.

(*i*) Note that you don't use **porque** at the beginning of a sentence; you should use **como** instead.

    <u>Como</u> estaba lloviendo, nos quedamos en casa.   <u>Because</u> or <u>As</u> it was raining, we stayed home.

> **Típ**
> Be careful not to mix up **porque** (meaning *because*) and **por qué** (meaning *why*).

- **que**   that
  Dice <u>que</u> me quiere.   He says <u>that</u> he loves me.
  Dicen <u>que</u> es millonario.   They say <u>that</u> he's a millionaire.
  Sabe <u>que</u> estamos aquí.   He knows <u>that</u> we are here.

⇨ *For more information on* **que** *followed by the subjunctive and* **que** (*meaning than*) *in comparisons, see pages 136 and 26.*

> **Típ**
> In English we can say both *He says he loves me* and *He says that he loves me*, or *She knows you're here* and *She knows that you're here*. In Spanish, you can <u>NEVER</u> omit **que** in the way that you can omit *that* in English.

- **si**   if, whether
  <u>Si</u> no estudias, no aprobarás.   <u>If</u> you don't study, you won't pass.
  ¿Sabes <u>si</u> tiene novio?   Do you know <u>if</u> or <u>whether</u> she has a boyfriend?
  Avísenme <u>si</u> no pueden venir.   Let me know <u>if</u> you can't come.

⇨ *For information on* **si** *followed by the subjunctive, see page 145.*

> **Típ**
> There is no accent on **si** when it means *if*. Be careful not to confuse **si** (meaning *if*) with **sí** (meaning *yes* or *himself/herself/yourself/themselves/yourselves*).

Some other common conjunctions

➤ Here are some other common Spanish conjunctions:

- **como**   as

Como es domingo, puedes quedarte en la cama.	<u>As</u> it's Sunday, you can stay in bed.

- **cuando**   when

Cuando entré estaba leyendo.	She was reading <u>when</u> I came in.

⇨ *For information on* **cuando** *followed by the subjunctive, see page 142.*

- **pues**   then, well

Tengo sueño. – ¡Acuéstate, pues!	I'm tired. – Go to bed <u>then</u>!
<u>**Pues**</u>**, no lo sabía.**	<u>Well</u>, I didn't know.
<u>**Pues**</u>**, como te iba contando …**	<u>Well</u>, as I was saying …

- **mientras**   while (*referring to time*)

Lava tú <u>mientras</u> yo seco.	You wash <u>while</u> I dry.
Canta <u>mientras</u> cocina.	He sings <u>while</u> he cooks.

⇨ *For information on* **mientras** *followed by the subjunctive, see page 142.*

- **mientras que**   whereas

Isabel es muy dinámica <u>mientras que</u> Ana es más tranquila.	Isabel is very dynamic <u>whereas</u> Ana is more laid-back.

- **aunque**   although, even though

Me gusta el francés, <u>aunque</u> prefiero el alemán.	I like French <u>although</u> I prefer German.
<u>**Aunque**</u> **estaba cansada, seguí trabajando.**	<u>Although</u> I was tired, I went on working.

Grammar Extra!

aunque is also used to mean *even if*. In this case, it is followed by the subjunctive.

⇨ *For more information on the* **Subjunctive**, *see page 136.*

Split conjunctions

In English we have conjunctions which are made up of two parts (*both ... and*, *neither ... nor*). Spanish also has conjunctions that have more than one part, of which the most common are probably **ni ... ni** (meaning *neither ... nor*) and **o ... o** (meaning *either ... or*):

- **ni ... ni**   neither ... nor

  <u>Ni</u> Carlos <u>ni</u> Sofía vinieron. *or*   <u>Neither</u> Carlos <u>nor</u> Sofía came.
  <u>No</u> vinieron <u>ni</u> Carlos <u>ni</u> Sofía.

[*i*] Note that if you're putting **ni ... ni** after the verb, you must put **no** before the verb.

  No tengo <u>ni</u> hermanos <u>ni</u> hermanas.   I have <u>neither</u> brothers <u>nor</u> sisters.

- **o ... o**   either ... or

  Puedes pedir <u>o</u> helado <u>o</u> yogur.   You can order <u>either</u> ice cream <u>or</u> yogurt.

Key points

✔ **y**, **o**, **pero**, **porque** and **si** are the most common Spanish conjunctions that you need to know.

✔ Use **e** rather than **y** before words beginning with **i** or **hi** (but not with **hie**).

✔ Use **u** rather than **o** before words beginning with **o** or **ho**.

✔ **que** very often means *that*. In English, *that* is often omitted, but **que** can never be omitted in Spanish.

✔ Some conjunctions such as **ni ... ni** and **o ... o** consist of two parts.

Spelling

1 Sounds that are spelled differently depending on the letter that follows

➤ In Spanish, certain sounds are spelled differently depending on what letter follows them. For example, the hard [k] sound heard in the English word *car* is usually spelled:

- **c** before **a**, **o** and **u**
- **qu** before **e** and **i**

➤ This means that the Spanish word for *singer* is spelled **cantante** (pronounced [*kan-tan-tay*]); the word for *coast* is spelled **costa** (pronounced [*ko-sta*]); and the word for *cure* is spelled **cura** (pronounced [*koo-ra*]).

➤ However, the Spanish word for cheese is spelled **queso** (pronounced [*kay-so*]) and the word for *chemistry* is spelled **química** (pronounced [*kee-mee-ka*]).

i Note that, although the letter **k** is not much used in Spanish, it is found in words relating to *kilos*, *kilometers* and *kilograms* (for example: **un kilo** (meaning *a kilo*); **un kilogramo** (meaning *a kilogram*); **un kilómetro** (meaning *a kilometer*).

➤ Similarly, the [g] sound heard in the English word *gone* is spelled:

- **g** before **a**, **o** and **u**
- **gu** before **e** and **i**

➤ This means that the Spanish word for *cat* is spelled **gato** (pronounced [*ga-toe*]); the word for *goal* is spelled **gol** (pronounced [*gol*]); and the word for *worm* is spelled **gusano** (pronounced [*goo-sa-no*]).

➤ However, the Spanish word for *war* is spelled **guerra** (pronounced [*gair-ra*]) and the word for *guitar* is spelled **guitarra** (pronounced [*ghee-tar-ra*]).

2 | Letters that are pronounced differently depending on what follows

➤ Certain letters are pronounced differently depending on what follows them. As we have seen, when **c** comes before **a**, **o** or **u**, it is pronounced like a [k]. When it comes before **e** or **i**, in Latin American Spanish it is pronounced like the [s] in *sing* and in European Spanish it is pronounced like the [th] in the English word *pith*.

➤ This means that **casa** (meaning *house*) is pronounced [ka-sa], but **centro** (meaning *center*) is pronounced [sen-tro] in Latin American Spanish and [then-tro] in European Spanish. Similarly, **cita** (meaning *date*) is pronounced [see-ta] in Latin American Spanish and [theeta] in European Spanish.

➤ In the same way, when **g** comes before **a**, **o** or **u**, it is pronounced like the [g] in *gone*. When it comes before **e** or **i**, however, it is pronounced like the strong [h] sound in the Spanish name *Geraldo* [He-ral-do].

➤ This means that **gas** (meaning *gas*) is pronounced [gas] but **gente** (meaning *people*) is pronounced [Hen-tay]. Similarly, **gimnasio** (meaning *gym*) is pronounced [Heem-na-see-o].

3 | Spelling changes that are needed in verbs to reflect the pronunciation

➤ Because **c** sounds like [k] before **a**, **o** and **u**, and like [s] (or [th] in European Spanish) before **e** and **i**, you sometimes have to alter the spelling of a verb when adding a particular ending to ensure the word reads as it is pronounced:

- In verbs ending in **-car** (which is pronounced [kar]), you have to change the **c** to **qu** before endings starting with an **e** to keep the hard [k] pronunciation. So the **yo** form of the preterite tense of **sacar** (meaning *to take out*) is spelled **saqué**. This spelling change affects the preterite and the present subjunctive of verbs ending in **-car**.

- In verbs ending in **-cer** and **-cir** (which are pronounced [ser] and [sir], or [ther] and [thir] in European Spanish), you have to change the **c** to **z** before endings starting with **a** or **o** to keep the soft [s/th] pronunciation. So while the **yo** form of the preterite tense of **hacer** is spelled **hice**, the **él/ella/usted** form is spelled **hizo**. This spelling change affects the ordinary present tense, as well as the present subjunctive of verbs ending in **-cer** or **-cir**.

➤ Because **g** sounds like the [g] of *gone* before **a**, **o** and **u**, and like the [H] of *Geraldo* before **e** and **i**, you also sometimes have to alter the spelling of a verb when adding a particular ending to ensure the verb still reads as it is pronounced:

- In verbs ending in **-gar** (which is pronounced [*gar*]), you have to change the **g** to **gu** before endings starting with an **e** or an **i** to keep the hard [g] pronunciation. So the **yo** form of the preterite tense of **pagar** (meaning *to pay*) is spelled **pagué**. This spelling change affects the preterite and the present subjunctive of verbs ending in **-gar**.

- In verbs ending in **-ger** and **-gir** (which are pronounced [*Her*] and [*Hir*]), you have to change the **g** to **j** before endings starting with **a** or **o** to keep the soft [H] pronunciation. So while the **él/ella/usted** form of the present tense of **escoger** (meaning *to choose*) is spelled **escoge**, the **yo** form is spelled **escojo**. This spelling change affects the ordinary present tense as well as the present subjunctive of verbs ending in **-ger** or **-gir**.

➤ Because **gui** sounds like [*ghee*] in verbs ending in **-guir**, but **gua** and **guo** sound like [*gwa*] and [*gwo*], you have to drop the **u** before **a** and **o** in verbs ending in **-guir**. So while the **él/ella/usted** form of the present tense of **seguir** (meaning *to follow*) is spelled **sigue**, the **yo** form is spelled **sigo**. This spelling change affects the ordinary present tense as well as the present subjunctive of verbs ending in **-guir**.

➤ Finally, although **z** is always pronounced [s] in Latin American Spanish and [th] in European Spanish, in verbs ending in **-zar** the **z** spelling is changed to **c** before **e**. So, while the **él/ella/usted** form of the preterite tense of **cruzar** is spelled **cruzó**, the **yo** form is spelled **crucé**. This spelling change affects the preterite and the present subjunctive of verbs ending in **-zar**.

4 Spelling changes that are needed when making nouns and adjectives plural

➤ In the same way that you have to make some spelling changes when modifying the endings of certain verbs, you sometimes have to change the spelling of nouns and adjectives when making them plural.

➤ This affects nouns and adjectives ending in **-z**. When adding the **-es** ending of the plural, you have to change the **z** to **c**.

una vez	once, one time	→	**dos veces**	twice, two times
una luz	a light	→	**unas luces**	some lights
capaz	capable, able (*sing*)	→	**capaces**	capable, able (*pl*)

For further explanation of grammatical terms, please see pages viii-xii.

➤ The following table shows the usual spelling of the various sounds discussed above:

	Usual spelling				
	before a	before o	before u	before e	before i
[k] sound (as in *cap*)	ca: casa house	co: cosa thing	cu: cuna crib	que: queso cheese	qui: química chemistry
[g] sound (as in *gap*)	ga: gato cat	go: gordo fat	gu: gusto taste	gue: guerra war	gui: guitarra guitar
[s] as in *sun** (pronounced [th] as in *pith* in European Spanish)	za: zapato shoe	zo: zorro fox	zu: zumo juice	ce: cero zero	ci: cinta ribbon
[H] sound (as in *Geraldo*)	ja: jardín garden	jo: joven young	ju: jugar to play	ge: gente people	gi: gimnasio gym

*[s] is also, of course, the pronunciation of the letter **s**, both in Latin American and European Spanish.

i Note that because **j** is also pronounced [H] even when it comes before **e** or **i**, there are quite a number of words that contain **je** or **ji**. For example:

el jefe/la jefa	the boss
el jerez	sherry
el jinete	jockey
la jirafa	giraffe
el ejemplo	the example
dije/dijiste	I said/you said
dejé	I left, I let

Similarly, because **z** is also pronounced [s] (or [th] in European Spanish) when it comes before **i** or **e**, there are one or two exceptions to the spelling rules described above. For example: **el zigzag** (meaning *zigzag*) and **la zeta** (the name of the letter **z** in Spanish).

Stress

Which syllable to stress

➤ Most words can be broken up into <u>syllables</u>. These are the different groups of sounds that make up a word. They are shown in this section by | and the stressed syllable is underlined.

➤ In Spanish, there are some very simple rules to help you remember which part of the word to stress, and when to use a written accent mark.

➤ In Spanish, words <u>DON'T</u> have a written acute accent if they follow the normal stress rules. If they do not follow the normal stress rules, they <u>DO</u> need an accent.

> *Tip*
>
> In Spanish, the written accent that shows stress is always an <u>acute</u> accent (´). To remember which way an acute accents slopes try thinking of this saying:
> *It's low on the left, with the height on the right.*

1 Words ending in a vowel or -n or -s

➤ Words ending in a vowel (*a, e, i, o* or *u*) or **-n** or **-s** are normally stressed on the <u>syllable before last</u>. If this is the case, they do <u>NOT</u> have any written accents.

<u>**ca**</u>**|sa**	house	<u>**ca**</u>**|sas**	houses
pa|<u>**la**</u>**|bra**	word	**pa|**<u>**la**</u>**|bras**	words
<u>**tar**</u>**|de**	afternoon	<u>**tar**</u>**|des**	afternoons
<u>**ha**</u>**|bla**	he/she speaks	<u>**ha**</u>**|blan**	they speak
<u>**co**</u>**|rre**	he/she runs	<u>**co**</u>**|rren**	they run

➤ Whenever words ending in a vowel or **-n** or **-s** are <u>NOT</u> stressed on the syllable before last, they have a written accent on the vowel that is stressed.

es|<u>**trés**</u>	stress
ra|<u>**tón**</u>	mouse
pin|<u>**té**</u>	I painted
<u>**úl**</u>**|ti|mo**	last
<u>**llá**</u>**|ma|los**	call them

For further explanation of grammatical terms, please see pages viii-xii.

2   Words ending in a consonant other than -n or -s

➤ Words ending in a consonant (a letter that isn't a vowel) other than **-n** or **-s** are normally stressed on the <u>last syllable</u>. If this is the case, they do <u>NOT</u> have an accent.

re|<u>loj</u>	clock, watch
ver|<u>dad</u>	truth
trac|<u>tor</u>	tractor

➤ Whenever words ending in a consonant other than **-n** or **-s** are <u>NOT</u> stressed on the last syllable, they have an accent.

ca|<u>rác</u>|ter	character
di|<u>fí</u>|cil	difficult
<u>cés</u>|ped	lawn

3   Accents on feminine and plural forms

➤ The same syllable is stressed in the plural form of adjectives and nouns as in the singular. To show this, you need to:

- add an accent in the plural in the case of unaccented nouns and adjectives of more than one syllable ending in **-n**

<u>or</u>|den	order	**<u>ór</u>|de|nes**	orders
e|<u>xa</u>|men	exam	**e|<u>xá</u>|me|nes**	exams
BUT: **tren**	train	**tre|nes**	trains

> *i* Note that in the case of one-syllable words ending in **-n** or **-s**, such as **tren** above, no accent is needed in the plural, since the stress falls naturally on the syllable before last thanks to the plural **-es** ending.

- drop the accent in the plural form of nouns and adjectives ending in **-n** or **-s** which have an accent on the last syllable in the singular

au|to|<u>bús</u>	bus	**au|to|<u>bu</u>|ses**	buses
re|vo|lu|<u>ción</u>	revolution	**re|vo|lu|<u>cio</u>|nes**	revolutions

➤ The feminine forms of nouns or adjectives whose masculine form ends in an accented vowel followed by **-n** or **-s** do <u>NOT</u> have an accent.

un franc<u>és</u>	a Frenchman
una franc<u>e</u>sa	a French woman

Tip

Just because a word has a written accent in the singular does not necessarily mean it has one in the plural, and vice versa.

jo|ven

Ends in **n**, so the rule is to stress the syllable before last; follows the rule, so <u>no</u> accent needed in the singular

jó|ve|nes

Ends in **s**, so the rule is to stress the syllable before last; breaks rule, so accent <u>is</u> needed in the plural to keep the stress on **jo-**

in|glés

Ends in **s**, so the rule is to stress the syllable before last; breaks the rule, so an accent <u>is</u> needed in singular

in|gle|ses

Ends in **s**, so the rule is to stress the syllable before last; follows the rule, so <u>no</u> accent needed in the plural to keep the stress on **-gle-**

4 Which vowel to stress in vowel combinations

➤ The vowels **i** and **u** are considered to be <u>weak</u>. The vowels **a**, **e** and **o** are considered to be <u>strong</u>.

➤ When a weak vowel (**i** or **u**) combines with a strong one (**a**, **e** or **o**), they form <u>ONE</u> sound that is part of the <u>SAME</u> syllable. Technically speaking, this is called a <u>diphthong</u>. The strong vowel is emphasized more.

bai|le	dance
cie|rra	he/she/it closes
boi|na	beret
pei|ne	comb
cau|sa	cause

Tip

To remember which are the weak vowels, try thinking of this saying: *U and I are weaklings and always lose out to other vowels!*

➤ When **i** is combined with **u** or **u** with **i** (the two weak vowels), they form <u>ONE</u> sound within the <u>SAME</u> syllable and there is more emphasis on the second vowel.

ciudad	city, town
fui	I went

For further explanation of grammatical terms, please see pages viii-xii.

➤ When you combine two strong vowels (**a, e** or **o**), they form <u>TWO</u> separate sounds and are part of <u>DIFFERENT</u> syllables.

ca|er	to fall
ca|os	chaos
fe|o	ugly

5   Adding accents to some verb forms

➤ When object pronouns are added to the end of certain verb forms, an accent is often required to show that the syllable stressed in the verb form does not change. These verb forms are:

- the <u>gerund</u>, when followed by one or more pronouns

compr<u>a</u>ndo	buying
compr<u>á</u>ndo(se)lo	buying it (for him/her/them)

- the <u>infinitive</u>, when followed by two pronouns

vend<u>e</u>r	to sell
vend<u>é</u>rselas	to sell them to him/her/them

- <u>imperative</u> forms

c<u>o</u>mpra	buy
c<u>ó</u>mpralo	buy it
m<u>a</u>nden	send
m<u>á</u>ndenselo	send it to him/her/them

➪ *For more information on **Gerunds**, **Infinitives** and the **Imperative**, see pages 128, 146 and 86.*

6   Accents on adjectives and adverbs

➤ Adjectives ending in **-ísimo** always have an accent on the first **-í** of the ending. This means that any other accents are omitted.

caro	→	**carísimo**
expensive		extremely expensive
difícil	→	**dificilísimo**
difficult		extremely difficult

➤ Accents on adjectives are <u>NOT</u> affected when you attach **-mente** to turn them into adverbs.

fácil	→	**fácilmente**
easy		easily

The accent used to show meaning

➤ An accent is often used to distinguish between the written forms of some words which are pronounced the same but have a different meaning or function.

Without an accent		With an accent	
mi	my	mí	me
tu	your	tú	you
te	you	té	tea
si	if	sí	yes; himself
el	the	él	he
de	of	dé	give
solo	alone; by oneself	sólo	only
mas	but	más	more

*The accent can also be used to distinguish the demonstrative pronouns, such as **éste** (meaning *this one*), from the corresponding adjective (e.g. **este**, meaning *this*) and the adverb **sólo** (meaning *only*) from the adjective **solo** (meaning *alone*), but this is only necessary in rare cases when there is a risk that the sentence might otherwise be misunderstood.

<u>Mi</u> hermano es médico.	My brother's a doctor.
A <u>mí</u> no me vio.	He didn't see me.
¿Te gusta <u>tu</u> trabajo?	Do you like your job?
¿<u>Tú</u>, qué opinas?	What do you think?
<u>Si</u> no viene, mejor.	If he doesn't come, so much the better.
<u>Sí</u> que lo sabe.	Yes, he does know.
<u>El</u> puerto está cerca.	The harbor's nearby.
<u>Solo</u> lo sabe él.	Only he knows.

➤ An accent is needed on question words in direct and indirect questions as well as after expressions of uncertainty.

¿<u>Cómo</u> estás?	How are you?
Dime <u>cómo</u> estás.	Tell me how you are.
Me preguntó <u>cómo</u> estaba.	He asked me how I was.
¿Con <u>quién</u> viajaste?	Who did you travel with?
¿<u>Dónde</u> encontraste eso?	Where did you find that?
No sé <u>dónde</u> está.	I don't know where it is.

⇨ *For more information on **Questions**, see page 162.*

For further explanation of grammatical terms, please see pages viii-xii.

➤ An accent is also needed on exclamation words.

¡**Qué** asco!	How disgusting!
¡**Qué** horror!	How awful!
¡**Qué** raro!	How strange!
¡**Cuánta** gente!	What a lot of people!

Key points

✔ When deciding whether or not to use a written accent mark on a word, think about how it sounds and what letter it ends in, as there are certain rules that dictate when an accent should be used.

✔ The vowels **i** and **u** are considered to be weak. The vowels **a**, **e** and **o** are considered to be strong. They can combine in a number of ways.

✔ Accents are added to written forms of words which are pronounced the same but have different meanings, for example, **mi/mí**, **tu/tú** and so on.

✔ Adjectives ending in **-ísimo** always have an accent on the first **-í** of the ending, but no accent is added when adverbs are formed by adding **-mente** to adjectives.

✔ Question words used in direct and indirect questions as well as exclamation words always have an acute accent.

Numbers

1	uno (un, una)		31	treinta y uno (un, una)
2	dos		40	cuarenta
3	tres		41	cuarenta y uno (un, una)
4	cuatro		50	cincuenta
5	cinco		52	cincuenta y dos
6	seis		60	sesenta
7	siete		65	sesenta y cinco
8	ocho		70	setenta
9	nueve		76	setenta y seis
10	diez		80	ochenta
11	once		87	ochenta y siete
12	doce		90	noventa
13	trece		99	noventa y nueve
14	catorce		100	cien (ciento)
15	quince		101	ciento uno (un, una)
16	dieciséis		200	doscientos/doscientas
17	diecisiete		212	doscientos/doscientas doce
18	dieciocho		300	trescientos/trescientas
19	diecinueve		400	cuatrocientos/cuatrocientas
20	veinte		500	quinientos/quinientas
21	veintiuno (veintiún, veintiuna)		600	seiscientos/seiscientas
22	veintidós		700	setecientos/setecientas
23	veintitrés		800	ochocientos/ochocientas
24	veinticuatro		900	novecientos/novecientas
25	veinticinco		1000	mil
26	veintiséis		1001	mil (y) uno (un, una)
27	veintisiete		2000	dos mil
28	veintiocho		2500	dos mil quinientos/quinientas
29	veintinueve		1.000.000	un millón
30	treinta			(*in English*: 1,000,000)

EJEMPLOS	EXAMPLES
Vive en el número diez.	He lives at number ten.
en la página diecinueve	on page nineteen
un/el diez por ciento	10%
un/el cien por cien(to)	100%

For further explanation of grammatical terms, please see pages viii-xii.

1   uno, un or una?

➤ Use **uno** when counting, unless referring to something or someone feminine.

➤ Use **un** before a masculine noun and **una** before a feminine noun even when the nouns are plural.

un hombre	one man
una mujer	one woman
treinta y **un** días	thirty-one days
treinta y **una** noches	thirty-one nights
veinti**ún** años	twenty-one years
veinti**una** mujeres	twenty-one women

2   cien or ciento?

➤ Use **cien** before both masculine and feminine nouns as well as before **mil** (meaning *thousand*) and **millones** (meaning *million* in the plural):

cien libros	one hundred books
cien mil hombres	one hundred thousand men
cien millones	one hundred million

➤ Use **ciento** before other numbers.

ciento un perros	one hundred and one dogs
ciento una ovejas	one hundred and one sheep
ciento cincuenta	one hundred and fifty

i   Note that you don't translate the *and* in 101, 220 and so on.

➤ Make **doscientos/doscientas**, **trescientos/trescientas**, **quinientos/quinientas** and so on agree with the noun in question.

doscientas veinte personas	two hundred and twenty people
quinientos alumnos	five hundred students

i   Note that **setecientos** and **setecientas** have no **i** after the first **s**. Similarly, **novecientos** and **novecientas** have an **o** rather than the **ue** you might expect.

3   Period, comma or space?

➤ A space should be used to separate thousands and millions when writing numbers **of more than four digits** in figures.

42 000 (cuarenta y dos mil)

100 500 (cien mil quinientos/-as)

BUT

2480 (dos mil cuatrocientos ochenta)

➤ However, in many Latin American countries, a comma is often used to separate thousands and millions in figures, just as it is in English.

700,000 (setecientos mil)	700,000 (seven hundred thousand)
5,000,000 (cinco millones)	5,000,000 (five million)

➤ Many Latin American countries use the decimal point to show decimals, just as we do in English.

0.5 (cero punto cinco)	0.5 (zero point five)
3.4 (tres punto cuatro)	3.4 (three point four)

➤ On the other hand, in Spain and in some South American countries, a period is used to separate thousands and millions and a comma is used to show decimals.

700. 000 (setecientos mil)	700,000 (seven hundred thousand)
0,5 (cero coma cinco)	0.5 (zero point five)

1st	**primero (1º), primer (1ᵉʳ), primera (1ª)**
2nd	**segundo (2º), segunda (2ª)**
3rd	**tercero (3º), tercer (3ᵉʳ), tercera (3ª)**
4th	**cuarto (4º), cuarta (4ª)**
5th	**quinto (5º), quinta (5ª)**
6th	**sexto (6º), sexta (6ª)**
7th	**séptimo (7º), séptima (7ª)**
8th	**octavo (8º), octava (8ª)**
9th	**noveno (9º), novena (9ª)**
10th	**décimo (10º), décima (10ª)**
100th	**centésimo (100º), centésima (100ª)**
101st	**centésimo primero (101º), centésima primera (101ª)**
1000th	**milésimo (1000º), milésima (1000ª)**

Es la cuarta vez que te lo digo.	This is the fourth time I've told you.
Llegó tercero.	He came in third.

> *Tip*
>
> Shorten **primero** (meaning *first*) to **primer**, and **tercero** (meaning *third*) to **tercer** before a masculine singular noun.
>
> | | |
> |---|---|
> | **su primer cumpleaños** | his first birthday |
> | **el tercer premio** | the third prize |

ℹ️ Note that when you are writing these numbers in figures, you must not write 1st, 2nd, 3rd as in English. Use 1º, 1ª, 1ᵉʳ, 2º, 2ª and 3º, 3ª, 3ᵉʳ as required by the noun.

For further explanation of grammatical terms, please see pages viii–xii.

4   <u>primero, segundo, tercero</u> or <u>uno, dos, tres?</u>

➤ Apart from **primero** (meaning *first*) up to **décimo** (meaning *tenth*), as well as **centésimo** (meaning *one hundredth*) and **milésimo** (meaning *one thousandth*), the ordinal numbers tend not to be used very much in Spanish. Cardinal numbers (ordinary numbers) are used instead.

> **Carlos III** (read as: **Carlos <u>tercero</u>**)
> **Alfonso XIII** (read as: **Alfonso <u>trece</u>**)

➪   *For numbers used in dates, see page 213.*

Time and date

LA HORA	THE TIME
¿Qué hora es?	What time is it?

To answer this question, you say **Son las dos/las tres/las cuatro**, etc. (It's two/three/four o'clock, etc.) BUT **Es la una** (It's one o'clock).

Es la una.	It's one o'clock.
Es la una y diez.	It's ten after one.
Es la una y cuarto.	It's a quarter after one.
Es la una y veinte.	It's twenty after one.
Es la una y media.	It's one thirty.
Son veinticinco para las dos.*	It's twenty-five to two.
Son cuarto para las dos.*	It's a quarter to two.
Son cinco para las dos.*	It's five to two.
Son las dos.	It's two o'clock.

*This is what you say in most of Latin America. In Spain, people say:

Son las dos menos veinticinco.	It's twenty-five to two.
Son las dos menos cuarto.	It's a quarter to two.
Son las dos menos cinco.	It's five to two.

¿A qué hora?	At what time?
a medianoche	at midnight
a mediodía	at midday/noon
a la una (del mediodía)	at one o'clock (in the afternoon)
a las tres (de la tarde)	at three o'clock (in the afternoon)
a las 9:25 *or* a las nueve (y) veinticinco	at nine twenty-five
a las 16:50 *or* a las dieciséis (y) cincuenta	at 16:50 *or* sixteen fifty

[i] Note that in Spanish, as in English, you can also tell the time using the figures you see on a digital clock or watch or on a 24-hour timetable.

LA FECHA	THE DATE
Los días de la semana	The days of the week
lunes	Monday
martes	Tuesday
miércoles	Wednesday
jueves	Thursday

For further explanation of grammatical terms, please see pages viii-xii.

viernes	Friday
sábado	Saturday
domingo	Sunday

¿Cuándo?	**When?**
el lunes	on Monday
los lunes	on Mondays
todos los lunes	every Monday
el martes pasado	last Tuesday
el viernes que viene	next Friday
el sábado que viene no, el otro	a week from Saturday
dentro de tres sábados	two weeks from Saturday

i Note that days of the week <u>DON'T</u> have a capital letter in Spanish.

Los meses del año	**Months of the year**
enero	January
febrero	February
marzo	March
abril	April
mayo	May
junio	June
julio	July
agosto	August
septiembre	September
octubre	October
noviembre	November
diciembre	December

¿Cuándo?	**When?**
en febrero	in February
el 1er (primero) *or* el 1 (uno) de diciembre	on December 1st
en 1998 (mil novecientos noventa y ocho)	in 1998
el 15 de diciembre de 2003 (dos mil tres)	on December 15th , 2003
el año dos mil	(the year) two thousand

¿Qué día es hoy?	**What day is it today?**
Es martes.	It's Tuesday.
lunes 26 de febrero	Monday, February 26th
domingo 3 de octubre	Sunday, October 3rd

i Note that, in Spanish, months of the year <u>DON'T</u> have a capital letter.

> ### Tip
> In English we use *first*, *second*, *third* and so on in dates. In Spanish, you use the equivalent of *two*, *three* and so on for all dates except the first of the month: **el 1° (primero) de abril**, **el 2 (dos) de abril**, **el 3 (tres) de abril** etc. (April 1st, 2nd, 3rd etc.). You may also come across **el 1 (uno) de abril**, particularly in European Spanish.

FRASES ÚTILES	USEFUL PHRASES
¿Cuándo?	**When?**
hoy	today
esta mañana	this morning
esta tarde	this afternoon/evening
esta noche	this evening/tonight
¿Con qué frecuencia?	**How often?**
todos los días	every day
cada dos días	every other day
una vez por semana	once a week
dos veces por semana	twice a week
una vez al mes	once a month
¿Cuándo pasó?	**When did it happen?**
en *or* por la mañana	in the morning
en *or* por la tarde	in the afternoon/evening
en *or* por la noche	in the evening/at night
ayer	yesterday
ayer en *or* por la mañana	yesterday morning
ayer en *or* por la tarde	yesterday afternoon/evening
ayer en *or* por la noche	yesterday evening/last night
anoche	last night
anteayer *or* antier	the day before yesterday
hace una semana	a week ago
hace quince días	two weeks ago
la semana pasada	last week
el año pasado	last year
¿Cuándo va a pasar?	**When is it going to happen?**
mañana	tomorrow
mañana en *or* por la mañana	tomorrow morning
mañana en *or* por la tarde	tomorrow afternoon/evening
mañana en *or* por la noche	tomorrow evening/night
pasado mañana	the day after tomorrow
dentro de dos días	in two days' time
dentro de una semana	in a week's time
dentro de quince días	in two weeks' time
el mes que viene	next month
el año que viene	next year

Main Index

Verb Tables

Introduction

The **Verb Tables** in the following section contain 120 tables of Spanish verbs (some regular and some irregular) in alphabetical order. Each table shows you the following forms: **Present**, **Present Perfect**, **Preterite**, **Imperfect**, **Future**, **Conditional**, **Present Subjunctive**, **Imperfect Subjunctive**, **Imperative** and the **Past Participle** and **Gerund**. For more information on these tenses and how they are formed you should look at the section on Verbs on pages 69-158.

In order to help you use the verbs shown in Verb Tables correctly, there are also a number of example phrases at the bottom of each page to show the verb as it is used in context.

In Spanish there are both **regular** verbs (their forms follow the normal rules) and **irregular** verbs (their forms do not follow the normal rules). The regular verbs in these tables that you can use as models for other regular verbs are:

hablar (regular -ar verb, Verb Table 340-341)
comer (regular -er verb, Verb Table 270-271)
vivir (regular -ir verb, Verb Table 456-457)

The irregular verbs are shown in full.

The **Verb Index** at the end of this section contains over 1,200 verbs, each of which is cross-referred to one of the verbs given in the Verb Tables. The table shows the patterns that the verb listed in the index follows.

abolir (to abolish)

	PRESENT		PRESENT PERFECT
(yo)			he abolido
(tú)			has abolido
(él/ella/usted)			ha abolido
(nosotros/as)	abolimos		hemos abolido
(vosotros/as)	abolís		habéis abolido
(ellos/ellas/ ustedes)			han abolido

Present tense only used in persons shown

	PRETERITE	IMPERFECT
(yo)	abolí	abolía
(tú)	aboliste	abolías
(él/ella/usted)	abolió	abolía
(nosotros/as)	abolimos	abolíamos
(vosotros/as)	abolisteis	abolíais
(ellos/ellas/ ustedes)	abolieron	abolían

GERUND	PAST PARTICIPLE
aboliendo	abolido

EXAMPLE PHRASES

Hay que **abolir** esta ley. This law should be abolished.

Habían abolido la pena de muerte. They had abolished the death penalty.

Abolieron la esclavitud. They abolished slavery.

Remember that subject pronouns are not used very often in Spanish.

abolir

	FUTURE	CONDITIONAL
(yo)	aboliré	aboliría
(tú)	abolirás	abolirías
(él/ella/usted)	abolirá	aboliría
(nosotros/as)	aboliremos	aboliríamos
(vosotros/as)	aboliréis	aboliríais
(ellos/ellas/ ustedes)	abolirán	abolirían

	PRESENT SUBJUNCTIVE	IMPERFECT SUBJUNCTIVE
(yo)	*not used*	aboliera *or* aboliese
(tú)		abolieras *or* abolieses
(él/ella/usted)		aboliera *or* aboliese
(nosotros/as)		aboliéramos *or* aboliésemos
(vosotros/as)		abolierais *or* abolieseis
(ellos/ellas/ ustedes)		abolieran *or* aboliesen

IMPERATIVE

abolid

EXAMPLE PHRASES

Prometieron que **abolirían** la censura. They promised they'd abolish censorship.

Remember that subject pronouns are not used very often in Spanish.

abrir (to open)

	PRESENT		PRESENT PERFECT
(yo)	abro		he abierto
(tú)	abres		has abierto
(él/ella/usted)	abre		ha abierto
(nosotros/as)	abrimos		hemos abierto
(vosotros/as)	abrís		habéis abierto
(ellos/ellas/ustedes)	abren		han abierto

	PRETERITE	IMPERFECT
(yo)	abrí	abría
(tú)	abriste	abrías
(él/ella/usted)	abrió	abría
(nosotros/as)	abrimos	abríamos
(vosotros/as)	abristeis	abríais
(ellos/ellas/ustedes)	abrieron	abrían

GERUND

abriendo

PAST PARTICIPLE

abierto

EXAMPLE PHRASES

Hoy **se abre** el periodo de inscripciones. Registration begins today.

Han abierto un nuevo restaurante cerca de aquí. They've opened a new restaurant near here.

¿Quién **abrió** la ventana? Who opened the window?

La llave **abría** el armario. The key opened the cupboard.

Remember that subject pronouns are not used very often in Spanish.

abrir

	FUTURE	CONDITIONAL
(yo)	abriré	abriría
(tú)	abrirás	abrirías
(él/ella/usted)	abrirá	abriría
(nosotros/as)	abriremos	abriríamos
(vosotros/as)	abriréis	abriríais
(ellos/ellas/ ustedes)	abrirán	abrirían

	PRESENT SUBJUNCTIVE	IMPERFECT SUBJUNCTIVE
(yo)	abra	abriera or abriese
(tú)	abras	abrieras or abrieses
(él/ella/usted)	abra	abriera or abriese
(nosotros/as)	abramos	abriéramos or abriésemos
(vosotros/as)	abráis	abrierais or abrieseis
(ellos/ellas/ ustedes)	abran	abrieran or abriesen

IMPERATIVE

abre / abrid

Use the present subjunctive in all cases other than these tú and vosotros affirmative forms.

EXAMPLE PHRASES

Abrirán todas las puertas de la catedral. They'll open all the doors of the cathedral.

Me dijo que hoy **abrirían** sólo por la tarde. He told me that today they'd be open only in the evening.

No creo que **abran** un nuevo supermercado por aquí. I don't think they'll open a new supermarket here.

No **abras** esa llave. Don't turn on that faucet.

Remember that subject pronouns are not used very often in Spanish.

actuar (to act)

	PRESENT	PRESENT PERFECT
(yo)	actúo	he actuado
(tú)	actúas	has actuado
(él/ella/usted)	actúa	ha actuado
(nosotros/as)	actuamos	hemos actuado
(vosotros/as)	actuáis	habéis actuado
(ellos/ellas/ustedes)	actúan	han actuado

	PRETERITE	IMPERFECT
(yo)	actué	actuaba
(tú)	actuaste	actuabas
(él/ella/usted)	actuó	actuaba
(nosotros/as)	actuamos	actuábamos
(vosotros/as)	actuasteis	actuabais
(ellos/ellas/ustedes)	actuaron	actuaban

GERUND

actuando

PAST PARTICIPLE

actuado

EXAMPLE PHRASES

Actúa de una forma muy rara. He's acting very strangely.

Actuó siguiendo un impulso. He acted on impulse.

Ha actuado en varias películas. He has been in several movies.

Actuaba como si no supiera nada. She was behaving as if she didn't know anything about it.

Remember that subject pronouns are not used very often in Spanish.

actuar

	FUTURE	**CONDITIONAL**
(yo)	actuaré	actuaría
(tú)	actuarás	actuarías
(él/ella/usted)	actuará	actuaría
(nosotros/as)	actuaremos	actuaríamos
(vosotros/as)	actuaréis	actuaríais
(ellos/ellas/ ustedes)	actuarán	actuarían

	PRESENT SUBJUNCTIVE	**IMPERFECT SUBJUNCTIVE**
(yo)	actúe	actuara *or* actuase
(tú)	actúes	actuaras *or* actuases
(él/ella/usted)	actúe	actuara *or* actuase
(nosotros/as)	actuemos	actuáramos *or* actuásemos
(vosotros/as)	actuéis	actuarais *or* actuaseis
(ellos/ellas/ ustedes)	actúen	actuaran *or* actuasen

IMPERATIVE

actúa / actuad

Use the present subjunctive in all cases other than these tú and vosotros affirmative forms.

EXAMPLE PHRASES

¿Quién **actuará** en su próxima película? Who will be in his next movie?

Yo nunca **actuaría** así. I'd never behave like that.

Si **actuara** de forma más lógica, sería más fácil atraparlo. It would be easier to catch him if he behaved in a more logical way.

Actúa como mejor te parezca. Do as you think best.

Remember that subject pronouns are not used very often in Spanish.

adquirir (to acquire, to obtain, to purchase)

	PRESENT	**PRESENT PERFECT**
(yo)	adquiero	he adquirido
(tú)	adquieres	has adquirido
(él/ella/usted)	adquiere	ha adquirido
(nosotros/as)	adquirimos	hemos adquirido
(vosotros/as)	adquirís	habéis adquirido
(ellos/ellas/ ustedes)	adquieren	han adquirido

	PRETERITE	**IMPERFECT**
(yo)	adquirí	adquiría
(tú)	adquiriste	adquirías
(él/ella/usted)	adquirió	adquiría
(nosotros/as)	adquirimos	adquiríamos
(vosotros/as)	adquiristeis	adquiríais
(ellos/ellas/ ustedes)	adquirieron	adquirían

GERUND

adquiriendo

PAST PARTICIPLE

adquirido

EXAMPLE PHRASES

Adquiere cada vez mayor importancia. It's becoming more and more important.

Está adquiriendo una reputación que no merece. It's getting a reputation it doesn't deserve.

Han adquirido más acciones. They've purchased more stock.

Con el tiempo **adquirió** madurez. Over the years he gained maturity.

Remember that subject pronouns are not used very often in Spanish.

adquirir

	FUTURE	CONDITIONAL
(yo)	adquiriré	adquiriría
(tú)	adquirirás	adquirirías
(él/ella/usted)	adquirirá	adquiriría
(nosotros/as)	adquiriremos	adquiriríamos
(vosotros/as)	adquiriréis	adquiriríais
(ellos/ellas/ustedes)	adquirirán	adquirirían

	PRESENT SUBJUNCTIVE	IMPERFECT SUBJUNCTIVE
(yo)	adquiera	adquiriera *or* adquiriese
(tú)	adquieras	adquirieras *or* adquirieses
(él/ella/usted)	adquiera	adquiriera *or* adquiriese
(nosotros/as)	adquiramos	adquiriéramos *or* adquiriésemos
(vosotros/as)	adquiráis	adquirierais *or* adquirieseis
(ellos/ellas/ustedes)	adquieran	adquirieran *or* adquiriesen

IMPERATIVE

adquiere / adquirid

Use the present subjunctive in all cases other than these tú and vosotros affirmative forms.

EXAMPLE PHRASES

Al final **adquirirán** los derechos de publicación. They will get the publishing rights in the end.

Adquiera o no la nacionalidad, podrá permanecer en el país. She'll be able to stay in the country whether she gets citizenship or not.

Tenía gran interés en que **adquiriera** el cuadro. He was eager that she should purchase the picture.

Remember that subject pronouns are not used very often in Spanish.

advertir (to warn, to notice)

	PRESENT		PRESENT PERFECT
(yo)	advierto		he advertido
(tú)	adviertes		has advertido
(él/ella/usted)	advierte		ha advertido
(nosotros/as)	advertimos		hemos advertido
(vosotros/as)	advertís		habéis advertido
(ellos/ellas/ ustedes)	advierten		han advertido

	PRETERITE		IMPERFECT
(yo)	advertí		advertía
(tú)	advertiste		advertías
(él/ella/usted)	advirtió		advertía
(nosotros/as)	advertimos		advertíamos
(vosotros/as)	advertisteis		advertíais
(ellos/ellas/ ustedes)	advirtieron		advertían

GERUND

advirtiendo

PAST PARTICIPLE

advertido

EXAMPLE PHRASES

Te **advierto** que no va a ser nada fácil. I must warn you that it won't be at all easy.

No **había advertido** nada extraño en su comportamiento. I hadn't noticed anything strange about his behavior.

Ya te **advertí** que no intervinieras. I warned you not to get involved.

Las señales **advertían** del peligro. The signs warned of danger.

Remember that subject pronouns are not used very often in Spanish.

advertir

	FUTURE	CONDITIONAL
(yo)	advertiré	advertiría
(tú)	advertirás	advertirías
(él/ella/usted)	advertirá	advertiría
(nosotros/as)	advertiremos	advertiríamos
(vosotros/as)	advertiréis	advertiríais
(ellos/ellas/ ustedes)	advertirán	advertirían

	PRESENT SUBJUNCTIVE	IMPERFECT SUBJUNCTIVE
(yo)	advierta	advirtiera *or* advirtiese
(tú)	adviertas	advirtieras *or* advirtieses
(él/ella/usted)	advierta	advirtiera *or* advirtiese
(nosotros/as)	advirtamos	advirtiéramos *or* advirtiésemos
(vosotros/as)	advirtáis	advirtierais *or* advirtieseis
(ellos/ellas/ ustedes)	adviertan	advirtieran *or* advirtiesen

IMPERATIVE

advierte / advertid

Use the present subjunctive in all cases other than these tú and vosotros affirmative forms.

EXAMPLE PHRASES

Si **advirtiera** algún cambio, llámenos. If you should notice any change, call us.

Adviértele del riesgo que entraña. Warn him about the risk involved.

Remember that subject pronouns are not used very often in Spanish.

amanecer (to get light, to wake up)

	PRESENT	PRESENT PERFECT
(yo)	amanezco	he amanecido
(tú)	amaneces	has amanecido
(él/ella/usted)	amanece	ha amanecido
(nosotros/as)	amanecemos	hemos amanecido
(vosotros/as)	amanecéis	habéis amanecido
(ellos/ellas/ ustedes)	amanecen	han amanecido

	PRETERITE	IMPERFECT
(yo)	amanecí	amanecía
(tú)	amaneciste	amanecías
(él/ella/usted)	amaneció	amanecía
(nosotros/as)	amanecimos	amanecíamos
(vosotros/as)	amanecisteis	amanecíais
(ellos/ellas/ ustedes)	amanecieron	amanecían

GERUND

amaneciendo

PAST PARTICIPLE

amanecido

EXAMPLE PHRASES

Siempre **amanece** nublado. The day always starts off cloudy.

Estaba **amaneciendo**. Dawn was breaking.

La ciudad **amaneció** desierta. In the morning the town was deserted.

Amanecía de un humor de perros. She would wake up in a really bad mood.

Remember that subject pronouns are not used very often in Spanish.

amanecer

	FUTURE	CONDITIONAL
(yo)	amaneceré	amanecería
(tú)	amanecerás	amanecerías
(él/ella/usted)	amanecerá	amanecería
(nosotros/as)	amaneceremos	amaneceríamos
(vosotros/as)	amaneceréis	amaneceríais
(ellos/ellas/ustedes)	amanecerán	amanecerían

	PRESENT SUBJUNCTIVE	IMPERFECT SUBJUNCTIVE
(yo)	amanezca	amaneciera or amaneciese
(tú)	amanezcas	amanecieras or amanecieses
(él/ella/usted)	amanezca	amaneciera or amaneciese
(nosotros/as)	amanezcamos	amaneciéramos or amaneciésemos
(vosotros/as)	amanezcáis	amanecierais or amanecieseis
(ellos/ellas/ustedes)	amanezcan	amanecieran or amaneciesen

IMPERATIVE

amanece / amaneced

Use the present subjunctive in all cases other than these tú and vosotros affirmative forms.

EXAMPLE PHRASES

Pronto **amanecerá**. It will soon be daylight.

Saldremos en cuanto **amanezca**. We'll get going as soon as it gets light.

Si **amanecieras** con fiebre, toma una de estas pastillas. If you should wake up with a fever, take one of these pills.

Remember that subject pronouns are not used very often in Spanish.

andar (to be, to work, to ride, to walk)

	PRESENT	PRESENT PERFECT
(yo)	ando	he andado
(tú)	andas	has andado
(él/ella/usted)	anda	ha andado
(nosotros/as)	andamos	hemos andado
(vosotros/as)	andáis	habéis andado
(ellos/ellas/ ustedes)	andan	han andado

	PRETERITE	IMPERFECT
(yo)	anduve	andaba
(tú)	anduviste	andabas
(él/ella/usted)	anduvo	andaba
(nosotros/as)	anduvimos	andábamos
(vosotros/as)	anduvisteis	andabais
(ellos/ellas/ ustedes)	anduvieron	andaban

GERUND

andando

PAST PARTICIPLE

andado

EXAMPLE PHRASES

¿Cómo **andas**? How are you?

La lavadora no **andaba** bien. The washing machine wasn't working properly.

Andaban mal de dinero. They were short of money.

No sabe **andar** en bicicleta. She doesn't know how to ride a bike.

Remember that subject pronouns are not used very often in Spanish.

andar

	FUTURE	**CONDITIONAL**
(yo)	andaré	andaría
(tú)	andarás	andarías
(él/ella/usted)	andará	andaría
(nosotros/as)	andaremos	andaríamos
(vosotros/as)	andaréis	andaríais
(ellos/ellas/ ustedes)	andarán	andarían

	PRESENT SUBJUNCTIVE	**IMPERFECT SUBJUNCTIVE**
(yo)	ande	anduviera *or* anduviese
(tú)	andes	anduvieras *or* anduvieses
(él/ella/usted)	ande	anduviera *or* anduviese
(nosotros/as)	andemos	anduviéramos *or* anduviésemos
(vosotros/as)	andéis	anduvierais *or* anduvieseis
(ellos/ellas/ ustedes)	anden	anduvieran *or* anduviesen

IMPERATIVE

anda / andad

Use the present subjunctive in all cases other than these tú and vosotros affirmative forms.

EXAMPLE PHRASES

Andará por los cuarenta. He must be about forty.

Yo **me andaría** con pies de plomo. I'd tread very carefully.

Si **anduvieras** con más cuidado, no te pasarían esas cosas. If you were more careful, this sort of thing wouldn't happen to you.

Remember that subject pronouns are not used very often in Spanish.

apoderarse de (to take control of)

	PRESENT	PRESENT PERFECT
(yo)	me apodero	me he apoderado
(tú)	te apoderas	te has apoderado
(él/ella/usted)	se apodera	se ha apoderado
(nosotros/as)	nos apoderamos	nos hemos apoderado
(vosotros/as)	os apoderáis	os habéis apoderado
(ellos/ellas/ustedes)	se apoderan	se han apoderado

	PRETERITE	IMPERFECT
(yo)	me apoderé	me apoderaba
(tú)	te apoderaste	te apoderabas
(él/ella/usted)	se apoderó	se apoderaba
(nosotros/as)	nos apoderamos	nos apoderábamos
(vosotros/as)	os apoderasteis	os apoderabais
(ellos/ellas/ustedes)	se apoderaron	se apoderaban

GERUND	PAST PARTICIPLE
apoderando	apoderado

EXAMPLE PHRASES

En esas situaciones, el miedo **se apodera** de mí. In situations like that, I find myself gripped by fear.

Poco a poco **se han ido apoderando** de las riquezas del país. Little by little, they've taken control of the country's riches.

Se apoderaron de las joyas y huyeron. They took the jewels and ran off.

Remember that subject pronouns are not used very often in Spanish.

apoderarse

	FUTURE	**CONDITIONAL**
(yo)	me apoderaré	me apoderaría
(tú)	te apoderarás	te apoderarías
(él/ella/usted)	se apoderará	se apoderaría
(nosotros/as)	nos apoderaremos	nos apoderaríamos
(vosotros/as)	os apoderaréis	os apoderaríais
(ellos/ellas/ ustedes)	se apoderarán	se apoderarían

	PRESENT SUBJUNCTIVE	**IMPERFECT SUBJUNCTIVE**
(yo)	me apodere	me apoderara or apoderase
(tú)	te apoderes	te apoderaras or apoderases
(él/ella/usted)	se apodere	se apoderara or apoderase
(nosotros/as)	nos apoderemos	nos apoderáramos or apoderásemos
(vosotros/as)	os apoderéis	os apoderarais or apoderaseis
(ellos/ellas/ ustedes)	se apoderen	se apoderaran or apoderasen

IMPERATIVE

apodérate / apoderaos

Use the present subjunctive in all cases other than these tú and vosotros affirmative forms.

EXAMPLE PHRASES

No dejes que la curiosidad **se apodere** de ti. Don't let curiosity get the better of you.

Remember that subject pronouns are not used very often in Spanish.

aprobar (to pass, to approve of)

	PRESENT	PRESENT PERFECT
(yo)	apruebo	he aprobado
(tú)	apruebas	has aprobado
(él/ella/usted)	aprueba	ha aprobado
(nosotros/as)	aprobamos	hemos aprobado
(vosotros/as)	aprobáis	habéis aprobado
(ellos/ellas/ ustedes)	aprueban	han aprobado

	PRETERITE	IMPERFECT
(yo)	aprobé	aprobaba
(tú)	aprobaste	aprobabas
(él/ella/usted)	aprobó	aprobaba
(nosotros/as)	aprobamos	aprobábamos
(vosotros/as)	aprobasteis	aprobabais
(ellos/ellas/ ustedes)	aprobaron	aprobaban

GERUND	PAST PARTICIPLE
aprobando	aprobado

EXAMPLE PHRASES

No **apruebo** esa conducta. I don't approve of that sort of behavior.

Este año lo **estoy aprobando** todo. So far this year I've passed everything.

Han aprobado una ley antitabaco. They've passed an anti-smoking law.

¿**Aprobaste** el examen? Did you pass the test?

La decisión **fue aprobada** por mayoría. The decision was approved by a majority.

Remember that subject pronouns are not used very often in Spanish.

aprobar

	FUTURE	CONDITIONAL
(yo)	aprobaré	aprobaría
(tú)	aprobarás	aprobarías
(él/ella/usted)	aprobará	aprobaría
(nosotros/as)	aprobaremos	aprobaríamos
(vosotros/as)	aprobaréis	aprobaríais
(ellos/ellas/ ustedes)	aprobarán	aprobarían

	PRESENT SUBJUNCTIVE	IMPERFECT SUBJUNCTIVE
(yo)	apruebe	aprobara or aprobase
(tú)	apruebes	aprobaras or aprobases
(él/ella/usted)	apruebe	aprobara or aprobase
(nosotros/as)	aprobemos	aprobáramos or aprobásemos
(vosotros/as)	aprobéis	aprobarais or aprobaseis
(ellos/ellas/ ustedes)	aprueben	aprobaran or aprobasen

IMPERATIVE

aprueba / aprobad

Use the present subjunctive in all cases other than these tú and vosotros affirmative forms.

Remember that subject pronouns are not used very often in Spanish.

arrancar (to pull up, to start)

	PRESENT	PRESENT PERFECT
(yo)	arranco	he arrancado
(tú)	arrancas	has arrancado
(él/ella/usted)	arranca	ha arrancado
(nosotros/as)	arrancamos	hemos arrancado
(vosotros/as)	arrancáis	habéis arrancado
(ellos/ellas/ ustedes)	arrancan	han arrancado

	PRETERITE	IMPERFECT
(yo)	arranqué	arrancaba
(tú)	arrancaste	arrancabas
(él/ella/usted)	arrancó	arrancaba
(nosotros/as)	arrancamos	arrancábamos
(vosotros/as)	arrancasteis	arrancabais
(ellos/ellas/ ustedes)	arrancaron	arrancaban

GERUND

arrancando

PAST PARTICIPLE

arrancado

EXAMPLE PHRASES

Lo tienes que **arrancar** de raíz. You must pull it up by its roots.

Estaba arrancando malas hierbas. I was pulling up weeds.

El viento **arrancó** varios árboles. Several trees were uprooted in the wind.

La moto no **arranca**. The motorcycle won't start.

Remember that subject pronouns are not used very often in Spanish.

arrancar

	FUTURE	CONDITIONAL
(yo)	arrancaré	arrancaría
(tú)	arrancarás	arrancarías
(él/ella/usted)	arrancará	arrancaría
(nosotros/as)	arrancaremos	arrancaríamos
(vosotros/as)	arrancaréis	arrancaríais
(ellos/ellas/ ustedes)	arrancarán	arrancarían

	PRESENT SUBJUNCTIVE	IMPERFECT SUBJUNCTIVE
(yo)	arranque	arrancara or arrancase
(tú)	arranques	arrancaras or arrancases
(él/ella/usted)	arranque	arrancara or arrancase
(nosotros/as)	arranquemos	arrancáramos or arrancásemos
(vosotros/as)	arranquéis	arrancarais or arrancaseis
(ellos/ellas/ ustedes)	arranquen	arrancaran or arrancasen

IMPERATIVE

arranca / arrancad

Use the present subjunctive in all cases other than these tú and vosotros affirmative forms.

EXAMPLE PHRASES

No **arranques** hojas del cuaderno. Don't tear pages out of the notebook.

Arranca y vámonos. Start the engine and let's get going.

Remember that subject pronouns are not used very often in Spanish.

arrepentirse (to be sorry, to change your mind)

	PRESENT	**PRESENT PERFECT**
(yo)	me arrepiento	me he arrepentido
(tú)	te arrepientes	te has arrepentido
(él/ella/usted)	se arrepiente	se ha arrepentido
(nosotros/as)	nos arrepentimos	nos hemos arrepentido
(vosotros/as)	os arrepentís	os habéis arrepentido
(ellos/ellas/ ustedes)	se arrepienten	se han arrepentido

	PRETERITE	**IMPERFECT**
(yo)	me arrepentí	me arrepentía
(tú)	te arrepentiste	te arrepentías
(él/ella/usted)	se arrepintió	se arrepentía
(nosotros/as)	nos arrepentimos	nos arrepentíamos
(vosotros/as)	os arrepentisteis	os arrepentíais
(ellos/ellas/ ustedes)	se arrepintieron	se arrepentían

GERUND

arrepintiéndose, etc

PAST PARTICIPLE

arrepentido

EXAMPLE PHRASES

¡Te vas a **arrepentir** de esto! You'll be sorry for this!

No **me arrepiento** de nada. I don't regret anything.

Se arrepintieron y decidieron no vender la casa. They changed their minds and decided not to sell the house.

Remember that subject pronouns are not used very often in Spanish.

arrepentirse

	FUTURE	CONDITIONAL
(yo)	me arrepentiré	me arrepentiría
(tú)	te arrepentirás	te arrepentirías
(él/ella/usted)	se arrepentirá	se arrepentiría
(nosotros/as)	nos arrepentiremos	nos arrepentiríamos
(vosotros/as)	os arrepentiréis	os arrepentiríais
(ellos/ellas/ ustedes)	se arrepentirán	se arrepentirían

	PRESENT SUBJUNCTIVE	IMPERFECT SUBJUNCTIVE
(yo)	me arrepienta	me arrepintiera or arrepintiese
(tú)	te arrepientas	te arrepintieras or arrepintieses
(él/ella/usted)	se arrepienta	se arrepintiera or arrepintiese
(nosotros/as)	nos arrepintamos	nos arrepintiéramos or arrepintiésemos
(vosotros/as)	os arrepintáis	os arrepintierais or arrepintieseis
(ellos/ellas/ ustedes)	se arrepientan	se arrepintieran or arrepintiesen

IMPERATIVE

arrepiéntete / arrepentíos

Use the present subjunctive in all cases other than these tú and vosotros affirmative forms.

EXAMPLE PHRASES

Algún día **se arrepentirá** de no haber estudiado una carrera. One day he'll be sorry he didn't go to college.

No **te arrepientas** nunca de haber dicho la verdad. Don't ever regret having told the truth.

Remember that subject pronouns are not used very often in Spanish.

atravesar (to cross, to go through)

	PRESENT	PRESENT PERFECT
(yo)	atravieso	he atravesado
(tú)	atraviesas	has atravesado
(él/ella/usted)	atraviesa	ha atravesado
(nosotros/as)	atravesamos	hemos atravesado
(vosotros/as)	atravesáis	habéis atravesado
(ellos/ellas/ ustedes)	atraviesan	han atravesado

	PRETERITE	IMPERFECT
(yo)	atravesé	atravesaba
(tú)	atravesaste	atravesabas
(él/ella/usted)	atravesó	atravesaba
(nosotros/as)	atravesamos	atravesábamos
(vosotros/as)	atravesasteis	atravesabais
(ellos/ellas/ ustedes)	atravesaron	atravesaban

GERUND	PAST PARTICIPLE
atravesando	atravesado

EXAMPLE PHRASES

Estamos atravesando un mal momento. We're going through a bad patch.

Atravesamos el río a nado. We swam across the river.

La bala le **atravesó** el cráneo. The bullet went through his skull.

Un camión **se** nos **atravesó** en la carretera. A truck came out into the road in front of us.

Remember that subject pronouns are not used very often in Spanish.

atravesar

	FUTURE	**CONDITIONAL**
(yo)	atravesaré	atravesaría
(tú)	atravesarás	atravesarías
(él/ella/usted)	atravesará	atravesaría
(nosotros/as)	atravesaremos	atravesaríamos
(vosotros/as)	atravesaréis	atravesaríais
(ellos/ellas/ ustedes)	atravesarán	atravesarían

	PRESENT SUBJUNCTIVE	**IMPERFECT SUBJUNCTIVE**
(yo)	atraviese	atravesara or atravesase
(tú)	atravieses	atravesaras or atravesases
(él/ella/usted)	atraviese	atravesara or atravesase
(nosotros/as)	atravesemos	atravesáramos or atravesásemos
(vosotros/as)	atraveséis	atravesarais or atravesaseis
(ellos/ellas/ ustedes)	atraviesen	atravesaran or atravesasen

IMPERATIVE

atraviesa / atravesad

Use the present subjunctive in all cases other than these tú and vosotros affirmative forms.

EXAMPLE PHRASES

El túnel **atravesará** la montaña. The tunnel will go under the mountain.

Remember that subject pronouns are not used very often in Spanish.

aunar (to join together)

	PRESENT	PRESENT PERFECT
(yo)	aúno	he aunado
(tú)	aúnas	has aunado
(él/ella/usted)	aúna	ha aunado
(nosotros/as)	aunamos	hemos aunado
(vosotros/as)	aunáis	habéis aunado
(ellos/ellas/ustedes)	aúnan	han aunado

	PRETERITE	IMPERFECT
(yo)	auné	aunaba
(tú)	aunaste	aunabas
(él/ella/usted)	aunó	aunaba
(nosotros/as)	aunamos	aunábamos
(vosotros/as)	aunasteis	aunabais
(ellos/ellas/ustedes)	aunaron	aunaban

GERUND

aunando

PAST PARTICIPLE

aunado

EXAMPLE PHRASES

En esta obra **se aúnan** imaginación y técnica. This play combines imagination and technique.

Aunaron esfuerzos. They joined forces.

Remember that subject pronouns are not used very often in Spanish.

aunar

	FUTURE	CONDITIONAL
(yo)	aunaré	aunaría
(tú)	aunarás	aunarías
(él/ella/usted)	aunará	aunaría
(nosotros/as)	aunaremos	aunaríamos
(vosotros/as)	aunaréis	aunaríais
(ellos/ellas/ ustedes)	aunarán	aunarían

	PRESENT SUBJUNCTIVE	IMPERFECT SUBJUNCTIVE
(yo)	aúne	aunara or aunase
(tú)	aúnes	aunaras or aunases
(él/ella/usted)	aúne	aunara or aunase
(nosotros/as)	aunemos	aunáramos or aunásemos
(vosotros/as)	aunéis	aunarais or aunaseis
(ellos/ellas/ ustedes)	aúnen	aunaran or aunasen

IMPERATIVE

aúna / aunad

Use the present subjunctive in all cases other than these tú and vosotros affirmative forms.

Remember that subject pronouns are not used very often in Spanish.

avergonzar (to shame)

	PRESENT	PRESENT PERFECT
(yo)	avergüenzo	he avergonzado
(tú)	avergüenzas	has avergonzado
(él/ella/usted)	avergüenza	ha avergonzado
(nosotros/as)	avergonzamos	hemos avergonzado
(vosotros/as)	avergonzáis	habéis avergonzado
(ellos/ellas/ustedes)	avergüenzan	han avergonzado

	PRETERITE	IMPERFECT
(yo)	avergoncé	avergonzaba
(tú)	avergonzaste	avergonzabas
(él/ella/usted)	avergonzó	avergonzaba
(nosotros/as)	avergonzamos	avergonzábamos
(vosotros/as)	avergonzasteis	avergonzabais
(ellos/ellas/ustedes)	avergonzaron	avergonzaban

GERUND

avergonzando

PAST PARTICIPLE

avergonzado

EXAMPLE PHRASES

Tendrías que **avergonzarte**. You should be ashamed of yourself.

La **avergüenza** no tener dinero. She's ashamed of having no money.

Cuando me lo dijo **me avergoncé**. I was embarrassed when he told me.

Se avergonzaba de su familia. He was ashamed of his family.

Remember that subject pronouns are not used very often in Spanish.

avergonzar

	FUTURE	**CONDITIONAL**
(yo)	avergonzaré	avergonzaría
(tú)	avergonzarás	avergonzarías
(él/ella/usted)	avergonzará	avergonzaría
(nosotros/as)	avergonzaremos	avergonzaríamos
(vosotros/as)	avegonzaréis	avergonzaríais
(ellos/ellas/ ustedes)	avergonzarán	avergonzarían

	PRESENT SUBJUNCTIVE	**IMPERFECT SUBJUNCTIVE**
(yo)	avergüence	avergonzara *or* avergonzase
(tú)	avergüences	avergonzaras *or* avergonzases
(él/ella/usted)	avergüence	avergonzara *or* avergonzase
(nosotros/as)	avergoncemos	avergonzáramos *or* avergonzásemos
(vosotros/as)	avergoncéis	avergonzarais *or* avergonzaseis
(ellos/ellas/ ustedes)	avergüencen	avergonzaran *or* avergonzasen

IMPERATIVE

avergüenza / avergonzad

Use the present subjunctive in all cases other than these tú and vosotros affirmative forms.

EXAMPLE PHRASES

Si de verdad **se avergonzaran**, no se comportarían así. They wouldn't behave like that if they were really ashamed.

Remember that subject pronouns are not used very often in Spanish.

averiguar (to find out)

	PRESENT	PRESENT PERFECT
(yo)	averiguo	he averiguado
(tú)	averiguas	has averiguado
(él/ella/usted)	averigua	ha averiguado
(nosotros/as)	averiguamos	hemos averiguado
(vosotros/as)	averiguáis	habéis averiguado
(ellos/ellas/ ustedes)	averiguan	han averiguado

	PRETERITE	IMPERFECT
(yo)	averigüé	averiguaba
(tú)	averiguaste	averiguabas
(él/ella/usted)	averiguó	averiguaba
(nosotros/as)	averiguamos	averiguábamos
(vosotros/as)	averiguasteis	averiguabais
(ellos/ellas/ ustedes)	averiguaron	averiguaban

GERUND

averiguando

PAST PARTICIPLE

averiguado

EXAMPLE PHRASES

Trataron de **averiguar** su paradero. They tried to find out his whereabouts.

Poco a poco **van averiguando** más cosas sobre su vida. They're gradually finding out more about his life.

¿Cómo **averiguaste** dónde vivo? How did you find out where I live?

¿Cuándo lo **averiguaron**? When did they find out?

Remember that subject pronouns are not used very often in Spanish.

averiguar

	FUTURE	CONDITIONAL
(yo)	averiguaré	averiguaría
(tú)	averiguarás	averiguarías
(él/ella/usted)	averiguará	averiguaría
(nosotros/as)	averiguaremos	averiguaríamos
(vosotros/as)	averiguaréis	averiguaríais
(ellos/ellas/ ustedes)	averiguarán	averiguarían

	PRESENT SUBJUNCTIVE	IMPERFECT SUBJUNCTIVE
(yo)	averigüe	averiguara *or* averiguase
(tú)	averigües	averiguaras *or* averiguases
(él/ella/usted)	averigüe	averiguara *or* averiguase
(nosotros/as)	averigüemos	averiguáramos *or* averiguásemos
(vosotros/as)	averigüéis	averiguarais *or* averiguaseis
(ellos/ellas/ ustedes)	averigüen	averiguaran *or* averiguasen

IMPERATIVE

averigua / averiguad

Use the present subjunctive in all cases other than these tú *and* vosotros *affirmative forms.*

EXAMPLE PHRASES

Lo **averiguaré** pronto. I'll find out soon.

Dijo que si le dábamos tiempo lo **averiguaría**. She said that she'd find out if we gave her time.

En cuanto lo **averigüe** te lo digo. I'll tell you as soon as I find out.

¡**Averígualo** inmediatamente! Check it out immediately!

Remember that subject pronouns are not used very often in Spanish.

bendecir (to bless)

	PRESENT	PRESENT PERFECT
(yo)	bendigo	he bendecido
(tú)	bendices	has bendecido
(él/ella/usted)	bendice	ha bendecido
(nosotros/as)	bendecimos	hemos bendecido
(vosotros/as)	bendecís	habéis bendecido
(ellos/ellas/ustedes)	bendicen	han bendecido

	PRETERITE	IMPERFECT
(yo)	bendije	bendecía
(tú)	bendijiste	bendecías
(él/ella/usted)	bendijo	bendecía
(nosotros/as)	bendijimos	bendecíamos
(vosotros/as)	bendijisteis	bendecíais
(ellos/ellas/ustedes)	bendijeron	bendecían

GERUND

bendiciendo

PAST PARTICIPLE

bendecido

EXAMPLE PHRASES

La vida me **ha bendecido** con unos hijos maravillosos. I've been blessed with wonderful children.

Jesús **bendijo** los panes y los peces. Jesus blessed the loaves and the fishes.

Bendecía el día en que lo conoció. She blessed the day she met him.

Remember that subject pronouns are not used very often in Spanish.

bendecir

	FUTURE	CONDITIONAL
(yo)	bendeciré	bendeciría
(tú)	bendecirás	bendecirías
(él/ella/usted)	bendecirá	bendeciría
(nosotros/as)	bendeciremos	bendeciríamos
(vosotros/as)	bendeciréis	bendeciríais
(ellos/ellas/ ustedes)	bendecirán	bendecirían

	PRESENT SUBJUNCTIVE	IMPERFECT SUBJUNCTIVE
(yo)	bendiga	bendijera or bendijese
(tú)	bendigas	bendijeras or bendijeses
(él/ella/usted)	bendiga	bendijera or bendijese
(nosotros/as)	bendigamos	bendijéramos or bendijésemos
(vosotros/as)	bendigáis	bendijerais or bendijeseis
(ellos/ellas/ ustedes)	bendigan	bendijeran or bendijesen

IMPERATIVE

bendice / bendecid

Use the present subjunctive in all cases other than these tú and vosotros affirmative forms.

EXAMPLE PHRASES

El Papa **bendecirá** a los fieles desde el balcón. The Pope will bless the faithful from the balcony.

Quieren que sea él quien **bendiga** su unión. They want him to marry them.

Pidieron a un sacerdote que **bendijera** su nueva casa. They asked a priest to bless their new house.

Remember that subject pronouns are not used very often in Spanish.

caber (to fit)

	PRESENT	PRESENT PERFECT
(yo)	quepo	he cabido
(tú)	cabes	has cabido
(él/ella/usted)	cabe	ha cabido
(nosotros/as)	cabemos	hemos cabido
(vosotros/as)	cabéis	habéis cabido
(ellos/ellas/ustedes)	caben	han cabido

	PRETERITE	IMPERFECT
(yo)	cupe	cabía
(tú)	cupiste	cabías
(él/ella/usted)	cupo	cabía
(nosotros/as)	cupimos	cabíamos
(vosotros/as)	cupisteis	cabíais
(ellos/ellas/ustedes)	cupieron	cabían

GERUND	PAST PARTICIPLE
cabiendo	cabido

EXAMPLE PHRASES

No te preocupes, que va a **caber**. Don't worry, it will fit.

Aquí no **cabe**. There isn't enough room for it here.

Al final **cupo** todo. In the end everything went in.

No le **cupo** la menor duda. She wasn't in any doubt.

No **cabía** en sí de dicha. She was beside herself with joy.

Remember that subject pronouns are not used very often in Spanish.

caber

	FUTURE	CONDITIONAL
(yo)	cabré	cabría
(tú)	cabrás	cabrías
(él/ella/usted)	cabrá	cabría
(nosotros/as)	cabremos	cabríamos
(vosotros/as)	cabréis	cabríais
(ellos/ellas/ustedes)	cabrán	cabrían

	PRESENT SUBJUNCTIVE	IMPERFECT SUBJUNCTIVE
(yo)	quepa	cupiera or cupiese
(tú)	quepas	cupieras or cupieses
(él/ella/usted)	quepa	cupiera or cupiese
(nosotros/as)	quepamos	cupiéramos or cupiésemos
(vosotros/as)	quepáis	cupierais or cupieseis
(ellos/ellas/ustedes)	quepan	cupieran or cupiesen

IMPERATIVE

cabe / cabed

Use the present subjunctive in all cases other than these tú and vosotros affirmative forms.

EXAMPLE PHRASES

¿Crees que **cabrá**? Do you think there will be enough room for it?

Cabría cuestionarse si es la mejor solución. We should ask ourselves whether it's the best solution.

Hizo lo imposible para que le **cupiera** la redacción en una página.
He did everything he could to fit the essay onto one page.

Remember that subject pronouns are not used very often in Spanish.

caer (to fall)

	PRESENT		PRESENT PERFECT
(yo)	caigo		he caído
(tú)	caes		has caído
(él/ella/usted)	cae		ha caído
(nosotros/as)	caemos		hemos caído
(vosotros/as)	caéis		habéis caído
(ellos/ellas/ ustedes)	caen		han caído

	PRETERITE		IMPERFECT
(yo)	caí		caía
(tú)	caíste		caías
(él/ella/usted)	cayó		caía
(nosotros/as)	caímos		caíamos
(vosotros/as)	caísteis		caíais
(ellos/ellas/ ustedes)	cayeron		caían

GERUND	PAST PARTICIPLE
cayendo	caído

EXAMPLE PHRASES

Su cumpleaños **cae** en viernes. Her birthday falls on a Friday.

Ese edificio **se está cayendo.** That building's falling down.

Se me **cayó** un guante. I dropped one of my gloves.

Me caí por las escaleras. I fell down the stairs.

Me caía muy bien. I really liked him.

Remember that subject pronouns are not used very often in Spanish.

caer

	FUTURE	CONDITIONAL
(yo)	caeré	caería
(tú)	caerás	caerías
(él/ella/usted)	caerá	caería
(nosotros/as)	caeremos	caeríamos
(vosotros/as)	caeréis	caeríais
(ellos/ellas/ustedes)	caerán	caerían

	PRESENT SUBJUNCTIVE	IMPERFECT SUBJUNCTIVE
(yo)	caiga	cayera or cayese
(tú)	caigas	cayeras or cayeses
(él/ella/usted)	caiga	cayera or cayese
(nosotros/as)	caigamos	cayéramos or cayésemos
(vosotros/as)	caigáis	cayerais or cayeseis
(ellos/ellas/ustedes)	caigan	cayeran or cayesen

IMPERATIVE

cae / caed

Use the present subjunctive in all cases other than these tú and vosotros affirmative forms.

EXAMPLE PHRASES

Tarde o temprano, **caerá** en manos del enemigo. Sooner or later, it will fall into enemy hands.

Yo **me caería** con esos tacones. I'd fall over if I wore heels like those.

Seguirá adelante **caiga** quien **caiga**. She'll go ahead no matter how many heads have to roll.

No **caigas** tan bajo. Don't stoop so low.

Remember that subject pronouns are not used very often in Spanish.

cambiar (to change)

	PRESENT		PRESENT PERFECT
(yo)	cambio		he cambiado
(tú)	cambias		has cambiado
(él/ella/usted)	cambia		ha cambiado
(nosotros/as)	cambiamos		hemos cambiado
(vosotros/as)	cambiáis		habéis cambiado
(ellos/ellas/ ustedes)	cambian		han cambiado

	PRETERITE		IMPERFECT
(yo)	cambié		cambiaba
(tú)	cambiaste		cambiabas
(él/ella/usted)	cambió		cambiaba
(nosotros/as)	cambiamos		cambiábamos
(vosotros/as)	cambiasteis		cambiabais
(ellos/ellas/ ustedes)	cambiaron		cambiaban

GERUND

cambiando

PAST PARTICIPLE

cambiado

EXAMPLE PHRASES

Necesito **cambiar** de ambiente. I need a change of scene.

Te **cambio** mi bolígrafo por tu goma. I'll swap my pen for your eraser.

Cambié varias veces de trabajo. I changed jobs several times.

Cambiaban de idea a cada rato. They kept changing their minds.

Remember that subject pronouns are not used very often in Spanish.

cambiar

	FUTURE	CONDITIONAL
(yo)	cambiaré	cambiaría
(tú)	cambiarás	cambiarías
(él/ella/usted)	cambiará	cambiaría
(nosotros/as)	cambiaremos	cambiaríamos
(vosotros/as)	cambiaréis	cambiaríais
(ellos/ellas/ ustedes)	cambiarán	cambiarían

	PRESENT SUBJUNCTIVE	IMPERFECT SUBJUNCTIVE
(yo)	cambie	cambiara *or* cambiase
(tú)	cambies	cambiaras *or* cambiases
(él/ella/usted)	cambie	cambiara *or* cambiase
(nosotros/as)	cambiemos	cambiáramos *or* cambiásemos
(vosotros/as)	cambiéis	cambiarais *or* cambiaseis
(ellos/ellas/ ustedes)	cambien	cambiaran *or* cambiasen

IMPERATIVE

cambia / cambiad

Use the present subjunctive in all cases other than these tú and vosotros affirmative forms.

EXAMPLE PHRASES

Cuando la conozcas, **cambiarás** de idea. You'll change your mind when you meet her.

Si pudiéramos, **nos cambiaríamos** de casa. If we could, we'd move.

No quiero que **cambies**. I don't want you to change.

Cámbiate, que se nos hace tarde. Get changed, it's getting late.

Remember that subject pronouns are not used very often in Spanish.

cazar (to hunt, to shoot)

	PRESENT	**PRESENT PERFECT**
(yo)	cazo	he cazado
(tú)	cazas	has cazado
(él/ella/usted)	caza	ha cazado
(nosotros/as)	cazamos	hemos cazado
(vosotros/as)	cazáis	habéis cazado
(ellos/ellas/ ustedes)	cazan	han cazado

	PRETERITE	**IMPERFECT**
(yo)	cacé	cazaba
(tú)	cazaste	cazabas
(él/ella/usted)	cazó	cazaba
(nosotros/as)	cazamos	cazábamos
(vosotros/as)	cazasteis	cazabais
(ellos/ellas/ ustedes)	cazaron	cazaban

GERUND

cazando

PAST PARTICIPLE

cazado

EXAMPLE PHRASES

Salieron a **cazar** ciervos. They went deer-hunting.

Caza las cosas al vuelo. She's very quick on the uptake.

Los **cacé** robando. I caught them stealing.

Cazaban con lanza. They hunted with spears.

Remember that subject pronouns are not used very often in Spanish.

cazar

	FUTURE	CONDITIONAL
(yo)	cazaré	cazaría
(tú)	cazarás	cazarías
(él/ella/usted)	cazará	cazaría
(nosotros/as)	cazaremos	cazaríamos
(vosotros/as)	cazaréis	cazaríais
(ellos/ellas/ ustedes)	cazarán	cazarían

	PRESENT SUBJUNCTIVE	IMPERFECT SUBJUNCTIVE
(yo)	cace	cazara or cazase
(tú)	caces	cazaras or cazases
(él/ella/usted)	cace	cazara or cazase
(nosotros/as)	cacemos	cazáramos or cazásemos
(vosotros/as)	cacéis	cazarais or cazaseis
(ellos/ellas/ ustedes)	cacen	cazaran or cazasen

IMPERATIVE

caza / cazad

Use the present subjunctive in all cases other than these tú and vosotros affirmative forms.

EXAMPLE PHRASES

¡Quién **cazara** a un millonario! I wish I could land myself a millionaire!

Remember that subject pronouns are not used very often in Spanish.

cerrar (to close, to shut)

	PRESENT	PRESENT PERFECT
(yo)	cierro	he cerrado
(tú)	cierras	has cerrado
(él/ella/usted)	cierra	ha cerrado
(nosotros/as)	cerramos	hemos cerrado
(vosotros/as)	cerráis	habéis cerrado
(ellos/ellas/ ustedes)	cierran	han cerrado

	PRETERITE	IMPERFECT
(yo)	cerré	cerraba
(tú)	cerraste	cerrabas
(él/ella/usted)	cerró	cerraba
(nosotros/as)	cerramos	cerrábamos
(vosotros/as)	cerrasteis	cerrabais
(ellos/ellas/ ustedes)	cerraron	cerraban

GERUND

cerrando

PAST PARTICIPLE

cerrado

EXAMPLE PHRASES

No puedo **cerrar** la maleta. I can't close this suitcase.

No **cierran** al mediodía. They don't close at midday.

Había **cerrado** la puerta con llave. She'd locked the door.

Cerró el libro. He closed the book.

Se le **cerraban** los ojos. She couldn't keep her eyes open.

Remember that subject pronouns are not used very often in Spanish.

cerrar

	FUTURE	CONDITIONAL
(yo)	cerraré	cerraría
(tú)	cerrarás	cerrarías
(él/ella/usted)	cerrará	cerraría
(nosotros/as)	cerraremos	cerraríamos
(vosotros/as)	cerraréis	cerraríais
(ellos/ellas/ ustedes)	cerrrarán	cerrarían

	PRESENT SUBJUNCTIVE	IMPERFECT SUBJUNCTIVE
(yo)	cierre	cerrara or cerrase
(tú)	cierres	cerraras or cerrases
(él/ella/usted)	cierre	cerraras or cerrases
(nosotros/as)	cerremos	cerráramos or cerrásemos
(vosotros/as)	cerréis	cerrarais or cerraseis
(ellos/ellas/ ustedes)	cierren	cerraran or cerrasen

IMPERATIVE

cierra / cerrad

Use the present subjunctive in all cases other than these tú and vosotros affirmative forms.

EXAMPLE PHRASES

No dejes que **se cierre** la puerta de golpe. Don't let the door slam shut.

No **cierres** la ventana. Don't close the window.

Cierra la llave. Turn off the faucet.

Remember that subject pronouns are not used very often in Spanish.

cocer (to boil, to cook)

	PRESENT		PRESENT PERFECT
(yo)	cuezo		he cocido
(tú)	cueces		has cocido
(él/ella/usted)	cuece		ha cocido
(nosotros/as)	cocemos		hemos cocido
(vosotros/as)	cocéis		habéis cocido
(ellos/ellas/ ustedes)	cuecen		han cocido

	PRETERITE		IMPERFECT
(yo)	cocí		cocía
(tú)	cociste		cocías
(él/ella/usted)	coció		cocía
(nosotros/as)	cocimos		cocíamos
(vosotros/as)	cocisteis		cocíais
(ellos/ellas/ ustedes)	cocieron		cocían

GERUND

cociendo

PAST PARTICIPLE

cocido

EXAMPLE PHRASES

El pescado **se cuece** en un momento. Fish takes no time to cook.

Aquí nos **estamos cociendo**. It's boiling in here.

Coció el pan en el horno. He baked the bread in the oven.

Remember that subject pronouns are not used very often in Spanish.

cocer

	FUTURE	**CONDITIONAL**
(yo)	coceré	cocería
(tú)	cocerás	cocerías
(él/ella/usted)	cocerá	cocería
(nosotros/as)	coceremos	coceríamos
(vosotros/as)	coceréis	coceríais
(ellos/ellas/ ustedes)	cocerán	cocerían

	PRESENT SUBJUNCTIVE	**IMPERFECT SUBJUNCTIVE**
(yo)	cueza	cociera *or* cociese
(tú)	cuezas	cocieras *or* cocieses
(él/ella/usted)	cueza	cociera *or* cociese
(nosotros/as)	cozamos	cociéramos *or* cociésemos
(vosotros/as)	cozáis	cocierais *or* cocieseis
(ellos/ellas/ ustedes)	cuezan	cocieran *or* cociesen

IMPERATIVE

cuece / coced

Use the present subjunctive in all cases other than these tú and vosotros affirmative forms.

EXAMPLE PHRASES

Te dije que lo **cocieras** tapado. I told you to cook it covered.

No lo **cuezas** demasiado. Don't overcook it.

Cuécelo a fuego lento. Cook it over a low heat.

Remember that subject pronouns are not used very often in Spanish.

colgar (to hang)

	PRESENT	PRESENT PERFECT
(yo)	cuelgo	he colgado
(tú)	cuelgas	has colgado
(él/ella/usted)	cuelga	ha colgado
(nosotros/as)	colgamos	hemos colgado
(vosotros/as)	colgáis	habéis colgado
(ellos/ellas/ ustedes)	cuelgan	han colgado

	PRETERITE	IMPERFECT
(yo)	colgué	colgaba
(tú)	colgaste	colgabas
(él/ella/usted)	colgó	colgaba
(nosotros/as)	colgamos	colgábamos
(vosotros/as)	colgasteis	colgabais
(ellos/ellas/ ustedes)	colgaron	colgaban

GERUND

colgando

PAST PARTICIPLE

colgado

EXAMPLE PHRASES

Hay telarañas **colgando** del techo. There are cobwebs hanging from the ceiling.

Te **colgué** la chaqueta en el clóset. I hung your jacket in the closet.

Me **colgó** el teléfono. He hung up on me.

De la pared **colgaba** un espejo. There was a mirror hanging on the wall.

Remember that subject pronouns are not used very often in Spanish.

colgar

	FUTURE	CONDITIONAL
(yo)	colgaré	colgaría
(tú)	colgarás	colgarías
(él/ella/usted)	colgará	colgaría
(nosotros/as)	colgaremos	colgaríamos
(vosotros/as)	colgaréis	colgaríais
(ellos/ellas/ ustedes)	colgarán	colgarían

	PRESENT SUBJUNCTIVE	IMPERFECT SUBJUNCTIVE
(yo)	cuelgue	colgara or colgase
(tú)	cuelgues	colgaras or colgases
(él/ella/usted)	cuelgue	colgara or colgase
(nosotros/as)	colguemos	colgáramos or colgásemos
(vosotros/as)	colguéis	colgarais or colgaseis
(ellos/ellas/ ustedes)	cuelguen	colgaran or colgasen

IMPERATIVE

cuelga / colgad

Use the present subjunctive in all cases other than these tú and vosotros affirmative forms.

EXAMPLE PHRASES

Colgaremos el cuadro en esa pared. We'll hang the picture on that wall.

No **cuelgue**, por favor. Please don't hang up.

Remember that subject pronouns are not used very often in Spanish.

comer (to eat)

	PRESENT	PRESENT PERFECT
(yo)	como	he comido
(tú)	comes	has comido
(él/ella/usted)	come	ha comido
(nosotros/as)	comemos	hemos comido
(vosotros/as)	coméis	habéis comido
(ellos/ellas/ ustedes)	comen	han comido

	PRETERITE	IMPERFECT
(yo)	comí	comía
(tú)	comiste	comías
(él/ella/usted)	comió	comía
(nosotros/as)	comimos	comíamos
(vosotros/as)	comisteis	comíais
(ellos/ellas/ ustedes)	comieron	comían

GERUND	PAST PARTICIPLE
comiendo	comido

EXAMPLE PHRASES

No **come** carne. He doesn't eat meat.

Se lo **comió** todo. He ate it all.

Comimos en un restaurante. We had lunch in a restaurant.

Siempre **comían** demasiado. They always ate too much.

Remember that subject pronouns are not used very often in Spanish.

comer

	FUTURE	**CONDITIONAL**
(yo)	comeré	comería
(tú)	comerás	comerías
(él/ella/usted)	comerá	comería
(nosotros/as)	comeremos	comeríamos
(vosotros/as)	comeréis	comeríais
(ellos/ellas/ ustedes)	comerán	comerían

	PRESENT SUBJUNCTIVE	**IMPERFECT SUBJUNCTIVE**
(yo)	coma	comiera *or* comiese
(tú)	comas	comieras *or* comieses
(él/ella/usted)	coma	comiera *or* comiese
(nosotros/as)	comamos	comiéramos *or* comiésemos
(vosotros/as)	comáis	comierais *or* comieseis
(ellos/ellas/ ustedes)	coman	comieran *or* comiesen

IMPERATIVE

come / comed

Use the present subjunctive in all cases other than these tú and vosotros affirmative forms.

EXAMPLE PHRASES

Me lo **comeré** yo. I'll eat it.

Si no fuera por mí, no **comeríamos**. We wouldn't eat if it weren't for me.

No **comas** tan deprisa. Don't eat so fast.

Remember that subject pronouns are not used very often in Spanish.

conducir (to lead, to drive, to take)

	PRESENT		PRESENT PERFECT
(yo)	conduzco		he conducido
(tú)	conduces		has conducido
(él/ella/usted)	conduce		ha conducido
(nosotros/as)	conducimos		hemos conducido
(vosotros/as)	conducís		habéis conducido
(ellos/ellas/ ustedes)	conducen		han conducido

	PRETERITE		IMPERFECT
(yo)	conduje		conducía
(tú)	condujiste		conducías
(él/ella/usted)	condujo		conducía
(nosotros/as)	condujimos		conducíamos
(vosotros/as)	condujisteis		conducíais
(ellos/ellas/ ustedes)	condujeron		conducían

GERUND

conduciendo

PAST PARTICIPLE

conducido

EXAMPLE PHRASES

Nos **condujo** a su habitación. He took us to his room.

Enojarte no **conduce** a nada. Getting angry doesn't get you anywhere.

La pista nos **condujo** hasta él. The clue led us to him.

Remember that subject pronouns are not used very often in Spanish.

conducir

	FUTURE	**CONDITIONAL**
(yo)	conduciré	conduciría
(tú)	conducirás	conducirías
(él/ella/usted)	conducirá	conduciría
(nosotros/as)	conduciremos	conduciríamos
(vosotros/as)	conduciréis	conduciríais
(ellos/ellas/ ustedes)	conducirán	conducirían

	PRESENT SUBJUNCTIVE	**IMPERFECT SUBJUNCTIVE**
(yo)	conduzca	condujera or condujese
(tú)	conduzcas	condujeras or condujeses
(él/ella/usted)	conduzca	condujera or condujese
(nosotros/as)	conduzcamos	condujéramos or condujésemos
(vosotros/as)	conduzcáis	condujerais or condujeseis
(ellos/ellas/ ustedes)	conduzcan	condujeran or condujesen

IMPERATIVE

conduce / conducid

Use the present subjunctive in all cases other than these tú and vosotros affirmative forms.

EXAMPLE PHRASES

Roberto los **conducirá** a su mesa. Roberto will show you to your table.

Remember that subject pronouns are not used very often in Spanish.

conocer (to know, to meet, to recognize)

	PRESENT	PRESENT PERFECT
(yo)	conozco	he conocido
(tú)	conoces	has conocido
(él/ella/usted)	conoce	ha conocido
(nosotros/as)	conocemos	hemos conocido
(vosotros/as)	conocéis	habéis conocido
(ellos/ellas/ ustedes)	conocen	han conocido

	PRETERITE	IMPERFECT
(yo)	conocí	conocía
(tú)	conociste	conocías
(él/ella/usted)	conoció	conocía
(nosotros/as)	conocimos	conocíamos
(vosotros/as)	conocisteis	conocíais
(ellos/ellas/ ustedes)	conocieron	conocían

GERUND
conociendo

PAST PARTICIPLE
conocido

EXAMPLE PHRASES

Conozco un restaurante donde se come bien. I know a restaurant where the food is very good.

La **conocí** en una fiesta. I met her at a party.

Nos **conocíamos** desde hacía años. We'd known each other for years.

Remember that subject pronouns are not used very often in Spanish.

conocer

	FUTURE	CONDITIONAL
(yo)	conoceré	conocería
(tú)	conocerás	conocerías
(él/ella/usted)	conocerá	conocería
(nosotros/as)	conoceremos	conoceríamos
(vosotros/as)	conoceréis	conoceríais
(ellos/ellas/ ustedes)	conocerán	conocerían

	PRESENT SUBJUNCTIVE	IMPERFECT SUBJUNCTIVE
(yo)	conozca	conociera or conociese
(tú)	conozcas	conocieras or conocieses
(él/ella/usted)	conozca	conociera or conociese
(nosotros/as)	conozcamos	conociéramos or conociésemos
(vosotros/as)	conozcáis	conocierais or conocieseis
(ellos/ellas/ ustedes)	conozcan	conocieran or conociesen

IMPERATIVE

conoce / conoced

Use the present subjunctive in all cases other than these tú and vosotros affirmative forms.

EXAMPLE PHRASES

No sé si la **conocerás** cuando la veas. I don't know if you'll recognize her when you see her.

No quiero que mis padres lo **conozcan**. I don't want my parents to meet him.

Si no la **conociera**, pensaría que lo hizo a propósito. If I didn't know her better, I'd think she had done it on purpose.

Remember that subject pronouns are not used very often in Spanish.

construir (to build)

	PRESENT		PRESENT PERFECT
(yo)	construyo		he construido
(tú)	construyes		has construido
(él/ella/usted)	construye		ha construido
(nosotros/as)	construimos		hemos construido
(vosotros/as)	construís		habéis construido
(ellos/ellas/ ustedes)	construyen		han construido

	PRETERITE		IMPERFECT
(yo)	construí		construía
(tú)	construiste		construías
(él/ella/usted)	construyó		construía
(nosotros/as)	construimos		construíamos
(vosotros/as)	construisteis		construíais
(ellos/ellas/ ustedes)	construyeron		construían

GERUND

construyendo

PAST PARTICIPLE

construido

EXAMPLE PHRASES

Construyen casas de madera. They build wooden houses.

Están construyendo una escuela. They're building a new school.

Construyó la casa él solo. He built the house on his own.

Su empresa **construía** puentes. His company built bridges.

Remember that subject pronouns are not used very often in Spanish.

construir

	FUTURE	CONDITIONAL
(yo)	construiré	construiría
(tú)	construirás	construirías
(él/ella/usted)	construirá	construiría
(nosotros/as)	construiremos	construiríamos
(vosotros/as)	construiréis	construiríais
(ellos/ellas/ ustedes)	construirán	construirían

	PRESENT SUBJUNCTIVE	IMPERFECT SUBJUNCTIVE
(yo)	construya	construyera *or* construyese
(tú)	construyas	construyeras *or* construyeses
(él/ella/usted)	construya	construyera *or* construyese
(nosotros/as)	construyamos	construyéramos *or* construyésemos
(vosotros/as)	construyáis	construyerais *or* construyeseis
(ellos/ellas/ ustedes)	construyan	construyeran *or* construyesen

IMPERATIVE

construye / construid

Use the present subjunctive in all cases other than these tú and vosotros affirmative forms.

EXAMPLE PHRASES

Construirán una nueva autopista. They're going to build a new highway.

Yo **construiría** la oración de otra forma. I'd construct the sentence differently.

Le pedí que lo **construyera** así. I asked him to build it like this.

Remember that subject pronouns are not used very often in Spanish.

contar (to tell, to count)

	PRESENT	PRESENT PERFECT
(yo)	cuento	he contado
(tú)	cuentas	has contado
(él/ella/usted)	cuenta	ha contado
(nosotros/as)	contamos	hemos contado
(vosotros/as)	contáis	habéis contado
(ellos/ellas/ ustedes)	cuentan	han contado

	PRETERITE	IMPERFECT
(yo)	conté	contaba
(tú)	contaste	contabas
(él/ella/usted)	contó	contaba
(nosotros/as)	contamos	contábamos
(vosotros/as)	contasteis	contabais
(ellos/ellas/ ustedes)	contaron	contaban

GERUND

contando

PAST PARTICIPLE

contado

EXAMPLE PHRASES

Sabe **contar** hasta diez. She can count up to ten.

Estoy contando los días. I'm counting the days.

Nos **contó** un secreto. He told us a secret.

Para él sólo **contaba** su carrera. The only thing that mattered to him was his career.

Remember that subject pronouns are not used very often in Spanish.

contar

	FUTURE	CONDITIONAL
(yo)	contaré	contaría
(tú)	contarás	contarías
(él/ella/usted)	contará	contaría
(nosotros/as)	contaremos	contaríamos
(vosotros/as)	contaréis	contaríais
(ellos/ellas/ ustedes)	contarán	contarían

	PRESENT SUBJUNCTIVE	IMPERFECT SUBJUNCTIVE
(yo)	cuente	contara or contase
(tú)	cuentes	contaras or contases
(él/ella/usted)	cuente	contara or contase
(nosotros/as)	contemos	contáramos or contásemos
(vosotros/as)	contéis	contarais or contaseis
(ellos/ellas/ ustedes)	cuenten	contaran or contasen

IMPERATIVE

cuenta / contad

Use the present subjunctive in all cases other than these tú and vosotros affirmative forms.

EXAMPLE PHRASES

Prométeme que no se lo **contarás** a nadie. Promise you won't tell anyone.

Quiero que me **cuente** exactamente qué pasó. I want you to tell me exactly what happened.

Quería que le **contara** un cuento. She wanted me to tell her a story.

No **cuentes** conmigo. Don't count on me.

Remember that subject pronouns are not used very often in Spanish.

crecer (to grow, to rise)

	PRESENT	PRESENT PERFECT
(yo)	crezco	he crecido
(tú)	creces	has crecido
(él/ella/usted)	crece	ha crecido
(nosotros/as)	crecemos	hemos crecido
(vosotros/as)	crecéis	habéis crecido
(ellos/ellas/ ustedes)	crecen	han crecido

	PRETERITE	IMPERFECT
(yo)	crecí	crecía
(tú)	creciste	crecías
(él/ella/usted)	creció	crecía
(nosotros/as)	crecimos	crecíamos
(vosotros/as)	crecisteis	crecíais
(ellos/ellas/ ustedes)	crecieron	crecían

GERUND

creciendo

PAST PARTICIPLE

crecido

EXAMPLE PHRASES

Esas plantas **crecen** en Chile. Those plants grow in Chile.

¡Cómo **has crecido**! Haven't you grown!

Crecimos juntos. We grew up together.

La ciudad **crecía** a pasos agigantados. The city was growing by leaps and bounds.

Sigue **creciendo** la inflación. Inflation is still rising.

Remember that subject pronouns are not used very often in Spanish.

crecer

	FUTURE	CONDITIONAL
(yo)	creceré	crecería
(tú)	crecerás	crecerías
(él/ella/usted)	crecerá	crecería
(nosotros/as)	creceremos	creceríamos
(vosotros/as)	creceréis	creceríais
(ellos/ellas/ ustedes)	crecerán	crecerían

	PRESENT SUBJUNCTIVE	IMPERFECT SUBJUNCTIVE
(yo)	crezca	creciera or creciese
(tú)	crezcas	crecieras or crecieses
(él/ella/usted)	crezca	creciera or creciese
(nosotros/as)	crezcamos	creciéramos or creciésemos
(vosotros/as)	crezcáis	crecierais or crecieseis
(ellos/ellas/ ustedes)	crezcan	crecieran or creciesen

IMPERATIVE

crece / creced

Use the present subjunctive in all cases other than these tú and vosotros affirmative forms.

EXAMPLE PHRASES

Este año la economía **crecerá** un 2%. The economy will grow by 2% this year.

Crecería mejor en un ambiente húmedo. It would grow better in a humid environment.

Quería que sus hijos **crecieran** en otro ambiente. She wanted her children to grow up in a different environment.

Remember that subject pronouns are not used very often in Spanish.

cruzar (to cross)

	PRESENT		PRESENT PERFECT
(yo)	cruzo		he cruzado
(tú)	cruzas		has cruzado
(él/ella/usted)	cruza		ha cruzado
(nosotros/as)	cruzamos		hemos cruzado
(vosotros/as)	cruzáis		habéis cruzado
(ellos/ellas/ustedes)	cruzan		han cruzado

	PRETERITE		IMPERFECT
(yo)	crucé		cruzaba
(tú)	cruzaste		cruzabas
(él/ella/usted)	cruzó		cruzaba
(nosotros/as)	cruzamos		cruzábamos
(vosotros/as)	cruzasteis		cruzabais
(ellos/ellas/ustedes)	cruzaron		cruzaban

GERUND

cruzando

PAST PARTICIPLE

cruzado

EXAMPLE PHRASES

Hace tiempo que no **me cruzo** con él. I haven't seen him for a long time.

La caravana **está cruzando** el desierto. The caravan is crossing the desert.

Cruzaron el puente. They crossed the bridge.

La carretera **cruzaba** el pueblo. The road went through the village.

cruzar

	FUTURE	CONDITIONAL
(yo)	cruzaré	cruzaría
(tú)	cruzarás	cruzarías
(él/ella/usted)	cruzará	cruzaría
(nosotros/as)	cruzaremos	cruzaríamos
(vosotros/as)	cruzaréis	cruzaríais
(ellos/ellas/ ustedes)	cruzarán	cruzarían

	PRESENT SUBJUNCTIVE	IMPERFECT SUBJUNCTIVE
(yo)	cruce	cruzara or cruzase
(tú)	cruces	cruzaras or cruzases
(él/ella/usted)	cruce	cruzara or cruzase
(nosotros/as)	crucemos	cruzáramos or cruzásemos
(vosotros/as)	crucéis	cruzarais or cruzaseis
(ellos/ellas/ ustedes)	crucen	cruzaran or cruzasen

IMPERATIVE

cruza / cruzad

Use the present subjunctive in all cases other than these tú and vosotros affirmative forms.

EXAMPLE PHRASES

Cruzarán varias especies distintas. They'll cross several different species.

Crucemos los dedos. Let's keep our fingers crossed.

Le dije que **cruzara** con cuidado. I told her to be careful crossing the street.

No **cruces** la calle con el semáforo en rojo. Don't cross the street when the signal's red.

Remember that subject pronouns are not used very often in Spanish.

cubrir (to cover)

	PRESENT	PRESENT PERFECT
(yo)	cubro	he cubierto
(tú)	cubres	has cubierto
(él/ella/usted)	cubre	ha cubierto
(nosotros/as)	cubrimos	hemos cubierto
(vosotros/as)	cubrís	habéis cubierto
(ellos/ellas/ ustedes)	cubren	han cubierto

	PRETERITE	IMPERFECT
(yo)	cubrí	cubría
(tú)	cubriste	cubrías
(él/ella/usted)	cubrió	cubría
(nosotros/as)	cubrimos	cubríamos
(vosotros/as)	cubristeis	cubríais
(ellos/ellas/ ustedes)	cubrieron	cubrían

GERUND
cubriendo

PAST PARTICIPLE
cubierto

EXAMPLE PHRASES

Esto no **cubre** los gastos. This isn't enough to cover expenses.

Lo **cubrieron** con una manta. They covered him with a blanket.

Se cubrió la cara con las manos. She covered her face with her hands.

La nieve **cubría** la montaña. The mountain was covered in snow.

Remember that subject pronouns are not used very often in Spanish.

cubrir

	FUTURE	**CONDITIONAL**
(yo)	cubriré	cubriría
(tú)	cubrirás	cubrirías
(él/ella/usted)	cubrirá	cubriría
(nosotros/as)	cubriremos	cubriríamos
(vosotros/as)	cubriréis	cubriríais
(ellos/ellas/ ustedes)	cubrirán	cubrirían

	PRESENT SUBJUNCTIVE	**IMPERFECT SUBJUNCTIVE**
(yo)	cubra	cubriera *or* cubriese
(tú)	cubras	cubrieras *or* cubrieses
(él/ella/usted)	cubra	cubriera *or* cubriese
(nosotros/as)	cubramos	cubriéramos *or* cubriésemos
(vosotros/as)	cubráis	cubrierais *or* cubrieseis
(ellos/ellas/ ustedes)	cubran	cubrieran *or* cubriesen

IMPERATIVE

cubre / cubrid

Use the present subjunctive in all cases other than these tú and vosotros affirmative forms.

EXAMPLE PHRASES

Los corredores **cubrirán** una distancia de 2 km. The runners will cover a distance of 2 km.

¿Quién **cubriría** la vacante? Who'd fill the vacancy?

Quiero que **cubras** la noticia. I want you to cover that news story.

Remember that subject pronouns are not used very often in Spanish.

dar (to give)

	PRESENT	PRESENT PERFECT
(yo)	doy	he dado
(tú)	das	has dado
(él/ella/usted)	da	ha dado
(nosotros/as)	damos	hemos dado
(vosotros/as)	dais	habéis dado
(ellos/ellas/ustedes)	dan	han dado

	PRETERITE	IMPERFECT
(yo)	di	daba
(tú)	diste	dabas
(él/ella/usted)	dio	daba
(nosotros/as)	dimos	dábamos
(vosotros/as)	disteis	dabais
(ellos/ellas/ustedes)	dieron	daban

GERUND

dando

PAST PARTICIPLE

dado

EXAMPLE PHRASES

Me **da** miedo la oscuridad. I'm afraid of the dark.

Nos **dieron** un par de entradas gratis. They gave us a pair of free tickets.

Mi ventana **daba** al jardín. My window looked out on the garden.

Remember that subject pronouns are not used very often in Spanish.

dar

	FUTURE	CONDITIONAL
(yo)	daré	daría
(tú)	darás	darías
(él/ella/usted)	dará	daría
(nosotros/as)	daremos	daríamos
(vosotros/as)	daréis	daríais
(ellos/ellas/ ustedes)	darán	darían

	PRESENT SUBJUNCTIVE	IMPERFECT SUBJUNCTIVE
(yo)	dé	diera or diese
(tú)	des	dieras or dieses
(él/ella/usted)	dé	diera or diese
(nosotros/as)	demos	diéramos or diésemos
(vosotros/as)	deis	dierais or dieseis
(ellos/ellas/ ustedes)	den	dieran or diesen

IMPERATIVE

da / dad

Use the present subjunctive in all cases other than these tú and vosotros affirmative forms.

EXAMPLE PHRASES

Te **daré** el número de mi celular. I'll give you my cell phone number.

Me **daría** mucha alegría volver a verla. It would be really good to see her again.

Quiero que me lo **des** ahora mismo. I want you to give it to me right now.

Déme 2 kilos. 2 kilos, please.

Remember that subject pronouns are not used very often in Spanish.

decir (to say, to tell)

	PRESENT	PRESENT PERFECT
(yo)	digo	he dicho
(tú)	dices	has dicho
(él/ella/usted)	dice	ha dicho
(nosotros/as)	decimos	hemos dicho
(vosotros/as)	decís	habéis dicho
(ellos/ellas/ ustedes)	dicen	han dicho

	PRETERITE	IMPERFECT
(yo)	dije	decía
(tú)	dijiste	decías
(él/ella/usted)	dijo	decía
(nosotros/as)	dijimos	decíamos
(vosotros/as)	dijisteis	decíais
(ellos/ellas/ ustedes)	dijeron	decían

GERUND

diciendo

PAST PARTICIPLE

dicho

EXAMPLE PHRASES

Pero ¿qué **dices**? What are you saying?

¿Te **dijo** lo de la boda? Did he tell you about the wedding?

Ya me lo había **dicho**. He had already told me.

Siempre nos **decía** que tuviéramos cuidado. She always used to tell us to be careful.

Remember that subject pronouns are not used very often in Spanish.

decir

	FUTURE	CONDITIONAL
(yo)	diré	diría
(tú)	dirás	dirías
(él/ella/usted)	dirá	diría
(nosotros/as)	diremos	diríamos
(vosotros/as)	diréis	diríais
(ellos/ellas/ ustedes)	dirán	dirían

	PRESENT SUBJUNCTIVE	IMPERFECT SUBJUNCTIVE
(yo)	diga	dijera *or* dijese
(tú)	digas	dijeras *or* dijeses
(él/ella/usted)	diga	dijera *or* dijese
(nosotros/as)	digamos	dijéramos *or* dijésemos
(vosotros/as)	digáis	dijerais *or* dijeseis
(ellos/ellas/ ustedes)	digan	dijeran *or* dijesen

IMPERATIVE

di / decid

Use the present subjunctive in all cases other than these tú and vosotros affirmative forms.

EXAMPLE PHRASES

Yo **diría** que miente. I'd say he's lying.

Si me **dijeras** lo que pasa, a lo mejor podría ayudar. If you told me what was going on, maybe I could help.

No le **digas** que me viste. Don't tell him you saw me.

Remember that subject pronouns are not used very often in Spanish.

despreocuparse (to stop worrying)

	PRESENT	PRESENT PERFECT
(yo)	me despreocupo	me he despreocupado
(tú)	te despreocupas	te has despreocupado
(él/ella/usted)	se despreocupa	se ha despreocupado
(nosotros/as)	nos despreocupamos	nos hemos despreocupado
(vosotros/as)	os despreocupáis	os habéis despreocupado
(ellos/ellas/ ustedes)	se despreocupan	se han despreocupado

	PRETERITE	IMPERFECT
(yo)	me despreocupé	me despreocupaba
(tú)	te despreocupaste	te despreocupabas
(él/ella/usted)	se despreocupó	se despreocupaba
(nosotros/as)	nos despreocupamos	nos despreocupábamos
(vosotros/as)	os despreocupasteis	os despreocupabais
(ellos/ellas/ ustedes)	se despreocuparon	se despreocupaban

GERUND

despreocupándose, etc

PAST PARTICIPLE

despreocupado

EXAMPLE PHRASES

Deberías **despreocuparte** un poco más de las cosas. You shouldn't worry so much about things.

Se despreocupa de todo. He shows no concern for anything.

Se despreocupó del asunto. He forgot about the matter.

Remember that subject pronouns are not used very often in Spanish.

despreocuparse

	FUTURE	CONDITIONAL
(yo)	me despreocuparé	me despreocuparía
(tú)	te despreocuparás	te despreocuparías
(él/ella/usted)	se despreocupará	se despreocuparía
(nosotros/as)	nos despreocuparemos	nos despreocuparíamos
(vosotros/as)	os despreocuparéis	os despreocuparíais
(ellos/ellas/ ustedes)	se despreocuparán	se despreocuparían

	PRESENT SUBJUNCTIVE	IMPERFECT SUBJUNCTIVE
(yo)	me despreocupe	me despreocupara or despreocupase
(tú)	te despreocupes	te despreocuparas or despreocupases
(él/ella/usted)	se despreocupe	se despreocupara or despreocupase
(nosotros/as)	nos despreocupemos	nos despreocupáramos or despreocupásemos
(vosotros/as)	os despreocupéis	os despreocuparais or despreocupaseis
(ellos/ellas/ ustedes)	se despreocupen	se despreocuparan or despreocupasen

IMPERATIVE

despreocúpate / despreocupaos

Use the present subjunctive in all cases other than these tú and vosotros affirmative forms.

EXAMPLE PHRASES

Yo **me despreocuparía** de él. I wouldn't worry about him.

Despreocúpate de todo. Don't worry about a thing.

Remember that subject pronouns are not used very often in Spanish.

detener (to stop, to arrest)

	PRESENT		PRESENT PERFECT
(yo)	detengo		he detenido
(tú)	detienes		has detenido
(él/ella/usted)	detiene		ha detenido
(nosotros/as)	detenemos		hemos detenido
(vosotros/as)	detenéis		habéis detenido
(ellos/ellas/ ustedes)	detienen		han detenido

	PRETERITE		IMPERFECT
(yo)	detuve		detenía
(tú)	detuviste		detenías
(él/ella/usted)	detuvo		detenía
(nosotros/as)	detuvimos		deteníamos
(vosotros/as)	detuvisteis		deteníais
(ellos/ellas/ ustedes)	detuvieron		detenían

GERUND

deteniendo

PAST PARTICIPLE

detenido

EXAMPLE PHRASES

Detuvieron a los ladrones. They arrested the thieves.

Nos detuvimos en el semáforo. We stopped at the light.

¡Queda **detenido**! You are under arrest!

Remember that subject pronouns are not used very often in Spanish.

detener

	FUTURE	**CONDITIONAL**
(yo)	detendré	detendría
(tú)	detendrás	detendrías
(él/ella/usted)	detendrá	detendría
(nosotros/as)	detendremos	detendríamos
(vosotros/as)	detendréis	detendríais
(ellos/ellas/ ustedes)	detendrán	detendrían

	PRESENT SUBJUNCTIVE	**IMPERFECT SUBJUNCTIVE**
(yo)	detenga	detuviera or detuviese
(tú)	detengas	detuvieras or detuvieses
(él/ella/usted)	detenga	detuviera or detuviese
(nosotros/as)	detengamos	detuviéramos or detuviésemos
(vosotros/as)	detengáis	detuvierais or detuvieseis
(ellos/ellas/ ustedes)	detengan	detuvieran or detuviesen

IMPERATIVE

detén / detened

Use the present subjunctive in all cases other than these tú and vosotros affirmative forms.

EXAMPLE PHRASES

Nada la **detendrá**. Nothing will stop her.

Si **te detuvieras** a pensar, nunca harías nada. If you stopped to think, you'd never do anything.

¡**Deténgase**! Stop!

¡No **te detengas**! Don't stop!

Remember that subject pronouns are not used very often in Spanish.

dirigir (to direct, to run)

	PRESENT	**PRESENT PERFECT**
(yo)	dirijo	he dirigido
(tú)	diriges	has dirigido
(él/ella/usted)	dirige	ha dirigido
(nosotros/as)	dirigimos	hemos dirigido
(vosotros/as)	dirigís	habéis dirigido
(ellos/ellas/ ustedes)	dirigen	han dirigido

	PRETERITE	**IMPERFECT**
(yo)	dirigí	dirigía
(tú)	dirigiste	dirigías
(él/ella/usted)	dirigió	dirigía
(nosotros/as)	dirigimos	dirigíamos
(vosotros/as)	dirigisteis	dirigíais
(ellos/ellas/ ustedes)	dirigieron	dirigían

GERUND

dirigiendo

PAST PARTICIPLE

dirigido

EXAMPLE PHRASES

Dirijo esta empresa desde hace dos años. I've been running this company for two years.

Ha dirigido varias películas. She has directed several movies.

No le **dirigió** la palabra. She didn't say a word to him.

Se **dirigía** a su casa. He was making his way home.

Remember that subject pronouns are not used very often in Spanish.

dirigir

	FUTURE	CONDITIONAL
(yo)	dirigiré	dirigiría
(tú)	dirigirás	dirigirías
(él/ella/usted)	dirigirá	dirigiría
(nosotros/as)	dirigiremos	dirigiríamos
(vosotros/as)	dirigiréis	dirigiríais
(ellos/ellas/ustedes)	dirigirán	dirigirían

	PRESENT SUBJUNCTIVE	IMPERFECT SUBJUNCTIVE
(yo)	dirija	dirigiera or dirigiese
(tú)	dirijas	dirigieras or dirigieses
(él/ella/usted)	dirija	dirigiera or dirigiese
(nosotros/as)	dirijamos	dirigiéramos or dirigiésemos
(vosotros/as)	dirijáis	dirigierais or dirigieseis
(ellos/ellas/ustedes)	dirijan	dirigieran or dirigiesen

IMPERATIVE
dirige / dirigid

Use the present subjunctive in all cases other than these tú and vosotros affirmative forms.

EXAMPLE PHRASES
Dirigirá la expedición. He'll be leading the expedition.

Para más información **diríjase** a la página 82. For more information turn to page 82.

Remember that subject pronouns are not used very often in Spanish.

distinguir (to distinguish)

	PRESENT	PRESENT PERFECT
(yo)	distingo	he distinguido
(tú)	distingues	has distinguido
(él/ella/usted)	distingue	ha distinguido
(nosotros/as)	distinguimos	hemos distinguido
(vosotros/as)	distinguís	habéis distinguido
(ellos/ellas/ustedes)	distinguen	han distinguido

	PRETERITE	IMPERFECT
(yo)	distinguí	distinguía
(tú)	distinguiste	distinguías
(él/ella/usted)	distinguió	distinguía
(nosotros/as)	distinguimos	distinguíamos
(vosotros/as)	distinguisteis	distinguíais
(ellos/ellas/ustedes)	distinguieron	distinguían

GERUND

distinguiendo

PAST PARTICIPLE

distinguido

EXAMPLE PHRASES

No lo **distingo** del azul. I can't tell the difference between it and the blue one.

Se **distinguió** por su valentía. He distinguished himself with his bravery.

Se **distinguía** desde lejos. You could see it from a distance.

Remember that subject pronouns are not used very often in Spanish.

distinguir

	FUTURE	CONDITIONAL
(yo)	distinguiré	distinguiría
(tú)	distinguirás	distinguirías
(él/ella/usted)	distinguirá	distinguiría
(nosotros/as)	distinguiremos	distinguiríamos
(vosotros/as)	distinguiréis	distinguiríais
(ellos/ellas/ ustedes)	distinguirán	distinguirían

	PRESENT SUBJUNCTIVE	IMPERFECT SUBJUNCTIVE
(yo)	distinga	distinguiera or distinguiese
(tú)	distingas	distinguieras or distinguieses
(él/ella/usted)	distinga	distinguiera or distinguiese
(nosotros/as)	distingamos	distinguiéramos or distinguiésemos
(vosotros/as)	distingáis	distinguierais or distinguieseis
(ellos/ellas/ ustedes)	distingan	distinguieran or distinguiesen

IMPERATIVE

distingue / distinguid

Use the present subjunctive in all cases other than these tú and vosotros affirmative forms.

EXAMPLE PHRASES

No los **distinguiría**. I wouldn't be able to tell them apart.

Nos **distinguirá** con su presencia. She will honor us with her presence.

Remember that subject pronouns are not used very often in Spanish.

divertir (to entertain, to amuse)

	PRESENT	PRESENT PERFECT
(yo)	divierto	he divertido
(tú)	diviertes	has divertido
(él/ella/usted)	divierte	ha divertido
(nosotros/as)	divertimos	hemos divertido
(vosotros/as)	divertís	habéis divertido
(ellos/ellas/ustedes)	divierten	han divertido

	PRETERITE	IMPERFECT
(yo)	divertí	divertía
(tú)	divertiste	divertías
(él/ella/usted)	divirtió	divertía
(nosotros/as)	divertimos	divertíamos
(vosotros/as)	divertisteis	divertíais
(ellos/ellas/ustedes)	divirtieron	divertían

GERUND

divirtiendo

PAST PARTICIPLE

divertido

EXAMPLE PHRASES

Cantamos sólo para **divertirnos**. We sing just for fun.

Me **divierte** verlos tan serios. It's amusing to see them looking so serious.

¿Se **divirtieron** en la fiesta? Did you enjoy the party?

Nos **divirtió** con sus anécdotas. He entertained us with his stories.

Nos divertíamos mucho jugando en la playa. We had a great time playing on the beach.

Remember that subject pronouns are not used very often in Spanish.

divertir

	FUTURE	CONDITIONAL
(yo)	divertiré	divertiría
(tú)	divertirás	divertirías
(él/ella/usted)	divertirá	divertiría
(nosotros/as)	divertiremos	divertiríamos
(vosotros/as)	divertiréis	divertiríais
(ellos/ellas/ ustedes)	divertirán	divertirían

	PRESENT SUBJUNCTIVE	IMPERFECT SUBJUNCTIVE
(yo)	divierta	divirtiera *or* divirtiese
(tú)	diviertas	divirtieras *or* divirtieses
(él/ella/usted)	divierta	divirtiera *or* divirtiese
(nosotros/as)	divirtamos	divirtiéramos *or* divirtiésemos
(vosotros/as)	divirtáis	divirtierais *or* divirtieseis
(ellos/ellas/ ustedes)	diviertan	divirtieran *or* divirtiesen

IMPERATIVE

divierte / divertid

Use the present subjunctive in all cases other than these tú and vosotros affirmative forms.

EXAMPLE PHRASES

Si fueras, **te divertirías** mucho. If you went, you'd have a great time.

Hizo lo posible por que **se divirtieran**. He did everything he could to make it fun for them.

¡Que **te diviertas**! Have a good time!

Remember that subject pronouns are not used very often in Spanish.

dormir (to sleep)

	PRESENT		PRESENT PERFECT
(yo)	duermo		he dormido
(tú)	duermes		has dormido
(él/ella/usted)	duerme		ha dormido
(nosotros/as)	dormimos		hemos dormido
(vosotros/as)	dormís		habéis dormido
(ellos/ellas/ ustedes)	duermen		han dormido

	PRETERITE		IMPERFECT
(yo)	dormí		dormía
(tú)	dormiste		dormías
(él/ella/usted)	durmió		dormía
(nosotros/as)	dormimos		dormíamos
(vosotros/as)	dormisteis		dormíais
(ellos/ellas/ ustedes)	durmieron		dormían

GERUND

durmiendo

PAST PARTICIPLE

dormido

EXAMPLE PHRASES

No **duermo** muy bien. I don't sleep very well.

Está **durmiendo**. She's asleep.

Dormí de un tirón. I slept like a log.

Se me **durmió** la pierna. My leg went to sleep.

Se **dormía** en clase. She would fall asleep in class.

Remember that subject pronouns are not used very often in Spanish.

dormir

	FUTURE	CONDITIONAL
(yo)	dormiré	dormiría
(tú)	dormirás	dormirías
(él/ella/usted)	dormirá	dormiría
(nosotros/as)	dormiremos	dormiríamos
(vosotros/as)	dormiréis	dormiríais
(ellos/ellas/ ustedes)	dormirán	dormirían

	PRESENT SUBJUNCTIVE	IMPERFECT SUBJUNCTIVE
(yo)	duerma	durmiera *or* durmiese
(tú)	duermas	durmieras *or* durmieses
(él/ella/usted)	duerma	durmiera *or* durmiese
(nosotros/as)	durmamos	durmiéramos *or* durmiésemos
(vosotros/as)	durmáis	durmierais *or* durmieseis
(ellos/ellas/ ustedes)	duerman	durmieran *or* durmiesen

IMPERATIVE

duerme / dormid

Use the present subjunctive in all cases other than these tú and vosotros affirmative forms.

EXAMPLE PHRASES

Si no tomo café, **me dormiré**. I'll fall asleep if I don't have some coffee.

Yo no **dormiría** en esa casa. I wouldn't sleep in that house.

Quiero que **duermas** la siesta. I want you to take a nap.

Si **durmieras** más horas, no estarías tan cansada. You wouldn't be so tired
   if you got more sleep.

Remember that subject pronouns are not used very often in Spanish.

elegir (to choose, to elect)

	PRESENT		PRESENT PERFECT
(yo)	elijo		he elegido
(tú)	eliges		has elegido
(él/ella/usted)	elige		ha elegido
(nosotros/as)	elegimos		hemos elegido
(vosotros/as)	elegís		habéis elegido
(ellos/ellas/ ustedes)	eligen		han elegido

	PRETERITE	IMPERFECT
(yo)	elegí	elegía
(tú)	elegiste	elegías
(él/ella/usted)	eligió	elegía
(nosotros/as)	elegimos	elegíamos
(vosotros/as)	elegisteis	elegíais
(ellos/ellas/ ustedes)	eligieron	elegían

GERUND

eligiendo

PAST PARTICIPLE

elegido

EXAMPLE PHRASES

Te dan a **elegir** entre dos modelos. You have a choice of two models.

Nosotros no **elegimos** a nuestros padres, ni ellos nos **eligen** a nosotros.
We don't choose our parents and they don't choose us either.

Creo que **eligió** bien. I think he made a good choice.

Salió **elegido** presidente. He was elected president.

Remember that subject pronouns are not used very often in Spanish.

elegir

	FUTURE	CONDITIONAL
(yo)	elegiré	elegiría
(tú)	elegirás	elegirías
(él/ella/usted)	elegirá	elegiría
(nosotros/as)	elegiremos	elegiríamos
(vosotros/as)	elegiréis	elegiríais
(ellos/ellas/ ustedes)	elegirán	elegirían

	PRESENT SUBJUNCTIVE	IMPERFECT SUBJUNCTIVE
(yo)	elija	eligiera or eligiese
(tú)	elijas	eligieras or eligieses
(él/ella/usted)	elija	eligiera or eligiese
(nosotros/as)	elijamos	eligiéramos or eligiésemos
(vosotros/as)	elijáis	eligierais or eligieseis
(ellos/ellas/ ustedes)	elijan	eligieran or eligiesen

IMPERATIVE

elige / elegid

Use the present subjunctive in all cases other than these tú and vosotros affirmative forms.

EXAMPLE PHRASES

Yo **elegiría** el más caro. I'd choose the most expensive one.

Elija una carta. Pick a card.

Remember that subject pronouns are not used very often in Spanish.

empezar (to begin, to start)

	PRESENT	PRESENT PERFECT
(yo)	empiezo	he empezado
(tú)	empiezas	has empezado
(él/ella/usted)	empieza	ha empezado
(nosotros/as)	empezamos	hemos empezado
(vosotros/as)	empezáis	habéis empezado
(ellos/ellas/ ustedes)	empiezan	han empezado

	PRETERITE	IMPERFECT
(yo)	empecé	empezaba
(tú)	empezaste	empezabas
(él/ella/usted)	empezó	empezaba
(nosotros/as)	empezamos	empezábamos
(vosotros/as)	empezasteis	empezabais
(ellos/ellas/ ustedes)	empezaron	empezaban

GERUND
empezando

PAST PARTICIPLE
empezado

EXAMPLE PHRASES

Está a punto de **empezar**. It's about to start.

¿Cuándo **empiezas** a trabajar en el sitio nuevo? When do you start work at the new place?

Empezó a nevar. It began to snow.

Las vacaciones **empezaron** el quince. The vacation started on the fifteenth.

Empezaba con *p*. It began with *p*.

Remember that subject pronouns are not used very often in Spanish.

empezar

	FUTURE	CONDITIONAL
(yo)	empezaré	empezaría
(tú)	empezarás	empezarías
(él/ella/usted)	empezará	empezaría
(nosotros/as)	empezaremos	empezaríamos
(vosotros/as)	empezaréis	empezaríais
(ellos/ellas/ ustedes)	empezarán	empezarían

	PRESENT SUBJUNCTIVE	IMPERFECT SUBJUNCTIVE
(yo)	empiece	empezara *or* empezase
(tú)	empieces	empezaras *or* empezases
(él/ella/usted)	empiece	empezara *or* empezase
(nosotros/as)	empecemos	empezáramos *or* empezásemos
(vosotros/as)	empecéis	empezarais *or* empezaseis
(ellos/ellas/ ustedes)	empiecen	empezaran *or* empezasen

IMPERATIVE

empieza / empezad

Use the present subjunctive in all cases other than these tú and vosotros affirmative forms.

EXAMPLE PHRASES

La semana que viene **empezaremos** un curso nuevo. We'll start a new course next week.

Yo **empezaría** desde cero. I'd start from scratch.

Quiero que **empieces** ya. I want you to start now.

Si **empezáramos** ahora, acabaríamos a las diez. If we started now, we'd be finished by ten.

Empieza por aquí. Start here.

Remember that subject pronouns are not used very often in Spanish.

enfrentarse (a/con to face)

	PRESENT	PRESENT PERFECT
(yo)	me enfrento	me he enfrentado
(tú)	te enfrentas	te has enfrentado
(él/ella/usted)	se enfrenta	se ha enfrentado
(nosotros/as)	nos enfrentamos	nos hemos enfrentado
(vosotros/as)	os enfrentáis	os habéis enfrentado
(ellos/ellas/ ustedes)	se enfrentan	se han enfrentado

	PRETERITE	IMPERFECT
(yo)	me enfrenté	me enfrentaba
(tú)	te enfrentaste	te enfrentabas
(él/ella/usted)	se enfrentó	se enfrentaba
(nosotros/as)	nos enfrentamos	nos enfrentábamos
(vosotros/as)	os enfrentasteis	os enfrentabais
(ellos/ellas/ ustedes)	se enfrentaron	se enfrentaban

GERUND

enfrentándose, etc

PAST PARTICIPLE

enfrentado

EXAMPLE PHRASES

Tienes que **enfrentarte** al problema. You have to face up to the problem.

Hoy **se enfrentan** los dos semifinalistas. The two semifinalists meet today.

Padre e hijo **se han enfrentado** varias veces. Father and son have had several confrontations.

Se enfrentaban a un futuro incierto. They faced an uncertain future.

Remember that subject pronouns are not used very often in Spanish.

enfrentarse

	FUTURE	CONDITIONAL
(yo)	me enfrentaré	me enfrentaría
(tú)	te enfrentarás	te enfrentarías
(él/ella/usted)	se enfrentará	se enfrentaría
(nosotros/as)	nos enfrentaremos	nos enfrentaríamos
(vosotros/as)	os enfrentaréis	os enfrentaríais
(ellos/ellas/ ustedes)	se enfrentarán	se enfrentarían

	PRESENT SUBJUNCTIVE	IMPERFECT SUBJUNCTIVE
(yo)	me enfrente	me enfrentara *or* enfrentase
(tú)	te enfrentes	te enfrentaras *or* enfrentases
(él/ella/usted)	se enfrente	se enfrentara *or* enfrentase
(nosotros/as)	nos enfrentemos	nos enfrentáramos *or* enfrentásemos
(vosotros/as)	os enfrentéis	os enfrentarais *or* enfrentaseis
(ellos/ellas/ ustedes)	se enfrenten	se enfrentaran *or* enfrentasen

IMPERATIVE

enfréntate / enfrentaos

Use the present subjunctive in all cases other than these *tú* and *vosotros* affirmative forms.

EXAMPLE PHRASES

Los dos equipos **se enfrentarán** mañana. The two teams will play each other tomorrow.

No **te enfrentes** con él. Don't confront him.

Remember that subject pronouns are not used very often in Spanish.

entender (to understand)

	PRESENT		PRESENT PERFECT
(yo)	entiendo		he entendido
(tú)	entiendes		has entendido
(él/ella/usted)	entiende		ha entendido
(nosotros/as)	entendemos		hemos entendido
(vosotros/as)	entendéis		habéis entendido
(ellos/ellas/ ustedes)	entienden		han entendido

	PRETERITE		IMPERFECT
(yo)	entendí		entendía
(tú)	entendiste		entendías
(él/ella/usted)	entendió		entendía
(nosotros/as)	entendimos		entendíamos
(vosotros/as)	entendisteis		entendíais
(ellos/ellas/ ustedes)	entendieron		entendían

GERUND

entendiendo

PAST PARTICIPLE

entendido

EXAMPLE PHRASES

No lo vas a **entender**. You won't understand.

No lo **entiendo**. I don't understand.

Estás **entendiéndolo** todo al revés. You're getting me all wrong.

¿**Entendiste** lo que dijo? Did you understand what she said?

Mi padre **entendía** mucho de caballos. My father knew a lot about horses.

Remember that subject pronouns are not used very often in Spanish.

entender

	FUTURE	CONDITIONAL
(yo)	entenderé	entendería
(tú)	entenderás	entenderías
(él/ella/usted)	entenderá	entendería
(nosotros/as)	entenderemos	entenderíamos
(vosotros/as)	entenderéis	entenderíais
(ellos/ellas/ustedes)	entenderán	entenderían

	PRESENT SUBJUNCTIVE	IMPERFECT SUBJUNCTIVE
(yo)	entienda	entendiera or entendiese
(tú)	entiendas	entendieras or entendieses
(él/ella/usted)	entienda	entendiera or entendiese
(nosotros/as)	entendamos	entendiéramos or entendiésemos
(vosotros/as)	entendáis	entendierais or entendieseis
(ellos/ellas/ustedes)	entiendan	entendieran or entendiesen

IMPERATIVE

entiende / entended

Use the present subjunctive in all cases other than these *tú* and *vosotros* affirmative forms.

EXAMPLE PHRASES

Con el tiempo lo **entenderás**. You'll understand one day.

Yo no lo **entendería** así. I wouldn't interpret it like that.

Si de verdad me **entendieras**, no habrías dicho eso. If you really understood me, you wouldn't have said that.

No me **entiendas** mal. Don't misunderstand me.

Remember that subject pronouns are not used very often in Spanish.

enviar (to send)

	PRESENT	PRESENT PERFECT
(yo)	envío	he enviado
(tú)	envías	has enviado
(él/ella/usted)	envía	ha enviado
(nosotros/as)	enviamos	hemos enviado
(vosotros/as)	enviáis	habéis enviado
(ellos/ellas/ ustedes)	envían	han enviado

	PRETERITE	IMPERFECT
(yo)	envié	enviaba
(tú)	enviaste	enviabas
(él/ella/usted)	envió	enviaba
(nosotros/as)	enviamos	enviábamos
(vosotros/as)	enviasteis	enviabais
(ellos/ellas/ ustedes)	enviaron	enviaban

GERUND	PAST PARTICIPLE
enviando	enviado

EXAMPLE PHRASES

¿Cómo lo vas a **enviar**? How are you going to send it?

Les **envío** el trabajo por correo electrónico. I send them my work by email.

Ya **está enviando** las invitaciones. She has already started sending out the invitations.

La **han enviado** a Guatemala. They've sent her to Guatemala.

Le **envió** el regalo por correo. He mailed her the present.

Remember that subject pronouns are not used very often in Spanish.

enviar

	FUTURE	**CONDITIONAL**
(yo)	enviaré	enviaría
(tú)	enviarás	enviarías
(él/ella/usted)	enviará	enviaría
(nosotros/as)	enviaremos	enviaríamos
(vosotros/as)	enviaréis	enviaríais
(ellos/ellas/ ustedes)	enviarán	enviarían

	PRESENT SUBJUNCTIVE	**IMPERFECT SUBJUNCTIVE**
(yo)	envíe	enviara or enviase
(tú)	envíes	enviaras or enviases
(él/ella/usted)	envíe	enviara or enviase
(nosotros/as)	enviemos	enviáramos or enviásemos
(vosotros/as)	enviéis	enviarais or enviaseis
(ellos/ellas/ ustedes)	envíen	enviaran or enviasen

IMPERATIVE

envía / enviad

Use the present subjunctive in all cases other than these tú and vosotros affirmative forms.

EXAMPLE PHRASES

Nos **enviarán** más información. They'll send us more information.

Yo lo **enviaría** por mensajero. I'd send it by courier.

Necesitamos que lo **envíes** inmediatamente. We need you to send it immediately.

Si lo **enviaras** ahora, llegaría el lunes. If you sent it now it would get there on Monday.

No lo **envíes** sin repasarlo antes. Don't send it in without checking it first.

Envíe sus datos personales. Send in your details.

Remember that subject pronouns are not used very often in Spanish.

equivocarse (to make a mistake, to be wrong)

	PRESENT	**PRESENT PERFECT**
(yo)	me equivoco	me he equivocado
(tú)	te equivocas	te has equivocado
(él/ella/usted)	se equivoca	se ha equivocado
(nosotros/as)	nos equivocamos	nos hemos equivocado
(vosotros/as)	os equivocáis	os habéis equivocado
(ellos/ellas/ ustedes)	se equivocan	se han equivocado

	PRETERITE	**IMPERFECT**
(yo)	me equivoqué	me equivocaba
(tú)	te equivocaste	te equivocabas
(él/ella/usted)	se equivocó	se equivocaba
(nosotros/as)	nos equivocamos	nos equivocábamos
(vosotros/as)	os equivocasteis	os equivocabais
(ellos/ellas/ ustedes)	se equivocaron	se equivocaban

GERUND	**PAST PARTICIPLE**
equivocándose, etc	equivocado

EXAMPLE PHRASES

Si crees que voy a dejarte ir, **te equivocas**. If you think I'm going to let you go, you're wrong.

Se equivocaron de tren. They took the wrong train.

Siempre **se equivocaba** de calle. He always took the wrong street.

Remember that subject pronouns are not used very often in Spanish.

equivocarse

	FUTURE	**CONDITIONAL**
(yo)	me equivocaré	me equivocaría
(tú)	te equivocarás	te equivocarías
(él/ella/usted)	se equivocará	se equivocaría
(nosotros/as)	nos equivocaremos	nos equivocaríamos
(vosotros/as)	os equivocaréis	os equivocaríais
(ellos/ellas/ ustedes)	se equivocarán	se equivocarían

	PRESENT SUBJUNCTIVE	**IMPERFECT SUBJUNCTIVE**
(yo)	me equivoque	me equivocara or equivocase
(tú)	te equivoques	te equivocaras or equivocases
(él/ella/usted)	se equivoque	se equivocara or equivocase
(nosotros/as)	nos equivoquemos	nos equivocáramos or equivocásemos
(vosotros/as)	os equivoquéis	os equivocarais or equivocaseis
(ellos/ellas/ ustedes)	se equivoquen	se equivocaran or equivocasen

IMPERATIVE

equivócate / equivocaos

Use the present subjunctive in all cases other than these tú and vosotros affirmative forms.

EXAMPLE PHRASES

Sobre todo, no **te equivoques** de hora. Above all, don't get the time wrong.

Si **te equivocaras**, quedarías eliminado del juego. If you made a mistake, you'd be out of the game.

Remember that subject pronouns are not used very often in Spanish.

erguir (to erect)

	PRESENT	PRESENT PERFECT
(yo)	yergo	he erguido
(tú)	yergues	has erguido
(él/ella/usted)	yergue	ha erguido
(nosotros/as)	erguimos	hemos erguido
(vosotros/as)	erguís	habéis erguido
(ellos/ellas/ ustedes)	yerguen	han erguido

	PRETERITE	IMPERFECT
(yo)	erguí	erguía
(tú)	erguiste	erguías
(él/ella/usted)	irguió	erguía
(nosotros/as)	erguimos	erguíamos
(vosotros/as)	erguisteis	erguías
(ellos/ellas/ ustedes)	irguieron	erguían

GERUND

irguiendo

PAST PARTICIPLE

erguido

EXAMPLE PHRASES

El perro **irguió** las orejas. The dog pricked up its ears.

La montaña **se erguía** majestuosa sobre el valle. The mountain rose majestically above the valley.

Tú mantén siempre la cabeza bien **erguida**. You must always hold your head high.

Remember that subject pronouns are not used very often in Spanish.

erguir

	FUTURE	CONDITIONAL
(yo)	erguiré	erguiría
(tú)	erguirás	erguirías
(él/ella/usted)	erguirá	erguiría
(nosotros/as)	erguiremos	erguiríamos
(vosotros/as)	erguiréis	erguiríais
(ellos/ellas/ustedes)	erguirán	erguirían

	PRESENT SUBJUNCTIVE	IMPERFECT SUBJUNCTIVE
(yo)	yerga	irguiera or irguiese
(tú)	yergas	irguieras or irguieses
(él/ella/usted)	yerga	irguiera or irguiese
(nosotros/as)	irgamos	irguiéramos or irguiésemos
(vosotros/as)	irgáis	irguierais or irguieseis
(ellos/ellas/ustedes)	yergan	irguieran or irguiesen

IMPERATIVE

yergue / erguid

Use the present subjunctive in all cases other than these tú and vosotros affirmative forms.

Remember that subject pronouns are not used very often in Spanish.

errar (to err)

	PRESENT	PRESENT PERFECT
(yo)	yerro	he errado
(tú)	yerras	has errado
(él/ella/usted)	yerra	ha errado
(nosotros/as)	erramos	hemos errado
(vosotros/as)	erráis	habéis errado
(ellos/ellas/ustedes)	yerran	han errado

	PRETERITE	IMPERFECT
(yo)	erré	erraba
(tú)	erraste	errabas
(él/ella/usted)	erró	erraba
(nosotros/as)	erramos	errábamos
(vosotros/as)	errasteis	errabais
(ellos/ellas/ustedes)	erraron	erraban

GERUND

errando

PAST PARTICIPLE

errado

EXAMPLE PHRASES

Errar es humano. To err is human.

Había errado en su decisión. She had made the wrong decision.

Erró el tiro. He missed.

Remember that subject pronouns are not used very often in Spanish.

errar

	FUTURE	CONDITIONAL
(yo)	erraré	erraría
(tú)	errarás	errarías
(él/ella/usted)	errará	erraría
(nosotros/as)	erraremos	erraríamos
(vosotros/as)	erraréis	erraríais
(ellos/ellas/ustedes)	errarán	errarían

	PRESENT SUBJUNCTIVE	IMPERFECT SUBJUNCTIVE
(yo)	yerre	errara or errase
(tú)	yerres	erraras or errases
(él/ella/usted)	yerre	errara or errase
(nosotros/as)	erremos	erráramos or errásemos
(vosotros/as)	erréis	errarais or erraseis
(ellos/ellas/ustedes)	yerren	erraran or errasen

IMPERATIVE

yerra / errad

Use the present subjunctive in all cases other than these tú *and* vosotros *affirmative forms.*

Remember that subject pronouns are not used very often in Spanish.

escoger (to choose, to pick)

	PRESENT		PRESENT PERFECT
(yo)	escojo		he escogido
(tú)	escoges		has escogido
(él/ella/usted)	escoge		ha escogido
(nosotros/as)	escogemos		hemos escogido
(vosotros/as)	escogéis		habéis escogido
(ellos/ellas/ ustedes)	escogen		han escogido

	PRETERITE		IMPERFECT
(yo)	escogí		escogía
(tú)	escogiste		escogías
(él/ella/usted)	escogió		escogía
(nosotros/as)	escogimos		escogíamos
(vosotros/as)	escogisteis		escogíais
(ellos/ellas/ ustedes)	escogieron		escogían

GERUND

escogiendo

PAST PARTICIPLE

escogido

EXAMPLE PHRASES

Escogió el más caro. He chose the most expensive one.

Escogía siempre al mismo alumno. She always picked the same student.

Remember that subject pronouns are not used very often in Spanish.

escoger

	FUTURE	CONDITIONAL
(yo)	escogeré	escogería
(tú)	escogerás	escogerías
(él/ella/usted)	escogerá	escogería
(nosotros/as)	escogeremos	escogeríamos
(vosotros/as)	escogeréis	escogeríais
(ellos/ellas/ ustedes)	escogerán	escogerían

	PRESENT SUBJUNCTIVE	IMPERFECT SUBJUNCTIVE
(yo)	escoja	escogiera or escogiese
(tú)	escojas	escogieras or escogieses
(él/ella/usted)	escoja	escogiera or escogiese
(nosotros/as)	escojamos	escogiéramos or escogiésemos
(vosotros/as)	escojáis	escogierais or escogieseis
(ellos/ellas/ ustedes)	escojan	escogieran or escogiesen

IMPERATIVE

escoge / escoged

Use the present subjunctive in all cases other than these tú and vosotros affirmative forms.

EXAMPLE PHRASES

Yo **escogería** el azul. I'd choose the blue one.

Escoja el que más le guste. Pick the one you like best.

Remember that subject pronouns are not used very often in Spanish.

escribir (to write)

	PRESENT		PRESENT PERFECT
(yo)	escribo		he escrito
(tú)	escribes		has escrito
(él/ella/usted)	escribe		ha escrito
(nosotros/as)	escribimos		hemos escrito
(vosotros/as)	escribís		habéis escrito
(ellos/ellas/ ustedes)	escriben		han escrito

	PRETERITE		IMPERFECT
(yo)	escribí		escribía
(tú)	escribiste		escribías
(él/ella/usted)	escribió		escribía
(nosotros/as)	escribimos		escribíamos
(vosotros/as)	escribisteis		escribíais
(ellos/ellas/ ustedes)	escribieron		escribían

GERUND

escribiendo

PAST PARTICIPLE

escrito

EXAMPLE PHRASES

¿Cómo se **escribe** su nombre? How do you spell your name?

¿**Estás escribiendo** la carta? Are you writing the letter?

Eso lo **escribí** yo. I wrote that.

Nos escribimos durante un tiempo. We wrote to each other for a while.

Escribía canciones. She wrote songs.

Remember that subject pronouns are not used very often in Spanish.

escribir

	FUTURE	CONDITIONAL
(yo)	escribiré	escribiría
(tú)	escribirás	escribirías
(él/ella/usted)	escribirá	escribiría
(nosotros/as)	escribiremos	escribiríamos
(vosotros/as)	escribiréis	escribiríais
(ellos/ellas/ ustedes)	escribirán	escribirían

	PRESENT SUBJUNCTIVE	IMPERFECT SUBJUNCTIVE
(yo)	escriba	escribiera or escribiese
(tú)	escribas	escribieras or escribieses
(él/ella/usted)	escriba	escribiera or escribiese
(nosotros/as)	escribamos	escribiéramos or escribiésemos
(vosotros/as)	escribáis	escribierais or escribieseis
(ellos/ellas/ ustedes)	escriban	escribieran or escribiesen

IMPERATIVE

escribe / escribid

Use the present subjunctive in all cases other than these tú and vosotros affirmative forms.

EXAMPLE PHRASES

¿Me **escribirás**? Will you write to me?

Yo lo **escribiría** con mayúscula. I'd write it with a capital letter.

No **escribas** en la mesa. Don't write on the table.

Si de verdad **escribiera** bien, ya le habrían publicado algún libro. If he really wrote well, he'd have had a book published by now.

Escríbelo en el pizarrón. Write it on the blackboard.

Remember that subject pronouns are not used very often in Spanish.

esforzarse (to make an effort)

	PRESENT		PRESENT PERFECT
(yo)	me esfuerzo		me he esforzado
(tú)	te esfuerzas		te has esforzado
(él/ella/usted)	se esfuerza		se ha esforzado
(nosotros/as)	nos esforzamos		nos hemos esforzado
(vosotros/as)	os esforzáis		os habéis esforzado
(ellos/ellas/ ustedes)	se esfuerzan		se han esforzado

	PRETERITE		IMPERFECT
(yo)	me esforcé		me esforzaba
(tú)	te esforzaste		te esforzabas
(él/ella/usted)	se esforzó		se esforzaba
(nosotros/as)	nos esforzamos		nos esforzábamos
(vosotros/as)	os esforzasteis		os esforzabais
(ellos/ellas/ ustedes)	se esforzaron		se esforzaban

GERUND

esforzándose, etc

PAST PARTICIPLE

esforzado

EXAMPLE PHRASES

Tienes que **esforzarte** si quieres ganar. You have to make an effort if you want to win.

No **te esfuerzas** lo suficiente. You don't make enough effort.

Se esforzó todo lo que pudo por aprobar el examen. He did everything he could to get through the test.

Me esforzaba por entenderla. I tried hard to understand her.

Remember that subject pronouns are not used very often in Spanish.

esforzarse

	FUTURE	**CONDITIONAL**
(yo)	me esforzaré	me esforzaría
(tú)	te esforzarás	te esforzarías
(él/ella/usted)	se esforzará	se esforzaría
(nosotros/as)	nos esforzaremos	nos esforzaríamos
(vosotros/as)	os esforzaréis	os esforzaríais
(ellos/ellas/ ustedes)	se esforzarán	se esforzarían

	PRESENT SUBJUNCTIVE	**IMPERFECT SUBJUNCTIVE**
(yo)	me esfuerce	me esforzara *or* esforzase
(tú)	te esfuerces	te esforzaras *or* esforzases
(él/ella/usted)	se esfuerce	se esforzara *or* esforzase
(nosotros/as)	nos esforcemos	nos esforzáramos *or* esforzásemos
(vosotros/as)	os esforcéis	os esforzarais *or* esforzaseis
(ellos/ellas/ ustedes)	se esfuercen	se esforzaran *or* esforzasen

IMPERATIVE

esfuérzate / esforzaos

Use the present subjunctive in all cases other than these tú and vosotros affirmative forms.

EXAMPLE PHRASES

No **te esfuerces**, no me vas a convencer. Don't bother trying, you're not going
to convince me.

Si **te esforzaras** un poco más, lo conseguirías. You'd manage it if you made
a little more effort.

Remember that subject pronouns are not used very often in Spanish.

establecer (to establish)

	PRESENT	PRESENT PERFECT
(yo)	**establezco**	**he establecido**
(tú)	**estableces**	has establecido
(él/ella/usted)	**establece**	ha establecido
(nosotros/as)	**establecemos**	**hemos establecido**
(vosotros/as)	**establecéis**	**habéis establecido**
(ellos/ellas/ ustedes)	**establecen**	**han establecido**

	PRETERITE	IMPERFECT
(yo)	**establecí**	**establecía**
(tú)	**estableciste**	**establecías**
(él/ella/usted)	**estableció**	**establecía**
(nosotros/as)	**establecimos**	**establecíamos**
(vosotros/as)	**establecisteis**	**establecíais**
(ellos/ellas/ ustedes)	**estableció**	**establecían**

GERUND
estableciendo

PAST PARTICIPLE
establecido

EXAMPLE PHRASES

Lograron **establecer** contacto con el barco. They managed to make contact
  with the boat.

La ley **establece** que... The law states that...

Se ha establecido una buena relación entre los dos países. A good relationship
  has been established between the two countries.

En 1945, la familia **se estableció** en Lima. In 1945, the family settled in Lima.

Remember that subject pronouns are not used very often in Spanish.

establecer

	FUTURE	CONDITIONAL
(yo)	estableceré	establecería
(tú)	establecerás	establecerías
(él/ella/usted)	establecerá	establecería
(nosotros/as)	estableceremos	estableceríamos
(vosotros/as)	estableceréis	estableceríais
(ellos/ellas/ ustedes)	establecerán	establecerían

	PRESENT SUBJUNCTIVE	IMPERFECT SUBJUNCTIVE
(yo)	establezca	estableciera *or* estableciese
(tú)	establezcas	establecieras *or* establecieses
(él/ella/usted)	establezca	estableciera *or* estableciese
(nosotros/as)	establezcamos	estableciéramos *or* estableciésemos
(vosotros/as)	establezcáis	establecierais *or* establecieseis
(ellos/ellas/ ustedes)	establezcan	establecieran *or* estableciesen

IMPERATIVE

establece / estableced

Use the present subjunctive in all cases other than these tú and vosotros affirmative forms.

EXAMPLE PHRASES

El año que viene **se establecerá** por su cuenta. Next year she'll set up on her own.

Remember that subject pronouns are not used very often in Spanish.

estar (to be)

	PRESENT	PRESENT PERFECT
(yo)	estoy	he estado
(tú)	estás	has estado
(él/ella/usted)	está	ha estado
(nosotros/as)	estamos	hemos estado
(vosotros/as)	estáis	habéis estado
(ellos/ellas/ ustedes)	están	han estado

	PRETERITE	IMPERFECT
(yo)	estuve	estaba
(tú)	estuviste	estabas
(él/ella/usted)	estuvo	estaba
(nosotros/as)	estuvimos	estábamos
(vosotros/as)	estuvisteis	estabais
(ellos/ellas/ ustedes)	estuvieron	estaban

GERUND

estando

PAST PARTICIPLE

estado

EXAMPLE PHRASES

Estoy cansado. I'm tired.

¿Cómo **estás**? How are you?

¿No **había estado** nunca en París? He'd never been to Paris?

Estuvimos en casa de mis padres. We were at my parents'.

¿Dónde **estabas**? Where were you?

Remember that subject pronouns are not used very often in Spanish.

estar

	FUTURE	CONDITIONAL
(yo)	estaré	estaría
(tú)	estarás	estarías
(él/ella/usted)	estará	estaría
(nosotros/as)	estaremos	estaríamos
(vosotros/as)	estaréis	estaríais
(ellos/ellas/ ustedes)	estarán	estarían

	PRESENT SUBJUNCTIVE	IMPERFECT SUBJUNCTIVE
(yo)	esté	estuviera or estuviese
(tú)	estés	estuvieras or estuvieses
(él/ella/usted)	esté	estuviera or estuviese
(nosotros/as)	estemos	estuviéramos or estuviésemos
(vosotros/as)	estéis	estuvierais or estuvieseis
(ellos/ellas/ ustedes)	estén	estuvieran or estuviesen

IMPERATIVE

está / estad

Use the present subjunctive in all cases other than these tú and vosotros affirmative forms.

EXAMPLE PHRASES

¿A qué hora **estarás** en casa? What time will you be home?

Dijo que **estaría** aquí a las ocho. She said she'd be here at eight o'clock.

Avísame cuando **estés** lista. Let me know when you're ready.

¡**Estáte** quieto! Keep still!

Si **estuviera** enfermo, habría llamado. If he were sick, he would have called.

Remember that subject pronouns are not used very often in Spanish.

evacuar (to evacuate)

	PRESENT	**PRESENT PERFECT**
(yo)	evacuo	he evacuado
(tú)	evacuas	has evacuado
(él/ella/usted)	evacua	ha evacuado
(nosotros/as)	evacuamos	hemos evacuado
(vosotros/as)	evacuáis	habéis evacuado
(ellos/ellas/ ustedes)	evacuan	han evacuado

	PRETERITE	**IMPERFECT**
(yo)	evacué	evacuaba
(tú)	evacuaste	evacuabas
(él/ella/usted)	evacuó	evacuaba
(nosotros/as)	evacuamos	evacuábamos
(vosotros/as)	evacuasteis	evacuabais
(ellos/ellas/ ustedes)	evacuaron	evacuaban

GERUND
evacuando

PAST PARTICIPLE
evacuado

EXAMPLE PHRASES

Van a **evacuar** a los heridos. They're going to evacuate the injured.

Han evacuado la zona. The area has been evacuated.

Remember that subject pronouns are not used very often in Spanish.

evacuar

	FUTURE	CONDITIONAL
(yo)	evacuaré	evacuaría
(tú)	evacuarás	evacuarías
(él/ella/usted)	evacuará	evacuaría
(nosotros/as)	evacuaremos	evacuaríamos
(vosotros/as)	evacuaréis	evacuaríais
(ellos/ellas/ ustedes)	evacuarán	evacuarían

	PRESENT SUBJUNCTIVE	IMPERFECT SUBJUNCTIVE
(yo)	evacue	evacuara *or* evacuase
(tú)	evacues	evacuaras *or* evacuases
(él/ella/usted)	evacue	evacuara *or* evacuase
(nosotros/as)	evacuemos	evacuáramos *or* evacuásemos
(vosotros/as)	evacuéis	evacuarais *or* evacuaseis
(ellos/ellas/ ustedes)	evacuen	evacuaran *or* evacuasen

IMPERATIVE

evacua / evacuad

Use the present subjunctive in all cases other than these tú and vosotros affirmative forms.

EXAMPLE PHRASES

Seguirá existiendo peligro mientras no **evacuen** el edificio. The danger won't be over while there are still people inside the building.

Remember that subject pronouns are not used very often in Spanish.

forzar (to force)

	PRESENT	PRESENT PERFECT
(yo)	fuerzo	he forzado
(tú)	fuerzas	has forzado
(él/ella/usted)	fuerza	ha forzado
(nosotros/as)	forzamos	hemos forzado
(vosotros/as)	forzáis	habéis forzado
(ellos/ellas/ ustedes)	fuerzan	han forzado

	PRETERITE	IMPERFECT
(yo)	forcé	forzaba
(tú)	forzaste	forzabas
(él/ella/usted)	forzó	forzaba
(nosotros/as)	forzamos	forzábamos
(vosotros/as)	forzasteis	forzabais
(ellos/ellas/ ustedes)	forzaron	forzaban

GERUND	PAST PARTICIPLE
forzando	forzado

EXAMPLE PHRASES

Nos **forzaron** a hacerlo. They forced us to do it.

Habían forzado la puerta de entrada. They had forced the front door.

Los **forzaban** a trabajar largas horas. They would force them to work long hours.

Remember that subject pronouns are not used very often in Spanish.

forzar

	FUTURE	CONDITIONAL
(yo)	forzaré	forzaría
(tú)	forzarás	forzarías
(él/ella/usted)	forzará	forzaría
(nosotros/as)	forzaremos	forzaríamos
(vosotros/as)	forzaréis	forzaríais
(ellos/ellas/ ustedes)	forzarán	forzarían

	PRESENT SUBJUNCTIVE	IMPERFECT SUBJUNCTIVE
(yo)	fuerce	forzara or forzase
(tú)	fuerces	forzaras or forzases
(él/ella/usted)	fuerce	forzara or forzase
(nosotros/as)	forcemos	forzáramos or forzásemos
(vosotros/as)	forcéis	forzarais or forzaseis
(ellos/ellas/ ustedes)	fuercen	forzaran or forzasen

IMPERATIVE

fuerza/forzad

Use the present subjunctive in all cases other than these tú and vosotros affirmative forms.

EXAMPLE PHRASES

No te **forzaremos** a ir. We won't force you to go.

No **fuerces** la cerradura. Don't force the lock.

Lo hizo sin que nadie lo **forzara**. He did it without anybody forcing him to.

Remember that subject pronouns are not used very often in Spanish.

freír (to fry)

	PRESENT		PRESENT PERFECT
(yo)	frío		he frito
(tú)	fríes		has frito
(él/ella/usted)	fríe		ha frito
(nosotros/as)	freímos		hemos frito
(vosotros/as)	freís		habéis frito
(ellos/ellas/ustedes)	fríen		han frito

	PRETERITE		IMPERFECT
(yo)	freí		freía
(tú)	freíste		freías
(él/ella/usted)	frió		freía
(nosotros/as)	freímos		freíamos
(vosotros/as)	freísteis		freíais
(ellos/ellas/ustedes)	frieron		freían

GERUND
friendo

PAST PARTICIPLE
frito

EXAMPLE PHRASES

No sabe ni **freír** un huevo. He can't even fry an egg.

Había frito el pescado. He had fried the fish.

Se está friendo demasiado por ese lado. It's getting overdone on that side.

Lo **frió** en mantequilla. She fried it in butter.

Nos **freíamos** de calor. We were roasting in the heat.

Remember that subject pronouns are not used very often in Spanish.

freír

	FUTURE	CONDITIONAL
(yo)	freiré	freiría
(tú)	freirás	freirías
(él/ella/usted)	freirá	freiría
(nosotros/as)	freiremos	freiríamos
(vosotros/as)	freiréis	freiríais
(ellos/ellas/ ustedes)	freirán	freirían

	PRESENT SUBJUNCTIVE	IMPERFECT SUBJUNCTIVE
(yo)	fría	friera or friese
(tú)	frías	frieras or frieses
(él/ella/usted)	fría	friera or friese
(nosotros/as)	friamos	friéramos or friésemos
(vosotros/as)	friáis	frierais or frieseis
(ellos/ellas/ ustedes)	frían	frieran or friesen

IMPERATIVE

fríe / freíd

Use the present subjunctive in all cases other than these tú and vosotros affirmative forms.

EXAMPLE PHRASES

Fríelo en aceite de oliva. Fry it in olive oil.

Me dijo que **friera** la cebolla. She told me to fry the onion.

Remember that subject pronouns are not used very often in Spanish.

gruñir (to grumble, to growl)

	PRESENT	PRESENT PERFECT
(yo)	gruño	he gruñido
(tú)	gruñes	has gruñido
(él/ella/usted)	gruñe	ha gruñido
(nosotros/as)	gruñimos	hemos gruñido
(vosotros/as)	gruñís	habéis gruñido
(ellos/ellas/ ustedes)	gruñen	han gruñido

	PRETERITE	IMPERFECT
(yo)	gruñí	gruñía
(tú)	gruñiste	gruñías
(él/ella/usted)	gruñó	gruñía
(nosotros/as)	gruñimos	gruñíamos
(vosotros/as)	gruñisteis	gruñíais
(ellos/ellas/ ustedes)	gruñeron	gruñían

GERUND	PAST PARTICIPLE
gruñendo	gruñido

EXAMPLE PHRASES

¿A quién le **gruñe** el perro? Who's the dog growling at?

Siempre **está gruñendo**. He's always grumbling.

El oso nos **gruñía** sin parar. The bear kept growling at us.

Remember that subject pronouns are not used very often in Spanish.

gruñir

	FUTURE	CONDITIONAL
(yo)	gruñiré	gruñiría
(tú)	gruñirás	gruñirías
(él/ella/usted)	gruñirá	gruñiría
(nosotros/as)	gruñiremos	gruñiríamos
(vosotros/as)	gruñiréis	gruñiríais
(ellos/ellas/ustedes)	gruñirán	gruñirían

	PRESENT SUBJUNCTIVE	IMPERFECT SUBJUNCTIVE
(yo)	gruña	gruñera or gruñese
(tú)	gruñas	gruñeras or gruñeses
(él/ella/usted)	gruña	gruñera or gruñese
(nosotros/as)	gruñamos	gruñéramos or gruñésemos
(vosotros/as)	gruñáis	gruñerais or gruñeseis
(ellos/ellas/ustedes)	gruñan	gruñeran or gruñesen

IMPERATIVE

gruñe / gruñid

Use the present subjunctive in all cases other than these tú and vosotros affirmative forms.

EXAMPLE PHRASES

¡No **gruñas** tanto! Don't grumble so much.

Remember that subject pronouns are not used very often in Spanish.

guiar (to guide)

	PRESENT	PRESENT PERFECT
(yo)	guío	he guiado
(tú)	guías	has guiado
(él/ella/usted)	guía	ha guiado
(nosotros/as)	guiamos	hemos guiado
(vosotros/as)	guiais	habéis guiado
(ellos/ellas/ ustedes)	guían	han guiado

	PRETERITE	IMPERFECT
(yo)	guie	guiaba
(tú)	guiaste	guiabas
(él/ella/usted)	guio	guiaba
(nosotros/as)	guiamos	guiábamos
(vosotros/as)	guiasteis	guiabais
(ellos/ellas/ ustedes)	guiaron	guiaban

GERUND
guiando

PAST PARTICIPLE
guiado

EXAMPLE PHRASES

Los perros **se guían** por su olfato. Dogs follow their sense of smell.

Me guié por el instinto. I followed my instinct.

Nos guiamos por un mapa que teníamos. We found our way using a map
we had.

Siempre me protegía y me **guiaba**. He always protected me and guided me.

Remember that subject pronouns are not used very often in Spanish.

guiar

	FUTURE	CONDITIONAL
(yo)	guiaré	guiaría
(tú)	guiarás	guiarías
(él/ella/usted)	guiará	guiaría
(nosotros/as)	guiaremos	guiaríamos
(vosotros/as)	guiaréis	guiaríais
(ellos/ellas/ ustedes)	guiarán	guiarían

	PRESENT SUBJUNCTIVE	IMPERFECT SUBJUNCTIVE
(yo)	guíe	guiara or guiase
(tú)	guíes	guiaras or guiases
(él/ella/usted)	guíe	guiara or guiase
(nosotros/as)	guiemos	guiáramos or guiásemos
(vosotros/as)	guieis	guiarais or guiaseis
(ellos/ellas/ ustedes)	guíen	guiaran or guiasen

IMPERATIVE

guía / guiad

Use the present subjunctive in all cases other than these tú and vosotros affirmative forms.

EXAMPLE PHRASES

Los **guiaré** hasta allí. I'll take you there.

Guíate por la razón. Use reason as your guide.

Remember that subject pronouns are not used very often in Spanish.

haber (to have – *auxiliary*)

	PRESENT	PRESENT PERFECT
(yo)	he	*not used except impersonally*
(tú)	has	*See* hay
(él/ella/usted)	ha	
(nosotros/as)	hemos	
(vosotros/as)	habéis	
(ellos/ellas/ustedes)	han	

	PRETERITE	IMPERFECT
(yo)	hube	había
(tú)	hubiste	habías
(él/ella/usted)	hubo	había
(nosotros/as)	hubimos	habíamos
(vosotros/as)	hubisteis	habíais
(ellos/ellas/ustedes)	hubieron	habían

GERUND	PAST PARTICIPLE
habiendo	habido

EXAMPLE PHRASES

De **haber**lo sabido, **habría** ido. If I'd known, I would have gone.

¿**Has** visto eso? Did you see that?

Eso nunca **había** pasado antes. That had never happened before.

Remember that subject pronouns are not used very often in Spanish.

haber

	FUTURE	CONDITIONAL
(yo)	habré	habría
(tú)	habrás	habrías
(él/ella/usted)	habrá	habría
(nosotros/as)	habremos	habríamos
(vosotros/as)	habréis	habríais
(ellos/ellas/ustedes)	habrán	habrían

	PRESENT SUBJUNCTIVE	IMPERFECT SUBJUNCTIVE
(yo)	haya	hubiera or hubiese
(tú)	hayas	hubieras or hubieses
(él/ella/usted)	haya	hubiera or hubiese
(nosotros/as)	hayamos	hubiéramos or hubiésemos
(vosotros/as)	hayáis	hubierais or hubieseis
(ellos/ellas/ustedes)	hayan	hubieran or hubiesen

IMPERATIVE

not used

EXAMPLE PHRASES

Como se **hayan** olvidado, los mato. I'll kill them if they've forgotten.

Si me lo **hubieras** dicho, te lo **habría** traído. I'd have brought it, if you'd told me.

Para esa hora ya **habremos** terminado. We'll have finished by that time.

Lo **habrías** logrado si **hubieras** intentado. You'd have succeeded if you'd tried.

Remember that subject pronouns are not used very often in Spanish.

hablar (to speak, to talk)

	PRESENT	PRESENT PERFECT
(yo)	hablo	he hablado
(tú)	hablas	has hablado
(él/ella/usted)	habla	ha hablado
(nosotros/as)	hablamos	hemos hablado
(vosotros/as)	habláis	habéis hablado
(ellos/ellas/ ustedes)	hablan	han hablado

	PRETERITE	IMPERFECT
(yo)	hablé	hablaba
(tú)	hablaste	hablabas
(él/ella/usted)	habló	hablaba
(nosotros/as)	hablamos	hablábamos
(vosotros/as)	hablasteis	hablabais
(ellos/ellas/ ustedes)	hablaron	hablaban

GERUND	PAST PARTICIPLE
hablando	hablado

EXAMPLE PHRASES

María no **habla** inglés. María doesn't speak English.

No **nos hablamos** desde hace tiempo. We haven't spoken to each other for a long time.

Está **hablando** por teléfono. He's on the phone.

Hoy **hablé** con mi hermana. I spoke to my sister today.

Hablaba rapidísimo. He spoke really fast.

Remember that subject pronouns are not used very often in Spanish.

hablar

	FUTURE	CONDITIONAL
(yo)	hablaré	hablaría
(tú)	hablarás	hablarías
(él/ella/usted)	hablará	hablaría
(nosotros/as)	hablaremos	hablaríamos
(vosotros/as)	hablaréis	hablaríais
(ellos/ellas/ ustedes)	hablarán .	hablarían

	PRESENT SUBJUNCTIVE	IMPERFECT SUBJUNCTIVE
(yo)	hable	hablara *or* hablase
(tú)	hables	hablaras *or* hablases
(él/ella/usted)	hable	hablara *or* hablase
(nosotros/as)	hablemos	habláramos *or* hablásemos
(vosotros/as)	habléis	hablarais *or* hablaseis
(ellos/ellas/ ustedes)	hablen	hablaran *or* hablasen

IMPERATIVE

habla / hablad

Use the present subjunctive in all cases other than these tú and vosotros affirmative forms.

EXAMPLE PHRASES

Luego **hablaremos** de ese tema. We'll talk about that later.

Recuérdame que **hable** con Daniel. Remind me to speak to Daniel.

¿Quieres que **hablemos**? Shall we talk?

Hay que darles una oportunidad para que **hablen**. We need to give them an opportunity to speak.

Remember that subject pronouns are not used very often in Spanish.

hacer (to do, to make)

	PRESENT	**PRESENT PERFECT**
(yo)	hago	he hecho
(tú)	haces	has hecho
(él/ella/usted)	hace	ha hecho
(nosotros/as)	hacemos	hemos hecho
(vosotros/as)	hacéis	habéis hecho
(ellos/ellas/ ustedes)	hacen	han hecho

	PRETERITE	**IMPERFECT**
(yo)	hice	hacía
(tú)	hiciste	hacías
(él/ella/usted)	hizo	hacía
(nosotros/as)	hicimos	hacíamos
(vosotros/as)	hicisteis	hacíais
(ellos/ellas/ ustedes)	hicieron	hacían

GERUND

haciendo

PAST PARTICIPLE

hecho

EXAMPLE PHRASES

¿Qué **hace** tu padre? What does your father do?

Están **haciendo** mucho ruido. They're making a lot of noise.

¿Quién **hizo** eso? Who did that?

Hicieron pintar la fachada del colegio. They had the front of the school painted.

Lo **hacía** para molestarme. He was doing it to annoy me.

Remember that subject pronouns are not used very often in Spanish.

hacer

	FUTURE	CONDITIONAL
(yo)	**haré**	haría
(tú)	**harás**	harías
(él/ella/usted)	**hará**	haría
(nosotros/as)	**haremos**	haríamos
(vosotros/as)	**haréis**	haríais
(ellos/ellas/ustedes)	**harán**	harían

	PRESENT SUBJUNCTIVE	IMPERFECT SUBJUNCTIVE
(yo)	**haga**	hiciera *or* hiciese
(tú)	**hagas**	hicieras *or* hicieses
(él/ella/usted)	**haga**	hiciera *or* hiciese
(nosotros/as)	**hagamos**	hiciéramos *or* hiciésemos
(vosotros/as)	**hagáis**	hicierais *or* hicieseis
(ellos/ellas/ustedes)	**hagan**	hicieran *or* hiciesen

IMPERATIVE

haz / haced

Use the present subjunctive in all cases other than these tú and vosotros affirmative forms.

EXAMPLE PHRASES

Lo **haré** yo mismo. I'll do it myself.

Dijiste que lo **harías**. You said you'd do it.

¿Quieres que **haga** las camas? Do you want me to make the beds?

Preferiría que **hiciera** menos calor. I wish it wasn't so hot.

Hazlo como te dije. Do it the way I told you.

Remember that subject pronouns are not used very often in Spanish.

hay (there is, there are)

PRESENT
hay

PRESENT PERFECT
ha habido

PRETERITE
hubo

IMPERFECT
había

GERUND
habiendo

PAST PARTICIPLE
habido

EXAMPLE PHRASES

Esta tarde va a **haber** una manifestación. There's going to be a demonstration this evening.

Hay una iglesia en la esquina. There's a church on the corner.

Ha habido muchos problemas. There have been a lot of problems.

Hubo una guerra. There was a war.

Había mucha gente. There were a lot of people.

Remember that subject pronouns are not used very often in Spanish.

hay

FUTURE

habrá

CONDITIONAL

habría

PRESENT SUBJUNCTIVE

haya

IMPERFECT SUBJUNCTIVE

hubiera *or* hubiese

IMPERATIVE

not used

EXAMPLE PHRASES

Habrá que repasarlo. We'll have to check it.

Habría que limpiarlo. We should clean it.

No creo que **haya** mucha gente en el recital. I don't think there'll be many
people at the concert.

Si **hubiera** más espacio, pondría un sofá. I'd have a sofa if there was more
room.

Remember that subject pronouns are not used very often in Spanish.

herir (to injure)

	PRESENT		PRESENT PERFECT
(yo)	hiero		he herido
(tú)	hieres		has herido
(él/ella/usted)	hiere		ha herido
(nosotros/as)	herimos		hemos herido
(vosotros/as)	herís		habéis herido
(ellos/ellas/ ustedes)	hieren		han herido

	PRETERITE		IMPERFECT
(yo)	herí		hería
(tú)	heriste		herías
(él/ella/usted)	hirió		hería
(nosotros/as)	herimos		heríamos
(vosotros/as)	heristeis		heríais
(ellos/ellas/ ustedes)	hirieron		herían

GERUND

hiriendo

PAST PARTICIPLE

herido

EXAMPLE PHRASES

Vas a **herir** sus sentimientos. You're going to hurt her feelings.

Me **hiere** que me digas eso. I'm hurt that you should say such a thing.

Lo **hirieron** en el pecho. He was wounded in the chest.

Su actitud la **hería** en lo más hondo. She was deeply hurt by his attitude.

herir

	FUTURE	**CONDITIONAL**
(yo)	heriré	heriría
(tú)	herirás	herirías
(él/ella/usted)	herirá	heriría
(nosotros/as)	heriremos	heriríamos
(vosotros/as)	heriréis	heriríais
(ellos/ellas/ustedes)	herirán	herirían

	PRESENT SUBJUNCTIVE	**IMPERFECT SUBJUNCTIVE**
(yo)	hiera	hiriera *or* hiriese
(tú)	hieras	hirieras *or* hirieses
(él/ella/usted)	hiera	hiriera *or* hiriese
(nosotros/as)	hiramos	hiriéramos *or* hiriésemos
(vosotros/as)	hiráis	hirierais *or* hirieseis
(ellos/ellas/ustedes)	hieran	hirieran *or* hiriesen

IMPERATIVE

hiere / herid

Use the present subjunctive in all cases other than these tú and vosotros affirmative forms.

Remember that subject pronouns are not used very often in Spanish.

huir (to escape, to run away, to flee)

	PRESENT	PRESENT PERFECT
(yo)	huyo	he huido
(tú)	huyes	has huido
(él/ella/usted)	huye	ha huido
(nosotros/as)	huimos	hemos huido
(vosotros/as)	huis	habéis huido
(ellos/ellas/ ustedes)	huyen	han huido

	PRETERITE	IMPERFECT
(yo)	hui	huía
(tú)	huiste	huías
(él/ella/usted)	huyó	huía
(nosotros/as)	huimos	huíamos
(vosotros/as)	huisteis	huíais
(ellos/ellas/ ustedes)	huyeron	huían

GERUND
huyendo

PAST PARTICIPLE
huido

EXAMPLE PHRASES

Salió **huyendo.** He ran away.

Huyeron del país. They fled the country.

Remember that subject pronouns are not used very often in Spanish.

huir

	FUTURE	**CONDITIONAL**
(yo)	huiré	huiría
(tú)	huirás	huirías
(él/ella/usted)	huirá	huiría
(nosotros/as)	huiremos	huiríamos
(vosotros/as)	huiréis	huiríais
(ellos/ellas/ ustedes)	huirán	huirían

	PRESENT SUBJUNCTIVE	**IMPERFECT SUBJUNCTIVE**
(yo)	huya	huyera *or* huyese
(tú)	huyas	huyeras *or* huyeses
(él/ella/usted)	huya	huyera *or* huyese
(nosotros/as)	huyamos	huyéramos *or* huyésemos
(vosotros/as)	huyáis	huyerais *or* huyeseis
(ellos/ellas/ ustedes)	huyan	huyeran *or* huyesen

IMPERATIVE

huye / huid

Use the present subjunctive in all cases other than these tú and vosotros affirmative forms.

EXAMPLE PHRASES

No quiero que **huyas** como un cobarde. I don't want you to run away like
   a coward.

¡**Huye**! Si te atrapan, te matarán. Run! If they catch you, they'll kill you.

Remember that subject pronouns are not used very often in Spanish.

imponer (to impose)

	PRESENT		PRESENT PERFECT
(yo)	impongo		he impuesto
(tú)	impones		has impuesto
(él/ella/usted)	impone		ha impuesto
(nosotros/as)	imponemos		hemos impuesto
(vosotros/as)	imponéis		habéis impuesto
(ellos/ellas/ ustedes)	imponen		han impuesto

	PRETERITE		IMPERFECT
(yo)	impuse		imponía
(tú)	impusiste		imponías
(él/ella/usted)	impuso		imponía
(nosotros/as)	impusimos		imponíamos
(vosotros/as)	impusisteis		imponíais
(ellos/ellas/ ustedes)	impusieron		imponían

GERUND

imponiendo

PAST PARTICIPLE

impuesto

EXAMPLE PHRASES

La minifalda **se está imponiendo** de nuevo. The miniskirt is coming back into fashion.

Habían impuesto la enseñanza religiosa. They had made religious education compulsory.

El corredor nigeriano **se impuso** en la segunda carrera. The Nigerian runner triumphed in the second race.

Mi abuelo **imponía** mucho respeto. My grandfather commanded a lot of respect.

Remember that subject pronouns are not used very often in Spanish.

imponer

	FUTURE	**CONDITIONAL**
(yo)	impondré	impondría
(tú)	impondrás	impondrías
(él/ella/usted)	impondrá	impondría
(nosotros/as)	impondremos	impondríamos
(vosotros/as)	impondréis	impondríais
(ellos/ellas/ ustedes)	impondrán	impondrían

	PRESENT SUBJUNCTIVE	**IMPERFECT SUBJUNCTIVE**
(yo)	imponga	impusiera *or* impusiese
(tú)	impongas	impusieras *or* impusieses
(él/ella/usted)	imponga	impusiera *or* impusiese
(nosotros/as)	impongamos	impusiéramos *or* impusiésemos
(vosotros/as)	impongáis	impusierais *or* impusieseis
(ellos/ellas/ ustedes)	impongan	impusieran *or* impusiesen

IMPERATIVE

impón / imponed

Use the present subjunctive in all cases other than these tú and vosotros affirmative forms.

EXAMPLE PHRASES

Impondrán cuantiosas multas. They'll impose heavy fines.

Remember that subject pronouns are not used very often in Spanish.

imprimir (to print)

	PRESENT		PRESENT PERFECT
(yo)	imprimo		he imprimido
(tú)	imprimes		has imprimido
(él/ella/usted)	imprime		ha imprimido
(nosotros/as)	imprimimos		hemos imprimido
(vosotros/as)	imprimís		habéis imprimido
(ellos/ellas/ ustedes)	imprimen		han imprimido

	PRETERITE		IMPERFECT
(yo)	imprimí		imprimía
(tú)	imprimiste		imprimías
(él/ella/usted)	imprimió		imprimía
(nosotros/as)	imprimimos		imprimíamos
(vosotros/as)	imprimisteis		imprimíais
(ellos/ellas/ ustedes)	imprimieron		imprimían

GERUND

imprimiendo

PAST PARTICIPLE

imprimido, impreso

EXAMPLE PHRASES

¿Puedes **imprimir** el documento? Can you print the document?

Se imprimieron sólo doce copias del libro. Only twelve copies of the book were printed.

Una experiencia así **imprime** carácter. An experience like that is character-building.

Remember that subject pronouns are not used very often in Spanish.

imprimir

	FUTURE	**CONDITIONAL**
(yo)	imprimiré	imprimiría
(tú)	imprimirás	imprimirías
(él/ella/usted)	imprimirá	imprimiría
(nosotros/as)	imprimiremos	imprimiríamos
(vosotros/as)	imprimiréis	imprimiríais
(ellos/ellas/ ustedes)	imprimirán	imprimirían

	PRESENT SUBJUNCTIVE	**IMPERFECT SUBJUNCTIVE**
(yo)	imprima	imprimiera *or* imprimiese
(tú)	imprimas	imprimieras *or* imprimieses
(él/ella/usted)	imprima	imprimiera *or* imprimiese
(nosotros/as)	imprimamos	imprimiéramos *or* imprimiésemos
(vosotros/as)	imprimáis	imprimierais *or* imprimieseis
(ellos/ellas/ ustedes)	impriman	imprimieran *or* imprimiesen

IMPERATIVE

imprime / imprimid

Use the present subjunctive in all cases other than these tú and vosotros affirmative forms.

EXAMPLE PHRASE

Imprímelo en blanco y negro. Print it in black and white.

Remember that subject pronouns are not used very often in Spanish.

ir (to go)

	PRESENT		PRESENT PERFECT
(yo)	voy		he ido
(tú)	vas		has ido
(él/ella/usted)	va		ha ido
(nosotros/as)	vamos		hemos ido
(vosotros/as)	vais		habéis ido
(ellos/ellas/ustedes)	van		han ido

	PRETERITE		IMPERFECT
(yo)	fui		iba
(tú)	fuiste		ibas
(él/ella/usted)	fue		iba
(nosotros/as)	fuimos		íbamos
(vosotros/as)	fuisteis		ibais
(ellos/ellas/ustedes)	fueron		iban

GERUND

yendo

PAST PARTICIPLE

ido

EXAMPLE PHRASES

¿Puedo **ir** contigo? Can I come with you?

Estoy yendo a clases de natación. I'm taking swimming classes.

Había ido a comprar el pan. She'd gone to buy the bread.

Anoche **fuimos** al cine. We went to the movies last night.

Remember that subject pronouns are not used very often in Spanish.

ir

	FUTURE	CONDITIONAL
(yo)	**iré**	iría
(tú)	**irás**	irías
(él/ella/usted)	**irá**	iría
(nosotros/as)	**iremos**	iríamos
(vosotros/as)	**iréis**	iríais
(ellos/ellas/ ustedes)	**irán**	irían

	PRESENT SUBJUNCTIVE	IMPERFECT SUBJUNCTIVE
(yo)	**vaya**	fuera or fuese
(tú)	**vayas**	fueras or fueses
(él/ella/usted)	**vaya**	fuera or fuese
(nosotros/as)	**vayamos**	fuéramos or fuésemos
(vosotros/as)	**vayáis**	fuerais or fueseis
(ellos/ellas/ ustedes)	**vayan**	fueran or fuesen

IMPERATIVE

ve / id

Use the present subjunctive in most cases other than these tú and vosotros affirmative forms.
However, in the 'let's' affirmative form, vamos is more common than vayamos.

EXAMPLE PHRASES

El domingo **iré** a verla. I'll go to see her on Sunday.

Dijeron que **irían** en tren. They said they'd go by train.

¡Que te **vaya** bien! Take care of yourself!

Quería pedirte que **fueras** en mi lugar. I wanted to ask you if you'd take my place.

No **te vayas** sin despedirte. Don't go without saying goodbye.

Remember that subject pronouns are not used very often in Spanish.

jugar (to play)

	PRESENT	PRESENT PERFECT
(yo)	juego	he jugado
(tú)	juegas	has jugado
(él/ella/usted)	juega	ha jugado
(nosotros/as)	jugamos	hemos jugado
(vosotros/as)	jugáis	habéis jugado
(ellos/ellas/ ustedes)	juegan	han jugado

	PRETERITE	IMPERFECT
(yo)	jugué	jugaba
(tú)	jugaste	jugabas
(él/ella/usted)	jugó	jugaba
(nosotros/as)	jugamos	jugábamos
(vosotros/as)	jugasteis	jugabais
(ellos/ellas/ ustedes)	jugaron	jugaban

GERUND

jugando

PAST PARTICIPLE

jugado

EXAMPLE PHRASES

Juego futbol todos los domingos. I play soccer every Sunday.

Están jugando en el jardín. They're playing in the yard.

Le **jugaron** una mala pasada. They played a dirty trick on him.

Se jugaba la vida continuamente. She was constantly risking her life.

Remember that subject pronouns are not used very often in Spanish.

jugar

	FUTURE	CONDITIONAL
(yo)	jugaré	jugaría
(tú)	jugarás	jugarías
(él/ella/usted)	jugará	jugaría
(nosotros/as)	jugaremos	jugaríamos
(vosotros/as)	jugaréis	jugaríais
(ellos/ellas/ ustedes)	jugarán	jugarían

	PRESENT SUBJUNCTIVE	IMPERFECT SUBJUNCTIVE
(yo)	juegue	jugara or jugase
(tú)	juegues	jugaras or jugases
(él/ella/usted)	juegue	jugara or jugase
(nosotros/as)	juguemos	jugáramos or jugásemos
(vosotros/as)	juguéis	jugarais or jugaseis
(ellos/ellas/ ustedes)	jueguen	jugaran or jugasen

IMPERATIVE

juega / jugad

Use the present subjunctive in all cases other than these tú and vosotros affirmative forms.

EXAMPLE PHRASES

Ambos partidos se **jugarán** el domingo. Both games will be played on Sunday.

Jugarías mejor si estuvieras más relajado. You'd play better if you were more relaxed.

No **juegues** con tu salud. Don't take risks with your health.

El médico le aconsejó que **jugara** más y leyera menos. The doctor advised him to play more and read less.

Remember that subject pronouns are not used very often in Spanish.

leer (to read)

	PRESENT		PRESENT PERFECT
(yo)	leo		he leído
(tú)	lees		has leído
(él/ella/usted)	lee		ha leído
(nosotros/as)	leemos		hemos leído
(vosotros/as)	leéis		habéis leído
(ellos/ellas/ ustedes)	leen		han leído

	PRETERITE		IMPERFECT
(yo)	leí		leía
(tú)	leíste		leías
(él/ella/usted)	leyó		leía
(nosotros/as)	leímos		leíamos
(vosotros/as)	leísteis		leíais
(ellos/ellas/ ustedes)	leyeron		leían

GERUND

leyendo

PAST PARTICIPLE

leído

EXAMPLE PHRASES

Hace mucho tiempo que no **leo** nada. I haven't read anything for ages.

Estoy leyendo un libro muy interesante. I'm reading a very interesting book.

No **había leído** nada suyo. I hadn't read anything by her

Lo **leí** hace tiempo. I read it a while ago.

Antes **leía** mucho más. I used to read much more than now.

Remember that subject pronouns are not used very often in Spanish.

leer

	FUTURE	**CONDITIONAL**
(yo)	leeré	leería
(tú)	leerás	leerías
(él/ella/usted)	leerá	leería
(nosotros/as)	leeremos	leeríamos
(vosotros/as)	leeréis	leeríais
(ellos/ellas/ ustedes)	leerán	leerían

	PRESENT SUBJUNCTIVE	**IMPERFECT SUBJUNCTIVE**
(yo)	lea	leyera *or* leyese
(tú)	leas	leyeras *or* leyeses
(él/ella/usted)	lea	leyera *or* leyese
(nosotros/as)	leamos	leyéramos *or* leyésemos
(vosotros/as)	leáis	leyerais *or* leyeseis
(ellos/ellas/ ustedes)	lean	leyeran *or* leyesen

IMPERATIVE

lee / leed

Use the present subjunctive in all cases other than these tú and vosotros affirmative forms.

EXAMPLE PHRASES

Si se portan bien, les **leeré** un cuento. If you behave yourselves, I'll read you a story.

Yo **leería** también la letra pequeña. I'd read the fine print as well.

Quiero que lo **leas** y me digas qué piensas. I want you to read it and tell me what you think.

No **leas** tan rápido. Don't read so fast.

Remember that subject pronouns are not used very often in Spanish.

levantar (to lift, to raise, to pick up)

	PRESENT	**PRESENT PERFECT**
(yo)	levanto	he levantado
(tú)	levantas	has levantado
(él/ella/usted)	levanta	ha levantado
(nosotros/as)	levantamos	hemos levantado
(vosotros/as)	levantáis	habéis levantado
(ellos/ellas/ustedes)	levantan	han levantado

	PRETERITE	**IMPERFECT**
(yo)	levanté	levantaba
(tú)	levantaste	levantabas
(él/ella/usted)	levantó	levantaba
(nosotros/as)	levantamos	levantábamos
(vosotros/as)	levantasteis	levantabais
(ellos/ellas/ustedes)	levantaron	levantaban

GERUND

levantando

PAST PARTICIPLE

levantado

EXAMPLE PHRASES

Fue la primera en **levantar** la mano. She was the first to raise her hand.

Siempre **se levanta** de mal humor. He's always in a bad mood when he gets up.

Hoy **me levanté** temprano. I got up early this morning.

Levantó la maleta como si no pesara nada. He lifted up the suitcase as if it weighed nothing.

Me levanté y seguí caminando. I got up and continued walking.

Remember that subject pronouns are not used very often in Spanish.

levantar

	FUTURE	**CONDITIONAL**
(yo)	levantaré	levantaría
(tú)	levantarás	levantarías
(él/ella/usted)	levantará	levantaría
(nosotros/as)	levantaremos	levantaríamos
(vosotros/as)	levantaréis	levantaríais
(ellos/ellas/ ustedes)	levantarán	levantarían

	PRESENT SUBJUNCTIVE	**IMPERFECT SUBJUNCTIVE**
(yo)	levante	levantara or levantase
(tú)	levantes	levantaras or levantases
(él/ella/usted)	levante	levantara or levantase
(nosotros/as)	levantemos	levantáramos or levantásemos
(vosotros/as)	levantéis	levantarais or levantaseis
(ellos/ellas/ ustedes)	levanten	levantaran or levantasen

IMPERATIVE

levanta / levantad

Use the present subjunctive in all cases other than these tú and vosotros affirmative forms.

EXAMPLE PHRASES

La noticia le **levantará** el ánimo. This news will raise her spirits.

Si pudiera me **levantaría** siempre tarde. I'd sleep in every day, if I could.

No me **levantes** la voz. Don't raise your voice to me.

Levanta la tapa. Lift the lid.

Levanten la mano si tienen alguna duda. Raise your hands if you are unclear about anything.

Remember that subject pronouns are not used very often in Spanish.

llover (to rain)

PRESENT
llueve

PRESENT PERFECT
ha llovido

PRETERITE
llovió

IMPERFECT
llovía

GERUND
lloviendo

PAST PARTICIPLE
llovido

EXAMPLE PHRASES

Hace semanas que no **llueve**. It hasn't rained in weeks.

Está **lloviendo**. It's raining.

Le **llovieron** las ofertas. He received a lot of offers.

Llovió sin parar. It rained nonstop.

Llovía a cántaros. It was pouring rain.

Remember that subject pronouns are not used very often in Spanish.

llover

FUTURE
lloverá

CONDITIONAL
llovería

PRESENT SUBJUNCTIVE
llueva

IMPERFECT SUBJUNCTIVE
lloviera *or* lloviese

IMPERATIVE
not used

EXAMPLE PHRASES

Sabía que le **lloverían** las críticas. She knew she would come in for a lot of criticism.

Espero que no **llueva** este fin de semana. I hope it won't rain this weekend.

Si no **lloviera**, podríamos salir a dar una vuelta. We could go for a walk if it weren't raining.

Remember that subject pronouns are not used very often in Spanish.

lucir (to look, to shine, to show off)

	PRESENT	PRESENT PERFECT
(yo)	luzco	he lucido
(tú)	luces	has lucido
(él/ella/usted)	luce	ha lucido
(nosotros/as)	lucimos	hemos lucido
(vosotros/as)	lucís	habéis lucido
(ellos/ellas/ ustedes)	lucen	han lucido

	PRETERITE	IMPERFECT
(yo)	lucí	lucía
(tú)	luciste	lucías
(él/ella/usted)	lució	lucía
(nosotros/as)	lucimos	lucíamos
(vosotros/as)	lucisteis	lucíais
(ellos/ellas/ ustedes)	lucieron	lucían

GERUND	PAST PARTICIPLE
luciendo	lucido

EXAMPLE PHRASES

Luces muy bien. You look very well.

Quería **lucir** sus conocimientos. He wanted to show off his knowledge.

Te **luciste** con la comida. You've outdone yourself with the meal.

Remember that subject pronouns are not used very often in Spanish.

lucir

	FUTURE	CONDITIONAL
(yo)	luciré	luciría
(tú)	lucirás	lucirías
(él/ella/usted)	lucirá	luciría
(nosotros/as)	luciremos	luciríamos
(vosotros/as)	luciréis	luciríais
(ellos/ellas/ ustedes)	lucirán	lucirían

	PRESENT SUBJUNCTIVE	IMPERFECT SUBJUNCTIVE
(yo)	luzca	luciera *or* luciese
(tú)	luzcas	lucieras *or* lucieses
(él/ella/usted)	luzca	luciera *or* luciese
(nosotros/as)	luzcamos	luciéramos *or* luciésemos
(vosotros/as)	luzcáis	lucierais *or* lucieseis
(ellos/ellas/ ustedes)	luzcan	lucieran *or* luciesen

IMPERATIVE

luce / lucid

Use the present subjunctive in all cases other than these tú and vosotros affirmative forms.

EXAMPLE PHRASES

Lucirá un traje muy elegante. She will be wearing a very elegant dress.

Luciría más con otros zapatos. It would look better with a different pair of shoes.

Quiero que esta noche **luzcas** tú el collar. I want you to wear the necklace tonight.

Remember that subject pronouns are not used very often in Spanish.

morir (to die)

	PRESENT	PRESENT PERFECT
(yo)	muero	he muerto
(tú)	mueres	has muerto
(él/ella/usted)	muere	ha muerto
(nosotros/as)	morimos	hemos muerto
(vosotros/as)	morís	habéis muerto
(ellos/ellas/ustedes)	mueren	han muerto

	PRETERITE	IMPERFECT
(yo)	morí	moría
(tú)	moriste	morías
(él/ella/usted)	murió	moría
(nosotros/as)	morimos	moríamos
(vosotros/as)	moristeis	moríais
(ellos/ellas/ustedes)	murieron	morían

GERUND	PAST PARTICIPLE
muriendo	muerto

EXAMPLE PHRASES

¡Me **muero** de hambre! I'm starving!

Se está **muriendo**. She's dying.

Se le **había muerto** el gato. His cat had died.

Se **murió** el mes pasado. He died last month.

Me **moría** de ganas de contárselo. I was dying to tell her.

Remember that subject pronouns are not used very often in Spanish.

morir

	FUTURE	CONDITIONAL
(yo)	moriré	moriría
(tú)	morirás	morirías
(él/ella/usted)	morirá	moriría
(nosotros/as)	moriremos	moriríamos
(vosotros/as)	moriréis	moriríais
(ellos/ellas/ustedes)	morirán	morirían

	PRESENT SUBJUNCTIVE	IMPERFECT SUBJUNCTIVE
(yo)	muera	muriera or muriese
(tú)	mueras	murieras or murieses
(él/ella/usted)	muera	muriera or muriese
(nosotros/as)	muramos	muriéramos or muriésemos
(vosotros/as)	muráis	murierais or murieseis
(ellos/ellas/ustedes)	mueran	murieran or muriesen

IMPERATIVE

muere / morid

Use the present subjunctive in all cases other than these tú and vosotros affirmative forms.

EXAMPLE PHRASES

Cuando te lo cuente **te morirás** de risa. You'll die laughing when I tell you.

Yo **me moriría** de vergüenza. I'd die of shame.

Cuando **me muera**... When I die...

¡Por favor, no **te mueras**! Please don't die!

Remember that subject pronouns are not used very often in Spanish.

mover (to move)

	PRESENT		PRESENT PERFECT
(yo)	muevo		he movido
(tú)	mueves		has movido
(él/ella/usted)	mueve		ha movido
(nosotros/as)	movemos		hemos movido
(vosotros/as)	movéis		habéis movido
(ellos/ellas/ ustedes)	mueven		han movido

	PRETERITE	IMPERFECT
(yo)	moví	movía
(tú)	moviste	movías
(él/ella/usted)	movió	movía
(nosotros/as)	movimos	movíamos
(vosotros/as)	movisteis	movíais
(ellos/ellas/ ustedes)	movieron	movían

GERUND
moviendo

PAST PARTICIPLE
movido

EXAMPLE PHRASES

El perro no dejaba de **mover** la cola. The dog kept wagging its tail.

Se está moviendo. It's moving.

No **se movieron** de casa. They didn't leave the house.

Antes **se movía** en esos ambientes. He used to move in those circles.

Remember that subject pronouns are not used very often in Spanish.

mover

	FUTURE	CONDITIONAL
(yo)	moveré	movería
(tú)	moverás	moverías
(él/ella/usted)	moverá	movería
(nosotros/as)	moveremos	moveríamos
(vosotros/as)	moveréis	moveríais
(ellos/ellas/ ustedes)	moverán	moverían

	PRESENT SUBJUNCTIVE	IMPERFECT SUBJUNCTIVE
(yo)	mueva	moviera or moviese
(tú)	muevas	movieras or movieses
(él/ella/usted)	mueva	moviera or moviese
(nosotros/as)	movamos	moviéramos or moviésemos
(vosotros/as)	mováis	movierais or movieseis
(ellos/ellas/ ustedes)	muevan	movieran or moviesen

IMPERATIVE

mueve / moved

Use the present subjunctive in all cases other than these tú *and* vosotros *affirmative forms.*

EXAMPLE PHRASES

Prométeme que no **te moverás** de aquí. Promise me you won't move from here.

No **te muevas**. Don't move.

Mueve un poco las cajas para que podamos pasar. Move the boxes a bit so that we can get past.

Remember that subject pronouns are not used very often in Spanish.

nacer (to be born)

	PRESENT	PRESENT PERFECT
(yo)	nazco	he nacido
(tú)	naces	has nacido
(él/ella/usted)	nace	ha nacido
(nosotros/as)	nacemos	hemos nacido
(vosotros/as)	nacéis	habéis nacido
(ellos/ellas/ ustedes)	nacen	han nacido

	PRETERITE	IMPERFECT
(yo)	nací	nacía
(tú)	naciste	nacías
(él/ella/usted)	nació	nacía
(nosotros/as)	nacimos	nacíamos
(vosotros/as)	nacisteis	nacíais
(ellos/ellas/ ustedes)	nacieron	nacían

GERUND	PAST PARTICIPLE
naciendo	nacido

EXAMPLE PHRASES

Nacen cuatro niños por minuto. Four children are born every minute.

Nació en 1980. He was born in 1980.

¿Cuándo **naciste**? When were you born?

Tu todavía no **habías nacido**. You hadn't been born yet.

Remember that subject pronouns are not used very often in Spanish.

nacer

	FUTURE	**CONDITIONAL**
(yo)	naceré	nacería
(tú)	nacerás	nacerías
(él/ella/usted)	nacerá	nacería
(nosotros/as)	naceremos	naceríamos
(vosotros/as)	naceréis	naceríais
(ellos/ellas/ ustedes)	nacerán	nacerían

	PRESENT SUBJUNCTIVE	**IMPERFECT SUBJUNCTIVE**
(yo)	nazca	naciera *or* naciese
(tú)	nazcas	nacieras *or* nacieses
(él/ella/usted)	nazca	naciera *or* naciese
(nosotros/as)	nazcamos	naciéramos *or* naciésemos
(vosotros/as)	nazcáis	nacierais *or* nacieseis
(ellos/ellas/ ustedes)	nazcan	nacieran *or* naciesen

IMPERATIVE

nace / naced

Use the present subjunctive in all cases other than these tú and vosotros affirmative forms.

EXAMPLE PHRASES

Nacerá el año que viene. It will be born next year.

Queremos que **nazca** en México. We want it to be born in Mexico.

Si **naciera** hoy, sería tauro. He'd be a Taurus if he were born today.

Remember that subject pronouns are not used very often in Spanish.

negar (to deny, to refuse)

	PRESENT		PRESENT PERFECT
(yo)	niego		he negado
(tú)	niegas		has negado
(él/ella/usted)	niega		ha negado
(nosotros/as)	negamos		hemos negado
(vosotros/as)	negáis		habéis negado
(ellos/ellas/ ustedes)	niegan		han negado

	PRETERITE		IMPERFECT
(yo)	negué		negaba
(tú)	negaste		negabas
(él/ella/usted)	negó		negaba
(nosotros/as)	negamos		negábamos
(vosotros/as)	negasteis		negabais
(ellos/ellas/ ustedes)	negaron		negaban

GERUND

negando

PAST PARTICIPLE

negado

EXAMPLE PHRASES

No lo puedes **negar**. You can't deny it.

Me **niego** a creerlo. I refuse to believe it.

Se **negó** a venir con nosotros. She refused to come with us.

Decían que era el ladrón, pero él lo **negaba**. They said that he was the thief, but he denied it.

Remember that subject pronouns are not used very often in Spanish.

negar

	FUTURE	CONDITIONAL
(yo)	**negaré**	**negaría**
(tú)	**negarás**	**negarías**
(él/ella/usted)	**negará**	**negaría**
(nosotros/as)	**negaremos**	**negaríamos**
(vosotros/as)	**negaréis**	**negaríais**
(ellos/ellas/ ustedes)	**negarán**	**negarían**

	PRESENT SUBJUNCTIVE	IMPERFECT SUBJUNCTIVE
(yo)	**niegue**	**negara** or **negase**
(tú)	**niegues**	**negaras** or **negases**
(él/ella/usted)	**niegue**	**negara** or **negase**
(nosotros/as)	**neguemos**	**negáramos** or **negásemos**
(vosotros/as)	**neguéis**	**negarais** or **negaseis**
(ellos/ellas/ ustedes)	**nieguen**	**negaran** or **negasen**

IMPERATIVE

niega / negad

Use the present subjunctive in all cases other than these tú and *vosotros* affirmative forms.

EXAMPLE PHRASES

No me **negarás** que es barato. You can't say it's not cheap.

Si lo **negaras**, nadie te creería. If you denied it, nobody would believe you.

No lo **niegues**. Don't deny it.

Remember that subject pronouns are not used very often in Spanish.

Oír (to hear, to listen)

	PRESENT	PRESENT PERFECT
(yo)	oigo	he oído
(tú)	oyes	has oído
(él/ella/usted)	oye	ha oído
(nosotros/as)	oímos	hemos oído
(vosotros/as)	oís	habéis oído
(ellos/ellas/ ustedes)	oyen	han oído

	PRETERITE	IMPERFECT
(yo)	oí	oía
(tú)	oíste	oías
(él/ella/usted)	oyó	oía
(nosotros/as)	oímos	oíamos
(vosotros/as)	oísteis	oíais
(ellos/ellas/ ustedes)	oyeron	oían

GERUND

oyendo

PAST PARTICIPLE

oído

EXAMPLE PHRASES

No **oigo** nada. I can't hear anything.

Estábamos oyendo las noticias. We were listening to the news.

¿**Oíste** eso? Did you hear that?

Lo **oí** por casualidad. I heard it by chance.

No **oía** muy bien. He couldn't hear very well.

Remember that subject pronouns are not used very often in Spanish.

oír

	FUTURE	CONDITIONAL
(yo)	oiré	oiría
(tú)	oirás	oirías
(él/ella/usted)	oirá	oiría
(nosotros/as)	oiremos	oiríamos
(vosotros/as)	oiréis	oiríais
(ellos/ellas/ustedes)	oirán	oirían

	PRESENT SUBJUNCTIVE	IMPERFECT SUBJUNCTIVE
(yo)	oiga	oyera or oyese
(tú)	oigas	oyeras or oyeses
(él/ella/usted)	oiga	oyera or oyese
(nosotros/as)	oigamos	oyéramos or oyésemos
(vosotros/as)	oigáis	oyerais or oyeseis
(ellos/ellas/ustedes)	oigan	oyeran or oyesen

IMPERATIVE

oye / oíd

Use the present subjunctive in all cases other than these tú and vosotros affirmative forms.

EXAMPLE PHRASES

Oye, ¿tú qué te crees? Listen, who do you think you are?

Oigan bien. Listen carefully.

Remember that subject pronouns are not used very often in Spanish.

oler (to smell)

	PRESENT	PRESENT PERFECT
(yo)	huelo	he olido
(tú)	hueles	has olido
(él/ella/usted)	huele	ha olido
(nosotros/as)	olemos	hemos olido
(vosotros/as)	oléis	habéis olido
(ellos/ellas/ ustedes)	huelen	han olido

	PRETERITE	IMPERFECT
(yo)	olí	olía
(tú)	oliste	olías
(él/ella/usted)	olió	olía
(nosotros/as)	olimos	olíamos
(vosotros/as)	olisteis	olíais
(ellos/ellas/ ustedes)	olieron	olían

GERUND	PAST PARTICIPLE
oliendo	olido

EXAMPLE PHRASES

Huele a pescado. It smells of fish.

El perro **estaba oliendo** la basura. The dog was sniffing the trash.

A mí el asunto me **olió** mal. I thought there was something fishy about it.

Olía muy bien. It smelled really nice.

Remember that subject pronouns are not used very often in Spanish.

oler

	FUTURE	CONDITIONAL
(yo)	oleré	olería
(tú)	olerás	olerías
(él/ella/usted)	olerá	olería
(nosotros/as)	oleremos	oleríamos
(vosotros/as)	oleréis	oleríais
(ellos/ellas/ ustedes)	olerán	olerían

	PRESENT SUBJUNCTIVE	IMPERFECT SUBJUNCTIVE
(yo)	huela	oliera _or_ oliese
(tú)	huelas	olieras _or_ olieses
(él/ella/usted)	huela	oliera _or_ oliese
(nosotros/as)	olamos	oliéramos _or_ oliésemos
(vosotros/as)	oláis	olierais _or_ olieseis
(ellos/ellas/ ustedes)	huelan	olieran _or_ oliesen

IMPERATIVE

huele / oled

Use the present subjunctive in all cases other than these **tú** and **vosotros** affirmative forms.

EXAMPLE PHRASES

Con esto ya no **olerá**. This will take the smell away.

Si estuviera fresco, no **olería** así. If it were fresh, it wouldn't smell like that.

Remember that subject pronouns are not used very often in Spanish.

pagar (to pay, to pay for)

	PRESENT	PRESENT PERFECT
(yo)	pago	he pagado
(tú)	pagas	has pagado
(él/ella/usted)	paga	ha pagado
(nosotros/as)	pagamos	hemos pagado
(vosotros/as)	pagáis	habéis pagado
(ellos/ellas/ ustedes)	pagan	han pagado

	PRETERITE	IMPERFECT
(yo)	pagué	pagaba
(tú)	pagaste	pagabas
(él/ella/usted)	pagó	pagaba
(nosotros/as)	pagamos	pagábamos
(vosotros/as)	pagasteis	pagabais
(ellos/ellas/ ustedes)	pagaron	pagaban

GERUND	PAST PARTICIPLE
pagando	pagado

EXAMPLE PHRASES

Se puede **pagar** con tarjeta de crédito. You can pay by credit card.

¿Cuánto te **pagan** al mes? How much do they pay you a month?

Lo **pagué** en efectivo. I paid for it in cash.

Me **pagaban** muy poco. I got paid very little.

Remember that subject pronouns are not used very often in Spanish.

pagar

	FUTURE	CONDITIONAL
(yo)	pagaré	pagaría
(tú)	pagarás	pagarías
(él/ella/usted)	pagará	pagaría
(nosotros/as)	pagaremos	pagaríamos
(vosotros/as)	pagaréis	pagaríais
(ellos/ellas/ ustedes)	pagarán	pagarían

	PRESENT SUBJUNCTIVE	IMPERFECT SUBJUNCTIVE
(yo)	pague	pagara or pagase
(tú)	pagues	pagaras or pagases
(él/ella/usted)	pague	pagara or pagase
(nosotros/as)	paguemos	pagáramos or pagásemos
(vosotros/as)	paguéis	pagarais or pagaseis
(ellos/ellas/ ustedes)	paguen	pagaran or pagasen

IMPERATIVE

paga / pagad

Use the present subjunctive in all cases other than these tú and vosotros affirmative forms.

EXAMPLE PHRASES

Yo te **pagaré** la entrada. I'll pay for your ticket.

¡Quiero que **pague** por lo que me ha hecho! I want him to pay for what he's done to me!

Si **pagara** sus deudas, se quedaría sin nada. He'd be left with nothing if he paid his debts.

No les **pagues** hasta que lo hayan hecho. Don't pay them until they've done it.

Págame lo que me debes. Pay me what you owe me.

Remember that subject pronouns are not used very often in Spanish.

partir (to leave)

	PRESENT	PRESENT PERFECT
(yo)	parto	he partido
(tú)	partes	has partido
(él/ella/usted)	parte	ha partido
(nosotros/as)	partimos	hemos partido
(vosotros/as)	partís	habéis partido
(ellos/ellas/ ustedes)	parten	han partido

	PRETERITE	IMPERFECT
(yo)	partí	partía
(tú)	partiste	partías
(él/ella/usted)	partió	partía
(nosotros/as)	partimos	partíamos
(vosotros/as)	partisteis	partíais
(ellos/ellas/ ustedes)	partieron	partían

GERUND

partiendo

PAST PARTICIPLE

partido

EXAMPLE PHRASES

¿Te **parto** un trozo de queso? Shall I cut you a piece of cheese?

Partiendo de la base de que... Assuming that...

El remo **se partió** en dos. The oar broke in two.

Remember that subject pronouns are not used very often in Spanish.

partir

	FUTURE	CONDITIONAL
(yo)	partiré	partiría
(tú)	partirás	partirías
(él/ella/usted)	partirá	partiría
(nosotros/as)	partiremos	partiríamos
(vosotros/as)	partiréis	partiríais
(ellos/ellas/ ustedes)	partirán	partirían

	PRESENT SUBJUNCTIVE	IMPERFECT SUBJUNCTIVE
(yo)	parta	partiera or partiese
(tú)	partas	partieras or partieses
(él/ella/usted)	parta	partiera or partiese
(nosotros/as)	partamos	partiéramos or partiésemos
(vosotros/as)	partáis	partierais or partieseis
(ellos/ellas/ ustedes)	partan	partieran or partiesen

IMPERATIVE

parte / partid

Use the present subjunctive in all cases other than these tú and vosotros affirmative forms.

EXAMPLE PHRASES

La expedición **partirá** mañana de París. The expedition is to leave from Paris tomorrow.

Eso le **partiría** el corazón. That would break his heart.

Pártelo por la mitad. Cut it in half.

Remember that subject pronouns are not used very often in Spanish.

pedir (to ask for, to ask)

	PRESENT		PRESENT PERFECT
(yo)	pido		he pedido
(tú)	pides		has pedido
(él/ella/usted)	pide		ha pedido
(nosotros/as)	pedimos		hemos pedido
(vosotros/as)	pedís		habéis pedido
(ellos/ellas/ ustedes)	piden		han pedido

	PRETERITE		IMPERFECT
(yo)	pedí		pedía
(tú)	pediste		pedías
(él/ella/usted)	pidió		pedía
(nosotros/as)	pedimos		pedíamos
(vosotros/as)	pedisteis		pedíais
(ellos/ellas/ ustedes)	pidieron		pedían

GERUND

pidiendo

PAST PARTICIPLE

pedido

EXAMPLE PHRASES

¿Cuánto **pide** por el carro? How much is he asking for the car?

La casa **está pidiendo** a gritos una mano de pintura. The house is crying out to be painted.

Pedimos dos cervezas. We ordered two beers.

No nos **pidieron** el pasaporte. They didn't ask us for our passports.

Pedían dos millones de rescate. They were demanding two million in ransom.

Remember that subject pronouns are not used very often in Spanish.

pedir

	FUTURE	CONDITIONAL
(yo)	pediré	pediría
(tú)	pedirás	pedirías
(él/ella/usted)	pedirá	pediría
(nosotros/as)	pediremos	pediríamos
(vosotros/as)	pediréis	pediríais
(ellos/ellas/ ustedes)	pedirán	pedirían

	PRESENT SUBJUNCTIVE	IMPERFECT SUBJUNCTIVE
(yo)	pida	pidiera or pidiese
(tú)	pidas	pidieras or pidieses
(él/ella/usted)	pida	pidiera or pidiese
(nosotros/as)	pidamos	pidiéramos or pidiésemos
(vosotros/as)	pidáis	pidierais or pidieseis
(ellos/ellas/ ustedes)	pidan	pidieran or pidiesen

IMPERATIVE

pide / pedid

Use the present subjunctive in all cases other than these tú and vosotros affirmative forms.

EXAMPLE PHRASES

Si se entera, te **pedirá** explicaciones. If he finds out, he'll ask you for an explanation.

Nunca te **pediría** que hicieras una cosa así. I'd never ask you to do anything like that.

Y que sea lo último que me **pidas**. And don't ask me for anything else.

Pídele el teléfono. Ask her for her phone number.

Remember that subject pronouns are not used very often in Spanish.

pensar (to think)

	PRESENT	PRESENT PERFECT
(yo)	pienso	he pensado
(tú)	piensas	has pensado
(él/ella/usted)	piensa	ha pensado
(nosotros/as)	pensamos	hemos pensado
(vosotros/as)	pensáis	habéis pensado
(ellos/ellas/ ustedes)	piensan	han pensado

	PRETERITE	IMPERFECT
(yo)	pensé	pensaba
(tú)	pensaste	pensabas
(él/ella/usted)	pensó	pensaba
(nosotros/as)	pensamos	pensábamos
(vosotros/as)	pensasteis	pensabais
(ellos/ellas/ ustedes)	pensaron	pensaban

GERUND

pensando

PAST PARTICIPLE

pensado

EXAMPLE PHRASES

¿**Piensas** que vale la pena? Do you think it's worth it?

¿Qué **piensas** del aborto? What do you think about abortion?

Está **pensando** en comprarse una casa. He's thinking about buying a house.

¿Lo **pensaste** bien? Have you thought about it carefully?

Pensaba que vendrías. I thought you'd come.

Remember that subject pronouns are not used very often in Spanish.

pensar

	FUTURE	CONDITIONAL
(yo)	pensaré	pensaría
(tú)	pensarás	pensarías
(él/ella/usted)	pensará	pensaría
(nosotros/as)	pensaremos	pensaríamos
(vosotros/as)	pensaréis	pensaríais
(ellos/ellas/ ustedes)	pensarán	pensarían

	PRESENT SUBJUNCTIVE	IMPERFECT SUBJUNCTIVE
(yo)	piense	pensara *or* pensase
(tú)	pienses	pensaras *or* pensases
(él/ella/usted)	piense	pensara *or* pensase
(nosotros/as)	pensemos	pensáramos *or* pensásemos
(vosotros/as)	penséis	pensarais *or* pensaseis
(ellos/ellas/ ustedes)	piensen	pensaran *or* pensasen

IMPERATIVE

piensa / pensad

Use the present subjunctive in all cases other than these tú and vosotros affirmative forms.

EXAMPLE PHRASES

Yo no me lo **pensaría** dos veces. I wouldn't think twice.

Me da igual lo que **piensen**. I don't care what they think.

Si **pensara** eso, te lo diría. If I thought that, I'd tell you.

No **pienses** que no quiero ir. Don't think that I don't want to go.

No lo **pienses** más. Don't think any more about it.

Remember that subject pronouns are not used very often in Spanish.

perder (to lose)

	PRESENT		PRESENT PERFECT
(yo)	pierdo		he perdido
(tú)	pierdes		has perdido
(él/ella/usted)	pierde		ha perdido
(nosotros/as)	perdemos		hemos perdido
(vosotros/as)	perdéis		habéis perdido
(ellos/ellas/ ustedes)	pierden		han perdido

	PRETERITE		IMPERFECT
(yo)	perdí		perdía
(tú)	perdiste		perdías
(él/ella/usted)	perdió		perdía
(nosotros/as)	perdimos		perdíamos
(vosotros/as)	perdisteis		perdíais
(ellos/ellas/ ustedes)	perdieron		perdían

GERUND

perdiendo

PAST PARTICIPLE

perdido

EXAMPLE PHRASES

Siempre **pierde** las llaves. He's always losing his keys.

Ana es la que saldrá **perdiendo**. Ana is the one who will lose out.

Había perdido dos kilos. He'd lost two kilos.

Perdimos dos a cero. We lost two-nothing.

Perdían siempre. They always used to lose.

Remember that subject pronouns are not used very often in Spanish.

perder

	FUTURE	CONDITIONAL
(yo)	perderé	perdería
(tú)	perderás	perderías
(él/ella/usted)	perderá	perdería
(nosotros/as)	perderemos	perderíamos
(vosotros/as)	perderéis	perderíais
(ellos/ellas/ ustedes)	perderán	perderían

	PRESENT SUBJUNCTIVE	IMPERFECT SUBJUNCTIVE
(yo)	pierda	perdiera *or* perdiese
(tú)	pierdas	perdieras *or* perdieses
(él/ella/usted)	pierda	perdiera *or* perdiese
(nosotros/as)	perdamos	perdiéramos *or* perdiésemos
(vosotros/as)	perdáis	perdierais *or* perdieseis
(ellos/ellas/ ustedes)	pierdan	perdieran *or* perdiesen

IMPERATIVE

pierde / perded

Use the present subjunctive in all cases other than these tú and vosotros affirmative forms.

EXAMPLE PHRASES

Apúrate o **perderás** el tren. Hurry up or you'll miss the train.

¡No **te** lo **pierdas**! Don't miss it!

No **pierdas** esta oportunidad. Don't miss this opportunity.

Remember that subject pronouns are not used very often in Spanish.

poder (to be able to)

	PRESENT	PRESENT PERFECT
(yo)	puedo	he podido
(tú)	puedes	has podido
(él/ella/usted)	puede	ha podido
(nosotros/as)	podemos	hemos podido
(vosotros/as)	podéis	habéis podido
(ellos/ellas/ustedes)	pueden	han podido

	PRETERITE	IMPERFECT
(yo)	pude	podía
(tú)	pudiste	podías
(él/ella/usted)	pudo	podía
(nosotros/as)	pudimos	podíamos
(vosotros/as)	pudisteis	podíais
(ellos/ellas/ustedes)	pudieron	podían

GERUND

pudiendo

PAST PARTICIPLE

podido

EXAMPLE PHRASES

¿**Puedo** entrar? Can I come in?

Puede que llegue mañana. He may arrive tomorrow.

No **pude** venir antes. I couldn't come before.

Pudiste haberte lastimado. You could have hurt yourself.

¡Me lo **podías** haber dicho! You could have told me!

Remember that subject pronouns are not used very often in Spanish.

poder

	FUTURE	CONDITIONAL
(yo)	podré	podría
(tú)	podrás	podrías
(él/ella/usted)	podrá	podría
(nosotros/as)	podremos	podríamos
(vosotros/as)	podréis	podríais
(ellos/ellas/ ustedes)	podrán	podrían

	PRESENT SUBJUNCTIVE	IMPERFECT SUBJUNCTIVE
(yo)	pueda	pudiera *or* pudiese
(tú)	puedas	pudieras *or* pudieses
(él/ella/usted)	pueda	pudiera *or* pudiese
(nosotros/as)	podamos	pudiéramos *or* pudiésemos
(vosotros/as)	podáis	pudierais *or* pudieseis
(ellos/ellas/ ustedes)	puedan	pudieran *or* pudiesen

IMPERATIVE

puede / poded

Use the present subjunctive in all cases other than these tú *and* vosotros *affirmative forms.*

EXAMPLE PHRASES

Estoy segura de que **podrá** conseguirlo. I'm sure he'll succeed.

¿**Podrías** ayudarme? Could you help me?

Ven en cuanto **puedas**. Come as soon as you can.

Me fui para que **pudieran** hablar. I left so they could talk.

Remember that subject pronouns are not used very often in Spanish.

poner (to put)

	PRESENT	PRESENT PERFECT
(yo)	pongo	he puesto
(tú)	pones	has puesto
(él/ella/usted)	pone	ha puesto
(nosotros/as)	ponemos	hemos puesto
(vosotros/as)	ponéis	habéis puesto
(ellos/ellas/ ustedes)	ponen	han puesto

	PRETERITE	IMPERFECT
(yo)	puse	ponía
(tú)	pusiste	ponías
(él/ella/usted)	puso	ponía
(nosotros/as)	pusimos	poníamos
(vosotros/as)	pusisteis	poníais
(ellos/ellas/ ustedes)	pusieron	ponían

GERUND

poniendo

PAST PARTICIPLE

puesto

EXAMPLE PHRASES

¿Dónde **pongo** mis cosas? Where shall I put my things?

¿Le **pusiste** azúcar a mi café? Did you put sugar in my coffee?

Todos **nos pusimos** de acuerdo. We all agreed.

Remember that subject pronouns are not used very often in Spanish.

poner

	FUTURE	**CONDITIONAL**
(yo)	pondré	pondría
(tú)	pondrás	pondrías
(él/ella/usted)	pondrá	pondría
(nosotros/as)	pondremos	pondríamos
(vosotros/as)	pondréis	pondríais
(ellos/ellas/ ustedes)	pondrán	pondrían

	PRESENT SUBJUNCTIVE	**IMPERFECT SUBJUNCTIVE**
(yo)	ponga	pusiera *or* pusiese
(tú)	pongas	pusieras *or* pusieses
(él/ella/usted)	ponga	pusiera *or* pusiese
(nosotros/as)	pongamos	pusiéramos *or* pusiésemos
(vosotros/as)	pongáis	pusierais *or* pusieseis
(ellos/ellas/ ustedes)	pongan	pusieran *or* pusiesen

IMPERATIVE

pon / poned

Use the present subjunctive in all cases other than these tú *and* vosotros *affirmative forms.*

EXAMPLE PHRASES

Lo **pondré** aquí. I'll put it here.

¿Le **pondrías** más sal? Would you add more salt?

Ponlo ahí. Put it over there.

Remember that subject pronouns are not used very often in Spanish.

prohibir (to ban, to prohibit)

	PRESENT	PRESENT PERFECT
(yo)	prohíbo	he prohibido
(tú)	prohíbes	has prohibido
(él/ella/usted)	prohíbe	ha prohibido
(nosotros/as)	prohibimos	hemos prohibido
(vosotros/as)	prohibís	habéis prohibido
(ellos/ellas/ ustedes)	prohíben	han prohibido

	PRETERITE	IMPERFECT
(yo)	prohibí	prohibía
(tú)	prohibiste	prohibías
(él/ella/usted)	prohibió	prohibía
(nosotros/as)	prohibimos	prohibíamos
(vosotros/as)	prohibisteis	prohibíais
(ellos/ellas/ ustedes)	prohibieron	prohibían

GERUND

prohibiendo

PAST PARTICIPLE

prohibido

EXAMPLE PHRASES

Deberían **prohibirlo**. It should be banned.

Te **prohíbo** que me hables así. I won't have you talking to me like that!

Le **prohibieron** la entrada. She was not allowed in.

El tratado **prohibía** el uso de armas químicas. The treaty prohibited the use of chemical weapons.

Remember that subject pronouns are not used very often in Spanish.

prohibir

	FUTURE	CONDITIONAL
(yo)	prohibiré	prohibiría
(tú)	prohibirás	prohibirías
(él/ella/usted)	prohibirá	prohibiría
(nosotros/as)	prohibiremos	prohibiríamos
(vosotros/as)	prohibiréis	prohibiríais
(ellos/ellas/ ustedes)	prohibirán	prohibirían

	PRESENT SUBJUNCTIVE	IMPERFECT SUBJUNCTIVE
(yo)	prohíba	prohibiera *or* prohibiese
(tú)	prohíbas	prohibieras *or* prohibieses
(él/ella/usted)	prohíba	prohibiera *or* prohibiese
(nosotros/as)	prohibamos	prohibiéramos *or* prohibiésemos
(vosotros/as)	prohibáis	prohibierais *or* prohibieseis
(ellos/ellas/ ustedes)	prohíban	prohibieran *or* prohibiesen

IMPERATIVE

prohíbe / prohibid

Use the present subjunctive in all cases other than these tú *and* vosotros *affirmative forms.*

EXAMPLE PHRASES

Tarde o temprano lo **prohibirán**. Sooner or later they'll ban it.

Yo esa música la **prohibiría**. If it were up to me, that music would be banned.

"**prohibido** fumar" "no smoking"

Remember that subject pronouns are not used very often in Spanish.

querer (to want, to love)

	PRESENT	PRESENT PERFECT
(yo)	quiero	he querido
(tú)	quieres	has querido
(él/ella/usted)	quiere	ha querido
(nosotros/as)	queremos	hemos querido
(vosotros/as)	queréis	habéis querido
(ellos/ellas/ ustedes)	quieren	han querido

	PRETERITE	IMPERFECT
(yo)	quise	quería
(tú)	quisiste	querías
(él/ella/usted)	quiso	quería
(nosotros/as)	quisimos	queríamos
(vosotros/as)	quisisteis	queríais
(ellos/ellas/ ustedes)	quisieron	querían

GERUND

queriendo

PAST PARTICIPLE

querido

EXAMPLE PHRASES

Lo hice sin **querer**. I didn't mean to do it.

Te **quiero**. I love you.

Quiero que vayas. I want you to go.

No **quería** decírmelo. She didn't want to tell me.

Remember that subject pronouns are not used very often in Spanish.

querer

	FUTURE	CONDITIONAL
(yo)	querré	querría
(tú)	querrás	querrías
(él/ella/usted)	querrá	querría
(nosotros/as)	querremos	querríamos
(vosotros/as)	querréis	querríais
(ellos/ellas/ ustedes)	querrán	querrían

	PRESENT SUBJUNCTIVE	IMPERFECT SUBJUNCTIVE
(yo)	quiera	quisiera or quisiese
(tú)	quieras	quisieras or quisieses
(él/ella/usted)	quiera	quisiera or quisiese
(nosotros/as)	queramos	quisiéramos or quisiésemos
(vosotros/as)	queráis	quisierais or quisieseis
(ellos/ellas/ ustedes)	quieran	quisieran or quisiesen

IMPERATIVE

quiere / quered

Use the present subjunctive in all cases other than these tú and vosotros affirmative forms.

EXAMPLE PHRASES

Siempre la **querré**. I will always love her.

Querría que no hubiera pasado nunca. I wish it had never happened.

¡Por lo que más **quieras**, cállate! For goodness sake, shut up!

Quisiera preguntar una cosa. I'd like to ask something.

Remember that subject pronouns are not used very often in Spanish.

reducir (to reduce)

	PRESENT	**PRESENT PERFECT**
(yo)	reduzco	he reducido
(tú)	reduces	has reducido
(él/ella/usted)	reduce	ha reducido
(nosotros/as)	reducimos	hemos reducido
(vosotros/as)	reducís	habéis reducido
(ellos/ellas/ustedes)	reducen	han reducido

	PRETERITE	**IMPERFECT**
(yo)	reduje	reducía
(tú)	redujiste	reducías
(él/ella/usted)	redujo	reducía
(nosotros/as)	redujimos	reducíamos
(vosotros/as)	redujisteis	reducíais
(ellos/ellas/ustedes)	redujeron	reducían

GERUND	**PAST PARTICIPLE**
reduciendo	reducido

EXAMPLE PHRASES

Al final todo **se reduce** a eso. In the end it all comes down to that.

Se había reducido la tasa de natalidad. The birth rate had fallen.

Sus gastos **se redujeron** a la mitad. Their expenses were cut by half.

Remember that subject pronouns are not used very often in Spanish.

reducir

	FUTURE	CONDITIONAL
(yo)	reduciré	reduciría
(tú)	reducirás	reducirías
(él/ella/usted)	reducirá	reduciría
(nosotros/as)	reduciremos	reduciríamos
(vosotros/as)	reduciréis	reduciríais
(ellos/ellas/ ustedes)	reducirán	reducirían

	PRESENT SUBJUNCTIVE	IMPERFECT SUBJUNCTIVE
(yo)	reduzca	redujera or redujese
(tú)	reduzcas	redujeras or redujeses
(él/ella/usted)	reduzca	redujera or redujese
(nosotros/as)	reduzcamos	redujéramos or redujésemos
(vosotros/as)	reduzcáis	redujerais or redujeseis
(ellos/ellas/ ustedes)	reduzcan	redujeran or redujesen

IMPERATIVE

reduce / reducid

Use the present subjunctive in all cases other than these tú and vosotros affirmative forms.

EXAMPLE PHRASES

Reducirán la producción en un 20%. They'll cut production by 20%.

Reduzca la velocidad. Reduce speed.

Remember that subject pronouns are not used very often in Spanish.

rehusar (to refuse)

	PRESENT	PRESENT PERFECT
(yo)	rehúso	he rehusado
(tú)	rehúsas	has rehusado
(él/ella/usted)	rehúsa	ha rehusado
(nosotros/as)	rehusamos	hemos rehusado
(vosotros/as)	rehusáis	habéis rehusado
(ellos/ellas/ ustedes)	rehúsan	han rehusado

	PRETERITE	IMPERFECT
(yo)	rehusé	rehusaba
(tú)	rehusaste	rehusabas
(él/ella/usted)	rehusó	rehusaba
(nosotros/as)	rehusamos	rehusábamos
(vosotros/as)	rehusasteis	rehusabais
(ellos/ellas/ ustedes)	rehusaron	rehusaban

GERUND	PAST PARTICIPLE
rehusando	rehusado

EXAMPLE PHRASES

Rehúso tomar parte en esto. I refuse to take part in this.

Había rehusado varias ofertas de trabajo. He had declined several job offers.

Su familia **rehusó** hacer declaraciones. His family refused to comment.

Remember that subject pronouns are not used very often in Spanish.

rehusar

	FUTURE	**CONDITIONAL**
(yo)	rehusaré	rehusaría
(tú)	rehusarás	rehusarías
(él/ella/usted)	rehusará	rehusaría
(nosotros/as)	rehusaremos	rehusaríamos
(vosotros/as)	rehusaréis	rehusaríais
(ellos/ellas/ ustedes)	rehusarán	rehusarían

	PRESENT SUBJUNCTIVE	**IMPERFECT SUBJUNCTIVE**
(yo)	rehúse	rehusara *or* rehusase
(tú)	rehúses	rehusaras *or* rehusases
(él/ella/usted)	rehúse	rehusara *or* rehusase
(nosotros/as)	rehusemos	rehusáramos *or* rehusásemos
(vosotros/as)	rehuséis	rehusarais *or* rehusaseis
(ellos/ellas/ ustedes)	rehúsen	rehusaran *or* rehusasen

IMPERATIVE

rehúsa / rehusad

Use the present subjunctive in all cases other than these tú *and* vosotros *affirmative forms.*

Remember that subject pronouns are not used very often in Spanish.

reír (to laugh)

	PRESENT		PRESENT PERFECT
(yo)	río		he reído
(tú)	ríes		has reído
(él/ella/usted)	ríe		ha reído
(nosotros/as)	reímos		hemos reído
(vosotros/as)	reís		habéis reído
(ellos/ellas/ ustedes)	ríen		han reído

	PRETERITE		IMPERFECT
(yo)	reí		reía
(tú)	reíste		reías
(él/ella/usted)	rió		reía
(nosotros/as)	reímos		reíamos
(vosotros/as)	reísteis		reíais
(ellos/ellas/ ustedes)	rieron		reían

GERUND

riendo

PAST PARTICIPLE

reído

EXAMPLE PHRASES

Se echó a **reír**. She burst out laughing.

Se ríe de todo. She doesn't take anything seriously.

¿De qué **te ríes**? What are you laughing at?

Siempre **están riéndose** en clase. They're always laughing in class.

Me reía mucho con él. I always had a good laugh with him.

Remember that subject pronouns are not used very often in Spanish.

reír

	FUTURE	CONDITIONAL
(yo)	reiré	reiría
(tú)	reirás	reirías
(él/ella/usted)	reirá	reiría
(nosotros/as)	reiremos	reiríamos
(vosotros/as)	reiréis	reiríais
(ellos/ellas/ ustedes)	reirán	reirían

	PRESENT SUBJUNCTIVE	IMPERFECT SUBJUNCTIVE
(yo)	ría	riera or riese
(tú)	rías	rieras or rieses
(él/ella/usted)	ría	riera or riese
(nosotros/as)	riamos	riéramos or riésemos
(vosotros/as)	riáis	rierais or rieseis
(ellos/ellas/ ustedes)	rían	rieran or riesen

IMPERATIVE

ríe / reíd

Use the present subjunctive in all cases other than these tú and vosotros affirmative forms.

EXAMPLE PHRASES

Te reirás cuando te lo cuente. You'll laugh when I tell you about it.

Que **se rían** lo que quieran. Let them laugh as much as they want.

No **te rías** de mí. Don't laugh at me.

¡Tú **ríete**, pero pasé muchísimo miedo! You may laugh, but I was really frightened.

Remember that subject pronouns are not used very often in Spanish.

reñir (to quarrel, to argue)

	PRESENT	PRESENT PERFECT
(yo)	riño	he reñido
(tú)	riñes	has reñido
(él/ella/usted)	riñe	ha reñido
(nosotros/as)	reñimos	hemos reñido
(vosotros/as)	reñís	habéis reñido
(ellos/ellas/ ustedes)	riñen	han reñido

	PRETERITE	IMPERFECT
(yo)	reñí	reñía
(tú)	reñiste	reñías
(él/ella/usted)	riñó	reñía
(nosotros/as)	reñimos	reñíamos
(vosotros/as)	reñisteis	reñíais
(ellos/ellas/ ustedes)	riñeron	reñían

GERUND

riñendo

PAST PARTICIPLE

reñido

EXAMPLE PHRASES

Se pasan el día entero **riñendo**. They spend the whole day quarreling.

Reñimos por una tontería. We argued over something stupid.

Remember that subject pronouns are not used very often in Spanish.

reñir

	FUTURE	**CONDITIONAL**
(yo)	reñiré	reñiría
(tú)	reñirás	reñirías
(él/ella/usted)	reñirá	reñiría
(nosotros/as)	reñiremos	reñiríamos
(vosotros/as)	reñiréis	reñiríais
(ellos/ellas/ustedes)	reñirán	reñirían

	PRESENT SUBJUNCTIVE	**IMPERFECT SUBJUNCTIVE**
(yo)	riña	riñera *or* riñese
(tú)	riñas	riñeras *or* riñeses
(él/ella/usted)	riña	riñera *or* riñese
(nosotros/as)	riñamos	riñéramos *or* riñésemos
(vosotros/as)	riñáis	riñerais *or* riñeseis
(ellos/ellas/ustedes)	riñan	riñeran *or* riñesen

IMPERATIVE

riñe / reñid

Use the present subjunctive in all cases other than these tú and vosotros affirmative forms.

EXAMPLE PHRASES

¡No **riñán** más! Stop fighting!

Remember that subject pronouns are not used very often in Spanish.

repetir (to repeat)

	PRESENT	PRESENT PERFECT
(yo)	repito	he repetido
(tú)	repites	has repetido
(él/ella/usted)	repite	ha repetido
(nosotros/as)	repetimos	hemos repetido
(vosotros/as)	repetís	habéis repetido
(ellos/ellas/ ustedes)	repiten	han repetido

	PRETERITE	IMPERFECT
(yo)	repetí	repetía
(tú)	repetiste	repetías
(él/ella/usted)	repitió	repetía
(nosotros/as)	repetimos	repetíamos
(vosotros/as)	repetisteis	repetíais
(ellos/ellas/ ustedes)	repitieron	repetían

GERUND	PAST PARTICIPLE
repitiendo	repetido

EXAMPLE PHRASES

¿Podría **repetir**lo, por favor? Could you repeat that, please?

Le **repito** que es imposible. I repeat that it is impossible.

Se lo **he repetido** mil veces, pero no escucha. I've told him hundreds of times but he won't listen.

Repetía una y otra vez que era inocente. He kept repeating that he was innocent.

Remember that subject pronouns are not used very often in Spanish.

repetir

	FUTURE	CONDITIONAL
(yo)	repetiré	repetiría
(tú)	repetirás	repetirías
(él/ella/usted)	repetirá	repetiría
(nosotros/as)	repetiremos	repetiríamos
(vosotros/as)	repetiréis	repetiríais
(ellos/ellas/ ustedes)	repetirán	repetirían

	PRESENT SUBJUNCTIVE	IMPERFECT SUBJUNCTIVE
(yo)	repita	repitiera or repitiese
(tú)	repitas	repitieras or repitieses
(él/ella/usted)	repita	repitiera or repitiese
(nosotros/as)	repitamos	repitiéramos or repitiésemos
(vosotros/as)	repitáis	repitierais or repitieseis
(ellos/ellas/ ustedes)	repitan	repitieran or repitiesen

IMPERATIVE

repite / repetid

Use the present subjunctive in all cases other than these tú and vosotros affirmative forms.

EXAMPLE PHRASES

Espero que no se **repita**. I hope this won't happen again.

Repitan el ejercicio. Repeat the exercise.

Remember that subject pronouns are not used very often in Spanish.

resolver (to solve)

	PRESENT		PRESENT PERFECT
(yo)	resuelvo		he resuelto
(tú)	resuelves		has resuelto
(él/ella/usted)	resuelve		ha resuelto
(nosotros/as)	resolvemos		hemos resuelto
(vosotros/as)	resolvéis		habéis resuelto
(ellos/ellas/ ustedes)	resuelven		han resuelto

	PRETERITE		IMPERFECT
(yo)	resolví		resolvía
(tú)	resolviste		resolvías
(él/ella/usted)	resolvió		resolvía
(nosotros/as)	resolvimos		resolvíamos
(vosotros/as)	resolvisteis		resolvíais
(ellos/ellas/ ustedes)	resolvieron		resolvían

GERUND

resolviendo

PAST PARTICIPLE

resuelto

EXAMPLE PHRASES

Trataré de **resolver** tus dudas. I'll try to answer your questions.

Enojarse no **resuelve** nada. Getting angry doesn't help at all.

Resolvimos el problema entre todos. We solved the problem together.

Remember that subject pronouns are not used very often in Spanish.

resolver

	FUTURE	CONDITIONAL
(yo)	resolveré	resolvería
(tú)	resolverás	resolverías
(él/ella/usted)	resolverá	resolvería
(nosotros/as)	resolveremos	resolveríamos
(vosotros/as)	resolveréis	resolveríais
(ellos/ellas/ustedes)	resolverán	resolverían

	PRESENT SUBJUNCTIVE	IMPERFECT SUBJUNCTIVE
(yo)	resuelva	resolviera or resolviese
(tú)	resuelvas	resolvieras or resolvieses
(él/ella/usted)	resuelva	resolviera or resolviese
(nosotros/as)	resolvamos	resolviéramos or resolviésemos
(vosotros/as)	resolváis	resolvierais or resolvieseis
(ellos/ellas/ustedes)	resuelvan	resolvieran or resolviesen

IMPERATIVE

resuelve / resolved

Use the present subjunctive in all cases other than these tú and vosotros affirmative forms.

EXAMPLE PHRASES

No te preocupes, ya lo **resolveremos**. Don't worry, we'll sort it out.

Yo lo **resolvería** de otra forma. I'd sort it out another way.

Hasta que no lo **resuelva** no descansaré. I won't rest until I've sorted it out.

Remember that subject pronouns are not used very often in Spanish.

reunir (to put together, to gather)

	PRESENT	PRESENT PERFECT
(yo)	reúno	he reunido
(tú)	reúnes	has reunido
(él/ella/usted)	reúne	ha reunido
(nosotros/as)	reunimos	hemos reunido
(vosotros/as)	reunís	habéis reunido
(ellos/ellas/ ustedes)	reúnen	han reunido

	PRETERITE	IMPERFECT
(yo)	reuní	reunía
(tú)	reuniste	reunías
(él/ella/usted)	reunió	reunía
(nosotros/as)	reunimos	reuníamos
(vosotros/as)	reunisteis	reuníais
(ellos/ellas/ ustedes)	reunieron	reunían

GERUND

reuniendo

PAST PARTICIPLE

reunido

EXAMPLE PHRASES

Hemos conseguido **reunir** suficiente dinero. We've managed to raise enough money.

Hace tiempo que no **me reúno** con ellos. I haven't seen them in ages.

Reunió a todos para comunicarles la noticia. He called them all together to tell them the news.

No **reunía** los requisitos. She didn't satisfy the requirements.

Remember that subject pronouns are not used very often in Spanish.

reunir

	FUTURE	**CONDITIONAL**
(yo)	reuniré	reuniría
(tú)	reunirás	reunirías
(él/ella/usted)	reunirá	reuniría
(nosotros/as)	reuniremos	reuniríamos
(vosotros/as)	reuniréis	reuniríais
(ellos/ellas/ ustedes)	reunirán	reunirían

	PRESENT SUBJUNCTIVE	**IMPERFECT SUBJUNCTIVE**
(yo)	reúna	reuniera or reuniese
(tú)	reúnas	reunieras or reunieses
(él/ella/usted)	reúna	reuniera or reuniese
(nosotros/as)	reunamos	reuniéramos or reuniésemos
(vosotros/as)	reunáis	reunierais or reunieseis
(ellos/ellas/ ustedes)	reúnan	reunieran or reuniesen

IMPERATIVE

reúne / reunid

Use the present subjunctive in all cases other than these tú and vosotros affirmative forms.

EXAMPLE PHRASES

Se reunirán el viernes. They'll meet on Friday.

Necesito encontrar un local que **reúna** las condiciones. I need to find premises that will meet the requirements.

Consiguió que su familia **se reuniera** tras una larga separación. She managed to get her family back together again after a long separation.

Remember that subject pronouns are not used very often in Spanish.

rogar (to beg, to pray)

	PRESENT	**PRESENT PERFECT**
(yo)	ruego	he rogado
(tú)	ruegas	has rogado
(él/ella/usted)	ruega	ha rogado
(nosotros/as)	rogamos	hemos rogado
(vosotros/as)	rogáis	habéis rogado
(ellos/ellas/ ustedes)	ruegan	han rogado

	PRETERITE	**IMPERFECT**
(yo)	rogué	rogaba
(tú)	rogaste	rogabas
(él/ella/usted)	rogó	rogaba
(nosotros/as)	rogamos	rogábamos
(vosotros/as)	rogasteis	rogabais
(ellos/ellas/ ustedes)	rogaron	rogaban

GERUND
rogando

PAST PARTICIPLE
rogado

EXAMPLE PHRASES

Les **rogamos** acepten nuestras disculpas. Please accept our apologies.

Te **ruego** que me lo devuelvas. Please give it back to me.

"Se **ruega** no fumar" "Please do not smoke"

Me **rogó** que lo perdonara. He begged me to forgive him.

Le **rogaba** a Dios que se curara. I prayed to God to make him better.

Remember that subject pronouns are not used very often in Spanish.

rogar

	FUTURE	**CONDITIONAL**
(yo)	rogaré	rogaría
(tú)	rogarás	rogarías
(él/ella/usted)	rogará	rogaría
(nosotros/as)	rogaremos	rogaríamos
(vosotros/as)	rogaréis	rogaríais
(ellos/ellas/ ustedes)	rogarán	rogarían

	PRESENT SUBJUNCTIVE	**IMPERFECT SUBJUNCTIVE**
(yo)	ruegue	rogara *or* rogase
(tú)	ruegues	rogaras *or* rogases
(él/ella/usted)	ruegue	rogara *or* rogase
(nosotros/as)	roguemos	rogáramos *or* rogásemos
(vosotros/as)	roguéis	rogarais *or* rogaseis
(ellos/ellas/ ustedes)	rueguen	rogaran *or* rogasen

IMPERATIVE

ruega / rogad

Use the present subjunctive in all cases other than these tú and vosotros affirmative forms.

EXAMPLE PHRASES

Ruega por mí. Pray for me.

Remember that subject pronouns are not used very often in Spanish.

romper (to break)

	PRESENT	PRESENT PERFECT
(yo)	rompo	he roto
(tú)	rompes	has roto
(él/ella/usted)	rompe	ha roto
(nosotros/as)	rompemos	hemos roto
(vosotros/as)	rompéis	habéis roto
(ellos/ellas/ ustedes)	rompen	han roto

	PRETERITE	IMPERFECT
(yo)	rompí	rompía
(tú)	rompiste	rompías
(él/ella/usted)	rompió	rompía
(nosotros/as)	rompimos	rompíamos
(vosotros/as)	rompisteis	rompíais
(ellos/ellas/ ustedes)	rompieron	rompían

GERUND	PAST PARTICIPLE
rompiendo	roto

EXAMPLE PHRASES

La cuerda **se** va a **romper**. The rope is going to snap.

Siempre **están rompiendo** cosas. They're always breaking things.

Se había roto una taza. A cup had gotten broken.

Se rompió el jarrón. The vase broke.

Remember that subject pronouns are not used very often in Spanish.

romper

	FUTURE	CONDITIONAL
(yo)	romperé	rompería
(tú)	romperás	romperías
(él/ella/usted)	romperá	rompería
(nosotros/as)	romperemos	romperíamos
(vosotros/as)	romperéis	romperíais
(ellos/ellas/ ustedes)	romperán	romperían

	PRESENT SUBJUNCTIVE	IMPERFECT SUBJUNCTIVE
(yo)	rompa	rompiera or rompiese
(tú)	rompas	rompieras or rompieses
(él/ella/usted)	rompa	rompiera or rompiese
(nosotros/as)	rompamos	rompiéramos or rompiésemos
(vosotros/as)	rompáis	rompierais or rompieseis
(ellos/ellas/ ustedes)	rompan	rompieran or rompiesen

IMPERATIVE

rompe / romped

Use the present subjunctive in all cases other than these tú and vosotros affirmative forms.

EXAMPLE PHRASES

Yo nunca **rompería** una promesa. I'd never break a promise.

Si lo **rompiera**, tendría que pagarlo. If you broke it, you'd have to pay for it.

Cuidado, no lo **rompas**. Careful you don't break it.

Remember that subject pronouns are not used very often in Spanish.

saber (to know)

	PRESENT	**PRESENT PERFECT**
(yo)	sé	he sabido
(tú)	sabes	has sabido
(él/ella/usted)	sabe	ha sabido
(nosotros/as)	sabemos	hemos sabido
(vosotros/as)	sabéis	habéis sabido
(ellos/ellas/ ustedes)	saben	han sabido

	PRETERITE	**IMPERFECT**
(yo)	supe	sabía
(tú)	supiste	sabías
(él/ella/usted)	supo	sabía
(nosotros/as)	supimos	sabíamos
(vosotros/as)	supisteis	sabíais
(ellos/ellas/ ustedes)	supieron	sabían

GERUND

sabiendo

PAST PARTICIPLE

sabido

EXAMPLE PHRASES

No lo **sé**. I don't know.

¿**Sabes** una cosa? Do you know what?

¿Cuándo lo **supiste**? When did you find out?

No **supe** qué responder. I didn't know how to answer.

Pensaba que lo **sabías**. I thought you knew.

Remember that subject pronouns are not used very often in Spanish.

saber

	FUTURE	CONDITIONAL
(yo)	sabré	sabría
(tú)	sabrás	sabrías
(él/ella/usted)	sabrá	sabría
(nosotros/as)	sabremos	sabríamos
(vosotros/as)	sabréis	sabríais
(ellos/ellas/ ustedes)	sabrán	sabrían

	PRESENT SUBJUNCTIVE	IMPERFECT SUBJUNCTIVE
(yo)	sepa	supiera or supiese
(tú)	sepas	supieras or supieses
(él/ella/usted)	sepa	supiera or supiese
(nosotros/as)	sepamos	supiéramos or suplésemos
(vosotros/as)	sepáis	supierais or supieseis
(ellos/ellas/ ustedes)	sepan	supieran or supiesen

IMPERATIVE

sabe / sabed

Use the present subjunctive in all cases other than these tú and vosotros affirmative forms.

EXAMPLE PHRASES

Nunca se **sabrá** quién la mató. We'll never know who killed her.

Si no le tuvieras tanto miedo al agua, ya **sabrías** nadar. If you weren't so afraid of water, you'd already be able to swim.

Que yo **sepa**, vive en París. As far as I know, she lives in Paris.

¡Si **supiéramos** al menos dónde está! If only we knew where he was!

Remember that subject pronouns are not used very often in Spanish.

sacar (to take out, to get)

	PRESENT	PRESENT PERFECT
(yo)	saco	he sacado
(tú)	sacas	has sacado
(él/ella/usted)	saca	ha sacado
(nosotros/as)	sacamos	hemos sacado
(vosotros/as)	sacáis	habéis sacado
(ellos/ellas/ ustedes)	sacan	han sacado

	PRETERITE	IMPERFECT
(yo)	saqué	sacaba
(tú)	sacaste	sacabas
(él/ella/usted)	sacó	sacaba
(nosotros/as)	sacamos	sacábamos
(vosotros/as)	sacasteis	sacabais
(ellos/ellas/ ustedes)	sacaron	sacaban

GERUND

sacando

PAST PARTICIPLE

sacado

EXAMPLE PHRASES

Voy a **sacar** la basura. I'm going to take out the trash.

¿Me **sacas** una foto? Will you take a photo of me?

Estás sacando las cosas de quicio. You're blowing things out of all proportion.

Ya **saqué** los boletos. I already bought the tickets.

¿De dónde **sacaba** tanto dinero? Where did he get so much money from?

Remember that subject pronouns are not used very often in Spanish.

sacar

	FUTURE	CONDITIONAL
(yo)	sacaré	sacaría
(tú)	sacarás	sacarías
(él/ella/usted)	sacará	sacaría
(nosotros/as)	sacaremos	sacaríamos
(vosotros/as)	sacaréis	sacaríais
(ellos/ellas/ustedes)	sacarán	sacarían

	PRESENT SUBJUNCTIVE	IMPERFECT SUBJUNCTIVE
(yo)	saque	sacara or sacase
(tú)	saques	sacaras or sacases
(él/ella/usted)	saque	sacara or sacase
(nosotros/as)	saquemos	sacáramos or sacásemos
(vosotros/as)	saquéis	sacarais or sacaseis
(ellos/ellas/ustedes)	saquen	sacaran or sacasen

IMPERATIVE

saca / sacad

Use the present subjunctive in all cases other than these tú and vosotros affirmative forms.

EXAMPLE PHRASES

Quiero que **saques** esa bicicleta de casa inmediatamente. I want you to get that bike out of the house immediately.

No **saques** la cabeza por la ventanilla. Don't lean out of the window.

Remember that subject pronouns are not used very often in Spanish.

salir (to go out, to work out)

	PRESENT		PRESENT PERFECT
(yo)	salgo		he salido
(tú)	sales		has salido
(él/ella/usted)	sale		ha salido
(nosotros/as)	salimos		hemos salido
(vosotros/as)	salís		habéis salido
(ellos/ellas/ ustedes)	salen		han salido

	PRETERITE		IMPERFECT
(yo)	salí		salía
(tú)	saliste		salías
(él/ella/usted)	salió		salía
(nosotros/as)	salimos		salíamos
(vosotros/as)	salisteis		salíais
(ellos/ellas/ ustedes)	salieron		salían

GERUND

saliendo

PAST PARTICIPLE

salido

EXAMPLE PHRASES

Hace tiempo que no **salimos**. We haven't been out for a while.

Está **saliendo** con un compañero de trabajo. She's dating a work colleague.

Su foto **salió** en todos los periódicos. Her picture appeared in all the newspapers.

Salía muy tarde de trabajar. He used to finish work very late.

Remember that subject pronouns are not used very often in Spanish.

salir

	FUTURE	CONDITIONAL
(yo)	**saldré**	**saldría**
(tú)	**saldrás**	**saldrías**
(él/ella/usted)	**saldrá**	**saldría**
(nosotros/as)	**saldremos**	**saldríamos**
(vosotros/as)	**saldréis**	**saldríais**
(ellos/ellas/ustedes)	**saldrán**	**saldrían**

	PRESENT SUBJUNCTIVE	IMPERFECT SUBJUNCTIVE
(yo)	**salga**	**saliera** or **saliese**
(tú)	**salgas**	**salieras** or **salieses**
(él/ella/usted)	**salga**	**saliera** or **saliese**
(nosotros/as)	**salgamos**	**saliéramos** or **saliésemos**
(vosotros/as)	**salgáis**	**salierais** or **salieseis**
(ellos/ellas/ustedes)	**salgan**	**salieran** or **saliesen**

IMPERATIVE

sal / salid

Use the present subjunctive in all cases other than these tú and vosotros affirmative forms.

EXAMPLE PHRASES

Te dije que **saldría** muy caro. I told you it would wind up being very expensive.

Espero que todo **salga** bien. I hope everything works out all right.

Si **saliera** elegido... If I were elected...

Por favor, **salgan** por la puerta de atrás. Please leave through the back door.

Remember that subject pronouns are not used very often in Spanish.

satisfacer (to satisfy)

	PRESENT	**PRESENT PERFECT**
(yo)	satisfago	he satisfecho
(tú)	satisfaces	has satisfecho
(él/ella/usted)	satisface	ha satisfecho
(nosotros/as)	satisfacemos	hemos satisfecho
(vosotros/as)	satisfacéis	habéis satisfecho
(ellos/ellas/ ustedes)	satisfacen	han satisfecho

	PRETERITE	**IMPERFECT**
(yo)	satisfice	satisfacía
(tú)	satisficiste	satisfacías
(él/ella/usted)	satisfizo	satisfacía
(nosotros/as)	satisficimos	satisfacíamos
(vosotros/as)	satisficisteis	satisfacíais
(ellos/ellas/ ustedes)	satisficieron	satisfacían

GERUND	**PAST PARTICIPLE**
satisfaciendo	satisfecho

EXAMPLE PHRASES

No me **satisface** nada el resultado. I'm not at all satisfied with the result.

Eso **satisfizo** mi curiosidad. That satisfied my curiosity.

Aquella vida **satisfacía** todas mis necesidades. That lifestyle satisfied all my needs.

Remember that subject pronouns are not used very often in Spanish.

satisfacer

	FUTURE	**CONDITIONAL**
(yo)	satisfaré	satisfaría
(tú)	satisfarás	satisfarías
(él/ella/usted)	satisfará	satisfaría
(nosotros/as)	satisfaremos	satisfaríamos
(vosotros/as)	satisfaréis	satisfaríais
(ellos/ellas/ ustedes)	satisfarán	satisfarían

	PRESENT SUBJUNCTIVE	**IMPERFECT SUBJUNCTIVE**
(yo)	satisfaga	satisficiera *or* satisficiese
(tú)	satisfagas	satisficieras *or* satisficieses
(él/ella/usted)	satisfaga	satisficiera *or* satisficiese
(nosotros/as)	satisfagamos	satisficiéramos *or* satisficiésemos
(vosotros/as)	satisfagáis	satisficierais *or* satisficieseis
(ellos/ellas/ ustedes)	satisfagan	satisficieran *or* satisficiesen

IMPERATIVE

satisfaz *or* satisface / satisfaced

Use the present subjunctive in all cases other than these tú *and* vosotros *affirmative forms.*

EXAMPLE PHRASES

Le **satisfará** saber que hemos cumplido nuestros objetivos. You'll be happy to know that we have achieved our objectives.

Tengo que aceptarlo aunque no me **satisfaga**. I have to accept it even though I'm not happy about it.

Remember that subject pronouns are not used very often in Spanish.

seguir (to follow, to go on)

	PRESENT	PRESENT PERFECT
(yo)	sigo	he seguido
(tú)	sigues	has seguido
(él/ella/usted)	sigue	ha seguido
(nosotros/as)	seguimos	hemos seguido
(vosotros/as)	seguís	habéis seguido
(ellos/ellas/ustedes)	siguen	han seguido

	PRETERITE	IMPERFECT
(yo)	seguí	seguía
(tú)	seguiste	seguías
(él/ella/usted)	siguió	seguía
(nosotros/as)	seguimos	seguíamos
(vosotros/as)	seguisteis	seguíais
(ellos/ellas/ustedes)	siguieron	seguían

GERUND

siguiendo

PAST PARTICIPLE

seguido

EXAMPLE PHRASES

Si **sigues** así, acabarás mal. If you go on like this you'll come to a bad end.

Siguió cantando como si nada. He went on singing as if there was nothing wrong.

Los **seguimos** mucho rato. We followed them for a long time.

Nos **habían seguido**. They had followed us.

Remember that subject pronouns are not used very often in Spanish.

seguir

	FUTURE	CONDITIONAL
(yo)	seguiré	seguiría
(tú)	seguirás	seguirías
(él/ella/usted)	seguirá	seguiría
(nosotros/as)	seguiremos	seguiríamos
(vosotros/as)	seguiréis	seguiríais
(ellos/ellas/ ustedes)	seguirán	seguirían

	PRESENT SUBJUNCTIVE	IMPERFECT SUBJUNCTIVE
(yo)	siga	siguiera *or* siguiese
(tú)	sigas	siguieras *or* siguieses
(él/ella/usted)	siga	siguiera *or* siguiese
(nosotros/as)	sigamos	siguiéramos *or* siguiésemos
(vosotros/as)	sigáis	siguierais *or* siguieseis
(ellos/ellas/ ustedes)	sigan	siguieran *or* siguiesen

IMPERATIVE

sigue / seguid

Use the present subjunctive in all cases other than these tú *and* vosotros *affirmative forms.*

EXAMPLE PHRASES

Nos seguiremos viendo. We will go on seeing each other.

Quiero que **sigas** estudiando. I want you to go on with your studies.

Si **siguieras** mis consejos, te iría muchísimo mejor. You'd be much better off if you followed my advice.

Siga por esta calle hasta el final. Go straight till you get to the end of the street.

Remember that subject pronouns are not used very often in Spanish.

sentir (to feel, to be sorry)

	PRESENT	PRESENT PERFECT
(yo)	siento	he sentido
(tú)	sientes	has sentido
(él/ella/usted)	siente	ha sentido
(nosotros/as)	sentimos	hemos sentido
(vosotros/as)	sentís	habéis sentido
(ellos/ellas/ustedes)	sienten	han sentido

	PRETERITE	IMPERFECT
(yo)	sentí	sentía
(tú)	sentiste	sentías
(él/ella/usted)	sintió	sentía
(nosotros/as)	sentimos	sentíamos
(vosotros/as)	sentisteis	sentíais
(ellos/ellas/ustedes)	sintieron	sentían

GERUND

sintiendo

PAST PARTICIPLE

sentido

EXAMPLE PHRASES

Te vas a **sentir** sola. You'll feel lonely.

Siento mucho lo que pasó. I'm really sorry about what happened.

Sintió mucho la muerte de su padre. He was greatly affected by his father's death.

No **sentí** nada. I didn't feel a thing.

Me **sentía** muy mal. I didn't feel well at all.

Remember that subject pronouns are not used very often in Spanish.

sentir

	FUTURE	CONDITIONAL
(yo)	sentiré	sentiría
(tú)	sentirás	sentirías
(él/ella/usted)	sentirá	sentiría
(nosotros/as)	sentiremos	sentiríamos
(vosotros/as)	sentiréis	sentiríais
(ellos/ellas/ ustedes)	sentirán	sentirían

	PRESENT SUBJUNCTIVE	IMPERFECT SUBJUNCTIVE
(yo)	sienta	sintiera *or* sintiese
(tú)	sientas	sintieras *or* sintieses
(él/ella/usted)	sienta	sintiera *or* sintiese
(nosotros/as)	sintamos	sintiéramos *or* sintiésemos
(vosotros/as)	sintáis	sintierais *or* sintieseis
(ellos/ellas/ ustedes)	sientan	sintieran *or* sintiesen

IMPERATIVE

siente / sentid

Use the present subjunctive in all cases other than these tú *and* vosotros *affirmative forms.*

EXAMPLE PHRASES

Al principio **te sentirás** un poco raro. You'll feel a bit strange at first.

Yo **sentiría** mucho que se fuera de la empresa. I'd be really sorry if you left the firm.

No creo que lo **sienta**. I don't think she's sorry.

Sería mucho más preocupante si no **sintiera** la pierna. It would be much more worrying if he couldn't feel his leg.

Remember that subject pronouns are not used very often in Spanish.

ser (to be)

	PRESENT		PRESENT PERFECT
(yo)	soy		he sido
(tú)	eres		has sido
(él/ella/usted)	es		ha sido
(nosotros/as)	somos		hemos sido
(vosotros/as)	sois		habéis sido
(ellos/ellas/ ustedes)	son		han sido

	PRETERITE		IMPERFECT
(yo)	fui		era
(tú)	fuiste		eras
(él/ella/usted)	fue		era
(nosotros/as)	fuimos		éramos
(vosotros/as)	fuisteis		erais
(ellos/ellas/ ustedes)	fueron		eran

GERUND

siendo

PAST PARTICIPLE

sido

EXAMPLE PHRASES

Soy colombiano. I'm Colombian.

Fue un duro golpe. It was a major blow.

¿**Fuiste** tú el que llamó? Was it you who called?

Era de noche. It was dark.

Había sido sacerdote. He had been a priest.

Remember that subject pronouns are not used very often in Spanish.

ser

	FUTURE	**CONDITIONAL**
(yo)	seré	sería
(tú)	serás	serías
(él/ella/usted)	será	sería
(nosotros/as)	seremos	seríamos
(vosotros/as)	seréis	seríais
(ellos/ellas/ ustedes)	serán	serían

	PRESENT SUBJUNCTIVE	**IMPERFECT SUBJUNCTIVE**
(yo)	sea	fuera or fuese
(tú)	seas	fueras or fueses
(él/ella/usted)	sea	fuera or fuese
(nosotros/as)	seamos	fuéramos or fuésemos
(vosotros/as)	seáis	fuerais or fueseis
(ellos/ellas/ ustedes)	sean	fueran or fuesen

IMPERATIVE

sé / sed

Use the present subjunctive in all cases other than these tú *and* vosotros *affirmative forms.*

EXAMPLE PHRASES

Será de Joaquín. Maybe it's Joaquín's.

Eso **sería** maravilloso. That would be wonderful.

O **sea**, que no vienes. So you're not coming.

No **seas** tan perfeccionista. Don't be such a perfectionist.

¡**Sean** buenos! Behave yourselves!

Remember that subject pronouns are not used very often in Spanish.

soler (to be wont to)

	PRESENT	PRESENT PERFECT
(yo)	suelo	*not used*
(tú)	sueles	
(él/ella/usted)	suele	
(nosotros/as)	solemos	
(vosotros/as)	soléis	
(ellos/ellas/ ustedes)	suelen	

	PRETERITE	IMPERFECT
(yo)	*not used*	solía
(tú)		solías
(él/ella/usted)		solía
(nosotros/as)		solíamos
(vosotros/as)		solíais
(ellos/ellas/ ustedes)		solían

GERUND	PAST PARTICIPLE
soliendo	*not used*

EXAMPLE PHRASES

Suele salir a las ocho. **He usually leaves at eight.**

Solíamos ir todos los años a la playa. **We used to go to the beach every year.**

Remember that subject pronouns are not used very often in Spanish.

soler

	FUTURE	**CONDITIONAL**
(yo)	*not used*	*not used*
(tú)		
(él/ella/usted)		
(nosotros/as)		
(vosotros/as)		
(ellos/ellas/ ustedes)		

	PRESENT SUBJUNCTIVE	**IMPERFECT SUBJUNCTIVE**
(yo)	suela	soliera *or* soliese
(tú)	suelas	solieras *or* solieses
(él/ella/usted)	suela	soliera *or* soliese
(nosotros/as)	solamos	soliéramos *or* soliésemos
(vosotros/as)	soláis	solierais *or* solieseis
(ellos/ellas/ ustedes)	suelan	solieran *or* soliesen

IMPERATIVE

not used

Remember that subject pronouns are not used very often in Spanish.

soltar (to let go of, to release)

	PRESENT	PRESENT PERFECT
(yo)	suelto	he soltado
(tú)	sueltas	has soltado
(él/ella/usted)	suelta	ha soltado
(nosotros/as)	soltamos	hemos soltado
(vosotros/as)	soltáis	habéis soltado
(ellos/ellas/ustedes)	sueltan	han soltado

	PRETERITE	IMPERFECT
(yo)	solté	soltaba
(tú)	soltaste	soltabas
(él/ella/usted)	soltó	soltaba
(nosotros/as)	soltamos	soltábamos
(vosotros/as)	soltasteis	soltabais
(ellos/ellas/ustedes)	soltaron	soltaban

GERUND

soltando

PAST PARTICIPLE

soltado

EXAMPLE PHRASES

Al final logró **soltarse**. Eventually she managed to break free.

¿Por qué no **te sueltas** el pelo? Why don't you wear your hair down?

Habían soltado a los rehenes. They had released the hostages.

Soltó una carcajada. He burst out laughing.

Remember that subject pronouns are not used very often in Spanish.

soltar

	FUTURE	**CONDITIONAL**
(yo)	soltaré	soltaría
(tú)	soltarás	soltarías
(él/ella/usted)	soltará	soltaría
(nosotros/as)	soltaremos	soltaríamos
(vosotros/as)	soltaréis	soltaríais
(ellos/ellas/ ustedes)	soltarán	soltarían

	PRESENT SUBJUNCTIVE	**IMPERFECT SUBJUNCTIVE**
(yo)	suelte	soltara *or* soltase
(tú)	sueltes	soltaras *or* soltases
(él/ella/usted)	suelte	soltara *or* soltase
(nosotros/as)	soltemos	soltáramos *or* soltásemos
(vosotros/as)	soltéis	soltarais *or* soltaseis
(ellos/ellas/ ustedes)	suelten	soltaran *or* soltasen

IMPERATIVE

suelta / soltad

Use the present subjunctive in all cases other than these tú *and* vosotros *affirmative forms.*

EXAMPLE PHRASES

Te **soltaré** el brazo si me dices dónde está. I'll let go of your arm if you tell me where he is.

Te dije que lo **soltaras**. I told you to let it go.

No **sueltes** la cuerda. Don't let go of the rope.

¡**Suéltame**! Let me go!

Remember that subject pronouns are not used very often in Spanish.

sonar (to sound, to ring)

	PRESENT	PRESENT PERFECT
(yo)	sueno	he sonado
(tú)	suenas	has sonado
(él/ella/usted)	suena	ha sonado
(nosotros/as)	sonamos	hemos sonado
(vosotros/as)	sonáis	habéis sonado
(ellos/ellas/ ustedes)	suenan	han sonado

	PRETERITE	IMPERFECT
(yo)	soné	sonaba
(tú)	sonaste	sonabas
(él/ella/usted)	sonó	sonaba
(nosotros/as)	sonamos	sonábamos
(vosotros/as)	sonasteis	sonabais
(ellos/ellas/ ustedes)	sonaron	sonaban

GERUND	PAST PARTICIPLE
sonando	sonado

EXAMPLE PHRASES

¿Te **suena** su nombre? Does her name sound familiar?

Justo en ese momento **sonó** el timbre. Just then the bell rang.

Sonabas un poco triste por teléfono. You sounded a bit sad on the phone.

Estaba sonando el teléfono. The phone was ringing.

Remember that subject pronouns are not used very often in Spanish.

sonar

	FUTURE	**CONDITIONAL**
(yo)	sonaré	sonaría
(tú)	sonarás	sonarías
(él/ella/usted)	sonará	sonaría
(nosotros/as)	sonaremos	sonaríamos
(vosotros/as)	sonaréis	sonaríais
(ellos/ellas/ ustedes)	sonarán	sonarían

	PRESENT SUBJUNCTIVE	**IMPERFECT SUBJUNCTIVE**
(yo)	suene	sonara or sonase
(tú)	suenes	sonaras or sonases
(él/ella/usted)	suene	sonara or sonase
(nosotros/as)	sonemos	sonáramos or sonásemos
(vosotros/as)	sonéis	sonarais or sonaseis
(ellos/ellas/ ustedes)	suenen	sonaran or sonasen

IMPERATIVE

suena / sonad

Use the present subjunctive in all cases other than these tú and vosotros affirmative forms.

EXAMPLE PHRASES

Hay que esperar a que **suene** un pitido. We have to wait until we hear a beep.

¡**Suénate** la nariz! Blow your nose!

Remember that subject pronouns are not used very often in Spanish.

temer (to be afraid)

	PRESENT	PRESENT PERFECT
(yo)	temo	he temido
(tú)	temes	has temido
(él/ella/usted)	teme	ha temido
(nosotros/as)	tememos	hemos temido
(vosotros/as)	teméis	habéis temido
(ellos/ellas/ustedes)	temen	han temido

	PRETERITE	IMPERFECT
(yo)	temí	temía
(tú)	temiste	temías
(él/ella/usted)	temío	temía
(nosotros/as)	temimos	temíamos
(vosotros/as)	temisteis	temíais
(ellos/ellas/ustedes)	temieron	temían

GERUND	PAST PARTICIPLE
temiendo	temido

EXAMPLE PHRASES

No le **teme** a nadie. He's not afraid of anyone.

Me temo que no. I'm afraid not.

Se temen lo peor. They fear the worst.

Empezó a llover. —**Me** lo **temía**. "It's started raining." – "I was afraid it would."

Temían por su seguridad. They feared for their safety.

Remember that subject pronouns are not used very often in Spanish.

temer

	FUTURE	CONDITIONAL
(yo)	temeré	temería
(tú)	temerás	temerías
(él/ella/usted)	temerá	temería
(nosotros/as)	temeremos	temeríamos
(vosotros/as)	temeréis	temeríais
(ellos/ellas/ ustedes)	temerán	temerían

	PRESENT SUBJUNCTIVE	IMPERFECT SUBJUNCTIVE
(yo)	tema	temiera *or* temiese
(tú)	temas	temieras *or* temieses
(él/ella/usted)	tema	temiera *or* temiese
(nosotros/as)	temamos	temiéramos *or* temiésemos
(vosotros/as)	temáis	temierais *or* temieseis
(ellos/ellas/ ustedes)	teman	temieran *or* temiesen

IMPERATIVE

teme / temed

Use the present subjunctive in all cases other than these tú and vosotros affirmative forms.

EXAMPLE PHRASES

No **temas.** Don't be afraid.

Remember that subject pronouns are not used very often in Spanish.

tener (to have)

	PRESENT		PRESENT PERFECT
(yo)	tengo		he tenido
(tú)	tienes		has tenido
(él/ella/usted)	tiene		ha tenido
(nosotros/as)	tenemos		hemos tenido
(vosotros/as)	tenéis		habéis tenido
(ellos/ellas/ ustedes)	tienen		ha tenido

	PRETERITE		IMPERFECT
(yo)	tuve		tenía
(tú)	tuviste		tenías
(él/ella/usted)	tuvo		tenía
(nosotros/as)	tuvimos		teníamos
(vosotros/as)	tuvisteis		teníais
(ellos/ellas/ ustedes)	tuvieron .		tenían

GERUND

teniendo

PAST PARTICIPLE

tenido

EXAMPLE PHRASES

Tengo dos hermanos. I have two brothers.

Había tenido una gripa muy fuerte. She'd had a very bad flu.

Tuvimos que irnos. We had to leave.

No **tenía** suficiente dinero. She didn't have enough money.

Estamos teniendo muchos problemas. We're having a lot of problems.

Remember that subject pronouns are not used very often in Spanish.

tener

	FUTURE	CONDITIONAL
(yo)	tendré	tendría
(tú)	tendrás	tendrías
(él/ella/usted)	tendrá	tendría
(nosotros/as)	tendremos	tendríamos
(vosotros/as)	tendréis	tendríais
(ellos/ellas/ ustedes)	tendrán	tendrían

	PRESENT SUBJUNCTIVE	IMPERFECT SUBJUNCTIVE
(yo)	tenga	tuviera *or* tuviese
(tú)	tengas	tuvieras *or* tuvieses
(él/ella/usted)	tenga	tuviera *or* tuviese
(nosotros/as)	tengamos	tuviéramos *or* tuviésemos
(vosotros/as)	tengáls	tuvierais *or* tuvieseis
(ellos/ellas/ ustedes)	tengan	tuvieran *or* tuviesen

IMPERATIVE

ten / tened

Use the present subjunctive in all cases other than these tú and vosotros affirmative forms.

EXAMPLE PHRASES

Tendrás que pagarlo tú. You'll have to pay for it yourself.

Tendrías que comer más. You should eat more.

No creo que **tenga** suficiente dinero. I don't think he has enough money.

Si **tuviera** tiempo, haría un curso de francés. If I had time, I'd take a French course.

Ten cuidado. Be careful.

No **tengas** miedo. Don't be afraid.

Remember that subject pronouns are not used very often in Spanish.

tocar (to touch, to play)

	PRESENT	PRESENT PERFECT
(yo)	toco	he tocado
(tú)	tocas	has tocado
(él/ella/usted)	toca	ha tocado
(nosotros/as)	tocamos	hemos tocado
(vosotros/as)	tocáis	habéis tocado
(ellos/ellas/ ustedes)	tocan	han tocado

	PRETERITE	IMPERFECT
(yo)	toqué	tocaba
(tú)	tocaste	tocabas
(él/ella/usted)	tocó	tocaba
(nosotros/as)	tocamos	tocábamos
(vosotros/as)	tocasteis	tocabais
(ellos/ellas/ ustedes)	tocaron	tocaban

GERUND	PAST PARTICIPLE
tocando	tocado

EXAMPLE PHRASES

Toca el violín. He plays the violin.

Te **toca** manejar. It's your turn to drive.

Me **tocó** el peor asiento. I ended up with the worst seat.

Me **tocaba** tirar a mí. It was my turn.

Tocaban muy bien. They played very well.

Remember that subject pronouns are not used very often in Spanish.

tocar

	FUTURE	**CONDITIONAL**
(yo)	tocaré	tocaría
(tú)	tocarás	tocarías
(él/ella/usted)	tocará	tocaría
(nosotros/as)	tocaremos	tocaríamos
(vosotros/as)	tocaréis	tocaríais
(ellos/ellas/ustedes)	tocarán	tocarían

	PRESENT SUBJUNCTIVE	**IMPERFECT SUBJUNCTIVE**
(yo)	toque	tocara *or* tocase
(tú)	toques	tocaras *or* tocases
(él/ella/usted)	toque	tocara *or* tocase
(nosotros/as)	toquemos	tocáramos *or* tocásemos
(vosotros/as)	toquéis	tocarais *or* tocaseis
(ellos/ellas/ustedes)	toquen	tocaran *or* tocasen

IMPERATIVE

toca / tocad

Use the present subjunctive in all cases other than these tú *and* vosotros *affirmative forms.*

EXAMPLE PHRASES

Sabía que me **tocaría** ir a mí. I knew I'd be the one to have to go.

No lo **toques**. Don't touch it.

Tócalo, otra vez. Play it again.

Remember that subject pronouns are not used very often in Spanish.

torcer (to twist)

	PRESENT	PRESENT PERFECT
(yo)	tuerzo	he torcido
(tú)	tuerces	has torcido
(él/ella/usted)	tuerce	ha torcido
(nosotros/as)	torcemos	hemos torcido
(vosotros/as)	torcéis	habéis torcido
(ellos/ellas/ ustedes)	tuercen	han torcido

	PRETERITE	IMPERFECT
(yo)	torcí	torcía
(tú)	torciste	torcías
(él/ella/usted)	torció	torcía
(nosotros/as)	torcimos	torcíamos
(vosotros/as)	torcisteis	torcíais
(ellos/ellas/ ustedes)	torcieron	torcían

GERUND

torciendo

PAST PARTICIPLE

torcido

EXAMPLE PHRASES

El sendero **tuerce** luego a la derecha. Later on the path curves around to the right.

Me **torció** la muñeca. He twisted my wrist.

Las cosas se empezaron a **torcer**. Things started to go wrong.

Remember that subject pronouns are not used very often in Spanish.

torcer

	FUTURE	**CONDITIONAL**
(yo)	torceré	torcería
(tú)	torcerás	torcerías
(él/ella/usted)	torcerá	torcería
(nosotros/as)	torceremos	torceríamos
(vosotros/as)	torceréis	torceríais
(ellos/ellas/ ustedes)	torcerán	torcerían

	PRESENT SUBJUNCTIVE	**IMPERFECT SUBJUNCTIVE**
(yo)	tuerza	torciera or torciese
(tú)	tuerzas	torcieras or torcieses
(él/ella/usted)	tuerza	torciera or torciese
(nosotros/as)	torzamos	torciéramos or torciésemos
(vosotros/as)	torzáis	torcierais or torcieseis
(ellos/ellas/ ustedes)	tuerzan	torcieran or torciesen

IMPERATIVE

tuerce / torced

Use the present subjunctive in all cases other than these tú and vosotros affirmative forms.

EXAMPLE PHRASES

Tuerza a la izquierda. Turn left.

Tuércelo un poco más. Twist it a little more.

Remember that subject pronouns are not used very often in Spanish.

traer (to bring)

	PRESENT		PRESENT PERFECT
(yo)	traigo		he traído
(tú)	traes		has traído
(él/ella/usted)	trae		ha traído
(nosotros/as)	traemos		hemos traído
(vosotros/as)	traéis		habéis traído
(ellos/ellas/ ustedes)	traen		han traído

	PRETERITE	IMPERFECT
(yo)	traje	traía
(tú)	trajiste	traías
(él/ella/usted)	trajo	traía
(nosotros/as)	trajimos	traíamos
(vosotros/as)	trajisteis	traíais
(ellos/ellas/ ustedes)	trajeron	traían

GERUND

trayendo

PAST PARTICIPLE

traído

EXAMPLE PHRASES

¿Me puedes **traer** una toalla? Can you bring me a towel?

Nos **está trayendo** muchos problemas. It's causing us a lot of trouble.

¿**Trajiste** lo que te pedí? Did you bring what I asked for?

Traía un vestido nuevo. She was wearing a new dress.

No **trajo** el dinero. He didn't bring the money.

Remember that subject pronouns are not used very often in Spanish.

traer

	FUTURE	**CONDITIONAL**
(yo)	traeré	traería
(tú)	traerás	traerías
(él/ella/usted)	traerá	traería
(nosotros/as)	traeremos	traeríamos
(vosotros/as)	traeréis	traeríais
(ellos/ellas/ ustedes)	traerán	traerían

	PRESENT SUBJUNCTIVE	**IMPERFECT SUBJUNCTIVE**
(yo)	traiga	trajera *or* trajese
(tú)	traigas	trajeras *or* trajeses
(él/ella/usted)	traiga	trajera *or* trajese
(nosotros/as)	traigamos	trajéramos *or* trajésemos
(vosotros/as)	traigáis	trajerais *or* trajeseis
(ellos/ellas/ ustedes)	traigan	trajeran *or* trajesen

IMPERATIVE

trae / traed

Use the present subjunctive in all cases other than these tú *and* vosotros *affirmative forms.*

EXAMPLE PHRASES

Me pregunto qué **se traerán** entre manos. I wonder what they're up to.

Dile que **traiga** a algún amigo. Tell him to bring a friend with him.

Le pedí que **trajera** las fotos. I asked her to bring the photos.

Remember that subject pronouns are not used very often in Spanish.

valer (to be worth)

	PRESENT	PRESENT PERFECT
(yo)	valgo	he valido
(tú)	vales	has valido
(él/ella/usted)	vale	ha valido
(nosotros/as)	valemos	hemos valido
(vosotros/as)	valéis	habéis valido
(ellos/ellas/ ustedes)	valen	han valido

	PRETERITE	IMPERFECT
(yo)	valí	valía
(tú)	valiste	valías
(él/ella/usted)	valió	valía
(nosotros/as)	valimos	valíamos
(vosotros/as)	valisteis	valíais
(ellos/ellas/ ustedes)	valieron	valían

GERUND

valiendo

PAST PARTICIPLE

valido

EXAMPLE PHRASES

¿Cuánto **vale** eso? How much is that?

No puede **valerse** por sí mismo. He can't look after himself.

No le **valió** de nada suplicar. Begging got her nowhere.

No **valía** la pena. It wasn't worth it.

Remember that subject pronouns are not used very often in Spanish.

valer

	FUTURE	CONDITIONAL
(yo)	valdré	valdría
(tú)	valdrás	valdrías
(él/ella/usted)	valdrá	valdría
(nosotros/as)	valdremos	valdríamos
(vosotros/as)	valdréis	valdríais
(ellos/ellas/ustedes)	valdrán	valdrían

	PRESENT SUBJUNCTIVE	IMPERFECT SUBJUNCTIVE
(yo)	valga	valiera or valiese
(tú)	valgas	valieras or valieses
(él/ella/usted)	valga	valiera or valiese
(nosotros/as)	valgamos	valiéramos or valiésemos
(vosotros/as)	valgáis	valierais or valieseis
(ellos/ellas/ustedes)	valgan	valieran or valiesen

IMPERATIVE

vale / valed

Use the present subjunctive in all cases other than these tú and vosotros affirmative forms.

EXAMPLE PHRASES

Valdrá unos 500 dólares. It must be worth around 500 dollars.

Valdría más si fuera antiguo. It would be worth more if it were an antique.

Remember that subject pronouns are not used very often in Spanish.

vencer (to win, to beat)

	PRESENT	**PRESENT PERFECT**
(yo)	venzo	he vencido
(tú)	vences	has vencido
(él/ella/usted)	vence	ha vencido
(nosotros/as)	vencemos	hemos vencido
(vosotros/as)	vencéis	habéis vencido
(ellos/ellas/ ustedes)	vencen	han vencido

	PRETERITE	**IMPERFECT**
(yo)	vencí	vencía
(tú)	venciste	vencías
(él/ella/usted)	venció	vencía
(nosotros/as)	vencimos	vencíamos
(vosotros/as)	vencisteis	vencíais
(ellos/ellas/ ustedes)	vencieron	vencían

GERUND

venciendo

PAST PARTICIPLE

vencido

EXAMPLE PHRASES

Tienes que **vencer** el miedo. You must overcome your fear.

Finalmente lo **venció** el sueño. He was finally overcome by sleep.

Lo **vencía** la curiosidad. His curiosity got the better of him.

Remember that subject pronouns are not used very often in Spanish.

vencer

	FUTURE	CONDITIONAL
(yo)	venceré	vencería
(tú)	vencerás	vencerías
(él/ella/usted)	vencerá	vencería
(nosotros/as)	venceremos	venceríamos
(vosotros/as)	venceréis	venceríais
(ellos/ellas/ ustedes)	vencerán	vencerían

	PRESENT SUBJUNCTIVE	IMPERFECT SUBJUNCTIVE
(yo)	venza	venciera *or* venciese
(tú)	venzas	vencieras *or* vencieses
(él/ella/usted)	venza	venciera *or* venciese
(nosotros/as)	venzamos	venciéramos *or* venciésemos
(vosotros/as)	venzáis	vencierais *or* vencieseis
(ellos/ellas/ ustedes)	venzan	vencieran *or* venciesen

IMPERATIVE

vence / venced

Use the present subjunctive in all cases other than these tú *and* vosotros *affirmative forms.*

EXAMPLE PHRASES

Nuestro ejército **vencerá**. Our army will be victorious.

No dejes que te **venza** la impaciencia. Don't let your impatience get the better of you.

Remember that subject pronouns are not used very often in Spanish.

venir (to come)

	PRESENT	PRESENT PERFECT
(yo)	vengo	he venido
(tú)	vienes	has venido
(él/ella/usted)	viene	ha venido
(nosotros/as)	venimos	hemos venido
(vosotros/as)	venís	habéis venido
(ellos/ellas/ ustedes)	vienen	han venido

	PRETERITE	IMPERFECT
(yo)	vine	venía
(tú)	viniste	venías
(él/ella/usted)	vino	venía
(nosotros/as)	vinimos	veníamos
(vosotros/as)	vinisteis	veníais
(ellos/ellas/ ustedes)	vinieron	venían

GERUND

viniendo

PAST PARTICIPLE

venido

EXAMPLE PHRASES

Vengo a menudo. I come here often.

La casa **se está viniendo** abajo. The house is falling apart.

Vino en taxi. He came by taxi.

Vinieron a verme al hospital. They came to see me in the hospital.

La noticia **venía** en el periódico. The news was in the paper.

Remember that subject pronouns are not used very often in Spanish.

venir

	FUTURE	**CONDITIONAL**
(yo)	vendré	vendría
(tú)	vendrás	vendrías
(él/ella/usted)	vendrá	vendría
(nosotros/as)	vendremos	vendríamos
(vosotros/as)	vendréis	vendríais
(ellos/ellas/ ustedes)	vendrán	vendrían

	PRESENT SUBJUNCTIVE	**IMPERFECT SUBJUNCTIVE**
(yo)	venga	viniera *or* viniese
(tú)	vengas	vinieras *or* vinieses
(él/ella/usted)	venga	viniera *or* viniese
(nosotros/as)	vengamos	viniéramos *or* viniésemos
(vosotros/as)	vengáis	vinierais *or* vinieseis
(ellos/ellas/ ustedes)	vengan	vinieran *or* viniesen

IMPERATIVE

ven / venid

Use the present subjunctive in all cases other than these tú and vosotros affirmative forms.

EXAMPLE PHRASES

¿Crees que **vendrá**? Do you think he'll come?

A mí me **vendría** mejor el sábado. Saturday would be better for me.

No **vengas** si no quieres. Don't come if you don't want to.

¡**Ven** aquí! Come here!

Remember that subject pronouns are not used very often in Spanish.

ver (to see)

	PRESENT		PRESENT PERFECT
(yo)	veo		he visto
(tú)	ves		has visto
(él/ella/usted)	ve		ha visto
(nosotros/as)	vemos		hemos visto
(vosotros/as)	veis		habéis visto
(ellos/ellas/ustedes)	ven		han visto

	PRETERITE		IMPERFECT
(yo)	vi		veía
(tú)	viste		veías
(él/ella/usted)	vio		veía
(nosotros/as)	vimos		veíamos
(vosotros/as)	visteis		veíais
(ellos/ellas/ustedes)	vieron		veían

GERUND

viendo

PAST PARTICIPLE

visto

EXAMPLE PHRASES

No **veo** muy bien. I can't see very well.

Están **viendo** la televisión. They're watching TV.

No la **había visto**. I hadn't seen her.

¿**Viste** lo que pasó? Did you see what happened?

Los **veía** a todos desde la ventana. I could see them all from the window.

Remember that subject pronouns are not used very often in Spanish.

ver

	FUTURE	CONDITIONAL
(yo)	veré	vería
(tú)	verás	verías
(él/ella/usted)	verá	vería
(nosotros/as)	veremos	veríamos
(vosotros/as)	veréis	veríais
(ellos/ellas/ustedes)	verán	verían

	PRESENT SUBJUNCTIVE	IMPERFECT SUBJUNCTIVE
(yo)	vea	viera or viese
(tú)	veas	vieras or vieses
(él/ella/usted)	vea	viera or viese
(nosotros/as)	veamos	viéramos or viésemos
(vosotros/as)	veáis	vierais or vieseis
(ellos/ellas/ustedes)	vean	vieran or viesen

IMPERATIVE

ve / ved

Use the present subjunctive in all cases other than these tú and vosotros affirmative forms.

EXAMPLE PHRASES

Eso ya se **verá**. We'll see.

¡Si **vieras** cómo ha cambiado todo aquello! If you could see how all that has changed!

Veamos, ¿qué le pasa? Let's see now, what's the matter?

Remember that subject pronouns are not used very often in Spanish.

verter (to pour)

	PRESENT	PRESENT PERFECT
(yo)	vierto	he vertido
(tú)	viertes	has vertido
(él/ella/usted)	vierte	ha vertido
(nosotros/as)	vertemos	hemos vertido
(vosotros/as)	vertéis	habéis vertido
(ellos/ellas/ustedes)	vierten	han vertido

	PRETERITE	IMPERFECT
(yo)	vertí	vertía
(tú)	vertiste	vertías
(él/ella/usted)	vertió	vertía
(nosotros/as)	vertimos	vertíamos
(vosotros/as)	vertisteis	vertíais
(ellos/ellas/ustedes)	vertieron	vertían

GERUND

vertiendo

PAST PARTICIPLE

vertido

EXAMPLE PHRASES

Primero **viertes** el contenido del sobre en un tazón. First you empty the contents of the package into a bowl.

Vertió un poco de leche en la cacerola. He poured some milk into the saucepan.

Se **vertían** muchos residuos radioactivos en el mar. A lot of nuclear waste was dumped in the sea.

Remember that subject pronouns are not used very often in Spanish.

verter

	FUTURE	CONDITIONAL
(yo)	**verteré**	**vertería**
(tú)	**verterás**	**verterías**
(él/ella/usted)	**verterá**	**vertería**
(nosotros/as)	**verteremos**	**verteríamos**
(vosotros/as)	**verteréis**	**verteríais**
(ellos/ellas/ ustedes)	**verterán**	**verterían**

	PRESENT SUBJUNCTIVE	IMPERFECT SUBJUNCTIVE
(yo)	**vierta**	**vertiera** or **vertiese**
(tú)	**viertas**	**vertieras** or **vertieses**
(él/ella/usted)	**vierta**	**vertiera** or **vertiese**
(nosotros/as)	**vertamos**	**vertiéramos** or **vertiésemos**
(vosotros/as)	**vertáis**	**vertierais** or **vertieseis**
(ellos/ellas/ ustedes)	**viertan**	**vertieran** or **vertiesen**

IMPERATIVE

vierte / verted

Use the present subjunctive in all cases other than these tú and vosotros affirmative forms.

EXAMPLE PHRASES

Se verterán muchas lágrimas por esto. A lot of tears will be shed over this.

Ten cuidado no **viertas** el café. Be careful you don't knock over the coffee.

Remember that subject pronouns are not used very often in Spanish.

vestir (to dress)

	PRESENT		PRESENT PERFECT
(yo)	visto		he vestido
(tú)	vistes		has vestido
(él/ella/usted)	viste		ha vestido
(nosotros/as)	vestimos		hemos vestido
(vosotros/as)	vestís		habéis vestido
(ellos/ellas/ ustedes)	visten		han vestido

	PRETERITE		IMPERFECT
(yo)	vestí		vestía
(tú)	vestiste		vestías
(él/ella/usted)	vistió		vestía
(nosotros/as)	vestimos		vestíamos
(vosotros/as)	vestisteis		vestíais
(ellos/ellas/ ustedes)	vistieron		vestían

GERUND

vistiendo

PAST PARTICIPLE

vestido

EXAMPLE PHRASES

Tengo una familia que **vestir** y alimentar. I have a family to feed and clothe.

Viste bien. She's a sharp dresser.

Estaba vistiendo a los niños. I was dressing the children

Me vestí en cinco minutos. I got dressed in five minutes.

Remember that subject pronouns are not used very often in Spanish.

vestir

	FUTURE	CONDITIONAL
(yo)	vestiré	vestiría
(tú)	vestirás	vestirías
(él/ella/usted)	vestirá	vestiría
(nosotros/as)	vestiremos	vestiríamos
(vosotros/as)	vestiréis	vestiríais
(ellos/ellas/ustedes)	vestirán	vestirían

	PRESENT SUBJUNCTIVE	IMPERFECT SUBJUNCTIVE
(yo)	vista	vistiera or vistiese
(tú)	vistas	vistieras or vistieses
(él/ella/usted)	vista	vistiera or vistiese
(nosotros/as)	vistamos	vistiéramos or vistiésemos
(vosotros/as)	vistáis	vistierais or vistieseis
(ellos/ellas/ustedes)	vistan	vistieran or vistiesen

IMPERATIVE

viste / vestid

Use the present subjunctive in all cases other than these tú and vosotros affirmative forms.

EXAMPLE PHRASES

Se vistió de princesa. She dressed up as a princess

Vestía jeans y una camiseta. He was wearing jeans and a shirt.

Su padre **vestirá** de uniforme. Her father will wear a uniform.

¡**Vístete** de una vez! For the last time, go and get dressed!

Remember that subject pronouns are not used very often in Spanish.

vivir (to live)

	PRESENT	PRESENT PERFECT
(yo)	vivo	he vivido
(tú)	vives	has vivido
(él/ella/usted)	vive	ha vivido
(nosotros/as)	vivimos	hemos vivido
(vosotros/as)	vivís	habéis vivido
(ellos/ellas/ ustedes)	viven	han vivido

	PRETERITE	IMPERFECT
(yo)	viví	vivía
(tú)	viviste	vivías
(él/ella/usted)	vivió	vivía
(nosotros/as)	vivimos	vivíamos
(vosotros/as)	vivisteis	vivíais
(ellos/ellas/ ustedes)	vivieron	vivían

GERUND

viviendo

PAST PARTICIPLE

vivido

EXAMPLE PHRASES

Me gusta **vivir** sola. I like living on my own.

¿Dónde **vives**? Where do you live?

Siempre **viveron** muy bien. They always had a very comfortable life.

Vivían de su pensión. They lived on his pension.

Remember that subject pronouns are not used very often in Spanish.

vivir

	FUTURE	CONDITIONAL
(yo)	viviré	viviría
(tú)	vivirás	vivirías
(él/ella/usted)	vivirá	viviría
(nosotros/as)	viviremos	viviríamos
(vosotros/as)	viviréis	viviríais
(ellos/ellas/ ustedes)	vivirán	vivirían

	PRESENT SUBJUNCTIVE	IMPERFECT SUBJUNCTIVE
(yo)	viva	viviera *or* viviese
(tú)	vivas	vivieras *or* vivieses
(él/ella/usted)	viva	viviera *or* viviese
(nosotros/as)	vivamos	viviéramos *or* viviésemos
(vosotros/as)	viváis	vivierais *or* vivieseis
(ellos/ellas/ ustedes)	vivan	vivieran *or* viviesen

IMPERATIVE

vive / vivid

Use the present subjunctive in all cases other than these tú *and* vosotros *affirmative forms.*

EXAMPLE PHRASES

Viviremos en el centro de la ciudad. We'll live downtown.

Si pudiéramos, **viviríamos** en el campo. We'd live in the country if we could.

Si **vivieran** más cerca, nos veríamos más a menudo. We'd see one another more often if you lived nearer.

!**Viva**! Hurray!

Remember that subject pronouns are not used very often in Spanish.

volcar (to overturn)

	PRESENT		PRESENT PERFECT
(yo)	vuelco		he volcado
(tú)	vuelcas		has volcado
(él/ella/usted)	vuelca		ha volcado
(nosotros/as)	volcamos		hemos volcado
(vosotros/as)	volcáis		habéis volcado
(ellos/ellas/ ustedes)	vuelcan		han volcado

	PRETERITE		IMPERFECT
(yo)	volqué		volcaba
(tú)	volcaste		volcabas
(él/ella/usted)	volcó		volcaba
(nosotros/as)	volcamos		volcábamos
(vosotros/as)	volcasteis		volcabais
(ellos/ellas/ ustedes)	volcaron		volcaban

GERUND

volcando

PAST PARTICIPLE

volcado

EXAMPLE PHRASES

La camioneta **volcó**. The van rolled over.

Se vuelca en su trabajo. She throws herself into her work.

Remember that subject pronouns are not used very often in Spanish.

volcar

	FUTURE	CONDITIONAL
(yo)	volcaré	volcaría
(tú)	volcarás	volcarías
(él/ella/usted)	volcará	volcaría
(nosotros/as)	volcaremos	volcaríamos
(vosotros/as)	volcaréis	volcaríais
(ellos/ellas/ ustedes)	volcarán	volcarían

	PRESENT SUBJUNCTIVE	IMPERFECT SUBJUNCTIVE
(yo)	vuelque	volcara *or* volcase
(tú)	vuelques	volcaras *or* volcases
(él/ella/usted)	vuelque	volcara *or* volcase
(nosotros/as)	volquemos	volcáramos *or* volcásemos
(vosotros/as)	volquéis	volcarais *or* volcaseis
(ellos/ellas/ ustedes)	vuelquen	volcaran *or* volcasen

IMPERATIVE

vuelca / volcad

Use the present subjunctive in all cases other than these tú *and* vosotros *affirmative forms.*

EXAMPLE PHRASES

Si sigues moviéndote, harás que **vuelque** el bote. If you keep on moving like that, you'll make the boat capsize.

Ten cuidado, no **vuelques** el vaso. Be careful not to knock over the glass.

Vuelca el contenido sobre la cama. Empty the contents onto the bed.

Remember that subject pronouns are not used very often in Spanish.

volver (to return, to go/come back)

	PRESENT		PRESENT PERFECT
(yo)	vuelvo		he vuelto
(tú)	vuelves		has vuelto
(él/ella/usted)	vuelve		ha vuelto
(nosotros/as)	volvemos		hemos vuelto
(vosotros/as)	volvéis		habéis vuelto
(ellos/ellas/ ustedes)	vuelven		han vuelto

	PRETERITE		IMPERFECT
(yo)	volví		volvía
(tú)	volviste		volvías
(él/ella/usted)	volvió		volvía
(nosotros/as)	volvimos		volvíamos
(vosotros/as)	volvisteis		volvíais
(ellos/ellas/ ustedes)	volvieron		volvían

GERUND

volviendo

PAST PARTICIPLE

vuelto

EXAMPLE PHRASES

Mi padre **vuelve** mañana. My father's coming back tomorrow.

Volvió a casa. He went back home.

Volvía agotado de trabajar. I used to come back from work exhausted.

Remember that subject pronouns are not used very often in Spanish.

volver

	FUTURE	CONDITIONAL
(yo)	volveré	volvería
(tú)	volverás	volverías
(él/ella/usted)	volverá	volvería
(nosotros/as)	volveremos	volveríamos
(vosotros/as)	volveréis	volveríais
(ellos/ellas/ ustedes)	volverán	volverían

	PRESENT SUBJUNCTIVE	IMPERFECT SUBJUNCTIVE
(yo)	vuelva	volviera or volviese
(tú)	vuelvas	volvieras or volvieses
(él/ella/usted)	vuelva	volviera or volviese
(nosotros/as)	volvamos	volviéramos or volviésemos
(vosotros/as)	volváis	volvierais or volvieseis
(ellos/ellas/ ustedes)	vuelvan	volvieran or volviesen

IMPERATIVE

vuelve / volved

Use the present subjunctive in all cases other than these tú and vosotros affirmative forms.

EXAMPLE PHRASES

Todo **volverá** a la normalidad. Everything will return to normal.

Yo **volvería** a intentarlo. I'd try again.

No quiero que **vuelvas** allí. I don't want you to go back there.

No **vuelvas** por aquí. Don't come back here.

¡**Vuelve** a la cama! Go back to bed!

Remember that subject pronouns are not used very often in Spanish.

zurcir (to darn)

	PRESENT	PRESENT PERFECT
(yo)	zurzo	he zurcido
(tú)	zurces	has zurcido
(él/ella/usted)	zurce	ha zurcido
(nosotros/as)	zurcimos	hemos zurcido
(vosotros/as)	zurcís	habéis zurcido
(ellos/ellas/ ustedes)	zurcen	han zurcido

	PRETERITE	IMPERFECT
(yo)	zurcí	zurcía
(tú)	zurciste	zurcías
(él/ella/usted)	zurció	zurcía
(nosotros/as)	zurcimos	zurcíamos
(vosotros/as)	zurcisteis	zurcíais
(ellos/ellas/ ustedes)	zurcieron	zurcían

GERUND

zurciendo

PAST PARTICIPLE

zurcido

EXAMPLE PHRASES

¿Quién le **zurce** los calcetines? Who darns his socks?

Las sábanas estaban **zurcidas**. The sheets had been mended.

Remember that subject pronouns are not used very often in Spanish.

zurcir

	FUTURE	CONDITIONAL
(yo)	zurciré	zurciría
(tú)	zurcirás	zurcirías
(él/ella/usted)	zurcirá	zurciría
(nosotros/as)	zurciremos	zurciríamos
(vosotros/as)	zurciréis	zurciríais
(ellos/ellas/ustedes)	zurcirán	zurcirían

	PRESENT SUBJUNCTIVE	IMPERFECT SUBJUNCTIVE
(yo)	zurza	zurciera or zurciese
(tú)	zurzas	zurcieras or zurcieses
(él/ella/usted)	zurza	zurciera or zurciese
(nosotros/as)	zurzamos	zurciéramos or zurciésemos
(vosotros/as)	zurzáis	zurcierals or zurcleseis
(ellos/ellas/ustedes)	zurzan	zurcieran or zurciesen

IMPERATIVE

zurce / zurcid

Use the present subjunctive in all cases other than these tú and vosotros affirmative forms.

Remember that subject pronouns are not used very often in Spanish.

How to use the Verb Index

The verbs in bold are the model verbs which you will find in the verb tables. All the other verbs follow one of these patterns, so the number next to each verb indicates which pattern fits this particular verb. For example, acampar (*to camp*) follows the same pattern as hablar (number 340 in the verb tables).

All the verbs are in alphabetical order. Superior numbers ([1] etc) refer you to notes on page 468. These notes explain any differences between verbs and their model.

abandonar	340	aficionar	340	animar	340	arropar	340
abastecer	280	afilar	340	anochecer[1]	280	arrugar	378
abolir	**224**	afiliarse	290	anotar	340	arruinar	340
abollar	340	afinar	340	anticipar	340	asaltar	340
abombar	340	afirmar	340	antojarse	290	asar	340
abonar	340	aflojar	340	anular	340	ascender	308
abortar	340	afrontar	340	anunciar	340	asegurar	340
abrasar	340	agachar	340	añadir	456	asesinar	340
abrazar	282	agarrar	340	apagar	378	asfixiar	340
abrigar	378	agitar	340	apañar	340	asimilar	340
abrir	**226**	aglomerarse	290	aparcar	416	asistir	456
abrochar	340	agobiar	340	aparecer	280	asociar	340
absorber	270	agotar	340	aparentar	340	asolear	340
abstenerse	436	agradar	340	apartar	340	asomar	340
abultar	340	agradecer	280	apasionarse	290	asombrar	340
aburrir	456	agrupar	340	apearse	290	asumir	456
abusar	340	aguantar	340	apellidar	340	asustar	340
acabar	340	ahogar	378	apestar	340	atacar	416
acampar	340	ahorcar	416	apetecer	280	atar	340
acariciar	340	ahorrar	340	aplastar	340	atardecer[1]	280
acatarrarse	340	ajustar	340	aplaudir	456	atender	308
acceder	270	alabar	340	aplazar	282	aterrizar	282
acelerar	340	alardear	340	aplicar	416	atiborrar	340
acentuar	228	alargar	378	**apoderarse**	**238**	atracar	416
aceptar	340	alcanzar	282	aportar	340	atraer	442
acercar	416	alegrar	340	apostar	278	atrapar	340
acertar	384	alejar	340	apoyar	340	**atravesar**	**246**
aclarar	340	aliarse	310	apreciar	340	atreverse	270
acobardarse	290	aligerar	340	aprender	270	atropellar	340
acoger	318	alimentar	340	apresurarse	290	aumentar	340
acompañar	340	aliviar	340	apretar	384	**aunar**	**248**
aconsejar	340	almacenar	340	**aprobar**	**240**	autorizar	282
acordar	278	almorzar	330	aprovechar	340	avanzar	282
acostar	278	alojar	340	aproximar	340	aventajar	340
acostumbrar	340	alquilar	340	apuntar	340	aventar	384
actuar	**228**	alterar	340	apuñalar	340	**avergonzar**	**250**
acudir	456	alternar	340	apurar	340	averiarse	310
acurrucarse	290	alucinar	340	arañar	340	**averiguar**	**252**
acusar	340	aludir	456	arar	340	avisar	340
adaptar	340	alzar	282	archivar	340	ayudar	340
adecuar	340	amamantar	340	arder	270	azotar	340
adelantar	340	**amanecer**	**234**	armar	340	bailar	340
adelgazar	282	amar	340	**arrancar**	**242**	bajar	340
adivinar	340	amargar	378	arrasar	340	bañar	340
admirar	340	amarrar	340	arrastrar	340	barnizar	282
admitir	456	amenazar	282	arrebatar	340	barrer	270
adoptar	340	amontonar	340	arreglar	340	basar	340
adorar	340	amortiguar	252	**arrepentirse**	**244**	bastar	340
adornar	340	ampliar	310	arrestar	340	batir	456
adquirir	**230**	amputar	340	arriesgar	378	beber	270
advertir	**232**	amueblar	340	arrimar	340	**bendecir**	**254**
afectar	340	analizar	282	arrodillarse	290	beneficiar	340
afeitar	340	**andar**	**236**	arrojar	340	besar	340

Notes

[1] The verbs anochecer, atardecer, granizar, helar, llover, nevar, nublarse and tronar are used almost exclusively in the infinitive and third person singular forms.

[2] The **past participle** of the verb pudrir is podrido.

Vocabulary

contents

contents

This section is divided into 50 topics, arranged in alphabetical order. This thematic approach enables you to learn related words and phrases together, so that you can become confident in using particular vocabulary in context.

Vocabulary within each topic is divided into nouns and useful phrases which are aimed at helping you to express yourself in idiomatic Spanish. Vocabulary within each topic is categorized to help you prioritize your learning. Essential words include the basic words you will need to be able to communicate effectively, important words help expand your knowledge, and useful words provide additional vocabulary which will enable you to express yourself more fully.

Nouns are grouped by gender: masculine ("el") nouns appear on the left-hand page, and feminine ("la") nouns on the right-hand page, enabling you to memorize words according to their gender. In addition, all feminine forms of adjectives are shown, as are irregular plurals.

At the end of the thematic section you will find a list of supplementary vocabulary, grouped according to parts of speech – adjective, verb, noun and so on. This is vocabulary which you will come across in many everyday situations.

ABBREVIATIONS

adj	adjective
adv	adverb
algn	alguien
conj	conjunction
f	feminine
inv	invariable
LAm	word used in Latin America
m	masculine
m+f	masculine and feminine form
Mex	word used in Mexico
n	noun
pl	plural
prep	preposition
sb	somebody
sing	singular
Sp	word used in Spain
sth	something

The swung dash ~ is used to indicate the basic elements of the compound and appropriate endings are then added.

PLURALS AND GENDER

In Spanish, if a noun ends in a vowel it generally takes –s in the plural (casa > casas). If it ends in a consonant (including y) it generally takes –es in the plural (reloj > relojes). If it doesn't follow these rules, then the plural will be shown in the text.

Although most masculine nouns use "el" and most feminine nouns use "la", you will find a few nouns grouped under feminine words which use "el" (el agua water; el arca chest; el aula classroom) because they are actually feminine. For more information, see Grammar section page 11.

ESSENTIAL WORDS *(masculine)*

el	**aduanero**	customs officer
el	**aeropuerto**	airport
el	**agente aduanal** *(Mex)*	customs officer
el	**agente de viajes**	travel agent
el	**alquiler de coches** *(Sp)*	car rental
el	**avión** *(pl* aviones)	plane
el	**boleto** *(LAm)*, el **billete** *(Sp)*	ticket
el	**bolso**	bag
el	**carné de identidad** *(Sp)*	ID
el	**duty free**	duty-free (shop)
el	**equipaje**	luggage
el	**equipaje de mano**	carry-on luggage
el	**horario**	schedule, timetable
el	**número**	number
el	**pasajero**	passenger
el	**pasaporte**	passport
el	**pase de abordar** *(Mex)*	boarding pass
el	**(precio del) boleto** *(LAm) or* **billete** *(Sp)*	fare
el	**retraso**	delay
los	**sanitarios**	restrooms
el	**taxi**	taxi
el	**turista**	tourist
el	**viaje**	trip
el	**viajero**	traveler

USEFUL PHRASES

viajar en avión to travel by plane

un boleto *(LAm) or* billete *(Sp)* de ida a one-way ticket

un boleto *(LAm) or* billete *(Sp)* de ida y vuelta, un boleto redondo *(Mex)*
  a round-trip ticket

reservar un boleto *(LAm) or* un billete *(Sp)* de avión to book a plane ticket

"por avión" "by airmail"

facturar el equipaje, checar *or* documentar el equipaje *(Mex)* to check in
  one's bags

el avión despegó/aterrizó the plane took off/landed

el panel de llegadas/salidas the arrivals/departures board

el vuelo número 776 procedente de Buenos Aires/con destino a Buenos Aires
  flight number 776 from Buenos Aires/to Buenos Aires

ESSENTIAL WORDS *(feminine)*

la	**aduana**	customs
la	**aduanera**	customs officer
la	**agente aduanal** *(Mex)*	customs officer
la	**agente de viajes**	travel agent
la	**cancelación** *(pl* cancelaciones)	cancelation
la	**conexión** *(pl* conexiones)	connection
la	**entrada**	entrance
la	**identificación**	ID
la	**información** *(pl* informaciones)	information desk; information
la	**llegada**	arrival
la	**maleta**	suitcase, bag
la	**pasajera**	passenger
la	**petaca** *(Mex)*	suitcase, bag
la	**puerta de embarque**	departure gate
la	**renta de autos** *(Mex)*	car rental
la	**reservación** *(LAm)*, **la reserva** *(Sp)*	reservation
la	**salida**	departure; exit
la	**salida de emergencia**	emergency exit
la	**tarifa**	fare
la	**tarjeta de embarque**	boarding pass
la	**terminal**	terminal
la	**turista**	tourist
la	**viajera**	traveler

USEFUL PHRASES

recoger el equipaje to pick up one's baggage
"recogida de equipajes" "baggage claim"
perdí la conexión I missed my connection
pasar por la aduana to go through customs
tengo algo que declarar I have something to declare
no tengo nada que declarar I have nothing to declare
registrar el equipaje to search the bags

IMPORTANT WORDS *(masculine)*

el	**accidente de avión**	plane crash
el	**boleto** (*LAm*) *or* el **billete** (*Sp*) **electrónico**	e-ticket
el	**carrito**	cart
el	**cinturón de seguridad** (*pl* cinturones ~~)	seat belt
el	**helicóptero**	helicopter
el	**mapa**	map
el	**mareo (en avión)**	airsickness
el	**piloto**	pilot
el	**reloj**	clock, watch
el	**vuelo**	flight

USEFUL WORDS *(masculine)*

el	**asiento**	seat
el	**aterrizaje**	landing
el	**auxiliar de vuelo**	flight attendant
el	**control de seguridad**	security check
el	**controlador aéreo**	air-traffic controller
los	**derechos de aduana**	customs duty
el	**despegue**	take-off
el	**detector de metales**	metal detector
el	**embarque**	boarding
el	**espacio para aseo para bebés**	baby change facility
el	**horario**	schedule, timetable
el	**jumbo**	jumbo jet
los	**mandos**	controls
el	**paracaídas** (*pl inv*)	parachute
el	**radar**	radar
el	**reactor**	jet plane/engine
el	**sobrecargo** (*Mex*)	flight attendant
el	**vacacionista** (*LAm*)	vacationer

USEFUL PHRASES

a bordo **on board**; "prohibido fumar" "**no smoking**"
"abróchense el cinturón de seguridad" "**fasten your seat belts**"
estamos sobrevolando la ciudad de México **we are flying over Mexico City**
estoy mareado **I feel nauseous**; secuestrar un avión **to hijack a plane**

IMPORTANT WORDS *(feminine)*

la **duración** (*pl* duraciones)	length; duration
la **escalera eléctrica** *or* **mecánica**	escalator
la **piloto**	pilot
la **sala de embarque**	departure lobby
la **velocidad**	speed

USEFUL WORDS *(feminine)*

el **ala** (*f pl* las alas)	wing
la **altitud**	altitude
la **altura**	height
la **auxiliar de vuelo**	flight attendant
la **barrera del sonido**	sound barrier
la **bolsa de aire**	air pocket
la **caja negra**	black box
la **cinta transportadora**	carousel
la **controladora aérea**	air-traffic controller
la **escala**	stopover
la **etiqueta**	label
la **hélice**	propeller
la **línea aérea**	airline
la **pista (de aterrizaje)**	runway
la **sobrecargo** (*Mex*)	flight attendant
la **terminal**	terminal
la **tienda libre de impuestos**	duty-free shop
la **torre de control**	control tower
la **tripulación** (*pl* tripulaciones)	crew
la **turbulencia**	turbulence
la **vacacionista** (*LAm*)	vacationer
la **ventanilla**	window

USEFUL PHRASES

"pasajeros del vuelo AB251 con destino a Lima embarquen por la puerta 51"
  "flight AB251 to Lima now boarding at gate 51"
hicimos escala en Nueva York **we stopped over in New York**
un aterrizaje forzoso *or* de emergencia **an emergency landing**
un aterrizaje violento **a crash landing**
cigarrillos libres de impuestos **duty-free cigarettes**

ESSENTIAL WORDS *(masculine)*

el	**animal**	animal
el	**buey** (*pl* ~es)	ox
el	**caballo**	horse
el	**cachorro**	puppy
el	**cerdo**	pig
el	**conejo**	rabbit
el	**cordero**	lamb
el	**elefante**	elephant
el	**gato**	cat
el	**gatito**	kitten
el	**hámster** (*pl* ~s)	hamster
el	**león** (*pl* leones)	lion
el	**pájaro**	bird
el	**pelaje**	fur, coat
el	**pelo**	coat, hair
el	**perro**	dog
el	**perrito**	puppy
el	**pescado**	fish
el	**pez** (*pl* peces)	fish
el	**potro**	foal
el	**ratón** (*pl* ratones)	mouse
el	**ternero**	calf
el	**tigre**	tiger
el	**zoo** (*pl* ~s)	zoo
el	**zoológico**	zoo

USEFUL PHRASES

me gustan los gatos, odio las serpientes, prefiero los ratones **I like cats, I hate snakes, I prefer mice**

tenemos 2 mascotas **we have 2 pets**

no tenemos mascotas **we have no pets**

los animales salvajes **wild animals**

los animales domésticos *or* las mascotas **pets**

el ganado **livestock**

poner un animal en una jaula **to put an animal in a cage**

liberar un animal **to set an animal free**

ESSENTIAL WORDS *(feminine)*

el	**ave** *(f pl* las aves)	bird
la	**gata**	cat (female)
la	**oveja**	ewe
la	**perra**	dog (female)
la	**tortuga**	turtle, tortoise
la	**vaca**	cow

IMPORTANT WORDS *(feminine)*

la	**cola**	tail
la	**jaula**	cage

USEFUL PHRASES

el perro ladra/gruñe the dog barks/growls
el gato maúlla/ronronea the cat meows/purrs
me gusta la equitación *or* andar a caballo I like horseback riding
a caballo on horseback
"cuidado con el perro" "beware of the dog"
"no se admiten perros" "no dogs allowed"
"¡quieto!" *(to a dog)* "down, boy!"
los derechos de los animales animal rights

USEFUL WORDS *(masculine)*

el	**asno**	donkey
el	**burro**	donkey
el	**camello**	camel
el	**canguro**	kangaroo
el	**caparazón** *(pl* caparazones)	shell *(of turtle)*
el	**casco**	hoof
el	**cerdo**	pig
el	**ciervo**	deer
el	**cocodrilo**	crocodile
el	**colmillo (de elefante)**	(elephant) tusk
el	**conejillo de Indias**	guinea pig
el	**cuerno**	horn
el	**erizo**	hedgehog
el	**guajolote** *(Mex)*	turkey
el	**hipopótamo**	hippopotamus
el	**hocico**	snout
el	**lobo**	wolf
el	**macho cabrío**	goat (male)
el	**mono**	monkey
el	**murciélago**	bat
el	**oso**	bear
el	**oso polar**	polar bear
el	**pavo**	turkey
el	**pony** *(pl* ~s)	pony
el	**rinoceronte**	rhinoceros
el	**sapo**	toad
el	**tiburón** *(pl* tiburones)	shark
el	**topo**	mole
el	**toro**	bull
el	**zorro**	fox

USEFUL WORDS *(feminine)*

la	ardilla	squirrel
el	asta *(fpl* las astas)	antler
la	ballena	whale
la	boca	mouth
la	bolsa	pouch *(of a kangaroo)*
la	cabra	goat *(female)*
la	crin	mane
la	culebra	(grass) snake
la	foca	seal
la	garra	claw
la	jirafa	giraffe
la	joroba	hump *(of a camel)*
la	leona	lioness
la	liebre	hare
la	melena	mane
la	mula	mule
la	pata	paw
la	pezuña	hoof
la	piel	fur; hide *(of a cow, elephant, etc)*
la	rana	frog
las	rayas	stripes *(of a zebra)*
la	serpiente	snake
la	tienda de animales	pet store
la	tigresa	tigress
la	trampa	trap
la	trompa	trunk *(of an elephant)*
la	yegua	mare
la	zebra	zebra

ESSENTIAL WORDS (*masculine*)

el	casco	helmet
el	ciclismo	cycling
el	ciclista	cyclist
el	faro	light
el	freno	brake
el	neumático (*Sp*)	tire

IMPORTANT WORDS (*masculine*)

el	pinchazo	flat tire

USEFUL WORDS (*masculine*)

el	ascenso	climb
el	asiento (*LAm*)	seat
el	candado	padlock
el	carril para bicicletas	bicycle lane
el	desviador *or* descarrilador	derailleur
el	descenso	descent
el	dínamo (*LAm*)	dynamo
el	eje	hub
el	guardabarros (*pl inv*) (*Sp*)	fender
el	kit de reparación de pinchazos (*pl* ~s ~ ~ ~ ~)	flat repair kit
el	kit de reparación de ponchaduras (*pl* ~s ~ ~ ~ ~) (*Mex*)	flat repair kit
el	manillar (*Sp*)	handlebars
el	manubrio (*LAm*)	handlebars
el	pedal	pedal
el	portaequipajes (*pl inv*)	rack
el	radio	spoke
el	reflector	reflector
el	sillín (*pl* sillines) (*Sp*)	seat
el	timbre	bell

USEFUL PHRASES

ir en bici(cleta) **to go by bike**
andar en bici(cleta) **to bike**
vine en bici(cleta) **I came by bike**

ESSENTIAL WORDS *(feminine)*

la **bici**	bike
la **bicicleta**	bicycle
la **bicicleta de montaña**	mountain bike
la **llanta** (*LAm*)	tire
la **salpicadera** (*Mex*)	fender

IMPORTANT WORDS *(feminine)*

la **ponchadura** (*Mex*)	flat tire
la **rueda**	wheel
la **velocidad**	speed; gear

USEFUL WORDS *(feminine)*

la **alforja**	saddlebag
la **barra**	crossbar
la **bomba**	pump
la **cadena**	chain
la **cuesta**	slope
la **cumbre**	top (*of a hill*)
la **dínamo** (*Sp*)	dynamo
la **luz delantera** (*pl* luces ~s)	front light
la **pendiente**	slope
la **subida**	climb
la **válvula**	valve

USEFUL PHRASES

ir a dar una vuelta *or* a pasear en bici(cleta) to go for a bike ride
se me ponchó una llanta (*Mex*) I had a flat
arreglar una ponchadura (*Mex*) *or* un pinchazo to fix a flat
la rueda delantera/trasera the front/back wheel
inflar las llantas (*LAm*) to inflate the tires
brillante, reluciente shiny
oxidado(a) rusty
fluorescente fluorescent

ESSENTIAL WORDS *(masculine)*

el	cielo	sky
el	gallo	rooster
el	ganso	goose
el	guajolote *(Mex)*	turkey
el	loro	parrot
el	pájaro	bird
el	pato	duck
el	pavo	turkey
el	periquito	parakeet
el	pollito	chick

USEFUL WORDS *(masculine)*

el	avestruz *(pl* avestruces)	ostrich
el	búho	owl
el	buitre	vulture
el	canario	canary
el	cardenal	cardinal
el	cisne	swan
el	cuervo	raven; crow
el	cuco	cuckoo
el	estornino	starling
el	faisán *(pl* faisanes)	pheasant
el	gorrión *(pl* gorriones)	sparrow
el	halcón *(pl* halcones)	falcon
el	huevo	egg
el	martín pescador	kingfisher
	(pl martines ~es)	
el	nido	nest
el	pájaro carpintero	woodpecker
el	pavo real	peacock
el	petirrojo	robin
el	pico	beak
el	pingüino	penguin
el	ruiseñor	nightingale
el	zopilote	black vulture

ESSENTIAL WORDS *(feminine)*

la	**gallina**	hen

USEFUL WORDS *(feminine)*

el	**águila** *(f pl* las águilas)	eagle
el	**ala** *(f pl* las alas)	wing
la	**alondra**	lark
el	**ave** *(f pl* las aves)	bird
el	**ave de rapiña** *(f pl* las ~s ~~)	bird of prey
el	**ave rapaz** *(f pl* las ~s rapaces)	bird of prey
la	**cigüeña**	stork
la	**codorniz** *(pl* codornices)	quail
la	**gaviota**	seagull
la	**golondrina**	swallow
la	**grulla**	crane
la	**jaula**	cage
la	**paloma**	pigeon; dove
la	**perdiz** *(pl* perdices)	partridge
la	**pluma**	feather
la	**urraca**	magpie

USEFUL PHRASES

volar to fly
levantar el vuelo to fly away
construir un nido to build a nest
silbar to whistle
cantar to sing
la gente los pone en jaulas people put them in cages
hibernar to hibernate
poner un huevo to lay an egg
un ave migratoria a migratory bird

ESSENTIAL WORDS *(masculine)*

el	**brazo**	arm
el	**cabello**	hair
el	**corazón** *(pl* corazones)	heart
el	**cuerpo**	body
el	**dedo**	finger
el	**diente**	tooth
el	**estómago**	stomach
el	**ojo**	eye
el	**pelo**	hair
el	**pie**	foot
el	**rostro**	face

IMPORTANT WORDS *(masculine)*

el	**cuello**	neck
el	**hombro**	shoulder
el	**mentón**	chin
el	**pecho**	chest; breast; bust
el	**pulgar**	thumb
el	**tobillo**	ankle

USEFUL PHRASES

parado(a) standing
sentado(a) sitting
acostado(a) lying

ESSENTIAL WORDS *(feminine)*

la	**boca**	mouth
la	**cabeza**	head
la	**espalda**	back
la	**garganta**	throat
la	**mano**	hand
la	**nariz** *(pl* narices)	nose
la	**oreja**	ear
la	**pierna**	leg
la	**rodilla**	knee

IMPORTANT WORDS *(feminine)*

la	**barbilla**	chin
la	**cara**	face
la	**ceja**	eyebrow
la	**frente**	forehead
la	**lengua**	tongue
la	**mejilla**	cheek
la	**piel**	skin
la	**sangre**	blood
la	**voz** *(pl* voces)	voice

USEFUL PHRASES

grande big
alto(a) tall
pequeño(a) small
bajo(a) short
gordo(a) fat
flaco(a) skinny
delgado(a) slim
bonito(a) pretty
feo(a) ugly

USEFUL WORDS *(masculine)*

el	**cerebro**	brain
el	**codo**	elbow
el	**cutis** *(pl inv)*	skin, complexion
el	**dedo del pie**	toe
el	**dedo índice**	forefinger
el	**dedo gordo**	the big toe
los	**dedos de los pies**	toes
el	**esqueleto**	skeleton
el	**gesto**	gesture
el	**hígado**	liver
el	**hueso**	bone
el	**labio**	lip
el	**músculo**	muscle
el	**muslo**	thigh
el	**párpado**	eyelid
el	**pulmón** *(pl pulmones)*	lung
el	**puño**	fist
el	**rasgo**	feature
el	**riñón** *(pl riñones)*	kidney
el	**seno**	breast
el	**talle**	waist
el	**talón** *(pl talones)*	heel
el	**trasero**	bottom

USEFUL PHRASES

sonarse (la nariz) to blow one's nose
cortarse las uñas to cut one's nails
cortarse el pelo to have one's hair cut
encogerse de hombros to shrug one's shoulders
asentir/decir que sí con la cabeza to nod one's head
negar/decir que no con la cabeza to shake one's head
ver to see; oír to hear; sentir to feel
oler to smell; tocar to touch; probar to taste
estrecharle la mano a alguien to shake hands with somebody
saludar a alguien con la mano to wave to somebody
señalar algo to point at something

USEFUL WORDS *(feminine)*

la	**arteria**	artery
la	**cadera**	hip
la	**carne**	flesh
la	**columna (vertebral)**	spine
la	**costilla**	rib
la	**facción** *(pl* facciones)	feature
la	**mandíbula**	jaw
la	**muñeca**	wrist
la	**nuca**	nape *(of the neck)*
la	**pantorrilla**	calf *(of the leg)*
la	**pestaña**	eyelash
la	**planta del pie**	sole of the foot
la	**pupila**	pupil *(of the eye)*
la	**sien**	temple *(of the head)*
la	**talla**	size
la	**tez** *(pl* teces)	complexion
la	**uña**	nail
la	**vena**	vein

USEFUL PHRASES

contorno de caderas hip measurement
cintura waist measurement
contorno de pecho chest measurement
sordo(a) deaf
ciego(a) blind
mudo(a) mute
discapacitado(a) disabled
disminuido(a) psíquico(a) person with learning disabilities
es más alto que tú he is taller than you
ha crecido mucho (s)he has grown a lot
estoy demasiado gordo(a) *or* tengo sobrepeso I am overweight
está más gorda/delgada she has put on/lost weight
mide 1,47 metros (s)he is 1.47 meters tall
pesa 40 kilos (s)he weighs 40 kilos

SEASONS

la	**primavera**	spring
el	**verano**	summer
el	**otoño**	fall, autumn
el	**invierno**	winter

MONTHS

enero	January	**julio**	July
febrero	February	**agosto**	August
marzo	March	**septiembre**	September
abril	April	**octubre**	October
mayo	May	**noviembre**	November
junio	June	**diciembre**	December

DAYS OF THE WEEK

lunes	Monday
martes	Tuesday
miércoles	Wednesday
jueves	Thursday
viernes	Friday
sábado	Saturday
domingo	Sunday

USEFUL PHRASES

en primavera/verano/otoño/invierno **in spring/summer/the fall/winter**
en mayo **in May**
el 10 de julio de 2006 **on July 10, 2006**
es 3 de diciembre **it's December 3rd**
los sábados voy al club **on Saturdays I go to the club**
el sábado fui al club **on Saturday I went to the club**
el próximo sábado/el sábado pasado **next/last Saturday**
el sábado anterior/siguiente **the previous/following Saturday**

CALENDAR

el	**calendario**	calendar
el	**día**	day
los	**días de la semana**	days of the week
el	**día festivo**	national holiday
la	**estación** (*pl* estaciones)	season
el	**mes**	month
la	**semana**	week

USEFUL PHRASES

el día de los Inocentes *celebrated on December 28 in the Spanish speaking world, similar to April Fools' Day*

la broma del día de los Inocentes *practical joke similar to an April fool*

el primero de mayo **May Day**

el día de la Hispanidad *or* de la raza **Columbus Day** (*October 12*)

el himno nacional **national anthem**

el día D **D-Day**

el día de los enamorados *or* de San Valentín **Valentine's Day**

el día de Todos los Santos **All Saints' Day** (*November 1*)

el día de muertos **All Souls' Day** (*November 2*)

la Semana Santa **Easter**

el Domingo de Resurrección *or* de Pascua **Easter Sunday**

el Miércoles de Ceniza **Ash Wednesday**

el Viernes Santo **Good Friday**

la Cuaresma **Lent**

la Pascua judía **Passover**

el Ramadán **Ramadan**

el Hanukkah **Hanukkah** *or* **Chanukah**

el Adviento **Advent**

la Nochebuena **Christmas Eve**

la Navidad **Christmas**

en Navidad **during Christmas**

el día de Navidad **Christmas Day**

la noche de Fin de Año **New Year's Eve**

el día de Año Nuevo **New Year's Day**

la cena *or* fiesta de Fin de Año **New Year's Eve dinner** *or* **party**

ESSENTIAL WORDS *(masculine)*

el	**aniversario de boda**	wedding anniversary
el	**cumpleaños** *(pl inv)*	birthday
el	**(día del) santo**	saint's day
el	**divorcio**	divorce
el	**matrimonio**	marriage
el	**regalo**	gift, present

IMPORTANT WORDS *(masculine)*

el	**compromiso**	engagement
el	**festival**	festival
los	**fuegos artificiales**	fireworks; fireworks display
el	**nacimiento**	birth
el	**parque de diversiones**	amusement park

USEFUL WORDS *(masculine)*

el	**bautismo**	baptism
el	**cementerio**	cemetery
el	**entierro**	burial
el	**festival folclórico**	folk festival
el	**funeral**	funeral
el	**testigo**	witness
el	**regalo de Navidad**	Christmas gift

USEFUL PHRASES

celebrar el cumpleaños to celebrate one's birthday
mi hermana nació en 1995 my sister was born in 1995
acaba de cumplir 17 años she's/he's just turned 17
me regaló esto (s)he gave me this
¡te lo regalo! I'm giving it to you!
gracias thank you
divorciarse to get divorced
casarse to get married
comprometerse (con algn) to get engaged (to sb)
mi padre murió hace dos años my father died two years ago
enterrar to bury

ESSENTIAL WORDS *(feminine)*

la **boda**	wedding
la **cita**	appointment; date
la **fecha**	date
la **fiesta**	festival, holiday; party

IMPORTANT WORDS *(feminine)*

las **fiestas**	festivities
la **feria**	fair
la **muerte**	death
la **hoguera**	bonfire

USEFUL WORDS *(feminine)*

la **ceremonia**	ceremony
la **dama de honor**	bridesmaid
la **invitación de boda** (*pl* invitaciones ~~)	wedding invitation
la **jubilación** (*pl* jubilaciones)	retirement
la **luna de miel**	honeymoon
la **procesión** (*pl* procesiones)	procession; march
la **tarjeta de felicitación**	greeting card
la **testigo**	witness

USEFUL PHRASES

bodas de plata/oro/diamante silver/golden/diamond wedding anniversary
desear a algn (un) Feliz Año to wish sb a Happy New Year
dar *or* hacer una fiesta to have a party
invitar a los amigos to invite one's friends
elegir un regalo to choose a gift
¡Feliz navidad! Merry Christmas!
¡Feliz cumpleaños! happy birthday!
(con) nuestros mejores deseos (with) best wishes
¡Felices Pascuas! Happy Easter!; Merry Christmas!

ESSENTIAL WORDS *(masculine)*

los	**aseos** *(Sp)*	restrooms
los	**baños** *(LAm)*	bathrooms; washrooms
el	**basurero** or el **bote de la basura** *(LAm)*	garbage can
el	**bote**	can
el	**camping** *(pl ~s)*	camping; campsite
el	**campista**	camper
el	**cerillo** *(LAm)*	match
el	**cubo de la basura** *(Sp)*	garbage can
el	**cuchillo**	knife
el	**emplazamiento**	site, location
el	**espejo**	mirror
el	**gas**	gas
el	**guarda**	warden
el	**lavabo**	sink
el	**plato**	plate
los	**servicios** *(Sp)*	restrooms
el	**suplemento**	extra charge
el	**tenedor**	fork
el	**trailer** *(pl ~s)* *(LAm)*	trailer
el	**vehículo**	vehicle

IMPORTANT WORDS *(masculine)*

el	**abrelatas** *(pl inv)*	can opener
el	**colchón inflable** *(pl* colchones *~s)*	airbed
el	**detergente**	detergent
el	**enchufe**	plug
el	**hornillo**	stove
el	**sacacorchos** *(pl inv)*	corkscrew
el	**saco de dormir**	sleeping bag
el	**tomacorriente** *(LAm)*	socket

USEFUL PHRASES

ir de or hacer camping to go camping
acampar to camp
armar una tienda or carpa to pitch a tent
hacer una hoguera to build a fire

ESSENTIAL WORDS *(feminine)*

el	agua (no) potable (f)	(non-)drinking water
la	alberca (*Mex*)	swimming pool
la	caja	box
la	cama plegable	cot
la	campista	camper
la	caravana (*Sp*)	trailer
la	carpa (*LAm*)	tent
la	cerilla (*Sp*)	match
la	cocina de camping-gas	gas stove
la	comida enlatada	canned food
la	cuchara	spoon
la	ducha	shower
la	estufa de camping-gas (*Mex*)	gas stove
la	lata	can
la	lavadora	washing machine
la	linterna	flashlight
la	mesa	table
la	navaja	penknife
la	noche	night
la	piscina (*Sp*)	swimming pool
la	sala	room; hall
la	silla reclinable	deckchair
la	tienda (de campaña)	tent
la	tumbona (*Sp*)	deckchair

IMPORTANT WORDS *(feminine)*

la	barbacoa	barbecue
la	bolsa de dormir	sleeping bag
las	instalaciones sanitarias	washing facilities
la	lavandería	Laundromat®
la	mochila	backpack
las	normas	rules
la	ropa lavada/para lavar	laundry
la	sala de juegos	gameroom
la	sombra	shade; shadow
la	toma de corriente	socket

ESSENTIAL WORDS *(masculine)*

el	**agricultor**	farmer
el	**auxiliar de vuelo**	flight attendant
el	**banco**	bank
el	**bombero**	firefighter, fireman
el	**cajero**	check-out clerk; cashier
el	**cartero**	mailman, postal carrier
el	**diseñador de páginas web**	web designer
el	**electricista**	electrician
el	**empleado**	employee
el	**empresario**	businessman; employer
el	**enfermero**	nurse
el	**farmacéutico**	chemist
el	**informático**	IT specialist
el	**jefe**	boss, superior
el	**maestro**	(elementary school) teacher
el	**mecánico**	mechanic
el	**médico**	doctor
el	**minero**	miner
el	**oficio**	trade
el	**policía**	policeman, police officer
el	**profesor**	teacher; professor
el	**redactor**	editor
el	**secretario**	secretary
el	**sobrecargo** *(Mex)*	flight attendant
el	**soldado**	soldier
el	**sueldo**	salary; wages
el	**taxista**	taxi driver
el	**trabajo**	job; work
el	**vendedor**	sales assistant

USEFUL PHRASES

interesante/poco interesante interesting/not very interesting
es cartero he is a mailman
trabajar to work
hacerse, volverse to become

ESSENTIAL WORDS *(feminine)*

la **agricultora**	farmer
la **ambición** (*pl* ambiciones)	ambition
la **auxiliar de vuelo**	flight attendant
la **cajera**	check-out clerk; cashier
la **cartera**	postal carrier
la **empleada**	employee
la **enfermera**	nurse
la **estrella** (*m+f*)	star
la **fábrica**	factory
la **informática**	IT specialist
la **jefa**	boss, superior
la **jubilación** (*pl* jubilaciones)	retirement
la **maestra**	(elementary school) teacher
la **mecanógrafa**	typist
la **médico** *or* la **médica**	doctor
la **oficina**	office
la **profesión** (*pl* profesiones)	profession
la **profesora**	teacher; professor
la **recepcionista**	receptionist
la **redactora**	editor
la **secretaria**	secretary
la **sobrecargo** (*Mex*)	flight attendant
la **vendedora**	sales assistant
la **vida**	life
la **vida laboral**	working life

USEFUL PHRASES

trabajar para ganarse la vida **to work for one's living**
mi ambición es ser juez(a) **it is my ambition to be a judge**
¿en qué trabajas? **what do you do (for a living)?**
solicitar un trabajo **to apply for a job**

IMPORTANT WORDS *(masculine)*

el	**aprendizaje**	apprenticeship
el	**asalariado**	wage earner
el	**aumento**	raise
el	**autor**	author
el	**cocinero**	cook
el	**colega**	colleague
el	**comerciante**	shopkeeper
el	**contrato**	contract
el	**conserje**	caretaker
el	**decorador**	interior designer
el	**desempleado**	unemployed person
el	**desempleo**	unemployment
el	**empleo**	job, position
el	**fontanero** *(Sp)*	plumber
el	**futuro**	future
el	**gerente**	manager
el	**hombre de negocios**	businessman
el	**mercado laboral**	job market
el	**negocio** *or* los **negocios**	business
el	**óptico**	optician
el	**peluquero**	hairdresser
el	**piloto**	pilot
el	**pintor**	painter
el	**plomero** *(LAm)*	plumber
el	**presidente**	president; chairperson
el	**sindicato**	trade union
el	**trabajador**	worker
el	**trabajo**	job

USEFUL PHRASES

estar desempleado(a) **to be unemployed**

contrato indefinido/temporal/a término fijo **permanent/temporary/fixed-term contract**

IMPORTANT WORDS *(feminine)*

la	**agencia de trabajo temporal**	temp agency
la	**asalariada**	wage earner
la	**biblioteca**	library
la	**carrera**	career
la	**carta adjunta**	cover letter
la	**cocinera**	cook
la	**colega**	colleague
la	**conserje**	caretaker
la	**entrevista (de trabajo)**	(job) interview
la	**gerente**	manager
la	**huelga**	strike
la	**mujer de negocios**	businessperson (female)
la	**oficina de empleo**	employment office
la	**peluquera**	hairdresser
la	**pintora**	painter
la	**política**	politics
la	**presidenta**	president; chairperson
la	**solicitud**	application
la	**trabajadora**	worker

USEFUL PHRASES

"empleos" **"seeking employment"**
"vacantes" **"help wanted"**
estar en/pertenercer a un sindicato **to be in a union**
ganar 600 dólares a la semana **to earn $600 a week**
una subida *or* un aumento de sueldo **a pay raise**
declararse en huelga *or* ir a la huelga **to go on strike**
estar en huelga **to be on strike**
trabajar jornada completa/media jornada **to work full-time/part-time**
trabajar horas extra(s) **to work overtime**
reducción de la jornada laboral **reduction in working hours**

USEFUL WORDS *(masculine)*

el	**abogado**	lawyer
el	**albañil**	construction worker
el	**arquitecto**	architect
el	**artista**	artist
el	**carpintero**	carpenter
el	**cirujano**	surgeon
el	**contador** *(LAm)*, el **contable** *(Sp)*	accountant
el	**cosmonauta**	cosmonaut
el	**cura**	priest
el	**curso de formación**	training course
el	**diputado**	representative, congressman
el	**diseñador**	designer
el	**ejecutivo**	executive
el	**escritor**	writer
el	**fotógrafo**	photographer
el	**funcionario público**	civil servant
el	**horario**	schedule
el	**ingeniero**	engineer
el	**intérprete**	interpreter
el	**investigador**	researcher
el	**juez** *(pl* jueces*)*	judge
el	**locutor**	announcer
el	**marinero**	sailor
el	**modelo**	model *(person)*
el	**monje**	monk
el	**notario**	notary public
el	**paro** *(Sp)*	unemployment benefit
el	**periodista**	journalist
el	**(período de) trabajo en prácticas**	work placement
el	**personal**	staff
el	**político**	politician
el	**procurador**	attorney
el	**religioso**	monk
el	**representante**	rep; sales rep
el	**sacerdote**	priest
el	**subsidio de desempleo**	unemployment benefit
el	**traductor**	translator
el	**veterinario**	veterinarian
el	**viticultor**	vintner, wine grower

USEFUL WORDS *(feminine)*

la **abogada**	lawyer
la **administración** (*pl* administraciones)	administration
el **ama de casa** (*f pl* amas ~ ~)	housewife
la **artista**	artist
la **compañía**	company
la **contadora** (*LAm*), la **contable** (*Sp*)	accountant
la **empresa**	company
la **formación**	training
la **funcionaria pública**	civil servant
la **indemnización por desempleo**	severance pay
la **intérprete**	interpreter
la **jueza**	judge
la **locutora**	announcer
la **modelo**	model (*person*)
la **modista**	dressmaker
la **monja**	nun
la **orientación profesional**	career counselling
la **periodista**	journalist
la **policía**	police officer, policewoman
la **religiosa**	nun
la **representante**	rep; sales rep
la **taquimecanógrafa**	shorthand typist
la **traductora**	translator

USEFUL PHRASES

el trabajo temporal **seasonal work**
un empleo temporal/permanente **a temporary/permanent job**
un trabajo a tiempo parcial *or* a medio tiempo **a part-time job**
contratar a algn **to hire sb**
echar a algn **to fire sb**
despedir a algn **to dismiss sb**
buscar trabajo **to look for work**
hacer un curso de formación profesional **to attend a training course**
marcar *or* checar (*Mex*) tarjeta al entrar a/al salir de trabajar **to clock in/out**
fichar (*Sp*) al entrar a/al salir de trabajar **to clock in/out**
trabajar en horario flexible **to work flextime**

ESSENTIAL WORDS *(masculine)*

el	**aceite**	oil
el	**agente de policía**	police officer, policeman
el	**aparcamiento** *(Sp)*	parking lot
el	**atasco**	traffic jam
el	**automóvil**	car
el	**aventón** *(Mex)*	ride
el	**camión** *(pl camiones)*	truck; *(Mex)* bus
el	**carnet** *or* **carné de conducir** *(Sp)* *(pl ~s or ~s ~~)*	driver's license
el	**carro** *(LAm)*	car
el	**chofer** *or* el **chófer** *(Sp)*	driver; chauffeur
el	**ciclista**	cyclist
el	**coche**	car
el	**conductor**	driver
el	**cruce**	intersection
el	**diesel**	diesel
el	**embotellamiento**	traffic jam
el	**estacionamiento** *(LAm)*	parking lot
los	**faros**	headlights
el	**freno**	brake
el	**garage** *(LAm)*, el **garaje** *(Sp)*	garage
el	**kilómetro**	kilometer
el	**litro**	liter
la	**llanta** *(LAm)*	tire
el	**mapa de carreteras**	road map
el	**mecánico**	mechanic
el	**neumático** *(Sp)*	tire
el	**número**	number
el	**parking** *(pl ~s)*	parking lot
el	**peaje**	toll
el	**peatón** *(pl peatones)*	pedestrian
el	**radar**	speed radar
el	**semáforo**	traffic light
el	**trailer** *(pl ~s) (LAm)*	trailer
el	**viaje**	journey

ESSENTIAL WORDS *(feminine)*

el	**agua** *(f)*	water
la	**autopista**	freeway, highway
la	**autopista de peaje**	toll road, turnpike
la	**caravana** *(Sp)*	trailer
la	**carretera**	road
la	**chofer** *(LAm)*, la **chófer** *(Sp)*	driver; chauffeur
la	**ciclista**	cyclist
la	**cochera**	garage
la	**conductora**	driver
la	**desviación** *(pl* desviaciones)	detour
la	**dirección** *(pl* direcciones)	direction; address
la	**dirección asistida** *(pl* direcciones ~s)	power steering
la	**distancia**	distance
la	**estación de servicio** *(pl* estaciones ~~)	gas station
la	**gasolina**	gasoline
la	**gasolina sin plomo**	unleaded gasoline
la	**licencia** *or* **libreta de manejar** *(LAm)*	driver's license
la	**placa** *(LAm)*, la **matrícula** *(Sp)*	license plate
la	**policía**	police
la	**póliza de seguros**	insurance policy
la	**ventanilla**	(car) window

USEFUL PHRASES

pedir aventón *(Mex)* to hitch a ride
viajar de aventón *(Mex)* to hitchhike
frenar bruscamente to brake suddenly
100 kilómetros por hora 100 kilometers an hour
¿tienes licencia de manejar? do you have a driver's license?
vamos a dar una vuelta (en coche/carro) we're going for a drive/ride (in the car)
¡lleno, por favor!, ¡llénelo, por favor! fill 'er up please!
tomar la carretera a/hacia Morelia take the road to Morelia
es un viaje de tres horas it's a 3-hour drive
de camino vimos ... on the way we saw ...
adelantar a algn/un carro to pass sb/a car
rebasar a algn *(Mex)* to pass sb

IMPORTANT WORDS *(masculine)*

el	**accidente (de tráfico** *or* **de tránsito)**	(traffic) accident
el	**automovilista**	driver, motorist
el	**camionero**	truck driver; *(Mex)* bus driver
el	**choque**	collision
el	**cinturón de seguridad**	seat belt
	(pl cinturones ~ ~)	
el	**claxon** *(pl* cláxones *or* ~s)	horn
el	**clutch** *(Mex)*	clutch
el	**daño**	damage
el	**embrague**	clutch
el	**maletero** *(Sp)*	trunk *(of a car)*
el	**motociclista**	motorcyclist
el	**motor**	engine
los	**papeles (del coche)**	license and registration
el	**pinchazo**	flat
el	**seguro**	insurance
el	**surtidor (de gasolina)**	gas pump
el	**tablero de mando**	dashboard
el	**tráfico** *or* **tránsito**	traffic
el	**túnel de lavado de coches**	car wash

USEFUL PHRASES

primero enciendes el motor *or* pones el motor en marcha **first you turn on the engine**

el motor arranca *or* se pone en marcha **the engine engages**

el coche se pone en marcha **the car moves off**

estamos circulando **we're driving along**

acelerar **to accelerate;** continuar **to continue**

reducir *or* aminorar la velocidad **to slow down**

detenerse **to stop;** estacionar (el coche) **to park (the car)**

apagar el motor **to turn off the engine**

parar con el semáforo en rojo **to stop at the red light**

IMPORTANT WORDS *(feminine)*

la	**autoescuela** *(Sp)*	driving school
la	**automovilista**	driver, motorist
la	**avería**	breakdown
la	**batería**	battery
la	**cajuela** *(Mex)*	trunk *(of a car)*
la	**calle de sentido único**	one-way street
la	**carrocería**	body work
la	**colisión** *(pl* colisiones*)*	collision
la	**documentación (del coche)**	license and registration
la	**escuela de conductores** *or* **de manejo** *(LAm)*	driving school
la	**frontera**	border
la	**glorieta**	traffic circle
la	**grúa**	tow truck
la	**marca**	make *(of car)*
la	**motociclista**	motorcyclist
la	**pieza de repuesto**	spare part
la	**póliza de seguros**	insurance policy
la	**ponchadura** *(Mex)*	flat
la	**prioridad**	right of way
la	**prueba del alcohol**	Breathalyzer® test
la	**puerta**	*(car)* door
la	**refacción** *(Mex)*	spare part
la	**rotonda**	traffic circle
la	**rueda**	tire; wheel
la	**rueda de repuesto**	spare tire
la	**velocidad**	speed; gear

USEFUL PHRASES

hubo un accidente **there was an accident**

hubo seis heridos en el accidente **six people were injured in the accident**

¿puedo ver la documentación *or* los papeles del coche, por favor? **may I see your license and registration, please?**

pinchar, tener un pinchazo **to have a flat;** arreglar **to repair** *or* **to fix**

se me ponchó una llanta *(Mex)* **I had a flat**

tener una avería **to break down**

me quedé sin gasolina **I ran out of gas**

USEFUL WORDS *(masculine)*

el acelerador	accelerator
el acotamiento *(Mex)*	shoulder
el (anillo) periférico *(LAm)*	beltway
el arcén *(pl arcenes) (Sp)*	shoulder
el autolavado	car wash
el botón de arranque *(pl botones ~ ~)*	starter
el capó	hood
el carburador	carburetor
el camellón *(Mex)*	median strip
el carril	lane
el catalizador	catalytic converter
el cofre *(Mex)*	hood
el consumo de gasolina	gas consumption
el cuentakilómetros *(pl inv)*	speedometer
el desvío	detour
el herido	casualty
el intermitente *(Sp)*	indicator
el lavacoches *(pl inv)*	car wash
el límite de velocidad	speed limit
el limpiador *(Mex)*	windshield wiper
el limpiaparabrisas *(pl inv)*	windshield wiper
el parabrisas *(pl inv)*	windshield
el paragolpes *(pl inv) (LAm)*	bumper
el parquímetro	parking meter
el pedal	pedal
el portaequipajes	roof rack
el profesor de manejo *(LAm)*	driving instructor
el remolque	trailer
el retrovisor	rear-view mirror
el (sistema de navegación) GPS	satellite navigation system
el volante	steering wheel

USEFUL PHRASES

en la hora pico *(LAm) or* punta *(Sp)* during rush hour
le pusieron una multa de 100 dólares he got a 100 dollar fine
¿está asegurado? are you insured?
está aprendiendo a manejar (s)he is learning to drive
ponerse el cinturón de seguridad to put on one's seat belt

USEFUL WORDS *(feminine)*

el	**área de servicio** (*f pl* las áreas ~~)	service area
la	**caja de cambios**	transmission
la	**carretera de circunvalación** (*Sp*)	beltway
la	**clase de manejo** (*LAm*)	driving lesson
la	**curva**	bend
la	**defensa** (*Mex*)	bumper
la	**direccional** (*LAm*)	indicator
la	**estación de servicio** (*pl* estaciones ~~)	gas station
la	**gasolinera**	gas station
la	**infracción de tráfico** *or* **tránsito** (*pl* infracciones ~~)	traffic offense
la	**matrícula**	license plate number
la	**mediana** (*Sp*)	median strip
la	**multa**	fine
la	**parada de emergencia**	emergency stop
la	**presión**	pressure
la	**profesora de manejo** (*LAm*)	driving instructor
la	**señal de tráfico** *or* **tránsito**	road sign
la	**vía de acceso**	access road
la	**víctima** (*m+f*)	casualty
la	**zona urbanizada**	developed area

USEFUL PHRASES

la rueda delantera/trasera the front/back wheel
tenemos que desviarnos we have to take a detour
una multa por exceso de velocidad a fine for speeding
contratar a un chofer (*LAm*) *or* a un chófer (*Sp*) to hire a driver
"ceda el paso" "yield"
"prohibido el paso" "no entry"
"prohibido estacionar" "no parking"
"obras" "road work" *or* "highway repairs"

ESSENTIAL WORDS (*masculine*)

el	abrigo	overcoat; coat
el	bañador (*Sp*)	swimsuit
el	bolsillo	pocket
el	bolso (*Sp*)	bag, purse
el	botón (*pl* botones)	button
el	calcetín (*pl* calcetines)	sock
los	calzoncillos	underpants; boxer shorts
el	calzón *or* los calzones (*LAm*)	panties
el	camisón (*pl* camisones)	nightgown
el	cuello	collar
el	impermeable	raincoat
los	jeans (*LAm*)	jeans
el	jersey (*pl* ~s) (*Sp*)	sweater
el	número (de zapato)	(shoe) size
el	pantalón (*pl* pantalones)	pants, trousers
los	pantalones de mezclilla (*Mex*)	jeans
los	(pantalones) vaqueros	jeans
el	pañuelo	handkerchief
el	paraguas (*pl inv*)	umbrella
el	pijama (*Sp*)	pajamas
el	sombrero	hat
el	suéter (*LAm*)	sweater
el	talle	waist
el	traje	suit (*for man*); costume
el	traje de baño	swimsuit
el	traje de chaqueta	suit (*for woman*)
el	vestido	dress
el	zapato	shoe

IMPORTANT WORDS (*masculine*)

el	cinturón (*pl* cinturones)	belt
el	guante	glove
los	shorts	shorts
el	uniforme	uniform

ESSENTIAL WORDS *(feminine)*

la	**bolsa**	bag; *(Mex)* purse; pocket
las	**bragas** *(Sp)*	panties
la	**camisa**	shirt
la	**camiseta**	t-shirt
la	**capucha**	hood
la	**chamarra** *(Mex)*	jacket
la	**chaqueta**	jacket
la	**corbata**	tie
la	**falda**	skirt
las	**medias**	pantyhose, stockings
la	**moda**	fashion
las	**pantaletas** *(Mex)*	panties
las	**pantimedias** *(Mex)*	pantyhose
la	**pijama** *(LAm)*	pajamas
la	**playera** *(Mex)*	t-shirt
la	**ropa**	clothes
la	**ropa interior**	underwear
la	**sandalia**	sandal
la	**talla**	size

IMPORTANT WORDS *(feminine)*

la	**americana** *(Sp)*	jacket *(for man)*
la	**blusa**	blouse
la	**bota**	boot
la	**pantufla** *(LAm)*	slipper
las	**prendas de vestir**	clothes, garments
la	**zapatilla** *(Sp)*	slipper
la	**zapatilla** *(Mex)*	shoe *(for woman)*

USEFUL PHRASES

en la mañana me visto **in the morning I get dressed**
en la noche me desvisto **in the evening I get undressed**
cuando llego a casa me cambio **when I get home, I get changed**
llevar, llevar puesto **to wear**
ponerse **to put on**
(eso) te queda bien **that suits you**
¿qué talla tienes (*or* tiene)? **what size do you wear?**

USEFUL WORDS *(masculine)*

los	**accesorios**	accessories
el	**bastón** (*pl* bastones)	walking stick
el	**brasier** (*LAm*)	bra
el	**cárdigan** (*pl* ~s)	cardigan
el	**chaleco**	vest
el	**chándal** (*pl* ~s) (*Sp*)	sweatsuit
los	**cordones**	(shoe)laces
el	**delantal**	apron
el	**desfile de modas**	fashion show
el	**foulard** (*pl* ~s)	scarf
el	**lazo**	bow
el	**mono** (*Sp*)	overalls
el	**ojal**	buttonhole
los	**pantis** (*Sp*)	tights
los	**pants** (*pl inv*) (*Mex*)	sweatsuit; sweatpants
el	**pañuelo**	scarf
el	**overol** (*LAm*)	overalls
el	**polar**	fleece jacket
el	**polo**	polo shirt
el	**probador**	fitting room
el	**sujetador** (*Sp*)	bra
los	**tenis** (*LAm*)	sneakers, running shoes
los	**tirantes**	suspenders
el	**traje de etiqueta**	dress suit
el	**traje de noche**	evening gown
el	**traje pantalón** (*pl* ~s ~)	pants suit
el	**vestido** *or* **traje de novia**	wedding gown
los	**zapatos de tacón**	high heels
los	**zapatos de tacón de aguja**	stiletto heels

USEFUL WORDS (*feminine*)

las	**agujetas** (*Mex*)	(shoe) laces
la	**alpargata**	espadrille
la	**alta costura**	high fashion, haute couture
la	**bata**	dressing gown
las	**bermudas**	Bermuda shorts
la	**boina**	beret
la	**bufanda**	scarf
las	**chanclas**	thongs (*sandals*)
la	**corbata de moño** (*LAm*)	bow tie
la	**cinta**	ribbon
la	**cremallera** (*Sp*)	zipper
la(s)	**enagua(s)**	slip, petticoat
la	**falda pantalón** (*pl ~s ~*)	culottes
la	**gorra**	cap
la	**limpieza en seco**	dry cleaning
la	**manga**	sleeve
la	**pajarita** (*Sp*)	bow tie
la	**rebeca** (*Sp*)	cardigan
la	**ropa lavada/para lavar**	laundry
la	**sudadera**	sweatshirt
la	**sudadera con capucha**	hooded top
la	**tintorería**	dry cleaner's
las	**zapatillas de deporte** (*Sp*)	sneakers, running shoes

USEFUL PHRASES

largo(a) **long**; corto(a) **short**
un vestido de manga corta/larga **a short-sleeved/long-sleeved dress**
estrecho(a), ajustado(a) **tight**
amplio(a), suelto(a) **loose**
una falda ajustada *or* ceñida **a tight skirt**
a rayas, de rayas **striped**; a cuadros, de cuadros **checkered**; de lunares
  polka-dotted
ropa de sport, ropa informal **casual clothes**
a la moda, de moda **fashionable**; moderno(a) **trendy**
pasado(a) de moda, anticuado(a) **old-fashioned**

amarillo(a)	yellow
azul	blue
azul celeste	sky blue
azul claro	pale blue
azul marino	navy blue
azul oscuro	dark blue
beige	beige
beis (*Sp*)	beige
blanco(a)	white
el color	color
crudo(a)	natural
dorado(a)	golden
granate	maroon
gris	gray
malva	mauve
marrón (*pl* marrones)	brown
naranja	orange
negro(a)	black
rojo(a)	red
rojo fuerte *or* intenso	bright red
rosa	pink
turquesa	turquoise
verde	green
violeta	purple

USEFUL PHRASES

¿de qué color tienes (*or* tiene) los ojos/el pelo? what color are your eyes/
   is your hair?

el azul te sienta bien blue looks good on you; the blue one looks good
   on you

pintar algo de azul to paint sth blue

los zapatos azules blue shoes

los zapatos azul claro light blue shoes

tiene los ojos verdes (s)he has green eyes

cambiar de color to change color

la Casa Blanca the White House

un (hombre) blanco a white man

una (mujer) blanca a white woman

un (hombre) negro a black man

una (mujer) negra a black woman

blanco como la nieve as white as snow

Blancanieves Snow White

Caperucita Roja Little Red Riding Hood

ponerse colorado(a) *or* rojo(a) to turn red

sonrojarse de vergüenza to blush with shame

blanco(a) como el papel as white as a sheet

un ojo morado a black eye

un filete rojo *or* a la inglesa (*Mex*) a rare steak

un filete muy poco hecho (*Sp*) a rare steak

ESSENTIAL WORDS *(masculine)*

el	**monitor**	monitor
el	**mouse** *(LAm)*	mouse
el	**ordenador (personal)** *(Sp)*	(personal) computer
el	**programa**	program
el	**programador**	programmer
el	**teclado**	keyboard
el	**ratón** *(pl* ratones) *(Sp)*	mouse

USEFUL WORDS *(masculine)*

el	**archivo**	file
el	**cartucho de tinta**	ink cartridge
el	**CD-ROM** *(pl inv)*	CD-ROM
el	**corrector ortográfico**	spellchecker
el	**correo electrónico**	email
el	**cursor**	cursor
los	**datos**	data
el	**disco duro**	hard disk
el	**documento**	document
el	**email**	email
el	**fichero** *(Sp)*	file
el	**fólder** *(LAm)*	folder
el	**icono**	icon
el	**internauta**	internet user
el	**juego de ordenador** *(Sp)*	computer game
el	**mail** *(pl ~s)*	email (message)
el	**menú**	menu
el	**módem** *(pl ~s)*	modem
el	**navegador**	browser
el	**paquete de programas**	software package
el	**pirata informático**	hacker
el	**portátil**	laptop
el	**procesador de textos**	wordprocessor
el	**servidor**	server
el	**sitio web**	website
el	**software** *(pl inv)*	software
el	**soporte (físico)**	hardware
el	**virus** *(pl inv)*	virus
el	**wifi**	wifi

ESSENTIAL WORDS *(feminine)*

la **computadora** (*LAm*)	computer
la **impresora**	printer
la **informática**	IT, computer science

USEFUL WORDS *(feminine)*

la **aplicación** (*pl* aplicaciones)	program
la **banda ancha**	broadband
la **base de datos**	database
la **carpeta** (*Sp*)	folder
la **computadora portátil** (*LAm*)	laptop
la **copia de seguridad**	back-up
la **copia impresa**	print out
la **dirección de correo (electrónico)** (*pl* direcciones ~~ (~))	email address
la **función** (*pl* funciones)	function
la **grabadora de DVD**	DVD burner
la **hoja de cálculo**	spreadsheet
la **interfaz** (*pl* interfaces)	interface
la **internauta**	internet user
(la) **Internet**	Internet
la **llave USB**	USB key
la **memoria**	memory
la **memoria RAM**	RAM, random access memory
la **memoria ROM**	ROM, read-only Memory
la **página de inicio**	homepage
la **pantalla**	screen
la **papelera de reciclaje**	recycle bin, trash
la **red**	network
la **unidad de disco**	disk drive
la **ventana**	window
la **Web** (*pl* ~s)	Web
la **webcam** (*pl* ~s)	webcam

USEFUL PHRASES

copiar to copy; eliminar, suprimir to delete; formatear to format
bajar *or* descargar un archivo to download a file
guardar to save; imprimir to print; teclear to key, to type
navegar por Internet to surf the internet

COUNTRIES (*masculine*)

	Brasil	Brazil
	Canadá	Canada
	Chile	Chile
	Ecuador	Ecuador
	EE.UU.	USA
	El Salvador	El Salvador
	Estados Unidos	United States
	Japón	Japan
	México	Mexico
el	país	country
	Panamá	Panama
	Paraguay	Paraguay
	Perú	Peru
	Puerto Rico	Puerto Rico
el	Tercer Mundo	the Third World
	Uruguay	Uruguay

USEFUL PHRASES

mi país de origen my native country

la capital de Argentina the capital of Argentina

¿de qué país eres (*or* es)? what country do you come from?

soy de (los) Estados Unidos/de Canadá I come from the United States/
from Canada

nací en Ecuador I was born in Ecuador

me voy a Chile I'm going to Chile

acabo de regresar de (los) Estados Unidos I have just come back from the
United States

los países en (vías de) desarrollo the developing countries

los países de habla hispana Spanish-speaking countries

COUNTRIES (*feminine*)

	Spanish	English
	África	Africa
	Alemania	Germany
	América	America
	América del Sur	South America
	Argentina	Argentina
	Asia	Asia
	Bolivia	Bolivia
	Centroamérica	Central America
(la)	China	China
	Colombia	Colombia
	Costa Rica	Costa Rica
	Cuba	Cuba
	España	Spain
	Europa	Europe
	Francia	France
	Gran Bretaña	Great Britain
	Guatemala	Guatemala
	Honduras	Honduras
(la)	India	India
	Inglaterra	England
	Irlanda	Ireland
	Italia	Italy
	Nicaragua	Nicaragua
la	República Dominicana	the Dominican Republic
	Sudamérica	South America
la	Unión Europea, la UE	the European Union, the EU
	Venezuela	Venezuela

NATIONALITIES

ESSENTIAL WORDS *(masculine)*

un	americano	an American
un	argentino	an Argentinian
un	boliviano	a Bolivian
un	chileno	a Chilean
un	colombiano	a Colombian
un	costarricense	a Costa Rican
un	cubano	a Cuban
un	dominicano	a Dominican
un	ecuatoriano	an Ecuadorean
un	español	a Spaniard
un	guatemalteco	a Guatemalan
un	hondureño	a Honduran
un	mexicano	a Mexican
un	nicaragüense	a Nicaraguan
un	panameño	a Panamanian
un	paraguayo	a Paraguayan
un	peruano	a Peruvian
un	puertorriqueño	a Puerto Rican
un	salvadoreño	a Salvadorian
un	uruguayo	a Uruguayan
un	venezolano	a Venezuelan

USEFUL PHRASES

es italiano he is Italian
es italiana she is Italian
la campiña italiana the Italian countryside
una ciudad italiana an Italian town

ESSENTIAL WORDS *(feminine)*

una	americana	an American
una	argentina	an Argentinian
una	boliviana	a Bolivian
una	chilena	a Chilean
una	colombiana	a Colombian
una	costarricense	a Costa Rican
una	cubana	a Cuban
una	dominicana	a Dominican
una	ecuatoriana	an Ecuadorean
una	española	a Spaniard
una	guatemalteca	a Guatemalan
una	hondureña	a Honduran
una	mexicana	a Mexican
una	nicaragüense	a Nicaraguan
una	panameña	a Panamanian
una	paraguaya	a Paraguayan
una	peruana	a Peruvian
una	puertorriqueña	a Puerto Rican
una	salvadoreña	a Salvadorian
una	uruguaya	a Uruguayan
una	venezolana	a Venezuelan

USEFUL PHRASES

soy americano – hablo inglés I am American – I speak English
soy americana I am American
un(a) extranjero(a) a foreigner
en el extranjero abroad
la nacionalidad nationality

USEFUL WORDS *(masculine)*

un **africano**	an African
un **alemán** *(pl* alemanes)	a German
un **árabe**	an Arab
un **brasileño**	a Brazilian
un **canadiense**	a Canadian
un **chino**	a Chinese
un **europeo**	a European
un **francés** *(pl* franceses)	a Frenchman
un **indio**	an Indian
un **inglés** *(pl* ingleses)	an Englishman
un **irlandés** *(pl* irlandeses)	an Irishman
un **italiano**	an Italian
un **japonés** *(pl* japoneses)	a Japanese

USEFUL WORDS *(feminine)*

una	**africana**	an African
una	**alemana**	a German
una	**árabe**	an Arab
una	**brasileña**	a Brazilian
una	**canadiense**	a Canadian
una	**china**	a Chinese
una	**europea**	a European
una	**francesa**	a Frenchwoman
una	**india**	an Indian
una	**inglésa**	an Englishwoman
una	**irlandesa**	an Irishwoman
una	**italiana**	an Italian
una	**japonesa**	a Japanese

ESSENTIAL WORDS *(masculine)*

el	**aire**	air
el	**albergue juvenil**	youth hostel
el	**árbol**	tree
el	**arroyo**	stream
el	**bastón** (*pl* bastones)	walking stick
el	**bosque**	wood; forest
el	**camino**	way
el	**campesino**	farmer; peasant
el	**campo**	country, countryside; field
el	**cazador**	hunter
el	**granjero**	farmer
el	**mercado**	market
el	**paisaje**	scenery
el	**paseo**	walk
el	**picnic** (*pl* ~s)	picnic
el	**pueblo**	village
el	**puente**	bridge
el	**río**	river
el	**ruido**	noise
el	**sendero**	path; track
el	**terreno**	soil; ground
el	**turista**	tourist
el	**valle**	valley

USEFUL PHRASES

al aire libre **in the open air**
sé el camino al pueblo **I know the way to the village**
(ir a) andar en bicicleta **to go cycling**
los vecinos *or* los habitantes de la zona **the locals**
fuimos de picnic **we had a picnic**

ESSENTIAL WORDS *(feminine)*

la	**camioneta**	van; station wagon
la	**campesina**	farmer; peasant
la	**carretera**	road
la	**cazadora**	hunter
la	**cerca**	fence
la	**excursión** (*pl* excursiones)	hike; excursion
la	**granja**	farm, farmhouse
la	**granjera**	farmer
la	**montaña**	mountain
la	**piedra**	stone; rock
la	**región** (*pl* regiones)	area; district
la	**tierra**	land; earth; soil; ground
la	**torre**	tower
la	**turista**	tourist
la	**vagoneta** (*Mex*)	van
la	**valla** (*Sp*)	fence

USEFUL PHRASES

en el campo **in the country**
ir (de excursión) al campo **to go to the country**
vivir en el campo/en la ciudad **to live in the country/in town**
cultivar la tierra **to cultivate the land**

IMPORTANT WORDS *(masculine)*

el	**agricultor**	farmer
el	**lago**	lake
el	**mesón** *(pl* mesones)	inn
el	**polvo**	dust
el	**ranchero** *(Mex)*	rancher
el	**rancho** *(Mex)*	ranch

USEFUL WORDS *(masculine)*

el	**arbusto**	bush
el	**barro** *or* el **lodo**	mud
los	**binoculares**	binoculars
el	**charco**	puddle
el	**estanque**	pond
el	**guijarro**	pebble
el	**heno**	hay
el	**matorral**	bushes
el	**maíz**	maize; corn
el	**molino (de viento)**	(wind)mill
el	**palo**	stick
el	**pantano**	marsh
el	**poste telegráfico**	telephone pole
los	**prismáticos**	binoculars
el	**seto**	hedge
el	**trigo**	wheat

USEFUL PHRASES

agrícola agricultural
apacible, tranquilo(a) peaceful, tranquil
en la cima de la colina at the top of the hill
caer en una trampa to fall into a trap

IMPORTANT WORDS *(feminine)*

la **agricultora**	farmer
la **agricultura**	agriculture
la **calzada**	road surface
la **cima**	top *(of a hill)*
la **colina**	hill
la **gente del campo**	country people
la **hoja**	leaf
la **posada**	inn
la **propiedad**	property; estate
la **ranchera** *(Mex)*	rancher
la **tranquilidad**	peace, tranquility

USEFUL WORDS *(feminine)*

la **aldea**	village
la **bota de goma**	rubber boot
la **bota de hule** *(Mex)*	rubber boot
la **cantera**	quarry
la **cascada**	waterfall
la **caza**	hunting; shooting
la **cosecha**	crop; harvest
la **fuente**	spring; source
la **llanura**	plain
la **orilla**	bank *(of a river)*
las **ruinas**	ruins
la **señal**	signpost
la **trampa**	trap
la **vendimia**	grape harvest
la **zanja**	ditch

USEFUL PHRASES

perderse to lose one's way; to get lost
recoger la cosecha to bring in the harvest
vendimiar, hacer la vendimia to harvest the grapes

ESSENTIAL WORDS *(masculine)*

el	**aspecto**	appearance
el	**bigote**	moustache
el	**cabello**	hair
el	**color**	color
los	**ojos**	eyes
el	**pelo**	hair
el	**talle**	waist

USEFUL PHRASES

alegre **cheerful**
alto(a) **tall**
amable **kind; nice**
antiguo(a) **old**
bajo(a) **short**
barbudo(a), de barba **bearded, with a beard**
bonito(a) **pretty**
bueno(a) **kind**
calvo(a) **bald**
canoso(a) **gray-haired**
culto(a) **well-educated, cultured**
delgado(a) **thin, slim**
desagradable **unpleasant**
divertido(a), entretenido(a) **amusing, entertaining**
educado(a) **polite**
esbelto(a) **slender, slim**
feliz (*pl* felices) **happy**
feo(a) **ugly**
flaco(a) **skinny**
gordo(a) **fat**
gracioso(a) **funny**
grosero(a) **rude**
guapo **handsome;** guapa **beautiful**
güero(a) (*Mex*) **blond(e)**
horrible **hideous**
infeliz (*pl* infelices), desgraciado(a) **unhappy, unfortunate**
inteligente **intelligent**
lindo(a) (*LAm*) **pretty, nice**
joven (*pl* jóvenes) **young**

ESSENTIAL WORDS *(feminine)*

la	**barba**	beard
la	**edad**	age
la	**estatura**	height; size
las	**gafas**	glasses
la	**identidad**	ID
la	**lágrima**	tear
la	**persona**	person
la	**talla**	size; height

USEFUL PHRASES

largo(a) **long**

malo(a) **naughty**

moreno(a) **dark-haired; dark-skinned**

mono(a) **cute**

nervioso(a), tenso(a) **nervous, tense**

optimista/pesimista **optimistic/pessimistic**

pequeno(a) **small, little**

rubio(a) **blond(e)**

serio(a) **serious**

tímido(a) **shy**

tonto(a) **stupid**

tranquilo(a) **calm**

viejo(a) **old**

parece triste **(s)he looks sad**

estaba llorando **(s)he was crying**

sonreía **(s)he was smiling**

la muchacha tenía lágrimas en los ojos **the girl had tears in her eyes**

un hombre de estatura mediana **a man of average height**

mido 1 metro 70 *or* uno setenta **I am 1 meter 70 tall**

¿de qué color son tus (*or* sus) ojos/es tu (*or* su) pelo? **what color are your eyes/ is your hair?**

soy rubia *or* (*Mex*) güera **I am blonde**

me/le están saliendo canas **I'm/(s)he's going gray**

tengo los ojos azules/verdes **I have blue/green eyes**

pelo moreno *or* castaño **dark *or* brown hair**

pelo castaño **light brown hair;** pelo rizado **curly hair**

pelirrojo(a) **red-haired**

pelo negro/canoso **black/gray hair**

pelo teñido **dyed hair**

IMPORTANT WORDS *(masculine)*

el	**carácter** *(pl* caracteres)	character; nature
el	**grano**	pimple
el	**humor**	mood

USEFUL WORDS *(masculine)*

el	**chino** *(Mex)*	curl
el	**defecto**	fault
el	**fleco** *(Mex)*	bangs
el	**flequillo** *(Sp)*	bangs
el	**gesto**	gesture
el	**gigante**	giant
los	**hoyuelos**	dimples
los	**lentes** *or* **anteojos**	glasses
los	**lentes de contacto**	contact lenses
el	**lunar**	mole, beauty mark
el	**parecido**	resemblance
el	**permanente** *(Mex)*	perm
el	**peso**	weight
el	**rizo**	curl

USEFUL PHRASES

tiene buen carácter (s)he is good-tempered
tiene mal genio *or* carácter (s)he is bad-tempered
tener la tez pálida *or* muy blanca to have a pale complexion
tener el pelo lacio to have straight hair
tener el pelo rizado *or* (*Mex*) chino to have curly hair
usar lentes *or* anteojos (*LAm*) to wear glasses
llevar gafas (*Sp*) to wear glasses
usar lentes de contacto to wear contact lenses

IMPORTANT WORDS *(feminine)*

la **belleza**	beauty
la **calidad**	(good) quality
la **costumbre**	habit
la **curiosidad**	curiosity
la **expresión** *(pl* expresiones)	expression
la **fealdad**	ugliness
la **mirada**	look
la **sonrisa**	smile
la **tez** *(pl* teces)	complexion
la **voz** *(pl* voces)	voice

USEFUL WORDS *(feminine)*

las **arrugas**	wrinkles
la **cicatriz** *(pl* cicatrices)	scar
la **dentadura**	teeth
la **dentadura postiza**	dentures, false teeth
las **pecas**	freckles
la **permanente**	perm
la **timidez**	shyness

USEFUL PHRASES

siempre estoy de buen humor **I am always in a good mood**
está de mal humor **(s)he is in a bad mood**
se enojó **(s)he got angry**
Marita se parece a su madre **Marita looks like her mother**
mi hermano se come *or* se muerde las uñas **my brother bites his nails**

ESSENTIAL WORDS *(masculine)*

el	alemán	German
el	alfabeto	alphabet
el	alumno	pupil; schoolboy
el	amigo	friend
el	aprendizaje	learning
el	club *(pl* ~s *or* ~es)	club
el	colegio	school
el	colegio de secundaria	secondary school
el	comienzo del curso	beginning of the semester
el	compañero de clase	school friend
el	concierto	concert
el	cuaderno	notebook
los	deberes	homework
el	día	day
el	dibujo	drawing
el	director	principal
el	dormitorio	dormitory
el	error	mistake
el	escolar	schoolboy
el	español	Spanish
el	estudiante	student
el	estudio (de)	study (of)
los	estudios	studies
el	examen *(pl* exámenes)	exam, test
el	experimento	experiment
el	francés	French
el	gimnasio	gym
el	grupo	group
el	horario	schedule, timetable
el	idioma	language
el	inglés	English
el	intercambio	exchange
el	italiano	Italian
el	laboratorio	laboratory
el	lápiz *(pl* lápices)	pencil
el	libro	book
el	maestro	elementary school teacher
el	mapa	map
el	ordenador *(Sp)*	computer

ESSENTIAL WORDS *(feminine)*

la	**alberca** *(Mex)*	swimming pool
la	**alumna**	pupil; schoolgirl
la	**amiga**	friend
el	**aula** *(f pl* las aulas*)*	classroom
la	**biología**	biology
la	**cafetería**	cafeteria
la	**calificación**	grade
las	**ciencias**	science
la	**clase**	class; year; classroom
las	**clases**	lessons
las	**clases prácticas**	lab
la	**compañera de clase**	school friend
la	**computadora** *(LAm)*	computer
la	**directora**	principal
la	**educación física**	PE
la	**electrónica**	electronics
la	**enseñanza**	education; teaching
la	**escolar**	schoolgirl
la	**escuela**	school
la	**escuela primaria**	elementary school
la	**estudiante**	student
la	**excursión** *(pl* excursiones*)*	trip; hike; outing
la	**física**	physics
la	**frase**	sentence
la	**geografía**	geography
la	**gimnasia**	gym
la	**goma (de borrar)**	eraser
la	**grabadora**	tape recorder
la	**guardería**	day care center
la	**historia**	history; story
la	**informática**	computer studies
la	**lección** *(pl* lecciones*)*	lesson
la	**lectura**	reading
las	**lenguas extranjeras**	foreign languages
la	**maestra**	elementary school teacher
las	**matemáticas**	mathematics
la	**materia (escolar)**	(school) subject
la	**música**	music
la	**natación**	swimming

ESSENTIAL WORDS (*masculine continued*)

el	**premio**	prize
el	**profesor**	teacher; professor
el	**progreso**	progress
el	**recreo**	recess
el	**resultado**	result
el	**semestre**	semester
el	**trabajo**	work
los	**trabajos manuales**	handicrafts, shop

USEFUL PHRASES

trabajar to work

aprender to learn

estudiar to study

¿cuánto tiempo hace que aprendes (*or* aprende) español? how long have you been studying Spanish?

aprenderse algo de memoria to learn sth by heart

hago la tarea todos los días I do my homework every day

mi hermana menor va a la escuela, yo voy a secundaria my kid sister goes to elementary school – I go to junior high

enseñar español to teach Spanish

el/la profesor(a) de alemán the German teacher

mejoré en matemáticas I've made progress in math

hacer *or* presentar un examen to take an exam *or* a test

aprobar un examen to pass an exam *or* a test

reprobar un examen (*LAm*) to fail an exam *or* a test

suspender un examen (*Sp*) to fail an exam *or* a test

sacar un aprobado to get a passing grade

ESSENTIAL WORDS (*feminine continued*)

la	**piscina**	swimming pool
la	**pizarra**	blackboard
la	**pregunta**	question
la	**prepa** *or* **preparatoria** (*Mex*)	high school; prep school
la	**preprimaria** (*Mex*)	kindergarten
la	**profesora**	teacher; professor
la	**química**	chemistry
la	**respuesta**	answer
la	**sala de profesores**	faculty room
la	**secundaria**	secondary education; junior high-school
la	**tarea** (*LAm*)	homework
la	**universidad**	college; university
las	**vacaciones**	vacation
las	**vacaciones de verano**	summer vacation

USEFUL PHRASES

fácil easy; difícil difficult

interesante interesting

aburrido(a) boring

leer to read; escribir to write

escuchar to listen (to)

mirar to look at, watch

repetir to repeat

contestar, responder to answer, to reply

hablar to speak

es la primera *or* la mejor de la clase she is top of the class

es la última *or* la peor de la clase she is bottom of the class

entrar a la clase to go into the classroom

cometer un error to make a mistake

corregir to correct

cometí un error gramatical I made a grammatical error

cometí una falta de ortografía I made a spelling mistake

me equivoqué I made a mistake

siempre saca buenas calificaciones (s)he always gets good grades

contesta (*or* contesten) la pregunta answer the question

¡levanten la mano! raise your hand!

IMPORTANT WORDS *(masculine)*

el	**bachillerato**	GED course/certificate
el	**certificado**	certificate
el	**colegio privado** *or* **particular**	private school
el	**colegio público** *or* **oficial**	public school
el	**corredor**	hall, corridor
el	**despacho**	office
el	**día libre**	day off
el	**diploma**	diploma
el	**estuche para lápices**	pencil case
el	**examen escrito** *(pl* exámenes ~s)	written exam
el	**examen oral** *(pl* exámenes ~es)	oral exam
el	**expediente**	file
el	**papel**	paper
el	**pasillo**	hall, corridor
el	**patio (de recreo)**	playground, schoolyard

USEFUL PHRASES

repasar to revise
repasaré otra vez la lección mañana I'll go over the lesson again tomorrow
hacer una composición to write a composition
hacer un trabajo sobre los mayas to do an assignment on the Mayas

IMPORTANT WORDS *(feminine)*

la	**carpeta**	file folder
la	**conferencia**	lecture
el	**fólder** (*LAm*)	folder
las	**normas**	rules
la	**regla**	rule; ruler
la	**selectividad** (*Sp*)	college entrance examination
la	**traducción** (*pl* traducciones)	translation
la	**versión** (*pl* versiones)	translation (*into a foreign language*)

USEFUL PHRASES

presente present

ausente absent

castigar a un(a) alumno(a) to punish a student

¡silencio! be quiet!

la maestra me puso falta the teacher marked me as absent

nunca falta a clase he never misses school

faltó a clase ayer (s)he didn't come/go to school yesterday

la Facultad de arquitectura the School of Architecture

un compañero de facultad a friend from college

USEFUL WORDS *(masculine)*

el	**block** *(pl ~s)*	notepad
el	**bolígrafo**	ballpoint pen
el	**borrador**	rough draft
el	**cálculo**	calculation
el	**castigo**	detention; punishment
el	**comportamiento**	behavior
el	**conserje**	janitor
el	**corrector (líquido)**	Wite-Out®, correction fluid
el	**diccionario**	dictionary
el	**ejercicio**	exercise
el	**examinador**	examiner
el	**gis** *(Mex)*	chalk, piece of chalk
el	**griego**	Greek
el	**inspector**	school inspector
el	**internado**	boarding school
el	**interno**	boarder
el	**latín**	Latin
el	**libro de texto**	textbook
el	**maletín** *(pl maletines)*	briefcase
el	**marcador** *(Mex)*	marker, magic marker
el	**plumón** *(Mex)*	felt-tip pen
el	**portafolios** *(pl inv)*	briefcase
el	**pupitre**	desk
el	**rotulador** *(Sp)*	felt-tip pen
el	**sacapuntas** *(pl inv)*	pencil sharpener
el	**test** *(pl ~s)*	test
el	**trabajo**	essay
el	**trimestre**	term
el	**vestuario**	changing room
el	**vocabulario**	vocabulary

USEFUL WORDS *(feminine)*

el	**álgebra** (*f*)	algebra
la	**aritmética**	arithmetic
la	**calculadora**	calculator
la	**caligrafía**	handwriting
la	**carpintería**	woodwork
las	**ciencias del medio ambiente**	natural science
las	**ciencias naturales**	natural history
la	**conserje**	janitor
la	**enseñanza religiosa**	religious instruction
la	**entrega de premios**	awards ceremony
la	**fila**	row (*of seats etc*)
la	**geometría**	geometry
la	**gramática**	grammar
la	**inspectora**	school inspector
la	**interna**	boarder
la	**mancha**	stain
la	**ortografía**	spelling
la	**pizarra (electrónica) interactiva**	interactive whiteboard
la	**poesía**	poetry; poem
la	**prueba**	test
la	**tinta**	ink
la	**tiza**	chalk
la	**traducción directa/inversa**	translation into one's own
	(*pl* traducciones ~s)	language/a foreign language

ESSENTIAL WORDS *(masculine)*

el	**aerogenerador**	windmill, wind turbine
el	**aire**	air
los	**animales**	animals
los	**árboles**	trees
el	**bosque**	wood
el	**calentamiento global**	global warming
el	**carro** *(LAm)*	car
el	**coche**	car
el	**diesel**	diesel
el	**ecologista**	environmentalist
el	**gas**	gas
los	**gases de escape**	exhaust fumes
el	**gasoil**	diesel
el	**generador eólico**	windmill, wind turbine
el	**mapa**	map
el	**mar**	sea
el	**medio ambiente**	environment
el	**mundo**	world
el	**país**	country
el	**parque eólico**	wind farm
el	**pescado**	fish
el	**tiempo**	weather; time
los	**Verdes**	the Greens
el	**vidrio**	glass

IMPORTANT WORDS *(masculine)*

el	**acontecimiento**	event
el	**aluminio**	aluminum
el	**calor**	heat
el	**clima**	climate
el	**contaminante**	pollutant
el	**daño**	damage
el	**detergente**	detergent
el	**futuro**	future
el	**gobierno**	government
el	**impuesto**	tax
el	**lago**	lake
el	**planeta**	planet
el	**río**	river

ESSENTIAL WORDS *(feminine)*

el	**agua** *(f)*	water
las	**botellas**	bottles
la	**contaminación**	pollution
la	**costa**	coast
la	**cuestión** *(pl* cuestiones)	question
la	**ecología**	ecology
la	**energía eólica**	wind energy
la	**energía nuclear**	nuclear power
la	**energía renovable**	renewable energy
la	**especie**	species
la	**fábrica**	factory
la	**flor**	flower
la	**fruta**	fruit
la	**gasolina**	gasoline
la	**isla**	island
la	**lluvia**	rain
la	**montaña**	mountain
la	**planta**	plant
la	**playa**	beach
la	**región** *(pl* regiones)	region; area
la	**temperatura**	temperature
la	**tierra**	earth
la(s)	**verdura(s)**	vegetables

IMPORTANT WORDS *(feminine)*

la	**central nuclear**	nuclear power plant
la	**crisis** *(pl inv)*	crisis
las	**legumbres**	pulses; vegetables
la	**selva**	forest; jungle
la	**solución** *(pl* soluciones)	solution
las	**verduras**	vegetables
la	**zona**	zone

USEFUL WORDS *(masculine)*

el	aerosol	aerosol
los	alimentos orgánicos	organic food
el	canal	canal
el	catalizador	catalytic converter
el	CFC (clorofluorocarbono)	CFC
los	científicos	scientists
el	combustible	fuel
el	continente	continent
el	desarrollo sustentable *or* sostenible	sustainable development
el	desierto	desert
el	ecosistema	ecosystem
el	fertilizante	(artificial) fertilizer
el	investigador	researcher
el	océano	ocean
el	OGM (organismo genéticamente modificado)	GMO
el	producto	product
los	productos químicos	chemicals
el	reciclado, el reciclaje	recycling
los	residuos nucleares/industriales	nuclear/industrial waste
el	universo	universe
el	vertedero	dumping ground

USEFUL PHRASES

es muy respetuoso con el medio ambiente **he's very environmentally-minded**
un producto ecológico **an eco-friendly product; an organic product**
un producto orgánico *or* biológico **an organic product**
en el futuro **in the future**
destruir **to destroy**
contaminar **to contaminate; to pollute**
prohibir **to ban**
salvar **to save**
reciclar **to recycle**
verde **green**

USEFUL WORDS *(feminine)*

las	**aguas negras** *(LAm)*	sewage
las	**aguas residuales**	sewage
la	**capa de ozono**	ozone layer
la	**catástrofe**	disaster
la	**contaminación acústica**	noise pollution
la	**lluvia ácida**	acid rain
la	**luna**	moon
la	**marea negra** *or* **la mancha de petróleo**	oil spill
la	**población** (*pl* poblaciones)	population
la	**selva tropical**	tropical rainforest

USEFUL PHRASES

biodegradable **biodegradable**
nocivo(a) *or* dañino(a) para el medio ambiente **harmful to the environment**
gasolina sin plomo **unleaded gasoline**
(las) especies en peligro de extinción **endangered species**

ESSENTIAL WORDS *(masculine)*

el	**abuelo**	grandfather
los	**abuelos**	grandparents
los	**adultos**	adults
el	**apellido**	surname
el	**apellido de soltera**	maiden name
el	**bebé**	baby
el	**hermano**	brother
el	**hijo**	son
el	**hombre**	man
el	**joven** (*pl* jóvenes)	young man
los	**jóvenes**	young people
el	**marido**	husband
los	**mayores**	grown-ups
el	**muchacho**	boy, young man
el	**niño**	child, boy
el	**nombre**	name
el	**nombre (de pila)**	first *or* Christian name
el	**novio**	boyfriend; bridegroom
el	**padre**	father
los	**padres**	parents
el	**papá**	dad, daddy
el	**pariente**	relative
el	**primo**	cousin
el	**prometido**	fiancé
el	**señor**	gentleman, man
el	**tío**	uncle

USEFUL PHRASES

¿qué edad tiene (*or* tienes)?, ¿cuántos años tiene (*or* tienes)? how old are you?
tengo 15 años – él tiene 40 años I'm 15 – he is 40
¿cómo se llama (*or* te llamas)? what is your name?
me llamo Daniela my name is Daniela
se llama Paco his name is Paco
prometido(a) engaged; casado(a) married
divorciado(a) divorced; separado(a) separated
casarse con algn to marry sb
casarse to get married; divorciarse to get divorced

ESSENTIAL WORDS *(feminine)*

la **abuela**	grandmother
la **edad**	age
la **esposa**	wife
la **familia**	family
la **gente**	people
la **hermana**	sister
la **hija**	daughter
la **joven** (*pl* jóvenes)	young girl
la **madre**	mother
la **mamá**	mom, mommy
la **muchacha**	girl, young woman
la **mujer**	woman; wife
la **niña**	child, girl
la **novia**	girlfriend; bride
la **persona**	person
la **prima**	cousin
la **prometida**	fiancée
la **señora**	lady, woman
la **tia**	aunt

USEFUL PHRASES

más joven/mayor que yo younger/older than me

¿tiene (*or* tienes) hermanos? do you have any brothers *or* sisters?

tengo un hermano y una hermana I have one brother and one sister

no tengo hermanos I don't have any brothers *or* sisters

soy hijo(a) único(a) I am an only child

toda la familia the whole family

crecer to grow

envejecer to get old, to age

me llevo bien con mis padres I get along with my parents

mi madre trabaja my mother works

IMPORTANT WORDS *(masculine)*

el	adolescente	teenager
el	esposo	husband
el	nieto	grandson
los	nietos	grandchildren
el	padrastro	stepfather
el	sobrino	nephew
el	soltero	bachelor
el	suegro	father-in-law
el	vecino	neighbor
el	viudo	widower

USEFUL WORDS *(masculine)*

el	ahijado	godson
el	anciano	elderly man
el	apodo	nickname
el	chaval *(Sp)*	kid
el	chavo *(Mex)*	kid
los	cuates *(Mex)*	twins; pals, buddies
el	cuñado	brother-in-law
los	gemelos (idénticos)	(identical) twins
el	hermanastro	stepbrother
el	hijastro	stepson
el	huérfano	orphan
el	jubilado	pensioner
los	mellizos	twins
el	mote	nickname
el	padrino	godfather
los	recién casados	newlyweds
los	trillizos	triplets
el	viejo	old man
el	yerno	son-in-law

USEFUL PHRASES

nacer to be born; vivir to live; morir to die; nací en 1990 I was born in 1990
mi abuela murió my grandmother is dead
murió en 1995 (s)he died in 1995

IMPORTANT WORDS *(feminine)*

la	**adolescente**	teenager
la	**madrastra**	stepmother
la	**nieta**	granddaughter
la	**sobrina**	niece
la	**soltera**	single woman
la	**suegra**	mother-in-law
la	**vecina**	neighbor
la	**viuda**	widow

USEFUL WORDS *(feminine)*

la	**ahijada**	goddaughter
el	**ama de casa** *(f pl* las amas ~ ~)	housewife
la	**anciana**	elderly woman
la	**chavala** *(Sp)*	kid
la	**chava** *(Mex)*	kid
las	**cuatas** *(Mex)*	twins
la	**cuñada**	sister-in-law
las	**gemelas (idénticas)**	(identical) twins
la	**hermanastra**	stepsister
la	**hijastra**	stepdaughter
la	**huérfana**	orphan
la	**jubilada**	pensioner
la	**madrina**	godmother
las	**mellizas**	twins, twin sisters
la	**niñera**	nanny
la	**nuera**	daughter-in-law
la	**pareja**	couple
la	**vejez**	old age
la	**vieja**	old woman

USEFUL PHRASES

es soltero(a) he/she is single
es viudo he is a widower; es viuda she is a widow
soy el/la menor I am the youngest; soy el/la mayor I am the eldest
mi hermana mayor my eldest sister

ESSENTIAL WORDS *(masculine)*

el	**agricultor**	farmer
el	**animal**	animal
el	**bosque**	forest
el	**buey**	ox
el	**caballo**	horse
el	**cabrito**	kid
el	**campo**	country, countryside; field
el	**cerdo**	pig
el	**chivo**	kid
el	**gato**	cat
el	**granjero**	farmer
el	**guajolote** *(Mex)*	turkey
el	**invernadero**	greenhouse
el	**pato**	duck
el	**pavo**	turkey
el	**perro**	dog
el	**perro pastor** *(pl ~s ~)*	sheepdog
el	**pollo**	chicken
el	**pueblo**	village
el	**rancho** *(Mex)*	ranch
el	**ranchero** *(Mex)*	rancher
el	**ternero**	calf

IMPORTANT WORDS *(masculine)*

el	**campesino**	farmer; peasant
el	**cordero**	lamb
el	**gallo**	rooster
el	**tractor**	tractor

USEFUL PHRASES

un maizal a cornfield; un trigal a wheat field
la agricultura ecológica *or* biológica *or* orgánica organic farming
los pollos ecológicos *or* criados en libertad free range chickens
los huevos ecológicos free range eggs
cuidar los animales to take care of the animals
recolectar to harvest
recoger la cosecha to harvest the crops

ESSENTIAL WORDS *(feminine)*

la **agricultora**	farmer
la **camioneta**	van; station wagon
la **cerca**	fence
la **cerda**	sow
la **finca**	farm
la **gallina**	hen
la **granja**	farm; farmhouse
la **granjera**	farmer; farmer's wife
la **oveja**	sheep; ewe
la **puerta**	gate
la **ranchera** *(Mex)*	farmer
la **tierra**	earth; ground
la **vaca**	cow
la **vagoneta** *(Mex)*	van
la **valla** *(Sp)*	fence
la **yegua**	mare

IMPORTANT WORDS *(feminine)*

la **campesina**	farmer; peasant
la **colina**	hill

USEFUL PHRASES

vivir en el campo to live in the country
trabajar en una granja to work on a farm
recolectar el heno to make hay

USEFUL WORDS *(masculine)*

el	abono	manure; fertilizer
el	arado	plow
el	barro *or* el lodo	mud
el	burro	donkey
el	carnero	ram
el	centeno	rye
el	cerdo	pig
el	cereal	cereal
el	chiquero *(LAm)*	pigsty
el	cobertizo	shed
el	corral	farmyard
el	elote *(Mex)*	corncob; corn
el	espantapájaros *(pl inv)*	scarecrow
el	establo	barn
el	estanque	pond
el	estiércol	manure
el	gallinero	henhouse
el	ganado	cattle
el	ganso	goose
el	granero	granary
el	grano	grain, seed
el	heno	hay
el	maíz	maize; corn
el	molino (de viento)	(wind)mill
el	paisaje	landscape
el	pajar	loft
el	páramo	moor, heath
el	pastor	shepherd
el	pollito	chick
el	potro	foal
el	pozo	well
el	rebaño	*(sheep)* flock; *(cattle)* herd
el	suelo	ground, earth
el	surco	furrow
el	toro	bull
el	trigo	wheat

USEFUL WORDS *(feminine)*

la	**avena**	oats
la	**cabra**	goat
la	**carretilla**	wheelbarrow
la	**cebada**	barley
la	**cosecha**	crop; harvest
la	**cosechadora**	combine harvester
la	**escalera**	ladder
la	**ganadería**	cattle farming
la	**lana**	wool
la	**paja**	straw
la	**pocilga** (*Sp*)	pigsty
la	**recolección** (*pl* recolecciones)	harvest
la	**uva**	grapes
la	**vendimia**	grape harvest, grape picking
la	**viña**	vine
la	**zanja**	ditch

ESSENTIAL WORDS (*masculine*)

el	**marisco** (*Sp*)	seafood
los	**mariscos** (*LAm*)	seafood
el	**pescado**	fish (*as food*)
el	**pez** (*pl* peces)	fish
el	**pez de colores** (*pl* peces ~ ~)	goldfish

IMPORTANT WORDS (*masculine*)

el	**cangrejo**	crab
el	**insecto**	insect

USEFUL WORDS (*masculine*)

el	**acuario**	aquarium
el	**arenque**	herring
el	**atún** (*pl* atunes)	tuna fish
el	**avispón** (*pl* avispones)	hornet
el	**bacalao**	cod
el	**calamar**	squid
el	**camarón** (*pl* camarones)	shrimp
el	**cangrejo de río**	crayfish
el	**grillo**	cricket
el	**gusano**	worm
el	**gusano de seda**	silkworm
el	**langostino**	jumbo shrimp
el	**lenguado**	sole
el	**mejillón** (*pl* mejillones)	mussel
el	**mosquito**	mosquito
el	**pulpo**	octopus
el	**renacuajo**	tadpole
el	**salmón** (*pl* salmones)	salmon
el	**saltamontes** (*pl inv*)	grasshopper
el	**tiburón** (*pl* tiburones)	shark
el	**zancudo** (*LAm*)	mosquito

USEFUL PHRASES

nadar to swim
volar to fly
vamos a ir a pescar **we're going fishing**

ESSENTIAL WORDS *(feminine)*

el **agua** (*f*)	water

IMPORTANT WORDS *(feminine)*

la **mosca**	fly
la **sardina**	sardine

USEFUL WORDS *(feminine)*

la **abeja**	bee
el **aguamala** (*f pl* las aguamalas) (*Mex*)	jellyfish
el **ala** (*f pl* las alas)	wing
la **anguila**	eel
la **araña**	spider
la **avispa**	wasp
la **catarina** (*Mex*)	ladybug
la **cigarra**	cicada
la **cucaracha**	cockroach
la **hormiga**	ant
la **langosta**	lobster
la **libélula**	dragonfly
la **mariposa**	butterfly
la **mariquita** (*Sp*)	ladybug
la **medusa**	jellyfish
la **merluza**	hake
la **mosca**	fly
la **oruga**	caterpillar
la **ostra**	oyster
la **polilla**	moth
la **pulga**	flea
la **rana**	frog
la **telaraña**	spider's web
la **trucha**	trout

USEFUL PHRASES

una picadura de abeja/avispa **a bee/wasp sting**

ESSENTIAL WORDS *(masculine)*

los	abarrotes *(Mex)*	groceries; grocery store
el	aceite	oil
el	alcohol	alcohol
el	almuerzo	lunch; *(Mex)* mid-morning snack
el	aperitivo	appetizer; aperitif
el	arroz	rice
el	azúcar	sugar
el	bar	bar
el	bistec *(pl ~es or ~s)*	steak
el	bote	can
el	café	coffee; café, coffee shop
el	café con leche	coffee with milk, light coffee
el	camarero *(Sp)*	waiter
el	caramelo	candy
los	cereales	cereals
el	chocolate (caliente)	(hot) chocolate
el	cocinero	cook
el	croissant *(Sp)*	croissant
el	cuarto	quarter *(bottle/liter etc)*
el	cuernito *(Mex)*	croissant
el	cuchillo	knife
el	desayuno	breakfast
el	dueño	owner
el	entrecot *(pl inv or ~s)*	sirloin steak
el	filete	tenderloin
el	helado	ice cream
el	huevo	egg
el	huevo duro *or* cocido	hard-boiled egg
el	huevo frito *or (Mex)* estrellado	fried egg
el	huevo pasado por agua *or* tibio	soft-boiled egg
los	huevos revueltos	scrambled eggs
el	jamón *(pl* jamones*)*	ham
el	jugo de fruta *(LAm)*	fruit juice
el	marisco *(Sp)*	seafood
los	mariscos *(LAm)*	seafood
el	menú del día	fixed-price menu
el	mesero *(LAm)*	waiter
el	pan	bread
el	pastel	cake; pie

ESSENTIAL WORDS *(feminine)*

la	**aceituna**	olive
el	**agua (mineral)** *(f)*	(mineral) water
la	**bandeja**	tray
la	**bebida**	drink
la	**botella**	bottle
la	**caja**	box
la	**carne**	meat
la	**carne de puerco** *(Mex)*	pork
la	**carne de res** *(Mex)*	beef
la	**carne de vaca**	beef
la	**carnicería**	butcher's
la	**carta**	menu
la	**cena**	dinner
la	**cerveza**	beer
la	**charola** *(LAm)*	tray
la	**Coca-Cola**® *(pl ~s)*	Coke®
la	**comida**	lunch; meal; food
la	**comida precocinada** *or* **preparada**	TV dinner
la	**copa**	glass (stemmed)
la	**cuchara**	spoon
la	**cuenta**	check, bill
la	**ensalada**	salad
la	**ensalada mixta**	mixed salad
la	**fruta**	fruit
el	**hambre** *(f)*	hunger
la	**hamburguesa**	hamburger
la	**lata**	can
la	**leche**	milk
las	**legumbres**	vegetables
la	**limonada**	lemonade
la	**mantequilla**	butter
la	**mermelada**	jam
la	**mermelada (de cítricos)**	marmalade
la	**mesa**	table
la	**mesera** *(LAm)*	waitress
la	**panadería**	baker's
las	**papas fritas** *(LAm)*	French fries; potato chips

ESSENTIAL WORDS (*masculine continued*)

el	**paté**	pâté
el	**pay** (*Mex*)	pie
el	**pescado**	fish
el	**picnic** (*pl* ~s)	picnic
el	**platillo**	saucer; (*Mex*) dish
el	**plato**	plate; dish; course
el	**plato del día**	today's special
el	**pollo (asado)**	(roast) chicken
el	**postre**	dessert
el	**primer plato**	first course, appetizer
el	**puerco** (*Mex*)	pork
el	**queso**	cheese
el	**restaurante**	restaurant
el	**salami**, el **salchichón** (*pl* salchichones)	salami
el	**sándwich** (*pl* ~es)	sandwich
el	**servicio**	service
el	**supermercado**	supermarket
el	**tazón**	bowl
el	**té**	tea
el	**tenedor**	fork
el	**vaso**	glass
el	**vinagre**	vinegar
el	**vino**	wine
el	**yogur(t)**	yogurt
el	**zumo de fruta** (*Sp*)	fruit juice

USEFUL PHRASES

cocinar to cook; comer to eat
beber to drink; tragar to swallow
mi plato favorito my favorite dish
¿qué vas (*or* va) a beber? what are you having to drink?
está bueno *or* rico it's nice
tener hambre to be hungry
tener sed to be thirsty

ESSENTIAL WORDS *(feminine continued)*

la	pastelería	pastries
las	patatas fritas *(Sp)*	French fries; potato chips
la	pescadería	fish shop
la	repostería	desserts
la	sal	salt
la	salchicha	sausage
la	sed *(pl inv)*	thirst
la	sidra	cider
la	sopa	soup
la	tarta	tart
la	taza	cup
la	ternera	veal
la	tienda de abarrotes *(Mex)*	grocery store
la	tortilla *(Mex)*	tortilla
la	tortilla de papas *(LAm)*	Spanish omelette
la	tortilla española	Spanish omelette
la	tostada	toast
las	verduras	vegetables

IMPORTANT WORDS *(feminine)*

la	barbacoa	*(Mex)* meat cooked in a hole in the ground; *(Sp)* barbecue
la	cafetería	cafeteria
la	camarera *(Sp)*	waitress
la	carne a la parrilla	grilled meat
la	cerveza de barril	draught beer
la	chef *(pl ~s)*	chef
la	chuleta de cerdo *(Sp)*	pork chop
la	chuleta de puerco *(Mex)*	pork chop
la	crema	cream
la	cucharita	teaspoon
la	cuchara (de postre)	dessert spoon
la	cuchara de servir	tablespoon
la	garrafa	carafe
la	harina	flour
la	jarra	pitcher

IMPORTANT WORDS *(masculine)*

el	**ajo**	garlic
el	**almíbar**	syrup
el	**asado**	roast meat; *(LAm)* barbecue
el	**bolillo** *(Mex)*	bread roll
los	**caracoles**	snails
el	**carrito**	cart
el	**chef** *(pl ~s)*	chef
el	**cocinero jefe**	chef
el	**conejo**	rabbit
el	**cordero**	lamb
el	**cubierto**	cover charge; place setting; piece of silverware
los	**cubiertos**	silverware
el	**gusto**	taste
el	**olor**	smell
el	**precio con todo incluido**	all-inclusive price
el	**precio fijo**	set price
el	**sabor**	flavor
el	**suplemento**	extra charge
el	**tentempié**	snack
el	**tocino** *(LAm)*	bacon

USEFUL WORDS *(masculine)*

el	**abrelatas** *(pl inv)*	can opener
el	**beicon** *(Sp)*	bacon
el	**bollo**	roll, sweet bun
el	**cacao**	cocoa
el	**catsup** *(LAm)*	ketchup
el	**champán** *(pl champanes)*	champagne
el	**coñac** *(pl ~s)*	brandy
el	**corcho**	cork
el	**cubito (de hielo)**	ice cube
el	**estofado**	stew
el	**hígado**	liver
el	**ketchup**	ketchup
el	**mantel**	tablecloth
los	**mejillones**	mussels
el	**panecillo** *(Sp)*	roll

IMPORTANT WORDS *(feminine continued)*

la **mayonesa**	mayonnaise
la **mostaza**	mustard
la **nata** *(Sp)*	cream
la **parrillada** *(LAm)*	barbecue
la **pimienta**	pepper
la **pizza**	pizza
la **propina**	tip
la **receta**	recipe
la **selección** *(pl* selecciones)	choice
la **telera** *(Mex)*	bread roll
la **tetera**	teapot
la **torta** *(Mex)*	sandwich (in a bread roll)
la **vainilla**	vanilla
la **vajilla**	dishes; dinner service

USEFUL WORDS *(feminine)*

las **aves**	poultry
la **botana** *(Mex)*	hors d'oeuvre, appetizer
la **carta de vinos**	wine list
la **caza**	game
la **champaña** *(LAm)*	champagne
la **chuleta**	chop
la **crema batida** *(LAm)*	whipped cream
la **gelatina**	Jell-O®

USEFUL PHRASES

lavar los platos **to do the dishes**
desayunar, tomar el desayuno **to have breakfast**
delicioso(a) **delicious**; repugnante **disgusting**
¡buen provecho! **enjoy your meal!**; ¡salud! **cheers!**
¡la cuenta, por favor! **the check please!**
"servicio (no) incluido" **"service (not) included"**
comer fuera **to eat out**
invitar a algn a comer **to invite sb to lunch**
tomar una copa **to have a drink**

USEFUL WORDS *(masculine continued)*

el	**paté de hígado**	liver pâté
el	**popote** *(Mex)*	(drinking) straw
el	**puré de papas** *(LAm)*	mashed potatoes
el	**puré de patatas** *(Sp)*	mashed potatoes
los	**riñones**	kidneys
el	**rosbif** *(pl inv or* ~s)	roast beef
el	**sacacorchos** *(pl inv)*	corkscrew
el	**tapón** *(pl* tapones)	cork
el	**termo**	flask
el	**whisky, whiskey** *(pl* ~s)	whisky

USEFUL PHRASES

poner la mesa **to set the table**; recoger la mesa **to clear the table**
probar algo **to taste sth**
¡eso huele bien! **that smells good!**
vino blanco/rosado/tinto **white/rosé/red wine**
un filete poco hecho/en su punto/bien hecho *(Sp)* **a rare/medium/ well-done steak**
un filete a la inglesa/a punto/bien cocido *(Mex)* **a rare/medium/well-done steak**

USEFUL WORDS *(feminine continued)*

la	**infusión** (*pl* infusiones)	herbal tea
la	**jalea**	jelly
la	**margarina**	margarine
la	**miel**	honey
la	**nata montada** (*Sp*)	whipped cream
las	**natillas**	custard
la	**pajita** (*Sp*)	(drinking) straw
la	**pasta**	pasta
la	**rebanada de pan**	slice of bread
la	**salsa**	sauce
la	**servilleta**	napkin
la	**tisana**	herbal tea
las	**tripas**	tripe
la	**vinagreta**	vinaigrette dressing

SMOKING

el	**cenicero**	ashtray
la	**cerilla** (*Sp*)	match
el	**cerillo** (*LAm*)	match
el	**cigarrillo**	cigarette
el	**cigarro**	cigar
el	**encendedor**	lighter
la	**pipa**	pipe
el	**tabaco**	tobacco

USEFUL PHRASES

una caja de cerillos **a box of matches**
¿tienes (*or* tiene) fuego? **do you have a light?**
encender un cigarrillo **to light up**
"prohibido fumar" **"no smoking"**
no fumo **I don't smoke**
tienes que dejar de fumar **you have to quit smoking**
fumar es perjudicial para la salud **smoking damages your health**

4

ESSENTIAL WORDS *(masculine)*

el	ajedrez	chess
el	amigo por correspondencia	penpal
el	baile	dance
el	billete *(Sp)*	ticket
el	boleto *(LAm)*	ticket
el	cantante	singer
el	canto	singing
el	canal de televisión	TV channel
el	CD *(pl inv or ~s)*	CD
el	celular *(LAm)*	cell phone
el	cine	movie theater, cinema
el	club *(pl ~s or ~es)*	club
el	concierto	concert
los	deportes	sports
el	disco	record *(LP, 45, etc)*
el	domingo *(Mex)*	allowance
el	DVD *(pl inv or ~s)*	DVD
el	espectáculo	show
el	fin de semana	weekend
el	folleto	leaflet
el	futbolín *(pl futbolines)*	foosball
el	hobby *(pl hobbies)*	hobby
el	juego	game
el	móvil *(Sp)*	cell phone
el	museo	museum; art gallery
los	naipes	cards
el	paseo	walk
el	periódico	newspaper
el	programa	program
el	radio *(LAm)*	radio *(set)*
el	recital	concert
el	reproductor *or* lector de CD/DVD/MP3	CD/DVD/MP3 player
el	socio	member *(of a club, etc)*
el	teatro	theater
el	televisor	TV *(set)*
el	tiempo libre	free time
el	videojuego	video game

ESSENTIAL WORDS *(feminine)*

la	**afición** (*pl* aficiones)	hobby
la	**amiga por correspondencia**	penpal
la	**cámara (de fotos)**	camera
la	**canción** (*pl* canciones)	song
la	**cantante**	singer
las	**cartas**	cards
la	**discoteca**	disco
la	**diversión** (*pl* diversiones)	entertainment
la	**estrella (de cine)** (*m+f*)	(movie) star
la	**excursión** (*pl* excursiones)	trip; outing; hike
la	**fiesta**	party
la	**foto**	photo
la	**historieta**	comic strip
	Internet	Internet
la	**lectura**	reading
la	**mesada** (*LAm*)	allowance
la	**música (pop/clásica)**	(pop/classical) music
las	**noticias**	news
la	**novela**	novel
la	**novela policíaca**	detective novel
la	**película**	movie; roll of film (*for a camera*)
la	**pista de patinaje**	skating rink
la	**prensa**	the press
la	**publicidad**	publicity
la	**radio**	radio
la	**revista**	magazine
la	**televisión**	television
la	**videoconsola**	video game console

USEFUL PHRASES

salgo con mis amigos I go out with my friends
leo el periódico I read the newspaper
veo la televisión I watch television
juego a las cartas *or* los naipes I play cards
juego al fútbol/al tenis I play soccer/tennis
juego fútbol/tenis (*LAm*) I play soccer/tennis
hacer bricolaje to do-it-yourself
hacer zapping to channel surf

IMPORTANT WORDS (masculine)

el	**anuncio**	notice; poster
los	**anuncios por palabras**	advertisements; small ads
el	**concurso**	competition
los	**dibujos animados**	cartoons
el	**juguete**	toy
el	**mensaje de texto**	text message
el	**noticiero** (*LAm*)	news
el	**novio**	boyfriend
el	**ordenador (personal)** (*Sp*)	(personal) computer
los	**pasatiempos**	leisure activities
el	**PC** (*pl ~s*)	PC
el	**programa**	program
el	**SMS** (*pl inv*)	text message
el	**telediario** (*Sp*)	news
el	**video** (*LAm*), el **vídeo** (*Sp*)	video
el	**website**	website

USEFUL WORDS (masculine)

el	**aficionado**	fan
el	**blog**	blog
el	**campamento de verano**	summer camp
el	**chat**	chat; chatroom
el	**club nocturno** (*pl ~s or ~es ~s*)	night club
el	**coro**	choir
el	**crucigrama**	crossword puzzle(s)
el	**juego de mesa**	board game
el	**monopatín** (*pl* monopatines) (*Sp*)	skateboard
el	**patín**	skate
el	**videoclub** (*pl ~s or ~es*)	video shop

USEFUL PHRASES

emocionante **exciting**
aburrido(a) **boring**
divertido(a) **funny**

IMPORTANT WORDS *(feminine)*

la	**cámara digital**	digital camera
la	**colección** (*pl* colecciones)	collection
la	**computadora (personal)** (*LAm*)	(personal) computer
la	**exposición** (*pl* exposiciones)	exhibition
la	**filmadora** (*LAm*)	camcorder
la	**grabadora de CD/DVD**	CD/DVD burner
la	**noche**	evening
la	**novia**	girlfriend
la	**pintura**	painting
la	**reunión** (*pl* reuniones)	meeting
la	**serie**	serial
la	**tarde**	afternoon, evening
la	**telenovela**	soap (opera)
la	**videocámara**	camcorder

USEFUL WORDS *(feminine)*

la	**aficionada**	fan
la	**diapositiva**	slide
la	**fotografía**	photograph; photography
la	**lista de éxitos**	charts
la	**patineta** (*LAm*)	skateboard

USEFUL PHRASES

no está mal **it's not bad**
bastante bien **quite good**
bailar **to dance**
sacar *or* tomar fotos **to take photos**
estoy aburrido(a) **I'm bored**
nos reunimos los viernes **we meet on Fridays**
estoy ahorrando para comprarme una impresora **I'm saving up to buy
  a printer**
me gustaría dar la vuelta al mundo **I'd like to go around the world**

ESSENTIAL WORDS *(masculine)*

el **albaricoque** *(Sp)*	apricot
el **árbol frutal**	fruit tree
el **chabacano** *(Mex)*	apricot
el **durazno** *(LAm)*	peach
el **jitomate** *(Mex)*	tomato
el **limón** *(pl* limones*)*	lemon
el **limón amarillo** *(pl* limones ~s*) (Mex)*	lemon
el **limón verde** *(pl* limones ~s*) (Mex)*	lime
el **melocotón** *(pl* melocotones*) (Sp)*	peach
el **melón** *(pl* melones*)*	melon
el **plátano**	banana
el **pomelo**	grapefruit
el **tomate**	tomato

USEFUL WORDS *(masculine)*

el **aguacate**	avocado
el **anacardo** *(Sp)*	cashew nut
el **arándano**	blueberry
el **cacahuate** *(Mex)*	peanut
el **cacahuete** *(Sp)*	peanut
el **coco**	coconut
el **dátil**	date
los **frutos secos**	nuts
el **higo**	fig
el **kiwi**	kiwi fruit
el **mango**	mango
el **maní** *(pl* ~es*) (LAm)*	peanut

USEFUL PHRASES

un jugo de naranja/piña *(LAm)* an orange/a pineapple juice
un zumo de naranja/piña *(Sp)* an orange/a pineapple juice
un racimo de uvas a bunch of grapes
maduro(a) ripe
verde unripe
pelar una fruta to peel a fruit
resbalar al pisar una cáscara de plátano to slip on a banana peel

ESSENTIAL WORDS *(feminine)*

la	castaña (asada)	(roasted) chestnut
la	cereza	cherry
la	frambuesa	raspberry
la	fresa	strawberry
la	fruta	fruit
la	lima	lime
la	manzana	apple
la	naranja	orange
la	pasa	raisin
la	pera	pear
la	piel	skin
la	piña	pineapple
la	toronja *(Mex)*	grapefruit
la	uva	grape(s)

USEFUL WORDS *(feminine)*

la	almendra	almond
la	avellana	hazelnut
la	baya	berry
la	ciruela	plum
la	ciruela pasa	prune
la	granada	pomegranate
la	grosella negra	blackcurrant
la	grosella (roja)	redcurrant
la	mandarina	tangerine
la	mora	blackberry
la	nuez *(pl* nueces)	walnut; *(Mex)* pecan nut
la	nuez de Castilla *(pl* nueces ~~) *(Mex)*	walnut
la	papaya	papaya
la	sandía	watermelon
la	vid	vine

ESSENTIAL WORDS *(masculine)*

el	**armario**	cupboard
el	**calefactor**	heater
el	**clóset** *(LAm)*	closet
el	**congelador** *or* el **freezer**	freezer
el	**equipo (de música)**	stereo
el	**espejo**	mirror
el	**estante**	shelf
el	**frigorífico** *(Sp)*	fridge, refrigerator
el	**mueble**	piece of furniture
los	**muebles**	furniture
el	**refrigerador** *(LAm)*	fridge
el	**reloj**	clock; watch
el	**sillón** *(pl* sillones*)*	armchair
el	**teléfono**	telephone

IMPORTANT WORDS *(masculine)*

el	**aparador**	sideboard; *(Mex)* store window
el	**aparato**	appliance
el	**celular** *(LAm)*	cell phone
el	**cuadro**	picture
el	**escritorio**	(writing) desk
el	**fregadero**	sink
el	**(horno) microondas**	microwave oven
el	**inalámbrico**	cordless phone
el	**lavavajillas** *(pl inv)*	dishwasher
el	**móvil** *(Sp)*	cell phone
el	**piano**	piano
el	**portátil**	laptop
el	**reproductor** *or* **lector de CD/DVD**	CD/DVD player
el	**sofá**	sofa
el	**trinchador** *(Mex)*	sideboard

ESSENTIAL WORDS *(feminine)*

la	**balda** *(Sp)*	shelf
la	**cama**	bed
la	**cocina (eléctrica/de gas)**	(electric/gas) stove
la	**estufa**	heater; *(Mex)* stove
la	**habitación** *(pl* habitaciones)	room
la	**lámpara**	lamp
la	**lavadora**	washing machine, washer
la	**mesa**	table
la	**nevera** *(Sp)*	fridge, refrigerator
la	**pantalla (de lámpara)**	lampshade
la	**radio**	radio
la	**silla**	chair
la	**televisión** *(pl* televisiones)	television

IMPORTANT WORDS *(feminine)*

la	**aspiradora**	vacuum cleaner
la	**biblioteca** *(LAm)*	bookcase
la	**librería** *(Sp)*	bookcase
la	**mesa de café**	coffee table
la	**pintura**	painting
la	**plancha**	iron
la	**secadora**	dryer; *(Mex)* hair dryer

USEFUL WORDS *(masculine)*

el	**asiento**	seat
el	**bafle**	speaker
el	**burro de planchar** *(Mex)*	ironing board
el	**cajón** *(pl* cajones)	drawer
el	**camión de mudanzas** *(pl* camiones ~~)	moving van
el	**colchón** *(pl* colchones)	mattress
el	**contestador**	answering machine
el	**control remoto** *(LAm)*	remote control
el	**horno**	oven
el	**mando a distancia** *(Sp)*	remote control
el	**marco**	frame
el	**mobiliario**	furniture
el	**paragüero**	umbrella stand
los	**postigos**	shutters
el	**robot de cocina** *(pl* ~ s ~~)	food processor, cuisinart®
el	**secador (de pelo)**	hairdryer
el	**teléfono inalámbrico**	cordless telephone
el	**tocador**	dressing table

USEFUL PHRASES

un departamento *(LAm) or* piso *(Sp)* amueblado a furnished apartment
encender/apagar la luz to turn the light on/off
haz tu cama make your bed
sentarse to sit down
poner *or* meter algo en el horno to put sth in the oven
correr las cortinas to draw the curtains
cerrar los postigos to close the shutters

USEFUL WORDS *(feminine)*

la	alfombra	rug
la	antena	antenna
la	antena parabólica	satellite dish
la	balanza	scale
la	báscula	(bathroom) scale
la	bocina *(Mex)*	speaker
la	cómoda	chest of drawers
la	contestadora *(Mex)*	answering machine
la	cuna	crib
la	estantería	shelves
la	lámpara de pie	floor lamp
la	lámpara halógena	halogen lamp
las	literas	bunk beds
la	máquina de coser	sewing machine
la	máquina de escribir	typewriter
la	mesilla de noche	nightstand
la	moqueta *(Sp)*	wall-to-wall carpet
la	mudanza	move
la	persiana	blind
la	tabla de planchar	ironing board
la	videocámara	video camera, camcorder

USEFUL PHRASES

un departamento de 4 habitaciones **a 4-room apartment**
¡ya está el desayuno/la comida/la cena! **breakfast/lunch/dinner is ready!**

ESSENTIAL WORDS

el	**Atlántico**	the Atlantic
el	**Distrito Federal (DF)**	Mexico City
el	**este**	the east
el	**norte**	the north
el	**oeste**	the west
el	**Pacífico**	the Pacific
el	**sur**	the south

USEFUL WORDS

	Atenas	Athens
	Berlín	Berlin
la	**capital**	capital
el	**Extremo Oriente**	the Far East
	Londres	London
	Moscú	Moscow
	Nueva York	New York
el	**Oriente Medio**	the Middle East
	París	Paris
	Pekín	Beijing
el	**Polo Norte/Sur**	the North/South Pole
	Roma	Rome

USEFUL PHRASES

ir a Londres/Nueva York **to go to London/New York**

soy de Oaxaca **I come from Oaxaca**

en el *or* al norte **in** *or* **to the north**

en el *or* al sur **in** *or* **to the south**

en el *or* al este **in** *or* **to the east**

en el *or* al oeste **in** *or* **to the west**

GREETINGS

hola hello
¿cómo está usted? *or* **¿cómo estás?** how are you?
¿qué tal? how are you?
bien fine (*in reply*)
encantado(a) pleased to meet you
hola hello (*on the telephone*)
bueno (*Mex*) hello (*on the telephone*)
buenas tardes good afternoon; good evening
buenas noches good evening; good night
adiós goodbye
hasta mañana see you tomorrow
hasta luego see you later

BEST WISHES

feliz cumpleaños happy birthday
feliz Navidad merry Christmas
feliz Año Nuevo happy New Year
felices Pascuas happy Easter; happy Christmas
recuerdos best wishes
saludos best wishes
bienvenido(a) welcome
enhorabuena congratulations
buen provecho enjoy your meal
que le (*or* te **) bien** all the best
que te diviertas (*or* se divierta**)** enjoy yourself
buena suerte good luck
buen viaje safe trip
¡salud! bless you (*after a sneeze*); cheers (*when drinking*)
a tu (*or* su, *etc***) salud** to your good health

SURPRISE

Dios mío my goodness
¿qué?, ¿cómo? what?
entiendo oh, I see
vaya well, well
pues… well…
(¿)de verdad(?), (¿)sí(?) really(?)
(¿)estás (*or* está) de broma(?) you're kidding; are you kidding?
¡qué suerte! how lucky!

POLITENESS

perdone I'm sorry; excuse me
por favor please
gracias thank you
no, gracias no, thank you
sí, gracias yes, please
de nada you're welcome, not at all, don't mention it
con mucho gusto la llevo I'd be delighted to take you there

AGREEMENT

sí yes
por supuesto of course
de acuerdo OK
okey (*LAm*) OK
vale (*Sp*) OK
bueno fine

DISAGREEMENT

no no
claro que no of course not
ni hablar no way
no estoy de acuerdo I don't agree
creo *or* **pienso que no** I don't think so; I think not
estoy en contra de la pena de muerte I am against the death penalty
en absoluto not at all
al contrario on the contrary
no te metas en lo que no te importa mind your own business

DIFFICULTIES

socorro help
fuego fire
ay ouch
perdón (I'm) sorry; excuse me; I beg your pardon
lo siento I'm sorry
qué pena what a pity
qué lata (*LAm*) what a nuisance; how boring
estoy harto(a) I'm fed up
no aguanto más I can't stand it any more
qué horror how awful

ORDERS

cuidado be careful
para (*or* **pare**) stop
oiga, usted hey, you there
fuera de aquí get lost
silencio shh
basta ya that's enough
prohibido fumar no smoking
vamos come on, let's go
sigue *or* **siga** go ahead, go on
vámonos let's go

OTHERS

no tengo (ni) idea I have no idea
quizá, quizás perhaps, maybe
no (lo) sé I don't know
¿qué desea? can I help you?
aquí tienes there; there you are
ya voy I'm coming
no te preocupes don't worry
no merece la pena it's not worth it
a propósito by the way
cariño, querido(a) darling, honey
el (*or* **la**) **pobre** poor thing
tanto mejor so much the better
no me importa I don't mind
a mí me da igual it's all the same to me
mala suerte too bad
depende it depends
¿qué voy a hacer? what shall I do?
¿qué sentido tiene? what's the point?
me molesta it annoys me
me saca de quicio it gets on my nerves

ESSENTIAL WORDS *(masculine)*

el	**accidente**	accident
el	**dentista**	dentist
el	**doctor**	doctor
el	**enfermero**	nurse
el	**enfermo**	patient
el	**estómago**	stomach
el	**hospital**	hospital
el	**médico**	doctor

IMPORTANT WORDS *(masculine)*

el	**algodón (hidrófilo)**	cotton wool
el	**antiséptico**	antiseptic
el	**comprimido**	pill, capsule
el	**dolor**	pain
el	**farmacéutico**	pharmacist
el	**jarabe**	syrup
el	**medicamento**	medicine, drug
el	**paciente**	patient
el	**resfriado**	cold
el	**seguro**	insurance
el	**yeso** *(LAm)*	plaster cast; plaster

USEFUL PHRASES

hubo un accidente there's been/there was an accident

la internaron *(LAm) or* ingresaron *(Sp)* en el hospital she was admitted to the hospital

debe permanecer en cama you/(s)he must stay in bed

estar enfermo(a) to be ill; sentirse mejor to feel better

cuidar to look after

me lastimé *(LAm)*, me he hecho daño *(Sp)* I have hurt myself

me enyesaron el brazo *(LAm)* they put my arm in a cast

me corté el dedo I cut my finger

me torcí el tobillo I sprained my ankle

se rompió el brazo (s)he broke his/her arm

me quemé I burnt myself

me duele la garganta/la cabeza/el estómago I have a sore throat/ a headache/a stomach ache

tener fiebre to have a temperature

ESSENTIAL WORDS *(feminine)*

la	**aspirina**	aspirin
la	**cama**	bed
la	**cita**	appointment
la	**curita** *(LAm)*	Band Aid®
la	**dentista**	dentist
la	**doctora**	doctor
la	**enferma**	patient
la	**enfermera**	nurse
la	**farmacia**	pharmacy, drug store
la	**médico/a**	doctor
la	**pastilla**	pill, capsule
la	**salud**	health
la	**temperatura**	temperature
la	**tirita** *(Sp)*	Band Aid®

IMPORTANT WORDS *(feminine)*

la	**ambulancia**	ambulance
la	**camilla**	stretcher
la	**clínica**	clinic, hospital
la	**consulta**	consultation
la	**crema**	cream, ointment
la	**cucharada**	spoonful
la	**diarrea**	diarrhea
la	**enfermedad**	illness
la	**escayola** *(Sp)*	plaster cast
la	**farmacéutica**	pharmacist
la	**gripa** *(Mex)*	flu
la	**gripe**	flu
la	**herida**	wound, injury
la	**insolación** *(pl insolaciones)*	sunstroke
la	**inyección** *(pl inyecciones)*	injection, shot
la	**medicina**	medicine
la	**operación** *(pl operaciones)*	operation
la	**paciente**	patient
la	**píldora**	pill; the Pill *(birth control)*
las	**quemaduras de sol**	sunburn
la	**receta**	prescription
la	**sangre**	blood
la	**tableta**	tablet
	urgencias	ER
la	**venda**	bandage

USEFUL WORDS *(masculine)*

el	absceso	abscess
el	acné	acne
el	arañazo	scratch
el	ataque	fit
el	ataque al corazón	heart attack
el	cáncer	cancer
el	cardenal *(Sp)*	bruise
el	embarazo	pregnancy
el	estrés	stress
el	mareo	dizzy spell; sickness
el	microbio	germ
el	moretón	bruise
el	nervio	nerve
el	preservativo	condom
los	primeros auxilios	first aid
el	pulso	pulse
el	régimen	diet
el	reposo	rest
el	sarampión	measles
el	shock	shock
el	sida	AIDS
el	tónico	tonic
el	vendaje	dressing
el	veneno	poison

USEFUL PHRASES

tengo sueño I'm sleepy
tengo naúseas I feel nauseous
adelgazar to lose weight
engordar to put on weight
tragar to swallow
sangrar to bleed
vomitar to vomit
estar en forma to be in good shape
reposar, descansar to rest

USEFUL WORDS *(feminine)*

la	**amigdalitis**	tonsillitis
	anginas	sore throat; tonsillitis
la	**apendicitis**	appendicitis
la	**astilla**	splinter
la	**cicatriz** (*pl* cicatrices)	scar
la	**dentadura postiza**	dentures, false teeth
la	**dieta**	diet
la	**epidemia**	epidemic
la	**fiebre del heno**	hay fever
la	**migraña**	migraine
la	**muleta**	crutch
la	**náusea**	nausea
las	**paperas**	mumps
la	**pomada**	ointment
la	**radiografía**	X-ray
la	**recuperación**	recovery
la	**rubeola**	German measles
la	**silla de ruedas**	wheelchair
la	**tos**	cough
la	**tos ferina**	whooping cough
la	**transfusión (de sangre)** (*pl* transfusiones (~~))	blood transfusion
la	**varicela**	chickenpox
la	**viruela**	smallpox

USEFUL PHRASES

curar to cure; curarse to get better
gravemente herido(a) seriously injured
¿tiene seguro? are you insured?
estoy resfriado(a) I have a cold
¡eso duele! that hurts!; me duele it hurts!
respirar to breathe
desmayarse to faint
toser to cough
morir to die
perder el conocimiento to lose consciousness
llevar el brazo en cabestrillo to have one's arm in a sling

ESSENTIAL WORDS *(masculine)*

el	**almuerzo**	lunch; *(Mex)* mid-morning snack
el	**ascensor**	elevator
el	**balcón** *(pl* balcones)	balcony
los	**baños públicos** *(LAm)*	restrooms
el	**bar**	bar
el	**camarero**	waiter
el	**cambio**	change
el	**cheque**	check
el	**cuarto de baño**	bathroom
el	**depósito**	deposit
el	**desayuno**	breakfast
el	**elevador** *(Mex)*	elevator
el	**equipaje**	luggage
el	**gerente**	manager
el	**hotel**	hotel
el	**huésped**	guest
el	**número**	number
el	**pasaporte**	passport
el	**piso**	floor, story
el	**precio**	price
el	**recepcionista**	receptionist
el	**restaurante**	restaurant
el	**ruido**	noise
los	**servicios**	services
el	**teléfono**	telephone

USEFUL PHRASES

quisiera reservar una habitación I would like to reserve a room
una habitación con ducha/con regadera *(Mex)* a room with a shower
una habitación con baño a room with a bath
una habitación individual a single room
una habitación doble a double room

ESSENTIAL WORDS *(feminine)*

la	**alberca** *(Mex)*	swimming pool
la	**cama de matrimonio**	double bed
la	**camarera** *(Sp)*	waitress
las	**camas separadas**	twin beds
la	**comida**	lunch; meal
la	**comodidad**	comfort
la	**cuenta**	bill
la	**ducha**	shower
la	**entrada**	entrance
la	**escalera**	stairs
la	**estancia**	stay
la	**fecha**	date
la	**ficha**	form
la	**gerente/a**	manager
la	**habitación** *(pl* habitaciones)	room
la	**huésped**	guest
la	**llave**	key
la	**maleta**	suitcase
la	**media pensión**	Modified American Plan
la	**noche**	night
la	**pensión** *(pl* pensiones)	guest house
la	**pensión completa**	American Plan
la	**petaca** *(Mex)*	suitcase
la	**piscina**	swimming pool
la	**recepción**	reception
la	**recepcionista**	receptionist
la	**salida de incendios**	fire escape
la	**tarifa**	rate, rates
la	**televisión** *(pl* televisiones)	television
la	**vista**	view

USEFUL PHRASES

¿lleva algún documento de identidad? **do you have any ID?**

¿a qué hora se sirve el desayuno? **what time is breakfast served?**

limpiar la habitación **to clean the room**

"se ruega no molestar" **"do not disturb"**

IMPORTANT WORDS *(masculine)*

el	**albergue**	hostel
el	**apagador** *(Mex)*	light switch
el	**baño**	bathroom
el	**interruptor**	switch
el	**lavabo**	sink (bathroom)
el	**precio total**	all-inclusive price
el	**recibo**	receipt
el	**switch** *(LAm)*	light switch

USEFUL WORDS *(masculine)*

el	**cocinero**	cook
el	**lobby**	lobby
el	**maître**	head waiter
el	**sommelier**	wine waiter

USEFUL PHRASES

ocupado(a) **occupied**

libre **vacant**

limpio(a) **clean**

sucio(a) **dirty**

dormir **to sleep**

despertarse **to wake up**

"con todas las comodidades" **"with all amenities"**

¿me pueden llamar mañana a las siete? **I'd like a wake-up call at 7 o'clock**

una habitación con vista al mar **a room overlooking the sea**

IMPORTANT WORDS *(feminine)*

la **bañera**	bathtub
la **bienvenida**	welcome
la **camarera** *or* **mucama (de hotel)**	maid
la **casa de huéspedes**	guest house
la **factura**	bill
la **guía turística**	guidebook
la **propina**	tip
la **reclamación** (*pl* reclamaciones)	complaint
la **regadera** (*Mex*)	shower
la **tina** (*Mex*)	bathtub

USEFUL WORDS *(feminine)*

la **cocinera**	cook

USEFUL PHRASES

el desayuno se sirve en el comedor breakfast is served in the dining room
una habitación con media pensión Modified American Plan
un hotel de tres/cinco estrellas a three-/five-star hotel

ESSENTIAL WORDS *(masculine)*

el	**aparcamiento** *(Sp)*	parking lot; parking space
el	**ascensor**	elevator
el	**balcón** *(pl* balcones)	balcony
el	**bloque de departamentos** *(LAm)*	apartment building
el	**bloque de pisos** *(Sp)*	apartment building
el	**comedor**	dining room
el	**cuarto de baño**	bathroom
el	**departamento** *(LAm)*	apartment
el	**dormitorio**	bedroom
el	**edificio**	building
el	**elevador** *(Mex)*	elevator
el	**estacionamiento** *(LAm)*	parking lot; parking space
el	**excusado** *(Mex)*	toilet
el	**exterior**	exterior
el	**garage** *(LAm) or* el **garaje** *(Sp)*	garage
el	**interior**	interior
el	**jardín** *(pl* jardines)	yard; garden
el	**mueble**	piece of furniture
los	**muebles**	furniture
el	**numéro de teléfono**	phone number
el	**patio**	yard
el	**piso**	floor, story; *(Sp)* apartment
el	**pueblo**	village
el	**sótano**	basement
el	**terreno**	plot of land

USEFUL PHRASES

estar en casa to be at home
ir a casa to go home
mirar por la ventana to look out of the window
en mi/tu/nuestra casa at my/your/our house
mudarse de casa to move *(to a new house or apartment)*
alquilar un departamento to rent an apartment

ESSENTIAL WORDS *(feminine)*

la	**avenida**	avenue
la	**calefacción (central)**	(central) heating
	(*pl* calefacciones (~es))	
la	**calle**	street
la	**casa**	house
la	**ciudad**	town; city
la	**cocina**	kitchen
la	**colonia (residencial)** *(Mex)*	suburb
la	**comodidad**	amenity
la	**dirección** (*pl* direcciones)	address
la	**ducha**	shower
la	**entrada**	entrance
la	**entrada para coches**	driveway
la	**escalera**	stairs
la	**habitación** (*pl* habitaciones)	room
la	**llave**	key
la	**parcela**	plot of land
la	**pared**	wall
la	**planta**	floor, story
la	**puerta**	door
la	**puerta principal** *or* **de calle**	front door
la	**recámara** *(Mex)*	bedroom
la	**regadera** *(Mex)*	shower
la	**sala**	living room
la	**urbanización** (*pl* urbanizaciones)	housing development
la	**ventana**	window
la	**vista**	view

USEFUL PHRASES

vivo en una casa/en un departamento **I live in a house/an apartment**
(en el piso de) arriba **upstairs**
(en el piso de) abajo **downstairs**
en el primer piso **on the first floor**

IMPORTANT WORDS (*masculine*)

el **alojamiento**	accommodations
el **alquiler** (*Sp*)	rent
el **baño**	bathroom
el **césped**	lawn
el **corredor**	hall, corridor
el **departamento amueblado**	furnished apartment
el **dueño**	landlord; owner
el **humo**	smoke
el **interfón** (*Mex*)	intercom
el **lavabo**	sink; toilet
el **mantenimiento**	maintenance
el **mobiliario**	furniture
el **pasillo**	hall, corridor
el **portero**	superintendent
el **portero automático**	electronic doorkeeper
el **propietario**	owner; landlord
el **rellano**	landing
el **techo** (*LAm*)	roof; ceiling
el **tejado** (*Sp*)	roof
el **vecino**	neighbor

USEFUL WORDS (*masculine*)

el **ático**	attic
el **cuarto de huéspedes**	guest room
el **despacho**	study
el **desván**	attic
el **escalón** (*pl* escalones)	step
el **estudio**	studio apartment
el **inquilino**	tenant; lodger
el **muro**	wall
el **parquet** (*pl* ~s)	parquet floor
el **seto**	hedge
el **suelo**	floor
el **timbre**	door bell
el **tragaluz** (*pl* tragaluces)	skylight
el **umbral**	doorstep
el **vestíbulo**	foyer
el **vidrio**	window pane

IMPORTANT WORDS *(feminine)*

la	cerca	fence
la	chimenea	chimney; fireplace
la	dueña	landlady; owner
la	mudanza	move
la	portera	superintendent
la	propietaria	owner; landlady
la	renta *(LAm)*	rent
la	señora de la limpieza	janitor
la	vecina	neighbor
la	vivienda	housing; dwelling; house

USEFUL WORDS *(feminine)*

el	ama de casa *(f pl* amas ~ ~)	housewife
la	antena	antenna
el	azulejo	(wall) tile
la	baldosa	(floor) tile
la	buhardilla	attic
la	caldera	boiler
la	contraventana	shutter
la	decoración *(pl* decoraciones)	decoration
la	fachada	front *(of a house)*
la	inquilina	tenant; lodger
la	persiana	blind
la	portería	doorkeeper's area
la	puerta ventana	French window
la	teja	roof shingle; slate

USEFUL PHRASES

llamar a la puerta **to knock on the door**
tocar el timbre **to ring the bell**
renovar/decorar una casa **to refurbish/to decorate a house**
llamar por el interfón *(Mex) or* el portero automático *(Sp)* **to call on the
  intercom**

ESSENTIAL WORDS *(masculine)*

el	**apagador** *(Mex)*	switch
el	**armario**	cupboard
el	**basurero** *or* el **bote de la basura** *(LAm)*	garbage can
el	**buzón** *(pl* buzones*)*	letterbox
el	**cenicero**	ashtray
el	**cepillo**	brush
el	**clóset** *(LAm)*	closet
el	**cuadro**	picture
el	**cubo de la basura** *(Sp)*	trash can
el	**despertador**	alarm clock
el	**espejo**	mirror
el	**fregadero**	sink
el	**frigorífico** *(Sp)*	fridge
el	**gas**	gas
el	**grifo** *(Sp)*	faucet
el	**interruptor**	switch
el	**jabón** *(pl* jabones*)*	soap
el	**lavabo**	(bathroom) sink; toilet
la	**pasta de dientes**	toothpaste
el	**póster** *(pl* ~es *or* ~s*)*	poster
los	**quehaceres domésticos** *or* **de la casa**	housework
el	**radiador**	radiator
el	**radio** *(LAm)*	radio (set)
el	**refrigerador** *(LAm)*	fridge
el	**reproductor** *or* **lector de CD/DVD/MP3**	CD/DVD/MP3 player
el	**switch** *(LAm)*	switch
el	**televisor**	television set

USEFUL PHRASES

darse un baño, bañarse to take a bath; to take a shower
darse una ducha, ducharse to take a shower
darse un regaderazo *(Mex)* to take a shower
hacer los quehaceres *or* las tareas de la casa to do the housework
me gusta cocinar I like cooking

ESSENTIAL WORDS (*feminine*)

el	**agua** (*f*)	water
la	**alfombra**	carpet, rug
la	**almohada**	pillow
la	**balanza**	scale
la	**báscula**	(bathroom) scale
la	**bandeja**	tray
la	**bañera**	bathtub
la	**cacerola**	saucepan
la	**cafetera**	coffee pot; coffee maker
la	**cobija** (*LAm*)	blanket
la	**cocina**	stove
las	**cortinas**	curtains, drapes
la	**ducha**	shower
la	**electricidad**	electricity
la	**estufa**	heater; (*Mex*) stove
la	**foto**	photo
la	**lámpara**	lamp
la	**lavadora**	washing machine, washer
la	**llave** (*LAm*)	faucet
la	**luz** (*pl* luces)	light
la	**manta**	blanket
la	**nevera** (*Sp*)	fridge, refrigerator
la	**radio**	radio
la	**regadera** (*Mex*)	shower
la	**sábana**	sheet
la	**servilleta**	napkin
las	**tareas domésticas** *or* **de la casa**	housework
la	**televisión** (*pl* televisiones)	television
la	**tina** (*Mex*)	bathtub
la	**toalla**	towel
la	**vajilla**	dishes

USEFUL PHRASES

ver la televisión **to watch television**
en televisión **on television**
prender *or* encender/apagar la tele **to turn on/off the TV**
tirar algo a la basura **to throw sth away**
lavar *or* fregar los platos **to do the dishes**

IMPORTANT WORDS *(masculine)*

el	**bidé**	bidet
los	**cubiertos**	silverware
el	**cuchillo**	knife
el	**detergente**	detergent
el	**enchufe**	plug; socket
el	**foco** *(LAm)*	light bulb
el	**horno**	oven
el	**lavavajillas** *(pl inv)*	dishwasher
el	**polvo**	dust
el	**sartén** *(pl* sartenes*)*	frying pan
el	**tenedor**	fork

USEFUL WORDS *(masculine)*

el	**adorno**	ornament
el	**almohadón** *(pl* almohadones*)*	cushion
el	**balde**	pail
el	**burro de planchar** *(Mex)*	ironing board
el	**cesto de la basura**	wastebasket
el	**cojín** *(pl* cojines*)*	cushion
el	**cubo** *(Sp)*	pail
el	**edredón** *(pl* edredones ~s*)*	quilt, duvet
el	**gancho (para colgar ropa)** *(LAm)*	coat hanger
el	**(horno) microondas**	microwave oven
el	**jarrón** *(pl* jarrones*)*	vase
el	**molinillo de café**	coffee grinder
el	**paño de cocina**	dishtowel
el	**papel tapiz**	wallpaper
el	**picaporte**	door handle
el	**sacudidor** *(Mex)*	dust cloth
el	**secador (para trastes)** *(Mex)*	dishtowel
el	**trapo (del polvo)**	dust cloth

USEFUL PHRASES

enchufar/desenchufar **to plug (in)/to unplug**
pasar la aspiradora **to vacuum**
lavar la ropa **to do the laundry**

IMPORTANT WORDS *(feminine)*

la	**aspiradora**	vacuum cleaner
la	**bombilla** *(Sp)*	light bulb
la	**cerradura**	lock
la	**cubeta** *(Mex)*	pail
la	**cuchara**	spoon
la	**estufa**	heater; *(Mex)* stove
la	**pintura**	paint; painting
la	**receta**	recipe
la	**ropa de cama**	sheets and pillowcases
la	**ropa para lavar**	laundry
la	**ropa sucia**	(dirty) laundry
la	**sartén** *(pl* sartenes*)*	frying pan
la	**señora de la limpieza**	cleaner

USEFUL WORDS *(feminine)*

la	**basura**	garbage, trash
la	**batidora**	mixer
la	**batería de cocina**	set of pots and pans
la	**escalera (de mano)**	ladder
la	**escoba**	broom
la	**esponja**	sponge
la	**licuadora**	blender
la	**manta eléctrica**	electric blanket
la	**moqueta** *(Sp)*	wall-to-wall carpet
la	**olla exprés** *or* **de presión**	pressure cooker
la	**percha** *(Sp)*	coat hanger
la	**plancha**	iron
la	**tabla de planchar**	ironing board
la	**tapa**	lid
la	**tapicería**	upholstery
la	**tostadora**	toaster

USEFUL PHRASES

barrer **to sweep (up)**
limpiar **to clean**

ESSENTIAL WORDS *(masculine)*

el	banco	bank
el	billete (de banco)	bank note
el	bolígrafo	ballpoint pen
el	buzón *(pl* buzones)	mailbox
el	cambio	change
el	carné de identidad *(Sp)*	ID card
el	cartero	postal carrier, mailman
el	celular *(LAm)*	cell phone
el	centavo	cent
el	cheque	check
el	código postal	zip code
el	contrato telefónico	phone contract
el	correo *(LAm)*	post office
el	correo eletrónico	email
el	documento de identidad	ID card
el	depósito *(LAm)*	deposit
el	dólar	dollar
el	empleado	clerk, teller
el	error	mistake
el	fax	fax
el	formulario	form
el	impreso *(Sp)*	form
el	indicativo (telefónico)	area code
el	ingreso *(Sp)*	deposit
el	justificante	written proof
el	mensaje de texto	text message
el	mostrador	counter
el	móvil *(Sp)*	cell phone
el	número	number
el	paquete	package
el	pasaporte	passport
el	precio	price
el	prefijo (telefónico)	area code
el	sello	postage stamp
el	sobre	envelope
el	teléfono	telephone
el	tono de marcado	dial tone

USEFUL PHRASES

cobrar un cheque to cash a check
cambiar dinero to change money

ESSENTIAL WORDS *(feminine)*

la	**bolsa**	bag, purse
la	**caja**	checkout
la	**carta**	letter
la	**cartera**	postal carrier; wallet, billfold
la	**clave LADA** *(Mex)*	area code
la	**compañía telefónica** *or* **de teléfonos**	phone company
la	**contestación**	reply
la	**dirección** *(pl* **direcciones)**	address
la	**empleada**	clerk, teller
la	**estampilla**	postage stamp; rubber stamp
la	**firma**	signature
la	**forma** *(Mex)*	form
la	**identificación**	ID
la	**información**	information; directory assistance
la	**llamada**	call
la	**oficina de correo** *(LAm) or* **de correos** *(Sp)*	post office
la	**oficina de turismo**	tourist information office
la	**pluma**	pen
la	**respuesta**	reply
la	**tarjeta de crédito**	credit card
la	**tarjeta de débito**	debit card
la	**(tarjeta) postal**	postcard

USEFUL PHRASES

una llamada telefónica **a phone call**

llamar a algn por teléfono, telefonear a algn **to call sb** *or* **make a call to sb**

descolgar el teléfono **to pick up the phone** *or* **to take the phone off the hook**

marcar (el número) **to dial (the number)**

hola – soy el Dr Pérez **hello, this is Dr. Pérez**

está ocupado *or* la linea está ocupada **the line is busy**

no cuelgue **hold the line**

me equivoqué de número **I got the wrong number**

colgar **to hang up**

quisiera hacer una llamada internacional **I'd like to make an international call**

IMPORTANT WORDS *(masculine)*

el	ADSL	broadband
el	archivo adjunto	attachment
el	cheque de viajero *or (Sp)* de viaje	traveler's cheque
el	cibercafé	cybercafé
el	contestador (automático)	answering machine
el	correo	mail
el	correo de voz	voicemail
el	crédito	credit, loan
el	directorio (telefónico) *(LAm)*	telephone book
el	domicílio	home address
el	gasto	expense
el	impuesto	tax
el	mail *(pl ~s)*	email
el	monedero	change purse
el	pago	payment
el	papel de carta	writing paper
el	recargo	extra charge
el	SMS *(pl inv)*	text message
el	talonario de cheques *(Sp)*	checkbook
el	telefonista	operator
el	(teléfono) fijo	landline
el	telegrama	telegram
el	tipo de cambio	exchange rate

USEFUL WORDS *(masculine)*

el	acceso al sistema	login
el	apartado postal	P.O. box
el	auricular	receiver
el	destinatario	addressee
el	documento adjunto	attachment
el	giro postal	postal money order
el	papel de envolver	wrapping paper
el	remitente	sender
el	tono de llamada	ringtone

IMPORTANT WORDS *(feminine)*

la	banda ancha	broadband
la	cabina telefónica	phone booth
la	chequera *(LAm)*	checkbook
la	contestadora (de teléfono) *(Mex)*	answering machine
la	contraseña	password
la	cuenta (bancaria)	(bank) account
la	guía telefónica	phone book
la	llamada telefónica	phone call
la	oficina de objetos perdidos	lost-and-found
la	ranura	slot
la	recogida	collection
la	recompensa	reward
la	tarjeta de recarga (del celular)	prepaid calling card
la	tarjeta telefónica	(prepaid) phone card
la	tasa de cambio	exchange rate
la	telefonista	operator

USEFUL WORDS *(feminine)*

la	bocina *(Mex)*	receiver
la	carta certificada	certified letter
la	casa de cambio	currency exchange office
la	destinataria	addressee
la	llamada de larga distancia	long-distance call
la	llamada internacional	international call
la	llamada local	local call
la	oficina de cambio	currency exchange office
la	remitente	sender
la	tarjeta SIM	SIM card

USEFUL PHRASES

perdí la cartera **I lost my wallet**
llenar un formulario **to fill out a form**
en mayúsculas **in block letters**
hacer una llamada a cobro revertido **to make a collect call**
llamar por cobrar *(Mex)* **to call collect**

GENERAL SITUATIONS

¿cuál es su dirección? what is your address?
¿cómo se escribe? how do you spell that?
¿tiene cambio de 100 dólares? do you have change for a hundred-dollar bill?
escribir to write
responder or contestar to reply
firmar to sign
¿me puede ayudar por favor? can you help me, please?
¿cómo se va a la estación? how do I get to the station?
todo derecho or todo recto straight ahead
a la derecha to or on the right; a la izquierda to or on the left

LETTERS

Querido Carlos Dear Carlos
Querida Ana Dear Ana
Estimado Señor Dear Sir
Estimada Señora Dear Madam
recuerdos, saludos best wishes
un abrazo de, un beso de, besos de love from
lo/la saluda atentamente or cordialmente sincerely yours
besos y abrazos love and kisses
atentamente sincerely
reciba un atento saludo, le saluda atentamente sincerely yours
sigue (al dorso) over (see the reverse side)

E-MAILS

mandarle un mail or un correo electrónico a algn to email sb

CELL PHONES

mandarle un mensaje de texto or un SMS a algn to text sb

PRONUNCIATION GUIDE

Pronounced approximately as:

A	ah
B	bay
C	thay, say
D	day
E	ay
F	efay
G	khay
H	atchay
I	ee
J	khota
K	kah
L	elay
LL	elyay
M	emay
N	enay
Ñ	enyay
O	oh
P	pay
Q	koo
R	eray
S	essay
T	tay
U	oo
V	bay korta (*LAm*), oobay (*Sp*)
W	doblay bay (*LAm*), oobay doblay (*Sp*)
X	ekees
Y	ee griayga
Z	seta (*LAm*), theta (*Sp*)

ESSENTIAL WORDS *(masculine)*

el	**abogado**	lawyer
el	**accidente**	accident
el	**carné de identidad** *(Sp)*	ID card
el	**documento de identidad**	ID card
el	**incendio**	fire
el	**policía**	police officer, policeman
el	**problema**	problem
el	**robo**	burglary; theft

IMPORTANT WORDS *(masculine)*

el	**atracador**	armed robber; mugger
el	**atraco**	hold-up; mugging
el	**consulado**	consulate
el	**control policial**	checkpoint; roadblock
el	**culpable**	culprit
el	**daño** *or* **los daños**	damage
el	**ejército**	army
el	**espía**	spy
el	**gobierno**	government
el	**impuesto a la renta**	income tax
los	**impuestos**	taxes
el	**ladrón** *(pl* ladrones)	burglar; thief; robber
el	**monedero**	change purse
el	**muerto**	dead man
el	**permiso**	permission
el	**propietario**	owner; landlord
el	**robo de identidad**	identity theft
el	**testigo**	witness

USEFUL PHRASES

llamar a la policía **to call the police**
robar **to burglarize; to steal; to rob**
¡me robaron la cartera! **someone has stolen my wallet!**
¡socorro! **help!**; ¡al ladrón! **stop, thief!**
encarcelar **to imprison**; fugarse, escapar **to escape**

ESSENTIAL WORDS *(feminine)*

la	**abogada**	lawyer
la	**culpa**	fault
la	**documentación**	papers
la	**identidad**	identity
la	**multa**	fine
la	**policía**	police; police officer, policewoman
la	**verdad**	truth

IMPORTANT WORDS *(feminine)*

la	**atracadora**	armed robber; mugger
la	**balacera**	shoot-out
la	**banda**	gang
la	**cartera**	wallet
la	**comisaría**	police station
la	**culpable**	culprit
la	**denuncia**	report
la	**espía**	spy
la	**ladrona**	burglar; thief; robber
la	**manifestación** *(pl* manifestaciones)	demonstration
la	**muerta**	dead woman
la	**muerte**	death
la	**pena de muerte**	death penalty
la	**póliza de seguros**	insurance policy
la	**propietaria**	owner; landlady
la	**recompensa**	reward
la	**testigo**	witness

USEFUL PHRASES

un atraco a mano armada **a hold-up**
raptar *or* secuestrar a un niño **to abduct a child**
en la cárcel **in prison**
pelearse **to fight;** detener *or* arrestar **to arrest**
acusar a algn de algo **to accuse sb of sth; to charge sb with sth**
estar fichado -a **to have a police record**
balacear a algn (*Mex*) **to shoot sb**

USEFUL WORDS (*masculine*)

el	arresto	arrest
el	asesinato	murder
el	asesino	murderer
el	botín (*pl* botines)	loot
el	cadáver	corpse
el	crimen (*pl* crímenes)	murder; crime
el	criminal	murderer; criminal
el	delincuente	criminal
el	detective privado	private detective
el	drogadicto	drug addict
el	encarcelamiento	imprisonment
el	estafador	crook
el	gamberro (*Sp*)	thug, hooligan
el	gángster (*pl* ~s)	gangster
el	guarda	guard; warden
el	guardia	guard; police officer
el	inmigrante ilegal	illegal immigrant
el	intento	attempt
el	juez (*pl* jueces)	judge
el	juicio	trial
el	jurado	jury
el	narcotraficante	drug trafficker
el	narcotráfico	drug trafficking
el	pandillero (*Mex*)	thug, hooligan
el	pirómano	arsonist
el	poli	cop
el	preso	prisoner
el	rehén (*pl* rehenes)	hostage
el	rescate	ransom; rescue
el	revólver	revolver
el	secuestrador	kidnapper; hijacker
el	secuestro	kidnapping
el	secuestro aéreo	hijacking
el	terrorismo	terrorism
el	terrorista	terrorist
el	traficante de drogas	drug dealer
el	tribunal	court

USEFUL WORDS *(feminine)*

la	**acusación** *(pl* acusaciones)	the prosecution; charge
el	**arma** *(fpl* las armas)	weapon
la	**asesina**	murderer
la	**bomba**	bomb
la	**cárcel**	prison
la	**celda**	cell
la	**criminal**	murderer; criminal
la	**declaración** *(pl* declaraciones)	statement
la	**defensa**	defence
la	**delincuencia**	crime
la	**delincuente**	criminal
la	**detective privada**	private detective
la	**detención** *(pl* detenciones)	arrest
la	**droga**	drug
la	**drogadicta**	drug addict
la	**estafadora**	crook
la	**fuga**	escape
la	**gamberra** *(Sp)*	thug, hooligan
la	**guarda**	guard; warden
la	**inmigrante ilegal**	illegal immigrant
la	**investigación** *(pl* investigaciones)	inquiry
la	**ley**	law
la	**narcotraficante**	drug trafficker
la	**pandillera** *(Mex)*	thug, hooligan
la	**pelea**	fight
la	**pirómana**	arsonist
la	**pistola**	gun
la	**poli**	the cops; cop
la	**prisión** *(pl* prisiones)	prison
la	**presa**	prisoner
la	**prueba**	proof
las	**pruebas**	evidence
la	**redada**	raid
la	**rehén** *(pl* rehenes)	hostage
la	**riña**	argument
la	**secuestradora**	kidnapper; hijacker
la	**terrorista**	terrorist
la	**traficante de drogas**	drug dealer

ESSENTIAL WORDS *(masculine)*

el	**acero**	steel
el	**algodón**	cotton
el	**caucho**	rubber
el	**cristal**	crystal; *(Sp)* glass
el	**cuero**	leather
el	**gas**	gas
el	**gasoil**	diesel
el	**hierro**	iron
el	**metal**	metal
el	**oro**	gold
el	**plástico**	plastic
el	**vidrio**	glass

IMPORTANT WORDS *(masculine)*

el	**acero inoxidable**	stainless steel
el	**aluminio**	aluminum
el	**cartón**	cardboard
el	**estado**	condition
el	**hierro forjado**	wrought iron
el	**ladrillo**	brick
el	**papel**	paper
el	**tejido**	fabric

USEFUL PHRASES

una silla de madera **a wooden chair**
una caja de plástico **a plastic box**
un anillo de oro **a gold ring**
en buen estado, en buenas condiciones **in good condition**
en mal estado, en malas condiciones **in bad condition**

ESSENTIAL WORDS *(feminine)*

la	**lana**	wool
la	**madera**	wood
la	**piedra**	stone
la	**piel**	fur; leather
la	**plata**	silver
la	**tela**	fabric

IMPORTANT WORDS *(feminine)*

la	**fibra sintética**	synthetic fiber
la	**seda**	silk

USEFUL PHRASES

un abrigo de piel **a fur coat**
un suéter de lana **a woolen jumper**
oxidado(a) **rusty**

USEFUL WORDS *(masculine)*

el	**acrílico**	acrylic
el	**alambre**	wire
el	**ante**	suede
el	**bronce**	bronze
el	**carbón**	coal
el	**cemento**	cement
el	**cobre**	copper
el	**concreto** (*LAm*)	concrete
el	**encaje**	lace
el	**estaño**	tin
el	**hilo**	thread
el	**hormigón**	concrete
el	**latón**	brass
el	**lino**	linen
el	**líquido**	liquid
el	**mármol**	marble
el	**material**	material
el	**mimbre**	wicker
el	**pegamento**	glue
el	**plomo**	lead
el	**satín**	satin
el	**terciopelo**	velvet
el	**tweed**	tweed
el	**yeso**	plaster

USEFUL WORDS *(feminine)*

la	**arcilla**	clay
la	**cera**	wax
la	**cerámica**	ceramic
la	**cola**	glue
la	**cuerda**	string
la	**escayola** *(Sp)*	plaster
la	**gomaespuma**	foam rubber
la	**hojalata**	tin, tinplate
la	**lona**	canvas
la	**loza**	pottery
la	**mezclilla** *(Mex)*	denim
la	**paja**	straw
la	**pana**	corduroy
la	**porcelana**	porcelain

ESSENTIAL WORDS (*masculine*)

el	**director de orquesta**	conductor
el	**grupo**	band
el	**instrumento musical**	musical instrument
el	**músico**	musician
el	**piano**	piano
el	**violín** (*pl* violines)	violin

USEFUL WORDS (*masculine*)

el	**acorde**	chord
el	**acordeón** (*pl* acordeones)	accordion
el	**arco**	bow
el	**atril**	music stand
el	**bajo**	bass
el	**bombo**	bass drum
el	**chelo**	cello
el	**clarinete**	clarinet
el	**contrabajo**	double bass
el	**estuche**	case
el	**estudio de grabación**	recording studio
el	**fagot**	bassoon
los	**instrumentos de cuerda**	string instruments
los	**instrumentos de percusión**	percussion instruments
los	**instrumentos de viento**	wind instruments
el	**jazz**	jazz
los	**metales**	brass
el	**micrófono**	microphone
el	**minidisco**	minidisc
el	**oboe**	oboe
el	**órgano**	organ
los	**platillos**	cymbals
el	**saxofón** (*pl* saxofones)	saxophone
el	**solfeo**	music theory
el	**solista**	soloist
el	**tambor**	drum
el	**triángulo**	triangle
el	**trombón** (*pl* trombones)	trombone
el	**violonchelo**	cello

ESSENTIAL WORDS *(feminine)*

la **banda**	band
la **batería**	drums, drum kit
la **directora de orquesta**	conductor
la **flauta**	flute
la **flauta dulce**	recorder
la **guitarra**	guitar
la **música**	music; musician
la **orquesta**	orchestra

USEFUL WORDS *(feminine)*

la **armónica**	harmonica
el **arpa** *(f pl* las arpas)	harp
la **batuta**	conductor's baton
la **composición** *(pl* composiciones)	composition
la **corneta**	bugle
la **cuerda**	string
la **gaita**	bagpipes
la **grabación digital** *(pl* grabaciones ~es)	digital recording
la **megafonía**	PA system
la **mesa de mezclas**	mixing deck
la **nota**	note
la **pandereta**	tambourine
la **solista**	soloist
la **tecla (de piano)**	(piano) key
la **trompeta**	trumpet
la **viola**	viola

USEFUL PHRASES

tocar *or* interpretar una pieza **to play a piece**
desafinar **to sing** *or* **play out of tune**
tocar el piano/la guitarra **to play the piano/the guitar**
tocar la batería **to play drums**
con Pedro en batería **with Pedro on drums**
practicar el piano **to practice the piano**
¿tocas en una banda? **do you play in a band?**

CARDINAL NUMBERS

cero	0	zero
uno (*m*), una (*f*)	1	one
dos	2	two
tres	3	three
cuatro	4	four
cinco	5	five
seis	6	six
siete	7	seven
ocho	8	eight
nueve	9	nine
diez	10	ten
once	11	eleven
doce	12	twelve
trece	13	thirteen
catorce	14	fourteen
quince	15	fifteen
dieciséis	16	sixteen
diecisiete	17	seventeen
dieciocho	18	eighteen
diecinueve	19	nineteen
veinte	20	twenty
veintiuno(a)	21	twenty-one
veintidós	22	twenty-two
veintitrés	23	twenty-three
treinta	30	thirty
treinta y uno(a)	31	thirty-one
treinta y dos	32	thirty-two
cuarenta	40	forty
cincuenta	50	fifty
sesenta	60	sixty
setenta	70	seventy
ochenta	80	eighty
noventa	90	ninety
cien	100	one hundred

CARDINAL NUMBERS (*continued*)

ciento uno(a)	101	a hundred and one
ciento dos	102	a hundred and two
ciento diez	110	a hundred and ten
ciento ochenta y dos	182	a hundred and eighty-two
doscientos(as)	200	two hundred
doscientos(as) uno(a)	201	two hundred and one
doscientos(as) dos	202	two hundred and two
trescientos(as)	300	three hundred
cuatrocientos(as)	400	four hundred
quinientos(as)	500	five hundred
seiscientos(as)	600	six hundred
setecientos(as)	700	seven hundred
ochocientos(as)	800	eight hundred
novecientos(as)	900	nine hundred
mil	1000	one thousand
mil uno(a)	1001	a thousand and one
mil dos	1002	a thousand and two
dos mil	2000	two thousand
dos mil seis	2006	two thousand and six
diez mil	10000	ten thousand
cien mil	100000	one hundred thousand
un millón	1000000	one million
dos millones	2000000	two million

USEFUL PHRASES

mil pesos **a thousand pesos**
un millón de dólares **one million dollars**
veintiún años **twenty-one years**
veintiuna páginas **twenty-one pages**
quinientos pesos **five hundred pesos**
quinientas veces **five hundred times**
el diez por ciento **ten per cent**

ORDINAL NUMBERS

primero(a)	1º, 1ª	first
segundo(a)	2º, 2ª	second
tercero(a)	3º, 3ª	third
cuarto(a)	4º, 4ª	fourth
quinto(a)	5º, 5ª	fifth
sexto(a)	6º, 6ª	sixth
séptimo(a)	7º, 7ª	seventh
octavo(a)	8º, 8ª	eighth
noveno(a)	9º, 9ª	ninth
décimo(a)	10º, 10ª	tenth
undécimo(a)	11º, 11ª	eleventh
duodécimo(a)	12º, 12ª	twelfth
decimotercero(a)	13º, 13ª	thirteenth
decimocuarto(a)	14º, 14ª	fourteenth
decimoquinto(a)	15º, 15ª	fifteenth
decimosexto(a)	16º, 16ª	sixteenth
decimoséptimo(a)	17º, 17ª	seventeenth
decimoctavo(a)	18º, 18ª	eighteenth
decimonoveno(a), decimonono(a)	19º, 19ª	nineteenth
vigésimo(a)	20º, 20ª	twentieth

Note:

Ordinal numbers are hardly ever used above 10th in spoken Spanish, and rarely at all above 20th. It's normal to use the cardinal numbers instead, except for milésimo(a).

milésimo(a)	1000º, 1000ª	thousandth
dos milésimo(a)	2000º, 2000ª	two thousandth
millonésimo(a)	1000000º, 1000000ª	millionth
dos millonésimo(a)	2000000º, 2000000ª	two millionth

FRACTIONS

Spanish	Fraction	English
un medio	$\frac{1}{2}$	a half
uno(a) y medio(a)	$1\frac{1}{2}$	one and a half
dos y medio(a)	$2\frac{1}{2}$	two and a half
un tercio, la tercera parte	$\frac{1}{3}$	a third
dos tercios, las dos terceras partes	$\frac{2}{3}$	two thirds
un cuarto, la cuarta parte	$\frac{1}{4}$	a quarter
tres cuartos, las tres cuartas partes	$\frac{3}{4}$	three quarters
un sexto, la sexta parte	$\frac{1}{6}$	a sixth
tres y cinco sextos	$3\frac{5}{6}$	three and five sixths
un séptimo, la séptima parte	$\frac{1}{7}$	a seventh
un octavo, la octava parte	$\frac{1}{8}$	an eighth
un noveno, la novena parte	$\frac{1}{9}$	a ninth
un décimo, la décima parte	$\frac{1}{10}$	a tenth
un onceavo, la onceava parte	$\frac{1}{11}$	an eleventh
un doceavo, la doceava parte	$\frac{1}{12}$	a twelfth
siete doceavos, las siete doceavas partes	$\frac{7}{12}$	seven twelfths
un centésimo, la centésima parte	$\frac{1}{100}$	a hundredth
un milésimo, la milésima parte	$\frac{1}{1000}$	a thousandth

USEFUL PHRASES

ambos (*f* ambas), los dos (*f* las dos) both of them
un bote *or* una lata de tomates a can of tomatoes
una botella de cerveza a bottle of beer
una caja de chocolates a box of chocolates
(gran) cantidad de gente lots of people
un grupo de muchachas a group of girls
un centenar de personas (about) a hundred people
miles de turistas thousands of tourists
la mayoría *or* la mayor parte de la población most of the population
una cucharada de azúcar a spoonful of sugar
media taza de harina half a cup of flour
cien gramos de jamón a hundred grammes of ham
un kilo de manzanas a kilo of apples
medio kilo de manzanas half a kilo of apples
una docena de huevos a dozen eggs
media docena de huevos half a dozen eggs
un litro de leche a liter of milk
medio litro de leche half a liter of milk

USEFUL PHRASES

un metro de tela a meter of fabric
medio metro de tela half a meter of fabric
la mitad del pastel half of the cake
un montón de ropa a pile of clothes
mucho ruido a lot of noise
mucha agua a lot of water
muchos/muchas estudiantes a lot of students
un paquete de galletas a packet of cookies
un par de zapatos a pair of shoes
un plato de arroz a plate of rice
un poco de crema a little cream; some cream
una porción de pollo a portion of chicken
una rebanada de pan a slice of bread
un rebaño de ovejas a flock of sheep
un sobre de sopa a packet of soup
n terrón de azúcar a lump of sugar
un trozo de papel/pastel a piece of paper/cake
un vaso de jugo a glass of juice

ESSENTIAL WORDS *(masculine)*

el	anillo	ring
el	cepillo	brush
el	cepillo de dientes	toothbrush
el	champú	shampoo
el	desodorante	deodorant
el	espejo	mirror
el	maquillaje	make-up
el	peine	comb
el	perfume	perfume
el	reloj	watch

USEFUL WORDS *(masculine)*

el	aftershave	aftershave
el	arete *(LAm)*	earring
el	bilet *(Mex)*	lipstick
el	broche	brooch
el	colgante	pendant
el	collar	necklace
el	diamante	diamond
los	efectos personales	personal effects
el	esmalte (de uñas)	nail polish
el	gemelo	cufflink
el	kleenex® *(pl inv)*	tissue
el	lápiz de labios *(pl* lápices ~~*)*	lipstick
el	llavero	keychain
el	maquillaje	make-up
el	neceser	toilet kit
el	papel higiénico	toilet paper
el	peinado	hairstyle
el	pendiente *(Sp)*	earring
los	polvos compactos	face powder
los	polvos para la cara	face powder
el	quitaesmalte	nail polish remover
el	rastrillo *(Mex)*	(safety) razor
el	rímel	mascara
el	rulo *(Sp)*	roller
el	secador	hairdryer
el	tubo *(LAm)*	roller

ESSENTIAL WORDS *(feminine)*

el	agua de colonia *(f)*	toilet water, eau de toilette
la	cadena	chain
la	crema para la cara	face cream
la	cuchilla de afeitar	razor
la	joya	jewel
la	máquina de afeitar *or* rasurar	elecrtic shaver
la	maquinilla de afeitar *(Sp)*	(safety) razor
la	navaja	razor
la	pasta de dientes	toothpaste
la	pulsera	bracelet
la	rasuradora *(LAm)*	electric razor

USEFUL WORDS *(feminine)*

la	alianza	wedding ring
la	base de maquillaje	foundation
la	brocha de afeitar *or* rasurar	shaving brush
la	crema de afeitar *or* rasurar	shaving cream
la	esponja	sponge
la	espuma de afeitar *or* rasurar	shaving foam
la	mancuerna *or* mancuernilla *(Mex)*	cufflink
la	manicura	manicure
la	perla	pearl
la	secadora *(Mex)*	hair dryer
la	sombra de ojos	eye shadow

USEFUL PHRASES

maquillarse **to put on one's make-up**
desmaquillarse **to take off one's make-up**
hacerse un peinado **to do one's hair**
peinarse **to comb one's hair**
cepillarse el pelo **to brush one's hair**
rasurarse *(LAm)* **to shave**
afeitarse **to shave**
lavarse/cepillarse los dientes **to brush one's teeth**

ESSENTIAL WORDS *(masculine)*

el	**árbol**	tree
el	**césped**	lawn
el	**jardín** (*pl* jardines)	garden
el	**jardinero**	gardener
el	**pasto** (*LAm*)	grass; lawn
el	**sol**	sun

IMPORTANT WORDS *(masculine)*

el	**arbusto**	bush; shrub
el	**banco**	bench
el	**camino**	path
el	**cultivo**	cultivation; growing
el	**ramo de flores**	bunch of flowers
el	**seto**	hedge

USEFUL PHRASES

plantar **to plant**
quitar las hierbas malas, deshierbar **to weed**
regalarle a algn un ramo de flores **to give sb a bunch of flowers**
cortar *or* podar el pasto *or* el césped **to mow the lawn**
"no pisar el césped" **"keep off the grass"**
a mi padre le gusta la jardinería **my father likes gardening**

ESSENTIAL WORDS *(feminine)*

la	**flor**	flower
la	**hierba**	grass; herb
la	**hoja**	leaf
la	**jardinera**	gardener; flower bed
la	**jardinería**	gardening
la	**lluvia**	rain
la	**planta**	plant
la	**rama**	branch
la	**rosa**	rose
la	**tierra**	land; soil; ground
las	**verduras**	vegetables

IMPORTANT WORDS *(feminine)*

la	**abeja**	bee
la	**avispa**	wasp
la	**cerca**	fence
las	**hierbas malas**	weeds
la	**raíz** *(pl* raíces*)*	root
la	**sombra**	shade; shadow

USEFUL PHRASES

las flores están creciendo **the flowers are growing**
en el suelo **on the ground**
regar las plantas **to water the flowers**
recoger flores **to pick flowers**
irse a la sombra **to go into the shade**
quedarse en la sombra **to remain in the shade**
a la sombra de un árbol **in the shade of a tree**

USEFUL WORDS *(masculine)*

el	**azafrán** (*pl* azafranes)	crocus
el	**brote**	bud
el	**clavel**	carnation
el	**cortacésped**	lawnmower
el	**crisantemo**	chrysanthemum
el	**diente de león**	dandelion
el	**estanque**	pond
el	**follaje**	leaves
el	**girasol**	sunflower
el	**gusano**	worm
el	**huerto**	vegetable garden
el	**invernadero**	greenhouse
el	**invierno**	winter
el	**jacinto**	hyacinth
el	**lirio**	lily; iris
el	**macizo de flores**	flower bed
el	**narciso**	daffodil
el	**otoño**	autumn, fall
el	**pensamiento**	pansy
el	**ranúnculo**	buttercup
el	**rocío**	dew
el	**rosal**	rose bush
el	**sendero**	path
el	**suelo**	ground; soil
el	**tallo**	stalk
el	**tronco**	trunk (*of tree*)
el	**tulipán** (*pl* tulipanes)	tulip
el	**verano**	summer

USEFUL WORDS *(feminine)*

la	amapola	poppy
la	baya	berry
la	campanilla	campanula, bellflower
la	carretilla	wheelbarrow
la	cosecha	crop
la	espina	thorn
la	herramienta	tool
la	hiedra	ivy
la	hortensia	hydrangea
las	lilas	lilac
la	madreselva	honeysuckle
la	manguera	hose
la	margarita	daisy
la	mariposa	butterfly
la	orquídea	orchid
la	peonía	peony
la	podadora de pasto *(Mex)*	lawn mower
la	primavera	spring; primrose
la	regadera	watering can
la	semilla	seed
la	violeta	violet

ESSENTIAL WORDS *(masculine)*

los	**anteojos** *or* **lentes de sol** *(LAm)*	sunglasses
el	**bañador** *(Sp)*	swimsuit, trunks
el	**bañista**	swimmer
el	**barco**	boat; ship
el	**barco de pesca**	fishing boat
el	**bikini** *or* **biquini**	bikini
el	**bote**	boat
el	**mar**	sea
el	**muelle**	pier, wharf, jetty
el	**paseo**	walk
el	**pescador**	fisherman
el	**pesquero**	fishing boat
el	**picnic** *(pl ~s)*	picnic
el	**puerto**	port, harbor
el	**puerto deportivo**	marina
el	**remo**	rowing; oar
el	**traje de baño**	swimsuit

IMPORTANT WORDS *(masculine)*

el	**cangrejo**	crab
el	**castillo de arena**	sandcastle
el	**fondo**	bottom
el	**horizonte**	horizon
el	**mareo**	seasickness
el	**vacacionista** *(LAm)*	vacationer

USEFUL PHRASES

en la playa **at the seaside; at** *or* **on the beach**
en el horizonte **on the horizon**
está mareado **he is seasick**
nadar **to swim**
ahogarse **to drown**
me voy a dar un baño **I'm going for a swim**
tirarse al agua, zambullirse **to dive into the water**
flotar **to float**

ESSENTIAL WORDS *(feminine)*

el	**agua** *(f)*	water
la	**arena**	sand
la	**bañista**	swimmer
la	**barca**	boat
la	**costa**	coast
las	**gafas de sol** *(Sp)*	sunglasses
la	**isla**	island
la	**natación**	swimming
la	**pescadora**	fisherwoman
la	**piedra**	stone
la	**playa**	beach; seaside
las	**quemaduras de sol**	sunburn
la	**toalla**	towel

IMPORTANT WORDS *(feminine)*

la	**colchoneta inflable**	airbed
la	**crema (de protección) solar**	sunscreen
la	**silla reclinable**	deckchair
la	**tabla de windsurf**	windsurfing board
la	**travesía**	crossing
la	**tumbona** *(Sp)*	deckchair
la	**vacacionista**	vacationer

USEFUL PHRASES

en el fondo del mar **at the bottom of the sea**
hacer la travesía en barco **to go across by boat**
broncearse **to get a tan**
tomar el sol **to sunbathe**
estar bronceado(a) **to be tanned**
sabe nadar **he can swim**

USEFUL WORDS *(masculine)*

el	acantilado	cliff
el	aire de mar	sea air
el	balde	bucket
el	(barco de) vapor	steamer
los	binoculares	binoculars
el	cabo	cape
el	crucero	cruise
el	cubo *(Sp)*	bucket
el	embarcadero	pier
el	estuario	estuary
el	faro	lighthouse
el	guijarro	pebble
el	marinero	sailor
el	marino	sailor; naval officer
el	mástil	mast
el	naufragio	shipwreck
los	náufragos	shipwrecked people, castaways
el	océano	ocean
el	oleaje	swell
los	prismáticos	binoculars
el	puente (de mando)	bridge *(of a ship)*
los	restos de un naufragio	wreckage
el	salvavidas *(pl inv)*	lifeguard; life jacket
el	socorrista	lifeguard
el	timón *(pl* timones)	rudder
el	transbordador	ferry

USEFUL WORDS *(feminine)*

las	**algas**	seaweed
el	**ancla** (*f pl* las anclas)	anchor
la	**bahía**	bay
la	**balsa**	raft
la	**bandera**	flag
la	**barca**	small boat
la	**boya**	buoy
la	**brisa marina**	sea breeze
la	**carga**	cargo
la	**concha**	shell
la	**corriente**	current
la	**desembocadura**	mouth (*of a river*)
la	**espuma**	foam
la	**gaviota**	seagull
la	**insolación** (*pl* insolaciones)	sunstroke
la	**marea**	tide
la	**marina**	navy; sailor; naval officer
la	**marinera**	sailor
la	**nave**	vessel
la	**ola**	wave
la	**orilla**	shore
la	**pala**	shovel
la	**pasarela**	gangway
la	**roca**	rock
la	**salvavidas** (*pl inv*) *or* socorrista	lifeguard
la	**sombrilla**	beach umbrella, parasol
la	**tripulación** (*pl* tripulaciones)	crew
la	**vela**	sail; sailing

USEFUL PHRASES

tuve una insolación **I had sunstroke**
con la marea baja/alta **at low/high tide**
ir a navegar/remar **to go sailing/rowing**

ESSENTIAL WORDS *(masculine)*

los	abarrotes *(Mex)*	grocery store
los	almacenes *(LAm)*	department store
el	banco	bank
el	billete (de banco)	banknote
el	cambio	change
el	centro comercial	mall, shopping center
el	cheque	check
el	cliente	customer
el	correo *(LAm)*	post office
el	departamento	department
el	dependiente	sales assistant
el	descuento	discount
el	dinero	money
el	dólar	dollar
el	estanco *(Sp)*	tobacconist's
el	euro	euro
los	grandes almacenes *(Sp)*	department store
el	hipermercado	hypermarket
el	mercado	market
el	número (de zapato)	(shoe) size
el	precio	price
el	regalo	present
el	souvenir *(pl ~s)*	souvenir
el	supermercado	supermarket
el	talonario de cheques *(Sp)*	checkbook
el	vendedor	salesman

USEFUL PHRASES

comprar/vender **to buy/sell**
¿cuánto cuesta? **how much does it cost?; how much is it?**
¿cuánto es? **how much is it?**
pagué veinte dólares por esto, esto me costó veinte dólares **I paid 20 dollars for this**
en la carnicería/la panadería **at the butcher's/bakery**

ESSENTIAL WORDS *(feminine)*

la	agencia de viajes	travel agent's
la	alimentación	food
la	barata *(Mex)*	sale, promotion
la	caja	checkout
la	carnicería	butcher's
la	clienta	customer
la	compra	purchase
la	dependienta	sales assistant
la	farmacia	pharmacy
la	florería *(LAm)*	florist
la	floristería *(Sp)*	florist
la	frutería	fruit vendor's
la	lista	list
la	oficina de correo *(LAm) or* de correos *(Sp)*	post office
la	panadería	bakery
la	pastelería	cake shop
la	perfumería	perfume shop/department
la	pescadería	fish shop
la	rebaja	price reduction
las	rebajas	sale, promotion
la	sección *(pl* secciones*)*	department
la	talla	size
la	tarjeta de crédito	credit card
la	tarjeta de débito	debit card
la	tienda	shop
la	tienda de abarrotes *(Mex)*	grocery store
la	tienda de alimentación	grocery store
la	tienda de departamentos *(Mex)*	department store
la	vendedora	saleswoman
la	verdulería	fruit and vegetable store
la	zapatería	shoe store

IMPORTANT WORDS *(masculine)*

el	**aparador** *(Mex)*	store window
el	**artículo**	article
el	**carnicero**	butcher
el	**comerciante**	shopkeeper
el	**comercio**	trade; store
el	**comercio justo**	fair trade
el	**encargado**	manager
el	**escaparate** *(Sp)*	store window
el	**frutero**	fruit vendor
el	**mercado**	market
el	**monedero**	change purse
el	**mostrador**	sales counter
el	**panadero**	baker
el	**pastelero**	confectioner, pastry chef
el	**peluquero**	hairdresser
el	**pescadero**	fish dealer
el	**recibo**	receipt
el	**tícket** *(pl ~s)*	receipt; ticket
el	**verdulero**	fruit and vegetable vendor
el	**zapatero**	shoemaker

USEFUL PHRASES

sólo estoy mirando **I'm just looking**
es demasiado caro **it's too expensive**
algo más barato **something cheaper**
es barato **it's cheap**
"pague en caja" **"pay at the checkout"**
¿lo quiere envuelto para regalo? **would you like it gift wrapped?**
debe de haber un error **there must be some mistake**

IMPORTANT WORDS *(feminine)*

la **biblioteca**	library
la **boutique**	boutique
la **calculadora**	calculator
la **carnicera**	butcher
la **cartera**	wallet
la **comerciante**	shopkeeper
la **encargada**	manager
la **escalera eléctrica** *or* **mecánica**	escalator
la **frutera**	fruit vendor
la **librería**	bookstore
la **marca**	brand
la **panadera**	baker
la **pastelera**	confectioner, pastry chef
la **peluquera**	hairdresser
la **pescadera**	fish dealer
la **promoción** (*pl* promociones)	special offer
la **reclamación** (*pl* reclamaciones)	complaint
la **tintorería**	dry cleaner's
la **verdulera**	fruit and vegetable vendor
la **vitrina** (*LAm*)	store window

USEFUL PHRASES

¿algo más? **anything else?**
S.A. (= *Sociedad Anónima*) **Inc.**
S.L. (= *Sociedad Limitada*) **limited liability company**
y Cía **& Co**
"en venta aquí" **"on sale here"**
en oferta, de oferta **on sale**
el café de comercio justo **fair-trade coffee**
de segunda mano **second-hand**

USEFUL WORDS *(masculine)*

el	**agente inmobiliario**	real estate agent
el	**color**	color
el	**gerente**	manager
el	**joyero**	jeweler; jewelery case
el	**librero**	bookseller
el	**mandado** *(LAm)*	errand
el	**óptico**	optician
el	**producto**	product
los	**productos**	produce
el	**recado** *(Sp)*	errand
el	**relojero**	watchmaker; clockmaker
el	**trato**	deal
el	**videoclub** *(pl ~s)*	video rental store

USEFUL PHRASES

horario opening hours
pagar en efectivo to pay cash
pagar con un cheque to pay by check
pagar con tarjeta de crédito to pay by credit card

USEFUL WORDS *(feminine)*

la	agencia de viajes	travel agent
la	agencia inmobiliaria	real estate agency
la	agente inmobiliaria	real estate agent
la	cola	line, queue
la	compra	purchase
las	compras	shopping
la	ferretería	hardware store
la	gerente	manager
la	joyera	jeweler
la	joyería	jewelery store
la	lavandería	laundry
la	librera	bookseller
la	mercancía	goods
la	óptica	optician; optician's
la	papelería	stationer's
la	rebaja	discount
la	relojera	watchmaker; clockmaker
la	relojería	watchmaker's; clockmaker's
la	sucursal	branch
la	talla de cuello	collar size
la	venta	sale

USEFUL PHRASES

ir de compras to go shopping
gastar to spend
ir a ver aparadores (*Mex*) to go window shopping
ir a ver escaparates, ir de escaparates (*Sp*) to go window shopping

ESSENTIAL WORDS *(masculine)*

el	**aerobics**	aerobics
el	**balón** (*pl* balones)	ball (*large*)
el	**baloncesto** (*Sp*)	basketball
el	**balonvolea** (*Sp*)	volleyball
el	**básquetbol** (*LAm*), el **basquetbol** (*Mex*)	basketball
el	**béisbol** (*LAm*), el **beisbol** (*Mex*)	baseball
el	**billar**	billiards
el	**campeón** (*pl* campeones)	champion
el	**campeonato**	championship
el	**campo**	field; (*golf*) course
el	**ciclismo**	cycling
el	**deporte**	sport
el	**equipo**	team
el	**esquí**	skiing; ski
el	**esquí acuático**	water skiing
el	**estadio**	stadium
el	**fútbol**, el **futbol** (*Mex*)	soccer
el	**fútbol** *or* **futbol** (*Mex*) **americano**	football
el	**gimnasta**	gymnast
el	**gol**	goal
el	**golf**	golf
el	**hockey**	hockey
el	**juego**	game; play
el	**jugador**	player
el	**partido**	game
el	**(método) Pilates**	Pilates
el	**portero**	goalkeeper, goalie
el	**puntaje** (*LAm*)	score
el	**resultado**	result
el	**rugby**	rugby
el	**tenis**	tennis
el	**vóleibol** (*LAm*), el **voleibol** (*Mex*)	volleyball

USEFUL PHRASES

jugar al tenis/al béisbol to play tennis/baseball
jugar tenis/beisbol (*Mex*) to play tennis/baseball
anotar un gol/un punto to score a goal/a point
¿cómo van? what's the score?
ganar/perder un partido to win/lose a match

ESSENTIAL WORDS *(feminine)*

la	**alberca** *(Mex)*	swimming pool
la	**campeona**	champion
la	**cancha**	*(basketball/tennis)* court; *(LAm)* field
la	**equitación**	horseback riding
la	**gimnasia**	gymnastics
la	**gimnasta**	gymnast
la	**jugadora**	player
la	**natación**	swimming
la	**pelota**	ball
la	**pesca**	fishing
la	**piscina**	swimming pool
la	**pista**	track
la	**portera**	goal keeper, goalie
la	**portería**	goal
la	**tabla de windsurf**	windsurfing board
la	**vela**	sailing; sail

USEFUL PHRASES

hacer deporte **to play sports**
empatar **to equalize; to tie**
correr **to run**; saltar **to jump**; lanzar **to throw**
derrotar *or* vencer a algn **to beat sb**
ganarle a algn **to beat sb**
nos ganaron cinco a dos **they beat us five-two**
van ganando cinco a dos **they are leading five -two**
un partido de tenis **a tennis match**
es socio de un club **he belongs to a club**
es socio del club de tenis **he's a member of the tennis club**
ir de pesca **to go fishing**
¿sabes nadar? **can you swim?**
ir a andar *(LAm) or* montar *(Sp)* en bicicleta **to go cycling**
ir a navegar *or* a hacer vela **to go sailing**
ir a correr *or* a hacer jogging **to go jogging**
patín de cuchilla/de ruedas/en línea **(ice)skate/rollerskate/Rollerblade®**
tiro al arco/al blanco **archery/target practice**
entrenar(se) **to train**

IMPORTANT WORDS (*masculine*)

los	**bolos**	skittles (*a type of bowling*)
el	**encuentro**	game, match

USEFUL WORDS (*masculine*)

el	**adversario**	opponent
el	**alpinismo**	mountaineering
el	**árbitro**	referee; umpire
el	**atletismo**	athletics
el	**bádminton**	badminton
el	**box** *or* el **boxeo**	boxing
el	**buceo**	diving
el	**chándal** (*Sp*)	sweatsuit; sweatpants
el	**cronómetro**	stopwatch
el	**descanso**	half-time
el	**entrenador**	trainer; coach
el	**espectador**	spectator
el	**ganador**	winner
el	**hipódromo**	racetrack
los	**Juegos Olímpicos**	Olympic Games
el	**Mundial de Fútbol**	Soccer World Cup
los	**pants** (*pl inv*) (*Mex*)	sweatsuit; sweatpants
el	**parapente**	paragliding
el	**patinaje sobre hielo**	(ice) skating
el	**perdedor**	loser
el	**principiante**	beginner
el	**remo**	rowing; oar
el	**salto con garrocha** (*LAm*) *or* **con pértiga** (*Sp*)	pole vault
el	**salto de altura**	high jump
el	**salto de longitud**	long jump
el	**squash**	squash
el	**tanto**	goal; point
los	**tenis** (*LAm*)	sneakers, running shoes
el	**tiro**	shooting
el	**torneo**	tournament
el	**trineo**	sledge

IMPORTANT WORDS *(feminine)*

la	**bola**	ball *(small)*
la	**carrera**	race
las	**carreras (de caballos)**	horse racing
la	**defensa**	defense
la	**pista de esquí**	ski slope

USEFUL WORDS *(feminine)*

la	**adversaria**	opponent
la	**árbitra**	referee; umpire
la	**camiseta (de deporte)**	jersey, shirt
la	**caña de pescar**	fishing rod
la	**caza**	hunting
la	**copa**	cup
la	**Copa del Mundo**	World Cup
la	**eliminatoria**	heat
la	**entrenadora**	trainer, coach
la	**esgrima**	fencing
la	**espectadora**	spectator
la	**estación de esquí**	ski resort
	(*pl* estaciones de ~)	
la	**etapa**	stage
la	**final**	final
la	**ganadora**	winner
la	**jabalina**	javelin
la	**lucha libre**	wrestling
la	**perdedora**	loser
la	**pesca**	fishing
la	**pista de hielo**	ice skating rink
la	**pista de patinaje**	skating rink
la	**principiante**	beginner
la	**prórroga**	extra time
la	**raqueta**	racket
la	**red**	net
la	**tribuna**	stand
las	**zapatillas de deporte** *(Sp)*	sneakers, running shoes

ESSENTIAL WORDS *(masculine)*

el **actor**	actor
el **ambiente**	atmosphere
el **asiento**	seat
el **auditorio**	auditorium; audience
el **boleto** *(LAm)*	ticket
el **cine**	movie theater
el **circo**	circus
el **cómico**	comedian
el **espectáculo**	show
el **payaso**	clown
el **programa**	program
el **público**	audience
el **show**	show
el **teatro**	theater
el **vestuario**	costumes
el **videoclip** *(pl ~s)*	music video
el **western** *(pl ~s)*	western

IMPORTANT WORDS *(masculine)*

el **acomodador**	usher
el **actor principal**	leading man
el **ballet** *(pl ~s)*	ballet
el **cartel**	notice; poster
el **director**	director
el **entreacto**	intermission
el **intermedio**	intermission
el **maquillaje**	make-up

USEFUL PHRASES

ir al teatro/al cine to go to the theater/to the movies
reservar un asiento to reserve a seat
mi actor preferido/actriz preferida my favorite actor/actress
durante el intermedio during the intermission
salir a escena to come on stage
interpretar el papel de to play the part of

ESSENTIAL WORDS *(feminine)*

la	**actriz** *(pl* actrices)	actress
la	**banda sonora**	soundtrack
la	**boletería** *(LAm)*	box office
la	**cómica**	comedian
la	**cortina**	curtain
la	**entrada**	ticket
la	**estrella de cine**	film star
la	**música**	music
la	**obra (de teatro)**	play
la	**ópera**	opera
la	**orquesta**	orchestra
la	**payasa**	clown
la	**película**	film
la	**sala**	auditorium; theater; screen *(at a multiplex)*
la	**salida**	exit
la	**sesión** *(pl* sesiones)	performance; showing, screening
la	**taquilla**	box office

USEFUL PHRASES

bailar to dance
cantar to sing
filmar una película to shoot a movie
"próxima sesión: 21 horas" "next showing: 9 p.m."
"versión original" "original version"
"subtitulada" "subtitled"
"localidades agotadas" "full house"
aplaudir to clap
¡otra! encore!
¡bravo! bravo!
una película de ciencia ficción/de amor a science fiction movie/a romance
una película de aventuras/de terror an adventure/a horror movie

IMPORTANT WORDS *(masculine continued)*

el	**primer actor**	leading man
el	**protagonista**	star; leading man; main character
el	**subtítulo**	subtitle
el	**título**	title

USEFUL WORDS *(masculine)*

los	**aplausos**	applause
el	**apuntador**	prompter
el	**argumento**	plot
los	**bastidores**	wings
el	**crítico**	critic
el	**decorado**	scenery
el	**director de escena**	producer; stage manager
el	**dramaturgo**	playwright
el	**ensayo (general)**	(dress) rehearsal
el	**escenario**	stage; scene
el	**espectador**	member of the audience
el	**estrado**	platform
el	**estreno**	opening night, premiere
el	**foco**	spotlight
el	**foso de la orquesta**	orchestra pit
el	**guardarropa**	checkroom
el	**guión** (*pl* guiones)	script
el	**guionista**	scriptwriter
el	**musical**	musical
el	**palco**	box
el	**papel**	part
el	**personaje**	character
el	**productor**	producer
el	**realizador**	director (*cinema*); producer (*TV*)
el	**reparto**	cast
el	**vestíbulo**	foyer

IMPORTANT WORDS *(feminine)*

la	**acomodadora**	usher
la	**actriz principal** *(pl* actrices ~es)	leading lady
la	**butaca**	seat
la	**cartelera**	billboard; listings
la	**comedia**	comedy
la	**directora**	director
la	**primera actriz** *(pl* ~s actrices)	leading lady
la	**propina**	tip
la	**protagonista**	star; leading lady; main character
la	**reservación** *(LAm)*, la **reserva** *(Sp)*	reservation

USEFUL WORDS *(feminine)*

la	**actuación** *(pl* actuaciones)	acting, performance
la	**apuntadora**	prompter
las	**candilejas**	footlights
la	**crítica**	review; critics; critic
la	**directora de escena**	producer; stage manager
la	**dramaturga**	playwright
la	**escena**	scene
la	**escenografía**	scenery
la	**espectadora**	member of the audience
la	**farsa**	farce
la	**función** *(pl* funciones)	performance
la	**guionista**	scriptwriter
la	**pantalla**	screen
la	**productora**	producer
la	**puesta en escena**	production
la	**realizadora**	director *(cinema)*; producer *(TV)*
la	**representación** *(pl* representaciones)	performance
la	**serie**	series; serial
la	**tragedia**	tragedy

ESSENTIAL WORDS *(masculine)*

el	**año**	year
el	**cuarto de hora**	quarter of an hour
el	**despertador**	alarm clock
el	**día**	day
el	**fin de semana**	weekend
el	**instante**	moment
el	**mes**	month
el	**minuto**	minute
el	**momento**	moment
el	**reloj**	watch; clock
el	**segundo**	second
el	**siglo**	century
el	**tiempo**	time

USEFUL PHRASES

a mediodía at midday *or* noon

a medianoche at midnight

pasado mañana the day after tomorrow

hoy today

hoy en día nowadays

anteayer, antes de ayer the day before yesterday

antier (*LAm*) the day before yesterday

mañana tomorrow

ayer yesterday

hace dos días 2 days ago

dentro de dos días in 2 days

una semana a week

una quincena two weeks

todos los días every day

¿qué día es hoy? what day is it?

¿qué fecha es hoy? what's the date?

en este momento at the moment

en el siglo XXI in the 21st century

ayer por *or* en la noche last night, yesterday evening

ESSENTIAL WORDS *(feminine)*

la **hora**	hour; time (*in general*)
la **mañana**	morning
la **media hora**	half an hour
la **noche**	night; evening
la **quincena**	two weeks
la **semana**	week
la **tarde**	afternoon; evening

USEFUL PHRASES

es la una **it's one o'clock**

son las dos **it's two o'clock**

son las dos en punto **it is 2 o'clock sharp**

son las dos y cuarto/y media **it's a quarter after two/two thirty**

son veinticinco para las tres (*LAm*)/las tres menos veinticinco (*Sp*) **it's twenty-five to three**

son cuarto para las tres (*LAm*)/las tres menos cuarto (*Sp*) **it's a quarter to three**

el año pasado/próximo **last/next year**

la semana/el año que viene **next week/year**

dentro de media hora **in half an hour**

una vez **once**

dos/tres veces **two/three times**

varias veces **several times**

tres veces al año **three times a year**

érase una vez **once upon a time there was**

diez a la vez **ten at a time**

¿qué hora es? **what time is it?**

¿tiene hora? **have you got the time?**

hace un rato **a while ago**

dentro de un rato **in a while**

temprano **early**

tarde **late**

esta noche **tonight**

IMPORTANT WORDS (*masculine*)

el	**día siguiente**	next day
el	**futuro**	future; future tense
el	**pasado**	past; past tense
el	**presente**	present (*time*); present tense
el	**retraso**	delay

USEFUL WORDS (*masculine*)

el	**año bisiesto**	leap year
el	**calendario**	calendar
el	**cronómetro**	stopwatch
el	**reloj de pie**	grandfather clock
el	**reloj de pulsera**	wristwatch
el	**reloj despertador**	alarm clock

USEFUL PHRASES

pasado mañana **the day after tomorrow**
dos días después **two days later**
el día antes *or* el día anterior **the day before**
un día sí y otro no **every other day**
en el futuro **in the future**
un día libre **a day off**
un día festivo *or* feriado **a national holiday**
un día laborable *or* de entre semana **a weekday**
(en) un día de lluvia, (en) un día lluvioso **on a rainy day**
al amanecer, al alba **at dawn**
(a) la mañana/tarde siguiente **the following morning/evening**
ahora **now**

USEFUL WORDS *(feminine)*

las	**agujas**	hands *(of a clock)*
la	**década**	decade
la	**Edad Media**	Middle Ages
la	**época**	time; era
la	**esfera**	face *(of a clock)*

USEFUL PHRASES

llegas tarde you are late
llegas temprano you are early
este reloj adelanta/atrasa this watch is fast/slow
llegar a tiempo, llegar a la hora to arrive on time
¿cuánto tiempo? how long?
el tercer milenio the third millennium
no levantarse hasta tarde to sleep in
de un momento a otro any minute now
dentro de una semana in a week's time
el lunes que viene no, el otro a week from Monday
la noche antes, la noche anterior the night before
en esa época at that time

ESSENTIAL WORDS *(masculine)*

el **bricolaje**	Do-It-Yourself
el **taller**	workshop

USEFUL WORDS *(masculine)*

el **alambre (de púas)**	(barbed) wire
el **alfiler**	pin
el **alicate** *or* los **alicates**	pliers
el **andamio**	scaffolding
el **candado**	padlock
el **celo** *(Sp)*	Scotch® tape
el **cincel**	chisel
el **clavo**	nail
el **desarmador** *(Mex)*	screwdriver
el **destornillador**	screwdriver
el **durex®** *or* **diurex®** *(LAm)*	Scotch® tape
el **martillo**	hammer
el **muelle**	spring
el **pico**	pickax
el **pincel**	paintbrush
el **resorte**	spring
el **taladro**	drill
el **tornillo**	screw

USEFUL PHRASES

clavar un clavo con el martillo to hammer in a nail
"recién pintado(a)" "wet paint"
pintar to paint
empapelar to wallpaper

ESSENTIAL WORDS *(feminine)*

la chinche *(LAm)*	thumbtack
la cuerda	rope
la herramienta	tool
la llave	key; *(LAm)* faucet
la llave inglesa	wrench
la máquina	machine
la reata *(Mex)*	rope

USEFUL WORDS *(feminine)*

la aguja	needle
la batería	battery *(in car)*
la caja de herramientas	toolbox
la cerradura	lock
la chincheta *(Sp)*	thumbtack
la cola	glue
la escalera (de mano)	ladder
la goma (elástica)	rubber band
la horca	pitchfork
la lima	file
la obra	construction site
la pala	shovel, spade; dustpan
la pila	battery *(in a radio, etc)*
la sierra	saw
la tabla	plank
la taladradora (neumática)	(pneumatic) drill
las tijeras	scissors

USEFUL PHRASES

"prohibido el paso a la obra" "construction site: keep out"
práctico(a) handy
cortar to cut
reparar to repair
atornillar to screw (in)
desatornillar to unscrew

ESSENTIAL WORDS *(masculine)*

los	**alrededores**	surroundings
el	**aparcamiento** *(Sp)*	parking lot; parking space
el	**autobús** *(pl* autobuses*)*	bus
el	**ayuntamiento**	town hall; town council
el	**banco**	bank; bench
el	**barrio**	district
el	**bloque de departamentos** *(LAm)*	apartment building
el	**bloque de pisos** *(Sp)*	apartment building
el	**café**	café, coffee shop; coffee
el	**camión** *(Mex)*	bus; truck
el	**carro** *(LAm)*	car
el	**centro de la ciudad**	downtown
el	**cine**	movie theater; cinema
el	**coche**	car
el	**correo** *(LAm)*	post office
el	**edificio**	building
el	**estacionamiento** *(LAm)*	parking lot; parking space
el	**habitante**	inhabitant
el	**hotel**	hotel
el	**mercado**	market
el	**metro**	subway
el	**museo**	museum; art gallery
el	**parking** *(pl* ~s*)*	parking lot
el	**parque**	park
el	**peatón** *(pl* peatones*)*	pedestrian
el	**policía**	police officer, policeman
el	**puente**	bridge
el	**restaurante**	restaurant
el	**suburbio**	suburb; slum area
el	**taxi**	taxi
el	**teatro**	theater
el	**tour** *(pl* ~s*)*	tour
el	**turista**	tourist

ESSENTIAL WORDS *(feminine)*

la	**alberca** *(Mex)*	swimming pool
la	**calle**	street
la	**carretera**	road
la	**catedral**	cathedral
la	**ciudad**	town, city
la	**colonia (residencial)** *(Mex)*	suburb
la	**comisaría**	police station
la	**contaminación**	air pollution
la	**esquina**	corner
la	**estación (de trenes)**	(train) station
	(*pl* estaciones (~~))	
la	**fábrica**	factory
la	**gasolinera**	gas station
la	**habitante**	inhabitant
la	**lavandería automática**	laundromat®
la	**oficina**	office
la	**oficina de correo**	post office
la	**parada (del autobús)**	bus stop
la	**parada (del camión)** *(Mex)*	bus stop
la	**parada de taxis**	taxi stand
la	**piscina**	swimming pool
la	**plaza**	square
la	**policía**	police officer, policewoman; police
la	**terminal de camiones** *(Mex) or* **de autobuses** *(Sp)*	bus station
la	**tienda**	shop
la	**torre**	tower
la	**turista**	tourist
la	**vista**	view

USEFUL PHRASES

voy a la ciudad *or* al centro **I'm going into town**
en el centro (de la ciudad) **downtown**
en la plaza **in the square**
una calle de un solo sentido **a one-way street**
"dirección prohibida" **"no entry"**
cruzar la calle **to cross the road**
tomar un taxi/el metro **to take a taxi/the subway**

IMPORTANT WORDS *(masculine)*

el	abono	season ticket
el	agente (de policía)	police officer
el	alcalde	mayor
el	atasco	traffic jam
el	cartel	notice; poster
el	castillo	castle
el	cibercafé	internet café
el	cruce	intersection
el	embotellamiento	traffic jam
el	lugar	place
el	monumento	monument
el	parquímetro	parking meter
el	quiosco de periódicos	newsstand
el	semáforo	traffic light
el	sitio	place
el	tráfico	traffic
el	transeúnte	passerby
el	tránsito	traffic
el	zoológico	zoo

USEFUL PHRASES

en la esquina de la calle **on the corner of the street**
vivir en las afueras **to live on the outskirts**
caminar **to walk**

IMPORTANT WORDS *(feminine)*

la	acera *(Sp)*	sidewalk
la	agente (de policía)	police officer
la	alcaldesa	mayor
la	banqueta *(Mex)*	sidewalk
la	biblioteca	library
la	calle principal	main street
la	calzada	road
la	circulación	traffic
la	desviación *(pl* desviaciones)	detour
la	estación de servicio	gas station
	(pl estaciones ~~)	
la	iglesia	church
la	máquina expendedora	ticket vending machine
	de boletos *(LAm) or* de billetes *(Sp)*	
la	mezquita	mosque
la	parte antigua	old town
la	polución	pollution
la	sinagoga	synagogue
la	transeúnte	passerby
la	zona azul	restricted parking zone
la	zona industrial	industrial park

USEFUL PHRASES

industrial **industrial**
histórico(a) **historic**
moderno(a) **modern**
bonito(a) **pretty**
feo(a) **ugly**
limpio(a) **clean**
sucio(a) **dirty**

USEFUL WORDS *(masculine)*

el	**adoquín** *(pl* adoquines)	cobblestone
el	**barrio residencial**	residential area
el	**callejón sin salida** *(pl* callejones ~ ~)	cul-de-sac, dead end
el	**camellón** *(Mex)*	median strip
el	**cementerio**	cemetery
el	**ciudadano**	citizen
el	**cochecito**	baby carriage; stroller
el	**concejo municipal**	town council
el	**cruce peatonal** *or* **de peatones**	crosswalk
el	**desfile**	parade
el	**distrito**	district
el	**edificio**	building
el	**folleto**	leaflet
los	**lugares de interés**	sights, places of interest
el	**parque de bomberos** *(Sp)*	firehouse
el	**paso peatonal** *or* **de peatones**	crosswalk
el	**pavimento**	road surface, pavement
el	**rascacielos** *(pl inv)*	skyscraper
el	**sondeo de opinión**	opinion poll

USEFUL WORDS *(feminine)*

las	**afueras**	outskirts
la	**alcantarilla**	sewer
la	**cafetería**	coffee shop, café; cafeteria
la	**calle sin salida**	cul-de-sac, dead end
la	**cárcel**	prison
la	**carreola** (*Mex*)	stroller
la	**ciclovía**	bicycle lane
la	**ciudadana**	citizen
la	**cola**	line, queue
la	**curva**	bend, curve
la	**estación de bomberos** (*pl* estaciones ~~) (*LAm*)	firehouse
la	**estatua**	statue
la	**flecha**	arrow
la	**galería de arte**	art gallery
la	**glorieta**	traffic circle
la	**mediana** (*Sp*)	median strip
la	**muchedumbre**	crowd
la	**multitud**	crowd
la	**población** (*pl* poblaciones)	town; village; population
la	**señal de tráfico** *or* **tránsito**	road sign

ESSENTIAL WORDS *(masculine)*

el	**aduanero**	customs officer
el	**agente aduanal** *(Mex)*	customs officer
el	**andén** *(pl andenes)*	platform
el	**asiento**	seat
el	**billete** *(Sp)*	ticket
el	**billete de ida** *(Sp)*	one-way ticket
el	**billete de ida y vuelta** *(Sp)*	round-trip ticket
el	**billete sencillo** *(Sp)*	one-way ticket
el	**boleto** *(LAm)*	ticket
el	**boleto de ida** *(LAm)*	one-way ticket
el	**boleto de ida y vuelta** *(LAm) or* **boleto redondo** *(Mex)*	round-trip ticket
el	**compartimento**	compartment
el	**descuento**	discount, price reduction
el	**equipaje**	luggage
el	**expreso**	express train
el	**freno**	brake
el	**horario**	timetable
el	**maletero**	porter
el	**metro**	subway
el	**número**	number
el	**pasaporte**	passport
el	**plano**	map
el	**precio del billete** *(Sp) or* **del boleto** *(LAm)*	fare
el	**puente**	bridge
el	**recargo**	surcharge
el	**retraso**	delay
el	**taxi**	taxi
el	**tícket** *(pl ~s)*	ticket; receipt
el	**tren**	train
el	**vagón** *(pl vagones)*	coach, car
el	**viaje**	journey
el	**viajero**	traveler

ESSENTIAL WORDS *(feminine)*

la	**aduana**	customs
la	**aduanera**	customs officer
la	**agente aduanal** *(Mex)*	customs officer
la	**bici**	bike
la	**bicicleta**	bicycle
la	**boletería** *(LAm)*	ticket office
la	**bolsa**	bag; *(Mex)* purse
la	**cartera**	wallet
la	**clase**	class
la	**conexión** *(pl* conexiones*)*	connection
la	**consigna**	baggage room
la	**consigna automática**	baggage locker
la	**dirección** *(pl* direcciones*)*	direction
la	**entrada**	entrance
la	**estación** *(pl* estaciones*)*	station
la	**estación de metro** *(pl* estaciones ~~*)*	subway station
la	**información**	information
la	**línea**	line
la	**llegada**	arrival
la	**maleta**	suitcase
la	**oficial de aduanas**	customs officer
la	**oficina de objetos perdidos**	lost and found office
la	**parada de taxis**	taxi stand
la	**petaca** *(Mex)*	suitcase
la	**reservación** *(LAm)*, **la reserva** *(Sp)*	reservation
la	**sala de espera**	waiting room
la	**salida**	departure; exit
la	**taquilla**	ticket office
la	**vía**	track, line
la	**viajera**	traveler

USEFUL PHRASES

reservar un asiento **to reserve a seat**

pagar un recargo, pagar un suplemento **to pay an extra charge, to pay a surcharge**

hacer/deshacer el equipaje **to pack/unpack**

IMPORTANT WORDS *(masculine)*

el **coche-cama** *(pl ~s~)*	sleeping car
el **coche-comedor** *(pl ~s~)*	dining car
el **conductor**	driver
el **destino**	destination
el **ferrocarril**	railroad

USEFUL WORDS *(masculine)*

el **abono**	season ticket
el **baúl**	trunk
el **descarrilamiento**	derailment
el **jefe de estación**	station master
el **maquinista**	engineer
el **paso a nivel**	grade crossing
el **silbato**	whistle
el **suplemento**	extra charge, surcharge
el **trayecto**	journey
el **(tren de) mercancías** *(pl (~es ~) ~)*	freight train

USEFUL PHRASES

tomar el tren **to take the train**
perder el tren **to miss the train**
subir al tren **to get on the train**
bajar del tren **to get off the train**
¿está libre este asiento? **is this seat taken?**
el tren lleva retraso **the train is late**
un vagón de fumadores/no fumadores **a smoking/non-smoking car**
"prohibido asomarse por la ventanilla" **"do not lean out of the window"**

IMPORTANT WORDS *(feminine)*

la	**barrera**	barrier
la	**conductora**	driver
la	**duración** *(pl* duraciones)	length (of time)
la	**escalera eléctrica** *or* **mecánica**	escalator
la	**frontera**	border
la	**litera**	couchette (*basic sleeping accommodations on a train*)
la	**propina**	tip
la	**tarifa**	fare

USEFUL WORDS *(feminine)*

la	**alarma**	alarm
la	**etiqueta**	label
la	**jefa de estación**	station master
la	**locomotora**	locomotive
la	**maquinista**	engineer
la	**vía férrea**	(railroad) line *or* track
las	**vías**	rails

USEFUL PHRASES

te acompañaré a la estación **I'll go to the station with you**
iré a buscarte a la estación **I'll pick you up at the station**
el tren de las diez con destino a/procedente de Oaxaca **the 10 o'clock train to/from Oaxaca**

ESSENTIAL WORDS *(masculine)*

el	árbol	tree
el	bosque	wood

USEFUL WORDS *(masculine)*

el	abedul	birch
el	abeto	fir tree
el	acebo	holly
el	albaricoque *(Sp)*	apricot tree
el	árbol frutal	fruit tree
el	arbusto	bush
el	arce	maple
el	brote	bud
el	castaño	chestnut tree
el	cerezo	cherry tree
el	chabacano *(Mex)*	apricot tree
el	chopo	poplar
el	duraznero *(LAm)*	peach tree
el	follaje	foliage
el	fresno	ash
el	huerto	orchard
el	limonero	lemon tree
el	manzano	apple tree
el	melocotonero *(Sp)*	peach tree
el	naranjo	orange tree
el	nogal	walnut tree
el	olmo	elm
el	peral	pear tree
el	pino	pine
el	platanero	banana tree
el	plátano	plane tree
el	roble	oak
el	sauce llorón *(pl ~s llorones)*	weeping willow
el	tejo	yew
el	tilo	lime tree
el	tronco	trunk
el	viñedo	vineyard

ESSENTIAL WORDS *(feminine)*

la	**hoja**	leaf
la	**rama**	branch
la	**selva** (tropical)	rainforest

USEFUL WORDS *(feminine)*

la	**baya**	berry
la	**corteza**	bark
la	**encina**	ilex, holm oak
el	**haya** *(f pl* las hayas)	beech
la	**higuera**	fig tree
la	**raíz** *(pl* raíces)	root
la	**viña**	vineyard

ESSENTIAL WORDS *(masculine)*

el	ajo	garlic
los	champiñones	mushrooms
los	chícharos *(Mex)*	peas
los	ejotes *(Mex)*	string beans
los	frijoles *(LAm)*	beans
los	guisantes *(Sp)*	peas
los	hongos *(LAm)*	mushrooms
el	jitomate *(Mex)*	tomato
el	pimiento	pepper
el	tomate	tomato

USEFUL WORDS *(masculine)*

el	apio	celery
el	berro	watercress
el	brócoli	broccoli
el	calabacín *(pl* calabacines*) (Sp)*	zucchini
el	col	cabbage
el	col de Bruselas	Brussel sprout
el	elote *(Mex)*	sweet corn
los	espárragos	asparagus
los	garbanzos	chickpeas
el	maíz (dulce *or* tierno) *(Sp)*	sweet corn
el	nabo	turnip
el	pepino	cucumber
el	perejil	parsley
el	poro *(Mex)*	leek
el	puerro	leek
el	rábano	radish
el	repollo	cabbage

USEFUL PHRASES

cultivar verduras to grow vegetables

un elote *(Mex)*, una mazorca de maíz *(Sp)* corncob

ESSENTIAL WORDS *(feminine)*

las	**arvejas** *(LAm)*	peas
la	**calabacita** *(Mex)*	zucchini
la	**cebolla**	onion
la	**coliflor**	cauliflower
la	**ensalada**	salad
las	**habichuelas** *(LAm)*	string beans
las	**judías verdes** *(Sp)*	string beans
la	**papa** *(LAm)*, la **patata** *(Sp)*	potato
las	**verduras**	vegetables
la	**zanahoria**	carrot

USESFUL WORDS *(feminine)*

la	**acelga** *or* las **acelgas**	Swiss chard
la	**alcachofa**	artichoke
las	**alubias**	navy beans
la	**berenjena**	eggplant
la	**calabaza**	pumpkin
la	**cebolleta**	scallion
la	**cebollita de Cambray** *(Mex)*	scallion
la	**endibia**	endive
la	**escarola**	escarole
la	**espinaca** *or* las **espinacas**	spinach
las	**judías** *(Sp)*	beans
la	**lechuga**	lettuce
las	**legumbres**	vegetables
las	**lentejas**	lentils
la	**remolacha**	beet

USEFUL PHRASES

zanahoria rallada grated carrot
orgánico(a), biológico(a), ecológico(a) organic
vegetariano(a) vegetarian

ESSENTIAL WORDS *(masculine)*

el **autobús** (*pl* autobuses)	bus
el **autocar** (*Sp*)	(long distance) bus
el **avión** (*pl* aviones)	airplane
el **barco de vela**	sailing ship; sailboat
el **bote**	boat
el **bote de remos**	rowboat
el **camión** (*pl* camiones)	truck; (*Mex*) bus
el **carro**	cart; (*LAm*) car
el **casco**	helmet
el **ciclomotor**	moped
el **coche**	car
el **helicóptero**	helicopter
el **medio de transporte**	means of transportation
el **metro**	subway
el **precio del boleto** (*LAm*) *or* **del billete** (*Sp*)	fare
el **taxi**	taxi
el **tráiler**	trailer
el **transbordador**	ferry
el **transporte público**	public transportation
el **tren**	train
el **vehículo**	vehicle
el **vehículo pesado**	heavy-duty vehicle

IMPORTANT WORDS *(masculine)*

el **camión de bomberos**	fire truck

USEFUL PHRASES

viajar **to travel**
fue a Dallas en avión **he flew to Dallas**
tomar el autobús/el metro/el tren **to take the bus/the subway/the train**
andar en bicicleta **to go cycling**
se puede ir en coche **you can get there by car**

ESSENTIAL WORDS *(feminine)*

la	**bici**	bike
la	**bicicleta**	bicycle
la	**camioneta**	van; station wagon
la	**distancia**	distance
la	**moto**	motorbike
la	**motocicleta**	motorcycle, motorbike
la	**parte de atrás/de adelante**	back/front
la	**parte delantera**	front
la	**parte trasera**	back
la	**vespa®**	scooter

IMPORTANT WORDS *(feminine)*

la	**ambulancia**	ambulance
la	**grúa**	tow truck

USEFUL PHRASES

reparar *or* arreglar el coche de algn to repair sb's car
un coche de alquiler a rental car
un coche *or* un carro de renta (*Mex*) a rental car
un coche deportivo a sports car
un coche de carreras a race car
arrancar to start, to move off

USEFUL WORDS *(masculine)*

el **aerodeslizador**	hovercraft
el **(barco de) vapor**	steamer
el **bulldozer** *(pl ~s)*	bulldozer
el **buque**	ship
el **camión articulado** *(pl* camiones ~s)	tractor-trailer, semi
el **camión cisterna** *(pl* camiones ~)	tanker
el **cohete**	rocket
el **hidroavión** *(pl* hidroaviones)	seaplane
el **jeep** *(pl ~s)*	jeep
el **navío**	ship
el **ovni (objeto volador no identificado)**	UFO *(unidentified flying object)*
el **petrolero**	oil tanker *(ship)*
el **planeador**	glider
el **platillo volador** *(LAm) or* **volante** *(Sp)*	flying saucer
el **portaaviones** *(pl inv)*	aircraft carrier
el **remolcador**	tug
el **remolque**	trailer
el **submarino**	submarine
el **tanque**	tank
el **teleférico**	cable car
el **telesilla**	chairlift
el **tranvía**	streetcar, tram
el **velero**	sailing ship; sailboat
el **yate**	yacht; pleasure cruiser

USEFUL WORDS *(feminine)*

la	**barcaza**	barge
la	**canoa**	canoe
la	**carreta**	wagon; cart
la	**lancha**	boat (*small*); launch
la	**lancha de motor**	motorboat
la	**lancha de salvamento**	lifeboat
la	**lancha de socorro**	lifeboat
la	**lancha neumática**	inflatable boat
la	**lancha rápida**	speedboat
la	**locomotora**	locomotive

ESSENTIAL WORDS *(masculine)*

el	**aire**	air
el	**boletín meteorológico**	weather report
	(*pl* boletines ~s)	
el	**calor**	heat
el	**cielo**	sky
el	**clima**	climate
el	**este**	east
el	**frío**	cold
el	**grado**	degree
el	**hielo**	ice
el	**invierno**	winter
el	**norte**	north
el	**oeste**	west
el	**otoño**	fall; autumn
el	**paraguas** (*pl inv*)	umbrella
el	**parte meteorológico**	weather report
el	**pronóstico del tiempo**	(weather) forecast
el	**sol**	sun; sunshine
el	**sur**	south
el	**tiempo**	weather
el	**verano**	summer
el	**viento**	wind

USEFUL PHRASES

¿qué tiempo hace? what's the weather like?
hace calor/frío it's hot/cold
hace un día precioso it's a lovely day
hace un día horrible it's a horrible day
al aire libre in the open air
hay niebla it's foggy
30° a la sombra 30° in the shade
escuchar el pronóstico del tiempo to listen to the weather forecast
llover to rain
nevar to snow
llueve *or* está lloviendo it's raining
nieva *or* está nevando it's snowing

ESSENTIAL WORDS *(feminine)*

la	**estación** *(pl* estaciones)	season
la	**lluvia**	rain
la	**niebla**	fog
la	**nieve**	snow
la	**nube**	cloud
la	**primavera**	spring
la	**región** *(pl* regiones)	region, area
la	**temperatura**	temperature

USEFUL PHRASES

brilla el sol **the sun is shining**
sopla el viento **the wind is blowing**
hace un frío glacial **it's freezing**
tengo las manos heladas **my hands are freezing**
helarse **to freeze**
derretirse **to melt**
soleado(a) **sunny**
tormentoso(a) **stormy**
lluvioso(a) **rainy**
fresco(a) **cool**
variable **changeable**
húmedo(a) **humid; damp**
nublado(a) **cloudy**

IMPORTANT WORDS *(masculine)*

el	**chubasco**	downpour, shower
el	**humo**	smoke
el	**polvo**	dust

USEFUL WORDS *(masculine)*

el	**aguacero**	downpour
el	**amanecer**	dawn, daybreak
el	**anochecer**	nightfall, dusk
el	**arco iris** *(pl inv)*	rainbow
el	**barómetro**	barometer
el	**cambio**	change
el	**charco**	puddle
el	**copo de nieve**	snowflake
el	**crepúsculo**	twilight
el	**deshielo**	thaw
el	**granizo**	hail
el	**huracán** *(pl huracanes)*	hurricane
el	**pararrayos** *(pl inv)*	lightning rod
el	**quitanieves** *(pl inv)*	snowplow
el	**rayo**	bolt of lightning
el	**rayo de sol**	ray of sunshine
el	**relámpago**	flash of lightning
(los)	**relámpagos**	lightning
el	**rocío**	dew
el	**trueno**	thunderclap
(los)	**truenos**	thunder

IMPORTANT WORDS *(feminine)*

las	**precipitaciones**	rainfall
la	**sombrilla**	parasol
la	**tormenta**	storm
la	**visibilidad**	visibility

USEFUL WORDS *(feminine)*

el	**alba** *(f pl* las albas)	dawn
la	**atmósfera**	atmosphere
la	**brisa**	breeze
la	**bruma**	mist
la	**corriente (de aire)**	draught
la	**escarcha**	frost *(on the ground)*
la	**gota de lluvia**	raindrop
la	**helada**	frost *(weather)*
la	**inundación** *(pl* inundaciones)	flood
la	**luz de la luna**	moonlight
la	**mejora**	improvement
la	**nevada**	snowfall
la	**ola de calor**	heatwave
la	**oscuridad**	darkness
la	**puesta de sol**	sunset
la	**ráfaga de viento**	gust of wind
la	**sequía**	drought
la	**tormenta eléctrica**	thunderstorm

ESSENTIAL WORDS *(masculine)*

el	**albergue juvenil**	youth hostel
los	**baños públicos** *(LAm)*	public restrooms
el	**bote de la basura** *(LAm)*	garbage can
el	**comedor**	dining room
el	**cuarto de baño**	bathroom
el	**cubo de la basura** *(Sp)*	garbage can
el	**desayuno**	breakfast
el	**dormitorio**	dormitory
los	**lavabos**	washrooms
el	**mapa**	map
los	**servicios** *(Sp)*	restrooms
el	**silencio**	silence
el	**visitante**	visitor

IMPORTANT WORDS *(masculine)*

el	**carnet de socio** *(pl ~s ~~)*	membership card
el	**lavabo**	washroom; lavatory
el	**saco de dormir**	sleeping bag

ESSENTIAL WORDS *(feminine)*

la	**bolsa de dormir**	sleeping bag
la	**cama**	bed
la	**litera**	bunk bed
la	**cocina**	kitchen; cooking
la	**comida**	meal
la	**ducha**	shower
la	**estancia**	stay
la	**lista de precios**	price list
la	**noche**	night
la	**oficina**	office
la	**regadera** *(Mex)*	shower
la	**sábana**	sheet
la	**sala de juegos**	gameroom
la	**tarifa**	rate(s)
la	**toalla**	towel
las	**vacaciones**	holidays
la	**visitante**	visitor

IMPORTANT WORDS *(feminine)*

la	**caminata**	hike
la	**excursión** *(pl* excursiones)	trip
la	**guía**	guidebook
la	**mochila**	backpack
las	**normas**	rules
la	**ropa de cama**	bed linens

USEFUL PHRASES

pasar una noche en el albergue juvenil to spend a night at the youth hostel

quisiera alquilar una bolsa de dormir *or* un saco de dormir I would like to rent a sleeping bag

está todo ocupado there's no more room

The vocabulary items on pages 670 to 707 have been grouped under parts of speech rather than topics because they can apply in a wide range of circumstances. Use them just as freely as the vocabulary already given.

ARTICLES AND PRONOUNS

What is an article?
In English, an **article** is one of the words *the*, *a* and *an* which is given in front of a noun.

What is a pronoun?
A **pronoun** is a word you use instead of a noun, when you do not need or want to name someone or something directly, for example, *it*, *you*, *none*.

algo something; anything
alguien somebody, someone; anybody, anyone
alguno/alguna one; someone, somebody
algunos/algunas some, some of them; some of us, some of you, some of them
ambos/ambas both
aquel/aquella that
aquellos/aquellas those
cada each; every
cual which; who; whom
  lo cual which
cuál what, which one
cualquiera any one; anybody, anyone
  cualquiera de los dos/las dos either (*see also* Adjectives)
cualesquiera (*pl*) any (*see also* Adjectives)
cuanto/cuanta as much as
cuánto/cuánta how much
cuantos/cuantas as many as
cuántos/cuántas how many
cuyo/cuya/cuyos/cuyas whose
  en cuyo caso in which case

demasiado/demasiada too much
demasiados/demasiadas too many
dos: los/las dos both
el/la the
él he; him; it
  de él his
ella she; her; it
  de ella hers
ello it
ellos/ellas they; them
  de ellos/ellas theirs
ese/esa that
esos/esas those
este/esta this
estos/estas these
la her; it; you
las them; you
le him; her; it; you
les them; you
lo him; it; you
los/las the
los them; you
me me; myself
mi/mis my
(el)mío/(la) mía/(los) míos/(las) mías mine

mismo/misma/mismos/mismas same
  mí mismo/misma; yo mismo/ misma myself; **nosotros mismos/ nosotras mismas** ourselves; **sí misma; ella misma** herself; **sí mismo; él mismo** himself; **sí mismos/sí mismas; ellos mismos/ellas mismas** themselves; **ti mismo/ti misma; tú mismo/ tú misma; usted mismo/usted misma** yourself; **vosotros mismos/vosotras mismas; ustedes mismos/ustedes mismas** yourselves; **uno mismo/ una misma** oneself

mucho/mucha a lot, lots; much (*see also* Adjectives; Adverbs)

muchos/muchas a lot, lots; many (*see also* Adjectives)

nada nothing
  nada más nothing else

nadie nobody, no one; anybody, anyone
  nadie más nobody else

ninguno/ninguna any; neither; either; none; no one, nobody
  ninguno de los dos/ninguna de las dos neither (*see also* Adjectives)

ningunos/ningunas any; none (*see also* Adjectives)

nos us; ourselves; each other

nosotros/nosotras we; us

nuestro/nuestra/nuestros/ nuestras our; ours
  el nuestro/la nuestra/los nuestros/las nuestras ours

os you; yourselves; each other

otro/otra another, another one (*see also* Adjectives)

otros/otras others (*see also* Adjectives)

poco/poca not much, little **un poco** a bit, a little
  dentro de poco shortly

pocos/pocas not many, few

que who; that

qué what; what a

quien/quienes who; whoever

quién/quiénes who

se him; her; them; you; himself; herself; itself; themselves; yourself; yourselves; oneself; each other

su/sus his; her; its; their; your; one's

(el) suyo/(la) suya/(los) suyos/ (las) suyas his; her; its; their; your; hers; theirs; yours; one's own

tal/tales such

tampoco not…either, neither

te you; yourself

ti you

todo/toda (it) all
  todo el mundo everybody, everyone (*see also* Adjectives)

todos/todas all; every; everybody; everyone (*see also* Adjectives)

tu/tus your

tú you

usted you

ustedes you

(el) tuyo/(la) tuya/(los) tuyos/(las) tuyas yours

un/una a; an; one

unos/unas some; a few; about, around

varios/varias several

vosotros/vosotras (*Sp*) you

vuestro/vuestra/vuestros/ vuestras (*Sp*) your; yours
  los vuestros/las vuestras (*Sp*) yours

yo I; me

CONJUNCTIONS

> **What is a conjunction?**
> A **conjunction** is a word such as *and*, *but*, *or*, *so*, *if* and *because*, that links two words or phrases of a similar type, or two parts of a sentence, for example, *Diane <u>and</u> I have been friends for years*; *I left <u>because</u> I was bored*.

ahora: ahora bien however;
  ahora que now that
antes: antes de que before
así: así (es) que so
aunque although, though
como as
conque so, so then
consiguiente: por consiguiente
  so, therefore
cuando when; whenever; if
cuanto: en cuanto as soon as; as
dar: dado que since
decir: es decir that is to say
desde: desde que since
después: después de que after
e and
embargo: sin embargo still,
  however
entonces then
fin: a fin de que so that, in order that
forma: de forma que so that
hasta: hasta que until, till
luego therefore
manera: de manera que so that
mas but
más: más que more than
menos: menos que less than
mientras while; as long as
  mientras que whereas;
  mientras (tanto) meanwhile

modo: de modo que so that
momento: en el momento en que
  just as
ni or; nor; even
  ni ... ni neither ... nor
o or
  o ... o ... either ... or ...
para: para que so that
pero but
porque because
pronto: tan pronto como as soon
  as
pues then; well; since
puesto: puesto que since
que that
ser: o sea that is
  a no ser que unless
si if; whether
  si no otherwise
siempre: siempre que whenever;
  as long as, provided that
sino but; except; only
tal: con tal (de) que as long as,
  provided that
tanto: por (lo) tanto so, therefore
u or
vez: una vez que once
vista: en vista de que seeing that
y and
ya: ya que as, since

ADJECTIVES

What is an adjective?
An **adjective** is a 'describing' word that tells you more about a person or thing, such as their appearance, colour, size or other qualities, for example, *pretty*, *blue*, *big*.

abierto(a) open
absoluto(a) absolute
absurdo(a) absurd
académico(a) academic
accesible accessible; approachable
aceptable acceptable
acondicionado(a) equipped
  con aire acondicionado
  air-conditioned
acostumbrado(a) accustomed; usual
activo(a) active
acusado(a) accused; marked
adecuado(a) appropriate
admirable admirable
aéreo(a) aerial
aficionado(a) enthusiastic
afilado(a) sharp
afortunado(a) fortunate, lucky
agitado(a) rough; upset; agitated;
  hectic
agotado(a) exhausted
agradable pleasant, agreeable
agresivo(a) aggressive
agrícola agricultural
agudo(a) sharp; acute
aislado(a) isolated
alegre happy; bright; lively; merry
alguno/alguna (*before masc sing*
  algún) some; any (*see also* Articles
  and Pronouns)
algunos/algunas some; several
  (*see also* Articles and Pronouns)

alternativo(a) alternating;
  alternative
alto(a) high; tall
amargo(a) bitter
ancho(a) broad; wide
anciano(a) elderly
animado(a) lively; cheerful
anónimo(a) anonymous
anormal abnormal
anterior former
antiguo(a) old; vintage; antique
anual annual
apagado(a) out; off; muffled; dull
aparente apparent
apasionado(a) passionate
apropiado(a) appropriate, suitable
aproximado(a) approximate,
  rough
arriba: de arriba top
asequible affordable
asombrado(a) amazed, astonished
asombroso(a) amazing, astonishing
áspero(a) rough, harsh
atestado(a) crowded; popular
atento(a) attentive; watchful
atractivo(a) attractive
automático(a) automatic
avanzado(a) advanced
bajo(a) low; short
barba: con *or* **de barba** bearded
barbudo(a) bearded
básico(a) basic

bastante enough; quite a lot of (*see also* Adverbs)
bien right; correct; fine
bienvenido(a) welcome
blando(a) soft
breve brief
brillante shining; bright
brutal brutal
bruto(a) rough; stupid; uncouth; gross
bueno(a) good
cada each; every
caliente hot; warm
callado(a) quiet
cansado(a) tired
capaz capable
cariñoso(a) affectionate
caro(a) expensive
cauteloso(a) cautious
central central
ceñido(a) tight
cercano(a) close; nearby
cerrado(a) closed; off
científico(a) scientific
cierto(a) true; certain
civil civil; civilian
claro(a) clear; light; bright
clásico(a) classical; classic
climatizado(a) air-conditioned
cobarde cowardly
comercial commercial
cómodo(a) comfortable
complejo(a) complex
completo(a) complete
complicado(a) complicated; complex
comprensivo(a) understanding
común common; mutual
concreto(a) specific; concrete
concurrido(a) crowded; popular
conmovedor(a) moving, touching

consciente conscious; aware
conservador(a) conservative
considerable considerable
constante constant
contemporáneo(a) contemporary
contento(a) happy; pleased
continuo(a) continuous
convencional conventional
correcto(a) correct, right
corriente ordinary; common
cortado(a) cut; closed; off; shy
creativo(a) creative
cristiano(a) Christian
crítico(a) critical
crudo(a) raw
cuadrado(a) square
cualquiera (*before masc and fem sing* **cualquier**) any (*see also* Articles and Pronouns)
cualesquiera any (*see also* Articles and Pronouns)
cuanto/cuanta as much as
cuánto/cuánta how much
cuantos/cuantas as many as
cuántos/cuántas how many
cultural cultural
curioso(a) curious
debido(a) due, proper
decepcionante disappointing
decidido(a) determined; decisive
delicado(a) delicate
delicioso(a) delicious
demasiado/demasiada too much
demasiados/demasiadas too many
democrático(a) democratic
derecho(a) right; straight
desafortunado(a) unfortunate
desagradable unpleasant
desconocido(a) unknown
desesperado(a) desperate

desierto(a) deserted

desnudo(a) naked; bare

despejado(a) clear

despierto(a) awake; sharp; alert

despreocupado(a) carefree; careless

destruido(a) destroyed

detallado(a) detailed

diestro(a) skilful; right-handed

difícil difficult

digno(a) dignified; **digno de** worthy of

diminuto(a) tiny

directo(a) direct

disgustado(a) upset; annoyed

disponible available

dispuesto(a) arranged; willing

distinguido(a) distinguished

distinto(a) different; various

divertido(a) funny, amusing; fun; entertaining

dividido(a) divided

divino(a) divine

doble double

domesticado(a) tame

doméstico(a) domestic

dos: los/las dos both

dulce sweet

duro(a) hard

económico(a) economic; economical

efectivo(a) effective

eficaz effective; efficient

eficiente efficient

eléctrico(a) electric

electrónico(a) electronic

elemental elementary

emocionante exciting

emotivo(a) emotional; moving

encantador(a) charming; lovely

enmascarado(a) masked

enorme enormous, huge

enterado(a) knowledgeable; well-informed; aware

entero(a) whole

equivalente equivalent

equivocado(a) wrong

escandaloso(a) shocking

esencial essential

especial special

específico(a) specific

espectacular spectacular

espeso(a) thick

espiritual spiritual

estrecho(a) narrow

estricto(a) strict

estropeado(a) broken (off); off

estupendo(a) marvellous, great

estúpido(a) stupid

étnico(a) ethnic

evidente obvious, evident

exacto(a) exact; accurate

excelente excellent

excepcional outstanding

exclusivo(a) exclusive

exigente demanding, exacting

experto(a) experienced

éxito: de éxito successful

exitoso(a) successful

exquisito(a) delicious; exquisite

extra extra; top-quality; bonus

extranjero(a) foreign

extraño(a) strange; foreign

extraordinario(a) extraordinary; outstanding; special

extremo(a) extreme

fácil easy

falso(a) false

familiar family; familiar

famoso(a) famous

federal federal

feroz fierce, ferocious

fijo(a) fixed; permanent
final final
financiero(a) financial
fino(a) fine; smooth; refined
firme firm; steady
físico(a) physical
flexible flexible
fluido(a) fluid; fluent
formal reliable; formal; official
frágil fragile; frail
frecuente frequent
fresco(a) fresh; cool; bold
fuerte strong; loud
futuro(a) future
general general
generoso(a) generous
genial brilliant; wonderful, great
gentil kind
genuino(a) genuine
global global
gordo(a) fat; big
grande (*before masc sing* **gran**) big; great
grandioso(a) grand; grandiose
habitual usual
herido(a) injured; wounded; hurt
hermoso(a) beautiful
histórico(a) historic; historical
holgado(a) loose
honrado(a) honest; respectable
horrible horrific; hideous; terrible
horroroso(a) dreadful; hideous; terrible
humano(a) human; humane
ideal ideal
idéntico(a) identical
igual equal
ilegal illegal
iluminado(a) illuminated, lit; enlightened

ilustrado(a) illustrated
imaginario(a) imaginary
impar odd
importante important
imposible impossible
imprescindible indispensable
impresionante impressive; moving; shocking
inaguantable unbearable
incapaz (de) incapable (of)
increíble incredible; unbelievable
inculto(a) uncultured
indefenso(a) defenseless
independiente independent
indiferente indifferent; unconcerned
individual individual; single
industrial industrial
inesperado(a) unexpected
inevitable inevitable
infantil childlike; childish
inflable inflatable
injusto(a) unfair
inmediato(a) immediate
inmenso(a) immense
inmune immune
inquieto(a) anxious; restless
intacto(a) intact
intencionado(a) deliberate
intenso(a) intense; intensive
interior interior; inside; inner; domestic
interminable endless
internacional international
interno(a) internal
interrumpido(a) interrupted
inútil useless
invisible invisible
izquierdo(a) left
junto(a) together

justo(a) just, fair; exact; tight
largo(a) long
legal legal
lento(a) slow
libre free
ligero(a) light; slight
limpio(a) clean
liso(a) smooth; straight; plain
listo(a) ready; bright
llamativo(a) bright; striking
llano(a) flat; straightforward
lleno(a) (de) full (of)
lluvioso(a) rainy, wet
loco(a) crazy, insane
lujo: de lujo luxurious
lujoso(a) luxurious
magnífico(a) magnificent;
  wonderful, superb
mal wrong, ill
maligno(a) malignant; evil,
  malicious
malo(a) bad
malvado(a) wicked
manso(a) meek; tame
maravilloso(a) marvelous,
  wonderful
marcado(a) marked
máximo(a) maximum
mayor bigger; elder, older
  el/la...mayor the biggest...;
  the eldest...; the oldest...
mecánico(a) mechanical
médico(a) medical
medio(a) half; average
medioambiental environmental
mejor better
  el/la mejor the best
menor smaller; younger
  el/la...menor the smallest;
  the youngest

mental mental
militar military
minucioso(a) thorough; very detailed
mismo(a) same
misterioso(a) mysterious
moderado(a) moderate
moderno(a) modern
mojado(a) wet; soaked
molesto(a) annoying; annoyed;
  awkward; uncomfortable
montañoso(a) mountainous
mucho/mucha a lot of, lots of;
  much (see also Pronouns; Adverbs)
muchos/muchas a lot of, lots of;
  many (see also Pronouns)
muerto(a) dead
mundial worldwide, global
mutuo(a) mutual
nacido(a) born
nacional national; domestic
nativo(a) native
natural natural
necesario(a) necessary
negativo(a) negative
ninguno/ninguna (before masc sing
  ningún) no; none, any (see also
  Pronouns)
ningunos/ningunas no; none, any
  (see also Pronouns)
normal normal; standard
nuclear nuclear
nuevo(a) new
numeroso(a) numerous
obediente obedient
objetivo(a) objective
obligatorio(a) compulsory,
  obligatory
obvio(a) obvious
ocupado(a) busy; taken; engaged;
  occupied

oficial official
oportuno(a) opportune; appropriate
original original
oscuro(a) dark; obscure
otro/otra another
  a/en otro lugar somewhere else;
  otra cosa something else;
  otra persona somebody else;
  otra vez again (*see also* Pronouns);
  otros/otras other (*see also* Pronouns)
pacífico(a) peaceful; peaceable
pálido(a) pale
par even
parado standing up
particular special; particular; private
patético(a) pathetic
peligroso(a) dangerous
peor worse
  el peor the worst
perdido(a) lost; stray; remote
perfecto(a) perfect
personal personal
pesado(a) heavy; tedious; boring
picante hot (spicy)
pie: de pie standing (up)
poco/poca not much, little
pocos/pocas not many, few
poderoso(a) powerful
polémico(a) controversial
polvoriento(a) dusty; powdery
popular popular
portátil portable
posible possible; potential
positivo(a) positive
práctico(a) practical
precioso(a) lovely, beautiful; precious

preciso(a) precise; **ser preciso** to be necessary
preferido(a) favorite
preliminar preliminary
presentable presentable
presunto(a) alleged
previo(a) previous
primario(a) primary
principal main
privado(a) private
privilegiado(a) privileged
profundo(a) deep
prometido(a) promised; engaged
propio(a) own
próximo(a) near, close; next
psicológico(a) psychological
público(a) public
pueril childish
pulcro(a) neat
puntiagudo(a) pointed; sharp
puntual punctual
puro(a) pure
qué what; which; what a
querido(a) dear
químico(a) chemical
racial racial
radical radical
rápido(a) fast, quick
raro(a) strange, odd; rare
razonable reasonable
reacio(a) reluctant
real actual; royal
reciente recent
recto(a) straight; honest
redondo(a) round
refrescante refreshing
regional regional
regular regular
religioso(a) religious
repentino(a) sudden

repuesto: de repuesto spare
reservado(a) reserved
resistente resistant; tough
responsable (de) responsible (for)
revolucionario(a) revolutionary
ridículo(a) ridiculous
rival rival
romántico(a) romantic
rubio(a) fair, blond
ruidoso(a) noisy
rural rural
sabio(a) wise
sagrado(a) sacred
salvaje wild
salvo: a salvo safe
sanitario(a) sanitary; health
sano(a) healthy
  sano(a) y salvo(a) safe and sound
santo(a) holy
satisfecho(a) (de) satisfied (with)
seco(a) dry
secreto(a) secret
secundario(a) secondary
seguro(a) safe; secure; certain;
  sure
semejante similar
sencillo(a) simple; natural; single
sensacional sensational
sentado(a) sitting, seated
señalado(a) special
separado(a) separate
servicial helpful
severo(a) severe
sexual sexual
significativo(a) significant;
  meaningful
siguiente next, following
silencioso(a) silent; quiet
sincero(a) sincere
singular singular; outstanding

siniestro(a) sinister
situado(a) situated
sobra: de sobra spare
sobrante spare
social social
solemne solemn
sólido(a) solid
solo(a) alone; lonely; black;
  straight, neat
soltero(a) single
sombrío(a) sombre; dim
sonriente smiling
soportable bearable
sorprendente surprising
sospechoso(a) suspicious
suave smooth; gentle; mild; slight
sucio(a) dirty
superior top; upper; superior
supremo(a) supreme
supuesto(a) assumed; supposed
tal/tales such
tanto/tanta so much
tantos/tantas so many
técnico(a) technical
terrible terrible
típico(a) typical
tirante tight; tense
todo/toda all (see also Pronouns)
todos/todas all; every (see also
  Pronouns)
tolerante broad-minded
total total
tradicional traditional
tremendo(a) tremendous
triste sad
último(a) last
  el último the latest
ultrajante offensive; outrageous
único(a) only; unique
urgente urgent

útil useful, helpful
vacante vacant
vacío(a) empty
valiente brave, courageous
valioso(a) valuable
valor: de valor valuable
variado(a) varied
varios/varias several
vecino(a) neighboring

verdad: de verdad real
verdadero(a) real; true
viejo(a) old
vil villainous; vile
violento(a) violent; awkward
visible visible
vital vital
vivo(a) living; alive; lively
voluntario(a) voluntary

ADVERBS AND PREPOSITIONS

> **What is an adverb?**
> An **adverb** is a word usually used with verbs, adjectives or other adverbs that gives more Information about when, how, where, or in what circumstances something happens, or to what degree something is true, for example, *quickly*, *happily*, *now*, *extremely*, *very*.
>
> **What is a preposition?**
> A **preposition** is a word such as *at*, *for*, *with*, *into* or *from*, which is usually followed by a noun, pronoun, or, in English, a word ending in -ing. Prepositions show how people or things relate to the rest of the sentence, for example, *She's at home; a tool for cutting grass; It's from David*.

a to; at; into: onto
abajo down; downstairs; below
　allá abajo down there;
　abajo de (*LAm*) under
absolutamente absolutely
acá here, over here; now
acerca: acerca de about
actualmente at present
acuerdo: de acuerdo OK, okay
adelante forward; in front;
　at the front; opposite
　en adelante from now on
　hacia adelante forward;
　adelante de (*LAm*) in front of ;
　opposite
además also; furthermore,
　moreover, in addition
　además de as well as; besides
adentro inside; **adentro de** (*LAm*)
　inside; in; within
admirablemente admirably
afortunadamente fortunately
afuera outside; out **afuera de** (*LAm*)
　outside, out of
agradablemente nicely

ahora now; in a minute
　hasta ahora so far
alcance: al alcance within reach
allá there, over there
allí there
alrededor de around
ansiosamente anxiously
ante before; in the face of; faced with
　ante todo above all
antemano: de antemano
　beforehand, in advance
anteriormente previously, before
antes before **antes de** before
　cuanto antes as soon as possible
　lo antes posible as soon as possible
apartado: apartado de away from
aparte: aparte de apart from
apenas hardly, scarcely; only
aproximadamente approximately
aquí here; now
arriba up; upstairs; above
　allá arriba up there; **arriba de**
　(*LAm*) on (top of)
así like that; like this
　así como as well as

atentamente attentively, carefully; kindly; yours sincerely (*in letters*)

atrás behind; at the back; backwards; ago

hacia atrás backwards; **atrás de** (*LAm*) behind

aun even

aun así even so

aun cuando even if

aún still, yet; even

azar: al azar at random

bajo low; quietly; under

básicamente basically

bastante enough; quite a lot; quite (*see also* Adjectives)

bien well; carefully; very; easily

brevemente briefly

bruscamente abruptly

cambio: a cambio de in exchange for; in return for

en cambio instead

camino: de camino on the way

casi almost, nearly

caso: en el caso de (que) in the case of

en todo caso in any case

casualidad: por casualidad by chance

causa: a causa de because of

cerca (de) close (to); near (to)

claramente clearly

cómo how

como like; such as; as; about

completamente completely

con with

concreto: en concreto specifically, in particular

continuamente constantly

contra against

correctamente correctly

cortésmente politely

cuando when

cuándo when

cuanto: en cuanto a as regards, as for

cuánto how much; how far; how

cuenta: a fin de cuentas ultimately

teniendo en cuenta considering

cuidado: con cuidado carefully

cuidadosamente carefully

curiosamente curiously

curso: en el curso de in the course of

de of; from; about; by; than; in; if

debajo underneath

debajo de under; **por debajo** underneath; **por debajo de** under; below

débilmente faintly; weakly

delante in front; at the front; opposite

delante de in front of; opposite

hacia delante forward

por delante ahead; at the front

demasiado too; too much

dentro inside

dentro de inside; in; within

derecha: a la derecha on the right

desde from; since

desgraciadamente unfortunately

despacio slowly

después later; after(wards); then

después de after

detrás behind; at the back; on the back; after

detrás de behind; **por detrás** from behind; on the back

día: al día per day; up to date

diariamente on a daily basis

diario: a diario daily

donde where; wherever

dónde where

dondequiera anywhere

duda: sin duda definitely, undoubtedly
dulcemente sweetly; gently
durante during; for
durante todo/toda throughout
efecto: en efecto in fact
ejemplo: por ejemplo for example
en in; on; at; into; by
encima on top
encima de above; on top of;
por encima over; **por encima de** over; above
enfrente (de) opposite
enseguida right away; immediately
entonces then
desde entonces since then;
hasta entonces until then
entre among(st); between
especialmente especially, particularly; specially
evidentemente obviously, evidently
exactamente exactly
excepción: con la excepción de with the exception of
excepto except (for)
extranjero: en el extranjero overseas; abroad
extremadamente extremely
fácilmente easily
fielmente faithfully
fin: por fin finally; at last
finalmente eventually
forma: de alguna forma somehow
de esta forma like that; like this;
de ninguna forma in no way;
de otra forma otherwise;
de todas formas anyway
francamente frankly; really
frecuentemente frequently
frente: frente a opposite, facing; against

fuera outside; out
fuera de outside; out of
gana: de buena gana willingly, happily
de mala gana reluctantly
general: por lo general as a rule
generalmente generally
gracias: gracias a thanks to
gradualmente gradually
hacia towards
hasta to, as far as; up to; down to; until
honradamente honestly
igualmente equally; likewise
incluido including
inmediatamente immediately
intensamente intensely
izquierda: a la izquierda on the left
jamás never; ever
junto: junto a close to, near; next to; together with
junto con together with
justamente just; exactly; justly
lado: al lado (de) next door (to); near
al lado de alongside; **al otro lado de** across; **de un lado a otro** to and fro; **por este lado (de)** on this side (of)
largo: a lo largo de along
lejos (de) far (from)
ligeramente lightly; slightly
luego then; later, afterwards
desde luego certainly
mal badly; poorly
manera: de alguna manera somehow
de esta manera like that; like this;
de ninguna manera in no way;
de otra manera otherwise;
de todas maneras anyway

más more; plus
   el/la más the most; más allá de beyond; más bien rather; más cerca closer; más lejos further; más o menos about; más...que more...than; no más no more
medio: en medio de in the middle of
   por medio de by means of
mejor better
   el/la mejor the best
menos less; minus el/la menos the least; menos...que less than; por lo menos at least
mentalmente mentally
menudo: a menudo often
misteriosamente mysteriously
modo: de algún modo somehow
   de este modo like that; like this; de ningún modo in no way; de otro modo otherwise; de todos modos anyway
momento: en este momento at the moment
   en ese mismo momento at that very moment
mucho a lot
   no mucho not much (*see also* Pronouns; Adjectives)
muy very; too
naturalmente naturally
nerviosamente nervously
no no; not
nombre: en nombre de on behalf of
normalmente normally; usually
novedad: sin novedad safely
nunca never; ever
paciencia: con paciencia patiently
para for; to
   para atrás backwards; para la derecha towards the right;

para siempre forever
parte: de mi parte on my behalf; from me
   en cualquier parte anywhere; en gran parte largely; en otra parte elsewhere; en parte partly, in part; en todas partes everywhere; por otra parte on the other hand
peligrosamente dangerously
peor worse
   el/la peor the worst
perfectamente perfectly
persona: por persona per person
personalmente personally
pesadamente heavily
pesar: a pesar de in spite of; despite
   a pesar de que even though
pie: a pie on foot
poco not very; not a lot; not much
   poco a poco little by little, bit by bit
por because of; for; by; through
   por qué why
precisamente precisely, exactly
primero first
principalmente mainly
principio: al principio at first
probable likely
probablemente probably
profundamente deeply
pronto soon; (*Sp*) early
propósito: a propósito deliberately; on purpose
qué how
querer: sin querer accidentally; unintentionally
quién: de quién/de quiénes whose
rápidamente fast, quickly
rápido quickly
realidad: en realidad in fact, actually
realmente really

recientemente recently, lately

regularmente regularly, on a
regular basis

relativamente relatively

repente: de repente suddenly

seguida: en seguida right away

seguido (*LAm*) often
todo seguido straight ahead

según according to; depending on

seguramente probably; surely

sencillamente simply

sentido: en este sentido in this
respect

separado: por separado separately

ser: a no ser que unless

serio: en serio seriously; really

sí yes

siempre always
como siempre as usual

siguiente: al/el día siguiente the
next day

silencio: en silencio quietly; in silence

silenciosamente quietly, silently

sin without **sin embargo** still,
however, nonetheless

siquiera: ni siquiera not even

sitio: en algún sitio somewhere
en ningún sitio nowhere

sobre on; over; about

solamente only; solely
solo only; solely
tan solo only, just

suavemente gently; softly; smoothly

sumamente highly, extremely

supuesto: por supuesto of course

tal: tal como just as
tal y como están las cosas
under the circumstances;
tal vez perhaps, maybe

también also, too

tampoco not ... either, neither

tan so; such
tan ... como as ... as

tanto so much; so often
tanto más all the more

tarde late
más tarde later; afterwards

temprano early
más temprano earlier

tiempo: a tiempo in time; on time
al mismo tiempo at the same
time; **mucho tiempo** long

todavía still; yet; even

todo: en todo/toda throughout
todo lo más at (the) most

total in short; at the end of the day
en total altogether, in all

totalmente totally, completely

través: a través de through; across

vano: en vano in vain

velocidad: a toda velocidad at full
speed, at top speed

ver: por lo visto apparently

vez: algunas veces sometimes
cada vez más more and more;
cada vez menos less and less;
de vez en cuando from time to time,
now and then; **en vez de** instead
of; **rara vez** rarely, seldom; **una vez**
once; **una vez más** once more

vía: en vías de on its way to
en vías de desarrollo developing;
en vías de extinción endangered

vista: de vista by sight
en vista de in view of

voz: en voz alta aloud; loudly
en voz baja in a low voice

ya already
ya mismo at once; **ya no** not any
more, no longer

SOME EXTRA NOUNS

> **What is a noun?**
> A **noun** is a 'naming' word for a living being, thing or idea, for example, *woman*, *desk*, *happiness*, *Andrew*.

la **abertura** opening
el **abismo** gulf
el **aburrimiento** boredom
el **abuso** abuse
el **acceso** access
la **acción** (*pl* acciones) action
el **acento** accent
el **ácido** acid
el **acontecimiento** event
la **actitud** attitude
la **actividad** activity
el **acuerdo** agreement; settlement
la **advertencia** warning
la **afirmación** (*pl* afirmaciones) claim
la **agencia** agency
la **agenda** diary
el/la **agente** agent
la **agitación** (*pl* agitaciones) stir
el **agujero** hole
la **alcantarilla** drain
la **alegría** joy
el **alfabeto** alphabet
el **alfiler** pin
el/la **aliado/a** ally
el **aliento** breath
el **alivio** relief
el **alma** (*f*) soul
el **almacén** (*pl* almacenes) department store; warehouse
el/la **amante** lover
la **ambición** (*pl* ambiciones) ambition
la **amenaza** threat

el/la **amigo(a)** friend
la **amistad** friendship
el **amor** love
el **análisis** (*pl inv*) analysis
la **anchura** breadth; width
el/la **anfitrión(ona)** host/hostess
el **ángel** angel
el **ángulo** angle
la **angustia** anguish
el **animal doméstico** pet
la **antigüedad** antique; ancient times; length of service
el **anuncio** announcement
el **anzuelo** hook
la **apertura** opening
el **apoyo** support
la **aprobación** (*pl* aprobaciones) approval
la **apuesta** bet; stake
la **armada** navy
el **arreglo** compromise
la **artesanía** craft
el **artículo** article; item
la **asociación** (*pl* asociaciones) association
el **asombro** astonishment
el **aspecto** aspect
la **astilla** splinter
el **asunto** matter; issue; affair
el **atajo** short-cut
el **ataúd** coffin
la **atención** (*pl* atenciones) attention
el **atentado** attempt

la **atracción**; el **atractivo** attraction
la **ausencia** absence
la **autoridad** authority
la **aventura** adventure; affair
el **aviso** notice
la **ayuda** assistance, help
el/la **ayudante** assistant
el **ayuntamiento** council
el **azar** chance
la **bala** bullet
la **barandilla** rail
la **barrera** barrier
el **barril** barrel
la **base** base
la **batalla** battle
la **batería** battery
la **beca** grant; scholarship
el **beso** kiss
la **Biblia** Bible
la **bomba** bomb
la **bondad** kindness
el **borde** edge
la **broma** joke
el **brote** outbreak; bud
el **bullicio** bustle
la **burbuja** bubble
el **cable** cable
la **caja** box
la **calcomanía** transfer
el **cálculo** calculation
el **caldo** stock
la **calidad** quality
la **calma** calm
el **camino** path; way
el **campamento** camp
la **campaña** campaign
el **camping** (pl ~s) site
el **canal** channel
la **canasta** basket
la **cantidad** amount

el **caos** chaos
la **capa** layer
la **capacidad** ability; capacity
el **capítulo** chapter
la **característica** characteristic; feature
la **caridad** charity
el/la **catedrático(a)** professor
los **celos** jealousy (sing)
el **centro** center; focus; middle
el **centro turístico** resort
el **cesto** basket
el **chiste** joke
el **cielo** heaven; sky
el **cierre** closure
la **cima** top
el **círculo** circle
las **circunstancias** circumstances
la **cita** quote; extract; appointment
el/la **civil** civilian
la **civilización** (pl civilizaciones) civilization
la **clase** sort; class, classroom
la **clasificación** (pl clasificaciones) classification
la **clave** code
la **codicia** greed
la **colegiatura** (Mex) school fees
la **columna** column
el **columpio** swing
la **combinación** (pl combinaciones) combination
el **combustible** fuel
el **comentario** comment, remark
el/la **comentarista** commentator
las **comillas: entre comillas** inverted commas: in quotes
la **comisión** (pl comisiones) commission
el **comité** (pl comités) committee

el/la compañero(a) classmate;
  partner
la comparación (*pl* comparaciones)
  comparison
la compasión (*pl* compasiones)
  sympathy
la competencia (*LAm*) contest;
  competition
la competición (*pl* competiciones)
  (*Sp*) contest; competition
el/la competidor(a) rival
la comprensión (*pl* comprensiones)
  sympathy
el compromiso commitment
la comunicación (*pl*
  comunicaciones) communication
la comunidad community
la concentración (*pl*
  concentraciones) concentration
la conciencia conscience
la condecoración (*pl*
  condecoraciones) honor
la condición (*pl* condiciones)
  condition; status
la conducta conduct
la conexión (*pl* conexiones)
  connection
la conferencia lecture; conference
la confianza confidence
el conflicto conflict
el confort comfort
el congreso conference
la conmoción (*pl* conmociones)
  shock; disturbance
el conocimiento knowledge;
  consciousness
la consecuencia consequence
el consejo (piece of) advice
la construcción (*pl* construcciones)
  construction; structure

el/la consumidor(a) consumer
el contacto contact
el contenido content
el contexto context
el contorno outline
el contraste contrast
la contribución (*pl* contribución)
  contribution
la conversación (*pl* conversaciones)
  conversation
la copia copy
el corazón (*pl* corazones) heart;
  core
la corona crown
el/la corresponsal correspondent
la corrupción (*pl* corrupciones)
  corruption
la cortesía politeness
la cosa thing
las cosas stuff (*sing*); things
la costumbre custom
el crecimiento growth
el/la criado(a) servant
la crisis (*pl inv*) crisis
la crítica criticism
el cuadro picture
el cubierto place (setting); piece of
  silverware
el cuchicheo whispering
la cuenta count
  por su cuenta of his own accord
el cuento tale
la cuestión (*pl* cuestiones) question
la cueva cave
el cuidado care
la culpa blame
la cultura culture
la cuota fee; (*LAm*) toll
la curiosidad curiosity
los datos data (*pl*)

el debate debate
el deber duty
la decepción (*pl* decepciones) disappointment
la decisión (*pl* decisiones) decision
el defecto fault
la definición (*pl* definiciones) definition
el/la dependiente(a) assistant
la depresión (*pl* depresiones) depression
el/la derecho(a) right
  los derechos fee
el desagüe drain
el desarrollo development
el desastre disaster
el descanso break
el/la desconocido(a) stranger
la desdicha unhappiness
el deseo desire; wish; urge
el desgarrón (*pl* desgarrones) tear
la desgracia misfortune
el desorden disorder; mess
el destino destiny; fate
la destreza skill
la destrucción (*pl* destrucciones) destruction
la desventaja disadvantage
el detalle detail
la devolución (*pl* devoluciones) refund; return
el diagrama diagram
el diálogo dialogue
la diana target
el diario diary; journal
la diferencia difference
la dificultad difficulty
la dimensión (*pl* dimensiones) dimension
el/la dios(a) god/goddess

el/la diplomático(a) diplomat
el/la diputado(a) deputy
la dirección (*pl* direcciones) direction; address
la disciplina discipline
el discurso speech
la discusión (*pl* discusiones) argument; discussion
el diseño design
el dispositivo device
la disputa dispute
la distancia distance
la división (*pl* divisiones) division
el drama drama
la duda doubt
el eco echo
la economía economics (*sing*); economy
la edición (*pl* ediciones) edition
el efecto effect
el ejemplar copy
el ejemplo example
  por ejemplo for instance
el/la elector(a) elector
la elegancia elegance
el elemento element
la encuesta survey
el/la enemigo(a) enemy
la energía energy
el entusiasmo enthusiasm; excitement
la envidia envy
la época period
el equilibrio balance
el equipo equipment
el error mistake
el escándalo scandal
el escape leak
la escasez shortage
la escritura writing

el esfuerzo effort
el espacio space
la espalda back
la especie species (*sing*)
el espectáculo show; sight
la esperanza hope
el espesor; la espesura thickness
el esquema outline; diagram
la estaca stake
la estancia stay
la estatua statue
el estilo style
la estrategia strategy
el estrés stress
la estructura structure
el estudio studio
la estupidez (*pl* estupideces)
  stupidity
la etapa stage
la excepción (*pl* excepciones)
  exception
el exceso excess
la excusa excuse
el/la exiliado(a) exile
el exilio exile
las existencias stock
el éxito success
la experiencia experience
el/la experto(a) expert
la explicación (*pl* explicaciones)
  explanation
la explosión (*pl* explosiones)
  explosion
  una explosión a bomb blast
las exportaciones exports
la exposición (*pl* exposiciones)
  exhibition
la expresión (*pl* expresiones)
  expression
la extensión (*pl* extensiones) extent

el extracto extract
el/la extranjero(a) foreigner
la fabricación (*pl* fabricaciones)
  manufacture
la facilidad facility
el factor factor
la falla flaw; defect; fault
la falta: absence
  falta (de) lack (of)
la fama reputation
el favor favor
la fe faith
la felicidad happiness
la fila row, line, rank
la filosofía philosophy
el fin end
la flecha arrow
el fondo background; bottom; fund
el/la forastero(a) stranger
la forma form; shape
la fortuna fortune
el fracaso failure
la frase sentence; phrase
la frente front
el frescor, la frescura freshness
la fuente source
la fuerza force; strength
la función (*pl* funciones) function
la ganancia gain
el gancho hook
los gastos expenses
la generación (*pl* generaciones)
  generation
el gol goal
el golfo gulf
el golpe bang; blow, punch; coup
la gotera leak
el grado degree
la gráfica, el gráfico chart
la grieta crack

el **grito** cry; scream
el **grupo** group
la **guía** guide
el **hambre** (*f*) hunger
el **hecho** fact
la **higiene** hygiene
la **hilera** row
el **honor** honor
los **honorarios** fees, honoraria
la **honra** honor
el **hueco** gap
la **huella** trace
el **humo** fumes (*pl*); smoke
el **humor** humor
la **idea** idea
  no tengo ni idea I haven't a clue
el **idioma** language
el/la **idiota** fool; idiot
la **imagen** (*pl* imágenes) image
la **imaginación** (*pl* imaginaciones)
  imagination
el **impacto** impact
el **imperio** empire
las **importaciones** imports
la **importancia** importance
la **impresión** (*pl* impresiones)
  impression
el **impuesto** tax; duty
el **impulso** urge
la **inauguración** (*pl* inauguraciones)
  opening
el **incidente** incident
la **independencia** independence
el **índice** index
la **indirecta** hint
la **infancia** childhood
el **infierno** hell
la **influencia** influence
los **ingresos** earnings
el/la **inspector(a)** inspector

el **instante** instant
la **institución** (*pl* instituciones)
  institution
el **instituto** institute
las **instrucciones** instructions
el **instrumento** instrument
la **intención** (*pl* intenciones)
  intention; aim
el **interés** (*pl* intereses) interest
la **interrupción** (*pl* interrupciones)
  interruption
el **intervalo** interval; gap
la **investigación** (*pl* investigaciones)
  research
la **invitación** (*pl* invitaciones)
  invitation
la **ira** anger
el/la **jefe(a)** boss; chief
el **juego** game; gambling
el **juguete** toy
la **lágrima** tear
la **lata** can
el/la **lector(a)** reader
la **leyenda** legend; caption
la **libertad** freedom
la **licenciatura** degree
el/la **líder** leader
la **liga** league
el **límite** boundary; limit
la **limpieza** cleanliness
la **línea** line
la **liquidación** (*pl* liquidaciones)
  sale; severance pay
la **lista** list
la **literatura** literature
el **local** premises (*pl*)
la **locura** madness, insanity
el **logro** achievement
la **longitud** length
el **lugar** place

el lujo luxury
la luz (*pl* luces) light
  luz de la luna moonlight
el/la maestro(a) (elementary
  school) teacher; master
la magia magic
la manera manner
la máquina machine
la marca brand; mark
el marco frame
el margen (*pl* márgenes) margin
la máscara mask
la matrícula registration;
  enrollment; license plate (number)
el máximo maximum
la mayoría majority
el medio (de) means (of)
la mejora, la mejoría improvement
la memoria memory
la mente mind
el método method
la mezcla mixture
el miedo fear
el milagro miracle
la mina mine
el mínimo minimum
la minoría minority
la mirada glance
la misa mass
la misión (*pl* misiones) mission
el misterio mystery
el mito myth
la moda fashion; trend
la molestia annoyance
el molino mill
el montón (*pl* montones) mass; pile
la moral morals (*pl*)
el mordisco bite
el motivo pattern
el motor motor

el muchacho boy; lad
la muchedumbre crowd
la muestra sample
la muñeca doll
la naturaleza nature
el naufragio wreckage
la(s) náusea(s) nausea
la negociación (*pl* negociaciones)
  negotiation
el nervio nerve
la niñez childhood
el nivel level
el nombramiento appointment
la nota note
el número number; issue
la objeción (*pl* objeciones) objection
el objetivo objective; purpose;
  target
el objeto object; goal
las obras works
el odio hate
el/la oficial officer
la olla pot
el olor smell
la opción (*pl* opciones) option
la opinión (*pl* opiniones) opinion
la oportunidad chance;
  opportunity
la oposición (*pl* oposiciones)
  opposition
la orden (*pl* órdenes) order
la organización (*pl* organizaciones)
  organization
  organización benéfica charity
el orgullo pride
el origen (*pl* orígenes) origin
la oscuridad darkness
la paciencia patience
la página page
la paja straw

la **palabra** word
el **palacio** palace
el **palo** stick
el **pánico** panic
el **paquete** pack; packet
la **pareja** couple
la **parte** part
  parte de arriba top; **parte delantera**
  front; **parte trasera** rear; **de parte**
  de algn on behalf of sb
el **parto** labor
  estar de parto to be in labor
el **pasaje**; el **pasillo** passage
la **pasión** (*pl* pasiones) passion
el **paso** (foot)step
el **patrón** (*pl* patrones) pattern
la **pausa** pause
el **payaso** clown
el **pedazo** piece
el **pedido** order; request
la **pelea** row
el **peligro** danger
la **pena** distress; penalty
el **penal** (*LAm*) penalty
el **penalty** (*pl* penalties) penalty
el **pensamiento** thought
el **periódico** newspaper; journal
el **periodo**, el **período** period
el/la **perito(a)** expert
el **permiso** permission
la **persona** person
el **personal** personnel
la **perspectiva** prospect
la **pesadilla** nightmare
la **picadura** bite; sting
la **pieza** piece; item; (*LAm*) room
la **pila** battery; pile
la **pista** clue
el **placer** delight; pleasure
el **plan** plan; scheme

el **platillo** (*Mex*) dish
el **plato** dish; plate
la **plaza** square
el **poder** power
el **poema** poem
la **política** politics (*sing*); policy
la **póliza** policy
el **polvo** dust
la **pompa** bubble
el **porcentaje** percentage
la **porción** (*pl* porciones) portion
el **portavoz** (*pl* portavoces)
  spokesman
la **posibilidad** possibility
la **posición** (*pl* posiciones) position
la **práctica** practice
la **preferencia** choice
la **pregunta** question
el **premio** award
la **preparación** (*pl* preparaciones)
  preparation
los **preparativos** arrangements;
  preparations
la **presencia** presence
la **presión** (*pl* presiones) pressure
el **presupuesto** budget; quote
la **princesa** princess
el **príncipe** prince
el **principio** beginning; principle
la **prioridad** priority
el **problema** problem; trouble
el **proceso** process
el/la **profesor(a)** teacher; professor
la **profundidad** depth
el **programa** schedule
la **prohibición** (*pl* prohibiciones)
  ban; prohibition
el **propósito** purpose
  a propósito on purpose
la **propuesta** proposal

la **prosperidad** prosperity

la **protección** (*pl* protecciones) protection

la **protesta** protest

las **provisiones** provisions

el **proyecto** plan; project

la **publicidad** publicity

la **punta** point

  la **puntería** aim

el **punto** item; point

punto de partida starting point;

  punto de vista point of view

el/la **querido(a)** darling

la **rabia** rage

la **raja** crack

el **rato** while

la **razón** (*pl* razones) reason

la **reacción** (*pl* reacciones) reaction;

  response

la **realidad** reality

la **rebanada** slice

el/la **rebelde** rebel

el **recado** message

la **recepción** (*pl* recepciones)

  reception

la **recesión** (*pl* recesiones) recession

la **reclamación** (*pl* reclamaciones)

  claim

el **recuerdo** memory; souvenir;

  keepsake

el **recurso** resource

  como último recurso as a last resort

la **red** network

la **reducción** (*pl* reducciones)

  reduction

la **reforma** reform

la **regla** ruler; period

la **reina** queen

la **relación** (*pl* relaciones)

  relationship

la **religión** (*pl* religiones) religion

el **remate** (*LAm*) auction

la **reputación** (*pl* reputaciones)

  status

el **requisito** requirement

la **reserva** fund; stock; reservation;

  booking

la **resistencia** resistance

la **resolución** (*pl* resoluciones)

  resolution

el **respecto: con respecto a** with

  regard to

el **respeto** respect

la **respiración** (*pl* respiraciones)

  breath

la **responsabilidad** responsibility

la **respuesta** reply; response

los **restos** remains; wreckage (*sing*)

el **resultado** outcome

el **reto** challenge

el **retrato** portrait; portrayal

la **reunión** (*pl* reuniones) meeting

la **revista** magazine; journal

el **rey** (*pl* ~es) king

el **riel** rail

el **ritmo** pace, rhythm

el/la **rival** rival

la **rodaja** slice

el **ruido** noise

la **ruina** ruin

el **rumor** rumor

la **ruptura** break

la **rutina** routine

el **sacrificio** sacrifice

el/la **santo(a)** saint

la **sección** (*pl* secciones) section

el **secreto** secret

el **sector** sector

la **sed** thirst

la **seguridad** security; safety

la **selección** (*pl* selecciones) selection; choice
el **sentido** sense; way; direction
el **sentimiento** feeling
la **señal** sign; mark
el **señor** man; gentleman; **el Señor** the Lord
el **servicio** service
la **sesión** (*pl* sesiones) session
el **significado** meaning
el **silbato** whistle
el **silencio** silence
el **símbolo** symbol
el **sindicato** trade union
el **sistema** system
el **sitio** place
la **situación** (*pl* situaciones) situation
el/la **sobreviviente** survivor
el/la **socio(a)** member
la **soledad** loneliness
el **sollozo** sob
la **solución** (*pl* soluciones) solution
la **sombra** shadow
el **sondeo (de opinión)** poll
el **sonido** sound
la **sorpresa** surprise
la **sospecha** suspicion
la **subasta** auction
el **subtítulo** caption
la **subvención** (*pl* subvenciones) grant
la **suciedad** dirtiness
el **sueño** sleep
la **suerte** luck
    buena/mala suerte good/bad luck
la **sugerencia** suggestion
el **suicidio** suicide
la **suma** sum
la **superficie** surface

la **supervisión** (*pl* supervisiones) supervision
el/la **superviviente** survivor
el/la **suplente** substitute
el **surtido** choice
la **sustancia** substance
el/la **sustituto(a)** substitute
la **táctica** tactics (*pl*)
el **talento** talent
la **tapa** lid; top
la **tapicería** upholstery
el **tapiz** (*pl* tapices) tapestry
el **tapón** (*pl* tapones) top
la **tarea** task
la **tarifa; la tasa** rate
el **teatro** theater; drama
la **técnica** technique
la **tecnología** technology
el **tema** theme; issue
la **tendencia** trend
la **tensión** (*pl* tensiones) tension; strain
la **tentativa** attempt; bid
la **teoría** theory
el **territorio** territory
el **terrón** (*pl* terrones) lump
el **texto** text
la **tienda** store
la **timidez** shyness
el **tipo** type; kind; fellow, guy
la **tirada, el tiraje** edition
el **título** title
el **tomo** volume
la **tortura** torture
el **total** total
la **tradición** (*pl* tradiciones) tradition
la **trampa** trap
la **tranquilidad** calmness
la **transferencia** transfer

el **tratamiento** treatment
el **trato** deal; treatment
la **tristeza** sadness
el **trozo** bit; piece; slice
el **truco** trick
el **tubo** tube
la **tumba** grave
el **tumor** tumor
el **turno** turn
la **unidad** unit
la **valentía** bravery, courage
el **valor** value
el **vapor** steam
la **variedad** variety; range
la **vela** candle
el **veneno** poison
la **ventaja** advantage; asset

la **verdad** truth
la **vergüenza** shame; embarrassment
la **versión** (*pl* versiones) version
la **victoria** victory
la **vida** life
el **vínculo** bond; link
la **violencia** violence
la **visita**; visit; visitor
el/la **visitante** visitor
la **vista** sight
el **volumen** (*pl* volúmenes) volume
el/la **voluntario(a)** volunteer
el/la **votante** voter
la **vuelta** turn; return
  dar una **vuelta** to go for a stroll;
  dar una **vuelta en bicicleta** to go
  for a bike ride

VERBS

> **What is a verb?**
> A **verb** is a 'doing' word which describes what someone or something does, what someone or something is, or what happens to them, for example, *be*, *sing*, *live*.

abandonar to abandon
abrigar(se) to shelter; to wrap up (in warm clothes)
abrir to turn on
  abrir(se) to open
abrochar to fasten
aburrir to bore
  aburrirse to get bored
acabar de hacer algo to have just done sth
acampar to camp
aceptar to accept
acercarse (a) to approach
  acercarse a to go towards
aclarar(se) to clear
acompañar to accompany; to go with
aconsejar to advise; to suggest
acordarse de to remember
acostarse to lie down
acostumbrarse a algo/algn to get used to sth/sb
actuar to act; to operate
acusar to accuse
adaptar to adapt
adelantar to go forward; to overtake
adivinar to guess
admirar to admire
admitir to admit
adoptar to adopt
adorar to adore

adquirir to acquire; to purchase
afectar to affect
afirmar to assert; to state
agarrar to catch; to grab; to grasp
agradecer to thank (for)
aguantar to bear
ahorrar to save
ahuyentar to chase (off)
alcanzar to reach
  alcanzar a algn to catch up with sb;
  alcanzar a ver to catch sight of
alimentar to feed; to nourish
aliviar to relieve
almacenar to store
alojarse to stay
alquilar to hire; to rent: to let
amar to love
amenazar to threaten
amontonar to stack
andar to walk
anhelar to long for
animar to encourage
  animar a algn a hacer algo to urge sb to do sth
anunciar to advertise; to announce
añadir to add
apagar to switch off; to turn off; to put out
apagar to turn off
  apagarse to fade
aparecer to appear

apetecer to feel like, to want
  me apetece un helado I would like
  an ice cream
aplastar to crush
aplaudir to applaud; to cheer;
  to clap
aplazar to postpone; to put back
aplicar a to apply to
apostar (a) to bet (on)
apoyar to support; to endorse
  apoyar(se) to lean
apreciar to appreciate
aprender to learn
apretar to press; to squeeze
aprobar to approve of; to endorse
aprovechar to take advantage (of)
apuntar to take down
arañar to scratch
arrancar to pull out
arrastrar to drag
  arrastrarse to crawl
arreglar to fix (up); to arrange;
  to settle
  arreglárselas to cope; to manage
arrepentirse de to regret
arriesgar to risk
arrojar to hurl, to throw
arruinar to ruin
asar to bake
ascender to promote
asegurar to assure; to ensure;
  to secure
  asentir con la cabeza to nod
asfixiar(se) to suffocate
asistir (a) to attend
asombrar to amaze; to astonish
asustar to alarm; to frighten;
  to startle
atacar to attack
atar to attach; to tie

atender to treat
  atender a to attend to
atraer to attract
atrasar to hold up
atreverse (a hacer algo) to dare
  (to do sth)
aumentar to increase; to raise
avanzar to advance
averiarse to break down
averiguar to check
avisar to warn
ayudar to help
azotar to whip
bailar to dance
bajar: to come down; to go down;
  to lower
  bajar (de): to get off; bajar de to
  get out of
balbucir to stammer
barrer to sweep
basar algo en to base sth on
batir to whip; to beat
besar to kiss
bombardear to bomb
brillar to shine; to sparkle
bromear to joke
burlarse de to make fun of
buscar to look for; to search; to seek
caerse to fall (down)
  se me cayó I dropped it
calcular to estimate
calentar(se) to heat (up)
callarse to be quiet
cambiar to alter; to exchange
  cambiar(se) to change
cancelar to cancel
cantar to sing
capturar to capture
carecer de to lack
cargar (de) to load (with)

causar to cause
cavar to dig
celebrar to celebrate
centellear to sparkle
cerrar: to turn off: to close; to fasten
  cerrar(se): to shut; cerrar con
  llave to lock
charlar to chat
chillar to scream
chismear to gossip
chocar con to bump into
chupar to suck
citar to quote
clasificarse to qualify
cobrar to claim; to get
coger to catch; to grab; to seize
colaborar to collaborate
coleccionar to collect
colgar to hang (up)
colocar to place
combinar to combine
comenzar (a) to start (to)
cometer to commit
compaginar to combine
comparar to compare
compartir to share
compensar to compensate (for)
  compensar por to make up for
competir en to compete in
complacer to please
completar to complete; to make up
comprar (a) to buy (from)
comprender to comprise
comunicar to communicate
conceder to grant
concentrarse to concentrate
concertar to arrange
concluir to conclude; to accomplish
condenar to condemn; to sentence
conducir to lead

conectar to connect
confesar to confess
confiar to trust
  confiar en to rely on
confirmar to confirm
confundir (con) to confuse (with)
  confundir a algn con to mistake
  sb for
congelar to freeze
conocer to know
conseguir to achieve; to get;
  to secure
  conseguir (hacer) to succeed
  (in doing)
considerar to consider; to rate
constar de to consist of
  hacer constar to record
constituir to constitute; to make up
construir to build; to put up
consultar to consult
consumir to consume
contar to count; to tell
  contar con to depend on
contemplar to contemplate
contener to contain; to hold
contestar to answer
continuar to continue; to keep;
  to resume
contribuir to contribute
controlar to control
convencer to convince
convenir to suit
convertir to convert
copiar to copy
correr to run
cortar to cut (off); to mow
costar to cost
crear to create
crecer to grow
creer to believe; to reckon

criar to bring up
criticar to criticize
cruzar to cross
cubrir (de) to cover (with)
cuchichear to whisper
cuidar to look after; to take care of;
  to mind
  cuidar de to take care of
cultivar to cultivate
cumplir to accomplish; to carry out
curar to heal
dañar to harm
dar to give:
  dar a to overlook; dar asco a to
  disgust; dar de comer a to feed;
  dar la bienvenida to welcome;
  dar marcha atrás to reverse;
  dar saltitos to hop; dar un paseo
  to go for a stroll; dar un puñetazo
  a to punch; dar una bofetada a
  to slap; dar vergüenza a to
  embarrass; dar vuelta a to turn;
  darse cuenta de algo to become
  aware of sth; darse por vencido
  to give up; darse prisa to hurry
deber must; to owe
  deber hacer algo to be supposed
  to do sth; debo hacerlo I must do it
decepcionar to disappoint
decidir(se) (a) to decide (to)
decidirse (a) to make up one's mind
  (to)
decir to say; to tell
declarar to declare
  declarar culpable to convict;
  declararse en huelga to (go on)
  strike
decorar to decorate
dedicar to devote
defender to defend

definir to define
dejar to leave
  dejar caer to drop
deletrear to spell
demorar(se) to delay
demostrar to demonstrate
depender de to depend on
derribar to demolish
desanimar to discourage
desaparecer to disappear
desarrollar(se) to develop
descansar to rest
descargar to unload
describir to describe
descubrir to discover; to find out
desear to desire; to wish
deshacerse de to get rid of
deslizar(se) to slip
desnudarse to strip
despedir to dismiss
despegar to take off
despejar(se) to clear
despertar(se) to wake up
desprenderse to come off
desteñirse to fade
destruir to smash; to destroy
desviar to divert
detener to arrest
determinar to determine
detestar to detest
devolver to bring back; to give back;
  to send back
  devolver a su sitio to put back
dibujar to draw
diferenciarse (de) to differ (from)
dimitir to resign
dirigir to conduct; to direct; to manage
disculparse (de) to apologise (for)
discutir to argue; to debate;
  to discuss

diseñar to design
disfrazar to disguise
disfrutar to enjoy
disminuir to decline; to decrease;
  to diminish
distinguir to distinguish
distribuir to distribute
divertir to divert
  divertirse to enjoy oneself
dividir to divide; to split
doblar to fold
  doblar(se) to double
dominar to dominate; to master
ducharse to shower
dudar to doubt
durar to last
echar to pour:
  echar a algn to throw sb out;
  echar a algn la culpa de algo
  to blame sb for sth; echar al correo
  to post; echar de menos to miss;
  echar una mirada a algo to glance
  at sth; echarse to lie; echarse a
  llorar to burst into tears;
  echarse a reír to burst out
  laughing
educar to bring up; to educate
ejecutar to execute
elegir to choose; to select; to elect
elogiar to praise
emocionar to excite
empatar to draw, to tie
empezar(a) to begin (to)
emplear to employ
empujar to push
encarcelar to imprison
encender to switch on; to turn on;
  to light
encerrar to shut in
encontrar to find; to meet

enfocar to focus
enjugar to wipe
enseñar to teach; to show
entender to understand
enterarse de to hear about
enterrar to bury
entrar (en) to enter
entregarse to give oneself up;
  to surrender
entrevistar to interview
enviar to send
envolver to wrap up
equivocarse to make a mistake;
  to be mistaken
erigir to erect
escapar (de) to escape (from)
escarbar to dig
escoger to choose; to pick
esconderse to hide
escuchar to listen (to)
especializarse en to specialize in
especular to gamble
esperar to wait (for); to expect;
  to hope
establecer to establish; to set up
  establecerse to settle
estallar to blow up
estar to be
  estar acostumbrado a algo/algn
  to be used to sth/sb; estar de
  acuerdo to agree; estar de pie
  to be standing; estar dispuesto a
  hacer algo to be prepared to do
  sth; to be willing to do sth;
  estar equivocado to be wrong;
  estar involucrado en algo to be
  involved in sth
estirar(se) to stretch (out)
estrecharse la mano to shake hands
estrellar(se) to crash

estropear to ruin
  estropear(se) to spoil
estudiar to study; to investigate
evitar (hacer) to avoid (doing)
exagerar to exaggerate
examinar to examine
  examinarse to take an exam
excitar to excite
exclamar to exclaim
excluir to exclude; to suspend
existir to exist
experimentar to experience
explicar to explain
explorar to explore
explotar to explode
exponer to display
exportar to export
expresar to express
exprimir to squeeze
expulsar temporalmente to suspend
extender to spread: to extend
  extender(se) to spread out
extrañar (*LAm*) to miss
fabricar to manufacture
faltar to be lacking; to fail
felicitar to congratulate
fiarse de to trust
financiar to finance
fingir to pretend (to)
firmar to sign
flotar to float
fluir to flow
formar(se) to form
forzar a algn a hacer (algo) to force
  sb to do (sth)
fotografiar to photograph
frecuentar to frequent
freír to fry
funcionar to work
  (hacer) funcionar to operate

fustigar to whip
ganar to earn; to gain
garantizar to guarantee
gastar to spend: to waste
  gastar(se) to wear (out)
gemir to groan
golpear to knock, to hit; to beat
grabar to record
gritar to shout; to scream; to cry
guardar to keep; to store
guiar to guide
gustar to like
haber to have
hablar to speak; to talk
hacer to do; to make; to bake
  hacer añicos to shatter;
  hacer campaña to campaign;
  hacer comentarios to comment;
  hacer daño a to hurt; **hacer las
  maletas** to pack; **hacer preguntas**
  to ask questions; **hacer público**
  to issue; **hacer señas** *or* **una señal**
  to signal; **hacer una lista de** to list;
  hacer una oferta to bid; **hacer
  una pausa** to pause; **hacer una
  señal con la mano** to wave;
  hacerse to become; to get;
  hacerse adulto to grow up;
  hacer(se) pedazos to smash
helarse to freeze
herir to injure
hervir to boil
huir to flee; to run away *or* off
identificar to identify
iluminar(se) to light
imaginar to imagine
impedir to prevent (from)
implicar to imply; to involve
imponer to impose
importar to matter; to mind;

to care
¡no me importa! I don't care!;
¿y a quién le importa? who cares?
impresionar to impress
imprimir to print
inclinar to bend
  inclinarse to bend down
incluir to include
indicar to point out; to indicate
influir to influence
informar to inform
inscribirse to register
insinuar to hint
insinuar to imply
insistir en to insist on
instruir to educate
insultar to insult
intentar to attempt to
interesar to interest
  interesarse por to be interested in
interrogar to question
interrumpir to interrupt
introducir to introduce
invadir to invade
investigar to investigate
invitar to invite
  invitar a algn a algo to treat sb to sth
ir to go
  ir a buscar a algn to fetch sb;
  ir bien a to suit; **ir deprisa** to dash;
  ir en bicicleta to ride a bike
irse to go away
irritar to irritate; to aggravate
jugar to play; to gamble
juntarse con to join
jurar to swear
justificar to justify
juzgar to judge
lamentarse to moan
lamer to lick

lanzar to throw; to launch
  lanzarse a to rush into
leer to read
levantar to raise; to put up; to lift
  levantarse to get up; to rise
limpiar to clean
llamar to call
  llamar por teléfono to ring;
  llamarse to be called
llegar to arrive
llenar (de) to fill (with)
llevar to carry; to bear; to wear
  llevar a cabo to carry out
  llevarse to take
llorar to cry, weep
llover to rain
  llover a cántaros to pour
luchar to fight; to struggle
maltratar to abuse
manchar to dirty
mandar to command, to order
manifestarse to demonstrate
mantener to maintain; to support
  mantener el equilibrio to balance
marcharse to depart; to leave
medir to measure
mejorar(se) to improve
mencionar to mention
mentir to lie
merecer to deserve, to merit
meterse en to get into
mezclar to mix
mimar to spoil
mirar to look (at); to watch
  mirar fijamente to stare at
modificar to adjust
molestar to annoy; to disturb;
  to trouble
montar a caballo to ride
morder to bite

morir to die
mostrar to display; to point out
  mostrar(se) to show
mover to move
multiplicar to multiply
nacer to be born
necesitar to need
negar to deny
  negarse(a) to refuse (to)
negociar to negotiate
notar to note
obedecer to obey
obligar a algn a to oblige sb to
observar to notice; to observe
obstruir to block
obtener to obtain
ocasionar to bring about
ocultar to hide
ocupar to occupy
  ocuparse de to deal with
ocurrir to occur
odiar to hate
ofender to offend
ofrecer to offer
  ofrecerse a hacer algo to volunteer
  to do sth
oír to hear
oler to smell
olvidar to forget
operar a algn to operate on sb
oponerse a to oppose; to object to
organizar(se) to organize
otorgar to award
pagar to pay
pararse to come to a halt, to stop
parecer to seem (to); to look
  parecerse a to look like, to resemble
participar en to take part in
partir to share
  partir(se) to split

pasar to pass; to overtake; to spend
pedir to request; to order
  pedir a algn que haga algo to ask
  sb to do sth; **pedir algo a algn** to
  ask sb for sth; **pedir algo prestado
  a algn** to borrow sth from sb
pegar to hit; to stick; to strike
pensar to think
  pensar en to think about;
  pensar hacer to intend to do
perder to miss
  perder a algn de vista to lose sight
  of sb
perdonar a to forgive
perdurar to survive
permitir to allow, to permit, to let
  permitirse to afford
perseguir to pursue
persuadir to persuade
pertenecer a to belong to
pesar to weigh
picar to bite
pinchar(se) to burst
planchar to iron
plegar to fold
poder to be able to; can; might
  ¿puedo llamar por teléfono?:
  may I use your phone?; **el profesor
  podría venir ahora**: the teacher
  might come now; **puede que
  venga más tarde** he might come
  later
poner to put; to lay
  poner de relieve to highlight;
  poner en duda to question;
  poner en el suelo to put down;
  poner en orden to tidy; **ponerse**
  to put on; **ponerse de pie** to stand
  up; **ponerse en contacto con**
  to contact

portarse to behave
poseer to own, to possess
practicar to practice
precipitarse to rush
predecir to predict
preferir to prefer
preguntar (por) to inquire (about)
  preguntarse to wonder
prender fuego to catch fire
preocupar to trouble; to bother
  preocuparse (por) to worry
  (about)
preparar(se) to prepare
prescindir de to do without
presentar to present; to introduce
prestar to lend
prevenir to warn
prever to foresee
privar to deprive
probar to prove
producir to produce
prohibir to ban, to prohibit; to forbid
prometer to promise
pronosticar to predict
pronunciar to pronounce
propagarse to spread
proponer to propose
proteger to protect
protestar to protest
proveer to provide
publicar to publish
quedar to remain
  quedarse to stay
quejarse (de) to complain (about)
quemar to burn
querer to want (to); to love; to like
quitar to remove
  quita ralgo a algn to take sth
  from sb; quitarse to take off
reaccionar to react; to respond

realizar to fulfil; to realize
reanudar to resume
recalcar to emphasize; to stress
rechazar to reject
recibir to receive
  recibirse (LAm) to qualify
reclamar to demand; to claim
recoger to pick (up); to collect;
  to gather
recomendar to recommend
reconocer to recognize
recordar to remember; to recall
  recordarle a algn to remind sb of
recuperarse to recover
reducir(se) to reduce
reembolsar to refund
referirse a to refer (to)
  en lo que se refiere a ... as regards ...
reflejar, reflexionar to reflect
reformar to reform
regañar to tell off
regar to water
registrar to register; to examine
regresar to return; to come back;
  to go back; (LAm) to give back;
  to send back
regresarse (LAm) to return; to come
  back; to go back
reír to laugh
  reírse de to laugh at
relajarse to relax
relatar to report
renovar to renew
rentar (LAm) to rent; to hire; to let
reñir to quarrel; to argue
reparar to repair, to mend
repartir to deal; to deliver
repetir(se) to repeat
reponer to replace
reponerse to recover

representar to perform; to represent
requerir to require
resbalar to slide
reservar to book; to reserve
resistir to hold out
  resistir(se) to resist
resolver to solve
respetar to respect
respirar to breathe
responder to reply, to answer;
  to respond
restaurar to restore
resultar to prove
retar to challenge
retirar(se) to withdraw
reunir(se) to collect
  reunirse to get together; to meet
revelar to reveal
rodear (de) to surround (with)
romper(se) to break; to tear; to burst
ruborizarse to blush
saber a to taste of
saber to know
  sé nadar I can swim
sacar to bring out; to take out
  sacar brillo to polish
sacudir to shake
salir to emerge
saltar to leap
saludar to greet
  saludar con la cabeza to nod
salvar to rescue; to save
secar(se) to dry
seguir to follow
  seguir haciendo algo to go on
  doing sth
sentarse to sit (down)
sentir to feel; to be sorry
  sentir(se) to feel
señalizar to indicate

ser to be
servir to serve
significar to mean
sobrevivir to survive
solicitar to apply to; to seek
soltar to release
sonar to sound; to ring
  (hacer) sonar to ring
sonreír to smile
sorprender to surprise
sospechar to suspect
subir to climb; to come up; to go up
  subir a to get on; to board
suceder to happen
sufrir (de) to suffer (from)
  sufrir un colapso to collapse
sugerir to suggest
sujetar to fix
suministrar to supply
suponer to assume; to suppose;
  to involve
surgir to emerge
suspender to suspend; to fail
suspirar to sigh
sustituir to replace
telefonear to telephone
temblar to shake
temer to fear
tener to have; to hold
  tener antipatía a to dislike;
  tener cuidado to be careful;
  tener éxito to be successful;
  tener frío to be cold; **tener**
  hambre to be hungry; **tener lugar**
  to take place; **tener mala suerte**
  to be unlucky; **tener miedo** to be
  afraid; **tener que** to have to;
  tener que ver con to concern;
  tener razón to be right; **tener sed**
  to be thirsty; **tener suerte** to be

lucky; **tener tendencia a hacer algo** to tend to do sth **tener trece/veinte años** to be thirteen/twenty years old
terminar to end; to finish
tirar to throw away
  tirar de to pull
tocar to touch; to play; to ring
tomar to take
torcer to twist
trabajar to work
traducir to translate
traer to bring
traicionar to betray
tranquilizar(se) to calm down
trasladar to transfer
tratar to treat
  tratar (de) to try (to);
  tratar con to deal with
unir to join
  unir(se) to unite
untar to spread
usar to use

vaciar(se) to empty
vacilar to hesitate
valer to be worth
variar to vary
vencer to conquer, to defeat, to overcome
vender to sell; to stock
venir to come
  venirse abajo to collapse
ver to see
visitar to visit
vislumbrar to catch sight of
vivir to live
volar to fly
volcar to overturn
volver to come back; to go back; to return
  volver(se) to turn round; to become; (*LAm*) to come back; to go back
  volverse hacia to turn towards
votar to vote